# AMERICAN PRESS OPINION
# WASHINGTON TO COOLIDGE

# AMERICAN PRESS OPINION

## Washington to Coolidge

A DOCUMENTARY RECORD OF EDITORIAL
LEADERSHIP AND CRITICISM
1785–1927

BY
### ALLAN NEVINS

Of Columbia University
and The New York
*World*

## D. C. HEATH AND COMPANY

| BOSTON | NEW YORK | CHICAGO |
| ATLANTA | SAN FRANCISCO | DALLAS |
| | LONDON | |

TO
WALTER  LIPPMANN

# PREFACE

The editor, no matter how distinguished, writes in water; his page is a palimpsest, on which he expends all his talents, wit, learning and judgment for the day alone, to be erased with the next sun. Nearly as much as the actor and more than the orator, his fame is based not on any achievement that succeeding generations can test for themselves, but simply upon contemporary records of his effect upon his own generation. At best, some small fragments — a few biting phrases, a fulmination which perhaps accidentally has made a distinct mark in history — are kept currently alive.

Hence it is that whereas everyone knows the names of our greatest editors — Greeley, Dana, Bennett, Raymond, Bowles — few except research workers in history have really read anything that they wrote; that while Bryant's poetry is familiar to every school-child, nobody has read the editorials into which Bryant actually put a much greater amount of time and effort. It is taken for granted that these men wrote admirably, as journalism goes; that for their passing day and purpose their work was valuable; but that it is as dead as the snows and blooms of those long past years.

With this verdict the present volume has a decided quarrel. That specimens of the best work of Greeley, Dana, and Godkin are of immediate present-day interest to journalists, students, and many general readers; that some outstanding American editorials possess qualities entitling them to permanent preservation in easily accessible form; above all, that a wide variety of typical editorials from representative journals, chronologically arranged, will furnish a valuable record of the history of public opinion — these are the beliefs upon which this collection is founded. It is not meant as an attempt at a mere selection of "famous" editorials. There are, to be sure, long-remembered editorials here included: Hamilton's attacks on Jefferson, Bache's diatribe against Washington, Bennett's announcement of his forthcoming marriage, the editorial in *Niles's Register* which gave Van Buren's candidacy in 1844 its death-blow, Greeley's exposure of the Kansas-Nebraska Bill, Bryant's denunciation of the Dred Scott decision, Greeley's "Prayer of Twenty Millions," the New York

v

*Times's* announcement of its Tweed Ring revelations, and so on down
to William Allen White's "What's the Matter with Kansas?" and
Henry Watterson's "Vae Victis." It is not meant as a collection of
model editorials, though many fine models are here. It is intended
as a representative body of the work of the best American editors, so
selected as to throw light on the chief events of American history.

There can be little doubt that the vigor, point, and shrewdness
of a great deal of this writing, from the early days of Cobbett and
Freneau, will surprise many readers. Probably nobody needs to be
told that Godkin was a master of English style, that for blunt, homely,
forcible exposition or argument Greeley was admirable, that Bryant
could attain moving heights of eloquence, and that Dana possessed
a wit which could sting or amuse, as he pleased. But the specimens
here reprinted will convince the ordinary man or woman of the truth
of these statements as mere assertion never could. It will also show
beyond any cavil that the work of some minor editors — for example,
Hezekiah Niles of *Niles's Register,* or Gales and Seaton of the *Intelligencer* — had excellent journalistic and even literary quality. The
sobriety and solidity of the editorials, taken as a whole, should be a
pleasing surprise to those who think this form of writing peculiarly
characterized by controversial intemperance, by sloppy sentimentality, and by inflated rhetoric. This is an impression which is widely
held, and which has not been lessened by certain recent peculiar
awards of the Pulitzer judges for the best editorial of each year. No
class of writers are less charitable to sentimental banalities or to
pompous rhetoric than hardened newspapermen. No class place
a greater value on terseness, lucidity, restraint, and genuine thought.

Some editorial pages wear well; some do not. The editor of this
compilation, who has turned over so many dusty, yellowing volumes
of files, may perhaps be pardoned a few expressions of personal
judgment upon the relative editorial merits of different journals.
One of these is that no other single American newspaper has quite
the long record of distinction which the *Evening Post,* under Coleman,
Bryant, Schurz, Godkin, Rollo Ogden, and Simeon Strunsky, almost
a century and a quarter, maintained. Another is that among American editors Horace Greeley stands preëminent for the vigor, vitality,
and persuasiveness of his writings, and that anyone who wishes to
study the best example of the editorial page as a great democratic
force must still go back to the New York *Tribune* of 1850–1860. A
third is that, admirable though the third Bowles was as an editor
and writer, his father, the second Bowles, stood head and shoulders

above him and above all but a few of his contemporaries. Another is that while E. L. Godkin is almost beyond praise in small doses, ordinary human nature rejects him if the dose be made too large or long-continued. Finally, he is convinced that, despite many lamentations over the sad estate of journalism, editorial leadership still vigorously survives, and that there are editors who are carrying on the great tradition of their calling in a way to give it fresh lustre; it is to one of these that this volume is dedicated.

## NOTE

Editorial titles which have been supplied — for in the early days titles were rare, and some of later periods proved unusable — have been indicated by brackets. Obvious errors of proofreading and grammar have been corrected, and the typographical form of the earlier editorials has been brought to sufficient conformity with modern usage to make them easily readable. Numerous editorials have been abbreviated, but excisions from the actual body of any piece of writing are always indicated by asterisks.

# CONTENTS

# CONTENTS

PAGE

## PART II

# CONTENTS

# CONTENTS

# CONTENTS

PAGE

# CONTENTS

PAGE

## PART IV

# CONTENTS

# CONTENTS

# CARTOONS

PART ONE

THE AMERICAN PRESS AND PUBLIC OPINION
1783–1835

# THE AMERICAN PRESS AND PUBLIC OPINION
## 1783–1835

The nineteenth century, to the historian of public opinion, is the century of the newspaper. The sphere of influence which had previously been shared by the preacher, the pamphleteer, and the politician was more and more largely engrossed, as the century wore on, by the journalist. When James Russell Lowell spoke in 1884 in London to the Provincial Newspaper Society he was able to declare that a revolution had taken place, in both America and Great Britain, in the methods of forming public opinion. "I am not sure that you are always aware," he said, "to how great an extent you have supplanted the pulpit, to how great an extent you have supplanted even the deliberative assembly. You have assumed responsibilities, I should say, heavier than ever man assumed before. You wield an influence entirely without precedent hitherto in human history." This was in essence what Carlyle had meant a generation earlier in writing that "the journalists are now the true kings and clergy," the "dynasts," of the earth. In America even more than England did the newspaper rise to a paramount position, and the greatest editors became figures almost as prominent and powerful as the greatest statesmen. This was hardly due to superior literacy in America — we should not forget that in 1840, for example, our republic of 17,000,000 people contained 500,000 illiterate adults. It was due to the diffused prosperity, enabling everyone to buy a newspaper, to our political democracy, giving every voter an interest in the newspaper discussion of politics, and to the editorial alertness which, taking advantage of the great distances and paucity of contacts in America, created a newspaper habit.

At the outset this alertness was not in evidence; for in 1783 the line between the editor and the pamphleteer was still very blurred. Historically, the editor had usually been a pamphleteer, and the greatest journalists, like Defoe in England, Franklin in America, and Cobbett in both, were the greatest of pamphleteers. The important newspapers in the generation after the Revolution, like the *Minerva*, the *Columbian Centinel*, the *Gazette of the United States*, and the *Aurora*,

3

were small, dingy, once-folded sheets which printed fragmentary commercial and political intelligence, some advertisements, and long editorials which usually resembled daily instalments of a pamphlet, or were actually such instalments. If written by the editor himself, they might unreservedly be called editorials. More often they were written by an outsider of political distinction, and signed Agricola, Publicola, or Cato. The style was that of a pamphlet: the writer thought of the cumulative effect of a series of articles, not of the individual effect of a single essay, and modeled himself upon Junius, Wilkes, or some other great pamphleteer.

The men who were interested in American public opinion between the Treaty of Paris and the Missouri Compromise were with few exceptions interested in it for political purposes. The birth of clear-cut, intensely antagonistic parties in Washington's first Administration was accompanied by the founding of a Federalist press by Hamilton, who assisted John Fenno and Noah Webster to establish newspapers, and whose papers signed "Camillus" and "Philo-Camillus" were as effective during the discussion of Jay's Treaty as his "Federalist" series had been during the debate on the Constitution; while Jefferson eagerly encouraged James T. Callender to set up a journal, and believing himself unfit for editorial controversies, wrote to Madison appealing that he answer Hamilton's fire. North and south, from Boston to Savannah, minor political leaders tended to establish, to assist, or to ally themselves with minor newspapers. Thus George Clinton in New York had his *American Citizen*, edited by the noted English immigrant James Cheetham, and Levi Lincoln in Massachusetts had his Worcester *National Ægis*. The true newspaper, independent of politics, had not yet been born even at the close of the second war with England, and the only sheets which were not supported by some party leader or party group were those which, led by the *Pennsylvania Packet*, devoted themselves to trade and markets. In these latter the editorial was almost entirely lacking; while in the other papers it dealt almost exclusively with politics.

The close connection between the political pamphlet and the newspaper editorial is amply illustrated by such journalists as Alexander Hamilton, William Cobbett, John Fenno, and J. T. Callender. The "Federalist" essays which Hamilton, Madison, and John Jay composed in 1787–1788 were essentially a pamphlet enterprise, published in a newspaper instead of pamphlet form for convenience and wide circulation, and then reprinted together. Appearing in the New York *Independent Journal* and another sheet friendly to the new Constitution, the New York *Packet*, they were copied by sympathetic newspapers throughout the country. Later Hamilton became virtually an over-editor or general supervisor of three journals in turn — Fenno's *Gazette of the United States*, Noah Webster's *Minerva*, and William Coleman's *Evening Post*. His "Camillus" series in the *Minerva* was practically a pamphlet — an argument for Jay's Treaty in thirty-six short chapters. In another aspect, they were a series of thirty-six editorials, for they had all the weight of the newspaper's editorial power behind them. Cobbett began his American career as a pamphleteer, and even after he had established *Porcupine's Gazette and Daily Advertiser* in 1797, he kept reprinting his material in pamphlet form. Callender first appears in history as the author of a pamphlet attack on William Pitt entitled "The Political Progress of Britain."

But a pamphlet, chopped into sections for the editorial page, had evident weaknesses from the standpoint of either the journalist or the party leader. Its sections sometimes lacked completeness; the length of the series made it dull; there was a lack of variety and vivacity. While the ponderous series of articles might serve as heavy artillery, small guns and rifle fire were needed. After 1795 the dashing franc-tireurs of journalism, such as William Duane of the *Aurora*, showed a marked preference for the brief editorial, peppered with denunciatory epithets and harsh accusations, and casting to the winds the dignity of the chief Federalist penmen. Their methods soon became characteristic of journalism. In the opposite camp such capable editors as Noah Webster of the *Minerva* and Coleman of the *Evening Post* began to intersperse the pamphlet-style articles by Hamilton, Rufus King, Oliver Wolcott, and other leaders with shorter, livelier comments of their own. Later, feeling that the public demands were best met by brief immediate comment, they concentrated their attention upon it, and the pamphlet matter began to fade away entirely from their pages. By 1815 there was little of it left. Meanwhile, such a versatile and talented journalist as Philip Freneau, who edited the *National Gazette* in Jefferson's behalf, made a contribution of different nature to the editorial page. Freneau, possessing high literary gifts and familiar with the best British essayists and poets, imparted sprightliness and grace to this journal and even more to his subsequent venture, the New York *Time-Piece*, by using poems, skits, dialogues, and epigram.

The really tremendous political influence of newspapers in this period — an influence attested by Hamilton, Jefferson, and Adams in emphatic language — was based largely upon the fact that the electorate was small. Property qualifications hedged it about, and all who voted read the press. These political journals, circulating among a small and very political-minded class, would even under favorable conditions have been slow to range outside the political field. But conditions were anything but favorable. It was impossible to present a varied editorial fare in an era which lacked varied social and intellectual interests. A raw young nation which had no independent literature, no drama, no art, no music, intent upon conquering a living from the wild forest and prairie — how much could this nation expect beyond politics; beyond underbred personalities, ill-tempered campaign harangues, and a none-too-intelligent discussion of fiscal topics? Certainly most journals gave it nothing better. In the larger cities, the obvious questions of municipal administration — paving, lighting, fires, the suppression of crime, epidemics, and accidents — obtained more and more attention, but their treatment lacked systematic energy. For the most part the editorials upon these subjects did not apply a definite reformative policy, but were casual in nature, and often did no more than supply the lack of news-stories upon them. Indeed, one function of the editorial columns until the thirties was to furnish news regarding even events of the greatest importance. When the Erie Canal was built, when the Baltimore & Ohio Railroad was opened, when John Quincy Adams was inaugurated, many newspapers had no way of treating the occurrence except by combining news with editorial comment. Reporting was in its infancy and correspondence was all but unknown, though letters were sometimes contributed by a benevolent friend. The most enterprising editors would either clip the needed news-story from some journal near the scene, or would furnish a second-hand account of the event in the guise of tepid comment; the unenterprising editors would print nothing at all.

The character of the editorial columns of the pre-Jacksonian era, it is clear, was determined by factors of environment that were slow to change. Those who turn over the yellowed files find the monotony of subject-matter, the woodenness of the treatment, and the lack of perspective painful. The shrillness of tone is often still more repugnant. Benjamin Russell, the Federalist editor of the *Columbian Centinel*, wrote in 1799 that his party had never employed Cobbett as a judicious writer in its cause, but had used him to assail the Democratic "foxes, skunks, and serpents" — the verminous newspapers which "ejected their mud, filth, and venom" upon even George Washington. John Fenno, in a moment of pique, wrote that same year that "the American newspapers are the most base, false, servile, and venal publications that ever polluted the fountains of society — their editors the most ignorant, mercenary, and vulgar automatons that ever were moved by the constantly rusting wires of sordid mercantile avarice." Yet again and again we do come, in the arid waste of governmental theorizing and intemperate political attacks, upon elevated and effective pieces of editorial writing, upon bits of eloquence and wit, upon utterances which arrest us by their sincerity or their lucid reasoning. We cannot help liking the directness and informality with which many editors, especially after 1800, wrote; addressing a familiar audience of perhaps 2,000 buyers they assumed no pontifical airs, but used the pronoun "I" and took an understanding of their personal crotchets for granted. Nor can we avoid being impressed by the intensity of conviction, the warmth of emotion, with which opinions upon political issues were often stated.

Of eminent editors in this period there were but a small number, and perhaps none of them can be said to have attained real greatness. The most important, viewed purely as a journalist, was indubitably William Cobbett — the irascible Englishman who, remaining but a few years (1794–1800), left nevertheless a deep imprint upon our newspapers. His ability lay in his earnestness, combativeness, and courage, in his homely, sinewy, picturesque English style, and in his reformative temper. Like every real publicist, he had an intense desire to make himself a power in the world. It was this which led him, a penniless ex-sergeant newly arrived in the United States, to challenge notice by his pamphlet upon Dr. Joseph Priestley, "Observations on the Emigration of a Martyr," and to follow it by his "Prospect from the Congress Gallery" and his "Political Censor." He gloried in the attention soon given him. In *Porcupine's Gazette* he published a naïve editorial which reveals how much he enjoyed the abuse he received. "'Dear father,'" (so it ran) — "'When you used to set me off in the morning, dressed in my blue smock-frock and woolen spatterdashes, with my bag of bread and cheese and bottle of small-beer swung over my shoulder on the little crook that my old godfather Boxall gave me, little did you imagine that I should one day become so great a man as to have my picture stuck in the windows, and have four whole books published about me in the course of one week.' Thus begins a letter which I wrote to my father yesterday morning, and which, if it reaches him, will make the old man drink an extraordinary pot of ale to my health. Heaven bless him! I think I see him now, by the old-fashioned fireside, reading the letter to his neighbors. 'Ay, ay,' says he. 'Will will stand his ground wherever he goes.' And so I will, father, in spite of all the hell of democracy." The pages of the *Gazette* show how this doughty John Bull did telling service for the Federalist party and for Mother England against France, and how he repaid the attacks of Franklin's grandson, Ben Bache, with shot in kind:

> Everyone will, I hope, have the goodness to believe that *my* grandfather was no philosopher. Indeed he was not. He never made a lightning rod, nor bottled up a single quart of sunshine, in the whole course of his life; he was no almanac-maker, nor quack, nor chimney-doctor, nor soap-boiler, nor ambassador, nor printer's devil; neither was he a deist; and all his children were born in wedlock. The legacies he left were his scythe, his reaping-hook, and his flail; he bequeathed no old and irrevocable debts to a hospital; he never cheated the poor during his life; nor mocked them at his death. He has, it is true, been suffered to sleep quietly beneath the green sward; but if his descendants cannot point to his statue over the door of a library, they have not the mortification of hearing him spoken of as a libertine, a hypocrite, and an infidel.

More combative still and even more vituperative, were two lesser men of British training, who remained in America permanently and who were identified with the Republican or anti-Federalist side — James T. Callender and William Duane. Of Callender, an Englishman born, it is sufficient to say that he founded the Richmond *Examiner* as an anti-Federalist organ, was imprisoned under the Sedition Act, and later in the columns of the Richmond *Reporter* foully slandered and abused his original patron Jefferson. Duane, a man of greater capacity and principle, was born in America, but spent more than a decade in India and England (1784–1795) before he became associated with Benjamin Franklin Bache in editing the *Aurora*. He succeeded to the chief editorship in 1798, and made the journal the leading Republican newspaper of the country, Jefferson ascribing his election as President largely to it. The *Aurora* remained of importance until 1822, when Duane resigned the editorship; but it lost its place as the head of the national Democratic press soon after the capital was removed from Philadelphia to Washington. Other of the most energetic editors of the time were foreign-born or foreign-trained: Thomas Cooper, James Cheetham, Joseph Gales, and Mathew Lyon. The chagrined John Adams, surveying this array of alien editors, wrote in 1801 after his defeat that "A group of foreign liars encouraged by a few ambitious native gentlemen have discomfited the education, the talents, the virtues, and the prosperity of the country."

One of the outstanding American newspapers of the nineteenth century commenced its career in Washington in the fall of 1800, when Samuel H. Smith founded the *National Intelligencer* to support Jefferson. The next year Hamilton and his friends brought into existence in New York a far greater journal, William Coleman's *Evening Post*. For three years Coleman, a man of talent who had left a Massachusetts editorship to join the New York bar, enjoyed the close collaboration of Hamilton himself. Inspired by these two men, the *Post* led in that editorial improvement in range, taste, and intellectual quality which was inevitable. Just a decade later, in 1811, a third distinguished newspaper appeared in the *Register* of Hezekiah Niles, published first in Baltimore and later in Washington; a weekly journal which is familiar to everyone as a repository of historical information, but which is not usually regarded as an organ of opinion. It was one, however — and a very effective one. Niles, who was of New England origin, made it a telling exponent first of Federalist and later of Whig doctrines, and argued unweariedly for a protective tariff. The second decade of the century brought in Thomas Ritchie's Richmond *Enquirer*, the vigorous editorials of which were soon read and discussed all over the country. In New England a little later (1814), Nathan Hale established the Boston *Daily Advertiser*, and gave special emphasis to editorials. He was an able, fearless, and responsible writer; but the claim sometimes made for Hale, that the unsigned editorial was his invention, is quite untenable.

A word of especial praise is due to the Washington *National Intelligencer* as conducted by Joseph W. Gales, Jr., and his brother-in-law, William Winston Seaton. Gales became editor in 1810, and remained in the harness till his death in 1860; Seaton joined him in 1812, and did not retire until 1864. Supporting Jefferson and Madison in its early years, the *Intelligencer* later turned to J. Q. Adams, and at the opening of the Jacksonian era adhered to Henry Clay and the American or Whig party of which he was one of the founders. It long derived a peculiar authority from the fact that, both Gales and Seaton being stenographers, it offered the only trustworthy report of the debates of Congress. Webster is quoted as having said that Gales and Seaton possessed the two wisest heads in the country, and that Gales's knowledge of our governmental history surpassed that of "all the other political writers of the day put together." Edward Everett late in life spoke of the *Intelligencer's* editorials as written "with an unsurpassed journalistic breadth of view and weight of authority"; and the *Atlantic Monthly* declared that the venerable editors had been for decades "a power and safety in the land." The influence of the *Intelligencer* was at its height in the thirties and early forties, declining when the slavery controversy overshot its mild and conciliatory views.

By the year 1830 journalism was showing greater breadth, elasticity, and energy in every department. It had spread far to the West. In New York William Cullen Bryant had joined the *Evening Post*, and James Watson Webb and M. M. Noah were making the *Courier and Enquirer* well known. The *Journal of Commerce*, established in 1827 by Arthur Tappan as a commercial journal of austerely moral standards, vied with the *Courier* in running pony expresses from Washington and in keeping news schooners off the harbor entrance. But despite the fresh and vigorous impulses of the time, politics still dominated the editorial pages. The most important of the newspapers which emerged into prominence with Jackson was the Washington *Globe*, which the stern old President decided to establish when Duff Green's *United States Telegraph*, previously the Administration organ, turned to follow the leadership of John C. Calhoun, with whom Green was connected by marriage. Jackson brought to Washington a Kentucky editor named Francis P. Blair, who issued the first number of the *Globe* on December 7, 1830. With the aid of the lucrative public printing contracts and of Federal officeholders throughout the country, the "government paper" flourished. Its editor was the shrewdest of politicians, and not a man of excessive scruple; and by virtue of his headship of the "Kitchen Cabinet," and of his contacts with the Albany "Regency" and Richmond "Junta," he played a part in what has been well called the most powerful political and journalistic cabal the nation has ever known.

It is interesting to note the close parallel which the relations between Andrew Jackson and Francis P. Blair furnished with those which had existed between Alexander Hamilton and William Coleman a generation earlier. Coleman had been wont, when any public question of importance was pending, to go — usually late at night — to Hamilton's home. "He (Hamilton) always keeps himself minutely informed upon all political matters," Coleman informed an acquaintance, Jeremiah Mason. "As soon as I see him he begins in a deliberate manner to dictate, and I to note down in shorthand; when he stops, my article is completed." In the same way, the chief editorial writer for the *Globe*, Amos Kendall, would come by night for a private conference with Andrew Jackson. The President would lie on a sofa and smoke, dictating his ideas as well as he could express them, while Kendall wrote, read, and rewrote his editorial until it approximated the model which the Chief Executive had in mind. Jackson, according to Henry A. Wise, needed just such an expert amanuensis. "He could think but could not write; he knew what nerve to touch, but he was no surgeon skilled in the instrument of dissection. Kendall was." In the same way that the *Evening Post* during and after Hamilton's time, till the close of the War of 1812, was the precentor of Hamiltonian Federalism, the *Globe* from 1830 to 1840 was the leader of the whole Jacksonian Democratic press.

Journalism developed mightily, in most material respects, in the first forty years of the republic; it improved its mechanical equipment, multiplied its offices and sheets, and strode to and beyond the Mississippi, till Illinois alone had more dailies in 1830 than the whole nation had possessed in 1790. It increased with greater slowness, but still steadily and creditably, in accuracy and editorial enterprise. Henry Adams was hardly too severe in characterizing the infant press of the country, about 1800, as simply a storehouse of political calumny; in saying that intermingled with its scanty advertisements, its marine lists, its extracts from English newspapers, one might find long dull columns of political disquisition, but hardly any real news or really pungent comment. However, even by 1812 this was no longer true. By 1830 a very decided turning point had been reached. The Washington correspondent had been invented, and James Gordon Bennett was about to make him important. A few newspapers in the largest cities were printing letters from other distant points. Reporting was beginning to become a profession. The basis was being laid for a newer, more popular, more broadly effective journalism, in touch with the strong currents of national life released by Jacksonian democracy; and the improvement in the news columns and distribution of intelligence was being already reflected in a greater vitality and strength in the editorial pages, and in a lessened dependence upon politics and politicians.

## [WILL NEW YORK REJECT THE IMPOST?] [1]

*Pennsylvania Packet*, March 22, 1786

The State of Rhode Island having at length acceded to the impost and the supplementary aids, according to the last proposition of Congress, and there remaining but little doubt of the same national spirit animating the councils of every other government on this side the Hudson, the eyes of the friends of the Union, the very existence of which has been brought into jeopardy by our past neglect of this salutary expedient to retrieve the credit of America, will now be turned to the State of New York, which, it is to be hoped, will not long be deficient in exhibiting this last proof of its attachment to our federal interest. It seems no less strange than remarkable that the influence of Congress should be least regarded in the place of their immediate residence: an argument, among others, in demonstrating the little probability there is of the authority of that truly respectable body being suddenly extended so as to endanger the existence of that democratic spirit which still, and we flatter ourselves will ever, flourish in full vigour throughout this continent. But at the same time, it is most ardently to be wished, that in guarding against this unhappy extreme, we should not run into all the horrors of anarchy and civil dissension, which are far more to be dreaded. A true American will feel for the reputation and interest of his country as keenly as for the immediate emolument of the State of which he is a member, and it is apparent beyond the necessity of language to explain it, that a government without the means of performing its engagements must soon be contemptible. There must therefore be some strong motives that immediately affect themselves to account for such a pointed opposition to the united views and wishes of almost every part of our federal government. If it proceeds from any little benefit which that State may derive from its peculiar situation as to commerce, it is an object so different from those which governed our conduct in the early days of our independence, and so repugnant to every principle of honor, policy, and the love of our country, that we must hope it will soon give place to a mode of procedure more consonant to their past glory and the present hopes of every real friend of America.

[1] The Pennsylvania *Packet* was the leading commercial newspaper of the United States and as such was heartily in favor of all measures to strengthen the Confederation. New York, swayed by Governor George Clinton, was successful in defeating the proposal for a national impost or customs tax. The measure was beaten in the Legislature in May, 1786 (though a much-mangled substitute, quite unsatisfactory in nature, did pass); and Governor Clinton refused to call a special session to take it up again. Many New Yorkers had just the selfish motive denounced by the *Packet*.

## [THE HARD TIMES ARE ONLY TEMPORARY] [1]

*Pennsylvania Gazette,* May 21, 1786

We see in the public newspapers of different States frequent complaints of *hard times, deadness of trade, scarcity of money,* and so on. It is not our intention to assert or maintain that these complaints are entirely without foundation. There can be no country or nation existing in which there will not be some people so circumstanced as to find it hard to gain a livelihood, people who are not in the way of any profitable trade, and with whom money is scarce because they have nothing to give in exchange for it. And it is always in the power of a small number to make a great clamor. But let us take a cool view of the general state of our affairs, and perhaps the prospect will appear less gloomy than has been imagined.

The great business of the continent is agriculture. For one citizen or merchant, I suppose we have at least one hundred farmers, by far the greatest part cultivators of their own fertile lands, from whence many of them draw not only the food necessary for their subsistence, but the materials of their clothing, so as to need very few foreign supplies; while they have a surplus of production to dispose of, whereby wealth is gradually accumulated. Such has been the goodness of Divine Providence to these regions, and so favorable the climate, that since the three or four years of hardship in the first settlement of our fathers here, a famine or scarcity has never been heard of among us; on the contrary, though some years may have been more, and others less plentiful, there has always been provision enough for ourselves, and a quantity to spare for exportation. And although the crops of last year were generally good, never was the farmer better paid for the part he can spare to commerce, as the published price currents abundantly testify. The lands he possesses are also continually rising in value with the increase of population. And on the whole, he is able to give such good wages to all who work for him that all who are acquainted with the Old World must agree that in no part of it are the laboring poor so generally well fed, well clothed, well lodged, and well paid as in the United States of America.

If we enter the cities, we find that since the Revolution the owners of houses and lots of ground there have had their interest vastly augmented in value; rents have risen to an astonishing height, and thence encouragement to increased building, which gives employment to an abundance of workmen, as does also the increased luxury and splendor of living among the inhabitants thus made

---

[1] The Revolution was followed by severe business depression, acutest in 1785–1786. Its subsidence coincided with the adoption of the Constitution in 1788.

richer.  These workmen all demand and obtain much higher wages than any other part of the world would afford them, and are paid in ready money.  This rank of people therefore do not or ought not to complain of hard times, and they make a very considerable part of the city inhabitants.

At the distance we live from the American fisheries, we cannot speak of them with certainty; but we have not heard that the labour of the valuable race of men employed in them is worse paid, or that they meet with less success than before the Revolution.  The whale-men indeed have been deprived of one market for their oil, but another we hear is opening for them, which it is hoped may be equally advantageous.  And the demand is constantly increasing for spermaceti candles, which therefore bear a much higher rate than formerly. . . .

Whoever has travelled through the various parts of Europe, and observed how small is the proportion of people in affluence or easy circumstances there, compared with those in poverty or misery, the few rich and haughty landlords, the multitude of poor, abject, rack-rented, tithe-paying tenants, and half-paid and half-starved ragged laborers;  and who views here the happy mediocrity that so generally prevails throughout these States, where the cultivator works for himself and supports his family in decent plenty, will, we think, feel abundant reason to bless Divine Providence for the evident and great difference in our favour, and be convinced that no nation known to us enjoys a greater share of human felicity.

## [PHILADELPHIA SHOULD BE THE NATIONAL CAPITAL]

*Pennsylvania Packet*, September 6, 1786

It seems a great hardship upon the people of the United States . . . that so great a majority as voted for Philadelphia should not determine the residence of Congress — New Hampshire, Connecti-cut, Pennsylvania, Maryland, Virginia, and North Carolina, having 1,480,000 people, according to the statements of the Federal Con-vention, voted for Philadelphia;  and Massachusetts, New York, New Jersey, and South Carolina, having only 920,000 people, were for New York.  Delaware and Georgia were divided.

We cannot but wonder at the want of reflection in the writer of a New York paragraph of August 30, who complains that Congress have not determined the question of the residence of the new govern-ment, although a ninth State has adopted the Constitution above two months.  Surely this gentleman will not complain as a New Yorker that Congress delayed for many weeks to determine the matter, when New York was not in a capacity to be fixed on, or even to be put in nomination. . . . This writer tells us that the sufferings of New York ought to influence Congress to fix the government there. Upon that principle it should go to New Jersey. But does he remember that half the ships and cargoes belonging to Philadelphia that were captured in the war would rebuild all they had lost? Our greater proportion of voluntary public loans, now reduced three-fourths in value, would also rebuild it. But they have been amply repaid for this loss by the confiscation of a great number of the most capital city estates. Philadelphia, he says, wishes to become the arbitress of the United States. This we deny and despise. Let New York remember how firmly she refused to make common cause even with her sister States, by refusing the impost; and let the worthy citizens of Connecticut and New Jersey remember how safe it would be for New York, with such an unjust spirit, to become the arbitress of America. The dispositions of this State are, and always have been, *national*. When Boston suffered before the war, Pennsylvania subscribed to their relief. When the South Carolinians were exiled, Pennsylvania subscribed for their poor and lent to their rich citizens. How much did New York do on these two occasions? They did not furnish in gifts or loans a tenth penny. When our Philosophical Society, or Bank, our Manufacturing Society, etc., were established, all America were publicly and heartily invited to partake. Our little societies have offered premiums for inventions, improvements, and new articles of produce to the citizens of the most distant States. Our spirit has always been Federal, both before and since the Revolution, as is well known.

## [VIRGINIA RATIFIES THE CONSTITUTION] [1]

### *Pennsylvania Packet*, August 9, 1788

It would be difficult to convey an adequate idea of the general enthusiastic happiness which this fortunate event has diffused. The acquisition of Virginia to the new confederated States would of itself have been highly important; but at this crisis, when it was considered that her accession, by being the ninth approving State, has established the liberty, independence, and public credit of this rising Western Union, our joy is not to be described. A general sympathy unites all. Hope, rational hope, animates every rank

[1] Virginia ratified the Constitution June 25, 1788, after a struggle in which Patrick Henry and George Mason led the opposition. She was the tenth State to take the step, and her action made the success of the new government certain. New Hampshire ratified only a few days earlier, which explains the *Packet's* erroneous reference to the "ninth State."

and profession.   The prospect of justice, parent of liberty and support of virtue, being speedily and impartially administered; public
faith and dignity supported; a consistent productive commerce
disseminating its happy consequences through every rank of citizens, arrested the attention and feelings of every lover of liberty
and mankind.

Shortly shall we begin to reap the blessings of the glorious revolution, purchased with difficulties and anxieties which none but a
sufferer can truly comprehend.   No longer shall the useful artisan
be paid with procrastinated promises;   no longer shall the planter
sweat for a hard-earned, narrow, uncertain competence, but receive
the just reward of his labor;   no longer shall we be insulted with the
tantalizing name of wealth, depreciated to a shadow, even while
we contemplate its nominal amount.   Specie (that valuable quid
pro quo attendant on all well-regulated efficient governments) will
again circulate;   the price of imports and exports will be regulated;
in short, it is to be expected as a natural consequence, that industry
and ingenuity will be rewarded with peace, plenty, and content
under this well-digested, approved confederation, framed by some
of the wisest and most virtuous men now existing, and by the most
strenuous supporters of liberty through the mazes of the late war.

## [THE FUNDING OF THE NATIONAL DEBT] [1]

*National Gazette*, September 11, 1792

Much declamation has been indulged against certain characters,
who are charged with advocating the pernicious doctrine, that
"public debts are public blessings," and with being friends to a
perpetuation of the public debt of the country.   Among these
characters, if the Secretary of the Treasury has not been named,
he has been pretty plainly alluded to.   It is proper to examine
what foundation there is then for these charges.

That officer, it is very certain, explicitly maintained, that the
*funding* of the existing debt of the United States would render it a
national blessing;   and a man has only to travel through the United
States with his eyes open, and to observe the invigoration of industry in every branch, to be convinced that the position is well
founded.

But, whether right or wrong, it is quite a different thing from
maintaining, as a general proposition, that a public debt is a public
blessing;   particular and temporary circumstances might render that
advantageous at one time, which at another might be hurtful.

It is known that prior to the Revolution, a great part of the cir-

1 Written by Alexander Hamilton, Secretary of the Treasury; signed " Fact."

culation was carried on by paper money; that in consequence of the events of the Revolution, that resource was in a great measure destroyed, by being discredited, and that the same events had destroyed a large proportion of the moneyed and mercantile capital of the country, and of personal property generally. It was natural to think that the chasm created by these circumstances required to be supplied, and a just theory was sufficient to demonstrate, that a funded debt would answer the end. To infer that it would have such an effect, was no more to maintain the general doctrine of "public debts being public blessings," than the saying, that paper emissions, by the authority of government, were useful in the early periods of the country, was the maintaining, that they would be useful in all the future stages of its progress. . . .

Extract from a report of the Secretary of the Treasury on the subject of a provision for the public debt, presented the 14th of January, 1790:

> Persuaded, as the Secretary is, that the proper funding of the *present* debt will render it a national blessing; yet he is *so far* from acceding to the position, in the latitude in which it is sometimes laid down, that 'Public debts are public benefits,' a position *inviting to prodigality, and liable to dangerous abuse*, that he ardently wishes to see it incorporated, as a *fundamental maxim* in the *system of public credit* of the United States, that the *creation of debt should be always accompanied with the means of extinguishment*. This he regards as the *true secret of rendering public credit immortal*.

## [DID JEFFERSON OPPOSE THE CONSTITUTION?] [1]

### Gazette of the United States, September 19, 1792

Mr. Pendleton represents a certain letter of Mr. Jefferson as containing these particulars — a strong wish that the *first nine conventions* may accept the new Constitution because it would secure the *good* it contains, which is *great* and *important*. 2d. A wish that the four latest, whichever they should be, might refuse to accede to it till *amendments were secured*. 3d. A caution to take care that no objection to the form of government should produce a schism in the Union; which Mr. Jefferson admits to be an incurable evil.

From this it appears, that though Mr. Jefferson was of opinion that the Constitution contained "great and important good," and was desirous that the first nine deliberating States should consent to it for the sake of preserving the existence of the Union, yet he had strong objections to the Constitution; so strong, that he was willing

[1] Written by Alexander Hamilton, and characteristic of the newspaper attacks which Jefferson, then Secretary of State, keenly resented; signed "Catullus."

to risk an *ultimate dismemberment* in an experiment to obtain the alterations which he deemed necessary.

If the four last deliberating States (particularly if they had happened to be States in geographical contiguity, which was very possible) had refused to ratify the Constitution, what might not have been the consequence? Who knows whether the assenting States would have been willing to have been *coerced* into the amendments which the non-assenting States might have been disposed to dictate? Calculating the intrigues and machinations which were to have been expected to stand in the way, who can say, if even two thirds of both houses of Congress should have been found willing to propose them, or that three fourths of the legislatures, or conventions, in three fourths of the States, would have been brought to adopt the required amendments?

Could anything but objections to the Constitution of the most *serious* kind have justified the hazarding an eventual schism in the Union, in so great a degree as would have attended an adherence to the advice given by Mr. Jefferson? Can there be any perversion of truth in affirming that the person who entertained those objections was opposed to the Constitution?

The opposition which was experienced in every part of the United States, acknowledged the necessity and utility of the Union; and, generally speaking, that the Constitution contained many valuable features; contending only that it wanted some essential alterations to render it upon the whole a safe and good government.

### [THE UNFAIR ATTACK ON JAY'S TREATY][1]
*American Minerva*, July 22, 1795

It was known, that the resentment produced by our revolution war with Great Britain, had never been entirely extinguished, and that recent injuries had rekindled the flame with additional violence. It was a natural consequence of this, that many should be disinclined to any amicable relation with Great Britain, and that many others should be prepared to acquiesce only in a treaty which should present advantages of so striking and preponderant a kind, as it was not reasonable to expect could be obtained, unless the United States were in a position to give the law to Great Britain, and as, if obtained under the coercion of such a situation, could only have been the short-lived prelude of a speedy rupture to get rid of them. . . .

It was not to be mistaken, that an enthusiasm for France and her revolution, throughout all its wonderful vicissitudes, has continued to possess the minds of the great body of the people of this country;

[1] By Alexander Hamilton; one of the Camillus series.

and it was to be inferred, that this sentiment would predispose to a jealousy of any agreement or treaty with her most persevering competitor — a jealousy so excessive, as would give the fullest scope to insidious arts to perplex and mislead the public opinion. It is well understood, that a numerous party among us, though disavowing the design, because the avowal would defeat it, have been steadily endeavoring to make the United States a party in the present European war, by advocating all those measures which would widen the breach between us and Great Britain, and by resisting all those which would tend to close it; and it was morally certain, that this party would eagerly improve every circumstance which could serve to render the treaty odious, and to frustrate it, as the most effectual road to their favorite goal.

It was also known beforehand, that personal and party rivalships, of the most active kind, would assail whatever treaty might be made, to disgrace, if possible, its organ. There are three persons prominent in the public eye, as the successor of the actual President of the United States, in the event of his retreat from the station, Mr. Adams, Mr. Jay, and Mr. Jefferson.

No one has forgotten the systematic pains which have been taken to impair the well-earned popularity of the first gentleman. Mr. Jay, too, has been repeatedly the object of attacks with the same view. His friends, as well as his enemies, anticipated that he could make no treaty which would not furnish weapons against him: and it were to have been ignorant of the indefatigable malice of his adversaries, to have doubted that they would be seized with eagerness and wielded with dexterity.

The peculiar circumstances which have attended the two last elections for governor of this State, have been of a nature to give the utmost keenness to party animosity. It was impossible that Mr. Jay should be forgiven for his double, and, in the last instance, triumphant success; or that any prominent opportunity of detaching from him the public confidence, should pass unimproved.[1] . . .

From the combined operation of these different causes, it would have been a vain expectation, that the treaty would be generally contemplated with candor and moderation, or that reason would regulate the first impressions concerning it. It was certain, on the contrary, that however unexceptionable its true character might be, it would have to fight its way through a mass of unreasonable opposition; and that time, examination, and reflection would be requisite to fix the public opinion on a true basis. It was certain

---

[1] Jay stood for Governor in 1792; but though he had an actual majority of votes, a partisan returning board so handled the returns of three counties as to elect George Clinton. But Jay obtained a clear majority at the election of May, 1795.

that it would become the instrument of a systematic effort against the national government and its administration; a decided engine of party to advance its own views at the hazard of the public peace and prosperity.

The events which have already taken place, are a full comment on these positions. If the good sense of the people does not speedily discountenance the projects which are on foot, more melancholy proofs may succeed.

Before the treaty was known, attempts were made to prepossess the public mind against it. It was absurdly asserted, that it was not expected by the people, that Mr. Jay was to make any treaty; as if he had been sent, not to accommodate differences by negotiation and agreement, but to dictate to Great Britain the terms of an unconditional submission.

Before it was published at large, a sketch, calculated to produce false impressions, was handed out to the public, through a medium noted for hostility to the administration of the government. — Emissaries flew through the country, spreading alarm and discontent: the leaders of clubs were everywhere active to seize the passions of the people, and preoccupy their judgments against the treaty.

At Boston it was published one day, and the next a town meeting was convened to condemn it; without ever being read, without any serious discussion, sentence was pronounced against it.

Will any man seriously believe, that in so short a time, an instrument of this nature could have been tolerably understood by the greater part of those who were thus induced to a condemnation of it? Can the result be considered as anything more than a sudden ebullition of popular passion, excited by the artifices of a party, which had adroitly seized a favorable moment to furorize the public opinion? This spirit of precipitation and the intemperance which accompanied it, prevented the body of the merchants and the greater part of the most considerate citizens, from attending the meeting, and left those who met wholly under the guidance of a set of men who, with two or three exceptions, have been the uniform opposers of the government.

The intelligence of this event had no sooner reached New York, than the leaders of the clubs were seen haranguing in every corner of the city, to stir up our citizens into an imitation of the example of the meeting at Boston. An invitation to meet at the city-hall quickly followed, not to consider or discuss the merits of the treaty, but to unite with the meeting at Boston to address the President against its ratification.

This was immediately succeeded by a handbill, full of invectives against the treaty, as absurd as they were inflammatory, and manifestly designed to induce the citizens to surrender their reason to the empire of their passions.

In vain did a respectable meeting of the merchants endeavor, by their advice, to moderate the violence of these views, and to promote a spirit favorable to a fair discussion of the treaty; in vain did a respectable majority of the citizens of every description attend for that purpose. The leaders of the clubs resisted all discussion, and their followers, by their clamors and vociferations, rendered it impracticable, notwithstanding the wish of a manifest majority of the citizens, convened upon the occasion.

Can we believe, that the leaders were really sincere in the objections they made to a discussion, or that the great and mixed mass of citizens then assembled, had so thoroughly mastered the merits of the treaty as that they might not have been enlightened by such a discussion?

It cannot be doubted that the real motive to the opposition, was the fear of a discussion; the desire of excluding light; the adherence to a plan of surprise and deception. Nor need we desire any fuller proof of the spirit of party which has stimulated the opposition to the treaty, than is to be found in the circumstances of that opposition.

## WASHINGTON LEAVES THE PRESIDENCY [1]

Philadelphia *Aurora*, March 6, 1797

"Lord, now lettest thou thy servant depart in peace, for mine eyes have seen thy salvation," was the pious ejaculation of a man who beheld a flood of happiness rushing in upon mankind. If ever there was a time that would license the reiteration of the exclamation, that time is now arrived; for the man who is the source of all the misfortunes of our country, is this day reduced to a level with his fellow citizens, and is no longer possessed of power to multiply evils upon the United States. If ever there was a period for rejoicing, this is the moment — every heart in unison with the freedom and happiness of the people ought to beat high, with exultation that the name of Washington from this day ceases to give a currency to political iniquity, and to legalize corruption. A new era is opening upon us, a new era which promises much to the people; for public measures must now stand upon their own merits, and nefarious projects can no longer be supported by a name.

---

[1] Long famous, or infamous, as the worst of the scurrilous attacks of extremist Anti-Federalists upon Washington. Written by Franklin's grandson, B. F. Bache, this classic of unseemly libel, as Worthington C. Ford calls it, reflects the family's resentment of Washington's frigid treatment of Franklin.

When a retrospect is taken of the Washingtonian Administration for eight years, it is a subject of the greatest astonishment, that a single individual should have canceled the principles of republicanism in an enlightened people, and should have carried his designs against the public liberty so far, as to have put in jeopardy its very existence. Such, however, are the facts, and with these staring us in the face, this day ought to be a *jubilee* in the United States.

## THE NATION'S NEW CAPITAL

### Washington *Gazette*, June 3, 1797

The city of Washington, or rather the site intended for the city, stands perhaps unrivalled by any in the world in point of advantages for becoming the emporium of a great nation. The scheme is grand and magnificent, and the funds intended for erecting public buildings *were* in the same proportion. But serious doubts are entertained in the minds of many persons, whose situations do not preclude them from examination, whether, in the execution, these funds have not been dissipated in wild and extravagant projects which, after having been carried on at an enormous expense, have been relinquished before being completed, so as not to be in any way beneficial. Instances need not be given; the facts speak for themselves, and are strongly imprinted in the memories of all who have had an opportunity for observing. . . . The enthusiastic spirit in which the operations of the city commenced opened a wide field for speculation, which has been practised in all its various forms, and has terminated in the ruin of all who were drawn into its vortex, and whose capital or talents were inferior to others'. Little is their failure to be regretted, were not a greater number of honest individuals, and useful mechanics and others, involved in its pernicious effects.

## [DANGERS OF THE WYOMING LAND DISPUTE][1]

### The *Time-Piece*, March 20, 1797

A bill is before the legislature of Pennsylvania for driving from their estates and burning the houses of the settlers under the Connecticut claims, at Wyoming. The severity of the proposed measure calls forth pointed animadversions in that State, and should the bill pass into a law, and the Executive attempt to enforce it, a civil commotion would probably be the consequence. The settlers on those lands have a strong sense of the justice of their claims, and

[1] These excerpts from the *Time-Piece* of Philip Freneau, a short-lived New York journal, are representative specimens of the editor's direct and telling style.

their right to the soil, which no legal decision has yet shaken; and to attempt to expel two, three, or perhaps five thousand hardy farmers from lands which they *firmly believe* to be their own property, would be a desperate undertaking. If the sword must be the ultimate arbiter between the parties, the blood of five thousand men might leave the controversy undecided. We trust the dreadful alternative will be avoided.

## [SLAVERY THE CURSE OF AMERICA]
### *Idem*, May 26, 1797

Mr. Rushton's address to the late President of the United States (see the first page of this paper) is an awful appeal to the moral sentiment of the world on the injustice and cruelty of man holding man in bondage; and in a country, too, that prides itself in having given the first spring to a universal emancipation from the fangs of tyrants. It is a lesson which cannot be soon forgot, and applies to every generous feeling of the heart that has not, from the accumulation of exorbitant wealth, become callous to the miseries of the far greater part of our species. There are not a few in these States who, notwithstanding all that has been said to the contrary, are still of the opinion that the patriotic Washington, who headed the Americans at a crisis that tried the heart of man, in the sublime cause of liberty and virtue, will come forward before the ingress of the approaching century (big with the most tremendous events) and shew an example to the world, that the people of republican America will not be the last to advance this grand object, the emancipation of slaves, by such means as the legislative wisdom of the Union shall deem it advisable to adopt. To suppose the continuance of the old *servile system* in this country, would be to suppose a halt in the progress of man towards that political perfection, which Plato of old and Condorcet in our own times, have given the world reason to believe is not wholly ideal.

## [PEACE WITH FRANCE SHOULD BE PRESERVED]
### *Idem*, June 9, 1797

Much is due to that description of men in Congress who have endeavored to prevent the flames of war from being kindled in these States; and it is to be hoped that their virtuous efforts will in the end defeat the hostile projects of the secret enemies of the peace of the United States, and the friends of the orders, checks, and balances of what is called the British Constitution. It is to be suspected that providing for friends in an American army and navy contributes in some degree to the thirst of certain persons for a war with France. Have all these people known what war is? or do they suppose it a frolic, that may be ended at pleasure? — have they ever witnessed the consequences of a battle either at sea or land, and the whole diabolical scene of broken bones, cleft skulls, and mangled carcasses — scenes which can only be justified in cases of resistance to oppression or invasion, and not from lighter considerations? If selfishness be the motive of some for warfare, let it be remembered that a whole nation is never selfish in this respect. It is for the interest of the few that men are turned into bulldogs and butchers — the selfishness of the many is their enjoyment of peace and quiet.

## [THE TALK OF NEW ENGLAND'S SECESSION]

*Idem*, July 7, 1797

On Saturday [in Congress] was exhibited striking evidence of the real designs and views of the party in New England, who are constantly struggling in the House of Representatives for an indefinite increase in the executive power in this country, in the declaration made by Mr. Sewell, a member from Massachusetts, in the reply to those members who opposed the equipping and manning of the three frigates, on the ground of their very great expense and the slight probability of their being of so great a national advantage as would justify such an expenditure under the present circumstances of the country with respect to revenue. The gentleman affected to consider this kind of reasoning as intended to throw out of the protection of the Union all those who were engaged in commerce; and [he] said, Let those States, or that part of the Union who live by commerce, *separate themselves from the Union*, if they are not to be protected by the agricultural part of the country, and they will then be able to defend themselves; or words to that effect. Declarations of this kind, we think, must convince every impartial person that if this party cannot succeed in carrying all their favorite points in the Federal Government (and almost all their projects require a great expenditure of money, which must fall upon the landed interest in pretty heavy taxes), they will not scruple to make attempts to separate themselves from the Union, and form a separate confederacy; and as such a confederacy must be in its nature weak, they will be more easily enabled by that circumstance to carry into effect that favorite object which they must have so long had in view, *the placing themselves under the protection of the British Government*. We are the more confirmed in this opinion, from a recollection of several publications which were not many months since made in the newspapers of Connecticut. . . . Can it be possible that the honest farmers of New England will long support such a party in such a system of measures?

## AMERICAN LOTTERIES: ADVICE TO THOSE WHO NEED IT [1]

*Porcupine's Gazette*, August 25, 1797

Have you an itching propensity to use your wits to advantage? Make a lottery. A splendid scheme is a bait that cannot fail to catch the gulls. Be sure to spangle it with rich prizes: the fewer blanks — on paper — the better; for on winding up the business, you know, it is easy to make as many blanks as you please. Witness a late lottery on the Potowmack. The *winding up*, however, is not absolutely necessary: you know what a noise the winding up of a certain clock once made. The better way is to delay the drawing; or should it *ever begin*, there is no hurry about the *end*, or rather, let it have no end at all. If, in either case, a set of discontented adventurers should happen to say hard things of you, show them that you despise their unmannerly insinuations, by humming the tune of *Yankee Doodle*. This may dumbfound them; but should they persist, there is a mode left that cannot fail to stop their mouths. The scheme of the lottery is your contract with the purchasers of tickets: produce this, and defy them to point out any breach of it on your part. *Entre nous;* I am supposing you discreet enough to avoid in your scheme anything that might look like a promise to commence the drawing on this or that particular day; or to finish at any given period. It would be enough to promise a beginning *when a sufficient number of tickets shall be sold;* of the sufficiency you would be the sole judge. Now they ought to know as well as you that, like Peter Pindar's razors, your tickets were "made to sell"; so that if but one ticket remained unsold, you are under no obligation to draw, a *sufficient number* not having been disposed of.

## JOHN ADAMS AND MONARCHY

Philadelphia *Aurora*, August, 1797

The British faction in Boston are making a very great parade with John Adams. It seems they have prepared a "feast of gratitude" to him — for what? What have been his achievements since he became President by three stolen votes? If the "illustrious Adams" has a claim upon the gratitude of a certain set of men in Boston, is it owing to his Whiggism or to the manifestation which he gave in

[1] By William Cobbett.

his war-whoop to the cause of Great Britain and of tyranny? If to his Revolutionary conduct, is it not extraordinary that the sentiment of gratitude should never have operated before? John Adams was Vice President of the United States for eight years, during which time he travelled to and from the dukedom of Braintree very often, and yet strange to tell, not one feast of gratitude was ever prepared for him by the faction at Boston. What an ungrateful set of monsters to let merit pass so long unnoticed and unrewarded.

. . . The farce of idolatry, however, it seems, must be kept up. The creator must worship the creature, or that order of things cannot be made to come to pass which a detestable and nefarious conspiracy in this country are seeking to bring about — *monarchy*.

## [AMERICAN FORBEARANCE TOWARDS FRANCE]

*Porcupine's Gazette*, September 9, 1797

There never was a nation on earth so unjustly and so contemptuously treated by another, as America has been by France. Nations have been invaded, laid under contribution, conquered, and enslaved; but this has been effected by force or by treachery; it has been the fortune of war, or the result of conspiracy. Never did we before hear of a nation at peace with all the world, and pretending to be in the full enjoyment of independence, suffering a millionth part of what we suffered from the French (even before a whimper of complaint escaped from our lips) without declaring war or making reprisals.

This tameness following so close upon the heels of that Revolution which in its origins, its progress, and its conclusion was so strongly marked with irascibility and stubbornness, will naturally excite astonishment in all those who shall read the American history. When they are told of the innumerable and inexpressible injuries and indignities we have received from the French; that this despicable race of beings lorded it over our bays and rivers; and, not content with plundering and chastising our mariners, made them put the seal to their degradation by exacting from them payment for the shot fired at them; when we are told this, and that we bore it all without even talking of revenge, will they not wonder what was become of the men of 1776 who, with the scroll of their imaginary rights in one hand, and the sword in the other, swore to preserve the full enjoyment of the former, or to perish by the latter? And what will be their astonishment when they are told that the greater part of those very men were still living, and were still the rulers of the land?

Were the bold, the undaunted, the haughty language of the first

Congress, in their public remonstrances and addresses, compared with the faltering, the timid, the tame, the humble, the whining tone of the answer to the President's firm and manly speech, what a contrast, great God! would it present!

Mr. Adams's speech seems to be the last gleam of the spirit of the old Whigs. It was his protest against the degradation of his country — as if he had said to the House of Representatives: "I see that you are resolved to blast your reputation and that of America, but you shall not blast mine."

## BENJAMIN FRANKLIN BACHE

*Porcupine's Gazette*, November 14, 1797

This atrocious wretch (worthy descendant of old Ben) knows that all men of any understanding set him down as an abandoned liar, as a tool and a hireling; and he is content that they should do so. He does not want to be thought anything else. As this *Gazette* is honored with many readers in foreign countries, it may not be improper to give them some little account of this miscreant.

If they have read the old hypocrite Franklin's will, they must have observed that part of his library, with some other things, are left to a certain *grandson;* this is the very identical Market-Street scoundrel. He spent several years in hunting offices under the Federal Government, and being constantly rejected, he at last became its most bitter foe. Hence his abuse of General Washington, whom, at the time he was soliciting a place, he panegyrized to the third heaven.

He was born for a hireling, and therefore when he found that he could not obtain employ in one quarter, he sought it in another. The first effect of his paw being greased, appeared soon after Genet's arrival, and he has from that time to this been as faithful to the cut-throats of Paris, as ever dog was to his master.

He is an ill-looking devil. His eyes never get above your knees. He is of a sallow complexion, hollow-cheeked, dead-eyed, and has a *tout ensemble* just like that of a fellow who has been about a week or ten days on a gibbet.

## [THE BENEFITS OF WAR WITH FRANCE]

*Porcupine's Gazette*, January, 1798

Let us see what would be gained by a war. The immediate effect would be, a free passage over the ocean, without the hazard of seizure, or even of examination.

The commerce of America would immediately raise its drooping head; the confidence of commercial men would be reëstablished, and the spirit of trade and enterprise renewed. American seamen would no longer be shot at, and flogged, within sight of their own shores; nor would the red-headed ruffians add to the twenty millions they have already seized: no peace should be made with them till they refund their plunder, which would amply discharge all the debts incurred by the war.

Louisiana they might be compelled to relinquish; and thus would these States be completely rid of the most alarming danger that ever menaced them; and which, if not soon removed, must and will, in a few years, effect their disunion and destruction.

But above all, the alliance with Great Britain would cut up the French faction here. It is my sincere opinion, that they have formed the diabolical plan of *revolutionizing* (to use one of their execrable terms) the whole continent of America. They have their agents and partizans without number, and very often where we do not imagine. Their immoral and blasphemous principles have made a most alarming progress. They have explored the community to its utmost boundaries and its inmost recesses, and have left a partizan on every spot, ready to preach up *the holy right of insurrection.*

They have no intention of invading these States with the fair and avowed purpose of *subjugating them.* No; they will come as they went to the Brabanters and the Dutch, as "friends and deliverers." A single spark of their fraternity would set all the Southern States in a flame, the progress of which, as far as Connecticut, would be as rapid as the chariot of Apollo. This dreadful scourge nothing can prevent but a war. That would naturally disarm and discredit their adherents; would expel their intriguing agents, who are now in our streets, in our houses, and at our tables. It would cut off the cankering, poisonous, *sans-culottes* connexion, and leave the country once more sound and really independent.

## PORCUPINE TO THE PUBLIC

*The Rushlight,* February 24, 1800

When I determined to discontinue the publication of *Porcupine's Gazette*, I intended to remain for the future if not an unconcerned, at least a silent spectator of public transactions and political events; but the unexpected and sweeping result of a lawsuit, since decided against me, has induced me to abandon my lounging intention. The suit to which I allude was an action of slander, commenced against me in the autumn of 1797 by Dr. Benjamin Rush, the noted bleeding physician of Philadelphia. I was tried on the 14th of December last, when "the upright, enlightened, and impartial

Republican jury" assessed, as damages, *five thousand dollars;* a sum surpassing the aggregate amount of all the damages assessed for all the torts of this kind, ever sued for in these States, from their first settlement to the present day. To the five thousand dollars must be added the costs of suit, the loss incurred by the interruption in collecting debts in Pennsylvania, and by the sacrifice of property taken in execution, and sold by the sheriff at public auction in Philadelphia, where a great number of books in sheets (among which was a part of the new edition of Porcupine's Works) were sold, or rather given away, as waste paper; so that the total of what has been, or will be, wrested away from me by Rush, will fall little short of eight thousand dollars.

To say that I do not feel this stroke, and very sensibly too, would be great affectation; but to repine at it would be folly, and to sink under it would be cowardice. I knew an Englishman in the Royal Province of New Brunswick, who had a very valuable house, which was, I believe, at that time nearly his all, burnt to the ground. He was out of town when the fire broke out, and happened to come just after it had exhausted itself. Everyone, knowing how hard he had earned the property, expected to see him bitterly bewail its loss. He came very leisurely up to the spot, stood about five minutes, looking earnestly at the rubbish, and then, stripping off his coat, *"here goes,"* said he, *"to earn another!"* and immediately went to work, raking the spikes and bits of iron out of the ashes. This noble-spirited man I have the honor to call my friend, and if ever this page should meet his eye, he will have the satisfaction to see that, should it be impossible for me to follow, I at least remember his example.

In the future exertions of my industry, however, pecuniary emolument will be, as it always has been with me, an object of only secondary consideration. Recent incidents, amongst which I reckon the unprecedented proceedings against me at Philadelphia, have imposed on me the discharge of a duty which I owe to my own country as well as this, and the sooner I begin the sooner I shall have done.

## NOAH WEBSTER [1]

### Philadelphia *Aurora*, July, 1800

There are some beings whose fate it seems to be to run counter from reason and propriety on all occasions. In every attempt

---

[1] Noah Webster's Dictionary, here derided, was successfully published in 1828 in two large volumes of more than 1,000 pages each, containing many more words and definitions than any previous dictionary of the language, and attaining a new level of the lexicographer's art.

which this oddity of literature has made, he appears not only to have made himself ridiculous, but to have rendered what he attempted to elucidate more obscure, and to injure or deface what he has intended to improve.

His spelling-book has done more injury in the common schools of the country than the genius of ignorance herself could have conceived a hope of, by his ridiculous attempts to alter the *syllable* division of words and to *new model* the spelling, by a capricious but utterly incompetent attempt of his own weak conception.

After involving the question of the yellow fever in deeper obscurity, and producing nothing but the profit by the sale of the work, he now appears as a legislator and municipal magistrate of Connecticut; writes nonsense pseudo-political and pseudo-philosophical for his newspaper at New York, and proposes to give to the American world no less than three dictionaries!

This man, who ought to go to school for the regulation of his understanding, has, it appears, undertaken to complete a *system of education*, and as part of these, we are told, is to give us a dictionary for *schools*, a dictionary for the *counting-house*, and a dictionary for the *learned!*

His motives, for they are truly *Gothic*, it appears are that a number of English words have been misapplied — new words introduced — and a considerable number exploded in America; for this reason he says it is necessary to make a new Dictionary. The plain truth is, for the reason given is preposterous, that he means to *make money* by a scheme which ought to be and will be discountenanced by every man who admires the classic English writers, who has sense enough to see the confusion which must arise from such a silly project — and the incapacity of a man who thus undertakes a work which, if it were at all necessary or eligible, would require the labor of a number of learned and competent men to accomplish it.

## [JEFFERSON BECOMES PRESIDENT]

### New York *American Citizen*, March 13, 1801

*Citizen* Adams arrived in town the day before yesterday on his way to the eastward. No bells were rung, no cannon were fired, no dinner was provided, no toasts were drunk on the occasion. As a citizen he arrived, as a citizen he was received, and as a citizen he was suffered to depart. Is it not mortifying that while Oliver Wolcott, the Secretary, is toasted and idolized, *Citizen* Adams is neglected? How shall we account for this? Mr. Adams is neglected by some for his political inconsistency in treating with France, and by a still greater proportion because he is no longer President.

## [DEMOCRATIC CONTRADICTIONS: MADISON VERSUS JEFFERSON]

New York *Evening Post*, November 23, 1801

To displace a man of high merit, and one who from his station may be supposed a man of extensive influence, will excite jealousies and create an interested opposition in the system, and in the people. He will have his friends, his dependants, and the public sympathy on his side, and if it should not give birth to an impeachment in the legislature, it would probably prove a fatal impeachment before the community at large. Can we suppose that a President of the United States, elected for four years only, dependent on the popular voice, impeachable by the legislature, and not perhaps distinguished in point of wealth or personal talents from the head of the department himself, can we suppose, I say, that in defiance of all these considerations, he will presume wantonly to dismiss a meritorious and virtuous officer from his service? I own it is *an abuse of power* which exceeds my imagination, and of which I can form no rational conception.

*Madison's Speech in Congress.*

How are vacancies to be obtained? Those by death are few, by resignation none. Can any other mode then but removal be proposed? This is a painful office, but it is made my duty, and I meet it as such.

*Jefferson's Reply to the New Haven Remonstrance.*

## [THE HORRID CUSTOM OF DUELLING]

New York *Evening Post*, November 24, 1801

Died, this morning, in the twentieth year of his age, PHILIP HAMILTON, eldest son of General Hamilton — murdered in a duel. As the public will be anxious to know the leading particulars of this deplorable event, we have collected the following, which may be relied upon as correct.

On Friday morning last, young Hamilton and young Price, sitting in the same box with Mr. George I. Eacker, began in levity a conversation respecting an oration delivered by the latter in July, and made use of some expressions respecting it, which were overheard by Eacker, who asked Hamilton to step into the lobby. Price followed. Here the expression, *damned rascal*, was used by

Eacker to one of them, and a little scuffle ensued; but they soon adjourned to a public house. An explanation was then demanded, which of them the offensive expression was meant for; after a little hesitation, it was declared to be meant for each. Eacker then said, as they parted, "I expect to hear from you;" they replied, "You shall;" and challenges followed. A meeting took place, between Eacker and Price, on Sunday morning; which, after their exchanging four shots each, was finished by the interference of the seconds.

Yesterday afternoon, the fatal duel was fought between young Hamilton and Eacker. Hamilton received a shot through the body at the first discharge, and fell without firing. He was brought across the ferry to his father's house, where he languished of the wound till this morning, when he expired.

He was a young man of an amiable disposition and cultivated mind; much esteemed and affectionately beloved by all who had the pleasure of his acquaintance.

Reflections on this horrid custom must occur to every man of humanity; but the voice of an individual or of the press must be ineffectual without additional, strong, and pointed legislative interference. Fashion has placed it upon a footing which nothing short of this can control.

### [MAKING TAMMANY VOTERS WHOLESALE]

New York *Evening Post*, December 15, 1801

Much public attention having been excited by the late election of charter officers, for the fourth and fifth wards of this city, and the scrutiny that succeeded, we have judged that it would be proper to publish a fair and correct statement of those transactions.

By the charter of the city, the aldermen and assistants are to be annually chosen by the freemen being inhabitants, and the freeholders of each respective ward; and by an act of the legislature the freehold must be of the value of $50 over and above all debts charged upon it, and have been possessed (unless acquired by descent or devise) at least one month before the day of such election. The elector is moreover obliged, if called upon for that purpose, to take an oath that he is not under any obligation or promise to convey to any other person after the election.

In the fourth ward, John Bogert and Nicholas Carmer were the federal, and Cornelius C. Roosevelt and Samuel Wendover the anti-federal candidates; and in the fifth ward the federal candidates were James Roosevelt and John P. Ritter, the anti-federal candidates were Arcularius and Drake.

The election according to law was to be held on the seventeenth day of November. But on the tenth day of October, Jasper Ward, a noted zealot of the anti-federal party, purchased from Abraham Bloodgood, the currier, another person of the same description, a lot of ground in the fifth ward, with a currier's shop upon it, at the price of $2,000, and took a conveyance for the same to thirty-nine persons, as tenants in common. On the same day a similar purchase was made in the fourth ward at the price of $3700, and a conveyance made in like manner to seventy-four persons; but the premises were subjected to a mortgage, upon which $1500, besides interest, were due. Both those purchases were clandestinely made for the sole and avowed purpose of procuring qualifications to vote at the next election of charter officers. In the fifth ward thirty-six of the persons named in the first deed, and in the fourth ward seventy-four named in the last, voted at the late election; and by their aid the anti-federal candidates had an apparent majority of six in the fifth, and of thirty-three in the fourth ward.

A scrutiny was demanded and the federal candidates in the fifth ward objected to the votes of the thirty-six persons named as grantees in the deed from Bloodgood, and to about thirty-three more. The federal candidates in the fourth ward at first objected to all the votes not given for themselves, except two; but being called on by the board to declare upon oath, how many they conscientiously believed to be proper subjects of challenge, they gave up one hundred, and then challenged the remainder, being eighty-one.

## [PRESIDENT JEFFERSON'S FIRST ANNUAL MESSAGE] [1]

### New York *Evening Post*, December 18, 1801

Instead of delivering a *speech* to the houses of Congress, at the opening of the present session, the President has thought fit to transmit a *message*. Whether this has proceeded from pride or from humility, from a temperate love of reform or from a wild spirit of innovation, is submitted to the conjectures of the curious. A single observation shall be indulged — since all agree that he is unlike his predecessors in essential points, it is a mark of consistency to differ from them in matters of form.

Whoever considers the temper of the day, must be satisfied that this message is likely to add much to the popularity of our chief magistrate. It conforms, as far as would be tolerated at this early stage of our progress in political perfection, to the bewitching tenets of that illuminated doctrine which promises man, ere long, an emancipation from the burdens and restraints of government;

[1] By William Coleman.

giving a foretaste of that pure felicity which the apostles of that doctrine have predicted. After having, with infinite pains and assiduity, formed the public taste for this species of fare, it is certainly right for those whom the people have chosen for their caterers to be attentive to the gratification of that taste. And should the viands which they offer prove baneful poisons instead of wholesome ailments, the justification is both plain and easy — *Good patriots must, at all events, please the people.* But those whose patriotism is of the old school, who differ so widely from the disciples of the new creed that they would rather risk incurring the displeasure of the people by speaking unpalatable truths, than betray their interest by fostering their prejudices, will never be deterred by an impure tide of popular opinion from honestly pointing out the mistakes or the faults of weak or wicked men, who may have been selected as guardians of the public weal.

The message of the President, by whatever motives it may have been dictated, is a performance which ought to alarm all who are anxious for the safety of our government, for the respectability and welfare of our nation. It makes, or aims at making, a most prodigal sacrifice of constitutional energy, of sound principle, and of public interest, to the popularity of one man.

## THE DEATH OF HAMILTON [1]

### Philadelphia *Political Register*, July 13, 1804

The mail from New York of this morning confirms the melancholy, the heart-rending intelligence of the DEATH of General Hamilton. The mourning countenance of our citizens — the anguish of his friends — the tears of his countrymen, proclaim their sense of his worth, and offer a just tribute of gratitude to his memory. To the honor of our character, let it be recorded, that those who entertained unceasing jealousy of his superior powers, while living — with honorable feeling lament him dead. After Washington (who alone surpassed him), after the first of men and greatest of heroes, who has rivalled Hamilton in usefulness to our country? — in attachment to its interests? in unceasing labour, in the exertion of the most splendid talents for its welfare? The generous and gallant soldier, the wise and virtuous statesman, the eloquent and accomplished orator, the ardent and magnanimous patriot, has fallen the victim of unyielding honor, and inflexible integrity.

His memory is embalmed in the esteem and affection of his con-

[1] By a fellow-soldier of Hamilton in the Revolution, Major Jackson. Its abstention from criticism of the custom of duelling, in contrast with the previous editorial, and from censure of Aaron Burr, are noteworthy.

temporaries, and will be consecrated by the gratitude of his country to future ages.

Thus has fallen, prematurely fallen, the Hero, to whose military ardor and accomplishments America confessed the highest obligation; the Civilian, from whose luminous and correct mind proceeded that invaluable commentary on the Constitution of the United States, which essentially contributed to secure its adoption; the Statesman, to whose talents we are indebted for the organization of our finances, and the establishment of our public credit; the Jurist and the Scholar, whose combination of intellectual powers formed the boast and ornament of our country; the Patriot, who gave, with glowing zeal, to that country, the increasing efforts of his superior mind; and the Man who, endeared to his friends by every tender and ennobled quality of the heart, received in return the truest affection, and the most respectful esteem.

## POLITICS FOR FARMERS: [THE FATUOUS CRY FOR WAR] [1]

Philadelphia *Aurora*, January, 1807

Foreign governments, whose institutions and interests are dissimilar from ours, *envy us, and endeavor to disturb our repose.*

Nations whose policy is a combination of commercial monopoly and war, to maintain that monopoly, look upon the United States as other sects look upon the *Quakers* — with *jealousy* — because our *Quaker policy* exempts us from all the variety of evils to which the *savage* and unchristian policy of war exposes them.

Our policy, so salutary for our own people, like all human things, admits of an alloy; it tempts numbers from those foreign governments to come hither merely for a temporary term — to profit by our policy, and being enriched, to go away; these persons spread through our seaports, with the various habits of their own citizen nations, and contaminate many of our own citizens.

Many of our citizens educated in the prejudices of the government which ruled us as colonies, still retain their early attachment and prejudices, and even the most peaceful sect exhibits too many examples of the blunders of prejudice which can maintain a *religious* and a *political* sentiment at variance, and destructive one of another.

A disposition is evident in many to be discontented with a calm and tranquil prosperity; and a solicitude in others to bow down the necks of their fellow citizens, over whom they fancy they possess

[1] By William Duane.

either greater talents or greater riches, which conveys to them a more important idea than talents, genius, or virtue.

Many persons educated after the prejudices and habits of foreign cities, and hostile to the simplicity and equality of a free state, become speculators in commerce and repay their commercial credits by infidelity to their country.

These various classes of men are wrought upon by foreign agents and emissaries — several in the receipt of *stipends* from foreign governments; numerous presses are indirectly bribed and kept in pay by mercantile and consular favor for the purpose of influencing our people, and forming interests, either to retard the growth of our own nation to maturity, or to create interests and alliances with foreign governments.

It is from these various and other subordinate sources that we hear the cry *for war — naval establishments —* and extravagant systems.

## THE RESPONSIBILITY FOR THE BRITISH OUTRAGE [1]

Washington *National Intelligencer*, July 10, 1807

We are pleased to observe the circumspection of the merchants. If they consult their own interests, or that of the country, they will for a time repress their spirit of adventure, and run as few risks as possible, until an explicit answer shall be given by the British Ministry. As yet it remains a point undetermined whether the late barbarous outrages have emanated directly from the British Cabinet, or are the acts exclusively of subordinate commanders. If they are directly authorized by the Cabinet, then we may calculate upon a scene of violence co-extensive with British power, and for another display of that perfidy so characteristic of its government. Every American vessel on the ocean will be seized and sent into some British port for adjudication, and the courts will take special care, if they do not forthwith proceed to condemnation, at any rate to keep the cases *sub judice*. Indeed, if the recent outrages do not emanate from the government, it is difficult to say whether they will not, notwithstanding, seize what they may consider a favorable opportunity to wreak their vengeance on this country. We know the hostility of the greater part of those who compose the British administration to our principles, and they may be Quixotic enough to imagine themselves able to crush these principles, or seriously arrest our commercial growth. They may, therefore, under some hollow pretext, refuse that satisfaction which we de-

[1] By Samuel Harrison Smith, the young editor whom Jefferson advised to remove from Philadelphia to Washington; his paper had by this date become the official organ of the Administration.

mand, the result of which will be war.    There is indeed no small color of truth in the supposition that this outrage has flowed from the change in the British Ministry, connected with the fate the treaty has received from our government, and that without meaning or expecting war, they have virtually authorized aggressions on us, which they fancied we would tamely submit to; and that however astonished they may be with the manifestation they will soon receive of the temper of the nation, their pride may prevent them from retracting.

Everything is, and must for some time remain, uncertain.    In the meantime it becomes our duty to husband all our strength.    But little injury can accrue to the merchant from a suspension of his export business for a few months, compared with the incalculable evils that might befall him from its active prosecution.    He is, therefore, under a double obligation to pursue this course, arising not only from a regard to his own interest, but likewise from a love of his country.    In the day of danger it will want all its resources, and all its seamen.    Were Congress in session, it is extremely probable that their first step would be the imposition of an embargo.    What they would do, were they sitting, it is the interest and duty of the merchant to do himself.    We have no doubt that the intelligence of this order of men may on this occasion, as it has on all former occasions, be relied on.

## [THE *CHESAPEAKE* AND THE *LEOPARD*]

### Washington *Federalist*, July 3, 1807

We have never, on any occasion, witnessed the spirit of the people excited to so great a degree of indignation, or such a thirst for revenge, as on hearing of the late unexampled outrage on the *Chesapeake*.    All parties, ranks, and professions were unanimous in their detestation of the dastardly deed, and all cried aloud for vengeance. The accounts which we receive from every quarter tend to show that these sentiments universally prevail.    The Administration may implicitly rely on the cordial support of every American citizen, in whatever manly and dignified steps they may take, to resent the insult and obtain reparation for the injury.

### New York *Evening Post*, July 24, 1807

We say and we once more repeat it, that the *Chesapeake, being a national ship,* was not liable to be searched for any purpose, nor to have any of her crew taken from her.    This is ground that ought to be maintained at every hazard.    But on the other hand, candor demands the concession, that it was in every way improper in the

American commodore to enlist four deserters from the British man of war, *knowing them to be such;* and whether they were English subjects, or had voluntarily enlisted and received their bounty (this being a conduct long since silently permitted by us), is immaterial. And we say further that if the Administration, on being applied to by the English consul, refused to accommodate the affair, but insisted on protecting the men by placing them under the national flag, the Administration thereby became criminal, and are answerable to the people for their culpable conduct.

Such are the sentiments we hold on this subject: they have been often revised, and are believed to be correct.

The result is that our own Administration are considered as having been to blame; but not so that their misconduct justified the resort to force on the part of the English. On this point, we are ready to say that we consider the national sovereignty has been attacked, the national honor tarnished, and that ample reparations and satisfaction must be given or that war ought to be resorted to by force of arms.

## [THE EVILS OF THE EMBARGO] [1]

*Columbian Centinel,* January 23, 1808

Since the promulgation of the British Order in Council — which has certainly been expected ever since the neutral nations have refused to resent or remonstrate against the abominable and unprecedented decrees of France — some men think the embargo not so bad a measure! Does not this betray a want of calculation? Let the following facts reply:

1. France cannot endanger our trade to England more than to the amount of about four or five per cent. Of course the embargo is not necessary against her.

2. Great Britain leaves open to us: —

Her own dominions and colonies throughout the world, to which we now export twenty-six millions per annum.

She relaxes her great Navigation Act in our favor.

She leaves open to us our trade to the colonies of France, Spain, and Holland, which will take off ten millions more of our produce.

She permits to us the free import of all our West India produce, which will still give us revenue and luxuries.

We can pursue the Russian, Swedish, African, and much of the Mediterranean trade; as well as all our India and China trade.

We can export all our present produce, and a very considerable part of our foreign importations.

[1] The Embargo Act, detested by such New England journals as the *Centinel,* was passed in December, 1807, and repealed March 1, 1809. The Federalists of New England and New York assailed it as a diabolical scheme to ruin the North while the South stood unharmed.

Is not this better than an embargo, which destroys all trade, all revenue, all employment? Let those who think it is not, discuss the subject; and they will find that this British decree, bad as it is, is not by far so bad as it was reported to be

## [THE EMBARGO AND THE FARMER'S STORY]

*Columbian Centinel*, May 25, 1808

A zealous Boston Democrat was lately in the country extolling the embargo to a plain farmer, as a wise as well as a strong measure, and urging the farmer to express his opinion upon it. The farmer, however, modestly declined, saying that he lived in the bush where he had not the means of information on which to ground an opinion on political measures; but if Boston folks, who knew more, said it was right, he supposed it was so; but, says he, I will tell you a story. Our minister one day sent his boy to the pasture after a horse. He was gone so long that the parson was afraid the horse had kicked his brains out; he went therefore with anxiety to look after him. In the field he found the boy standing still with his eyes steadily fixed upon the ground. His master inquired with severity what he was doing there. Why, sir, said he, I saw a woodchuck run into this hole, and so I thought I would stand and watch for him until he was starved out; but *I declare I am almost starved to death myself.*

## [HATEFUL MEASURES FOR ENFORCING THE EMBARGO]

Boston *Gazette*, February 2, 1809

Within a few days past Colonel Boyd, commanding at the Castle, received orders from the Secretary of War to interdict all vessels from passing Fort Independence; in consequence of this edict the acting Collector has been placed under the necessity of withholding clearances to every description of vessels.

This aggravated repression was not generally known until yesterday, when the vessels in the harbor bound their colors in black, and hoisted them half-mast. The circumstance has created some considerable agitation in the public mind, but to the honor of the town has been yet unattended with any serious consequences.

It is to be presumed that this new edict will at least continue to be enforced until Secretary Dearborn is at leisure to come on, to mark out his favorites, and take upon himself the office, so long reserved for him, of the Customs.

The spirit of our citizens is rising and may burst into a flame. Everything should therefore be done to calm them till the Legislature has had time to mature its plans of redress. It is feared that the caution necessary in such an assembly may protract our relief too long; but we must wait patiently the aid of our *Constitutional Guardians*, rather than stain the character of this metropolis by mobs and riots. If our government cannot do anything now that shall afford full and complete relief, they may at least do enough to calm the public mind and lead the citizens to wait for events, which must place the means for a radical cure completely in our hands.

The spirit of New England is slow in rising; but when once inflamed by oppression, it will never be repressed by anything short of complete *justice*.

## THE EMBARGO EXPERIMENT ENDED[1]

Baltimore *Federal Republican*, March, 1809

The embargo now ceases to be in force, and every merchant who can give a bond with good sureties to double the amount of vessel and cargo, is entitled to clear out for any port except in France or England or the dependency of either of them. After depriving government of its means of support for sixteen months, and preventing the people of the United States from pursuing a lawful and profitable commerce, and reducing the whole country to a state of wretchedness and poverty, our infatuated rulers, blinded by a corrupt predilection for France, have been forced to acknowledge their fatal error, and so far to retrace their steps. To the patriotism of the New England States is due the praise of our salvation. By their courage and virtue have we been saved from entanglements in a fatal alliance with France. The whole system of fraud and corruption has been exposed to the people, and those very men who were the first to cast off the yoke of England, have lived to save their country from falling under the command of a more cruel tyrant. The patriot who had the courage to encounter the fury of the political storm, who stepped forth in the hour of danger to give the first alarm to his country, we trust will one day be rewarded with the highest honors in the gift of a grateful people.

[1] The Republican caucus in Congress decided on February 7, 1809, in favor of dropping the embargo and returning to the old non-intercourse plan. President Jefferson signed the repeal on March 1, just before he left office. The opposition "patriot" to whom the Baltimore *Republican* refers was Senator Timothy Pickering of Massachusetts.

## EX-PRESIDENT ADAMS ON NATIONAL UNITY AND FOREIGN AFFAIRS [1]

*Columbian Centinel,* March 25, 1809

The Democrats have attempted to make much electioneering use of their old friend the late President Adams. For nearly a year past they have put their wits in requisition to extract something from the venerable patriot which should serve them as a lift. Numerous demagogues were selected to write to him, to send him pamphlets, and to ask his advice on public affairs; knowing that politeness, etiquette, and habit would induce him to answer them. The mere correspondence they knew would *tell* something; but their chief hope was that good use might be made, at a proper time, of mutilated parts of the answer, and perhaps the escape of a hasty or unguarded expression. Though the impudence of this attempt was without parallel in the annals of Machiavellism, yet as the case was desperate, the attempt must be made. It did not deter these Democratic demagogues that they and the world well knew that only four or five short years ago they themselves, and their hirelings, had branded this same John Adams — this *new* correspondent — with every invective which the lexicography of hatred, malice, and billingsgate could furnish; that he was by them unblushingly proclaimed a "hoary-headed traitor"; an upstart tyrant, the son of a shoemaker, who wished to lord it over an American heritage; whose aim *totis viribus* was to introduce Monarchy, Aristocracy, and Slavery into the United States; who for this purpose was the father of the Alien and Sedition laws, the introducer of a standing army, excise and land taxes, and of eight per cent loans; that he, John Adams, had sold himself to Great Britain; that he had defended, in a book written for the purpose, a government of kings, lords, and commons; and that he was the venal tool of the British Ministry. Nay more, these demagogues knew that there was no epithet too degrading which they had not applied to this same Mr. John Adams; and that of the nicknames they had bestowed on him, that of the "French War-Hawk," "Duke of Braintree," and "skulking, crazy John" were not the most opprobrious. A record of these scurrilities, and of many others, will be found in the files of the Democratic papers.

The new correspondence between Mr. Adams and these demagogues was at first heard of only in rumors and privately shewn to confidential persons. Not one of the old friends of the President

---

[1] By Benjamin Russell, the stout Federalist who had founded the *Centinel* in 1784, and kept it for more than thirty years the leading Boston newspaper, and one of the greatest of the Federalist organs. His arguments against the Embargo were warmly applauded throughout New England.

who had supported him through thick and thin was allowed to take a peep at them.   It was thought not quite up to the mark for general publication, and was, perhaps, too strongly tinctured with old-fashioned political morality.   Still the names of John Adams and the Embargo were linked together, and capitalized in many a caucus resolution.   But the approaching election called for something to cheer up the drooping spirits of Democracy;  and two of the Hampshire County managers were selected to write to Mr. Adams and request an answer.   The answer was prompt, but only extracts from it have been permitted to meet the public eye.   The extracts follow:

Quincy, March 13, 1809.

Gentlemen:

I have received your very civil letter of the third of this month with emotions very similar to those which I felt many years ago.

I have neither power nor influence to do anything for my country, to assist her in her present distresses, or guard her against future calamities.   Nothing now remains to me but the right of private judgment, and that I exercise freely, and communicate my sentiments as freely to those who wish to know them.

I am *totis viribus* against any division of the Union, by the North River, or by Delaware River, or by the Potomac, or any other river, or by any chain of mountains.   I am for maintaining the independence of the nation at all events. [1]

I am no advocate for Mr. Gore's declaration of war against France.   Knowing as I do from personal experience the mutually friendly dispositions between the people of France and the people of America, Bonaparte out of the question, I should be very sorry to see them converted into ill-will, and our old English prejudices revived.   Lasting injuries and misfortunes would arise to this country from such a change. [2]

I am averse also to a war with England, and wish to maintain our neutrality as long as possible, without conceding important principles.   If either of the belligerent powers force us into a war, I am for fighting that power, whichever it may be. [3]

I always consider the whole nation as my children: but they have almost all been undutiful to me.   You two gentlemen are almost the only ones, out of my own house, who have for a long time, and I thank you for it, expressed a filial affection for

JOHN ADAMS. [4]

(1) And who, pray, has ever advocated a dissolution of the Union, excepting indeed Mr. Giles and some other Virginia demagogues during Mr. Adams's Administration?   We do not know why this remark was lugged in here.   But we defy anyone to produce

a single act adopted, or a single line written by any Federalist, in which a dissolution of the Union has been threatened or advocated. The idea is an absurdity; and the charge one of the most contemptible ever propagated. We appeal to the hundreds of spirited resolutions of the people of New England recently adopted in their primary assemblies; to the resolutions, reports, and addresses of the legislature of Massachusetts for proof of the attachment of the Federalists to the union and independence of the United States.

(2) What does all this mean? Can it be possible that Mr. Adams has adopted the newspaper slang of the day — "Mr. Gore's declaration of War"? O tempora! O mores! The legislature appointed a large committee to report on a certain subject; Mr. Gore signed the report as chairman. The report was in favor of a repeal of the embargo laws, and as the Democrats demanded a substitute, for they insisted upon war or embargo, the report recommended the entire repeal of the embargo laws; and if we must have war with one of the European aggressors, it ought to be with France, who was first aggressor and the enemy likely to do us the least harm. This opinion was not merely that of the committee and Mr. Gore as one of them, but of the Legislature and the people at large. At the town meeting in Boston Mr. Eustis, now Secretary of War, and Mr. Blake, both declared not merely that if war was made it ought to be with France, but that we ought to, and should be, at war with France. Thousands heard and can remember this declaration.

(3) Mr. Adams's aversion to war seems to be among the new doctrines he has embraced. Does he recollect the answer he gave to the young men of Boston in 1798–1799? "*To arms, my young friends, to arms!*" We have not the files before us to copy the war articles of those days. But the language is rather of a different nature from the present, though a war then would have been made against the French people themselves; whereas a war now would be against the Tyrant who governs them.

(4) We have heretofore preserved an unabated respect for the character of the late President. But we must say that thus to lend himself to a party which has loaded him with their execrations and charges, and which he has repeatedly denounced as the worst enemies of their country, solely to serve *electioneering purposes*, is a degradation of conduct unworthy a statesman and a philosopher; and which must blast his fame to all posterity. We say nothing of gratitude due his old friends, and particularly to Mr. Gore, who never injured him in thought, word, or deed.[1]

---

[1] Both John Adams and John Quincy Adams were bitterly opposed to England in these years, denouncing her interferences with neutral trade. Their support of the embargo aroused all Federalist New England against them.

## [FRENCH OUTRAGES AGAINST OUR SHIPS AND SAILORS][1]

### New York *Evening Post*, July, 1809

Fellow Citizens, for more than two years has your flag been struck on the ocean whenever it has been met with by the flag of France; your vessels have been scornfully burnt or scuttled in the ocean; your property has been seized or confiscated; your sailors robbed and manacled, or forced by cruelties to serve against their own country; the worthless part of them suborned by a public decree to commit perjury, and on their evidence, though charging no crime, the wretched remainder of the crew condemned as prisoners of war, landed as such and marched without shoes to their feet or clothing to their backs in the most inclement weather some hundreds of miles into the interior of France; lashed along the highway like slaves, treated with every possible indignity, and then immured in the infernal dungeons of Arras or Verdun. There, deprived of every comfort and of all intercourse with the rest of the world, there, fellow citizens, have they been lying, some for months and some for years! There they now lie, wasting away the best vigor of their days, counting the hours of their captivity as they turn in vain their imploring eyes towards their own government, and etching down another and another week of grief and despondence. Nineteen cents a day allowed them for subsistence and clothing and medicine! Allow them seven a day, or $25 a year for clothing, and you leave them four cents to purchase each meal. Think of this, ye who live in luxury here, and read their story with more indifference than you listen to the fictitious sorrows of a Robinson Crusoe; think of this, and let it at length engage your attention, and induce you to demand of your government to interfere in earnest.

But after all, what is to be expected? If any one of these wretched men, more fortunate than his fellow sufferers, escapes and brings the tale of their situation, and makes it known to his countrymen, a set of inhuman wretches here, more cruel than the French themselves, turn their wrongs into derision, or exert their miserable faculties in cavillings and criticisms to shew that all these statements are fabrications, because they have not been drawn up by some special pleader. The barbarous impudence of some editors pronounces them forgeries, and every fellow who can set a type repeats the infamous calumny, till the public voice that had begun to raise itself in their favor is stilled, and sympathy extinguished.

---

[1] Under the Bayonne Decree of April 17, 1808, the Napoleonic Government seized many American ships and imprisoned their men, and French frigates even sank American ships at sea.

## [THE FOLLY OF JOINING THE ARMY] [1]

New York *Evening Post*, January 24, 1812

"*Tricks upon Travellers*," or "*More Ways than one to kill a Cat.*" — Old saws. We are certainly now to have a war, for Congress have voted to have an army. But let me tell you, there is all the difference in the world between an army on paper, and an army in the field. An army on paper is voted in a whiff, but to raise an army, you must offer men good wages. The wages proposed to be given to induce men to come forward and enlist for five years, leave their homes and march away to take Canada, is a bounty of $16, and $5 a month; and at the end of the war, if they can get a certificate of good behavior, 160 acres of wild land and three months' pay; for the purpose, I presume, of enabling the soldier to walk off and find it, if he can. Now I should really be glad to be informed, whether it is seriously expected that, in a country where a stout able-bodied man can earn $15 a month from May to November, and a dollar a day during mowing and harvesting, he will go into the army for a bounty of $16, $5 a month for five years, if the war should last so long, and 160 acres of wild land, if he happens to be on such good terms with his commanding officer as to obtain a certificate of good behavior? Let the public judge if such inducements as these will ever raise an army of 25,000 men, or ever were seriously expected to do it? If not, can anything be meant more than "sound and fury signifying nothing"? This may be called humbugging on a large scale.

## [THEY CALL IT A WAR FOR COMMERCE!]

New York *Evening Post*, January 26, 1812

*Look for yourselves, good people all.* — The administration tell me that the object for which they are going to war with Great Britain, is to secure our commercial rights; to put the trade of the country on a good footing; to enable our merchants to deal with Great Britain on full as favorable terms as they deal with France, or else not deal at all. Such is the declared object for which all further intercourse is to be suspended with Great Britain and her allies, while we proceed to make war upon her and them until we compel her to pay more respect to American commerce: and, as Mr. Stow truly observed in his late excellent speech, the anxiety of members of Congress to effect this object is always the greater in proportion

---

[1] By William Coleman; his efforts to prevent army enlistments and subscriptions to the national loan on the eve of the War of 1812 explain why he and his newspaper were threatened with mob attack.

to the distance any honorable member lives from the seaboard.  To
enable you, good people, to judge for yourselves, I have only to
beg of you to turn your eyes to Mr. Gallatin's letter in a succeeding
column, stating the amount of the exports of the United States for
the last year [actually the year ending October 1, 1811]; the
particular country to which these exports were sent, and specifying
the amount received from us by each.  If you will just cast a glance
at this document, you will find of the articles of our own growth
or manufactures we in that time carried or sent abroad (in round
numbers) no less than $45,294,000 worth.  You will next find that
out of this sum, all the rest of the world (Great Britain and her allies
excepted) took about $7,719,366, and that Great Britain and her
allies took the remainder, amounting to $38,575,627.  Now, after this,
let me ask you what you think of making war upon Great Britain
and her allies, for the purpose of benefiting commerce?

## [WAR SHOULD BE DECLARED]

### Washington *National Intelligencer*, April 14, 1812

The public attention has been drawn to the approaching arrival
of the *Hornet*, as a period when the measures of our government
would take a decisive character, or rather their final cast.  We are
among those who have attached to this event a high degree of
importance, and have therefore looked to it with the utmost solicitude.

But if the reports which we now hear are true, that with England
all hope of honorable accommodation is at an end, and that with
France our negotiations are in a forwardness encouraging expecta-
tions of a favorable result, where is the motive for longer delay?
The final step ought to be taken, and that step is WAR.  *By what
course of measures we have reached the present crisis, is not now a question
for patriots and freemen to discuss.*  It exists: and it is by open and manly
war only that we can get through it with honor and advantage to
the country.  Our wrongs have been great; our cause is just; and
if we are decided and firm, success is inevitable.

Let war therefore be forthwith proclaimed against England.
With her there can be no motive for delay. Any further discussion,
any new attempt at negotiation, would be as fruitless as it would
be dishonorable.  With France we shall be at liberty to pursue the
course which circumstances may require.  The advance she has
already made by a repeal of her decrees; the manner of its reception by the government, and the prospect which exists of an amicable
accommodation, entitle her to this preference.  If she acquits herself to the just claims of the United States, we shall have good cause

to applaud our conduct in it, and if she fails we shall always be in time to place her on the ground of her adversary.

But it is said that we are not prepared for war, and ought therefore not to declare it. This is an idle objection, which can have weight with the timid and pusillanimous only. The fact is otherwise. Our preparations are adequate to every essential object. Do we apprehend danger to ourselves? From what quarter will it assail us? From England, and by invasion? The idea is too absurd to merit a moment's consideration. Where are her troops? But lately she dreaded an invasion of her own dominions from her powerful and menacing neighbor. That danger, it is true, has diminished, but it has not entirely and forever disappeared. The war in the Peninsula, which lingers, requires strong armies to support it. She maintains an army in Sicily; another in India; and a strong force in Ireland, and along her own coast, and in the West Indies. Can anyone believe that, under such circumstances, the British government could be so infatuated as to send troops here for the purpose of invasion? The experience and the fortune of our Revolution, when we were comparatively in an infant state, have doubtless taught her a useful lesson that she cannot have forgotten. Since that period our population has increased threefold, whilst hers has remained almost stationary. The condition of the civilized world, too, has changed. Although Great Britain has nothing to fear as to her independence, and her military operations are extensive and distant, the contest is evidently maintained by her rather for safety than for conquest. Have we cause to dread an attack from her neighboring provinces? That apprehension is still more groundless. Seven or eight millions of people have nothing to dread from 300,000. From the moment that war is declared, the British colonies will be put on the defensive. and soon after we get in motion must sink under the pressure.

## AN ADDRESS TO THE PEOPLE OF THE EASTERN STATES

New York *Evening Post*, April 21, 1812

In a war with England we shall need numerous armies and ample treasuries for their support. The war-hounds that are howling for war through the continent are not to be the men who are to force entrenchments, and scale ramparts against the bayonet and the cannon's mouth; to perish in sickly camps, or in long marches through sultry heats or wastes of snow. These gowned warriors, who are so loudly seconded by a set of fiery spirits in the great towns, and by a set of office hunters in the country, expect that their influence with the great body of the people, the honest yeomanry of our country, is such that every farmer, every mechanic, every laborer, will send off his sons, nay, will even shoulder his firelock himself and march to the field of blood. While these *brave men* who are "designing or exhorting glorious war," lodged safe at Monticello or some other secure retreat, will *direct and look on;* and will receive such pay for their services as they shall see fit to ask, and such as will answer their purposes.

Citizens, if pecuniary redress is your object in going to war with England, the measure is perfect madness. You will lose millions when you will gain a cent. The expense will be enormous. It will ruin our country. Direct taxes must be resorted to. The people will have nothing to pay. We once had a revenue; — that has been destroyed in the destruction of our commerce. For several years past you have been deceived and abused by the false pretenses of a full treasury. That phantom of hope will soon vanish. You have lately seen fifteen millions of dollars wasted in the purchase of a province we did not want, and never shall possess. And will you spend thousands of millions in conquering a province which, were it made a present to us, would not be worth accepting? Our territories are already too large. The desire to annex Canada to the United States is as base an ambition as ever burned in the bosom of Alexander. What benefit will it ever be to the great body of the people, after their wealth is exhausted, and their best blood is shed in its reduction? — "We wish to clear our continent of foreign powers." So did the *Madman* of Macedon wish to clear the world of his enemies, and such as would not bow to his sceptre. So does Bonaparte wish to clear Europe of all his enemies; yea, and Asia too. Canada, if annexed to the United States, will furnish offices to a set of hungry villains, grown quite too numerous for our present wide limits; and that is *all* the benefit we ever shall derive from it.

These remarks will have little weight with men whose interest leads them to advocate war. Thousands of lives, millions of money, the flames of cities, the tears of widows and orphans, with *them* are light expedients when they lead to wealth and power. But to the people who must fight, if fighting must be done, — who must pay if money be wanted — who must march when the trumpet sounds, and who must die when the "battle bleeds," — to the people I appeal. To them the warning voice is lifted. From a war they are to expect nothing but expenses and sufferings; — expenses disproportionate to their means, and sufferings lasting as life.

In our extensive shores and numerous seaports, we know not where the enemy will strike; or more properly speaking, we know they will strike when a station is defenceless. Their fleets will hover on our coasts, and can trace our line from Maine to New Orleans in a few weeks. *Gunboats* cannot repel them, nor is there a fort on all our shores in which confidence can be placed. The ruin of our seaports and loss of all vessels will form an item in the list of expenses. Fortifications and garrisons numerous and strong must be added. As to the main points of attack or defence, I shall only say that an efficient force will be necessary. A handful of men cannot *run up* and take Canada, in a few weeks, for mere diversion. The conflict will be long and severe: resistance formidable, and the final result doubtful. A nation that can debar the conqueror of Europe from the sea, and resist his armies in Spain, will not surrender its provinces without a struggle. Those who advocate a British war must be perfectly aware that the whole revenue arising from all British America for the ensuing century would not repay the expenses of that war.

## THE GALLATIN LOAN

New York *Evening Post*, April 28, 1812

It has been whispered that two or three merchants here have expressed an inclination to dabble in the Gallatin loan. If so, I dare say these gentlemen know how to calculate better than I do; six per cent they doubtless find to be a good premium, although they can now purchase government six per cent stock at three per cent under par. As to the security, those who subscribe must be such friends of the Administration as to advance their money without even thinking of that. Not a cent of revenue is pledged, and for a very good reason; they have none to pledge. But even if they had pledged it, will it not be as easy to destroy the pledge whenever they please, as it was for the same party to destroy the excise after it had been solemnly pledged to the public creditors under the Washington Administration? As it will very much depend on the filling up of this loan whether we shall or shall not go to war, it is evident that no man who is averse to that calamity can ever, consistently, lend his assistance to enable the government to plunge us into it. Let those who are for war subscribe — let those who dread it avoid doing so, as they value all they hold dear.

## [THE SURRENDER OF HULL AT DETROIT]

New York *Evening Post*, August 31, 1812

On the disgraceful and deplorable results of our first military efforts in Canada, we are not in a temper to say much. How much soever we deprecated this ruinous war at the outset; however satisfied we were that the whole plan of the campaign was miserably imbecile and must be utterly inefficient — yet such a catastrophe as is just announced was beyond our most gloomy apprehensions. Mr. Madison, Mr. Gallatin, Dr. Eustis, and Dr. Hamilton, it was evident, must be utterly unequal to cope with the experienced veteran British officers in Canada. And when, besides this disheartening fact, we beheld how small a force was relied upon, what could reasonable men feel but despair? With inferior numbers and inferior skill, the odds were fearful indeed.

Yet we did not expect so deep a stain upon our country's character.[1] A nation, counting eight millions of souls, deliberating and planning for a whole winter and spring and part of a summer, the invasion and conquest of a neighboring province; at length making that invasion; and in one month its army retiring — captured — and captured almost without firing a gun! Miserably deficient in practical talent must that Administration be which formed the plan of that invasion; or the army which has thus surrendered must be a gang of more cowardly poltroons than ever disgraced a country. A parallel to this melancholy defeat is not to be found in all history. But we do not, we cannot brand our countrymen in General Hull's army with cowardice. We shall not till we are compelled. For when were Americans known to shrink from danger? — when have they not been heroes? But the folly, the weakness, the utter incapacity of our Administration to conduct affairs of difficulty to a successful issue, has not only been the tedious theme of many an appeal to our fellow-citizens, but is felt in the privations and distresses of almost every man, woman, and child in this once happy and prosperous country. And he who can longer doubt that incapacity, would not believe though one should rise from the dead.

What! March an army *into* a country where there were not more than seven or eight hundred soldiers to oppose them, and not make the army large enough! March them *from* a country which is the granary of the world, and let them famish on the very frontiers for want of provisions! Issue a gasconading proclamation threatening to exterminate the enemy, and surrender your whole army to them! If there be judgment in this people, they will see the utter unfitness of our rulers for anything beyond management, intrigue, and electioneering. They have talents enough to inflame a misguided populace against their best friends; but they cannot protect the nation from insult and disgrace. They have talents enough to persecute the pupils and disciples of Washington, but not to meet the enemies whom they have called into the field. "Woe to the people whose King is a child!"

[1] General William Hull marched into Canada with a small American army, laid siege to Malden, hastily retreated to Detroit when British reinforcements approached, and on August 16, 1812, ignominiously surrendered his whole army.

## THE *CONSTITUTION* AND THE *GUERRIERE*

New York *Evening Post*, September 2, 1812

After the gloomy accounts which have crowded upon us for some days past, we are happy to be able this day to give our readers something in favor of the courage and activity of our countrymen. We have always contended that our people would fight whenever they should have a chance, and that on an equal footing they would be beaten by no men on earth; the naval action, the particulars of which we publish this day, proves our assertion. Captain Hull, who has immortalized himself in the capture of the *Guerriere*, is a relation of General Hull, who has been sacrificed by an imbecile Administration on the borders of Canada. We have no doubt that General Hull would have fought as manfully as his kinsman, and that the result would have been as favorable, had he been placed in a situation where there had been the least chance of success; but without provisions or munitions of war, what could be done against a veteran and well-appointed army?

Though very little present benefit is to be expected from the war, commenced as it *has been* and carried on as it *will be*, under the present Administration, yet it may have one good effect: it will prove that in a contest where the *freedom of the seas* is the object, a naval force is much superior to an army on the land. It will prove what the Federalists have always advocated, and what the present ruling party have always opposed, the necessity of a maritime force to a commercial people. It will in fact settle the question practically which has so often been debated in our councils, whether a nation can exist as a powerful maritime nation without a well-appointed navy?

We shall not attempt to heap applauses upon Captain Hull and his gallant crew; after what they have achieved, our approbation can be of but little use to them. The thing shows for itself: it shows that man to man and gun to gun, even the veteran British tars can get no advantage over the Americans.

## [THE BLAME FOR HULL'S SURRENDER: TWO VIEWS] [1]

Washington *National Intelligencer*, September 3, 1812

The government is not as yet, that we are informed, in possession of any official advices relating to the disaster which seems to have befallen our Northwestern army. The rumor of it has struck every-

[1] By either William Seaton or Joseph Gales, who had taken over the *National Intelligencer* and kept it the Administration organ under Madison and Monroe as it had been under Jefferson.

one here, as it must everywhere, with astonishment. That at the moment the country was looking with the best-founded and most justified hope for the intelligence of the success of our arms in that quarter, we should hear of defeat — of the total surrender of an army of 2,500 men without a battle — probably without firing a gun — to a force not greater, perhaps much less, than its own, is equally extraordinary and mysterious. It might, perhaps, be premature, in us, at such a moment as this, to hazard any opinion on an event so vitally important to the character of the commanding general; but we share largely in the public astonishment which manifests itself upon the occasion. A very little time must unravel the cause of this utterly unexpected reverse. We think we do not misunderstand the character of that army when we say it was abundantly strong under every calculation of safety and prudence, and in the previous estimation of the general himself, for the contemplated objects of the expedition on which it set out; that it was also abundantly supplied with every requisite of ammunition, arms, stores, provisions, to secure, under judicious and prompt movements, all the advantages that were looked to from its march.

New York *Evening Post*, September 5, 1812[1]

The government gazette has, at last, published the articles of capitulation by which General Hull surrendered himself and his army to the British. It will be seen by the editorial article which we copy from the same paper that the Administration intend to shift the disgrace of this shameful affair from their own shoulders to those of General Hull and his abused officers and men. The *Intelligencer* says the army was "abundantly strong for the contemplated objects of the expedition on which it set out; that it was also abundantly supplied with every requisite of ammunition, arms, stores, and provisions, to secure, under judicious and prompt movements, all the advantages that were looked to from its march." By letters from General Hull and his officers dated previous to the capture and inserted in the same *Intelligencer*, it appears that such was not the case: they all agree in stating that the army was without provisions — and was so weak that if reinforcements did not soon arrive, the most fatal consequences were to be expected. Now on which statement are we to depend: on the accounts of General Hull and his officers, written on the spot, or on the speculations of the government editor, written five hundred miles from the scene of action?

---

[1] The best historical opinion is that, as Henry Adams says, "a good general would have saved Detroit for some weeks, if not altogether." But he was wretchedly supplied.

## THE NEW ENGLAND THREAT OF SECESSION

*Columbian Centinel*, January 13, 1813

North of the Delaware, there is among all who do not bask or expect to bask in the Executive sunshine but one voice for *Peace*. South of that river, the general cry is "Open war, O peers!" There are not two hostile nations upon earth whose views of the principles and polity of a perfect commonwealth, and of men and measures, are more discordant than those of these two great divisions. There is but little of congeniality or sympathy in our notions or feelings; and this small residuum will be extinguished by this withering war.

The sentiment is hourly extending, and in these Northern States will soon be universal, that we are in a condition no better in relation to the South than that of a *conquered people*. We have been compelled without the least necessity or occasion to renounce our habits, occupations, means of happiness, and subsistence. We are plunged into a war, without a sense of enmity, or a perception of sufficient provocation; and obliged to fight the battles of a Cabal which, under the sickening affectation of republican *equality*, aims at trampling into the dust the weight, influence, and power of Commerce and her dependencies. We, whose soil was the hotbed and whose ships were the nursery of Sailors, are insulted with the hypocrisy of a devotedness to Sailors' rights, and the arrogance of a pretended skill in maritime jurisprudence, by those whose country furnishes no navigation beyond the size of a ferryboat or an Indian canoe. We have no more interest in waging this sort of war, at this period and under these circumstances, at the command of Virginia, than Holland in accelerating her ruin by uniting her destiny to France. We resemble Holland in another particular. The officers and power of government are engrossed by executive minions, who are selected on account of *their known infidelity to the interest of their fellow citizens*, to foment divisions and to deceive and distract the people whom they cannot intimidate. The land is literally taken from its Old Possessors and given to strangers. The Cabinet has no confidence in those who enjoy the confidence of this people, and on the other hand the solid mass of the talents and property of this community is wholly unsusceptible of any favorable impressions or dispositions towards an Executive in whose choice they had no part, and by whom they feel that they shall be, as they always have been, degraded and marked as objects of oppression and resentment. The consequence of this state of things must then be, either that the Southern States must *drag* the Northern States farther into the war, or we must *drag* them out of it; or the chain will break. This will be the "imposing attitude" of the next year.

We must no longer be deafened by senseless clamors about a separation of the States. It is an event we do not desire, not because we have derived advantages from the compact, but because we cannot foresee or limit the dangers or effects of revolution. *But the States are separated in fact*, when one section assumes an *imposing attitude*, and with high hand perseveres in measures fatal to the interests and repugnant to the opinions of another section, by dint of a geographical majority.

## NEW ORLEANS[1]

### New York *Evening Post*, February 7, 1815

We have today the official account of General Jackson, which makes the loss of the enemy much greater than it was reported to be, and on our side still less.

On the subject of this gallant, this extraordinary defence, it is due to truth and justice to observe that on no pretence whatever, are the Administration entitled to the least share of the honor attending this very brilliant affair, or to partake in the smallest of the glory acquired. After being three years at war with a powerful enemy, who had the means of transporting his forces to any part of our sea-coast, the Administration has been so utterly neglectful of this important place, the depôt of immense property belonging to the trading part of the community, that it was not until his forces were actually on the point of landing, that any measures of defence were taken. New Orleans was left to itself. And when at last the militia of the neighboring states voluntarily turned out to defend it, the Administration had not even provided arms, for their use, nor clothing to protect them from the cold. Whatever, therefore, of honor or glory the militia have acquired in this achievement, they alone are exclusively entitled to it; it would be the highest injustice to attempt to divide it with the President or with the Secretary of War. Had New Orleans fallen, I have no doubt that Mr. Madison would have been impeached by his own party. Report is very erroneous if he would not, and surely a different result, not owing to any measure of his, cannot materially alter the complexion of his conduct.

We cannot omit this opportunity to express how much we are pleased, at the unstudied simplicity and modesty of General Jackson's official letter; and we recommend it to American officers as a model for imitation.

---

[1] Jackson's victory of January 8, 1815, over the British army under Pakenham, was one of the few events of the war in which Americans could take pride. It came at a moment when, as Coleman hints, the government of Madison trembled on the brink of disaster. Jackson rightly received the entire credit.

## PEACE

New York *Evening Post*, February 13, 1815

On Saturday evening, about eight o'clock, arrived the British sloop of war, *Favorite*, bringing Mr. Carroll, one of the Secretaries attached to the American legation, bearer of a treaty of PEACE between the United States and Great Britain.  He came not unexpected to us: Ever since the receipt of the October dispatches, we have entertained and expressed, as our readers know, but one opinion.  A critical examination of those dispatches convinced us that the negociations would, nay, must terminate in the restoration of a speedy peace; and the speech of the Prince Regent, in November, contained an implied assurance that the preliminaries waited for little else than the form of signatures.  It has come, and the public expressions of tumultuous joy and gladness that spontaneously burst forth from all ranks and degrees of people on Saturday evening, without stopping to enquire the conditions, evinced how really sick at heart they were, of a war that threatened to wring from them the remaining means of subsistence, and of which they could neither see the object nor the end.  The public exhilaration shewed itself in the illumination of most of the windows in the lower part of Broadway and the adjoining streets in less than twenty minutes after Mr. Carroll arrived at the City Hotel.  The street itself was illuminated by lighted candles, carried in the hands of a large concourse of the populace;  the city resounded in all parts with the joyful cry of a peace! a peace! and it was for nearly two hours difficult to make one's way through unnumbered crowds of persons of all descriptions, who came forth to see and to hear and to rejoice.  In the truth, the occasion called for the liveliest marks of sincere congratulations.  Never, in our opinion, has there occurred so great a one since we became an independent nation.  Expresses of the glad tidings were instantly dispatched in all directions, to Boston, Philadelphia, Providence, Albany, &c., &c.  The country will now be convinced that the federalists were right in the opinion they have ever held, that during the despotism of Bonaparte, no peace was ever to be expected for their own country, and therefore they publickly rejoiced at his downfall, and celebrated the restoration of the Bourbons.  Men of property, particularly, should felicitate themselves, for they may look back upon the perils they have just escaped with the same sensations that the passenger in a ship experiences, when, driving directly on the breakers through the blunders of an ignorant pilot, he is unexpectedly snatched from impending destruction by a sudden shifting of the wind.  Fears were entertained, that it was really intended, like losing and desperate gamblers, to find a pretence for never paying the public debt, in the magnitude of the sum: that a spunge would be employed in the last resort, as the favorite instrument to wipe off all scores at once. A principle nearly bordering on this, was, not long ago, openly avowed on the floor of Congress by a member from Virginia. Neither is it a small cause of congratulation that we are now to be delivered from that swarm of leeches that have so long fastened upon the nation, and been sucking its blood. Their day is over. Let the nation rejoice.

What the terms of the peace are, we cannot tell; they will only be made known at Washington, by the dispatches themselves. But one thing I will venture to say now and before they are opened, and I will hazard my reputation upon the correctness of what I say, that when the terms are disclosed, it will be found that the government have not by this negociation obtained one single avowed object for which they involved the country in this bloody and expensive war.

## [EFFECTS OF THE NEWS OF PEACE]

New York *Evening Post*, February 14, 1815

In yesterday's paper we gave a rapid sketch of the effects of war; today we give one of the effects of the prospect of peace even before the ratification. Our markets of every kind experienced a sudden and to many a shocking change. Sugar, for instance, fell from $26 per hundredweight to $12.50; tea, which sold at $2.25 on Saturday, yesterday was purchased at $1; specie, which had got up to the enormous rate of 22 per cent premium, dropped down to two. The article in particular of tin fell from the height of $80 the box to $25. Six per cent bonds rose from 76 to 86, or ten per cent, and Treasury notes rose from 92 to 98 per cent. This difference between the two kinds of stock is owing to the interest being the same on both, while the price of the former is much less to the holder; that is, the holder of the former receives six per cent on $100, while the holder of the latter receives the same interest, but the principal costs him 96.

Bank stock rose generally from five to ten per cent. *Sailors' Rights* beat time to the sound of the hammer at every wharf, and *free trade* looked briskly up; no longer did it live in toasts alone. On the other hand, wagons creaked their dying groans on their dry axle-trees. Ships swarm in the columns of our friends Lang & Turner, and glisten in a row in Crooks & Butler's; even a few, from some friendly hand, here and there adorn the *Evening Post* and help to make up a show. We are grateful for what we have received.

It is really wonderful to see the change produced in a few hours in the city of New York. In no place has the war been more felt nor proved more disastrous, putting us back in our growth at least ten years; and no place in the United States will more experience the reviving blessings of a peace. Let us be grateful to that merciful Providence who has kindly interposed for our relief and delivered us from all our fears.

## [PRESIDENT MONROE'S TOUR AND THE ERA OF GOOD FEELING]

Washington *National Intelligencer*, April 23, 1817

It has been already intimated in several papers that the President proposes, within a short time, to commence a tour through a part of the United States. . . .

By the Constitution of our country, it is made the duty of the President of the United States to give to Congress information of the state of the Union, and to recommend from time to time such measures as he shall judge necessary and expedient. One of the principal objects of the association of these States, under a Federal head, was to secure adequate provision for the national defence. Such attention has always been paid to that object heretofore as the best information authorized and required. But there is no information so satisfactory, nor upon which so much reliance can be placed, as that obtained by personal observation. It is therefore believed, in the present quiet state of our foreign and domestic concerns, not requiring the presence of the President at the seat of government, that he could not do a more valuable service to his country than by personally inspecting the state of the public works, of the military and naval posts and depots, and all the establishments connected with national defence.

*Idem*, July 24, 1817

We trace the path of the President by means of the newspapers as far east as Portland, Maine, the remotest point in that direction, and the remotest in any direction ever before visited by a President of the United States. Wherever the President passes, concord attends his steps. So extraordinary is the unanimity of sentiment, and the fraternity of intercourse which the progress of the President has developed, that we are led to believe that an excuse only was wanting for the harmony of society for which the President's conciliating deportment is assigned as a reason. Mr. Monroe was always the same as he now is, and his predecessor was certainly distinguished for urbanity and freedom from the asperities of political controversy.

Let us not, however, too nicely scan the motive when the effect is so valuable. Never before, perhaps, since the institution of civil government, did the same harmony, the same absence of party spirit, the same national feeling, pervade a community. The result is too consoling to dispute too nicely about the cause.

## [EFFECTS OF THE PANIC OF 1819][1]

### *Niles's Register*, September 16, 1820

A large part of the present dullness of trade and "scarcity of money" is owing to a diminished consumption of costly articles for food and raiment, or for ornament and show, whether of foreign or domestic product. It is a hard thing to retrograde in these, but — *necessitas non habet leges;* what "can't be cured must be endured." There are few even of the most wealthy (except some steady-habited old fellows who never conformed to the times), who now live as they did a few years ago, so far as my observation and information extend. Pride, pomp, and splendor, as well as sheer luxury and what is sometimes called comfort, derive much of their real value (if anything they have) from comparison. The black broth of the Lacedemonians was their greatest enjoyment, though the humblest stranger could hardly keep it on his stomach. A little while ago, I frequently saw the streets crowded in an evening with a bustling multitude dashing in carriages to Mrs. Anything's party. An orderly man could hardly get along for them. I have heard of three hundred persons taking tea with the wife of the servant of a bank! But "madam's husband" can't afford it any longer, or so much respects common decency that he won't allow it. So those who may afford it receive the same comparative *éclat* for having thirty or forty which they used to derive from having three or four hundred at their parties; and it is much better, because in a company of the former dimensions you may find a satisfaction not to be expected in the other, designed *only to make a noise.* It is thus also with gentlemen's dinners and suppers — ten or twenty are occasionally invited, instead of having twenty or forty frequently. The style is still maintained, but *fashion* does not call for its exhibition so extensively nor so often. "The top of the wheel" is still held, and that is enough.

But the general retrenchment spoken of may be proven from a multitude of facts. In the New York, Philadelphia, and Baltimore newspapers you may often see the grocers puffing their wines by saying that certain particular pipes were expressly imported for

[1] By Hezekiah Niles. The war with England was followed by severe commercial distress, culminating in something like a financial panic in 1819.

private use. Their sayings are true. The gentlemen who ordered it had found out that there was an end to paper credit when the wine arrived, and though they might have retained some money, it would look too bad to see a pipe of wine going into a bankrupt's cellar; and the fact is that our grocers hardly sell one gallon of their costly wines for ten which they used to dispose of. So also it is for every business, trade, or profession which furnishes us with luxuries, from the wine merchant to the confectioner; and if it was known that a man in an ordinary trade gave his wife a shawl which cost $500, his note would certainly be "turned down" at bank.

## SLAVERY AND THE MISSOURI COMPROMISE [1]

*Niles's Register*, December 23, 1820

It is established (so far as large majorities in both houses of Congress can establish it) that the power to check the progress of a slave population within the territories of the United States exists by the Constitution; but admitted that it was not expedient to exert that power in regard to Missouri and Arkansas. The latter depended on many considerations of no ordinary importance: the safety and feelings of the white population in several of the States appeared to be involved in it, and the rights and feelings of others were as deeply concerned in the subject at large. In this conflict of interests, among persons who possibly desired the same ultimate issue, though their views of it were diametrically opposed, a spirit of conciliation prevailed and a compromise was effected. The people of those sections of country in which there are few or no slaves or persons of color, very imperfectly appreciate the wants, necessity, or general principle of others differently situated.

Collectively, the latter deprecate slavery as severely as the former, and deprecate its increase; but individual cupidity and rashness acts against the common sentiment, in the hope that an event which everybody believes must happen, will not happen in their day. It is thus that too many of us act about death; we are sure it must come, yet we commit wrong to acquire property, just as if we should hold and enjoy it forever. That the slave population will, at some certain period, cause the most horrible catastrophe, cannot be doubted; those who possess them act defensively in behalf of all that is nearest and dearest to them, when they endeavor to acquire all the strength and influence to meet that period which they can; and hence the political and civil opposition of these to

[1] A characteristic expression of the strong nationalism of Niles, of his New England aversion to slavery, though his newspaper was conducted in a slave State, Maryland, and in its prophecy of a "horrible catastrophe," of his political shrewdness. The *Register* agreed with Jefferson that the Missouri discussion was like "a firebell in the night."

the restriction which was proposed to be laid on Missouri.   They *have* the offensive population, and no feasible plan has yet been contrived to rid them of it, if they were disposed so to do.   Will the people of any of the States, so much alive to humanity, pass acts to encourage emancipation by agreeing to receive the emancipated?   What will they do, what can they do, to assist the people of others to relieve themselves of their unfortunate condition?   It is easy to use severe terms against the practise of slavery;  but let us first tell the Southern people what they can safely do to abolish it, before we condemn them wholesale.

No one can hate slavery more than I do — it is a thing opposed to every principle that operates on my mind as an individual — and in my own private circle I do much to discourage it.   I am also exceedingly jealous of it, so far as it affects my political rights as a citizen of the United States, entitled to be fairly and fully represented, and no more.   But I can make great allowances for those who hold slaves in districts where they abound — where, in many cases, their emancipation might be an act of cruelty to them, and of most serious injury to the white population.   Their difference of color is an insuperable barrier to their incorporation within the society;  and the mixture of free blacks with slaves is detrimental to the happiness of both, the cause of uncounted crimes.   Yet I think that some have urged their defensive character too far;  without a proper respect for the rights and feelings of others, as applicable to an extension of the evil.   But we advocated the compromise, as fixing certain points for the future government of all the parties concerned;  believing that the moral and political evil of spreading slavery over Missouri and even in Arkansas was not greater than that which might have risen from restriction, though to restrict was right in itself.   The harmony of the Union, and the peace and prosperity of the white population, most excited our sympathies. We did not fear the dreadful things which some silly folks talked of, but apprehended geographical oppositions which might lead to the worst of calamities.   We had no pleasant feeling on the Compromise, for bad was the best that could be done.   Nevertheless, we hoped that the contest was at an end, and that things would settle down and adapt themselves to the agreement which necessity imposed.

### [CRUELTY TO DUMB ANIMALS]

*Niles's Register*, July 7, 1821

A person was taken up and committed to prison in New York for so fastening the tongue of a calf that it could not suck its mother, both of which were for sale.   Now in Baltimore it is quite a common thing, when cows and calves are driven through our streets for sale, to see the mouths of the latter severely tied up with string; but what is much worse, in passing the Centre market every Wednesday and Saturday, we see calves with their four feet bound together with ropes, and so suffered to lie for hours together on the public pavements, exposed to a burning sun!  If there is no law to punish such cruelty, the people might soon check it, if they would act as I do. I inquire what butchers are in the habit of this cruelty, and avoid their stalls as if their meat was as putrid as their hearts are callous to humanity and disregardful of decency.

## WHY WE NEED A PROTECTIVE TARIFF [1]

*Niles's Register*, June 23, 1821

The Waltham manufactory is the largest and probably the most prosperous in the United States.  Too much credit cannot be given to the managers for the economy and skill with which it is conducted, or the good order and morality which are so conspicuous among the workmen, women and children.  It is a magnificent and truly national establishment, presenting a splendid matter-of-fact illustration of the true principles of political economy; imparting to the mind of one who views its structure, machinery, and management, more conviction and practical information than could be drawn from all the books which its walls could contain.

When foreign or hireling writers tell us, your country is not fit for manufactures, we can with pride tell them — look at Waltham; that manufactures are injurious to morals and agriculture — look at Waltham and its neighborhood; that they will destroy commerce — ask the merchants of Boston and Providence; that they will destroy the market for our produce — look at Mr. Jackson's books; that the Southern planter will suffer — count the bales of cotton in store; that they tax the many and oppress the few — compare the price and quality of their fabrics with the imported; that we have not sufficient capital — examine the list of stockholders and their bankbooks ($600,000 paid in, $600,000 more ready if it could be employed).  In short, there is not an objection to the encouragement of manufactures among us that is not put down by an inspection of this establishment, without reasoning

[1] Francis Lowell in 1814 invented a power-loom which was at once used successfully in textile manufacturing in Waltham.  Here the Boston Manufacturing Company established the first modern factory in the United States.  It performed all operations by central power, used specialized labor, organized the workers into departments, and standardized the product.  The idea of the factory as America now knows it was thus first demonstrated, and the success of the establishment, with its benefits to the surrounding country, was much used by writers like Niles in the argument for tariffs.

or books, except the book we all neglect too much — the book of observation, practical experience, and active life. It would give me much pleasure to seat myself on an eminence near Waltham with some honest anti-tariffite, and for one day watch the motions of all the in-comers and out-goers at the village and factory; to take a note of what they brought in and took out; to ask the passing farmer what he took to market, the price he obtained, and what he brought home in exchange; to ask the fond mother who had been to see her children, whether their habits were industrious, frugal, moral, and how much of their earnings went to the comforts of their aged parents. I would ask one of the worthy mercantile proprietors what effect it had on his commercial pursuits; and I would cheerfully agree to give up all my tariff doctrines, if the answers of all would not be as I could wish.[1]

If my anti-tariff friend would not be convinced, I would put him this case: Suppose this fine factory should be destroyed by fire, and the proprietors should not rebuild it. We will suppose ourselves sitting on this same hill one year after the establishment had been in ruins, and the same farmer, the same mother, and the same merchant should all join us, and we should join in the conversation, comparing the past with the present, the farmer's market, the mother's children, the merchant's business. Reader, I need not detail our remarks to you, for you will imagine them all: you know there is not one of the group that would not look at the unemployed waterfall, the ruins of the factory, and say there it stood; things were not so when the factory was going. Suppose we come down to the village. It is quiet — a few people seen about the taverns and retail stores, houses decaying, children ragged, old people begging. "What is the matter? It was not so last year." "O, no! but the factory is burnt!" This answer would break from every mouth, and I am much mistaken if any anti-tariff man could stand the scene unconvinced. Every man of this description ought to go to Waltham, or some other manufactory, and imagine to himself the difference between *a factory at work and a factory burnt*. This is the mode of settling questions of political economy and national policy. What Waltham is on a large scale every manufacturing establishment is on a small one; and those are the books which the people must study or they will never understand the subject. When they see the practical difference between a factory stopped and a factory active, the nation will cease to be divided and Congress indifferent.

---

[1] The tariff act passed in the spring of 1824 placed protective duties, as Niles desired, upon the textile and other industrial interests of the North. Northern shipping interests and Southern agriculturists both opposed such legislation.

# [THE ERIE CANAL: "THE MEETING OF THE WATERS"][1]

New York *Commercial Advertiser*, October 11, 1822

*Ye shades of ancient heroes! Ye who toiled,*
*Through long successive ages, to build up*
*A laboring plan of state; behold, at once,*
*The wonder done!*

Wednesday of the present week was not only a proud day for New York, but for the Union; for although the joyous festival at Albany was a celebration of an event in the achievement of which New York has exerted her enterprise and physical energies single-handed and alone, yet the stupendous object is not the less important in a national point of view. In addition to the incalculable benefits it will confer on our State in respect to commercial affairs, the canal will long serve as a chain to bind together rich and populous territories, far distant from each other, and whose real or imaginary diversity of interests might otherwise, and at no very remote period, cause a dissolution, alike injurious and disastrous to all. By means of this great artificial river, and others which will be formed in consequence of our example, the Atlantic States and the rich and widely extended regions of the West will become neighbors, and a close community of interests will induce them to cling together with a degree of tenaciousness and constancy which even a daily recollection of their consanguinity would not otherwise have produced. . . .

Whatever party rules, whatever political chief rises or falls, agriculture, manufactures, and commerce must still remain the greatest of our concerns, and by the opening of the canal these three great vital interests are all most eminently promoted. What a widespread region of cultivated soil has already been brought within the near vicinity of the greatest market on our continent! How many manufacturing establishments have had the value of everything connected with them doubled by this "meeting of the waters"! How vastly have the internal resources of this metropolis been, in one day,

[1] An interesting example of the literary treatment of a commercial topic. The Erie Canal was begun in 1817 and completed in November, 1825; the celebration here noted marked the completion of its most important stage. DeWitt Clinton was primarily responsible for beginning and pushing the work, but in 1822 he was forced by the opposition to his administration to decline to seek a third term as Governor. Later he was reëlected triumphantly, serving from 1825 till his death in 1828. The editor of the *Commercial Advertiser* alludes to this temporary retirement in a tactful way. At this date steam navigation was rapidly increasing on all rivers and along the coast; while the ship *Savannah* had crossed the Atlantic under sail and steam in 1819. Americans were greatly interested in the subject. The Erie Canal was of course destined to make New York the metropolis of the continent.

practically extended! Without adverting to any long vista of future times, how much has already, at this present hour, been effected in the enhancement of the total value of the whole State! If we justly consider the Hudson, flowing through the densest population and best-cultivated territory, an invaluable blessing, and a leading feature of our local advantages, what must be the opening of a new and additional river, twice the navigable length of the Hudson, and traversing a region whose population and agricultural wealth will soon rival and even surpass those of its banks? A river which, in one year more, will carry our trade to the foot of the falls of St. Mary, and will eventually give us access to the remotest shore of Lake Superior!

Thus has closed one of the greatest, happiest, proudest, most propitious scenes our State has ever witnessed. Excepting that day on which she joined the national confederacy, there is none like it in her history; nor is there likely to be, save that which will commemorate the completion of the same grand design, now so near its consummation. The prominent figure in this scene of the public exultation is a man whose name will be preserved from the stroke of time by the benedictions of remotest posterity; one of those men whom one age is insufficient to appreciate; whose thoughts and purposes run through many ages — and whose minds are never fully developed till their conceptions have been embodied in plans and measures which go on to bless a nation from generation to generation. It is in vain that the efforts of the weak, who cannot comprehend, or the malignant, who comprehend only to hate and envy true greatness, are combined to bring such men into the dust:

> Like ancient oaks, superior in power,
> To all the warring winds of heaven, they rise;
> And from their stony promontory tower,
> And toss their giant arms amid the skies,
> While each assailing blast increase of strength supplies.

De Witt Clinton, whatever may be his public career, is now a private man; and none of those feelings which public life, in a free country, never fail to arouse, have anything to do with claims to his country's gratitude which rest upon his measures for internal improvement. These claims are clear, acknowledged, irresistible. They have borne down opposition of party feeling, except in heads and hearts which nothing can penetrate; and they will be owned, and paid too, when we are dead and our squabbles forgotten.

## [STATES WHICH REFUSE POLITICAL EQUALITY][1]

*Niles's Register*, November 29, 1823

Delaware, Maryland, Virginia, and North Carolina are the only States whose representation, in their several legislatures, depends upon the long-laughed-at and truly ridiculous, though abominable and unjust, rotten-borough system of England.  That is, a certain district of country, or space of land, whether inhabited by whites, blacks, or mulattoes, or a mixture of all — or by bucks and does, or bears and wolves, or even frogs and mosquitoes, provided it hath certain qualified bipeds enough in it to fill the place of representatives of the people — is entitled to an equal degree of power in the passage of laws to regulate the affairs of the several commonwealths.  It is no matter whether a district is fertile or barren, large or small, ten feet square or an hundred miles — whether it contains five militiamen or fifty thousand, or pays one dollar tax or one million — such is the virtue of the Constitution that the very pine-trees and stunted oaks, whortleberry bushes or chestnut sprouts, are transformed into somethings that make great men out of very little ones, investing them with the sovereign power of legislation!

One county in Delaware has 22,360 citizens, and another only 14,180, and yet they are represented by an equal number of members.

One city in Maryland, which sends two members to the house of delegates, has much more effective strength of population and pays nearly as much tax as ten counties which send forty members.

One county in Virginia, entitled to two members, contains a greater number of citizens than nine counties which send eighteen members.

One county in North Carolina, with two members, is equal in its number of citizens to seven counties sending fourteen members.

And yet we smile at the English system!  That has the plea of antiquity, the danger of "reform" in its favor;  but what have we to plead for our equally ridiculous delegations of power?  We prate about liberty and declaim in favor of our just laws;  we say that taxation without representation is tyranny!  How shall we be judged? — by that which we chatter about, or that which we suffer to be and sanction by our sufferance?

---

[1] The demand for equitable representation in Virginia was one of the chief causes for the holding of a constitutional convention in that State in 1829; yet this convention refused the equality sought.  Hezekiah Niles's editorial is an interesting expression of one of the impulses which lent strength to Jacksonian Democracy.

## [THE MONROE DOCTRINE ENUNCIATED]

*Niles's Register*, December 6, 1823

The message of the President of the United States, delivered on Tuesday last, is remarkable for the amplitude and simplicity of its details, and suggests many subjects that will engage the serious attention of the representatives of the people, if they shall not be too much occupied with electioneering to attend to them. Instead of pointing out these things, or attempting to explain what the President means, the readers of this work are referred to the message itself, in a belief that the document may be understood without the aid of editorial interpretations. I would only invite a careful perusal of it.

There is one part of the message, however, that will attract particular attention. It is where the President suggests the possibility that the Allied Powers may attempt an extension of their "political system" to Mexico and the South American states; which, he declares, ought to be regarded as "dangerous to our peace and safety." Every thinking American will accord in this opinion. But the expression of it, on an occasion like the present, convinces us that there must be some special reason for putting it forth. It has been universally believed that the members of the Holy Alliance entertained the design of reducing all governments to their own standard of right, as Procrustes stretched or chopped off the limbs of persons that they might fit the measure of his bed; and we recollect also, that a work was published at Verona, dedicated by permission to the emperor of Austria, in which it was recommended, as necessary to the repose of Europe, that even England should be compelled to fall into their system. But we hardly thought that they had proceeded so far as we are now disposed to believe they have done. Be this as it may, the present is not a time to trifle or tamper with our means of defense. They should be cherished, as we love ourselves or our children. An increased power in them may not be necessary just now, but their *efficiency* should be kept up and increased.

[1] What has since become famous as the Monroe Doctrine was announced in President Monroe's annual message to Congress, December 2, 1823. Its main assertions were that the American continents " are henceforth not to be considered as subjects for future colonization by any European Powers," and that, as regards the Powers of the Holy Alliance, America "should consider any attempt on their part to extend their system to any portion of this hemisphere as dangerous to our peace and safety." The primary impulse in the announcement of this doctrine was furnished by the British Foreign Minister, Canning. In its final form it owed most to J. Q. Adams.

## [ALBERT GALLATIN AS A "FOREIGNER"][1]

*Niles's Register*, April 17, 1824

I am not one of those who think all's fair in politics. "Jokes may be free in harvest," but truth is the same the whole year round. Nominated as Mr. Gallatin was by a *minority* of that political interest with which I have steadily acted from the year 1795 until the present day, no obligation whatever presents itself to my mind why, on account of that interest, I should support him for the Vice-Presidency of the United States; but an evident duty to principle urges me to reprove the practise of some who, whether friendly or unfriendly to the late caucus, speak of him as a *foreigner*. Indeed, judging from what I have seen on both sides, the nomination was an unfortunate one for the caucus party, for its design of operating on Pennsylvania has totally failed, as was predicted at the moment when it was made; and on every account it has rather taken from than added to the strength of the ticket. But Mr. Gallatin arrived in this country, not then the "United States," long before the present Constitution was formed, or even the war had ended; and, in the letter or spirit of that instrument, and in the fitness of things, he cannot be regarded any more as a foreigner than those of us who happened to be born in this land before the fourth of July, 1776, unless long enough before that period to have taken some part in ratifying the Declaration of Independence by the force of arms or otherwise. And in the very year that the government of the United States went into operation, Mr. Gallatin, as a member of the Pennsylvania convention, took an active part in the formation of the Constitution of that great State.

I escaped the honor of being a subject of his Britannic Majesty, but all the past Presidents were so; so was the present President, and all who are held up as candidates to succeed him. Were they or are they on that account to be suspected of having anti-American feelings? Or does the accident of birth under King George afford a better assurance that a person is more a friend of liberty than the accident of birth under the dominion of any other king? Is English royalty, that raised the tomahawk of the savage, that slaughtered our people, conflagrated our towns, and so on, in the Revolution, more deserving of respect than French royalty, which aided and assisted us in gaining our freedom? Is the much-esteemed and

---

[1] Gallatin's nomination for the Vice-Presidency in the spring of 1824, on the ticket of William H. Crawford, was the signal for bitter attacks upon him as a foreigner; he was born in Switzerland in 1761. Ultimately Martin Van Buren, who was one of the Crawford managers, decided that Gallatin weakened the ticket, and his retirement was arranged that autumn. Niles expresses the feeling of men of principle regarding the attacks.

venerable Colonel Paul Bentalou, now Federal marshal of the district of Maryland, less a citizen than I myself am, because he pronounces many English words with a French accent? No, no; he belongs to the small fragment of those who hewed out citizenship with their swords; he was a gallant captain in his youth in the celebrated legion of Pulaski, and there are few men living who saw more service in our country than he; and since the termination of the Revolutionary War, his home has been in the land that he helped to wrest from the hands of a tyrant. No one would have spoken of General Montgomery as a foreigner were he yet living among us; yet Col. Bentalou is frequently called a Frenchman, though many Englishmen or renegade Americans who actually fought against the republic are unhesitatingly accepted as citizens thereof. Nay, thousands lately imported seem willing to suspect the descendants of the original German and Dutch settlers of Pennsylvania and New York as foreigners, because perhaps they may use *und* for *and*, instead of saying *hand* for *and*, or *Hamos* for *Amos;* but the former is a language spoken by many millions of intelligent beings, and the other is local and not belonging to any language at all. Yes, and there are some of them, though possibly named Sheepshanks or Shufflebottom, "Clutterbuck or Higgenbottom," who laugh at the names of our German brethren and find others, native citizens, foolish enough to join in it with them!

The matters here spoken of come out of the host of miserable prejudices which have descended to us from our British ancestors; and concerning some of these I have often felt myself bound to speak freely. I will yet battle with them until a *national* feeling is established, that shall not regard imported doctrines and notions any more if received from England than from Japan.

## [THE DEATH OF ADAMS AND JEFFERSON]

*Niles's Register*, July 15, 1826

We had hardly announced the decease of the patriot who drafted the Declaration of Independence than news arrived of the death of his venerable compatriot, who more than any other man, perhaps, urged the adoption of that famous measure, and supported it through every change of time and circumstance, himself unchanged. Thomas Jefferson departed this life between twelve and one o'clock on the fiftieth anniversary of the Declaration of Independence, and nearly if not precisely at the same hour of the day when it was first reading before Congress; and John Adams, who was also the committee who reported that Declaration, left us between five and six o'clock of the same jubilee-anniversary, at nearly if not precisely the very hour when the contents of that memorable paper were first proclaimed to the people in the State-House yard in Philadelphia, and when the United States were first saluted as "free, sovereign, and independent;" when the thunder of cannon and the loud huzza of the multitude first ratified the solemn and august act of representatives of the people, appealing to Heaven and resting confidently in the virtues of their fellow-citizens, for the accomplishment of the mighty work which had just then been planned.

It was a fearful time. But "there were giants in those days." And none were more conspicuous for ardent devotion and unlimited zeal, fixed resolution and steady perseverance, than John Adams of Massachusetts and Thomas Jefferson of Virginia. They both lived to grow old, if we may be allowed the expression, in the glories of the nation which they labored so faithfully to establish; they both died on the same day, and that was the jubilee-anniversary of the nation's existence! What a torrent of thought rushes on the mind when these things are mentioned — recollections of the past seemingly overwhelm us by the importance of events that have happened — we greatly wonder at what has taken place and endeavor to look into futurity; saying to ourselves, what will the next fifty years produce? — will anyone now living behold such mighty marches of mind and power as Adams and Jefferson witnessed? With what pleasure do we dwell on the past — with what pride do we look at the present and anticipate the future — with what delighted feeling we remember the services of these venerable and venerated friends, and of others who have long passed from works to rewards — and with what profound respect and grateful tenderness should we cherish the few, the very few oaks of the Revolution that remain, palsied by age, if not withered by neglect, and rendered helpless by former suffering and present privations!

## ASPECTS OF AMERICAN SOCIAL HISTORY, 1827[1]

### Washington *National Intelligencer*

*General Washington's Works:* January 29, 1827.

It is with great satisfaction that we have learnt that Mr. Jared Sparks, editor of the *North American Review*, has made arrangements with Judge Washington for publishing an entire edition of "General Washington's Works," to consist of his letters to the Governor of Virginia during the French War, his State Papers, Official Cor-

[1] No other newspaper in the country exhibited quite so fully the various phases of American life in its editorial columns, at this period, as the *National Intelligencer*. As the chief Washington newspaper, to which the whole press looked for full reports of Congressional debates, it was in large degree a national clearing-house of information.

respondence, both civil and military, and such of his private letters as may be deemed suited for publication; the whole to be comprised in a series of volumes, with notes and illustrations by the esteemed editor.  It is well known that General Washington preserved, with scrupulous care, copies of his own letters, as well as the prodigious number of originals which he received from other persons.  In addition to a full use of these papers, which are now at Mount Vernon, Mr. Sparks will profit by a mass of material for Revolutionary History, which he has gathered by a personal inspection of the several public offices in the old States, as well as from various private sources.  The records, correspondence, and other papers of the old Congress are preserved in the Department of State, to which he will also have access.  With these advantages and resources in aid of the editor, it may be expected that the work will possess a national interest, and constitute a most valuable addition to our political history.

*A Railway Project:*  March 5, 1827.

A great Railway is spoken of in Baltimore, to extend from Baltimore to the Ohio, and many capitalists are said seriously to patronize the thought.  They had better patronize the Ohio and Chesapeake Canal, which appears to us much more feasible than a railway *three hundred miles long.*  We cannot conceive of the practicability of such work, as a regular everyday line of transportation.  We shall, however, lay before our readers the arguments in favor of the measure, which we should be far from opposing from any mean motive of jealousy or envy, if the work be practicable.  There would be trade enough leave the road, whenever it found a water communication — at Cumberland, for example — to make the part of the road which crosses the mountain ridge a very important work to this District.

*Imprisonment for Debt:*  May 29, 1827.

. . . We need not cross the Atlantic for evidences of barbarity worthy of the ages from which it has descended.  Imprisonment for debt yet exists by our laws — even by the laws of the United States, which exclusively govern this District.  Yes, in sight of the splendid dome, the interior of which is adorned with the pictured story of the *triumph of Liberty,* and on the exterior of which proudly float the symbols of National Sovereignty, it is but a few months since a man was immured for *six months* for a debt of *three dollars!*  It is almost incredible, but we arrive at the fact in a manner which leaves no doubt of it.  Legislators of the Union, how long will you sanctify by your laws such outrages upon human rights?  Let it not be said that it is the fault of our community that this man was suffered to lie so long in such durance. It is not *their* fault. The law must have its way; and it is one of the curses of the system that it shuts up its victim from the view of his fellow-men, and he might rot there for years without his situation being known, otherwise than by accident; and it is another of the worst features of the system that the more destitute and miserable a man is, the more so he is sure to become, under its operation.

*Our Public Hotels:* June 18, 1827.

There is no city in the Union, we believe, so well supplied with hotels of the first class, both in extent and style of keeping, as the city of Washington now is. The large number of these establishments, compared with the resident population of the place, is owing, of course, to the great influx of visitors for several months of every year, during the session of Congress, and the considerable number brought here at all seasons of public business, or by curiosity. The splendor of modern hotels has obtained for them the appellation of "the palaces of the public;" and really the elegance of some of them here and elsewhere almost justifies the phrase. A few years ago a casual visitor of this city, in winter, might think himself well off if he could squeeze himself into a comfortable lodging, and there was no little risk, some times, of getting none at all. Now, besides numerous genteel and excellent boarding-houses, there are three principal hotels that will vie with any others in the Union in extent, elegance, good keeping, and comfort. The Mansion Hotel of Mr. Williamson, and the Indian Queen of Mr. Brown, are long established and well known houses; both of them have lately been enlarged, particularly the latter, and highly improved. In addition to these commodious and excellent hotels, there has lately been erected a new establishment, of surpassing magnitude and elegance, the National Hotel . . . opened under the superintendence of our old friend Gadsby.

*A Southern Lynching:* July 23, 1827.

Some time during the last week one of those outrageous transactions — and we really think, disgraceful to the character of civilized man — took place near the northeast boundary line of Perry, adjoining Bibb and Autauga Counties, Georgia. The circumstances, we are informed by a gentleman from that county are, that a Mr. McNeily having lost some clothing or some other property of no great value, the slave of a neighboring planter was charged with the theft. McNeily in company with his brother found the negro driving his master's wagon; they seized him and either did or were about to chastize him, when the negro stabbed McNeily so that he

died in an hour afterwards.  The negro was taken before a justice
of the peace, who after serious deliberation waived his authority —
perhaps through fear, as the crowd of persons from the above
counties had collected to the number of seventy or eighty near Mr.
Peoples' (the justice) house.  He acted as president of the mob and
put the vote, when it was decided he should be immediately executed by *being burnt to death*.  The sable culprit was led to a tree
and tied to it, and a large quantity of pine knots collected and placed
around him, and the fatal torch was applied to the pile even against
the remonstrances of several gentlemen who were present:  and the
miserable being was in a short time burnt to ashes.  An inquest was
held over the remains, and the sheriff of Perry County, with a company of about twenty men, repaired to the neighborhood where this
barbarous act took place, to secure those concerned, with what
success we have not heard:  but we hope he will succeed in bringing
the perpetrators of so high-handed a measure to account. . . .

*New England Morals:*  August 8, 1827.

A theatre is about to be opened in Salem, and fifty dollars are
offered by the manager for the best poetic address.  A theatre in
Salem!  *Tempora Mutantur.*

*The Evils of Drink:*  August 16, 1827.

Intemperance, with all its shocking consequences, seems to gain
upon society, notwithstanding the laudable efforts made to arrest
its destructive march.  Domestic wretchedness and ruin are its
general, if not invariable, consequences;  but to these are not infrequently added murder and suicide.  In fact, it is heart-sickening
to read the accounts which almost every day's mail brings us, of
instances of these dreadful fruits of the prevalent vice.  We do not
often notice these occurrences in our paper, because if their exhibition rouses public attention to the evil, it on the other hand
tends to deaden the public horror and sensibility to the most revolting crimes, by rendering them familiar;  but we really believe
that there have been more murders committed in the United States
within the last two years (most of them the effect of intemperance)
than took place in all Great Britain during the same period.

## [THE ARGUMENT AGAINST GENERAL JACKSON]

Washington *National Intelligencer*, August 4, 1827

Of the seductiveness of military fame in popular governments, if
we had ever doubted it, the last Presidential election has given us
instructive illustration.  Mr. Adams, Mr. Crawford, Mr. Clay, and
Mr. Calhoun, all distinguished civilians, were familiarly spoken of

as candidates for the Presidency before General Jackson was seriously announced. The moment he was brought forward, the soldiers whom he had led to battle rallied under his standard. It was by them, in fact, that he was formally presented as a candidate. The military fervor, created by the arrival and triumphal progress of the good Lafayette through the land, aided the spread of the contagion; and in some populous districts of the interior, the militia, exalted into enthusiasm by the militia victory at New Orleans, marched almost literally in embattled legions to the polls. Had the election taken place three months later, it is quite possible that the experiment would have been made, which we have been taught by all history to deprecate, of a successful general arriving, by means solely of a military achievement, at the highest station of the republic.

Such an experiment we deprecate, not because we have any apprehension for the form of our government from any leader, military or civil. The Constitution will be found strong enough to check the boldest and most daring attempt at usurpation. But we object to placing a military man in the chief authority because, having once tasted of the pleasure of absolute command, as on the field of battle, he may retain the relish for it, and is too likely, in the exercise of public duties, to substitute for the injunctions of law, or the suggestions of policy, his own sovereign will and pleasure. He cannot endanger the existence of the government, but he may endanger the public peace, at home as well as abroad. We object to such elevation of a military man especially when his military fame is the only argument in favor of it, and when his civil qualifications are either not inquired into, or not established.

## [THE ARGUMENT AGAINST J. Q. ADAMS][1]

Natchez *Gazette*, November 1, 1827

John Quincy Adams has passed the principal part of his life in Europe, amid the luxury and splendor of regal governments. Surrounded by all that was enervating in manners, and seductive in pleasure, by the glitter of dress and the fascination of voluptuousness, it is not at all astonishing that he has contracted a few of the vices which disgrace the age. Intercourse with a licentious nobility, whose profligacy of habit, insatiable avarice, and turpitude of heart are concealed by the "star, garters, and ribands" with which they are adorned, must exercise a deleterious influence upon a man who bows to every vicissitude, swims upon the tide of every revolution,

[1] This curious and absurd editorial represented a type of attack upon John Quincy Adams which had immense potency throughout the South and West, and which was accepted by many rough voters of the Jackson following as gospel truth.

and is the acknowledged creature of circumstances.    The courtly
voluptuary, refined in all the stratagems of sensuality; the privileged
libertine, at whose approach innocence trembles and the blushing
cheek grows pale, who considers virtue as the *ignis fatuus* of imagination, and health and happiness as his lawful prey — the deceit-
ful diplomatist, the fawning sycophant, the superannuated beggar,
ecclesiastics without religion, and councillors without learning, are
the characters who surround the thrones of Europe.    These have
been the associates of Mr. Adams, and those who idolize him add
it to the catalogue of his qualifications.    He went abroad, it is
presumed, before his principles had been formed — in the imma-
turity of youth, when the mind is ductile and susceptible of impression.    It was there that he learned the superiority of a monarchical
over a democratic or federative government — that the people were
not calculated to govern themselves — that republics wanted energy
— that orders of nobility should be instituted, and Senators entrusted with their official functions for life.

## PRESIDENT ADAMS'S REGARD FOR MERIT

### Washington *National Intelligencer*, November 27, 1827

As for the madness of this Administration, we know wherein
what is called its "madness" has consisted.   What we have approved
in this Administration — what convinced us of the political honesty
and integrity of the President — has been this very thing;   namely,
that he has filled the great offices in his gift not with personal friends,
or political parasites and office-seekers, but with high-minded and
honorable men — with such men as Henry Clay, his associate in
negotiating the Treaty of Ghent, and the fearless and free advocate
of measures without regard to men;   Richard Rush, the confidential
friend and worthy pupil of the illustrious Madison during his
Administration;   James Barbour, the independent and enthusiastic
supporter of the Madison Republican Administration, and of Mr.
Monroe's, which followed it, and the true and conscientious friend
of William H. Crawford;   Rufus King, the venerable Federalist
who stood forward for his country during the late war, and was for
that reason placed by the Republicans of New York in the seat of
honor;   Albert Gallatin, a Republican of 1798 and a Republican
now, whose talents, integrity, and valuable experience the President
had the sense to appreciate and avail himself of . . . This loftiness of
conduct of the President is the "madness" with which he is afflicted.
We know, and probably he knows, how this imputation of madness
might have been prevented;   but, if the remedy were even now to
be applied as a cure, having been neglected as a preventive, we
should condemn the resort to it.

**FANCIED SECURITY, OR THE RATS ON A BENDER.**

**JACKSON CLEARING THE KITCHEN.**

(Two old campaign broadsides. The upper shows Fillmore, the Whig candidate, guarding the government crib against Frémont and Buchanan in 1856; the lower shows Jackson at the time of his Cabinet reorganization in 1830).

## [THE BALTIMORE AND OHIO RAILROAD][1]

Baltimore *Gazette*, April 30, 1828

When the Baltimore and Ohio Railroad Company first embarked in the undertaking of constructing the proposed road, it was their desire, if practicable, to procure the necessary iron in the United States; and they accordingly advertised extensively for proposals for the requisite supplies, in order to ascertain the quantities that could be furnished and at what prices it would be delivered. The result of this effort convinced them that it would be necessary to look abroad for this indispensable material, as but two offers were made to the company, both of which were for very limited quantities and at prices above 100 per cent dearer than is paid by the Liverpool & Manchester Railroad Company.

From the best information that has been obtained, it appears that there is already a deficiency in the home supplies of iron, for the ordinary purposes of this country, of twenty to thirty thousand tons annually. The lowest price at which iron rails could be obtained in the United States would be about $100 per ton; and should the company have to go into the market here for the quantity wanted, a considerable rise would unavoidably be the consequence, to the serious prejudice of both the manufacturing and agricultural interests of the country.

Iron manufactured in England to suit the purposes of the railroad company . . . would cost delivered here, exclusive of duty upon it, about $57 per ton; and with a duty of twenty-five per cent ad valorem it would cost about $70 per ton. It is therefore obvious that the company must obtain their supplies from abroad, and the iron-masters of this country, under existing circumstances, can have no interest whatever in the matter of a rebate of duty; the only question being in fact whether the government will deem it judicious to burden an undertaking, in the success of which the whole nation has a deep and vital interest, with a heavy and grievous incumbrance, or will at once come forward and promote its accomplishment by the very reasonable and moderate encouragement its friends solicit. No one who has reflected on the subject can fail to appreciate the importance of the great work before us, as it regards the political, commercial, and social relations of our country; and it is on all hands admitted that the enterprise has a strong claim upon the most liberal patronage of the nation. The mere amount of the duty

---

[1] Despite the doubts of the *National Intelligencer*, there was a heavy rush for shares in the Baltimore and Ohio Railroad as soon as the stock-books were opened, and ground was broken July 4, 1828, by Charles Carroll of Carrollton. The first division of the railroad was ready for use in 1830.

which the government would derive from the iron to be employed upon the road could be of no importance to the country, but at the same time it would be severely felt by the individuals who have so generously committed their fortunes in the undertaking.

## [JOHN QUINCY ADAMS GIVES WAY TO JACKSON] [1]

New York *Evening Post*, March 5, 1829

"The long agony is over," as the *American* says, and the new Administration, the strongest ever seen in this country since the days of Washington, has entered upon its career. Of the past we will not say much, since we can say no good. The country has been rendered contemptible abroad and distracted at home. Of Mr. Adams himself we must be permitted to state that his acts have all shown that we were not wide of the truth when we said, as may be seen in our files, that although not deficient in literary acquirements, he has certain defects of character that unfitted him for directing the affairs of a great empire; and that his prejudices against that nation, with which it more behooves us to be on good and amicable terms than with all Europe besides, were so blind and so inveterate that we ventured to predict that no satisfactory settlement could ever be effected with it during his Administration. The event has proved that our fears were not chimerical. As to his Cabinet friends and advisers, we shall dismiss them from our consideration at this time by congratulating the country on its escape from what was once called by an eminent English statesman "the worst of evils that could predominate in our country: men without popular confidence, public opinion, or general trust, invested with all the powers of government."

## A DECLARATION OF ANTI-MASONIC PRINCIPLES [2]

Albany *Evening Journal*, March 22, 1830

The public sentiment which spontaneously demanded the establishment of this journal is pregnant with interest and instruction. The "speck" which three years since appeared on the western horizon has magnified itself into a mighty cloud, overshadowing the whole State, and preparing to pour out healthful showers to refresh and vivify the civil and political institutions of our country.

---

[1] Probably one of the early editorials by William Cullen Bryant, who this year became editor-in-chief of the *Evening Post*.

[2] Written by Thurlow Weed, and taken from the first issue of this long-powerful newspaper. It began as an Anti-Masonic Organ, with the support of William H. Seward, Francis Granger, and other men just becoming prominent in New York State politics; it developed into one of the important newspapers of the Whig Party.

The abduction, imprisonment, and murder of a citizen, by an association of men sufficiently numerous and influential to hold our Tribunals of Justice at bay, naturally awakened a public investigation.[1] The offences were found to have been committed by Free Masons, for the protection of their order. Further investigation established the fearful fact that the laws were too feeble to vindicate themselves against Masonic aggression. Still further inquiry proved that the executive, legislative, judicial, and municipal departments of the government were in the hands of Free Masons and under the influence of their institutions. These startling disclosures provoked a searching investigation into the principles, tendency, and aims of the Masonic institution. They will soon be unfolded, and found to be utterly inconsistent with private rights, and fraught with manifold dangers to the public welfare. . . .

The mode adopted by the people to overthrow Free Masonry is at once the most effective and least exceptionable of any that could have been resorted to. It accomplishes a great public good, without inflicting any private wrongs. None suffer with Free Masonry except such as voluntarily elect to maintain her cause and abide its fate. The friends of the order generally admit that it is *useless* — while its opponents, having clearly proved it to be *dangerous*, call upon its thousand virtuous members to renounce it and place themselves upon an equality with their fellow-citizens. There is nothing of constraint in this. Those who prefer the swelling titles, the bauble sceptres, the mock majesty, and the mystic honors and emoluments of Free Masonry, to the simple, unostentatious duties of Republican citizens — who take and obey her unearthly oaths, certainly have no title to reproach the people for withdrawing *their* confidence from the sworn subjects of another government.

There is too much frankness in the character of our people, too little guile in the nature of our institutions, to tolerate the existence of secret societies. Studied secrecy always awakens doubts and distrust. The country has everything to apprehend and nothing to hope from formidable secret societies. Shame, vice, and treason are engendered by night, and woo concealment; but charity, science, and religion love the light, and seek to be reflected in its rays. The ancients aspired to a state of moral perfection which would enable them to walk with a window in their breasts. But from this test of heathen virtue the vaunting "*Hand-maid of Religion*" shrinks, toad-like, into her dark and loathsome lodge-room, from which the genial light and wholesome air are excluded.

[1] This is of course a reference to the disappearance of William Morgan, who had published a book on the secrets of Masonry. It was alleged that the Masons had murdered him. So stern became the indignation against him that the Anti-Masonic Party polled 128,000 votes in 1830.

This paper, while laboring to disrobe Free Masonry of its assumed vestments, and to exhibit it to the world in its assumed garb, will aim to disabuse the public mind in relation to the origins, progress, and purpose of anti-Masonry. The Masonic institution, when truly presented to the understandings of men, will be found to be barren and bald of all the virtues and wisdom with which it has been invested by fable and tradition.

## [PRESIDENT JACKSON'S TOAST: A SOUTHERN INTERPRETATION [1]

### Charleston *Mercury*, April 24, 1830

The President's toast at the late Jeffersonian banquet was, "The Federal Union — it must be preserved!" To this we respond, amen. But how preserved? There is but one mode, and that is by inducing the majority to respect the rights and feelings of the minority, or, in other words, by inducing the North and East to repeal or modify the iniquitous measures by which the South is impoverished and enslaved. And that the President alludes to this mode is too evident, we think, to admit the shadow of a doubt. His message to Congress distinctly recognizes the rights of the States, and solemnly cautions Congress to beware of encroachments on them. He is a disciple of Jefferson, whose whole life was devoted to State Rights doctrines, and who first pointed out the mode by which alone Federal usurpation can be resisted and repressed. He had met with numerous other disciples of the same great man, to do honor to his memory and to revive and perpetuate his political principles. When the President, therefore, under such circumstances says that "the Union must be preserved," it follows necessarily that he refers to the mode of preservation pointed out by Mr. Jefferson. And that is, by the exercise of the sovereignty of the States and by their interposing in their highest capacity, to arrest the progress of tyranny and injustice. The President's toast, we think, taken in connection with his well-known principles, and the peculiar circumstances under which it was announced, completely puts an end to whatever little doubt may heretofore have existed as to his feelings or opinions in relation to the momentous question, now at issue between the Federal government and the whole Southern section of the Union. Indeed, it is a distinct recognition of Jeffersonian principles, as contradistinguished from the consolidation doctrines advocated by Mr. Webster.

[1] This editorial, from the chief organ of the South Carolina Nullificationists, was a transparent misinterpretation for propagandist purposes; Jackson's famous toast at the Jefferson Day dinner this year, uttered as he looked John C. Calhoun, the Vice-President, straight in the eye, was a direct defiance of the Nullifiers.

## PRESIDENT JACKSON AND INTERNAL IMPROVEMENTS [1]

Richmond *Enquirer*, June 1, 1830

The President has negatived the Maysville road bill; and he has assigned the grounds of his objections in the eloquent and memorable message which we this day lay before our readers. We do not exactly agree with all its propositions; but we hail with pleasure the defeat of the bill which he has rejected — and we hail with gratitude the spirit he displays in favor of restoring the true principles of the Constitution. He assumes the construction of the Constitution set up by the old Republican party in 1798 as its "true reading in relation to the power under consideration." He wishes to bring us back to that reading through the agency of the people. He protests directly against the passage of any bill for works of internal improvement, which "bears upon the sovereignty of the States within whose limits their execution is contemplated, if *jurisdiction* of the territory which they occupy be claimed as necessary to their preservation and use." He disclaims especially such a work as the Maysville road, as being of a *local*, not *general*, of a *State*, not a *national*, character. He objects, on the strongest grounds of expediency, to the undertaking at this time of even "such works as are *authorized* by the States, and are *national* in their character." He insists, 1st, upon the propriety of paying off the national debt, leaving our resources unfettered, reducing the taxes and burdens of the people; and 2dly, after this grand event is consummated, he urges the expediency of embarking in no "system of internal improvements without a previous amendment of the Constitution, explaining and defining the precise powers of the Federal government over it."

Throughout the whole of this interesting document, we see the spirit of a man who is desirous of bringing back the Constitution to its true reading, and of limiting the Federal government to its specified powers — of arresting the rage of encroachment — of protecting the States against any further extension of Federal jurisdiction, and of saving as much of the money power as other Administrations have left — and thus arresting, as far as such precedents would permit, the alarming course of events which has set in to the augmentation and abuse of the Federal authority.

[1] By Thomas Ritchie, the founder of the *Enquirer*. Henry Clay, who favored internal improvements at Federal expense, had a bill passed in May, 1830, to build a turnpike from Maysville to Lexington, Ky. Jackson vetoed it, bringing the era of national internal improvements to an end.

## THE ARGUMENT AGAINST FREE PUBLIC SCHOOLS
Philadelphia *National Gazette*, July 10, 1830

It is an old and a sound remark, that government cannot provide for the necessities of the People; it is they who maintain the government, and not the latter the People. Education may be among their necessities; but it is one of that description which the State or national councils cannot supply, except partially and in a limited degree. They may endow public schools for the indigent, and colleges for the most costly and comprehensive scheme of instruction. To create and sustain seminaries for the tuition of all classes — to digest and regulate systems; to adjust and manage details, to render a multitude of schools effective, is beyond their province and power. Education in general must be the work of the intelligence, need, and enterprise of individuals and associations. At present, in nearly all the most populous parts of the United States, it is attainable for nearly all the inhabitants; it is comparatively cheap, and if not the best possible, it is susceptible of improvememt and likely to be advanced. Its progress and wider diffusion will depend, not upon government, but on the public spirit, information liberality, and training of the citizens themselves, who may appreciate duly the value of the object as a national good, and as a personal benefit for their children. Some of the writers about universal public instruction and discipline, seem to forget the constitution of modern society, and declaim as if our communities could receive institutions or habits like those of Sparta. The dream embraces grand Republican female academies, to make Roman matrons!

*Idem*, August 19, 1830

We can readily pardon the editor of the *United States Gazette* for not perceiving that the scheme of Universal Equal Education at the expense of the State, is virtually "Agrarianism." It would be a compulsory application of the means of the richer, for the direct use of the poorer classes; and so far an arbitrary division of property among them. The declared object is, to procure the opportunity of instruction for the child or children of every citizen; to elevate the standard of the education of the working classes, or equalize the standard for all classes; which would, doubtless, be to lower or narrow that which the rich may now compass. But the most sensible and reflecting possessors of property sufficient to enable them to educate their children in the most liberal and efficacious way, and upon the broadest scale, would prefer to share their means for any other purpose, or in any other mode, than such as would injuriously affect or circumscribe the proficiency of their own offspring.

## THE PROTECTIVE TARIFF AND THE SOUTH

Richmond *Enquirer*, March 15, 1831

It is impossible that the people of the oppressed sections of the United States *can submit much longer to so oppressive a system.* The extinguishment of the public debt is rapidly approaching. We tell our tariff brethren of the North in the frankest and most friendly spirit that it is impossible to remain in this durance vile for many years longer. When that debt is sponged away (and we go for that consummation even more anxiously than they do), the question must be settled — and we trust to heaven with the mutual consent of all the partners in the compact. Union, harmony, the most cordial fellowship with our brethren, are objects dear, very dear, to our hearts. But we cannot tolerate oppression — a subjection to a system so absurd, so much at war with every principle of our Federal system, the unfettering institutions of a young and a free people, and with the very spirit of the age itself.

## TOKENS OF NATIONAL GROWTH

Philadelphia *Gazette*, February 23, 1832

*The Centennial Anniversary (of Washington's Birth).* — Yesterday will be ever memorable in the annals of our city. . . . The civic and military procession in honor of it, to which we particularly refer, was the most imposing, and altogether the most curious and respectable, that has taken place perhaps in modern times. If the remains of Washington had been the prize in a competition of effort throughout the land, to pay the most jealous and signal homage to his memory, they would, we think, have been allotted to this community. The procession embraced nearly 20,000 persons; it was between three and four miles in length; it consumed upwards of two hours in moving steadily past any particular spot; it must have marched about eight miles; it drew forth to the streets, or attracted to the windows, nearly the whole population of Philadelphia; and many thousands came in from the country to witness the extraordinary spectacle.

Washington *National Intelligencer*, April 19, 1832

*Bustle at the Capital.* — Crowds flock to the city as much as ever. There is no end to visitors. They are coming and going every hour in the day. All the lines between this city and Baltimore are full every day. We have several fresh beauties from the East; Philadelphia and New York parties are as frequent as ever. We had the other night three parties at the selfsame hour, and tonight two splendid ones. We don't know what the world is coming to. It is very evident it is not coming to an end, however.

## A LEAF FROM MRS. TROLLOPE'S MEMORANDUM BOOK[1]

New York *Evening Post*, July 9, 1832

(Found among some loose papers accidentally left at her lodgings)

New York is rather a charming little city, containing from 100,000 to 150,000 inhabitants, mostly black. The streets are altogether monopolized by these sons and daughters of Africa, who take the wall of you on all occasions; and it would be entirely useless, as well as extremely dangerous, to notice any insult which they may offer you, as they all carry long daggers concealed in their bosoms, and use them, too, with utter impunity, under the very nose of the public authorities. Indeed, I once saw a little black boy carried to Bridewell for stealing, and that very afternoon the whole negro male population turned out in a procession, consisting of twenty thousand, with banners which bore the words "Wilberforce Philanthropic Society." From this I presume the boy's name was Wilberforce; at all events, the Court of Sessions (which, by the way, is here held in a little grocery store in William Street, called Harmony Hall) acquitted the culprit, in consequence of the sensation his imprisonment had produced.

This took place in the month of August, and so great was the alarm that immense numbers fled from the city, fearing another *insurrection*. Whole families departed at once. The steamboats (of which there are two tolerable good ones, one plying to Albany, the other to New Orleans on Long Island) were every day crowded with trembling passengers, who sought refuge from the bloody and atrocious scenes which yearly disgrace the streets, and retired to Saratoga, Communipaw, Brooklyn in New Jersey, Charleston in North Carolina, and Greenwich Village on Lake George. Scarcely a night passes without the negroes setting two or three of the houses

[1] Frances Trollope had come to the United States in 1827, and remained until 1831; a business venture — a small shop — of hers in Cincinnati failed, and her impressions of the country were colored by the fact. She published her "Domestic Manners of the Americans" in both England and America early in 1832, and its caustic and unfair picture of American life created great resentment. Bryant here satirizes its foolish exaggerations and inaccuracies. Not a single sentence in the memorandum "leaf" fails to include some wild absurdity. The names of the theatrical personages are ridiculously confused. At the same time, in other editorials the *Evening Post* admitted that Mrs. Trollope had hit some disagreeable facts squarely on the head. It credited her book with reforming a number of prevalent vulgarities; and declared that the mere cry "A Trollope! A Trollope!" would correct public misbehavior.

on fire with the view of destroying the inhabitants. As the best mansions are made of light pine wood, it may be easily imagined that they are universally combustible; but fortunately the city of New York has really a copious supply of water, which prevents much damage.

Their theatres are positively amusing, and I must say I laughed very heartily, although to confess the truth, it was only at their tragedies and their operas. The Park Theatre was originally an old barn; its outside is disgraceful, and its interior more so. It has been burnt down *fourteen times*, probably by the religious party, which form the majority, and have now elected Jackson to the Presidency. The establishment stands opposite the Roman Catholic Cathedral, and is under the management of Messrs. Pierson and Drurie. I am indebted to my kind friend for many of these particulars. He knows that I am writing a book of travels, and although himself only an American, has kindly volunteered his services to collect materials for me, giving me sketches of character and authentic anecdotes, and has corrected, with the most scrupulous care, all of my geographical and typographical illustrations, in which the reader may consequently repose the most implicit reliance. The theatres have, however, two or three decent performers. Mr. Barnes is the principal tragedian. I saw him one evening in Romeo to Mrs. Keppel's Juliet, and I must say I thought his conception of the character rather good. He is quite small, with large melancholy eyes, and features expressive of tenderness and passion. Mrs. Keppel, as Juliet, was not sufficiently poetic, but was nevertheless pretty well. This was, however, afterwards accounted for by the discovery that she was an English lady. I afterwards saw Mr. Hilson in Young Norval. The greatest attraction they have, however, is Mr. Povey, a distinguished vocalist. He plays the Prince in Cinderella, and Masaniello, quite delightfully; all the rest are not worth mentioning. A fellow by the name of H. Placide undertook to personate the Baron, but I was thoroughly disgusted.

There are some peculiar customs prevailing among the audience here, which are apt to provoke a smile on the lips of a rational stranger. All their ladies dress in the most tasteless and extravagant style, and yet betray the most incontrovertible evidences of vulgarity, sitting on the banisters with their backs to the stage, between the acts, eating Carolina potatoes, and drinking ginger pop. This is done every night at the Park Theatre, and some good society females smoke "long nines" with a degree of audacious ease and familiarity that are really shocking.

## JACKSON'S VETO OF THE BANK RECHARTER[1]

New York *Evening Post*, July 30, 1832

We want words to express our sympathy with our worthy friends of the opposition at discovering that the veto message of the President is likely to increase his popularity, instead of destroying it as they had intended it should. That the opposition meant to give him a bill which should produce a veto, there is no question; but now they have got the veto, they are puzzled what to do with it; and the majority of them, we have no doubt, repent the haste they were in to get it. Their first manoeuvre was an attempt to excite the people against it by all sorts of opprobrious epithets bestowed upon the document, the President, and his Administration. Unluckily this had no effect. The great meeting at Pittsburgh — the great meeting at Philadelphia, in which the course of the President was approved in the warmest terms — the public rejoicings in various places in the State of Ohio — the general voice of the press in favor of this act of the President — these circumstances together soon convinced them how different is the effect of the veto from what they had expected with so much confidence.

Now take one of the leading opposition papers, and see what are its principal topics. They are full of railing against the Jackson party for supporting, indiscriminately, all the acts of the Administration; they are in a transport of indignation at the blindness of the people; and they abuse, in the bitterest terms, the presses which uphold the Chief Magistrate in refusing his signature, styling them "slavish" and "pensioned." Then they set their "ready and exact calculators" to work to ascertain how many people the area which contained the great Jackson meeting at Philadelphia could hold, with a view to reducing the supposed number of persons present. What is the fair inference from all this? Why, that the opposition are disappointed, and that the veto is popular.

## THE CHOLERA IN NEW YORK

New York *Courier and Enquirer*, August 7, 1832

The cholera first made its appearance in this city about the 25th of June, in the family of a poor woman and her two children, said to be from Quebec, who lived in Cherry near James Street. It made

---

[1] Henry Clay, in an effort to provide his party with an issue, had a Senate bill introduced in the spring of 1832 for the recharter of the Bank of the United States. Passing both houses, this bill went to President Jackson on July 4, and six days later was returned with a veto. Clay had his issue, but it proved fatal to the hopes of his party. Bryant's editorial is characteristic of the Democratic rejoicings over the popularity of the veto message.

but little progress until the 3d of July, when the Board of Health first made their official report, announcing that several deaths had occurred of a disease resembling in some measure the cholera then prevailing in Canada. The disease lingered where it first broke out for several days, when it appeared in another section of the city, and on the opposite side of it, at the foot of Reed near Washington Street. In a few days after, it broke out in Lawrence Street, and the streets in that vicinity, and almost immediately afterwards at Greenwich Village, Orange, and other streets about the Five Points, and in the lower part of Manhattan Island. These different sections are distant from each other, some half a mile, and some one or two miles. They are all inhabited by a crowded population.

The cases have been by far the most numerous in Orange, Mulberry, and Lawrence Streets, each of which have had reported from one to two hundred cases. For instance, in Orange Street, No. 20 had ten; Nos. 27 seven, 33 ten, 61 twelve, 89 nine; and many other dwellings four and five each. Four houses in Little Water Street, Nos. 2, 4, 5, and 7, have thirty-six cases. The streets in the Sixth Ward at and near the Five Points furnished about eight hundred cases within the last four weeks; and if those taken to the various hospitals from that ward were added, it is probable that the number would amount to full twelve hundred. By the late census, the Sixth Ward contained 13,570 inhabitants. If we deduct those residing in the ward in high and respectable streets, and also the number that have left the city or ward, the number left in the crowded and filthy portions will probably be about 10,000. Of this number at least 1200 have had the disease, and fully half have died; a degree of mortality seldom equalled in any country. On an examination of the sections of the city where the disease has prevailed the most, it will be found that they are all principally made ground, or ground that has been filled in. Lawrence Street, the Five Points, and lower Manhattan Island are all of this description.

If the city authorities profit by past experience, they will, we think, make some law regulating the number of persons who may occupy a house. It is a notorious fact that a number of individuals, some of whom are wealthy, in this city employ their capital by covering their lots with tenements to shelter the greatest possible number of poor families, renting them by the month, week, or day, and compelling them to pay enormously for these miserable accommodations. We have the fact from an authentic source, that on two lots in a certain street in this city, 370 miserable poor persons were found at one time, being a population exceeding that of many country villages, who were crowded together on two lots of forty by one hundred feet, or a little more. We refer to the degraded population of St. Giles on London with no small degree of disgust, when we have sections of our city inhabited by equally debased and miserable blacks and whites, as deeply sunk in crime and filth as any that can be found within any of the parishes in London.

## [A CITY EMPTIED BY THE CHOLERA PLAGUE]

New York *Evening Post*, August 20, 1832

The appearance which New York presents to one who views it at the present time from the midst of the Hudson or from the opposite shores of New Jersey is a spectacle scarcely less unusual and solemn than to one who visits what were two months since its crowded and noisy places of business.   The number of persons who have left the city is estimated at upwards of one hundred thousand people, including all classes and occupations.   So many domestic fires have been put out, and the furnaces of so many manufactories have been extinguished, that the dense cloud of smoke which always lay over the city, inclining in the direction of the wind, is now so thin as often to be scarcely discernible, and the buildings of the great metropolis appear with unusual clearness and distinctness.   On a fair afternoon the corners of the houses, their eaves and roofs, appear as sharply defined as if the spectator stood close by their side, and from the walks of Hoboken you may count the dormer windows in any given block of buildings.   The various colors of the edifices appear also with an astonishing vividness, while the usual murmur from the streets is scarcely heard.

## THE UNITED STATES BANK AS THE ELECTION ISSUE

Washington *Globe*, August 30, 1832

A day or two since we spoke of the course taken by the opposition in making the Bank question the great engine of their party by which to eject the present Chief Magistrate and instal Mr. Clay in his place.   Every mail brings a new confirmation of our remarks. The opposition relies on the Bank question to revolutionize the politics of Pennsylvania, to secure Kentucky to Mr. Clay, to remove all doubt of the vote of Ohio, and to alienate Maryland and Missouri from the Hero of New Orleans.   It is impossible for one who does not daily look over the newspapers published in the various parts of the country to form an idea of the extent to which this devotion to the Bank is carried, and how completely the Clay party have identified their cause with that institution.   All questions of public policy — all considerations relating to national character, public virtue, free institutions, taxation, commerce, foreign relations — all are forgotten in the zeal to perpetuate the privilege of a great and overshadowing association of money lenders. A whole party have put on the badge of mammon, and have taken his mark on their forehead. Let any candid man belonging to the National Republican Party pass in review the journals of his side, as we have done this morning, and it would be cruelty to ask him whether he did not feel ashamed of the position in which they have placed themselves — harnessed and toiling in the yoke of a monied institution — contending perpetually in that sordid cause, as if the things that make the true glory and happiness of a nation had no existence.

If the fate of the United States Bank has become a question between itself and the people, it is the Bank which has made it so. If that institution had refused to lend itself to the plans of the opposition, if it had contented itself with making the application for a new charter at a time favorable to impartial discussion, if it had followed the fair and usual course of business transactions, if it had kept itself clear of the suspicion of purchasing men and presses, it would have escaped an immense load of odium which now rests upon its cause, and which even the whole weight of the opposition party brought to its aid cannot counterbalance. The people will now demand that it shall come before them with clean hands. They will ask what is the meaning of this and that "ugly smutch" upon a palm which should be stainless, and they will not take long-winded, rhetorical explanations of the matters filling a whole newspaper; they will be satisfied only with direct plain answers, such as have not yet been given.

## THE CORRUPTING INFLUENCE OF THE BANK

New York *Evening Post*, October 4, 1832

The election has now, we say it with feelings of the strongest regret, become little else than a battle between the United States Bank and the friends of the administration. Hitherto the warfare of elections has been carried on by the discussion of public measures and plans of policy, by the attack and defense of the characters and qualifications of the candidates, their acts, their opinions and their promises — by appeals to preconceived prejudices or partialities — but now, an element of a hitherto unknown and most dangerous nature is mingled with our party struggles. A monied institution, headed by an active, subtle and insinuating lender, has thrown itself with its capital of thirty millions, into the arena of political strife. What may be affected by such an institution, with such a means of influence, by the distribution of its favors among those from whom services are expected, of those whose enmity is feared, may be easily imagined. The Saviour of the world was betrayed for thirty pieces of silver. The influence of the "root of all evil" is not lessened by the lapse of eighteen hundred years, and the interests of the Union may be betrayed for thirty millions of dollars.

Sober and good men are alarmed at seeing the manner in which the Bank has intermeddled with the politics of the country. The regular organized system of corruption on which it has proceeded, the application it has made of pecuniary persuasion to men possessed of political influence — to members of Congress and conductors of the public press — while it has corrupted some enemies into friends, has caused hundreds of honest men who were its friends to become its enemies. We are yet, however, to see what will be the effect of all this upon public opinion. We are to see whether the detestation of corruption is strong enough among the mass of the people to cause them to rise in their might and prostrate, by a total and ignominious defeat, both the buyers and sellers engaged in the infamous traffic.

In the meantime, our readers may ask what the Bank is doing since the investigations of the Committee. We can assure them that it has intermitted none of its activity. The disgrace of exposure has had no influence upon its transactions. We take from the Washington *Globe* the following list of pecuniary favours distributed by it among those whose services are not to be undervalued. We have been assured from a respectable source that it is substantially correct. The accuracy of the statement that the Bank had *contracted* its loans may be judged of from this statement.

Innumerable *political* loans have been made by the principal Bank since the investigating Committee made their report.

To Gales and Seaton a new loan of $20,000 has been made, half covered up by a little indirection to give them a pretence for denial.

The faithless Senator from Mississippi has gotten at least $10,000, with mere nominal security.

About the sum of $14,000 was loaned to a member of the House of Representatives, supposed to be opposed to the Bank, who was not at his post to vote against the Bank.

Another member, always before opposed to the Bank, voted for the bill, and, with a friend who had taken care to be absent on the passage of the bill, went to Philadelphia shortly after, and the Bank loaned them on a mutual endorsement, $7,500.

After the veto, Daniel Webster, on his return home, got from the Bank about $10,000 — swelling his debt to about $40,000.

Other loans have been made, even *recently*, to members of Congress and public officers, to a considerable amount.

## JACKSON'S VICTORY OVER HENRY CLAY

New York *Evening Post*, November 12, 1832

The question who is to be our President for the next four years is now universally allowed to be settled. Popular opinion has declared itself in a manner not to be misunderstood or explained away. The most obstinate and the most prejudiced of our adversaries no longer venture to question the fact that the present Chief Magistrate has, by some means or other, obtained a fast hold upon the affections and confidence of the people of the United States. They like his character, they like his manner of administrating the affairs of the nation, and they have made up their minds to have him for their President for another term. There has prevailed in the great mass of the people a deeply-rooted conviction that the principles of foreign and domestic policy adopted and avowed by him are essential to the peace and prosperity of the Union. This conviction did not manifest itself by any clamor, because there was no occasion for any; but when the time came for declaring itself through the ballot-boxes, it came forward with a strength which nothing could resist. The opposition were swept before it like stubble before the whirlwind. We look around us and wonder how so feeble a minority could have contrived to make so much noise, and by what means they could have inoculated themselves so universally — even to the shrewdest and most experienced in their ranks — with the delusion that they should prevail in the contest. . . .

For our own part, we rejoice at the result for manifold reasons independent of the ordinary pleasure attending the victory of one's own party. We rejoice because a man clear-minded, honest, and decided far beyond the majority of those who fill high political stations in the various States, is triumphantly sustained by the people against the malice of his enemies. We rejoice that the only man under whom there can exist a prospect of pacifying the discontents of the South, and of preserving the Union, is continued in power. We are glad that a pacific settlement of the Indian question is now certain, and that a civil war with Georgia, into which the declared policy of either of General Jackson's competitors would have inevitably plunged the nation, will be avoided. We congratulate the nation that so large a majority of its citizens have concurred with the President in placing the seal of reprobation on that folly which would have exhausted the resources of the nation in a series of wasteful and ill-considered projects of internal improvement, and which would have produced perhaps perpetual collisions between the national government and that of the States. We congratulate all honest men that the league between the opposition and the Bank, and the attempt to elect a President by pecuniary corruption, has been defeated in such a signal manner that it will serve as a fearful warning for the future. In the election of Mr. Van Buren to the Vice Presidency, we are gratified to see that the people have passed a solemn censure on that Senate which, listening only to the promptings of party hatred, endeavored to proscribe one of our ablest and most deserving citizens. Finally, we rejoice to witness with what an intelligent and fortunate unanimity the people have ratified the sound, wise, and healing principles of public policy adopted by the present Administration.

## MR. VAN BUREN'S RETURN FROM ENGLAND [1]

### New York *Evening Post*, November 22, 1832

The compliment paid by our city authorities to Mr. Van Buren has been consummated at a moment when, from every quarter of the land, every mail brings to him the most gratifying assurances that his private virtues and public services, the moderation of his temper, the integrity of his heart, the fortitude of his mind, and the zeal of his patriotism, are justly estimated by the people. At such a moment, an avowal of regard from a single city can hardly be supposed to produce the deep effect upon his feelings which, a short while since, such an expression from the metropolis of his native State could not but have occasioned. But let it be remembered, in justice to the Corporation, that they are not timeservers in this respect. They have not waited till the sentiments of other cities and other States could be ascertained. They have not hesitated to act until a land's united cry should speak, with an emphasis not to be misunderstood, the sense of the whole people as to the character of Van Buren, and as to that proceeding of the United States Senate by which, without cause, and on the most unfounded pretence that was ever alleged against a statesman, he was called from a diplomatic mission which his talents promised to render of great value to the nation. New York was not so tardy to do honor to her insulted son. As long ago as March, 1829, the compliment yesterday paid was determined upon, as will be seen by the resolution which will be found in its place in the account below of the proceedings upon this interesting occasion. Why this resolution was not carried into effect immediately upon Mr. Van Buren's return from Europe, all our readers will remember; and the conduct of that gentleman then, in declining the ceremonial of a public re-

[1] Martin Van Buren was appointed Minister to England on August 1, 1831; his enemies in the Senate, led by Vice-President Calhoun, and actuated by unworthy reasons of political enmity, rejected the nomination. Their act redounded to the political advantage of Van Buren, and Bryant's editorial recognizes the fact.

ception, and the various honors which were intended him, gratifying as under the circumstances they must have been, was justly looked upon as another instance, added to the many he had before given, of his readiness at all times to sacrifice personal advantages to considerations of public good.

How significant, how beautiful, how fine a comment on the character of our people and the nature of our institutions, is the act of political retribution paid the Senate for their malignant course to Mr. Van Buren! Who now are the rebuked? To the same chair, lately occupied by the ambitious Lepidus when he dared to throw his casting vote into the political balance against a man his equal in acquirements, his superior in talents, and oh, how greatly his superior in honesty, in singleness of motive, in elevation of character, and in all those qualities which give the greatest value to talents and learning — to that high seat the rejected is raised! The rebuked of Clay and Calhoun is the honored of the people! The very act that was intended to prostrate him forever, has made him Vice-President of the United States! In contemplating such an act of retributive justice, one might almost be excused for exclaiming, "Vox populi, vox Dei!"

## THE UNION [1]

### Washington *Globe*, November 29, 1832

Can there be a doubt of the purpose of the Nullifiers to carry it to a civil war? Why the recent language of their leading partizans? Why do we hear of pledges of life, fortune, and sacred honor, "to carry into effect the resolves of the Convention"? Why has Governor Hamilton been so assiduously courting and drilling the militia? Why has he recently, by the most extraordinary means, procured himself to be elevated to the military rank of a brigadier-general? What is all this but preparation for war? What does Hamilton mean, but to be the military hero of Nullification, while Hayne shall hold the civil power, and Calhoun, the desperate author of the whole scheme, watch to profit by their hazards and their perils?

This, then, is Nullification: — *It is* CIVIL WAR AND DISUNION!

Let each American now ask himself, *Shall the Federal Union be preserved?* Shall these desperate men be permitted to entail on this happy land, or on South Carolina itself, the miseries of Civil War and the everlasting evils which will flow from the destruction of this confederacy? Who is ready to have the blood of millions, the oppression of this beautiful continent, and the slavery of its in-

[1] This long article is characteristic of the best editorial utterances of the *Globe*, and is unquestionably one of those upon which the editors carefully consulted President Jackson.

habitants, born and unborn, laid at his door? Let no man promise himself that these States can be riven asunder, and the fragments exist alongside each other in perpetual peace. Any anticipation of that sort is contradicted by all history, by the dispositions of men, and by the peculiar circumstances in which the new States or confederacies would be placed. As family quarrels are most bitter, so animosities as deep as can torture the human heart would actuate the disjointed remains of the confederacy, urging them into frequent conflicts, the most persevering and embittered. The North would rise up against the South, and the South against the North. The West would send her hordes over the mountains in search of glory and conquest. Instead of being a land of peace, plenty, and happiness, our country would present scenes of war, want, and wretchedness. From the points of millions of bayonets, liberty would fly to other lands, and leave us ages of blood, extortion, and misery, in the place of that Union whose blessings are now treated with derision.

Is it asked how the career of the Nullifiers is to be cut short and their fatal designs defeated? It may be done without the shedding of one drop of blood. Let the whole country rise up as one man and denounce them. Let the whole people out of the limits of South Carolina, and the true hearts within, form themselves at once into a great UNION PARTY, and say to them, in a language which they shall understand, THIS UNION SHALL NOT BE DISSOLVED. Let them resolve, one and all, that while they will make every concession to remove all just causes of complaint, they will rally round the government in support of the Union which *must be preserved at every hazard*. Let them tell the Nullifiers, it is not for you that we step forward in this crisis; it is for ourselves, for our children, for your children, for generations unborn, for the cause of freedom and the happiness of mankind.

A language like this from the other States, and especially from States in the South — from Virginia — from North Carolina — from Georgia — from Alabama — would make these men pause in their mad career, and suspend the hand of violence. Deprived of all hope from without, and resolutely opposed within, they would see only their own immediate ruin in a forward step, and would return to the path of duty and of moderation.

Will the States and the people in the South, the West, the North or the East, withhold the expression of their firm resolves not to permit the dissolution of the Union? Will they omit to do an act of peace, when they may prevent an act, or acts, which their country will mourn for ages to come? Will they not concentrate public opinion upon this horrible design with an intensity which shall make its projectors shrink appalled from their own imaginings before they are bodied forth in acts of violence?

Let no one say the expression of public opinion, through legislative bodies, public meetings, and the press, will not produce the desired result. It is *the hope of aid from abroad* which gives the Nullifiers courage. Deprived of that, they sink into despair and abandon designs which can end only in their own ruin.

No time is to be lost. The edict of Nullification has already appeared, as prepared by the conspirators for the adoption of the convention. With rapid pace, the attempt to execute it will follow. Unless public opinion do its work in a few weeks and awe the factious into submission, the mind cannot conceive the woes which these men may bring upon South Carolina and their own country. Let every legislature, every public meeting, every editor, and every American patriot, hasten to make his voice heard, that the warning may come in time to prevent the first act of violence.

## SOUTH CAROLINA MUST YIELD

New York *Evening Post*, December 7, 1832

Letters from Washington assure us that notwithstanding the calm tone of the message in relation to South Carolina, the President, with his usual decision, is taking the *most efficient measures* to secure the due execution of the revenue laws in that State. No language has been employed the effect of which might be only to irritate, and it is not the manner of the President to bandy words with anyone. A course of legislation in relation to the tariff has been recommended which, if adopted, cannot fail to appease all discontentment in the South, and even to satisfy every man in South Carolina whose excitement on this question has not run away with his reason, or who has not suffered the views of a guilty ambition to make him forget his duty to the Federal Republic, and his regard to the welfare of his own State. This recommendation every true patriot must earnestly hope to see adopted — that it will be so, we cannot permit ourselves to doubt — if not by the present Congress, at least by the next. For our own part, we believe that the recommendation will of itself go a great way towards pacifying the excitement which exists in South Carolina, and that it will dispose the majority of her citizens to pause in the rash and violent career upon which they have entered. If it does not in a good degree operate as a sedative upon the inflamed feelings of that State — if many of the leaders of the Nullification party, worthy by their talents and their previous standing in the councils of the nation to take the lead in a better cause, are not influenced by it to use their exertions in calming the storm they have raised, they will give the strongest confirmation of what has been laid to their charge, that they are guilty of a previous and deliberate design to dismember the Union.

In the meantime, however, while South Carolina remains a member of the Union, she must expect to obey its laws and contribute to support its burdens. The utter confusion into which the suspension of the revenue laws in one State, and that a State possessing one of our most important ports, would throw the affairs of the nation, the multiplied embarrassments in which it would involve the trade and revenue, make it a matter of imperious duty on the part of the government to see that those laws are strictly enforced.

## [SOUTH CAROLINA RISKING RUIN]

New York *Evening Post*, December 21, 1832

The Union party of South Carolina are no less ardent and determined in support of the execution of the laws of the Federal government, than the dominant party in taking measures to resist them. A letter from Columbia dated December 10, published in the Charleston *Courier*, says that "if there is any difference between the Unionists of Charleston and those of the interior, it is that the latter exceed the former in warmth and violence." The people of Greenville have raised the flag of the United States in the village, and declare that it shall remain flying while they have lives to defend it. Hamilton and Calhoun, it is said, have been hung and burnt in effigy in Spartansburg District. A similar spirit prevails in other quarters of the State, and the tyrannical decrees held over their heads by the majority seem to have inflamed the excitement which already existed into a feeling of fierce indignation. The resolutions already before the Union Convention in that State recognize most solemnly an undivided allegiance to the real government, and propose a military organization of the Union Party to defend, if necessary, their rights by force.

Should a civil war break out in consequence of resistance to the revenue laws, we have no doubt that it will first begin among the citizens of South Carolina. Any feeling of jealousy, animosity, or indignation with which the people of two portions of the Union may regard each other is complacency itself to that which subsists between the two parties in South Carolina. An attempt to carry the Ordinance of the convention into effect with the terrible array of penalties by which it is accompanied, much as it might be regretted for the sake of the Union at large, would be unutterably calamitous for the State itself.

## [NULLIFICATION AND THE TARIFF COMPROMISE]
### Washington *Globe*, January 17, 1833

It is somewhat remarkable that Mr. Calhoun should feel himself called on to thrust his nullifying ordinance into Congress as a sort of firebrand at a moment when that body, from respect to the changed condition of the whole country, was temperately discussing the best means of accommodating the tariff to the various interests concerned. Did Mr. Calhoun imagine that, by waving the torch of civil war in the eyes of the Senate, and by giving intensity to its flame, he could drive that body into submission? We think not. It is probable rather that he took this course to arrest the progress of calm discussion, and to mar the spirit of conciliation which portended a sudden termination of the excitememt that gives him temporary importance — "a bad eminence!" It certainly required a good deal of hardihood in the former Vice-President to introduce into the Senate the snares which he has been preparing for two years to destroy its dignity — nay, its authority — its existence as the representative of a glorious confederacy of States. Catiline, we believe, although he held his seat in the Senate while without its walls he was conspiring its overthrow and that of the Republic, had not the hardihood to call on the body to sanction his designs and consent to self-immolation. Mr. Calhoun comes forth from the scene in which he has arrayed an armed force against the government, and has the audacity to present himself in the Senate chamber with the sword in one hand, and the nullification ordinance in the other, to demand submission — an acquiescence in the annihilation of the best government in the world; and this from the august assembly to which the States of the Union have most especially confided its preservation! We trust some Cicero will be found in that body, who will mark the assailant of our sacred institutions with more than the fire of the Consul's eloquence, and hand his own name and that of the public enemy down to posterity in the noblest strains of patriotic inspiration.

## THE NULLIFICATION COMPROMISE OF 1833[1]
### Washington *Globe*, March 22, 1833

The Nullifiers, for the sake of the political objects of their leaders, will conceal from the honest and deluded people the fact which Mr. Clay declared to be his strongest motive for entering into an

[1] Clay's compromise tariff bill, designed to allay the resentment of South Carolina, and providing for a gradual reduction of the tariff duties, extending over nine years, was passed by Congress on March 1, 1833, and signed by Jackson on March 2. The *Globe* here taunts Calhoun with having accepted a very bad bargain in order to save his face.

agreement; that he foresaw that at the next session the South would get all it asked. Were the Nullifiers to confess that if they had waited until the coming of the new Congress they would have obtained the same gradual reduction of the tariff, unclogged by the hard conditions imposed by Mr. Clay in the cash duties, the home valuation, and the increase of the duty on coarse woollens from five to fifty per cent, what would the planters say to their Representatives, who were in such haste to make sacrifices at the shrine of a political coalition? And especially when they find themselves in shackles to adhere to the terms, however willing a subsequent Congress may be to make the adjustment more favorable; and when the adjustment concluded is not to take effect in the way of reduction till after the next Congress shall have been convened, whereas the increase on the woollens begins, as we understand it, before any reduction takes place. Thus Mr. Calhoun has bargained for an immediate increase of duties, and remote reductions coupled with hard conditions; and all, as Mr. Clay says, to prevent the next Congress from granting a relief that would at once have been fatal to his system, for which he has obtained a reprieve of nine years.

## ANDREW JACKSON VISITS NEW YORK

New York *Evening Post*, June 13, 1833

The reception of the President yesterday was one of the most striking public ceremonies ever witnessed by the people of the city. It did not derive its interest from any splendour of preparation, though in this respect there was no deficiency, and the arrangements were made generally in good taste, and executed with admirable order, but from the spirit of cordial good-will and the enthusiasm of welcome which pervaded the vast population of the metropolis and the multitude of strangers assembled to witness his arrival, and which manifested itself in a thousand spontaneous demonstrations of personal kindness and respect. The inhabitants of the city seemed to have deserted all the other quarters for the Battery and Broadway. The approach of the steamboats and vessels in company made a noble and picturesque appearance from the shore, proceeding as they did, slowly and in beautiful order, decorated with coloured flags, and the decks covered so thickly with passengers that they seemed like vast animated masses, while the water around them was covered with smaller craft, which seemed with difficulty to subdue their speed to the deliberate and majestic progress of the steamers. The people stood waiting in the perfect silence on the Battery and the neighboring wharves until the moment he landed,

when the salutes and the music were followed by deafening acclamations from the multitude.   But the most striking part of the
spectacle was the progress of the President through Broadway.  The
street from the Battery to the City Hall was thronged with spectators;  the sidewalks were closely crowded;  rows of carriages were
drawn up on each side, and the narrow passage in the midst was
less densely filled with a shifting multitude.   Every perch that could
sustain a spectator was occupied, the lamp posts, the trees, the
awnings, the carriage tops, — every window showed a group of fair
faces, — the house tops were also crowded with spectators wherever
a footing could be obtained — men were seen sitting on the eaves
and clinging to the chimneys.   To those who looked from an elevated
position on this vast and crowded aggregate of human life, the
spectacle was inexpressibly imposing.   The number of persons collected between the Park and the Battery has been estimated at a
hundred thousand, but if we include those who occupied the windows and the house tops, the number must have been scarcely less
than twice as great.   As the President appeared, his white head
uncovered, sitting easily on his horse and bowing gracefully on
either side, the recollection of his military and civic service, of his
manly virtues and chivalric character, rose in the minds of the
people, and their enthusiasm was not to be restrained.   They
crowded about him so as often for a few minutes to impede his
progress, they broke through the circle of armed cavalry that surrounded him, they rushed between the legs of his escorts' horses to
touch his hand or some part of his person.   The ladies waved their
handkerchiefs from the windows, and his course was attended with
perpetual acclamations.

## [THE BANK'S PROSTITUTION OF THE AMERICAN PRESS]

Washington *Globe*, July 4, 1833

The Bank of the United States has put out a new set of feelers.
The Swiss Corps of Editors, who upon a search were taken with the
money of the people as well as of the private stockholders, picked
most dexterously from Mr. Biddle's breeches' pocket, have lost all
influence with the public.  As *mere mercenaries*, it was soon perceived
that the patriotism of the enlisted body of editors was proportioned
to the momentum derived from the Bank.   Eighty thousand dollars
threw the *National Intelligencer* into ecstacies, and its zeal sparkled
out in thousands and tens of thousands of gratuitous extras.   Fifty-
two thousand dollars turned the *Courier and Enquirer* topsy-turvy,
and when fairly upon its legs again, it ran off in a direction directly

opposite to that which it had previously pursued. Those who supported the Bank (it had previously told us) were "bought as cattle in the market;" but the sum of $52,000, tendered to Mr. Webb, convinced him that the price given was quite too much for bullocks. It was found that the Bank was able and liberal enough to enter upon Sir Robert Walpole's traffic and buy *honorable men*. To get into such good company was always Webb's ambition, so he took the Bank's title and its pension; and a hard bargain the Bank has had of him.

Thirty thousand dollars metamorphosed the Pennsylvania *Inquirer*, and twenty thousand brought the *Telegraph* to renounce vows against the Bank more terrible than those of Hannibal against the Romans; and this, too, notwithstanding Mr. Biddle's written agreement that the money was not to be taken as a consideration for the abandonment of his principles. The notorious prostitution of the press to the Bank, although not yet half revealed, has brought its editorial corps into complete disgrace; and it has therefore fallen upon the expedient of setting its stipendiaries to work under disguises. One of its hirelings has disgraced the name of "Patrick Henry," another that of "Cato," and before all's over, we shall have every incorruptible patriot of antiquity and every illustrious name of our own times dishonored in the Bank's service.

## THE UNITED STATES BANK

### Cincinnati *Republican*, August 6, 1833

There remains not the least doubt that a desperate effort will be made by the Bank, at the ensuing session of Congress, to obtain a re-charter. Great hopes of success are founded upon the adhesion of the Nullifiers to the cause of the institution. In addition to the strength of this accession, it is well understood that her gold will be scattered with a liberal hand, on the theory of Horace Walpole, that *"every man has his price."* How many members she may be able to buy remains yet to be told. How many may yet yield up their principles and their honors to the graspings of avarice, and prostrate themselves before this modern temple of Plutus, cannot be conjectured now. History will inform posterity of the facts. Some of the honorable members may, Judas-like, betray their master, the people's will; but let not the fancied security arising from a secret sale of their conscience be relied upon to screen them from that punishment which will assuredly follow their crime.

The attempt will be made to carry the Bank bill over the head of the President by procuring its reconsideration by two-thirds of each house of Congress. The scheme is not even concealed. But it will not avail the Bank. However successful she may prove herself next winter, at the ensuing elections she will be compelled again to enter the field. The people who in 1832 decided this question by an overwhelming verdict, in the election of Andrew Jackson, are not to be trifled with by hollow-hearted agents. Those members of Congress who shall dare to become the purchased partisans of the Bank will meet with the full measure of that chastisement which the people can so effectually inflict. A new Congress, fresh from the fountain of power, will not hesitate to reverse an act that has been carried by corruption and political treachery.

Let the Bank, and the friends of the Bank, rest assured that if the veto of the people's President will not stay them in their attempts to obtain a renewal of their monopolies, the people, themselves, will pronounce that *veto*. They will pronounce it in a voice that cannot be misunderstood, and in a manner that will settle the question forever. Let the Bank and its mercenary tools look to it.

## THE REMOVAL OF THE DEPOSITS [1]

New York *Evening Post*, September 23, 1833

*Hung be the heavens with black! Yield day to night!*
*Comets, importing change of time and states,*
*Brandish your crystal tresses in the sky,*
*And with them scourge the bad revolting stars,*
*That let the public be removed*
*From Biddle's bank — too famous to live long!*

Of this tenor are the jeremiads of the Bank journals. It is heart-rending to hear their doleful lamentations on the occasion of the removal of the deposits. They lift up their voices and weep aloud. From the depths of their affliction come sounds of sublime denunciation. They grieve with an exceeding great grief over the fallen glory of their temple, and refuse to be comforted. The tears which stream from their eyes seem to have cleared their mental vision, and they see future events as through a glass darkling. "A field of the dead rushes red on their sight." They foretell the ruin of their country, for "the Cabinet improper have triumphed!" and woe! woe! woe! is now the burden of their prediction. "The die is cast!" exclaims the *National Intelligencer;* "the evil counsellors by whom the President is surrounded have prevailed!" "The star of Olivier le Vain is in the ascendant!" "The evil consequences which we predicted *must* result from it to all the interests, public and private,

[1] The somewhat excessively literary tone of this editorial betrays Bryant's hand before he had learned restraint: but its description of the wailings of the Whig newspapers is hardly overdrawn.

of the country!" "If this be not tyranny — if this be not usurpation, what under heaven can constitute tyranny and usurpation?" "The law openly trampled on!" "its pernicious effects!" — "bankruptcy and ruin must result from it!" "Will the people stand by and calmly see their authority thus spurned? — We asked if the people will quietly witness the restraints of the law broken down, and trodden under feet by their own servants. Will the Secretary of the Treasury suffer the sanctity of the law to be violated in his person?"

The *National Gazette* is not less sublimely dolorous, nor less fearfully prophetic. But however great its patriotic grief for the evil that has befallen the country, the event does not excite its surprise. "It was to be expected," says that pure and single-minded journal, "that the scheme of profligate and rancorous hostility against the Bank would be implacably pursued;" and it added that "the case is fitted to awaken lively alarm and the gravest reflection." "To what does this lead? — to the result that the President of the United States will have usurped the command of the whole twenty-five millions of revenue! and the power of distributing that revenue to whomsoever he pleases, whether to Banks *or to individuals at Washington or elsewhere, as managers of a political game!*" "This affair is equal in fearful import to anything that has occurred in our country;" it is "outrageous law!" and is a "scheme of usurpation."

The rest of the purchased presses of the Bank are not less lachrymose and lugubrious, and all of them partake of a spirit of prescience. They all exclaim, almost in the words of Lord Byron,

> *The day of our destiny's over,*
> *The star of our fate has declined!*

— "the times are out of joint," they say — a disaster has befallen the country from which it can never recover — we are ruined, lost, utterly undone! — and like the misshapen dwarf in the "Lay of the Last Minstrel," they wave their lean arms on high and run to and fro, crying "lost! lost! lost!" Who can doubt the sincerity of their lamentations at the death-blow which has been given to the United States Bank, when it is remembered how munificent a patron that institution has been to them? Who can wonder that they appear at the head of the funeral train as chief mourners, and raise so loud their solemn wail, when he reflects how well their grief is paid for? No hired mourner at a New England funeral ever earned his wages by so energetic a wail, or so lachrymose an aspect. They seem as woe-begone as pilgrims from the Cave of Trophinious, when

> — *the sad sage, returning, smiled no more.*

But their wailing is in vain — "vainly they heap the ashes on their heads" — the fate of the Bank is sealed; and we, who are not paid to wet our cheeks with artificial tears, who have no cause to be a mourner, must be permitted to congratulate the country that a monopoly which, in the corrupt exercise of its dangerous power threatened to sap the foundation of American independence, has by this firm and timely act of the general government been reduced to a state of feebleness which, we trust, is only the precursor of its final dissolution.

## THE PENNSYLVANIA PRISON SYSTEM[1]

*American Quarterly Review*, September, 1833

The idea of expiation does not belong to it. It is humane in all its operations, and the deprivation of liberty and of intercourse with others, is only to afford proper facilities for reflection and moral culture. It has no relation to society at large, further than the knowledge of the belief in the necessity of seclusion, to remove criminal propensities, may deter those whom the fear of the penalty, and not upright principles, keep in the path of honesty. What is the amount of atonement rendered to society by the confinement of the offender under discipline more or less rigorous? What gratification can the community derive from any amount of bodily pain which can be inflicted upon an individual? The prisoner in his cell is lost sight of by the world, and the whole operation of the system relates to himself. The causes which led to the crime are removed from him. The morbid influences of evil habits, associations, and passions are withdrawn — he is thrown back upon himself — he sees only those who are reputable, and learns to compare his present condition with theirs. When he leaves the prison, the finger of scorn is not pointed to him to throw him again into the paths of vice, and there is nothing to prevent the success of his exertions in the way of uprightness. . . .

After using language decidedly approbatory of the discipline in Pennsylvania, and stating it as that which offers the least embarrassment, the French commissioners are brought to speak of the discipline of the Auburn system. The infliction of stripes is the compulsory process of the plan last named. Stripes were once the punishment for offences committed in Pennsylvania. The whipping

[1] The Pennsylvania prison system was built upon solitary confinement with labor, and marked an epochal advance in American penal methods. The Auburn system in New York was based upon labor in common, but in silence, with corporal punishment for breaches of discipline. This semi-editorial article in a Pennsylvania review was called forth by De Tocqueville's report to the French Government, and defends the Pennsylvania system as the better.

post was once the great scandal of our humane community.  Our old citizens advert to that period as that in which society had not emerged from barbarism.  Humanity was outraged, and the system exploded as unworthy the age.  It was almost the last remnant of the retributive system, but it was a material part of it.  Our public men held the opinion that it degraded the moral sense, and that it was calculated to plunge men still deeper, who were already low enough in the moral estimate.  They held that it produced vindictive feelings in the sufferer, and added malice and malignity to crime.  The unhappy sufferer saw no means of regaining his station, after having undergone this degradation.  He truly felt that the honest community was no community for him.

## THREE OPPOSITION LEADERS: CLAY, CALHOUN, AND WEBSTER[1]

### New York *Evening Post*, March 31, 1834

When an intelligent and rational people is called upon in a contest between two great political parties, it is proper for them to know who are their opponents and what they are fighting for; whether for something or nothing; principles or men.  Although the question of restoring the deposits and perpetuating the monopoly of the Bank of the United States is inseparably associated with the result of the coming election, it is by no means the only point involved in the contest.  The party we have to contend with is manifold; it is headed by the most discordant leaders, wielding the opposite weapons; each marching under his own banner, and each laboring in his own cause.  Let us then pass in review their avowed principles and purposes, that the people may judge whether such discordant materials could possibly be kept together except by the strong cement of a common interest.

In the first place stands Henry Clay.  He is the parent and champion of the tariff and internal improvements; of a system directly opposed to the interests and prosperity of every merchant in the United States, and devised for the purpose of organizing an extensive scheme through which the different portions of the United

[1] Bryant's hand is here plainly visible; these three characterizations represent the prevailing Democratic attitude, and that of Webster alone is excessively unfair and misleading.  The essential disharmony of Calhoun and Clay was palpable.  For a time after the settlement of the Nullification troubles Calhoun, acting with the Whigs though still independent, was as warmly opposed to Jackson as were Webster and Clay.  But he shortly left the Whigs.  When Van Buren proposed the sub-treasury scheme after the panic of 1837, Calhoun supported the President.  Clay was much chagrined by his defection.

States might be bought up in detail. By assuming the power of dissipating the public revenue in local improvements, by which one portion of the community would be benefited at the expense of many others, Congress acquired the means of influencing and controlling the politics of every State in the Union, and of establishing a rigid, invincible consolidated government. By assuming the power of protecting any class or portion of the industry of this country, by bounties in the shape of high duties on foreign importations, they placed the labor and industry of the people entirely at their own disposal, and usurped the prerogative of dispensing all the blessings of Providence at pleasure. They could at any time decide what class of industry should be enriched, and what class impoverished; whether commerce should flourish or decay; whether the manufacturer of cotton, wool, or iron should become a king, while the common laborer sank into a pauper. Out of this system grew those great manufacturing establishments which have monopolized almost all the pursuits of simple mechanics, and converted them from independent men presiding over their own homes, masters of their own shops, and proprietors of their own earnings, into the pale, sickly, and half-starved slaves of companies and corporations.

It is against this great system of making the rich richer, the poor poorer, and thus creating those enormous disproportions of wealth which are always the forerunner of the loss of freedom; it is against this great plan of making the resources of the general government the means of obtaining the control of the States by an adroit specie of political bribery, that General Jackson has arrayed himself. He has arrested the one by his influence, the other by his veto.

In the second place stands John C. Calhoun. Reflecting and honest men may perhaps wonder to see this strange alliance between the man by whom the tariff was begotten, nurtured, and brought to a monstrous maturity, and him who carried his State to the verge of rebellion in opposition to that very system. By his means and influence, this great Union was all but dissolved, and in all probability would at this moment lie shattered into fragments had it not been for the energetic and prompt patriotism of the stern old man who then said, "The Union: it must be preserved!" Even at this moment Mr. Calhoun still threatens to separate South Carolina from the confederacy if she is not suffered to remain in it with the privilege of a *veto* on the laws of the Union. It is against these dangerous doctrines, which have been repudiated by every other State in the Union, which find no kindred or responsive feeling in the hearts of the people, that General Jackson stands arrayed, in behalf of the integrity of this great confederation. He appears as a

champion of Union, and appeals to the people to support him in
the struggle for their happiness.

The third of the triumvirate of this strange confederacy of contradictions is Daniel Webster. Without firmness, consistency, or
political courage to be a leader, except in one small section of the
Union, he seems to crow to any good purpose only on his own dung-
hill, and is a much greater fowl in his own barnyard than anywhere
else. He is a good speaker at the bar and in the House; but he is
a much greater lawyer than statesman, and far more expert in
detailing old arguments than fruitful in inventing new ones. He is
not what we should call a great man, much less a great politician;
and we should go so far as to question the power of his intellect,
did it not occasionally disclose itself in a rich exuberance of contradictory opinions. A man who can argue so well on both sides
of a question cannot be totally destitute of genius.

And here these three gentlemen, who agree in no one single
principle, who own no one single feeling in common, except that of
hatred to the old hero of New Orleans, stand battling side by side.
The author and champion of the tariff, and the man who on every
occasion denounced it as a violation of the Constitution; the oracle
of nullification and the oracle of consolidation; the trio of antipa-
thies; the union of contradictions; the consistency of inconsistencies; the coalition of oil, vinegar, and mustard; the dressing in which
the great political salad is to be served up to the people.

We must not deny, however, that these gentlemen have a sort of
paternal, or maternal, influence watching over them and coöperating in the great cause of domestic industry and internal improvements; nullification and consolidation; State rights and Federal
usurpations, thus inharmoniously jumbled together higgledy-pig-
gledy. It is the Mother Bank, the Alma Mater, under whose petti-
coats they are fighting the great battle, every one for himself and
Mother Bank for all. Nicholas Biddle, the paramour of the old
lady, who has the sole management of her business, is connected
with the partnership as a sort of Commissary-General of purchases.
He holds the purse-strings, which are equivalent to both bridle and
spur, arms and ammunition, in modern political warfare. To all
these mighty powers and potentates the honest Democracy of this
country have nothing to oppose but their ancient, invariable principles; their inflexible integrity of purpose; and their invincible old
leader, Andrew Jackson. Is not this enough? We think it is, and
await the issue without a single throb of apprehension.

PART TWO

THE AMERICAN PRESS AND PUBLIC OPINION
1835–1865

# THE AMERICAN PRESS AND PUBLIC OPINION
## 1835–1865

A series of steps, each with a special significance, marked during the thirties — the decade of Jacksonian democracy — the advent of a new journalism. The first of these was the adaptation to American conditions of the English "penny paper," which was introduced to Boston and New York as a one-cent newspaper for the masses, filled with police court news, anecdotes, scraps of gossip, and other lively materials. The second was the establishment, under the leadership of the New York *Herald*, of the cheap newspaper appealing to a wide public not by sensational gossip, but rather through unprecedented enterprise in the publication of all news, political, mercantile, criminal, financial, and even religious, and through a new impudence and independence in editorial opinion. The third, partly a result of and partly a reaction against the two previous phenomena, was the emergence of newspapers which were as cheap as the *Sun* and the *Herald*, and as enterprising in securing news, but which were highly respectable in moral tone and serious in their attitude toward all current problems. The chief exemplar of this enterprising but moral journalism was Horace Greeley, who had begun editing the weekly *New Yorker* in 1834, had written editorials for the *Daily Whig*, and who in the spring of 1841 began the publication of the New York *Tribune*.

The first of the "penny papers," with Benjamin H. Day's New York *Sun* (launched on September 3, 1833) at their head, paid little attention to editorial utterance and influenced opinion only through their treatment of the news. They excluded from their columns all but a brief outline of the political happenings in Congress and the legislatures, and nearly all political discussions and events outside. What few editorials they did print commented briefly upon the latest sensation, upon municipal affairs, and upon questions of morals and manners. Thus the *Sun* loved to deal with drunkenness, duelling, gambling, reckless driving, and the relations between the sexes; it combined a frank portrayal of the vices and dissipations of the day in its news columns with a vigorous reprehension of them in its editorials — a combination always effective, and probably certain to live as long as journalism itself.

Nor was the *Herald*, either in its first struggling years before 1840, or in the later period when its wealth and energy gave it a measure of grudging respect, a newspaper of real editorial force. It attracted attention by its swagger, its cynicism, its recklessness, and its flippancy. It boasted of its independence upon all questions, political or otherwise, James Gordon Bennett declaring that he would avoid party commitments as if they were "steel traps." The founder loved himself to write brief editorials of an impudent nature, and astonished and scandalized the town by his pithy and Machiavellian paragraphs. Himself a Catholic, in writing of the Holy Roman Catholic Church he could add, "All we Catholics are devilish holy." Describing the commencement of an enterprise which ruined thousands, he remarked: "Ground was broken for the Erie Railroad yesterday; we hope it breaks nothing else." Again, his editorial columns contained the observation: "Great excitement among the Presbyterians just now. The question in dispute is, whether or not a man can do anything towards saving his own soul." He paraded his personality in the editorial columns after a manner which sometimes verged upon indecency, and which perhaps only the psychopath could fully explain. Thus he boasted of his intense industry; described his confidence in the paper's future — "Nothing can prevent its success but God Almighty, and he happens to be entirely on my side"; spoke of his contempt for speculators, pickpockets, and the sixpenny editors, "whose crimes and immoralities I have exposed, and shall continue to expose as long as the God of Heaven gives me a soul to think, and a hand to execute"; expatiated upon his joy in the prospect of marriage to "one of the most splendid women in intellect, in heart, in soul"; and dwelt upon his domestic felicity after the birth of his son.

Bennett knew that these materials helped to sell his newspaper; he knew that many readers were amused by the reckless levity of such editorials as that which James Parton quotes from an issue of 1836, in which he advocated the election of Jackson, Harrison, Martin Van Buren, Hugh White, or Anybody, as "the Emperor of this great Republic for life." At a later date Bennett, feeling himself firmly established, became somewhat more sober. He was also able to employ capable editorial writers, and one of his assistants, Isaac Pray, has left us a graphic account of how he used them:

The papers marked for Mr. Bennett are . . . taken to his own private room, where he is seated ready to receive them, as soon as he has finished reading the private correspondence and letters for publication which have been brought in from the post office. . .

In this way an hour is passed. The next hour will be devoted to the newspapers, and, perhaps, to a breakfast or luncheon or dry toast and tea, as an accompaniment. The editorials of the newspapers particularly are scrutinized, and every now and then dot, dot goes down a mysterious word as a peg to hang a thought or an article upon. If any political profligate or statesman has made a speech, or written a letter, the points in it are all seized with rapidity, and designated by a sign upon the memorandum. This work being done, and the tea and toast having been exhausted, the tray is removed by the boy who has been summoned for the purpose, and one of the gentlemen who phonographizes is requested to make his appearance. He arrives and takes his seat by Mr. Bennett's side, who passes the compliments of the day and asks if anything new has taken place worthy of notice. He then begins to talk; first giving the caption of the leading article. He speaks with some rapidity, making his points with effect, and sometimes smiling as he raps one of his dear political friends over the knuckles. Having concluded his article with, "that will do," he gives the head of another article and dictates it in a similar way, and then, perhaps, another and another, till the reporter sighs at the amount of the work he has before him, and he is told that that will be enough for "today."

The presence of another gentleman is now required. He may not be a phonographer, but one who is able to seize the points of a discourse, and fashion them with some force and elegance of expression, or even to illustrate them. Mr. Bennett invites him to a conversation on a particular topic upon which both have been thinking, and then gives his own view, which he desires to see written out. All the while his assistant editor takes notes, so as not to miss the points or spirit of the desired article, and thus having prepared himself with matter enough to fill two columns, he is permitted to withdraw.

Yet while the *Herald* prospered, printing early in 1840 some 17,000 copies of the daily and 19,000 of the weekly edition, and reaching during the Civil War a circulation of 100,000, its influence upon opinion remained slight. James Parton at the close of the Civil War declared that it was the chief newspaper of the metropolis. But, he added, it has singularly little power to sway the public view, as was demonstrated when its support of Lincoln against McClellan in the election of 1864 proved perfectly futile in New York city. "Influence over opinion no paper can have which has itself no opinion, and cares for none. It is not as a vehicle of opinion

that the *Herald* has importance, but solely as a vehicle of news."
This statement might well have been qualified, for at various junc-
tures and with various social groups the *Herald* really did exercise
some power. Having been consistently Democratic for years, its
support of John C. Frémont in 1856 was highly valuable to that
candidate. Soon afterward it became a vociferous mouthpiece for
the Southern slaveholders, and was read with much comfort and
satisfaction both by people of the Cotton Kingdom, and by the
commercial elements in New York which depended upon Southern
trade. During the Civil War the *Herald* made itself almost indispensable to close students of the conflict by its admirable field correspondence, upon which Bennett spent nearly half a million dollars.
As a result the *Herald* had genuine respect in England, where Goldwin Smith noted that it was regarded as *the* American newspaper;
while Lincoln was glad to placate it by offering Bennett the post of
Minister to France.

But it was the "respectable" new journalism of this period, and
not the disreputable *Herald*, which led in the formation of public
opinion. Above all, it was the New York *Tribune* and *Times* (joining the older *Evening Post*), the Springfield *Republican*, and in the
fifties, the Chicago *Tribune* as well. To Horace Greeley's great
newspaper we may unhesitatingly ascribe the development of the
editorial page in its modern American character: that is, a page
treating a wide variety of topics in a variety of manners, though
pursuing a consistent policy; achieving a level of genuine literary
merit; produced by a body of editors, not by a single man, and
representing their united judgment and information; and earnestly
directed to the elevation and rectification of public opinion. The
editorial page of Bryant's *Post* answered, in the thirties, to some of
these requirements. It had a high purpose, and flashes of fine
literary quality. But Bryant's heart was not fully in it until he returned, in 1836, from a European tour which he had hoped might
last indefinitely, and he had but one editorial assistant; first that
fiery reformer William Leggett, and later Parke Godwin. Their
energies were largely consumed by tasks connected with the news
and the counting-room, and until after Greeley led the way the
*Evening Post* seldom contained more than one or two editorial articles
daily — these being almost exclusively political.

The New York *Tribune* for a whole generation, the fateful generation in which the struggle against slavery rose to a climax, stood
preëminent among the organs of opinion in the United States; it

was one of the great leaders of the nation, and its rôle in the particular drama which ended with the Emancipation Proclamation was as great as any statesman's save Lincoln.  No free soil leader — not Chase, not Sumner, not Seward, and probably not all three combined — did as much to rally the North in unyielding opposition to the spread of slavery.  Like all great newspapers, it became far greater than its editor.  Indeed, the tragedy of Greeley's career is essentially that before 1861 he had created a magnificent instrument of democratic leadership which he proved quite unable to use wisely and safely in the four years of agony and effort which followed; and yet much of its greatness was drawn from Greeley.  In his autobiography the editor writes that his leading idea in 1841 was "the establishment of a journal removed alike from servile partisanship on the one hand and from gagged, mincing neutrality on the other" — a journal which might heartily advocate the general principles of its own party, and yet "frankly dissent from its course on a particular question, and even denounce its candidates if they were shown to be deficient in capacity or (far worse) in integrity."  But no mere idea would have carried the paper far without the qualities which he brought to it.  These included a passionate moral earnestness; an ability to divine with marvelous clarity the deeper convictions of his readers; an unshakable faith in principles; and, as E. L. Godkin said, "an English style which, for vigor, terseness, clearness, and simplicity, has never been surpassed except perhaps by Cobbett."

Greeley quickly collected about him the ablest staff yet known in the history of American journalism.  Early in 1847, when the combined daily and weekly circulation was 26,000, Charles A. Dana became city editor and shortly afterward managing editor, in which capacities he contributed to the editorial page.  So did George Ripley, who in 1849 became literary editor, a post previously held by the gifted Margaret Fuller;  so did Bayard Taylor, who in 1844 had begun to contribute travel sketches, and in 1848 became a regular member of the staff;  and so did Solon Robinson, the agricultural editor and author of those remarkable "human interest" sketches of New York life which were collected into book form under the title of "Hot Corn."  James S. Pike, the Washington correspondent, was frequently also invaluable.  By 1854 there were, besides the editor and managing editor, ten so-called associate-editors, and fourteen reporters, while the regularly paid correspondents numbered no fewer than thirty-eight.  In the years following the

agitation of the Wilmot Proviso the *Tribune* came into the plenitude
of its power.  Its weekly edition penetrated to the remotest hamlets
of the West, and in a day when popular magazines were few and
costly, it was read from beginning to end and passed from household
to household; with the result that Greeley and his staff spoke to all
the free-soil States and Territories, as James Ford Rhodes states,
"with a power never before or since known in this country."  By
1853 the circulation of the weekly *Tribune* had risen to 51,000; by
1854 it was 112,000.  Bayard Taylor, on a lecture trip in the fifties,
could write that "The *Tribune* comes next to the Bible all through
the West."

From the beginning, Greeley's conduct of the editorial page was
characterized by the general absence of that autocracy which usually
marks the strong editor.  Having chosen associates in whose judgment he had confidence, he permitted them the utmost freedom in
expressing their opinions.  An examination of James S. Pike's "First
Blows of the Civil War," a book which reprints many of the Washington articles, office letters, and editorials of the fifties, shows
Greeley repeatedly expostulating with his sub-editors, especially
Dana, for the way in which they ignored his views.  He permitted
one editorial writer, against his better judgment, to reiterate in 1861
the cry "On to Richmond!"  At various times before or during the
Civil War he explained to his readers that this or that article had
been inserted despite his disapproval.  Yet upon occasion he did
exercise his dominant authority in a ruthless way.  A wartime
division of views between him and Dana led him, with some characteristic wabbling, to cut that lieutenant summarily from his staff.

We are fortunate in having from the pen of James Parton, himself
a born journalist, a description of the methods of work pursued by
the *Tribune's* editorial staff in the early fifties.  The chief sub-editors
— Bayard Taylor, Dana, Solon Robinson, Ripley — he says, arrived
at eleven o'clock in the morning.  For a time all was leisure.  Taylor,
"pale, delicate-featured, with a curling beard and subdued mous-
tache," could be seen reading a newspaper; W. H. Fry, another
editorial writer, slowly paced the carpet; Ripley took off his coat,
and with deliberate care began examining the day's grist of twenty-
four new books and nine magazines; and Dana, entering with
quick, decided step, went to his desk in the central sanctum, and
was soon reading Karl Marx.  Between twelve and one Greeley
came in, his pockets distended with papers, and after some chat in
the outer rooms, seated himself at his desk to look over the letters,

clippings, and newspapers which covered it, and to listen to a miscellaneous pack of visitors.  Towards four o'clock, this preliminary business disposed of, he went out for dinner.  When he came back the work of the day was taken up in earnest, and by nine o'clock in the evening it was in full swing:

> The editorial rooms . . . have become intense.  Seven desks are occupied with silent writers, most of them in the *Tribune* uniform — shirt sleeves and moustache.  The night-reader is looking over the papers last arrived, with scissors ready for any paragraph of news that catches his eye.  An editor occasionally goes to the copy-box, places in it a page or two of the article he is writing, and rings the bell;  the box slides up to the composing room, and the pages are in type and corrected before the article is finished.  Such articles are those which are prompted by the event of the hour;  others are more deliberately written;  some are weeks in preparation;  and of some the keel is laid months before they are launched upon the public mind.  The Editor-in-Chief is at his desk writing in a singular attitude, the desk on a level with his nose, and the writer sitting bolt upright.  He writes rapidly, with scarcely a pause for thought, and not once in a page makes an erasure.  The foolscap leaves fly from under his pen at the rate of one in fifteen minutes.  He does most of the *thinking* before he begins to write, and produces matter about as fast as a swift copyist can copy.  Yet he leaves nothing for the compositor to guess at, and if he makes an alteration in the proof, he is careful to do it in such a way that the printer loses no time in "overrunning;"  that is, he inserts as many words as he erases.  Not infrequently he bounds up into the composing room, and makes a correction or adds a sentence with his own hand.  He is not patient under the infliction of an error;  and he expects men to understand his wishes by intuition;  and when they do *not*, but interpret his half-expressed orders in a way exactly contrary to his intention, a scene is likely to ensue. . . .
>
> Midnight.  The strain is off.  Mr. Greeley finished his work about eleven, chatted a while with Mr. Dana, and went home.  Mr. Dana has received from the foreman the list of the articles in type, the articles now in hand, and the articles expected;  he has designated those which *must* go in;  those which it is highly desirable *should* go in, and those which will keep.  He has also marked the order in which the articles are to appear;  and, having performed this last duty, he returns the list to the compositor, puts on his coat, and departs.

Three years after Greeley founded the *Tribune*, an eighteen-year-old lad in Springfield, Massachusetts, working on his father's weekly newspaper, became responsible for the founding and management of the daily *Republican* of that city.  Within a decade Samuel Bowles had made it the best provincial journal in the country. It was enterprising, keen, independent, and soundly conservative. Like Bryant and Greeley, Bowles laid emphasis upon the moral, agricultural, and literary departments of his newspaper, and in the weekly edition particularly produced a sheet which was valued not merely in western Massachusetts, but by New Englanders scattered all over the Middle West. The young editor's chief assistant, Dr. J. G. Holland, who had been a preacher and a teacher, struck a rich vein when he began to contribute to the columns what he called lay-sermons, writing three series of "Timothy Titcomb's Letters to Young People." But more important than the wealth of New England news, the vigorous literary and religious departments, and the didactic and historical articles from Holland's pen, was the editorial page. Bowles made a specialty of brief, crisp, telling editorial paragraphs, printed alongside extended and careful articles which avoided all pedantry, but which emphasized principles dear to the anti-slavery party of the North. In 1848 he, like Bryant of the *Evening Post*, supported the Free Soil Party, and declaring immediately after the passage of the Kansas-Nebraska Act that the Whig Party was dead, he made the *Republican* one of the pillars of the new Republican party. His editorials never quite achieved the superb heights of ringing eloquence reached by Bryant and John Bigelow in the *Evening Post* of the late fifties, nor did they have quite the Saxon strength of Greeley's best work; but clear, nervous, shrewd in their reasoning, and of unfailing elevation, they commanded respect throughout the North, and exercised a far wider influence than the circulation of the *Republican* (in 1860 some 5,700 for the daily edition, and 11,280 for the weekly) might have seemed to imply.

Henry Jarvis Raymond, who founded the New York *Times* on September 18, 1851, had begun his career in 1841 as assistant to Greeley at $8 a week. Late in life Greeley wrote of him that he had never known a person who "evinced so signal and such versatile ability in journalism," or who was "cleverer, readier, or more generally efficient." Raymond quickly saw that the expanding population of New York, and the fact that people had to choose between the highly moralistic Greeley and the highly cynical Bennett, furnished an opportunity for a fresh type of newspaper. His design, he announced, was to present all the news of the day from all parts of the world in the fairest manner, and to discuss public questions without "passion," in a just and good-tempered way. Unquestionably he had in mind not merely a middle line between the mental eccentricity of the *Tribune* and the moral eccentricity of the *Herald*, as Dana later put it, but an imitation of the London *Times* of Delane, trustworthy, authoritative, and complete. Founded with a capital of $100,000, a figure which contrasts strikingly with the $1,000 which Greeley had deemed to be all that he needed just a decade earlier, Raymond's *Times* quickly became a success. Its editor was a man of the world, who possessed strong political ambitions of his own, and who commanded valuable personal sources of information. He was well acquainted with Europe, and he shortly went far beyond his competitors in finding and publishing foreign news. His newspaper contained few innovations, but in its nice balance, its harmony of parts, its pervasive accuracy, and its abstentation from coarseness and abuse, it was a model of journalism.

Editorially, Raymond exercised less power than his great contemporaries just named. The very fact of his temperance, of his constitutional inability not to see both sides of most questions, of his quietness and courtesy, made his editorial page seem to some readers laodicean and half-hearted. His writing was cautious, rational, and impersonal. He eschewed fervor as well as violence. But moderate men of his own bent of mind liked his freedom from bias, and respected his opinions as those of an editor devoted solely and broadmindedly to the truth.

Throughout the fifteen years before the Civil War newspapers in foreign tongues, with the German press most prominent, increased rapidly throughout the North and West. Journals championing special causes, the chief being William Lloyd Garrison's abolitionist *Liberator*, which was founded in 1831, gained a national hearing. Beyond the Alleghenies rose a series of powerful newspapers, such as the Chicago *Tribune*, which first appeared in 1847, and which became widely known after Joseph Medill purchased an interest in 1855, and the Louisville *Journal* (1830), which George D. Prentice made distinctive by his epigrammatic paragraphs, ironical or satirical — "stinging, hissing bolts of scorn," Bryant called them. News was being steadily broadened; the war correspondent had come in with the Mexican conflict; and we have only to turn to some of the travel letters of the time — Bayard Taylor's sketches of California in gold rush days for the *Tribune*, F. L. Olmsted's pictures of Southern slavery in the *Times*, and Bryant's letters from Europe in the *Evening Post* are salient examples — to see how excellent the general correspondence had become. If the telegraph after 1844 did much to kill such publications as *Niles's Weekly*, it contributed immensely to the improvement of journalism in general. It was against the background of these changes, and with the advantages which they afforded, that the editorial giants of the time spoke to the country.

## [JAMES GORDON BENNETT'S SELF–EXPLOITATION][1]

New York *Herald*

*May 10, 1836.*

As I was leisurely pursuing my business yesterday, in Wall Street, collecting the information which is daily disseminated in the *Herald*, James Watson Webb came up to me, on the northern side of the street — said something which I could not hear distinctly, then pushed me down the stone steps, leading to one of the broker's offices, and commenced fighting with a species of brutal and demoniac desperation characteristic of a fury.

My damage is a scratch, about three quarters of an inch in length, on the third finger of my left hand, which I received from the iron railing I was forced against, and three buttons torn from my vest, which any tailor will reinstate for a sixpence. His loss is a rent from top to bottom of a very beautiful black coat, which cost the ruffian $40, and a blow in the face, which may have knocked down his throat some of his infernal teeth for anything I know. Balance in my favor, $39.94.

As to intimidating me or changing my course, the thing cannot be done. Neither Webb nor any other man shall, or can, intimidate me. I tell the honest truth in my paper, and leave the consequences to God. Could I leave them in better hands? I may be attacked, I may be assailed, I may be killed, I may be murdered, but I never will succumb. I never will abandon the cause of truth, morals, and virtue.

*August 16, 1836.*

We published yesterday the principal items of the foreign news, received by the *Sheffield*, being eight days later than our previous arrivals. Neither the *Sun* nor the *Transcript* had a single item on the subject. The *Sun* did not even know of its existence. The large papers in Wall Street had also the news, but as the editors are lazy, ignorant, indolent, blustering blockheads, one and all, they did not

---

[1] These are the three best-known of a long list of editorials in which Bennett advertised himself and his paper and catered to the public appetite for personal gossip. James Watson Webb, an explosive graduate of West Point, edited the six-penny *Courier and Enquirer*.

pick out the cream and serve it out as we did. The *Herald* alone knows how to dish up the foreign news, or indeed domestic events, in a readable style. Every reader, numbering *between thirty and forty thousand daily*, acknowledges this merit in the management of our paper. We do not, as the Wall Street lazy editors do, come down to our office about ten or twelve o'clock, pull out a Spanish cigar, take up a pair of scissors, puff and cut, cut and puff for a couple of hours, and then adjourn to Delmonico's to eat, drink, gormandize, and blow up our contemporaries. We rise in the morning at five o'clock, write our leading editorials, squibs, sketches, etc., before breakfast. From nine till one we read all our papers and original communications, the latter being more numerous than those of any other office in New York. From these we pick out facts, thoughts, hints, and incidents sufficient to make up a column of original spicy articles. We also give audiences to visitors, gentlemen on business, and some of the loveliest ladies in New York, who call to subscribe — Heaven bless them! At one we sally out among the gentlemen and *loafers* of Wall Street — find out the state of the money market, return, finish the next day's paper — close every piece of business requiring thought, sentiment, feeling, or philosophy, before four o'clock. We then dine moderately and temperately — read our proofs — take in cash and advertisements, which are increasing like smoke — and close the day always by going to bed at ten o'clock, seldom later. That's the way to conduct a paper with spirit and success.

*June 1, 1840.*

*To The Readers of the Herald — Declaration of Love — Caught At Last — Going To Be Married — New Movement in Civilization.* — I am going to be married in a few days. The weather is so beautiful; times are getting so good; the prospects of political and moral reform so auspicious, that I cannot resist the divine instinct of honest nature any longer; so I am going to be married to one of the most splendid women in intellect, in heart, in soul, in property, in person, in manner, that I have yet seen in the course of my interesting pilgrimage through human life.

. . . I cannot stop in my career. I must fulfill that awful destiny which the Almighty Father has written against my name, in the broad letters of life, against the wall of heaven. I must give the world a pattern of happy wedded life, with all the charities that spring from a nuptial love. In a few days I shall be married according to the holy rites of the most holy Christian church, to one of the most remarkable, accomplished, and beautiful young women of the age. She possesses a fortune. I sought and found a fortune — a large fortune. She has no Stonington shares or Manhattan stock, but in purity and uprightness she is worth half a million of pure gold. Can any swindling bank show as much? In good sense and elegance another half a million; in soul, mind, and beauty, millions on millions, equal to the whole specie of all the rotten banks in the world. Happily the patronage of the public to the *Herald* is nearly twenty-five thousand dollars per annum, almost equal to a President's salary. But property in the world's goods was never my object. Fame, public good, usefulness in my day and generation; the religious associations of female excellence; the progress of true industry — these have been my dreams by night and my desires by day.

In the new and holy condition into which I am about to enter, and to enter with the same reverential feelings as I would enter heaven itself, I anticipate some signal changes in my feelings, in my views, in my purposes, in my pursuits. What they may be I know not — time alone can tell. My ardent desire has been through life, to reach the highest order of human intelligence, by the shortest possible cut. Association, night and day, in sickness and in health, in war and in peace, with a woman of the highest order of excellence, must produce some curious results in my heart and feelings, and these results the future will develop in due time in the columns of the *Herald*.

## THE SURPLUS AND THE TARIFF[1]

### Washington *Globe*, March 2, 1836

The disposable fund of the nation, the surplus revenue, has now become a bone of contention in Congress. Messrs. Clay and Calhoun, with their penchant for aristocratical abuses — the scheme of Hamilton to save the government from the dangers of democracy by corrupt influence — have seized with avidity upon the surplus as a fund to apply to such sinister purposes. By the settlement for which they obtained the guarantee of Congress up to 1842, these politicians have provided against a reduction of the tariff to the ordinary wants of the government, and the fund to be accumulated under this arrangement they are anxious to scatter among the States from the hand of Congress. The habit fostered by this system before 1842 will go to make Congress always collector, through its indirect taxation, of immense sums from the people generally, to be squandered by the leading men of the different States to promote their various objects of political ambition or pecuniary interest. The

[1] Characteristic of the *Globe's* attacks upon the "American system" of Henry Clay, which called for a combination of high tariff and internal improvements.

**MR. CLAY TAKING A NEW VIEW OF THE TEXAS QUESTION.**

Now for one I certainly am not willing to involve this country in a foreign war for the object of acquiring Texas. Honor and good faith, and justice, are equally due from this country toward the weak as toward the strong.—*Mr. Clay's Raleigh Letter.*

FA, FE, FI, FO FUM: I SMELL THE BLOOD OF A MEXICUN! DEAD OR ALIVE I WILL HAVE SOME!

I feel as if I yet must go and slay a Mexican! *Mr. Clay's Speech at New Orleans.*

From *Yankee Doodle*, February 6, 1847.

power which has the responsibility of bringing in the immense tax will not have the responsibility of disposing of it; and the divided responsibility will in the end prove to be no responsibility. The State legislatures, like heirs inheriting property without encountering the difficulties of acquisition, will waste it prodigally. The Congress, plied on all sides by the members from the States to provide for the unchecked expenditure, will draw lavishly through its indirect channel of supply, the custom-house, upon the productive classes of the country, who make up the mass of consumers, to afford means to answer this new demand. The result will be an everenduring and increasing tariff, to feed the vices of aristocracy in all the shapes which it may assume among us.

## TEXAS TRIUMPHANT.

### Washington *Globe*, May 23, 1836

The gratifying confirmation of the defeat and capture of Santa Anna by General Houston has reached us under New Orleans dates of the 9th. Now the tone of the New York *American*, of the *National Gazette*, of the *National Intelligencer*, of the Richmond *Whig*, of the Louisiana *Advertiser*, the leading organs of the Webster, Harrison, and White combination, will be changed. They will now probably admit that to march out four hundred men to execution, after a solemn capitulation, was not altogether reconcilable to the laws of civilized nations, or even to the humanity of barbarians. They will cease to excuse the deliberate slaughter to which four columns, of one hundred victims each, were led, half famished but tantalized with hope, to unresisting destruction. Some were told that they were about to embark for their friends; others, that they were marched out to bring up beeves; others, that they were going to receive rations already prepared. This formal and coolly contrived butchery the Richmond *Whig* imputes (for Santa Anna's sake) to the uncontrollable fury of the Mexican soldiery!

The author of this monstrous cruelty is now in the hands of General Houston. Houston retains the Mexican Chief Magistrate and all his officers as hostages for the abandonment of the country by the Mexican troops, without shedding more blood. It would seem that he has made no pledges to Santa Anna; but we trust that whatever may be the determination as to the Mexican leader, no retribution will be allowed to fall upon the heads of such portions

---

[1] Samuel Houston surprised Santa Anna at San Jacinto on April 21, 1836, and crushed his army, capturing its leader. The *Globe* expresses the pleasure which the Jackson Administration, and the South generally, took in the now certain establishment of Texan independence. The massacre mentioned was that of Goliad.

of the officers and troops as had no participation in the councils which decided the fate of the brave and unfortunate men who suffered with the brave Fannin.

## THE RIGHT OF WORKMEN TO STRIKE[1]

New York *Evening Post*, June 13, 1836

Sentence was passed on Saturday on the twenty "men who had determined not to work." — They have committed the crime of unanimously declining to go to work at the wages offered to them by their masters. They had said to one another, "Let us come out from the meanness and misery of our caste. Let us begin to do what every order more privileged and more honored is doing every day. By the means which we believe to be the best, let us raise ourselves and our families above the humbleness of our condition. We may be wrong, but we cannot help believing that we might do much if we were true brothers to each other, and would resolve not to sell the only thing which is our own, the cunning of our hands, for less than it is worth." What other things they may have done is nothing to the purpose: it was for this they were condemned; it is for this they are to endure the penalty of the law.

We call upon a candid and generous community to mark that the punishment inflicted upon these twenty "men who had determined not to work" is not directed against the offence of conspiring to prevent others by force from working at low wages, but expressly against the offence of settling by pre-concert the compensation which they thought they were entitled to obtain. It is certainly superfluous to repeat, that this journal would be the very last to oppose a law levelled at any attempt to molest the labourer who chooses to work for less than the prices settled by the union. We have said, and to cut off cavil, we say it now again, that a conspiracy to deter, by threats of violence, a fellow-workman from arranging his own terms with his employers, is a conspiracy to commit a felony — a conspiracy which, being a crime against liberty, we should be the first to condemn — a conspiracy which no strike should, for its own sake, countenance for a moment — a conspiracy already punishable by the statute, and far easier to reach than the one of which "the twenty" stood accused; but a conspiracy, we must add, that has not a single feature in common with the base and barbarous prohibition under which the offenders were indicted and condemned.

[1] Workmen in New York City and elsewhere had formed unions, and a number of journeymen tailors had commenced a strike. They were indicted under the laws against conspiracy and after a trial in the court of oyer and terminer, twenty-one of them were heavily fined. Bryant here expresses his indignation over this blow at the rights of workingmen.

They were condemned because they had determined not to work for the wages that were offered them! Can any thing be imagined more abhorrent to every sentiment of generosity or justice, than the law which arms the rich with the legal right to fix, by assize, the wages of the poor? If this is not SLAVERY, we have forgotten its definition. Strike the right of associating for the sale of labour from the privileges of a freeman, and you may as well at once bind him to a master, or ascribe him to the soil. If it be not in the colour of his skin, and in the poor franchise of naming his own terms in a contract for his work, what advantage has the labourer of the north over the bondsman of the south? Punish by human laws a "determination not to work," make it penal by any other penalty than idleness inflicts, and it matters little whether the task-masters be one or many, an individual or an order, the hateful scheme of slavery will have gained a foothold in the land.

"Self-created societies," says Judge Edwards, "are unknown to the constitution and laws, and will not be permitted to rear their crest and extend their baneful influence over any portion of the community." If there is any sense in this passage, it means that self-created societies are unlawful, and must be put down by the courts. Down then with every literary, every religious, and every charitable association not incorporated! — Gather up then and sweep to the penitentiary all those who are confederated to carry on any business or trade in concert, by fixed rules, and see how many you would leave at large in this city. The members of every partnership in the place will come under the penalties of the law, and not only these, but every person pursuing any occupation whatever, who governs himself by a mutual understanding with others that follow the same occupation.

## THE SPECULATION IN WESTERN LANDS

### Washington *Globe*, July 21, 1836

Within a very short time, notwithstanding the denunciations of the *Intelligencer* and the dismal croakings of the learned and lugubrious editor of the *National* (late United States Bank) *Gazette*, the salutary effects of the late Treasury regulation will be perceptible. The all grasping and monopolizing spirit of the speculators will be restrained; the public lands will be reserved for actual settlers, and purchasers, to a reasonable amount; gold and silver will become more abundant in the West, where in the natural course of events there must soon be a demand for it, and caution and economy will take the place of the recklessness and extravagance which have of late been but too common in some speculating communities.

Twenty years ago, we recollect there was a rush after the public lands very similar to the recent and present movements, except that it was not upon so great a scale. The money was obtained in the same way (from the banks), and made of the same material (rags), and the consequences were the same that we shall witness again, unless some check is given to this inordinate grasping after the public domain; thousands of individuals will be ruined, and millions of dollars will be lost to the United States.

Congress will, it is to be presumed, take up this subject and act upon it at the next session. It is one of vital importance to the community, and should not be lost sight of. The question is simply whether it is best to regulate the sales of public lands by the wants of the community, and the demands of emigration, or to let them fall, all at once, into the hands of speculators, who by a combination (which will certainly take place) may compel the purchaser who purchases to cultivate to pay four or five times the price fixed by the government.

## [THE RIGHT TO FORM TRADE-UNIONS] [1]

### New York *Plaindealer*, December 10, 1836

Some days ago we observed in one of the newspapers a paragraph stating that a meeting of mechanics and laborers was about to be held in this city for the purpose of adopting measures of concerted or combined action against the practise, which we have reason to believe exists to a very great extent, of paying them in the uncurrent notes of distant or suspected banks. No such meeting, however, as far as we can learn, has yet been held. We hope it soon will be; for the object is a good one, and there is no other way of resisting the rapacious and extortionate custom of employees paying their journeymen and laborers in depreciated paper, half so effectual as combination.

There are some journalists who affect to entertain great horror of combinations, considering them as utterly adverse to the principles of free trade; and it is frequently recommended to make them penal by law. Our notions of free trade were acquired in a different school, and dispose us to leave men entirely at liberty to effect a proper object either by concerted or individual action. The character of combinations, in our view, depends entirely upon the intrinsic character of the end which is aimed at. In the subject under consideration, the end proposed is good beyond all possibility of

---

[1] William Leggett, one of the leaders of the radical Loco-foco Democracy in New York City, and a passionate believer in greater social and political equality, was editor of the short-lived *Plaindealer*. Though the weekly lasted but ten months, he made it genuinely influential.

question. There is high warrant for saying that *the laborer is worthy of his hire;* but the employer who takes advantage of his necessities and defencelessness to pay him in a depreciated substitute for money, does not give him his hire; he does not perform his engagement with him; he filches from the poor man a part of his hard-earned wages and is guilty of a miserable fraud. Who shall say that this sneaking species of extortion ought not to be prevented? Who will say that separate individual action is adequate to that end? There is no one who will make so rash an assertion.

The only effectual mode of doing away the evil is by attacking it with the great instrument of the rights of the poor — *associated effort.* There is but one bulwark behind which mechanics and laborers may safely rally to oppose a common enemy, who, if they ventured singly into the field against him, would cut them to pieces: that bulwark is the *Principle of Combination.* We would advise them to take refuge behind it only in extreme cases, because in their collisions with their employers, as in those between nations, the manifold evils of a siege are experienced, more or less, by both parties, and are therefore to be incurred only in extreme emergencies. But the evil of being habitually paid in a depreciated currency; of being daily cheated out of a portion of the just fruits of honest toil; of having a slice continually clipped from the hard-earned crust, is one of great moment, and is worthy of such an effort as we propose.

## THE EXPUNGING PROCESS [1]

### Washington *National Intelligencer*, January 15, 1837

We believe that no question before Congress has ever been viewed with so solemn and painful a feeling by the thinking public, as the proposition which there is too much reason to fear is about to be adopted by the Senate. For our own part, we declare, in all sincerity, that we look upon it with more oppressed feelings than we should upon a proposition heedlessly to involve the nation in the calamities of war. We shall look upon its passage with a more painful emotion than we experienced when, many years ago, we saw the Capitol in flames, and our own individual property committed to the torch of an invading enemy. Time can obliterate the evils of war, and industry repair its ravages. But what time can heal a wound inflicted by the Senate on its own honor? It savors, we know, of arrogance, to interpose our humble voice in a question upon which the greatest minds of our country are exerting their

[1] Thomas Hart Benton's long fight to expunge from the Senate journals the censure of that body upon Andrew Jackson was successfully ended in the final days of the Jackson Administration, 1837.

powers. But in the fullness of the heart the mouth speaketh; and it is not without the hope of inducing some of those more considerate gentlemen who are conscientiously approaching this act as an act of duty, to pause and reflect whether there are not some sacrifices too fearful to be yielded to the vindictive exactions of party, or of vindictive party leaders, that we have said thus much. There is indeed scarcely a personal sacrifice which we would not cheerfully make to avert the impending calamity; and God knows that the sacrifice would be made by us with feelings untainted by party influence, and with the sole and only earthly motive of saving the Constitution of our country from a wound, and the Senate of that country from a dishonor, which we have no surety that the Senate itself would long survive.

## THE BLESSINGS OF SLAVERY

New York *Plaindealer*, February 25, 1837

An extraordinary colloquy took place in the United States Senate some short time since between Mr. Rives and Mr. Calhoun, in which the latter Senator maintained with much vehemence that slavery is not an evil, but "a good, a great good," and reproached Mr. Rives, in sharp terms, for admitting the contrary. As his remarks were reported by the stenographers at the time, they contained some very insulting allusions to the free laborers of the Northern States, whom Mr. Calhoun spoke of in the most contemptuous terms as serfs and vassals, far beneath the negro bondmen of the South in moral degradation. An elaborate report was some days afterward published in the Washington papers, which probably had undergone the revision of the several speakers; and from that the offensive expressions relative to the free citizens of the North were wholly omitted. . . .

We have Mr. Calhoun's own warrant for attacking his positions with all the fervour which a high sense of duty can give; for we do hold from the bottom of our soul that slavery is an evil, a deep, detestable, damnable evil; an evil in all its aspects; an evil to the blacks and a greater evil to the whites; an evil, moral, social, and political; an evil which shows itself in the languishing condition of agriculture at the South, in its paralyzed commerce, and in the prostration of the mechanic arts; an evil that stares you in the face from uncultivated fields, and howls in your ears through the tangled recesses of the Southern swamps and morasses. Slavery is such an evil that it withers what it touches. Where it is once securely established, the land becomes desolate, as the tree inevitably perishes which the sea-hawk chooses for its nest; while freedom, on the contrary, flourishes like the tannen, on the loftiest and least sheltered rocks, and clothes with its refreshing verdure what without it would frown in naked and incurable sterility.

If anyone desires an illustration of the opposite influences of slavery and freedom, let him look at the two sister States of Kentucky and Ohio. Alike in soil and climate, and divided only by a river whose translucent waters reveal, through nearly the whole breadth, the sandy bottom over which they sparkle, how different are they in all the respects over which man has control! On the one hand, the air is vocal with the mingled tumult of a vast and prosperous population. Every hillside smiles with an abundant harvest; every valley shelters a thriving village; the click of a busy mill drowns the prattle of every rivulet, and all the multitudinous sound of business denote happy activity in every branch of social occupation.

This is the State which, but a few years ago, slept in the unbroken solitude of nature. The forest spread an interminable canopy of shade over the dark soil, on which the fat and useless vegetation rotted at ease, and through the dusky vistas of the wood only savage beasts and more savage men prowled in quest of prey. The whole land now blossoms like a garden. The tall and interlacing trees have unlocked their hold, and bowed before the woodman's axe. The soil is disencumbered of the mossy trunks which had reposed upon it for ages. The rivers flash in the sunlight and the fields smile with waving harvests. This is Ohio, and this what *freedom* has done for it.

Let us turn to Kentucky, and note the opposite influences of *slavery*. A narrow and unfrequented path through the close and sultry canebrake conducts us to a wretched hovel. It stands in the midst of an unweeded field, whose dilapidated enclosure scarcely protects it from the lowing and hungry kine. Children half-clad and squalid, and destitute of the buoyancy natural to their age, lounge in the sunshine, while their parent saunters apart to watch his languid slaves drive the ill-appointed team afield. This is not a fancy picture. It is a true copy of one of the features which make up the aspect of the State — and of every State where the moral leprosy of slavery covers the people with its noisome scales. A deadening lethargy benumbs the limbs of the body politic. A stupor settles on the arts of life. Agriculture reluctantly drags the plough and harrow to the field, only when scourged by necessity. The axe drops from the woodman's nerveless hand the moment his fire is scantily supplied with fuel; and the fen, undrained, sends up its noxious exhalations to rack with cramps and agues the frame already too much enervated by a moral epidemic, to creep beyond the sphere of the material miasma.

Heaven knows we have no disposition to exaggerate the deleterious influences of slavery. We would rather pause far within the truth, than transgress it ever so little. There are evils which it invariably generates a thousand times more pernicious than those we have faintly touched. There are evils which affect the moral character, and poison the social relations, of those who breathe the atmosphere of slavery, more to be deplored than its paralyzing influence on their physical condition. Whence comes the hot and imperious temper of Southern statesmen, but from their unlimited domination over their fellow-men? Whence comes it that "the church-going bell" so seldom fills the air with its pleasant music, inviting the population to religious worship? Whence comes it that Sabbath schools diffuse to so small a number of their children the inestimable benefits of education? Whence comes it that the knife and the pistol are so readily resorted to for the adjustment of private quarrel?

The answer to these and many kindred questions will sufficiently show that slavery is indeed an evil of the most hideous and destructive kind; and it therefore becomes the duty of every wise and virtuous man to exert himself to put it down.


## THE SQUATTERS[1]

### New York *Evening Post*, March, 1837

We see pretty frequently in the party prints, expressions of scorn concerning the squatters of the western country, and attempts to scout the notion of passing a general pre-emption law for their benefit. We know well what class of persons are designated by this title, for we have seen them amid the broad prairies, where they raise their harvests, and beside the noble woods where they hunt their game, and we have shared the hospitality of their cabins. They are our old friends and neighbors; men who have emigrated from the Atlantic States, men who are perhaps a little more adventurous and restless, but quite as moral and intelligent, as those they have left behind; nay, if we take into the estimate the inhabitants of the larger towns, more moral and intelligent. We have known among these squatters some of the best and purest men it has ever been our fortune to be acquainted with. No man who has once visited the West, scruples, if his convenience should lead him, to seat himself upon the unoccupied territory belonging to Government, the

[1] Of more than ordinary interest as embodying Bryant's personal reminiscences of a journey to visit his brother on the Illinois prairies.

sale of which is not yet permitted.   Here he builds his log cabin, in the edge of a grove, splits his trees into rails, fences in a portion of the wide and rich prairie, turns up the virgin soil, which yields a hundred fold for the seeds which he casts upon it, and pastures his herd upon the vast, unenclosed, flowery champaign before his dwelling.   One emigrant arrives after another, and in this way neighborhoods are formed, communities of honest, kind, and religious people, with their schools and places of worship, before a single inch is offered for sale.   This is the universal and well understood custom of the West — not a custom of yesterday, but of a century's growth; a custom which dates back to the time when the first hunter raised his cabin in the rich natural meadows of Kentucky.   It is a custom which the government itself has tolerated; we may use a still stronger term — it is a custom which the government has recognised and sanctioned, by passing from time to time pre-emption laws giving the settler the first right to purchase the soil he has occupied.

And these laws are consonant with natural equity.   The cabin of the settler is the work of his own hands; and he has made the prairie valuable by surrounding it with fences, and breaking up the green sward.   The neighborhoods formed by squatters give a value to the unclaimed lands around them which they otherwise would not have.   The speculator and the newcomer both reap the benefit of a settlement already formed, instead of selling or settling upon lands in the midst of a wilderness.   It is just that they who founded the colonies from which the lands derive their subsequent value should be compensated in some way or other for the hardships and inconveniences they have undergone.

If local and temporary pre-emption laws are just in principle, then is also a general pre-emption law.   What is right in one case is right in all.


## THE MASSACHUSETTS MADMAN[1]

New York *Plaindealer*, January 21, 1837

Though this be madness, yet there's method in it. — *Hamlet.*

The phrase which we make use of as a title for this article is furnished by the Albany *Argus:*

[1] The American Antislavery Society, Garrison's *Liberator*, and other Abolitionist activities had caused the presentation to Congress of numerous petitions praying for the destruction or restriction of slavery.   Speaker James K. Polk of the House ruled that the constitutional right of petition did not oblige the House to *receive* a petition, and that it might be thrown into the wastebasket without being even referred to a committee for burial. John Quincy Adams at once took up the fight for the Anglo-Saxon right of petition in its full meaning, and rallied a great part of the North behind him.   William Leggett's editorial shows how one Northern Democrat felt.

It will be seen, by the Congressional report, that Mr. Adams and the Abolition members of Congress have started the old game of agitation in the House of Representatives. No doubt the design is to waste as much as possible of the public time, at this short session, upon a question not less fruitless than mischievous. How discreditable it is to the country, that the *Massachusetts madman* is permitted, not only to outrage all order and decorum in the House, but to scatter incendiary evil and excitement throughout the country!

What an exquisite sense of "order and decorum" the Albany *Argus* displays! What dignity, what respect for the character which should distinguish the State paper, and what deference for a man who has filled the highest office in our republic, this modestly worded paragraph evinces! There is something in the circumstance of Mr. Adams being *permitted* to make a motion in the House of Representatives which, we must confess, deserves strong rebuke; and our only wonder is that the Albany *Argus* could so admirably command its temper, as to confine itself to so gentle a reprimand. "The Massachusetts Madman" merits harsher treatment. He should have been denounced, in the bitterest terms, as a baldheaded and paralytic dotard for the unparalleled audacity he has been guilty of in presenting a petition of his constituents to the House of Representatives, and asking that it might be appropriately referred.

That Mr. Adams is a madman there is medical authority for asserting. A physician being called on as a witness, not long since, in this city, in the case of a trial before one of our courts in which an attempt was made to prove one of the parties insane, defined madness to consist in conduct or opinions differing from those of the mass of mankind. Mr. Adams differs very widely, alas! from the mass of mankind, both in conduct and opinions, if we are to take the House of Representatives as a fair criterion of public sentiment. He strangely believes that slavery is an evil; that Congress has constitutional jurisdiction, in all respects, over the District of Columbia; that the right of petition is guaranteed to all citizens by the federal compact; and that the right of speech justifies him in expressing his sentiments, even on the tabooed question of abolishing involuntary servitude. To these crazy questions, he adds the crazy conduct of persisting in expressing them; and thus comes doubly within the category of madman. . . . The man who is so utterly frantic as to express unpopular opinions should be dealt with somewhat after the fashion that keepers of insane hospitals deal with their raving and delirious patients. Instead of ordinary habiliments, his limbs should be swathed in a species of straight waistcoat — an unguentous integument, composed of molasses and boiling tar; he should be placed on a diet of rotten eggs; and for exercise, ridden a few miles at a sharp trot on a wooden rail.  This is the mode of treatment which the madness of uttering unpopular opinions is considered as calling for, and we faithfully copy the inscription from the latest edition of the Political Pharmacopœia, a chapter of which was transcribed from the Westchester *Spy* in the last number of our paper.

It has been discovered, we believe, of late years in Great Britain, that a free use of the *halter* is not the best possible mode of preventing petty crimes; and there are some who will probably question whether *tar and feathers* are a sovereign specific for the disease of abolitionism.  Insanity, of the kind which the Massachusetts Madman displays, is certainly wonderfully on the increase.  It has got to be an epidemic in the land; and what is most surprising, cases of the most aggravated description, and in the greatest numbers, occur in those neighborhoods where the remedial measures have been most energetically applied.  We have our doubts even, if some patriotic practitioner should administer a dose of tar and molasses to Mr. Adams, whether the result would not be, not to effect a cure, but to spread the disease.  The operation seems to be somewhat like that of the means adopted by the British Government to plant the Episcopal Church in Ireland, which, according to the London *Examiner*, have done more to advance the cause of Popery than could have been effected by a hundred *Colleges de Propaganda*.  A hundred thousand undisturbed lecturers on abolition, at all events, could not have done half so much to spread their doctrines, as has been effected by the violence of those who sought to suppress them.  They have but pricked the sides of their intent.  They have but spurred them to more rapid progress.  Their opposition has but inflamed the spirit which it could not vanquish.

## THE INAUGURATION OF MR. VAN BUREN[1]
### Washington *Globe*, March 5, 1837

All the concomitants which attended the inauguration were in happy keeping with the principal and attracting objects.  A lovely day of brightest sunshine gladdened every heart — a soft spring snow, which had fallen two days before, in virgin purity reflected from the surrounding hills the cheering light and benignity of the heavens — the paved avenue, of more than a mile in extent, was thronged with citizens from every quarter of the Union, all dressed in holiday suits and cheering each other with eager salutations.  At twelve o'clock the late venerable chief magistrate, with his successor by his side, took his seat in the beautiful phaeton built of the wood

[1] An excellent example of the common descriptive editorial of the period, combining news and comment.  The *Globe* of course rejoiced in Van Buren's inaug-

of the frigate *Constitution*, and lately presented to him by the Democracy of the city of New York, and preceded by a splendid escort of cavalry and infantry, and a fine band of martial music, proceeded to the Capitol through the Pennsylvania Avenue. An immense crowd filled the square on the east front of the Capitol.

An opening was readily made for the late and present President, and the family of the former and of Chief Justice Taney (who are at present inmates of the President's mansion), and under the conduct of Messrs. Grundy, Parker, and Tallmadge, the committee appointed by the Senate, they proceeded to the Senate chamber. On ascending the steps of the eastern portico, cheers of unanimous greeting rose from the surrounding people, and were repeated with an effecting emphasis when the whitened head of the toil-worn general was seen, for the first time since his sickness, and probably for the last time, rising above the rest as he ascended the portico of the Capitol. After reaching the Senate, the procession was formed as set down in the published arrangements; and President Van Buren, attended by his predecessor, the members of the Senate, of the Cabinet, and of the diplomatic corps of foreign nations, led the way to the rostrum erected on the ascent to the eastern portico. He then delivered his inaugural address in clear and impressive tones, and in an easy and eloquent manner. At the close of it, the oath of office was administered by Chief Justice Taney.

There never was a more sublime spectacle presented to the reflecting mind than was exhibited in the fixed attention, the perfect order and quiet, which held the immense auditory in view of the rostrum as still as the sea in a perfect calm. Nothing disturbed the profound interest which those within the reach of the speaker's voice gave to the address. Those beyond it stood with a steady gaze on the objects elevated by the public confidence to the high station which the one was about to abandon, and the other to enter upon. So absorbing and riveting was the sense of the immediate transaction that many, we are told, did not even hear the peals of the cannon firing at the time a Federal salute at the navy yard, though it reverberated in the surrounding hills like the sounds of distant thunder. How beautifully this fact illustrates the feeling of our countrymen! The maxim that *inter arma leges silent* had its counterpart strongly displayed on the late occasion. While the organ of our civil institutions spoke in the gentlest tones, and was listened to with rapt attention, the thunder of the cannon which speaks the prowess of our country abroad rolled over the Capitol and was unheard.

uration. But the incoming New Yorker — whom some called the "Mistletoe Politician," nourished upon Old Hickory — attracted less attention than Jackson. The cheers both before and after the inaugural address were all an ovation for the retiring President.

## THE PANIC OF 1837[1]

New York *Journal of Commerce*, April 8, 1837

The past week will long be remembered by our merchants as a season of trial and difficulty, such as has not before been experienced for many years. It will be remembered also, we trust, as the crisis of the great financial troubles which have been gathering for more than a year past, from the combined influence of speculation, the surplus revenue, bad government, and so on. The first three days of the week were indeed gloomy: a number of failures occurred, chiefly however of houses essentially sound, but which were unable to sustain themselves under the tremendous money pressure which existed; and what was worse than all in some of its bearings, *confidence*, that essential element of credit, appeared to be entirely at an end. It was a glorious time for panic-makers, croakers, and assassins of credit, and well did they improve the opportunity afforded them. We could mention a dozen of our largest and best houses who were reported among the fallen, but who still survive unharmed. The temporary suspension of payments by Messrs. E. M. Morgan & Co., who were agents for twenty or thirty country banks, gave opportunity to the enemies of such institutions to propagate suspicions concerning them; and all these troubles were aggravated by a portion of the press.

Thus things were proceeding, when by a concerted movement between the United States Bank and our local institutions, measures were adopted for the relief of the community; and from that moment the state of the money market has been evidently improving. During the last three days of the week we did not hear of a single failure. Stocks which had been rapidly declining began to rally; and confidence, though still scarce, was perceptibly gaining ground. We feel assured that these encouraging indications will continue and increase, until the money market shall recover its usual healthy condition. Perfect restoration is not, however, to be expected in a day; the disease was too deeply seated, and some of the exciting causes still remain. But with prudence and moderation on the part of the patients, and careful management by the physicians, a complete recovery is certain, and cannot be far remote. To drop the figure, nothing could more fully prove the substantial basis on which our mercantile credit rests — the resources, even in the worst of times, which a vast proportion of our merchants are

---

[1] The cataclysmic panic of 1837 struck New York on March 17; by May the number of failures in the East was appalling, and in that month the banks stopped specie payments. The optimism of the *Journal of Commerce* was hollowly professional.

able to command — than the fiery ordeal through which they have passed.

The result of the whole matter, instead of destroying confidence, ought to increase it: — confidence, we mean, in the general soundness of the business community of New York, and their ability, under any supposable circumstances, to meet their engagements. We can say without fear of contradiction that there is no other mercantile body, equally numerous, in the world, which could have met such a storm with so few disasters. And as to the banks, there has not been a single failure, far or near. This speaks well for their condition, since to them also, as well as to the merchants, the ordeal has been severe.

We think it is now time for people to "thank God and take courage." Down with the panic-makers, and down with the prevalent mistrust! The resources of the country are vast, and no financial embarrassments, in time of peace, can be more than temporary. A bright sun will soon dispel the remaining darkness, and days of prosperity and glory will be ours. In the meantime we shall have learned lessons of wisdom which experience alone can teach, and which will tend greatly to restrain speculation in times to come. What we learn from our fathers we soon forget; but what we learn by experience, we are apt to remember. Nobody, says Dr. Johnson, ever forgot a man that kicked his shins.

## [THE EFFECTS OF THE GREAT PANIC]

Salem (Mass.) *Gazette,* April 14, 1837

We regret to learn that the failure of several houses in New York, extensively engaged in the shoe business, has occasioned a great number of failures in Lynn, and has affected the other shoe-manufacturing towns in this county to some extent. In this city we have fortunately passed through the storm thus far unscathed, and we believe not a whisper or a doubt has been circulated in disparagement of the credit of any mercantile house. Retrenchment, both in business and expenditure, has been the order of the day for many months in Salem, and we regret to learn that one operation of this excellent system has been to occasion the suspension of labor on several whale-ships which are getting ready for sea. So far as this suspension extends to the employment of laboring men, it is a misfortune; but it is the only effectual way to meet the extraordinary crisis produced by Gen. Jackson's mad experiments upon the business of the country. The cessation of new expenditures and engagements is a great evil, but far less than the results of an opposite course.

Kennebec *Journal*, April 12, 1837

The prospects for the demand for lumber this year look rather blue. We shall have enough of it, though but little has been cut the past winter. There will be but very little building in any of our Atlantic cities this season, and therefore small demand for lumber. The price of wool will keep up as well as anything, for most of the factories will probably continue in operation. But few if any new ones will be built, however, while the business of the country is in its present condition, and especially while we are threatened with a repeal of the protecting duties. Hence it is that the waterpower which will be created this summer in this town will be of little use until a new order of things is brought about. Last year near one hundred buildings were erected in Augusta; this year all building is nearly suspended. In Bangor it is much worse. We are told that there are at least sixty stores to let, which have been occupied. Of course with no new buildings being erected, our mechanics are going away. Such are the fruits of the "golden experiment" — such the consequences of placing political mountebanks in power. And the worst has not yet come.

New Orleans *True American*, April 14, 1837

Not a bale of cotton, not a hogshead of tobacco, was shipped yesterday from this port. The failures still continue. On Wednesday the largest cotton house in the Southern country went by the board for fifteen millions of dollars. . . . The storm will have its way, and as yet the patches of blue sky that now and then break upon us are but signs of increasing violence.

## [THURLOW WEED PROTESTS AGAINST SLANDER][1]

Albany *Evening Journal*, May 9, 1838

A word in relation to the "grossness and unfairness of personal assault that characterize the *Evening Journal*." When the *Evening Journal* made its first appearance here eight years ago, the Albany *Argus* commenced a series of gross and wanton "personal assaults" upon its editor, such as has "characterized" few public journals. Nothing in the shape of personal vituperation was too bitter for the taste of the *Argus*. It was the daily habit of the State Printer to represent us as a man of infamous character, unworthy even of the ordinary courtesies of society. This system of personal reproach

---

[1] Between Thurlow Weed's Albany *Evening Journal* and the Albany *Argus* of Edwin Croswell there long existed a bitter feud. Weed relates in his autobiography that the only time he ever stood plaintiff in a libel suit was against the *Argus* and that he made Croswell retract.

and assault was continued for years. We acted on the defensive. If we indulged in personalities, it was only because we were personally assailed.

Finally, about a year since, the *Argus* changed its course. The controversy became, as the readers of both papers must have observed, divested of its unpleasant personal character. Our statement that we had not seen Mr. Biddle's letter was pronounced a falsehood by the editor of the *Argus*. Unwilling to renew the personal warfare, we repeated the statement, with the explanation that the letter of Mr. Biddle only came to this city in the *National Gazette*, a paper with which we do not exchange, and which we had not seen. But Mr. Croswell saw fit to reiterate his charge of falsehood against us. The *Argus* has elected the terms upon which it chooses to stand with the *Evening Journal*. Let it not complain of us for "personal assaults" which were provoked by itself.

## [THE DEFALCATION OF SAMUEL SWARTWOUT][1]

Albany *Evening Journal*, November 15, 1828

A strong sensation has been created in New York by the report that Samuel Swartwout, late Collector of the Port of New York, has proved a defaulter to the government to the amount of a million and a quarter of dollars! We know nothing of the foundation of this story, but presume there is some truth in it. What can the government have been about, to let one man embezzle the public money at this rate? Who has audited his accounts? Who has kept track of them? Has his own simple statement of the amount of money collected at New York been deemed sufficient? Where has slept the vigilance of the Secretary of the Treasury? How long is it since General Jackson assured Congress that his officers were performing their duties admirably, and resisted all attempts to investigate their conduct as an impeachment of *his* veracity? Now, one of these officers, appointed by General Jackson and continued in office through his entire eight years, proves a public defaulter and the Tory organs not only "deny the responsibility," but turn him off upon the Whigs!

But the *Evening Post* labors to twist this defalcation into an argument for the Sub-Treasury plan, and the *Argus* in its sneaking way follows in its footsteps. Let us look at this view of the case.

General Jackson appointed Mr. Swartwout Collector at New York and exacted such securities as were deemed sufficient. His instructions were positive, to deposit every dollar of the public revenue in

[1] The horror created among all good Whigs by the enormous embezzlements of Samuel Swartwout, who was appointed by Andrew Jackson over the protests of Martin Van Buren, is best reflected in the pages of Philip Hone's Diary.

the deposit banks, thence to be drawn only on the deposit warrant of the Treasurer of the United States. In point of fact, very little of it should ever have come into the Collector's hands at all, but should have been paid directly to the banks by the merchants as their bonds fell due — an account of it only being kept by the Collector. Now if the requisitions of law had been obeyed and the money deposited in the banks, not a sixpence of it would ever have been lost. But instead of this, Mr. Swartwout has constituted himself a sub-treasury, in advance of the passage of Mr. Cambreleng's bill, and diverted the moneys to his own pockets, whence it has been spent or lost. And this, say the *Post* and *Argus*, is an argument against putting any money into banks and in favor of keeping it all in the custody of public officers. We do not see the force of this — does anyone?

## THE FRUITS OF JACKSONIAN MISGOVERNMENT

### Washington *National Intelligencer*, March 20, 1840

Had General Jackson been wisely distrustful of his own capacity, he would have found in the example of his illustrious predecessors the chart of safety. He had but to throw himself on the wave that was carrying the whole country on to its proud and enviable destiny, and all would have been well. But the infirmities of his character prevailed over the dictates of reason. With daring courage, indeed, but yet with presumption which ignorance alone could excuse, he approached the most delicate and vital principles in the science of government, and determined to reform them, though the wisdom of nations had declared them good, and the experience of ages had proclaimed them settled. He took hold of the currency and the finances of the country, and in the absence of both information and experience on the subject, resolved to change them from their settled foundations. And this purpose he accomplished, in violation of the sanctity of the Constitution, and in disregard of law. Without a faltering step he pursued his determination, which has been the prolific source of so much mischief. The warning of wise counsel, the remonstrances of friends, and the predictions of evil, only made his resolves the more inflexible, and his means of accomplishing them the more desperate.

Thus was laid the foundation of all the evils which now scourge the country; and our present Chief Magistrate, by following in the footsteps of his illustrious predecessor, has consummated the work of mischief and ruin.

From the beginning of General Jackson's crusade against the currency, the finances, and the institutions upon which their suc-

cessful management essentially depended, must be dated the downfall of our national prosperity and happiness.  And if the wit of
mankind had been taxed to work out a scheme of the quickest and
most successful ruin, none could have been devised more fatal and
efficient than that whose success General Jackson's flatterers made
him believe was to crown his fame with glory.  We have but to cast
our eyes over our continent, and we behold in all directions the sad
memorials of a desperate and fatal maladministration of public
affairs.  Our commerce, that once floated on every sea, has dwindled
down to a mere remnant.  Our manufactures, which erewhile were
enlivened with the busy movements of industry and profit, are
lingering out an unprofitable existence.  Our agriculture, that until
lately was rewarded with a rich return, seeks in vain for a market.
Our internal improvements, that recently stretched out their thousand arms to embrace the Union in one bond of fellowship and intercourse, are abandoned, and many millions of their cost are
already lost to the country in consequence.  The stream of capital
that was flowing in from its capacious reservoir in the Old World
to seek employment in the enterprises of the new is already cut off.
Our credit, that once stood with proud respect in all the marts of
the world, is now dishonored.  Our enterprise, that was wont to
explore every avenue for profit, is stricken down in hopeless despair.
Labor, that brought its return of happiness and comfort to tens of
thousands of families, now wanders about in rags begging for employment.  The exchanges of our country, which ten years ago
stood at less than one per cent between the extremes of the Union,
are now ranging, between places only a hundred or two hundred
miles apart, at from six and seven to fifteen and twenty per cent.
In fine, a national paralysis, ruined fortunes, gloom, suffering, and
a bankrupt treasury, are the prints of General Jackson's footsteps,
in which Mr. Van Buren has faithfully followed.

### [MAJOR JACK DOWNING'S LETTERS] [1]

New York *Express*, April 19, April 27, 1840

Washington, March 20, 1840.

To the Moderator of the Downingville Convention,
Respected Sir:

I don't mean to take things by hearsay, as some folks did a spell
ago with tother Old Hero.  Times have got so now, I am determined

---

[1] The original " Jack Downing" was Seba Smith, whose letters first attracted wide
attention in the Portland *Courier* in 1830.  They were extensively imitated, and
Charles A. Davis published a series of "Jack Downing Letters" which in some respects surpassed those of Smith.  It is from Davis's downright Whig series that the
above extracts are taken.  In intent, if not in form, they may be regarded as editorials.

to recommend no man for President till I have got a chance to measure him. The People are entitled to a good man — one who will do justice by *all parties*, and go by the *Constitution and the Laws*. The country has had enuf of party Presidents, and as the party in power have had it all their own way now for nigh twelve years, and got things pretty considerable starn foremost (as any party will that goes more for *party* than the good of the hull country) I think it's about time to tack ship and see if we can't make things *go ahead*. Folks in office, I suppose, won't agree to this principle; and as there are a good many on 'em, and all drawing good pay in hard currency, too, they will work like beavers to keep things as they are — but I hope they will remember that they are not all creation.

There is one thing, when I think on't, makes me crawl all over, and lifts my dander considerable: that a set of men filling all kinds of offices, from the highest to the lowest, with wages from $70 a day down to $3 a day, all turn to and spend more time and labor in working for the purpose of keeping in office than in performing the duty of their office; and so, instead of being the people's sarvents, claim to be the people's masters. This will never do; and the longer things are left so, the worse it gits, till the President himself don't dare to turn 'em out, for fear that they in turn will hitch teams and turn him out. This will never do; I for one can't stand it any longer.

———

Log Cabin, North Bend, March 29, 1840 [1].

I got here yesterday and enquired for the Old Hero, and was told he was out attending to plowing up some bottom land, and I went off looking for him; and sure enuf I found him as busy as a bee in a tar-bucket, and twice as spry. I hadn't got my regimentals on and he took me for a settler. "Well, stranger," says he, "how do you do?" "Right smart," says I; "how is it with you?" "From the East?" says he, "and goin' West?" "Yes and no," says I. "Well," says he, "that sounds right, and makes me hope you will stop in these parts." I had never seen him afore, and as I had come to measure him thru and thru, I got eyeing him, and we had considerable conversation afore I let on who I was; and when I did tell him I guess all Downingville, and especially our family and name, would like to see the right down hearty shake of

---

[1] William Henry Harrison, the "Old Hero" of the battles of Tippecanoe and the Thames, lived at North Bend, Ohio, near Cincinnati. A part of his home here had formerly been a log cabin, but it was really a commodious and elegant mansion. Harrison's political availability rested largely upon the fact that he was non-committal upon most political issues. It will be noted that Major Downing deals in patriotic generalities. It will also be noted that he describes Harrison as a hard-working farmer.

the hand the Old Hero gave me. "Why," says he, "Major, a rise in the Ohio arter a long dry spell was never more pleasing to me than to see you." . . .

There are some things I like to see here in The Cabin, and which look about right. There are four pictures hanging up here, which the Old Hero says ought to hang in every cabin in the country, and Congress ought to have printed and framed and sent round to every cabin that can't affird to buy 'em (a leetle saving out o' the public printing would pay the hull expense), and they be: 1st, *the Declaration of Independence;* 2d, *the Constitution of the United States;* 3d, *Gineral Washington's Farewell Address;* 4th, *the Map of the United States.* Now with these, the Gineral says many a good honest Democrat — looking well to 'em — will straighten the crooks of party.

## LOG CABINS[1]

### Newark *Advertiser,* May 16, 1840

Log Cabins were the dwelling places of the founders of our republic. It was a Log Cabin that received the daring pioneers of liberty who exchanged the dangers of the half-sinking *Mayflower* for the dangers and perils of an inhospitable clime. It was in view of the Rock of Plymouth that the Puritans of New England first erected their Log Cabins. It was in Log Cabins that the pioneers of the mighty West — the Boones, the Worthingtons, the McArthurs, the Shelbys — of the vast region that stretches from the Appalachian chain to and beyond the shores of the Mississippi, reared the race of statesmen and heroes who have since civilized it. It was in a Log Cabin that the illustrious Harrison, the governor of a territory equal almost in extent to the dominions of the Russian Autocrat, learned the lessons of wisdom, moderation, and courage which have placed him in the foremost rank of the great men of the nation, and are destined to invest him with the first honors of the republic. Log Cabins were the early homes of the first settlers of every State in the Union. Log Cabins were the garrisons of the frontiers when every acre was won from the wilderness and the savage by the sacrifice of a human life. Honored, then, through all time, be these memorials of the trials, the sufferings, the triumphs of our forefathers. Thrice honored be he whom the splendid palaces, the seduction of official station, the blaze of military and civic renown, could never allure from his attachment to the republican simplicity which he learned between the unhewn rafters of his log cabin.

[1] Immediately after the Harrisburg convention of December, 1839, which nominated William Henry Harrison, a Baltimore newspaper quoted a friend of the disappointed Henry Clay as saying that if Harrison were given a barrel of hard cider and a pension of $2,000 a year, he would spend the rest of his days in his log cabin by the side of the fire, studying moral philosophy. This editorial is typical of the Whig response to the sneer.

## [WHY HARRISON SHOULD NOT BE ELECTED PRESIDENT]

New York *Evening Post*, September 11, 1840

We promised yesterday to explain in what respect we differed from our correspondent Veto, when he said that "General Harrison has been all his life a brave, well-meaning, and honest man."

Animal courage we will not deny General Harrison to possess. He would probably at any time of his life, if engaged in a contest of physical force, stand his ground like most other men. This is a very common and not a very exalted kind of merit. So far Veto is right. The higher kind of courage, moral courage, we see no ground for ascribing to him. He is not the man who will boldly avow an unpopular opinion. He is too fond of being on good terms with everybody, too desirous of getting everybody's good word, and when he is a candidate, of obtaining every man's vote, to have any of that sort of boldness. His attempt to secure the votes of the Northern abolitionists, by writing letters representing himself favorable to their cause, while he was endeavoring to obtain the support of the Southern States by making different representations in that quarter, is an act of the grossest moral cowardice.

"Well-meaning" in certain respects Harrison may be. He is not, we believe, very select in his morals; it would not do to compile a code of ethics from his example. Yet he is hospitable, and probably in the main friendly in his dealings with mankind. He has good nature we doubt not, but his very good nature, being accompanied with a weak intellect, only makes him the easier tool of others. The most convenient and supple instruments of profligate politicians are often good natured. In a higher sense, that of governing his conduct by a steady and rigid conscientiousness, he is not well-meaning, as is evident from the course he has pursued towards Colonel Croghan, of which an account has already been published in this paper; and the same remark may be made on the course he has pursued in regard to the abolition question.

"Honest" in some respects, probably Harrison is. We hope he would not attempt to cheat anybody in driving a bargain, and that he punctually pays such debts as he contracts. He is probably a man who, if he had never been thought of for any place of honor or trust, might have passed through the world with the reputation of average honesty. But his conduct in the case of Croghan, to which we have alluded, and his concealment and double-dealing in regard to his political opinions since he was last nominated for the Presidency, are at variance with every principle of honesty. When his incapacity for places of high responsibility is threatened with exposure, as in Croghan's case, or when his popularity is concerned, as in the present canvass for the Presidency, he is neither brave enough nor well-meaning enough to be honest. His pliancy of temper and dullness of moral perception are such that when advised to play the knave by those who are about him, he does so without much hesitation.

We take no pleasure in discussing these matters. We have spoken of Harrison's personal character in this article in as mild terms as conscience would allow us to use, and we should not have written it had not the words of our correspondent been falsely imputed to us. The great objection, after all, to General Harrison is that he is set up by a party who are governed by pernicious maxims of government and who propose pernicious measures, and that his election is their victory. Another objection which certainly deserves great consideration is that made by Governor Tazewell, that even allowing him to be "brave, well-meaning and honest," he is "both physically and intellectually incompetent to the duties of the Presidency."

## FEDERAL CENTRALIZATION UNDER THE DEMOCRATS

*Kennebec Journal*, October 1, 1840

We formerly held the opinion that the predictions of Patrick Henry and other Anti-Federalists, who opposed our present Federal Constitution, were visionary and not well considered. They apprehended that too much power was conferred on the general government and particularly upon the Executive. We could see no such danger, and looking at the doctrines of Nullification as eminently mischievous and dangerous, and many other State Rights doctrines which have been broached in our time as absurd, we rather apprehended that the centrifugal power was the greatest; that there was the most danger of the Union falling to pieces. These opinions were formed, however, when the Federal power was used under Monroe and Adams for beneficent purposes only. But the experience of the last ten years has entirely changed the face of things.

It has for several years been apparent to us, as we see by General Harrison's latest speech that it has been to him, and as it has been to thousands of others, that the principle of monarchy in our Federal Government, so much dreaded by Patrick Henry, Luther Martin, and others, has been steadily developing itself under the present Administration. The power and patronage of the Federal Government have been immeasurably extended within a few years. The patronage of the State governments has been brought in to swell that of the Federal Government. Governors and State officers are made obsequious partisans of the great Federal head at Washington. These State offices have become stepping stones to lucrative appointments under the President, and have, of course, been administered to meet the royal favor. There is nothing like State independence in any commonwealth which supports the Administration. The rulers of our own State, for instance, on the great question of our boundary, dare take no step which is not acceptable to Martin Van Buren.

The principle of Federalism, therefore, as it was understood by the old Democrats of 1798, has been expanding its proportions within the last few years far beyond all previous example, and this has been done altogether in the abused name of Democracy. Had it professed to be what it is — had it assumed no false disguise — it would not have been tolerated so long; more especially when connected with a ruinous administration of the finances of the country. But the people are now beginning to inquire more universally what Federalism really is, and what Democracy is, and whether the present Administration will stand a severe scrutiny. It will be found — it is found — that everything that was odious in ancient Federalism has been adopted and enlarged upon by the present dynasty, without any of its higher motives, its honorable purposes, or its pure integrity; and for that the true principles of Democracy have been disregarded to a most culpable extent.

## THE PRESIDENTIAL ELECTION

New York *Courier and Enquirer*, November 7, 1840

The polls of our election closed last evening at sundown, and the result is a Van Buren majority, in this city, of about twelve thousand, being two thousand less than was claimed at Tammany Hall, and one thousand less than it was supposed the Democrats had received when the voting ceased. Although we have lost four members of Congress, and the results on the other nominations are the same as before, yet the anticipated majority of our opponents has been so greatly reduced that the Whigs may well regard the result as a substantial victory.

The defect of our registry law which allows the process of registration to be continued until the closing of the polls alone prevented the success of the entire Whig ticket. The great object of a registration of voters is to require that every voter should have "a local habitation and a name," at some given period before the opening of the polls. And by such registration only can an election be conducted in this city with an approach to fairness. Not a particle of doubt is now entertained but that the Whigs would have carried the city under the registration, large as it was, had not the doors been left open for the "certificate voters" who were yesterday manufactured to order for the occasion. We are informed that about two thousand of these voters were created in this way.

## [HARRISON'S ELECTION IS BUT A TEMPORARY DEFEAT]

New York *Evening Post*, November 9, 1840

General Harrison is the President-elect of the United States; the returns from the western counties of New York have decided that question. The time for a "change" has at last arrived; the time when the people, in order to be convinced of the benefits of a Democratic policy, must try a taste of its opposite.

There is no teacher like experience. No man values the blessing of health like him who has just risen from a sick bed — no man enjoys the sweets of liberty like him who has tasted the bitterness of oppression. We suppose that it is just so with nations; to keep up their attachment to a wise and liberal government, which respects the rights and liberties of all alike, it may be necessary that now and then they should submit to see their affairs administered on principles which exalt the few at the expense of the many.

The Democratic party will watch the conduct of the new Administration, we hope, in a spirit of fairness, but with a determination to contest every inch of ground, in the attempt which will doubtless be made to revive exploded principles and pernicious measures. If they succeed in forcing a national bank upon us, we shall never cease to call for a repeal of its charter. If they return to the policy of internal improvements which prevailed under the younger Adams, we shall demand that they be abandoned the moment a Democratic party is again in the ascendency. If they revive a protective tariff, we shall claim that it be rescinded. Every step that is taken in violation of the Constitution and the principles of equal rights will be retraced the moment their brief hour of authority is past.

The first step will undoubtedly be to propose a national bank. They see that the commerce of the country is rapidly reviving, and the money market gradually recovering from the state of confusion into which it was thrown by the failure of our banking system, and they will be in haste to apply their grand remedy, in order that it may have the credit of bringing about the favorable results which must infallibly take place, and in fact, are now taking place without it. Let them create their national bank and let those subscribe in its stock who are willing to contribute their capital to an institution which has only four years at most to live! Its charter will scarcely outlive the period prescribed for filling up its stock.

We enter upon the contest which lies before us, not only with a firm resolution, but with the most cheerful hopes of the issue. Democratic principles have taken deep root in the hearts even of many who have been led, by a popular delusion, to assist in the overthrow of the present administration. The young men of the country, with no very numerous exceptions, are indoctrinated in democratic principles, friends to the freedom of trade, inclined to those plans of legislation which interfere least with men's employments, which create fewest offices, and which are founded on an honest and rigid construction of the Constitution. The moment the Whig party begin to move in those projects which their leaders, have darkly hinted at, but which they dared not distinctly proclaim because they knew them to be unpopular, we shall have this class of young men instantly on our side.

## SECTIONS AND VOTES IN 1840

Washington *National Intelligencer*, November 14, 1840

A view of the political complexion of the different States of the Union, as indicated by their votes at the recent election, will show how little is the influence which sectional prejudices exert in the formation of parties. For example, in the midst of New England stands New Hampshire, one State of the six, voting for the Democratic candidate which the other five reject. At the other extremity of the Union, South Carolina declines the sisterly association which her neighbors proffer on the north and south of her, and chooses her ally far away among the White Mountains. Louisiana prefers to go with Maine rather than with Arkansas; Ohio reaches out a long arm over Virginia and shakes hands with North Carolina.

But these results may show also the power of party discipline and of political alliances. In asking why South Carolina has adhered to the Administration, one need be at no loss for an answer. If there be one State in the Union which formerly displayed more than usual hostility against the men and the measures of the dominant party, that State was South Carolina. The language of the press, the speeches of her public men, abounding in denunciations and invective, fierce, bitter, unrelenting, demonstrated this. Whether Mr. Calhoun has abused the influence which his great abilities and personal authority gave him in his native State, in drawing her over to continue a coalition between herself and the Administration which he had so unsparingly condemned, is a question which the people of the State themselves must judge of. Perhaps the personal influence of a prominent citizen in Missouri, of another in New Hampshire, constituted the principal bond of coalescence which united those States also with the political fortunes of Mr. Van Buren rather than any natural affinity between their interests and the policy of his administration.

But if these individual instances show the force of party organization and of alliances among leaders, the grand result demonstrates how ineffectual are such devices to keep down or control the mighty power of the popular will.  The cunning and the wise in their own conceit are confounded in the midst of their stratagems.  They leave out in their calculations an item which proves large enough to overbalance the whole sum of their estimates, an item indeed which cannot be reckoned in figures — that spirit of independence in the people, the determination to vindicate their own power of rule when those to whom they entrust it have abused it.  To this we are to look if we would ascertain the operative cause of the great and glorious revolution just accomplished.

## THE CHANGES IN PRESIDENT TYLER'S CABINET[1]

New York *Tribune*, September 18, 1841

We heartily approved the course of Mr. Webster in remaining in the Cabinet after the retirement of his colleagues, believing that considerations of the highest national importance imperatively dictated the course he has taken.  In saying this, we by no means imply that no other man is fully competent to the discharge of the duties of Secretary of State, under the most critical circumstances. But Mr. Webster has a standing as a statesman on both sides of the Atlantic which very few Americans enjoy; his character and talents command a respect and esteem in Europe which are of the highest consequence in the present state of our relations with England; he can proffer and obtain terms of adjustment which a new man could not, for the English will believe that he but asks what is right, while our people know that he will submit to nothing less than that; and even those who have spent the summer in foully reviling and libelling him as a truckler and traitor would at heart regret to see his de-

[1] The death of Harrison immediately after his inauguration gave the Presidency to John Tyler, who was far more nearly a Democrat than a Whig, and who fell once under the influence of a coterie of fellow-Virginians led by Henry A. Wise. In consequence he refused to promote the principal Whig measures, and vetoed the bill for a third United States Bank, upon which the Whigs had set their hearts. Nearly all the Whig members of his Cabinet, feeling personally affronted by this veto, resigned; but Daniel Webster remained, declaring that he did so in order to carry through the negotiations with Great Britain over the northeastern boundary line. Most of the Whig press stood by him in this decision, and so did Horace Greeley.

partment now confided to any other man.  If he were to resign and
any other man but Henry Clay be appointed in his stead, the nation
would feel that it had sustained a serious loss at a moment least
opportune — that, from some cause or other, the public interest
had been put at hazard by personal differences on points of comparatively no moment.  We have rejoiced, therefore, that Mr.
Webster has remained at his post, and we doubt not that he will be
found fully competent to the guardianship of the national rights
and his own honor.

But we are not well pleased with the tenor of his letter of Monday
to the editor of the *National Intelligencer*.  His letter states that he
has "seen no sufficient reasons for the dissolution of the late Cabinet,"
and that "if I had seen reason to resign my office, I should not have
done so without giving the President reasonable notice," etc., etc.
We think all this better unsaid by Mr. Webster.  What *he* has seen,
we cannot positively say; but we have seen, among other things,
the following:

> We have seen the obnoxious Jacksonian claim of exclusive ex-
> ecutive power in the President asserted in behalf of President
> Tyler by the journal most devoted to him in Washington, with
> the corollary that his Cabinet Ministers ought to reflect and sus-
> tain his views or resign. . . .
> We have seen a disreputable journal, which has notoriously
> been honored with too large a share of the President's considera-
> tion, clamoring for the resignation of the Cabinet (Mr. Webster
> included), accusing them of meanness in clinging to their places,
> and threatening that they would soon be kicked out if they did
> not resign.
> We have seen a "Tyler" Congressman from Virginia, elected
> as a Whig but opposing every Whig measure of the session, sub-
> mit to the House approvingly the resolutions of a Loco-foco
> meeting in Louisa County declaring that they accorded in opinion
> with the Administration proper (to wit, John Tyler), at the other
> end of the Avenue (the White House), but not with the Admin-
> istration improper (the representatives of the people) at this end
> (the Capitol).  The Cabinet were known to sympathize with the
> Administration improper — we had before hoped Mr. Webster
> did also. . . .

One word now of Mr. Webster's position.  There are very many
clamoring for his resignation.  But to what end?  To resign *now* is
to sacrifice himself irredeemably, and to no good purpose whatever.
Mr. Webster occupies a position of fearful responsibility and peril.
He stands virtually pledged to the country that the Administration
of John Tyler shall, in spite of seductions, jealousies, and abstrac-
tions, be a Whig Administration, and that a satisfactory plan of

adjustment of the currency question shall be proposed, or at least approved, by the President at the approaching session. Should he prove to have been deceived in this, his position is lamentable. What lover of his country, what lover of fairness, can considerately seek to embarrass him in his position or his course?

## A DEFENCE OF PRESIDENT TYLER [1]

Philadelphia *American Sentinel*, June, 1843

No President has been more fiercely denounced by the rancor of party hatred than John Tyler. Professing Democratic principles, it is his misfortune to have been indebted for his election to "Federal Whigs" — to have been the head of a party whose measures he was forced to negative, and he in turn be denounced as guilty of inconsistency, vacillation, ingratitude, and treachery.

And yet, notwithstanding this denunciation, few statesmen of any distinction in this country have been guilty of less political tergiversation than Mr. Tyler. The very acts for which he is now condemned by his former Whig friends are the best proofs of the general consistency of his political conduct.

When selected by the Whigs as their candidate for the Vice-Presidency he was, like Mr. Rives, a prominent member of the conservative Democratic party; his uniform hostility to the great leading doctrines of Federal Whiggery was matter of history. He was selected by the Whigs *as a Democrat* — because they believed his nomination would secure the defeat of the regular Democratic candidates.

They knew that Mr. Tyler, as governor of Virginia, was a faithful Democrat who had never wavered from the creed of Jefferson; that in 1819, as one of the Congressional committee of investigation into the abuses of the United States Bank, he joined in Mr. Spencer's able report convicting the Bank of a forfeiture of charter, and took an active part in the subsequent discussions, which finally resulted in placing Mr. Cheves at the head of its reform direction.

They knew that in the succeeding ten years, Mr. Tyler's conduct was marked by the same consistent support of Democratic doctrines; that from 1830 to 1834 he occupied a seat in the United States Senate as a State Rights Jackson man, where his votes were generally recorded for the measures of the Administration; that his consistent attachment to State Rights principles led him to oppose the famous proclamation of General Jackson against South Carolina, and finally

[1] By 1843 Tyler had no friends in the Whig party, and few who really respected him in the Democratic ranks, though the Democrats were willing to make use of him. This defence is from a Democratic newspaper. The Whigs united in regarding him as a traitor of particularly low sort.

occasioned the resignation of his seat in 1836, when the legislature of Virginia instructed him to vote for the "expunging resolutions."

The Whigs knew all this when in 1840 they drew him from his retirement, and with the assistance of the conservative Democrats elected him to the Vice-Presidency of the United States. By the death of General Harrison he became President, and since that event has continued to manifest the same consistent attachment to the Democratic State Rights principles which marked his career in Congress up to the time of his resignation.

The Whigs, we have said, when they nominated Mr. Tyler well knew the principles by which he had been uniformly guided in his long public career. His nomination was intended for political effect; it was shrewdly calculated that his known hostility to a United States Bank would secure a vast increase of political capital. But they never dreamed that he might be called to exercise the duties of chief magistrate. His nomination was the result of a factious combination, willing to compromise principles to obtain power — one of those alliances which look only to "expediency" — and the profligacy of the spirit which impelled the policy has been well rebuked.

We are by no means certain, from the aspect of things, that a change in 1844 is desirable. The policy of Mr. Tyler's administration is developed and generally approved. That his leading measures have been essentially Democratic is universally admitted. His appointments have been the worst feature of his Administration; for by the appointment of Whigs to office, that party seemed to have a conceded right to demand that he should sanction Whig measures. Political principles apply as much to men as to measures, and a Democratic President can be well served only by Democratic officers.

## [MR. TYLER'S POLITICS: A REPLY]

### The Pennsylvanian, June, 1843

The *Sentinel* insists upon it that at the time of his nomination to the Vice Presidency, Mr. Tyler was a conservative Democrat of the Rives school, hostile to the doctrines of Federal Whiggery, and that he was on this account selected to strengthen the Whig ticket, "without a why or a wherefore." Even if all this were true, we do not regard it as being much to the credit of the same John Tyler, to have been thus a trimmer between parties, and to allow his name to be used to operate against the party which he regarded as soundest in principles. Taking it for granted that the *Sentinel's* assertions are correct, Mr. Tyler is made out, on the showing of his friends, to be a very paltry politician. But the *United States Gazette* denies the statements of the *Sentinel* in toto, and in the following terms declares that John Tyler received the nomination as a professor of Clay Whiggism.

"He was selected by the Whigs. He declared himself to be a Whig, and a Clay man, and he was selected or rather nominated on these professions, as a compliment to the Clay men, who, though a *majority*, had given up their candidate — had given up against their better sense, and the *tears* of John Tyler.

"Mr. Tyler's uniform hostility to the doctrines of Federal Whiggery is, we suppose, to be inferred from his Pittsburgh letter."

## THE WEBSTER–ASHBURTON SETTLEMENT [1]

*Niles's Register*, June 10, 1843

That a war of blood and devastation would speedily ensue between Great Britain and the United States, in consequence of any of the difficulties which lately existed, many of which have been happily settled by the treaty of Washington, our readers must well remember we have never conceded as probable. At every recurrence of dispute we have maintained that between two nations whose people were as intelligent, who had as much influence in controlling their own governments through the force of public sentiment, and who had such manifest inducements to remain at peace and such reason to apprehend direful results in case of resorting to "the unpleasant alternative of trying which could do the other the most harm," there was too much *good sense* to allow their governments to get into a war with each other for any considerations so comparatively trifling as they were to war about. Kings as well as people have learned within the last half century that war is a dangerous and expensive game to play at. Mr. Webster and Lord Ashburton were entitled to and have received the thanks of their countrymen for most faithfully representing and carrying out the public disposition in their negotiations and adjustments of difficulties, so far as they have succeeded in adjusting them. None could have better done that which the occasion required — few if any could have done it as handsomely — yet it would be injustice to the great body of the people of both England and America to insinuate that the restoration of harmony in the case was dependent upon any two men. When peace was so manifestly the interest of both countries, and was so desired by the people of both, agents could surely be found qualified to carry the desires into effect.

[1] The Webster-Ashburton Treaty settling the Maine boundary and questions of extradition and the slave trade was ratified by the Senate in the late summer of 1842. *Niles's Register* reflects the relief of conservative and thoughtful men over the disappearance of a dangerous crisis.

## THE INCONSISTENCIES OF JOHN C. CALHOUN[1]

Macon *Messenger*, July, 1843

In 1816, the godfather of a protective tariff; in 1833, the advocate of nullification to overthrow it — in 1832, the supporter of the compromise act; in 1841, the violent opponent of it — in 1816, the advocate of a national bank; in 1834, proposing to extend its charter twelve years; in 1838 and 1841, denouncing it as unconstitutional — in 1816, the advocate of a system of internal improvements; in 1819, the moving spirit that breathed life into it; in 1832 the denouncer of it as entailing all the evils of the tariff; in 1843, again its advocate — in 1836, the advocate of distributing the proceeds of the sales of public lands among the States, and the author of the scheme; in 1841, the reviler of the scheme as unconstitutional; in 1842, the advocate of the proceeds of the public lands being continued in the Treasury, as the only constitutional mode of application; in 1834, the author of the proposition to take them from the old States, and to cede them to the States in which they lie — in 1816, the author of the proposition to appropriate the bonus of the United States Bank to works of internal improvement; in 1840, the reviler of those who voted for his proposition — in 1825, the proud boaster of his great services in giving being to the "American system"; now the traducer of those who acted with him and followed his lead — the author of the system of internal improvements, which has squandered so many millions of dollars for no good end, and now the prosecuting reviler of those who attempt to carry out the schemes he planned — the opponent of the sub-treasury in 1834, and the great advocate of it now — the advocate of every measure hated by the South, and the bold Senator who declared in 1842 that he had not changed any of these principles, and yet the suppliant for their votes. The blustering advocate now of "free trade," in his whole Congressional career before his connection with Mr. Monroe's cabinet, he was the ultra advocate of protection both by his votes and speeches. A member of the Senate since 1832, amidst all the excitement of the tariff question he has never yet presented to the American people the first free trade proposition.

This is the politician who never yet raised a party around him, and this is the political weathercock whose friends have established a press at Macon to persuade the people of Georgia to follow him. This is the Presidential aspirant who cannot get the vote of any two States in the Union. What an imposition upon common sense!

[1] Calhoun in 1843, and indeed throughout his life, coveted the Presidency as ardently as did Henry Clay. In details, his policy was often inconsistent. But he never wavered in his central aim — the welding of a solid South. He sought to unite the Southern people behind the great sectional interest of slavery.

## THE TRADE OF THE MISSISSIPPI VALLEY

Baltimore *American*, August 19, 1843

The increase of trade on the Mississippi waters in the last thirty years furnishes a most striking indication of the astonishing progress of the country in wealth and prosperity. The July number of *Hunt's Merchant's Magazine*, in an article on this subject, sets forth a series of facts which are truly wonderful.

In 1817, less than thirty years ago, the entire tonnage on all the waters of the Mississippi was only 6,500 tons. Steamers were then newly in use; they were heavy and slow — almost as far behind the steamers of the present day in construction and rapidity as the keel boat was inferior to the early steamer. A Louisville paper quotes the *Commercial Chronicle* for May, 1818, of the port of Louisville, from which it appears that the steamboat *Etna* arrived at Shippingport at the falls of the Ohio, a few miles below Louisville, in thirty-two days from New Orleans. The steamboat *Governor Shelby* arrived at Shippingport from New Orleans in twenty-two days running-time. On the first of May, 1818, a hermaphrodite-rigged barge arrived at Shippingport in seventy-one days from New Orleans. A keel boat arrived there on the same day in one hundred and one days from New Orleans. The time now occupied in making a trip from New Orleans to Louisville is between five and six days.

In 1834 there were two hundred and fifty steamboats afloat on the Mississippi waters with an aggregate tonnage of thirty-nine thousand tons. In the eight years following this tonnage was more than doubled; for in 1842 there were on the western waters four hundred and fifty steamers, averaging two hundred tons each, and making an aggregate of ninety thousand tons, built at a cost of seven millions of dollars. To this vast amount of steamboat tonnage there must be added, in the great account of the Mississippi trade for that year, four thousand flatboats of some seventy-five tons each. The whole amount for 1842 shows an increase of 130 per cent over the tonnage of 1834; an increase in eight years most remarkable.

When it is recollected that the great west is yet in its infancy — that millions of acres traversed by its mighty rivers are yet unproductive, awaiting the hand of culture — that vast works of internal improvement in that fertile region are but just beginning to aid in the development of its exhaustless resources — how immense is the swelling aggregate of future trade which rises to the mind's eye! Let the view extend to the Western tributaries of the Mississippi, and to the fertile countries watered by them; and in contemplation of the results which succeeding years must bring to pass on the banks of the Missouri, the Arkansas, the Red and other great rivers, all pouring their rich freights into the Mississippi, it is not in the power of imagination to take in the incalculable and ever-increasing mass of trade which is destined to give wealth, splendor, and magnificence to that portion of the republic and to all other parts also as participants in its diffusion.

## [THE DEMOCRATS SHOULD NOMINATE MR. VAN BUREN]

### Richmond *Enquirer*, August, 1843

We have no selfish ends in view. We shall gain not a feather's weight by the election of Mr. Van Buren. As for a glass of wine which he would give us when we visited Washington, it is no more than Mr. Calhoun, or Mr. Buchanan, would give us. As to Mr. Van Buren's declining the office, we frankly express the sentiment we entertain, that he is less anxious to obtain it than any of the other candidates. He will bear his defeat with as much philosophy as any of them. He might gain some credit for magnanimity by the act of withdrawing; but would not Messrs. Calhoun, Buchanan, and others gain honor by it also? and would not their biding time give them a higher claim upon the democracy than either of them now possesses? We repeat our impression, that Mr. Van Buren is among the least anxious for his personal elevation, and that rather than endanger his party, he would magnanimously decline the nomination.

But can he do so? His numerous friends throughout the country would consider him bound to act as the instrument for restoring those principles which were struck down with him, and would they consent to his withdrawal? Mr. Van Buren has, it is true, been covered with honors, and he has worn them well; but there is one other and last reward which the Democracy wish to bestow upon him for his fidelity. They desire to rescue his name from the stains so unjustly cast upon it in 1840, and to restore him to that elevation from which he was overturned on account of his steady devotion to republican principles. Say rather, what is more strictly the truth, they wish the true principles of the government, cloven down with him in 1840, to be restored in 1844. They wish the cloud which was thrown over the capacity of the people for self-government through the tricks of the Whigs to be now dispersed by their signal defeat.

Though Mr. Van Buren be kept before the people twelve years, did not the same thing occur with Jefferson and Jackson; and can the Democracy ever regret that the public mind was engaged so long in the elevation of these true patriots? There were peculiar circumstances in each case; and in the present instance, it would be far from an "injustice."

## THE DEFAULT OF STATES ON THEIR DEBTS

*Niles's Register*, August 5, 1843

Two of the States and one of the territories have officially equivo-
cated as to their obligations. Mississippi disputes paying five
millions which was obtained for banking purposes, as her governor
alleges, in violation of the Constitution of the State; Michigan
disputes $2,200,000 which was negotiated for purposes of internal
improvement through the United States Bank. And Florida has
repudiated three millions which she obtained for banking purposes;
making a total, in disputed debts, of $11,200,000.

Without referring to the pretexts alleged for disowning their
obligations in these cases, it is sufficient for the present that we
recognize the seal and signature of the constituted authorities, as
the act of the States respectively. And we have no doubt that the
people of the States, without exception, will compel their own
governments to redeem those evidences of indebtedness. Disputing
a claim is always injurious to the credit of the debtor, but can never
invalidate a debt; neither refusing payment, "repudiating," nor
any act of "limitation," can invalidate a just claim upon a government. The binding obligation of *contract* is more sacredly insured
by the moral obligation in such a case than even by the letter and
spirit of a constitutional provision.

There is no form of government which is more likely to retrace an
error than the form under which Americans are now reposing.
Florida, one of the disputing three named above, is not yet one of
the States of this Union. She is still in her minority, and Uncle
Sam is her guardian. Is there a sensible man in this Union that
doubts either the *disposition* or the *authority* of the guardian to have
justice done in the case of her debtors? Michigan is the youngest
sister in the Union. Her people assumed the power of self-government at the unfortunate instant when speculation was at its acme,
and the first exercise of her sovereignty was to make an imprudent
adventure for such a moment. She was for the moment overwhelmed by the crash which ensued. But the circumstances of
Michigan are most rapidly improving. What will two millions of
debt be to such a State as Michigan will be seven years hence?
What are her resources even now? Look at the teeming products of
her soil that are already seeking every market!

Mississippi was the first to contest her liability for her bonds.
What Mississippi has *suffered*, instead of gained by that act, let her
melancholy condition answer. How long she will continue in an
attitude so unenviable, we can only conjecture. That a change will
speedily be wrought looks probable from the fact that whilst one of

the political parties there in unbroken column is exerting every nerve to have the State redeem their bonds, the party heretofore in majority were so far divided upon the subject at their State convention held a few days since that those who insisted upon the State paying, actually seceded and withdrew from the convention. Whether the change is at hand, or is to be yet delayed, it will eventually come. We do not mean a change of party, but a change of the State policy. Mississippi can and will redeem her character, and we verily believe that no party will continue long in power there that neglects the means of retrieving it. See, in another part of this number, Governor Hamilton's admirable speech upon repudiation in that State.

So much for the two States and one territory which dispute paying their debts. Six other of the States, though admitting their indebtedness, have for some time past been unable to pay regularly the whole of the interest accruing thereon. Each one of them, however, has evinced more than anxiety to do so, and most of them have resorted to measures that in a short time will insure their future punctuality.

Most of the debtor States have the improvements for which the debts were contracted. These will in a few years be able to relieve the States of any charge on their account, and many of them will in process of time no doubt pay off the principal, and then remain a source of profit to the State, as well as of convenience to their communities. . . . Maryland, our own State, is in this dilemma, and according to her means as deeply involved as any State in the Union, yet even if her vast public works, in constructing which the debt was incurred, and which are yet incomplete, should fail to produce anything — even in that case an annual tax of one per cent upon the assessable property in the State would redeem the whole of her obligations in a few years. Who believes that her people would not rather endure such a tax than endure the opprobrium themselves, and bequeath to their descendants the disgrace of dishonoring the faith of the State? Whoever so judges of Maryland has mistaken her character, and forgotten her history.

## THE ANNEXATION OF TEXAS[1]

### Washington *National Intelligencer*, April 4, 1844

Our objections at the threshold of the project of annexation, that that question has been sprung upon us without any regard whatever to the wishes of the country; that its present agitation is the result

[1] At the time this editorial appeared, the treaty annexing Texas to the United States was about to be signed. John C. Calhoun, an ardent annexationist, had become Secretary of State in February, 1844. He at once entered upon negotiations

of the mere individual will of the President, independent of any expression of the national will, such as ought to have preceded it, or of the President's constitutional advisers, whom he did not deign to consult on the subject; that it is, in short, an act of the President *per se*, have lost none of their force by further reflection upon them. The President, entering upon this negotiation, appears to us to have acted upon a misconception of the nature and extent of the executive authority in reference to the treaty-making power. Reasoning from analogy, probably, the President appears to have considered the treaty-making power to be in his hands an independent self-existent power, for the exercise of which, so far as the President is concerned, he is responsible only to his own will and pleasure; instead of its being a representative power, in the exercise of which he is bound to obey the national will when ascertained, and for that purpose, before he embarks in any new adventure, to take all proper means to ascertain that will. Much more is he bound, in all practicable cases, if not under all possible circumstances, before undertaking negotiations of such possible consequence as the annexation to the United States of a foreign country, or even the mere purchase of territory from a foreign power, to consult the Senate, that body without whose consent and coöperation in such matters the Presidential office is a mere pageant. For such purposes the President has the power to convene the Senate if the public service requires it. He could have obtained the advice of the Senate on this subject in the recess of Congress, in less time than it took to make his first ineffectual overture to the President of Texas. But when the last overture was made, the Senate was in session, and nothing could have been easier than for the President to have taken the sense of the Senate before proceeding to extremities which, he knew, involved the question of war — a question which he had not the shadow of a right to determine.

We object to the institution of this negotiation, further, because the public opinion, so far as there had been any expression of it, was decidedly more against it than for it; because there was no public necessity, nor any plausible excuse, for this forced march in diplomacy; and because it was against the national dignity to depart, in such strange haste as characterized the opening of this negotiation, from the ground heretofore solemnly and wisely taken by this government in relation to it.

What sort of a moral spectacle should we exhibit to the gaze of

with the Texas government, and signed the treaty April 12. The *Intelligencer's* editorial is a very moderate expression of the opposition sentiment. Old J. Q. Adams wrote in his Diary on April 22 that "The treaty for the annexation of Texas to the Union was this day sent to the Senate, and with it went the freedom of the human race."

the world in possessing ourselves of the territory of Texas (putting its government and population out of the question) under the circumstances, which the world understands as well as we? Here is a territory wrested from Mexico — so far as it is actually severed from that republic — by citizens of the United States, who emigrated to it in military array against the laws and in defiance of instructions by the Executive of the United States to its law-officers to "prosecute, without respect to persons, all who might attempt to violate the obligations of our neutrality;" Mexico, our sister republic, being then in perfect peace and amity with us. With what face can this government — now that the emigrants above-mentioned have possessed themselves, in defiance of the civil authority of the United States, of the territory of Texas — turn round and buy from these very persons the territory which they wrested from the republic of Mexico, we being still in the same relations of perfect amity with that republic that we were at the date of the message of President Jackson referred to? What would the world say of us were we, under existing circumstances, to do this thing?

## [TEXAS SHOULD BE ANNEXED AT ONCE]

### Washington *Globe*, April 20, 1844

Texas will come in at the right door, for she will be cordially received by the family to which she belongs. We have said before that we looked upon Texas, in right, as a territory of the Union. The guardian who once had the disposal of this fair patrimony in his hands made way with it wrongfully by throwing it into the arms of the Spanish potentate. A revolution made it the possession of another power on this continent — Mexico; another revolution makes it the appanage of a young branch of our own family. These children of the American Union now come forward and say: "The inheritance which was divorced from us by unworthy management has been honestly regained. It is ours and we are yours. We ask the annexation of Texas 'on a footing in all respects equal with the other States of the Union.'" Is there a State in the Union prepared to repel this fair proposal? — a proposal which brings to us innumerable benefits, and confers on them all the blessings of our glorious nation.

It is said that President Houston and the patriotic men who have redeemed Texas will, in yielding their acquisitions to us, make a conquest of the United States for themselves. This is a proud achievement, worthy of their ambition. The Roman citizens who gave new States to their country were indulged with a triumph at the seat of their empire. We should be glad to welcome, in the same way, the conquerors of Texas in the capital of the United States. And who will object, if they thus receive back their own country by winning for it again the fine regions dissevered by faithlessness? But we think the people of Texas will deserve more than a triumphant welcome for the services they have rendered. We would be glad to see an ample, nay a noble dowry put at the disposal of the State; one not only commensurate with its sacrifices and its sufferings, its expenditure of money and of blood, but sufficient to requite her for the full value of the lands she brings into the common stock, and to make some advance for the rich contributions which must be derived from imposts upon the consumption of her people.

## [MR. VAN BUREN'S CANDIDACY LOSING STRENGTH] [1]

*Niles's Register*, May 11, 1844

The Democratic national convention for nominating candidates for the Presidency and Vice-Presidency is to meet at Baltimore on the 27th instant, and notwithstanding the apparent certainty three weeks ago that Mr. Van Buren would be the nominee of that convention, there is now great uncertainty of the result. The defeat of his party in the Virginia elections seems to have convinced many of his warmest friends in Congress and elsewhere that there remains little hope of success with him as their candidate for the Presidency. If we may judge by the language of the *Globe*, the *Pennsylvanian*, and other leading journals in favor of Mr. Van Buren, there must be at this moment a warm contest in the ranks of the party as to the course best for them to adopt. A Congressional caucus is spoken of as having been held, at which it was proposed and we rather think must have been carried, to induce the reconsideration of instructions which have been given to the delegates to the national convention to vote for Mr. Van Buren as the candidate. This is indicated by a movement made where we should have least expected to see it; we mean at Richmond, and made too by Mr. Ritchie himself, who has been regarded on all hands as the senior field marshal of Mr. Van Buren's party — the first and the warmest of his advocates, and with whom, if we mistake not, he had proposed to "sink or swim."

Mr. Ritchie's sincere devotion to Mr. Van Buren has been too well established throughout many a well-fought campaign to admit

[1] This editorial struck a fatal blow at Van Buren's already tottering candidacy for the Democratic nomination; see G. P. Garrison's "Westward Extension," page 129. James K. Polk, the first "dark horse," was named instead.

of doubt. He led in the late severe electioneering contest in Virginia, and sustained the banner of his party with all his accustomed tact and untiring vigilance, nor once wavered in regard to Mr. Van Buren as the Democratic nominee. He could not command success, however his efforts may have deserved it. He was fairly beaten. He has been beaten before and few politicians ever evinced more skill than Mr. Ritchie has in rallying from a defeat, mustering munitions, and supplying magazines for renewed operations. His present movement has been influenced, no doubt, by what he now deems a certainty that Mr. Van Buren stands no chance of being elected, if nominated, and he thinks it better for the party to be at liberty to look for a more available candidate.

A letter from Mr. Dromgoole of the House of Representatives, addressed to Mr. Ritchie, was published in the *Globe* of the fourth instant, full of remonstrances and complaints at the course which Mr. Ritchie has thought proper to pursue. Mr. Dromgoole says that "if Mr. Van Buren, who has evidently been preferred, must be withdrawn because he cannot be elected by the party, then it is manifest that no one, with an inferior share of the confidence and favor of the party, can be elected by it as at present constituted and organized." These demonstrations have quickened all kinds of political fermentation at Washington. The Tyler Committee have put out an address in which this appeal is sounded:

Democrats! arouse to a sense of your danger. Listen not to the siren song of those who would delude you with assurances of security. Behold the precipice on the brink of which you are standing. Calculate calmly and soberly the awful stakes in this unequal game. Consider well what you are doing. Think before you act. Do not suffer yourselves by any unworthy prejudices to be betrayed into self-destruction. Consider well that the interests involved in the struggle of 1840 are as nothing compared to those of 1844. What were the questions then agitated, compared to the readmission of Texas into the Union, to the settlement of the Oregon question, to our last and final independence of Great Britain, and the expulsion of English influence and English intrigue from our soil?

The address recommends to the Democracy to carry a banner inscribed with "Tyler, Texas, America, and the Vetoes, against Clay, the Bank, Van Buren, and England."

The *Spectator*, Mr. Calhoun's organ at Washington, says: "We have, for six months, looked to Mr. Van Buren as the candidate of the Democratic party for the Presidency, and expected as such to support him, as we had done at the last election. Mr. Calhoun's friends in Virginia coöperated with all their zeal with his friends in the late elections. But Texas has destroyed him; and considering him as beside the Presidential canvass, we shall hereafter say but little concerning him in connection with this high office. We thank the Richmond *Enquirer* for its frank acknowledgment of the course of Mr. Calhoun's friends in Virginia."

The Washington *Globe* preserves a bold and determined front in the midst of the confusion which this movement produces in the ranks of the party. Its language is, "If the Richmond movement is persisted in, the Democratic party in that State is separated from the body of the party and disbanded." But the Washington correspondent of the New York *American*, dated on Saturday last, says: "Pandemonium is in deep conclave at the moment that I write, and the destinies of Locofocoism form the subject of the deep debate. The proceedings of the Whig convention at Baltimore, the letter of Van Buren against annexation, and generally the signs of the times have struck dismay to the hearts of the party here. There is such absolute confusion and fear of coming events, that the leaders know not what to do."

## A NEW PUBLIC PARK [1]

New York *Evening Post*, July 3, 1844

The heats of summer are upon us, and while some are leaving the town for shady retreats in the country, others refresh themselves with short excursions to Hoboken and New Brighton, or other places among the beautiful environs of our city. If the public authorities who spend so much of our money in laying out the city would do what is in their power, they might give our vast population an extensive pleasure ground for shade and recreation in these sultry afternoons, which we might reach without going out of town.

On the road to Harlem, between Sixty-eighth Street on the south and Seventy-seventh on the north, and extending from Third Avenue to the East River, is a tract of beautiful woodland, comprising sixty or seventy acres, thickly covered with old trees, intermingled with a variety of shrubs. The surface is varied in a very striking and picturesque manner, with craggy eminences and hollows, and a little stream runs through the midst. The swift tides of the East River sweep its rocky shores, and the fresh breeze of the bay comes in, on every warm summer afternoon, over the restless waters. The trees are of almost every species that grows in our woods — the different varieties of ash, the birch, the beech, the linden, the mulberry, the tulip tree and others; the azalea, the

[1] To this editorial, the first important demand for an uptown park in New York is to be traced the inception of the movement which led to the creation of Central Park. It was written by William Cullen Bryant.

kalmia, and other flowering shrubs are in bloom here in their season, and the ground in spring is gay with flowers. There never was a finer situation for the public garden of a great city. Nothing is wanting but to cut winding paths through it, leaving the woods as they now are, and introducing here and there a jet from the Croton aqueduct, the streams from which would make their own waterfalls over the rocks, and keep the brooks running through the place always fresh and full.

As we are now going on, we are making a belt of muddy docks all round the island. We should be glad to see one small part of the shore without them, one place at least where the tides may be allowed to flow pure, and the ancient brim of rocks which borders the waters left in its original picturesqueness and beauty. Commerce is devouring inch by inch the coast of the island, and if we would rescue any part of it for health and recreation, it must be done now.

All large cities have their extensive public grounds and gardens; Madrid and Mexico City their Alamedas, London its Regent's Park, Paris its Champs Elysees, and Vienna its Prater. There are none of them, we believe, which have the same natural advantages of the picturesque and beautiful which belong to this spot. It would be of easy access to the citizens, and the public carriages which now rattle in almost every street of this city would take them to its gates. The only objection which we can see to the plan would be the difficulty of persuading the owners of the soil to part with it — and this rich city can easily raise the means.

## THE ANNEXATION OF TEXAS CARRIED![1]

### New York *Tribune*, March 1, 1845

By the midnight mail, we have the astounding intelligence of the passage of annexation through the Senate by a vote of 27 to 25; every Locofoco voting in the affirmative, with just the three necessary Whigs: Johnson of Louisiana, Henderson of Mississippi, and Merrick, the purchased traitor of Maryland. The two former were constrained by the popular sentiment of constituents, but Merrick knew that *his* constituents thought as he did when he seemed to be an honest man, and had just been told so by the legislature. So black a perfidy as his has not been known since Tyler's.

Yes, the mischief is done and we are now involved in war! We have adopted a war ready made, and taken upon ourselves its prosecution to the end. We are to furnish the bodies to fill trenches

---

[1] Texas was annexed by joint resolution; this resolution passing the Senate by a vote of 27 to 25, and the House (February 28, 1845) by a vote of 132 to 76. The anguish of the Whigs opposed to the expansion of slavery was intense, and Greeley gave it its best expression.

and the cash to defray its enormous expense. Mexico, despoiled of one of her fairest provinces by our rapacity and hypocrisy, has no choice but to resist, however ineffectively, the consummation of our flagitious designs. If she should not resist now on the Rio Del Norte, she will soon be forced to struggle against our marauders in Sonora and California. Already it is openly declared at Washington that we must and will have all North America in due season; that the question is one of time only. If therefore Great Britain should see fit to stand up for the feeble and unoffending people upon whom we are making war, she will be but obeying the instinct of self-preservation. By our proceedings in getting possession of Texas, we have declared ourselves the enemies of the civilized world, or are only constrained from becoming such by the lowest considerations of self-interest. Surely there must come a reckoning for this. If those who are driving us on to untold expenditure and carnage were themselves to pay the taxes and stop the bullets, it would be a different matter.

People of the United States! what shall yet be done to turn aside this storm of unjust war from our borders? Say not that Mexico is feeble; the God of justice is with her, and we have proved how powerful is a just cause against the greatest disparity of physical force. Ought we not to hold public meetings to consider and determine what is incumbent on us in this crisis?

## CITY EMBELLISHMENTS[1]

### New York *Mirror*, April 26, 1845

You may remember the marble mantelpieces in the Verandah parlors in New Orleans. They are of the color of snow, with the soft semi-transparency of alabaster, covered all over with sculptured ornaments — vines, with trunks, leaves, and fruits, wrought in full relief with the cunning skill peculiar to the Italian! Each piece cost $1,000 in Florence.

Not long ago, we saw a respectable sugar planter from St. Landry, whilst discussing the general question of "protection," raise a heavy, metal-heeled boot to a level with the lowest button of his waistcoat, and place it firmly against a cluster of these leaves, bracing back his chair upon two of its legs! We ran up an estimate in our own minds, directly, of the probable damage, fixing it at one hundred and twenty-five dollars. Presently a leaf crumbled, and the bits of white marble fell upon the carpet. It was just as we had anticipated.

[1] This Jefferson Brick editorial was by either G. P. Morris or N. P. Willis; probably the latter. The Fountain Mirabeau was an exceptionally massive and ugly fountain temporarily placed in Battery Park, New York City.

Feeling his footing give way, the gentleman brought his foot to the floor. Our estimate, we thought a remarkably close one. But to our surprise, and in the face of all probability, whilst the gentleman grew warm upon the "sugar duty," he replaced his boot higher up the column, and let it down by hitches over the delicate sculpture. We were obliged to admit that the damages were, in the end, about two hundred and fifty dollars!

We are afraid the "ten thousand" will speak harshly of the St. Landry planter. Softly, my friends! This much you may say of the planter of the parish St. Landry: — In matters of art, he has an indifferent taste. You may go further. You may say the same thing of the mass of his countrymen. You may go further. You may say the same thing of the mass of Englishmen. But, of the St. Landry planter, it is to be observed that he is educated. He possesses a vigorous judgment, general intelligence, and a spirit of independence and courage that becomes him well. There is about the St. Landry man a certain noble peculiarity. He has the *bearing of an American.* I will venture a small wager he cannot fiddle. But I will wager again that he has made a thousand acres of wild forest blossom like the rose. *Like the fountain Mirabeau is your American.* In the little, nothing. In the great, incomparable.


## THE ASTOR CATACOMBS[1]

### New York *Mirror*, May 17, 1845

These mysterious caverns under the portico and vast vestibule of our great granite caravanserai have been conjured, during the last week, into a garden pavilion looking out upon flowers and a fountain. Herein, hereafter, the Astorians will gossip and smoke — as luxuriously quartered as a Turk in a kiosk of Constantinople. The large inner court of the Astor was, till lately, a place for house-rubbish, clothes to dry, and unhappy dogs — unsightly to look into, and devoted to the establishment's inevitable lumber. Strangers wished for the rooms which *look outward*, for the *look inward* was a wet blanket to the spirits. Now — all this is felicitously changed. The quadrangle court is made into a garden — balsam firs planted in the green sward — a beautiful fountain sending up its sparkling uselessness in the centre, and the low windows of a pillar'd saloon looking *inward* upon all. It is a hotel built around a garden — the most desirable windows looking *inward.* The guest in his solitary room sits and dreams pleasantly of his home, beguiled by the restless upgush and music of the fountain, and the thoughtful smoker goes down into the catacombs, when weary of Broadway and out-of-

[1] By N. P. Willis.

doors, and puffs away with his eyes on green grass and bright water.

These changes in the Astor have been, to our thinking, a most significant sign of American progress. It is the defect in our national character — a defect we are just now ready to remedy — to make all our culture look *outward*. Away from business and away from friends, the American is as vacant as a monomaniac in a lucid interval, and the interior of his mind is a place for unsightly lumber which he has no pleasure in returning inwards to contemplate. The education of a gentleman makes the same improvement in a man that this garden and fountain have made in the Astor — making *his windows that look inward the most desirable*. A city is a vastly pleasanter place when it is only an accessory to a mind that is pleasantest when the city is shut out, and New York is a tiresome place (as any other would be) when the gloom and rubbish of a *man's inner court* compel his attention to be only occupied out of doors.

We did not think we should preach such a sermon when we began, however!

## TEXAN ANNEXATION AND ITS CONSEQUENCES

### New York *Tribune*, March 3, 1846

The thunder of cannon, the shouts of exhilarated thousands, no less than the silence of anxious, thoughtful tens of thousands, apprise us that so far as the preliminary action of Congress is concerned, the cause of annexation is triumphant, and Texas is in a fair way to be incorporated with our country. The evil which the illustrious, pure-minded, philanthropic Channing foresaw and so eloquently reprehended years ago — which was more widely proclaimed by some faithful members of the Twenty-seventh Congress — which had been in a hundred ways most lucidly exposed to all who were not resolved to be blind — has been put in train of consummation. We have seen the beginning, but who shall show us the end?

Disguise it as we may under the cant of extending the area of freedom and the like phrases wherein gigantic crime and rapacity have in all ages invested themselves, this drama of annexation, taking into view all its acts and scenes from the migration to Texas of Houston and his confederates with the purpose which they have at length so nearly effected, cannot fail to startle the civilized world. We had before been seen to break faith with and practise hideous cruelties upon the poor aboriginal tribes within our geographical limits, but we haughtily repelled all foreign inquiry into their treatment, as a matter of purely domestic concern. Soon our border adventurers cross our well-ascertained, solemnly-established national boundary, rifle and bowie-knife in hand, drive out the national authorities, and establish their own dominion. Our government is appealed to and pretends to discountenance and frown upon the irruption, while pleading inability to act more effectively. But at length the mask is thrown off; our Executive first shows his hand in a treaty of annexation, next in a diplomatic declaration that for twenty years we have been intent on acquiring Texas, and at last, by the use of fraudulent disguises in a Presidential election and a most unconstitutional appliance of Presidential power and patronage in aid of party discipline after it, we have the measure barely screwed through the Senate by the smallest possible majority. In a most unconstitutional manner, we have an acquiescence put in for the Union to the accession of Texas to the confederacy. *She* will consent — no fear of that. She is at war and will gladly see us taxed and shot, if need be, to finish her war. The resolutions of annexation leave her in absolute possession of her public lands.

## DISPOSITION OF THE PUBLIC LANDS[1]

New York *Weekly Tribune*, March 6, 1847

What we would have done by legislation with regard to lands may be summed up as follows: 1. Let the Public Lands, whether of the Union or of any State, be disposed of to actual settlers only. 2. Let each man who needs land be permitted to take without price so much as he actually needs. 3. Let no man be authorized to acquire and hold more than a fixed maximum of arable land, say 160,320 feet, or 540 acres. 4. Take from no man that which is lawfully his; but let him who falls heir to lands above the legal maximum be required to sell the excess to someone who has less, within a year after coming into possession. 5. Let the Homestead of a family, to the extent of forty acres, not including more than one dwelling, be rendered inalienable by mortgage, execution, or otherwise than by the voluntary deed of the occupying owner and his wife, if such there be. These measures, though various, are parts of one system, of which the end is to enable every industrious man to sit under his own vine and fig-tree, with none to molest nor make him afraid. That the idea will encounter vehement hostility and misrepresentation was inevitable from the outset, but the day of its triumph "Is coming yet for a' that." It needs but to be discussed and understood to secure it an overwhelming approval and support.

---

[1] The demand for free homesteads, of which Thomas Hart Benton was the first great champion, and which was to prove victorious in 1862, was vigorously supported by Greeley, who added some curious ideas of his own.

## THE PHILOSOPHY OF FERRIES[1]

Brooklyn *Eagle*, August 13, 1847

Our Brooklyn ferries teach some sage lessons in philosophy, gentle reader (we like that time-honored phrase), whether you ever knew it or not. There is the *Fulton*, now, which takes precedence by age, and by a sort of aristocratic seniority of wealth and business, too. It moves on like iron-willed destiny. Passionless and fixed, at the six-stroke the boats come in; and at the three-stroke, succeeded by a single tap, they depart again, with the steadiness of nature herself. Perhaps a man, prompted by the hell-like delirium tremens, has jumped overboard and been drowned; still the trips go on as before. Perhaps some one has been crushed between the landing and the prow (ah, that most horrible thing of all!); still no matter, for the great business of the mass must be helped forward as before. A moment's pause — the quick gathering of a curious crowd (how strange that they can look so unshudderingly on the scene) — the paleness of the more chicken-hearted — and all subsides, and the current sweeps as it did the moment previously. How it deadens one's sympathies, this living in a city!

But the "most moral" part of the ferry sights is to see the conduct of the people, old and young, fat and lean, gentle and simple, when the bell sounds three taps. Then follows a spectacle indeed — particularly on the Brooklyn side, at from seven o'clock to nine in the morning. At the very first moment of the sound, perhaps some sixty or eighty gentlemen are plodding along the sidewalks, adjacent to the ferry boat — likewise some score or so of ladies — with that brisk pace which bespeaks the "business individual." Now see them as the said three-tap is heard! Apparently moved by an electric impulse, two thirds of the whole number start off on the wings of the wind! Coat-tails fly high and wide. You get a swift view of the phantom-like semblance of humanity as it is sometimes seen in dreams — but nothing more — unless it be you are on the walk yourself, when the chances are in favor of a breath-destroying punch in the stomach. In their insane fury, the rushing crowd spare neither age nor sex. Then the single stroke of the bell is heard; and straightway what was rage before comes to be a sort of ecstatic fury! Aware of his danger, the man that takes the toll has ensconced himself behind a stout oaken partition, which seems only to be entered through a little window-looking place; but we think he must have more than ordinary courage to stand even there. We seriously recommend the ferry superintendent to have this place as strong as iron bars can make it.

[1] By Walt Whitman; a characteristic subject, characteristically treated.

This rushing and raging, however, is not inconsistent with other items of the American character.  Perhaps it is a part of the "indomitable energy" and "chainless enterprise" which we get so much praise for.  But it is a very ludicrous thing, nevertheless.  If the trait is remembered down to posterity, and put in the annals, it will be a bad thing for us.  Posterity surely cannot attach anything of the dignified and august to a people who run after steamboats with their hats flying off, and shirts streaming behind!  Think of any of the Roman senators, or the worthies of Greece, in such a predicament. — (The esteem which we had for a certain acquaintance went up at least a hundred per cent, one day, when we found that, though a daily passenger over the ferry, he never accelerated his pace in the slightest manner, even when by so doing he could "save a boat.")

A similar indecorum and folly are exhibited when a boat approaches the wharf.  As if some avenging fate were behind them, and the devil was going to "take the hindmost," the passengers crowd to the very verge of the forward parts, and wait with frightful eagerness till they are within three or four yards of the landing — when the front row prepare themselves for desperate springs.  Among many there is a rivalry as to who shall leap on shore over the widest stretch of water!  The boat gets some three or four feet from the wharf, and then the springing begins — hop!  hop!  hop! — those who are in the greatest hurry generally stopping for several minutes when they get on the dock to look at their companions behind on the boat, and how *they* come ashore!  Well:  there is a great deal of inconsistency in this world.

## THE  MEXICAN  WAR:  HOW  END  IT? [1]

### Springfield *Republican*, October 14, 1847

The point at which the war with Mexico has now arrived is one which ought to call out the unbiassed and patriotic judgment of every citizen who is unwilling to see the national character dimmed in the light of national glory — the glory of arms.  To maintain our claims to a vast desert, we have carried our victorious eagles round nearly the whole circuit of Mexico.  At the threshold of her proud and ancient capital we stopped to talk of peace; we demanded of her the surrender of half her territory;  but she determined not to

---

[1] When this editorial was written General Scott had won the victories of Molino del Ray and Chapultepec, had occupied Mexico City on September 14, 1847, and had compelled the abdication of Santa Anna.  A new Mexican government was about to reopen negotiations with Nicholas Trist, the American commissioner.  But by this time many Americans, including Secretaries Buchanan and Walker of the Polk Cabinet and some prominent Democratic Senators, wished to annex the whole of Mexico.

yield even the desert.  She did propose to abandon all claim to Texas, and to give us a strip of territory equal to five such States as Virginia, and containing on the Pacific a jewel which we had long coveted to place in our casket.  Now hostilities are resumed; and from our own capital goes forth the proclamation that we will no longer ask for half the territory of Mexico; let us proceed forthwith to take the whole.  "We must talk less," says the Administration organ at Washington, "of the exercise of humanity!"

Has it indeed come to this?  In the land of Washington, Franklin and Jefferson, all of whom deeply deplored the influence of a love of war on our institutions, are we now officially told that "the exercise of humanity" is not to be talked of, and must be abandoned? "The inhabitants of her towns," says the Administration organ, "must be laid under stringent contributions."  And for what? Simply because she refuses to surrender one-half of her territory. And who are the inhabitants upon whom these contributions are to be laid?  Are they a bold, spirited, intelligent, enlightened body of freemen?  Are they a flourishing, thriving, wealthy population? Are they a class of inhabitants who are worthy to meet the foe that falls upon them for contributions?  Nothing like it; nothing like it. They are like the Sikhs, upon whom England in the plenitude of her warrior-fame levied contributions in the East — debased, ignorant, idolatrous, unthrifty.  Is this worthy of a nation that lays claim to so lofty a position as the American Union?  We are strong and powerful; Mexico is weak and distracted.  We have a population of twenty millions; Mexico, not more than one-third of that number. We are the giant; Mexico the dwarf.  We stand high — Mexico! none so low to do her reverence.

What then is the dictate of generosity; what the voice of humanity?  What is due from us to the sentiment of the world?  What is due to our own great principles?  What is due to liberty?  What is to be the influence of our example on the progress which free institutions are making?  Is there nothing in all this?  Are we, on the other hand, to stifle the pleadings of humanity and forego its exercise?  Are we, with barbaric ambition, to seek for barbaric conquest, and thus to cover ourselves with barbaric fame?  All this can easily be done; we can easily blot out Mexico from the list of republics — easily, because we have the power.

But what is to be the issue then?  The "exercise of humanity" laid aside and Mexico conquered! — all this will be but the prelude to scenes upon which no thoughtful mind can dwell without anguish.  How is the country thus gained to be governed, disposed of, parcelled out?  In the "Instructions of the Ministerial Council to the Mexican Commissioners," appointed to negotiate for peace, the thirteenth article of the instructions was: "The United States shall engage not to permit slavery in any part of the territory acquired from Mexico." But suppose the result to be that the United States conquer and appropriate to their own use the whole territory of Mexico; what will the engagement then be on the part of the United States with regard to slavery? Who can look unmoved at the prospect spread before us by such an inquiry?

## ZACHARY TAYLOR AND THE PRESIDENCY[1]

### Springfield *Republican*, December 29, 1847

Since General Taylor's return to the United States, the fervor seems to have increased in his behalf as a candidate for the Presidency. Nobody can doubt the strength of the popular feeling towards him; and he certainly seems destined to be a stumbling block in the way of politicians. Those wary agents in the Keystone State, Mr. Vice President Dallas and Mr. Secretary Buchanan, are pushing themselves forward, through the instrumentality of their friends, for the favor of the next Baltimore convention of the Locofoco Party. What progress these gentlemen make out of their own peculiar precincts, we do not know; enough only is known to render it certain that they are striving each for the mastery. On the score of subserviency to the slave power, it would be difficult to say which has the advantage. They are both without any conscientious or constitutional scruples on that head; they seem perfectly willing to toe the mark indicated by the "patriarchal" dictators; and under their auspices slavery would flourish in all its greenness. Their worthy compeers, Cass in the West and Woodbury in the East, are equally pliable and docile.

The South, *per se*, manifests no indications of its usual forthputting. It names no candidate; but as far as appearances go, will be very willing to come under the rule of a Northern man with Southern principles. Yet at the same time General Taylor has unquestionably the hearts of the Southern people; and the Southwest and most of the Western States are equally devoted to him. The hero of Buena Vista has declared, since his arrival at New Orleans, that he is and means to be a candidate for the highest *civil* post in the country. But he eschews all conventions. He says the people have taken him up, and he will not consent to be put down by the politicians; none but the people shall make him budge an inch.

So far as political or party caste is concerned, it is beyond dispute that General Taylor is, as he always has been, a Whig. This he makes avowal of himself; and that, too, since the speculations on

[1] By the first Samuel Bowles.

that point have ceased to bother the public mind. He has made the statement very deliberately. What all this may amount to everyone will say for himself. At all events, it does not augur very favorably for the continued ascendancy of those schemes of party despotism of which the party in power have always been singularly enamored, and of which the Baltimore Convention that nominated Mr. Polk is a pregnant example. We are free to say that we shall regard it as a great point gained if by means of General Taylor the despotic practises of such a convention and of the party which upholds it can be shattered. But this is not all that is to be kept in view in the movements toward a right result at the next Presidential election. The continued ascendancy of the slave power is a greater evil than the domineering rule of party. If both can be put down, happy, happy indeed will it be for the country!

The power of slavery is to be overturned only by a steadfast, perhaps long-continued conflict — a conflict already begun, and to be most vigilantly maintained, in order that it may be gloriously ended. The contest against slavery will not cease or be relaxed until slavery itself shall be extinguished; of this we may feel perfectly assured. Is General Taylor identified with the slave power? If not, will he identify himself with it? These are questions which will agitate the free States during the coming Presidential campaign. He is known to be a slaveholder; how does he stand as to the power which slavery gives, and how as to slavery itself?

## MR. WEBSTER'S SPEECH [1]

New York *Evening Post*, March 30, 1848

The speech lately delivered by Mr. Webster in the Senate on the Ten Regiment bill is mainly, as it appears to us, a defence of his vote for rejecting the Mexican treaty. Mr. Webster, it appears, is an enemy to all further acquisitions of territory in the Southwestern quarter. His objection is two-fold. In the first place, he urges that the States which will be formed out of this territory will possess but a small population, and will therefore be represented in the Senate by two members, while they will not send any more, or perhaps not so many, members to the House of Representatives, which, he says, "will inevitably break up the relation existing between the two branches of the legislature and destroy its balance." In the second place, he objects that the character of the inhabitants, whom

[1] The Ten Regiment bill was a bill to increase the army engaged in Mexico by ten new regiments; and it gave Webster an opportunity to declare himself opposed to the enlargement of the Union in any direction. In this he was largely actuated by his perception that the new territories would involve the question of slavery extension, and that this would endanger the nation's harmony.

the annexation of New Mexico and California will introduce into the Union, is so degraded, that their morals are so depraved, and their ignorance so gross, that we shall debase our national character by admitting them as citizens.

The first of these objections certainly has very little force. If what Mr. Webster calls a balance between the two branches of the national legislature be what is wanted, it is what we never have had. There has never been a time, since the adoption of the Constitution, when there was anything like an equality of representation in the Senate. In 1790 Virginia had eight times as many inhabitants as Georgia, and Pennsylvania seven times as many as Rhode Island, yet the Constitution which gave each of these States two members, and two only, in the Senate, was adopted in spite of these differences. . . .

We do not get rid of the inequality concerning which he declaims so loudly by refusing to receive New Mexico and California into the Union. It is an inequality which was born with us as a nation; a congenital distemper, which was with us at first, has been with us till now, and which will not be done away with till the Constitution is essentially changed. Mr. Webster's argument is therefore, if it be worth anything, an argument against the Constitution, and not an argument against the acquisition of new territory. It is as good a reason for a dissolution of the present Union as it is against extending that Union to new States.·

To alarm us by the prospect of the future, Mr. Webster affirms that California and New Mexico can never sustain a considerable population. New Mexico, he says, contains sixty thousand inhabitants — an exaggerated estimate doubtless — and cannot contain any more. Let us see how this is. New Mexico, it is admitted, abounds in mines; it is known also that Mexican agriculture is the most slovenly and superficial in the world. When emigrants from the North work the mines will there be no essential addition to the population? If there be not, the result will be contrary to all former experience. When our modes of agriculture are introduced, under the direction of our industry, will the soil be able to support no more inhabitants than now? Mr. Webster, we think, would be obliged to answer this question in the affirmative. New Mexico, says Mr. Webster, is an old settlement, and therefore must have nearly all the inhabitants it can well contain. We remind him that Florida is as old a settlement as that, and has just begun to be peopled.

Mr. Webster takes it for granted that the soil of California is barren and incapable of affording sustenance to a large population. He is mistaken in this, so far at least as relates to a tract of land one hundred and fifty or two hundred miles in width, running the whole length of the coast.   Here a population as large, if not larger, than that of all New England, might be supported in comfort from the produce of a fertile soil which only requires occasional irrigation to make it as fertile as the valley of the Mississippi.   We speak from the information of intelligent persons who have seen the country.

The morals of the people who are to be taken into the Union, if the treaty with Mexico goes into effect, occasion Mr. Webster much anxiety.   The Boston Cato certainly does well to be vigilant in this matter, and we applaud the zealous severity with which he exercises his censorship.   We do not think much of the authority he has quoted, the book of the traveller Ruxton, but we are willing to admit that the morals of the people of that country are not what they ought to be.   Under better institutions they will doubtless improve — those of the whites at least — while for the Indian portion of the population, we see nothing to prevent the gradual waste and early extinction of their race, a fate which has fallen upon the Northern tribes.   Both New Mexico and California will shortly be as fully Americanized as Florida has been.

Thus it will appear that two objections raised by the great Eastern champion of the Whig party against the treaty, even if we admit that they have any present application, are but objections which the lapse of a few years will remove.   They are not of sufficient permanence to form the elements from which the statesman of large views, "looking before and after," estimates the unfolding of that destiny which lies wrapped up in the present as the leaf lies sheathed in the bud.   We recollect that when Mr. Webster made his treaty with Great Britain concerning the Maine boundary, he endured many attacks on account of his concessions to that Power.   The time for retaliation has arrived; his political adversary of that day has made a treaty, and he is paying off the old debt.   We cannot congratulate him upon having added anything to his reputation as a statesman by the choice he has made of the grounds for his attack.

## [THE NOMINATION OF LEWIS CASS][1]

Springfield *Republican*, June 1, 1848

At first blush, the nominations of the Loco-foco national convention — General Lewis Cass for President, and General William O. Butler for Vice-President — appear the weakest that could possibly be made; but reflection and experience will prove that it could have settled upon no stronger candidates.   Their strength

---

[1] The nomination of Lewis Cass by the Democratic national convention in 1848 was the signal for a revolt by those Democrats who were unalterably opposed to the extension of slavery, and who gave their votes to Taylor or to the Free Soil candidate, Martin Van Buren.

lies not so much in the personal ability of the men themselves, as in the power of the party which nominated them. General Cass is a thorough party man; he is in close fellowship with the Administration in all its acts and purposes; his Administration if chosen would be but a continuation of Mr. Polk's. It was the power of the Administration, undoubtedly, that secured his selection by the convention in preference to his competitors.

General Cass, moreover, is a base intriguer, an unprincipled demagogue; he sacrifices means to the ends. These are strong terms, but they are deserved; they are such as men of his own party apply to him — such as we have heard them apply to him since his nomination. And yet these men will probably vote for him, so overpowering to their subservient souls, is the strength of party discipline and fealty. General Cass is a "Northern man with Southern principles." None have played the sycophant, none have bended in abject submission to the South, more basely than he; none have more completely turned the back upon their former professions, and deserted the interests of the section in which they live and which they represent, for the purpose of gaining favor and strength with the enemies of those they so meanly betray, than has he. A year or two since, the Michigan Legislature adopted resolutions in favor of the Wilmot Proviso, which were dictated and strengthened by him; within the past few months he has written a crouching, slavish epistle, denouncing the Proviso as unconstitutional, inoperative, improper, and inadvisable. He stands forth, therefore, as the representative of the pro-slavery party — the defender of the war — the friend of territorial acquisition — the opponent of true freedom — and in every thing prepared to be the successor of the present Executive in all his objects, purposes and wishes, his weakness and his political deformity.

On the river and harbor question, although a Western man, he has wrongly betrayed the interests of the West in apologizing for and defending the President's vetoes, and thus aiding in the defeat of all efforts during the present administration to improve the great inland seas of the Union, on which in so immense a degree depend the individual and public prosperity and wealth of the country. His non-committal six-line letter to the Chicago Convention on this subject excited unmeasured contempt and ridicule among all friends of internal improvements. One would think that this would be almost a death-blow to his prospects at the West, yet there his main strength is said to lie. What he has done to secure the affections of the Western people, we are not able to perceive, and must doubt the truth of his boasted personal popularity among them, till we have better evidence of it. He is a Western man, it is true, has long lived in that section, and held responsible offices, and was an officer in the army in the War of 1812, without, however distinguishing himself by any remarkable deeds; farther than this, what claims he can urge for their especial support it is not in us to see. Certain it is that he has betrayed their highest interests on the river and harbor and free-Territory questions. If they can forgive him for this, their charity must be unbounded.

General Butler of Kentucky, the candidate for the second office, is a less objectionable person, and within his own State, at least, will add strength to the ticket. He served in the War of 1812, as aid to General Jackson, and was an early volunteer in the war with Mexico, where he has served with distinction, been rapidly pushed forward by Executive power, and now, in the recall of General Scott, occupies the post of Commander-in-Chief of the United States forces in that country. He was the candidate of his party for Governor of Kentucky a year or two since, and pressed Judge Owsley, the Whig candidate, who was unpopular, quite hard, but did not secure an election. We cannot conceive of a nomination by the Whigs against which he can carry the State for Cass and himself.

Out of New York, we do not perceive that there is any reason to expect that these candidates will not get the main strength of their party. New York is irrecoverably lost to the ticket. The Barnburners utterly repudiate the convention and its deeds; most especially and most pointedly the nomination of General Cass, who is scouted by all the Barnburning papers in the State, of which there is at least one in every large city, and their number is increasing rather than diminishing. We doubt whether the convention could have made any nomination that would have carried New York; certainly none, which in so doing, would not have endangered a far greater number of electoral votes in other States.

## THE RESULT OF THE ELECTION[1]

New York *Evening Post*, November 8, 1848

The electoral ticket nominated by the friends of General Taylor has carried the city of New York by a large majority over all the other candidates. The preference for this ticket has secured the success of the other Whig candidates in the city; members of Congress, members of the Assembly, and county officers, including the recorders, though by smaller majorities. The returns from different

[1] Bryant had taken a leading part in the Free Soil nomination of Van Buren, and the *Evening Post* energetically supported the Free Soil ticket. The Van Buren candidacy threw New York State to the Whig nominee, Taylor; while the Free Soilers elected thirteen Congressmen, who held the balance of power in the House between the Democrats and Whigs.

parts of the State show also that the Taylor electoral ticket has been chosen, and the vote of this State is certain for Taylor by a huge majority.

The causes of this result lie upon the surface; everybody who attended yesterday at the polls, whether in the city or in the country, saw and felt that Taylor had carried the State, not on account of any high personal popularity, not on account of any strong confidence which the people have in the ability or wisdom with which his Administration will be conducted, but because they believe the contest to be between Cass and Taylor, and they preferred the latter. Cass had declared himself against the prohibition of slavery in the territories. Taylor had said nothing on the subject, with the exception of some general declarations concerning his veto power, from which, however, numbers, with little ground in our opinion, drew the inference that he would not apply the veto power to any future edition of the Wilmot Proviso.

With those who regarded the matter in this light, the desire to express their disapprobation of the nomination of General Cass overbalanced every other motive. Hundreds of Whigs, known to be free soil men, appeared yesterday at the polls with votes for Taylor in their hands. "We know that your principles are right," said they in answer to the remonstrances of other Whigs who had heartily espoused the Free Soil party. "We esteem your cause to be just, and we prefer your candidate for the Presidency. We should be glad to vote for Van Buren, but we do not believe that he can possibly be elected. We regard this as a struggle between Cass and Taylor; the choice lies between these two, and we cannot afford to take a course which will in any way increase the chance that Cass will be elected."

To secure the votes of the two parties for Taylor and Polk, the friends of these candidates found it necessary to make the most profuse expressions of their zeal for the cause of free soil. We believe it will be found that not a single member of Congress has been elected in this State who has not probably pledged himself to resist the extension of slavery. John A. King, who is elected as the Taylor candidate to Congress from Queens County by a thousand majority, came out in the papers with a declaration of his devotion to the cause of free soil just before the election. Such declarations made by the Whig candidates no doubt had the effect of confirming the vague idea which numbers of both parties entertained that Taylor was not personally hostile to the Wilmot Proviso.

In spite of all these influences, in spite of the newness of our party, a party yet in its cradle, in spite of the difficulty of creating a large vote for any party at the very first election after it makes its appearance, we have, according to all indications, polled a large vote in the State, unprecedentedly large, considering the short time allowed us to organize and to employ the means of influencing public opinion. We have laid the foundation of a mighty party, with a great principle for its basis. The establishment of this party has already effected great results.

It has determined, indirectly but most effectually, the Presidential election between the two candidates of the Baltimore and the Philadelphia conventions.

It has compelled both parties to do homage to the principle of freedom in the Territories, and to acknowledge it as an established maxim of political conduct.

It has emancipated the Democratic party from the control of the slave power.

It has so disturbed the torn position of the Democratic party of the North, that it will compel it to reorganize with the principle of free soil in its creed as a settled doctrine.

It has taught an emphatic lesson to all politicians who are disposed to sell themselves to the South. That trade is broken up and Mr. Cass is the last adventurer in it.

Lastly, it has in all probability decided the question of freedom or slavery in the Territories. The agitation of that question by the Free Soil party, has, we believe, made the success of the slaveholders in this controversy impossible.

## A WASHINGTON MONUMENT[1]

*National Anti-Slavery Standard*, December 28, 1848

If one must needs have something to remember our great men by, statues would be better than anything else. For not only is there a natural desire in men to see how a famous person looked, but this kind of remembrance has also the farther advantage that we have a great and original sculptor of our own to make them for us. Probably the world has never had five such sculptors as Powers, and we ought to see to it that he has enough to do. Our present statues of Washington are poor. There is not one of them which we can look at with so much pleasure as upon that of Penn in front of the hospital in Philadelphia. However wanting in other respects, that figure has a simplicity and integrity about it which we miss in all the stone that has been chiselled in honor of Washington. The statue by Houdon has a vulgar swagger. That by Chantrey has a certain English dignity and solidity about it well befitting the subject, but the sculptor was afraid to make an American without

[1] By James Russell Lowell; for seven years, 1844–1850, Lowell was associated with Abolitionism. The Washington Monument was actually begun in 1848.

a kind of apology to ancient art in the drapery. Greenough's we have never seen, but we should consider the size as sufficient objection to it. Great men do not require to be represented as giants. The costume also is bad. The clothes that were good enough for the man are good enough for the marble. The objection of familiarity has no force, for it is merely one of time — a transient consideration of which a fine work of art is entirely independent. Nothing could be uglier than court-dress of the time of Charles the First, nothing more unbecoming than a suit of armor. Yet in Van Dyke's pictures they seemed natural, graceful, and dignified.

After all, Washington is not our representative American man. He is rather English than American. Daniel Boone is more like it — adventurous, forever pushing westward, annexing by dint of long rifle and longer head, yet carrying with him a kind of law, and planting the seed of a commonwealth. Our art is likely to do better things with such a man than with Washington. But the monument at present proposed to be built to Washington is an obelisk five hundred feet high, springing from a square base presenting on every side a columned front. The Anglo-Saxon race have never shown much aptitude for any kind of architecture except that of colonies and states. With stone and mortar they have done little, and that meagre and imitative. Not sentimental nor eminently imbued with religious feeling, they have housed their religion worse than any other race. The cathedrals and abbeys of England and Scotland sprang from Norman brains. Use and not sentiment has been the Saxon characteristic. Accordingly their dwellings have been the most comfortable, their ideas of government the most practical, and their criticism (till inoculated from Germany) the coldest and most meagre in the world.

The Pilgrims who came to New England in 1620 represented in tolerable completeness the Saxon element of English life. They built up a state and a commerce forthwith. Ere long they began to send out colonies. They could not have elbow-room enough on the continent while the French were seated to the north of them. They made a religion hard, square, and unyielding, and then constructed square boxes to hold it where they might be sure to find it once a week. For religion was a job of downright hard work, which they went at with their coats off. Organization, trade, and the sending out of new colonies — these were their play. From such a race architecture for architecture's sake was not to be looked for. They have built best what was useful and practical, as ships, railroads, and aqueducts. In all the United States there is not a beautiful church — or, if beautiful, it is not in any sense American. But we have handsome shops enough.

No nation should be more cautious in undertaking to erect a monument. The drawing of the one now proposed for Washington does not strike us favorably. We can perceive no peculiar appropriateness in it, and consequently no peculiar beauty. On the other hand, we find many incongruities. What is the meaning, for example, of the figure in front of the obelisk driving four horses abreast? There are such figures on some other monuments, perhaps, borrowed from the antique, and there is something like it in Guido's Aurora, but where is its fitness? Sensible people do not drive horses in this manner, nor did we ever see anything like the chariot to which they are attached, except an ox cart or a dray. Then, too, the inscription is in Latin. Why? Because it is more generally understood? Then why not in French, which is more generally understood still? Or perhaps it is Classic? In that case, why did not the Romans use Greek in their inscriptions — a language more classic than their own, and which was the French of the ancient world beside?

But we do not see the need of any monument at all, least of all in such an out of the way place as the city of Washington. . . We would not forget that he held slaves, but neither would we forget that he was Washington, and, even if we were anxious that a pile of stones should be heaped up to his memory, we could never consent to give any the least aid toward building it in the District of Columbia. Let no shaft rise for so great and good a man in a market-place for human flesh! If our Whig friends must keep reminding us that Washington held his fellow-men in bondage, they cannot, at least, say that he was a slave-trader. Let no man, Abolitionist or not, contribute to rear an obelisk within hearing of the man-seller's hammer, and in front of which the wretched slave-coffle shall be driven to the hopeless South!

## THE FUTURE OF THE SOUTH

Boston *Atlas*, May, 1849

We fully agree with the statement which is often made that so far as natural advantages are concerned, the South altogether leads the North in facilities for manufacturing, especially in the manufacture of cotton. She has waterpower in abundance. She has coal and iron in inexhaustible supplies, of which the New England States have none; and more than all, she possesses the soil and climate on which to grow the raw material, and which no law, no capital, no enterprise, can take from her. In this last particular, the cotton-growing States need fear no competition. Not all the free trade laws in the world, or all the protective tariffs that ever filled the

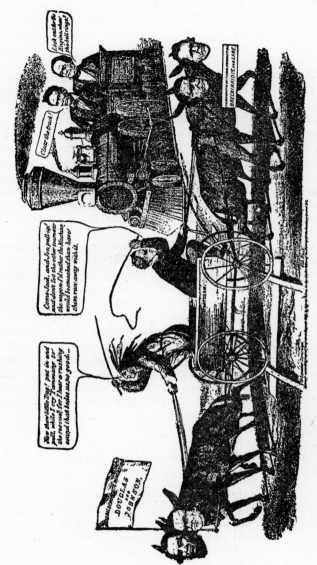

**PROGRESSIVE DEMOCRACY—PROSPECT OF A SMASH UP.**

(An old campaign broadside, picturing the Lincoln-Hamlin triumph of 1860.)

pages of a statute book, can transfer the immense business of cotton growing from the South to the North. It remains there, fixed by the immutable laws of Providence. Possessing all these advantages, what is to hinder the South from outstripping the North in the manufacture of cotton? Nothing but the very thing which our South Carolina friend is so anxious to preserve and perpetuate, slavery.

## [THE FUTURE OF THE SOUTH: A REJOINDER]

Augusta [Georgia] *Sentinel*, May, 1849

The holders of slaves owe it to themselves to demonstrate, in a large way, that cotton can be picked, carded, spun, and woven, as well as grown at the South. Nothing short of this will stop the ceaseless reproaches and unjust imputations cast upon the relation of master and servant, as it exists in this quarter of the Union. It is the duty of all cotton planters to take hold of this great question of manufacturing and mechanical industry in good earnest. Of all men, you are most deeply interested in creating a steady home market for your great staple. Of all men, you are most to be benefited by proving that slave labor in Georgia is as profitable to you, and as useful to the world, as free labor is at the North or can be at the South. The whole matter will turn in the end on the one pivot of dollars and cents. Slavery was abolished in New York because experience proved that the relation of master and slave was not profitable to the master. The people of the non-slaveholding States firmly believe that institution is unprofitable at the South; that every planting State would be much better off if its citizens would emancipate their servants. This is also the deliberate opinion of ninety-nine in every one hundred of the hundreds of thousands of emigrants from Europe, who annually flock to this country, remain permanently, and become a portion of its sovereign rulers.

We must show by visible results that slavery is not incompatible with improvement of the soil; is not inimical to common schools and a high standard of general intelligence; and is not hostile to the most successful manufacturing, mechanical, and commercial industry. We can influence and control public opinion on all these points if we will only set ourselves properly and steadily at work to attain the objects indicated. Our sectional movements, our empty resolutions and "committees of safety," are taken by the civilized world as a confession of weakness; a consciousness of wrong which cannot endure the searching light of truth and a free discussion.

So far is slavery from being naturally opposed to all progress and improvement in rural and mechanical arts, in internal trade and foreign commerce, in popular education and moral instruction, that it can easily be made auxiliary to all these important ends. It is the perfection of human wisdom to make the best possible use of all the means which a good Providence has placed at our disposal. To whom much is given, much will also be required. Because God has given us much, it will not do to say in practise that we need do nothing for ourselves. Our abundant means for labor, our great advantages of climate, soil, and waterpower, demand the most skilful use, the most profitable employment.

## [FIRST STEPS TOWARDS THE INDUSTRIAL FUTURE]
### Baltimore *American*, May, 1849

It is not generally known that within the last year or two steps have been taken at the South to supply the home market with domestic flour. Several large flouring establishments have been put in operation in the States of Georgia and Alabama, by which good merchantable flour is produced from Southern grain. The "Mobile City Mills," of Messrs. Anderson & Company, are capable of turning out six hundred barrels a week, and the papers state that they find a ready sale for all the flour they can make. These mills are supplied with wheat from New Orleans, but during the past year they consumed about 3,000 bushels of Alabama wheat, bought at $1 to $1.25 a bushel. There are at present in Georgia several extensive mills producing flour, which finds a ready home market and is rapidly reducing the amount of importations from the Northern markets. In addition to those now in operation, it is contemplated to erect one or more large flouring mills at Augusta, on the immense waterpower which has been recently introduced there for manufacturing purposes.

## MR. WEBSTER'S SPEECH [1]
### New York *Evening Post*, March 8, 1850

The *Journal of Commerce* exults at Mr. Webster's declaration that he will not support any measure to prohibit slavery in the territories.

We did not suppose that he would. We knew that the Administration had been generous to the family of the Massachusetts Senator, and that he is, by temperament, grateful, and sensible of the obligations which those who receive benefits are under to those by whom they are bestowed. It was for that, among other reasons, that we so confidently assured our readers, the other day, that he would

[1] Webster's Seventh of March speech in favor of the Compromise of 1850 brought down upon his head a storm of abuse from anti-slavery newspapers and leaders.

not fail to support the Administration in its recommendation not to apply the proviso of 1787 to the new territories. It was as natural to suppose that he would do this, as that he could abandon, in the manner he has done, the doctrines of free trade, once maintained by him in their fullest extent, and taking the money of the eastern mill-owners, enroll himself as the champion of protection for the rest of his life.

We take no pleasure in making these animadversions, but they are forced upon us. Mr. Webster stands before the public as a man who has deserted the cause which he lately defended, deserted it under circumstances which force upon him the imputation of a sordid motive, deserted it when his apostasy was desired by the Administration, and immediately after an office had been conferred upon his son, to say nothing of what has been done by the Administration for his other relatives. It is but a little more than two years since that he declared himself the firmest of friends to the Wilmot Proviso, professing himself its original and unvarying champion, and claiming its principles as a Whig doctrine. In a speech which he made at a Whig convention held at Springfield in Massachusetts, in the year 1847, he said:

> There is not a man in this hall who holds to the principles of the Wilmot Proviso more firmly than I do, no one who adheres to it more than another. I feel some little interest in this matter, sir. Did I not commit myself in 1838 to the whole doctrine, fully, entirely? And I must be permitted to say that I cannot quite consent that more recent discoverers should claim the merit and take out a patent. I deny the priority of their invention. Allow me to say, sir, that it is not their thunder.

But now, in the speech delivered yesterday on the floor of the Senate, in reply to Mr. Calhoun, of which our readers will find the telegraphic report in our columns, he ridicules the Wilmot Proviso as the invention of Northern Democracy, and declares that he "will not vote for the insertion, into any bill giving territorial government to the new Territory, of any provision prohibiting slavery."

Of course there is a pretext for this shameful renunciation of a principle once so zealously professed; no apostasy is ever without its pretext. Mr. Webster now pretends that it is impossible that slavery should exist in the new Territories, and says that the adoption of the Wilmot Proviso would be "a re-enactment of the law of God."

What would he have? Would he have an enactment contrary to the law of God? But what are his reasons for supposing that slavery cannot be transplanted to New Mexico and the portions of California not included in the new State? He states none; he *can*

state none: there are none.  Let it be once understood that Congress
will not interpose to forbid the introduction of slavery into the new
Territory, and it will migrate thither as readily as it did into Missouri.
Any man who has passed much time at Washington during the
sessions of Congress knows that such is the opinion of the Southern
members, and that they express it freely in private conversations.
"Sugar and cotton," they say, "can be raised in the new Territories,
and we mean to go thither with our slaves."   In a speech, delivered
last February in the Senate, Mr. Foote said that, were slaves to be
introduced into California and employed in mining, their owners
would derive from their labors "pecuniary profits not heretofore
realized by the most successful cotton and sugar planters of the
South." . . .

But the catalogue of Mr. Webster's concessions to the slave interest is not yet closed.  He offers up all Texas, if his speech is fairly
reported.  We quote the words:

> Texas had been admitted with all her territory, with the in-
> stitution of slavery, and an irrepealable law by which, if new
> States are erected out of any portion of her territory, they shall
> be slave States, and he wished it to be distinctly understood, that
> he considered this government solemnly bound by law to create
> new slave States out of Texas, when her territory shall contain a
> sufficient population.

For aught we see, Mr. Webster is prepared to accept Mr. Bell's
scheme of a compromise by balancing the introduction of California
into the Union with the immediate admission of a slave State from
the domain of Texas.  It is singular, however, that he should have
paid no heed to the resolution of Congress under which Texas was
admitted, pretending to provide that slavery should not be lawful
above 36° 30′ north latitude.

We leave Mr. Webster's speech here.  It is sordidly timorous and
temporizing in spirit, and if the report we have of it be not a perfect
caricature, deplorably feeble in argument.  He had an opportunity
of replying nobly to Mr. Calhoun, and of taking ground upon which
he might stand with the port and attitude of a leader in this great
battle of opinion.  He prefers to stand by the baggage wagons.

## [FUGITIVE SLAVES AND THE OMNIBUS BILL]

### New York *Tribune*, May 17, 1850

"But the passage of the Omnibus Bill will not settle the slavery
agitation."  You never said a truer thing than that!  Neither Mr.
Clay's, the President's, nor any other plan can stop the slavery

agitation so long as slavery shall not merely exist but insist on extending its dominion.  With Cuban invasions, Haytian conquests,
and New Mexican subjugations imminent, he must be green indeed
who expects any abatement even of the slavery excitement.  On the
contrary, it is morally certain to swell and spread until it overrrides
and overrules everything else.  If the South were as wise now as
were its great statesmen in 1787, when they joined heartily in
excluding slavery forever from the territory northwest of the Ohio,
there might be a lull in the tempest;  but the Ruler of Nations
would seem to have other designs, and they will be accomplished.
This slave-catching bill now pressed upon Congress will make a
hundred Abolitionists oftener than it catches one slave.  But is there
any use in throwing up rockets to warn the wilfully blind?

## THE SOUTH AND THE COMPROMISE

*De Bow's Review*, July, 1850

The Union is the source of our greatness and strength; its dismemberment will probably be of our impotence and ruin, whilst
all the world will look on, with amazement, upon the dissolution of
a fabric so fair and beautiful in its proportions.

Thus we should feel and think.  Yet there must be an end, some-
where, of concessions.  If not a *voluntary* end, a *necessary* one, when
everything to be conceded is gone.  It becomes the South to determine how far its safety will admit of concession.  The stand should
be made there.  None can mistake the *anti-slavery* growth — it has
no resting place.  The cry is onward!  When was there ever a step
backward in its history?  It will sweep over Mr. Webster as the
whirlwind sweeps over the reed.  Every concession made to it will
induce a more imperious tone — every success will embolden and
pave the way for a new and higher triumph.  "Will you interpose
the Constitution?"  There is a voice higher than the Constitution!
Will you make a compromise and hold up its sacred assurances?
Majorities rule — numbers have assumed the sway — the edict of
Congress goes out upon the land, backed by its fleets and its armies,
potent as the nod of the autocrat of Russia, and unalterable as the
law of the Medes and the Persians.  The path is clear, the end
undisputed.  The protection of the national flag will be withheld
from the slave, in his passage from one port to another in the Union.
His arrest in a free State impossible.  Slavery will go by the board
in the District of Columbia — in the forts and navy yards.  The
trade between the States will be prohibited.  The final act is not
yet, but soon.  There is a precedent in the British Parliament and
the West Indies.  *They will use the precedent.*  We know the rest

## [THE DELIVERANCE OF THE SLAVE SHADRACH IN BOSTON] [1]

*The Liberator,* February, 1851

"The head and front of the offending," in this instance — what is it? A sudden rush of a score or two of unarmed friends of equal liberty — an uninjurious deliverance of the oppressed out of the hands of the oppressor — the quiet transportation of a slave out of this slavery-ruled land to the free soil of Upper Canada! Nobody injured, nobody wronged, but simply a chattel transformed into a man, and conducted to a spot whereon he can glorify God in his body and spirit, which are his!

And yet, how all the fiends of the pit are writhing and yelling! Not tormented before their time, but just at the right time. Truly, "devils with devils damned firm concord hold!" The President of the United States is out with his Proclamation of Terror, conveying it to us in tones of thunder and on the wings of the lightning; even as though in the old Bay State chaos had come again, and a million of foreign myrmidons were invading our shores! A poor, hunted, entrapped fugitive slave is dexterously removed from the courtroom, and the whole land is shaken! A hundred free white citizens of the North may be thrown into prison, or tarred and feathered, or compelled to flee for their lives at the South, on suspicion of being morally averse to the slave system; but who cares? A thousand colored seamen of the North may be incarcerated in loathsome cells, and compelled to pay for their imprisonment, though guiltless of crime, and even sold into slavery on the auction-block at the South; but whose breast burns with indignation, or what voice calls for redress? Official State Commissioners, venerable for their years and esteemed for their worth, sent to the South to test the constitutionality of such acts, are driven away by lawless violence, and not allowed to remain on the soil; but where is the Presidential proclamation calling on the people to obey the laws and observe their Constitutional obligations? But a solitary slave in Boston is plucked as a brand from the burning, and forthwith a Cabinet council is held, and behold a menacing proclamation, bearing the signature of Millard Fillmore, President of the United States! Henry Clay — with one foot in the grave, and just ready to have both body and soul cast into hell — as if eager to make his damnation doubly sure, rises in the United

---

[1] The fugitive slave, Shadrach, was rescued in Boston from the United States deputy marshal on March 16, 1851, this being the first important Northern defiance of the new Fugitive Slave Act. The incident showed that in Massachusetts and other Northern states the law would be enforced with difficulty if at all. Congress took up the affair, and President Fillmore issued a proclamation demanding obedience to the Act. William Lloyd Garrison here angrily replies to it.

States Senate and proposes an inquiry into the expediency of passing yet another law, by which everyone who shall dare peep or mutter against the execution of the Fugitive Slave Bill shall have his life crushed out!

## UNCLE TOM'S CABIN[1]

*The Liberator*, March 26, 1852

In the execution of her very difficult task, Mrs. Stowe has displayed rare descriptive powers, a familiar acquaintance with slavery under its best and its worst phases, uncommon moral and philosophical acumen, great facility of thought and expression, and feelings and emotions of the strongest character. Intimate as we have been, for a score of years, with the features and operations of the slave system, and often as we have listened to the recitals of its horrors from the lips of the poor hunted fugitives, we confess to the frequent moistening of our eyes, the making of our heart grow liquid as water, and the trembling of every nerve within us, in the perusal of the incidents and scenes so vividly depicted in her pages. The effect of such a work upon all intelligent and humane minds coming in contact with it, and especially upon the rising generation in its plastic condition, to awaken the strongest compassion for the oppressed and the utmost abhorrence of the system which grinds them to dust, cannot be estimated; it must be prodigious, and therefore eminently serviceable in the tremendous conflict now waged for the immediate and entire suppression of slavery upon American soil.

The appalling liabilities which constantly impend over such slaves as have "kind and indulgent masters," are thrillingly illustrated in various personal narratives; especially in that of "Uncle Tom," over whose fate every reader will drop the scalding tear, and for whose character the highest reverence will be felt. No insult, no outrage, no suffering, could ruffle the Christlike meekness of his spirit, or shake the steadfastness of his faith. Towards his merciless oppressors he cherished no animosity, and breathed nothing of retaliation. Like his Lord and Master, he was willing to be "led as a lamb to the slaughter," returning blessing for cursing and anxious only for the salvation of his enemies. His character is sketched with great power and rare religious perception. It triumphantly exemplifies the nature, tendency, and results of Christian non-resistance.

[1] Following serial publication in the Washington *National Era*, "Uncle Tom's Cabin" was issued in book form in March, 1852. William Lloyd Garrison's editorial is an expression not only of his admiration for it, but of his strong pacifist convictions.

We are curious to know whether Mrs. Stowe is a believer in the duty of non-resistance for the white man, under all possible outrage and peril, as well as for the black man; whether she is for self-defence on her own part, or that of her husband or friends or country, in case of malignant assault, or whether she impartially disarms all mankind in the name of Christ, be the danger or suffering what it may. We are curious to know this, because our opinion of her as a religious teacher would be greatly strengthened or lessened as the inquiry might terminate. That the slaves of the South ought, "if smitten on the one cheek, to turn the other also," — to repudiate all carnal weapons, shed no blood, "be obedient to their masters," wait for a peaceful deliverance, and abstain from all insurrectionary movements — is everywhere taken for granted because the victims are black. *They* cannot be animated by a Christian spirit and yet return blow for blow, or conspire for the destruction of their oppressors. *They* are required by the Bible to put away all wrath, to submit to every conceivable outrage without resistance, to suffer with Christ if they would reign with Him. None of *their* advocates may seek to inspire *them* to imitate the example of the Greeks, the Poles, the Hungarians, our Revolutionary sires. . . . But for those whose skin is of a different complexion, the case is materially altered. When they are spit upon and buffeted, outraged, and oppressed, talk not to them of a non-resisting Saviour — it is fanaticism! Talk not of overcoming evil with goodness — it is madness! Talk not of peacefully submitting to chains and stripes — it is base servility! Talk not of servants being obedient to their masters — let the blood of tyrants flow! How is this to be explained or reconciled? Is there one law of submission and non-resistance for the black man, and another law of rebellion and conflict for the white man? When it is the whites who are trodden in the dust, does Christ justify them in taking up arms to vindicate their rights? And when it is the blacks who are thus treated, does Christ require them to be patient, harmless, long-suffering, and forgiving? Are there two Christs?

## [MRS. STOWE'S PERNICIOUS SENTIMENTALITY][1]

### De Bow's Review, March, 1853

It is useless for us to tell the benevolent ladies and gentlemen who have undertaken to instruct us in our catechism of humanity that they are entirely ignorant of the condition of the negro. "Uncle Tom's Cabin" tells them differently. It is useless for us to tell them

[1] While this utterance may be regarded as editorial, and was accompanied by an explicit endorsement by the editor himself, it was written by an anonymous woman contributor to the *Review*, and not by James D. B. De Bow himself.

that our slaves are not "interdicted education in the truths of the gospel and the ordinances of Christianity;" it is useless for us to repeat that their family ties and social affections are respected and indulged in a greater degree than those of any laboring class in the world. "Uncle Tom's Cabin" says differently; and the negrophilists have very nearly reached the point of pronouncing sentence of excommunication, on the ground of infidelity, against all who dispute the authenticity of so high an authority. It is useless for us to point to the comparative census of the nations of the earth; it is useless for us to show that in none are the tables of crime, of deformity, and insanity so low as in our slave population. Mrs. Stowe and Uncle Tom! Mrs. Stowe and Uncle Tom! Mrs. Stowe and Uncle Tom! ding, ding, dong. What is the use of reasoning, what is the use of facts, when those who should hear us deafen themselves with this eternal "ding, dong" of superstitious prejudice and pharisaical cant? As regards the condition of our slaves, compared with that of the white population of our own free States (than which, avowedly, no population in the world enjoys greater advantages), ten minutes' investigation of our late census returns, with about so much arithmetical knowledge as any boy of ten years old can command, will suffice to show that, for every insane slave, there are from eight to ten insane whites; and that this is not an exception resulting from any physical peculiarity of the negro, is proved by the fact that among the *free* blacks the proportion of insane is, within a very small fraction, equal to that among the whites. This fact alone speaks volumes. The number of deaf mutes and of blind, though the disproportion is not so great, shows largely in favor of the slave, and are worth dwelling upon as indicating the comforts of his position; but, would men consent to open their eyes and hearts to the truth, volumes of argument and cartloads of Uncle Tom's Cabins would not weigh a feather against the indisputable fact which we have just noted of the disparity in the numbers of the insane presented in the different positions referred to.

## A GREAT OLD SUNSET[1]

### The *Ohio Statesman*, 1853

What a stormful sunset was that of last night! How glorious the storm and how splendid the setting of the sun! We do not remember ever to have seen the like on our round globe.

[1] Reprinted all over the country, this long-famous editorial by S. S. Cox gave him his sobriquet of "Sunset" Cox. It is a fair example of the tawdry rhetoric which innumerable readers of the time thought really admirable. The *Ohio Statesman* was published in Columbus. Cox, after retiring from the editorship, served for many years as a Democratic Representative in Congress, first from Ohio and later from New York.

The scene opened in the West, with a whole horizon full of golden interpenetrating luster, which colored the foliage and brightened every object into its own rich dyes.  The colors grew deeper and deeper until the golden luster was transfused into a storm cloud full of the finest lightnings, which leaped into dazzling zigzags all around over the city.

The wind arose with fury, the slender shrubs and giant trees made obeisance to its majesty.  Some even snapped before its force.  The strawberry beds and grass plots turned up their whites to see Zephirus march by.  As the rain came and the pools formed and the gutters hurried away, thunder rolled grandly and the firebells caught the excitement and rang with hearty chorus.

The south and the east received the copious showers, and the west all at once brightened up in a long polished belt of azure, worthy of a Sicilian sky.  Presently a cloud appeared in the azure belt in the form of a castellated city.  It became more vivid, revealing strange forms of peerless fanes and alabaster temples and glories rare and grand in this mundane sphere.  It reminded us of Wordsworth's splendid verse in his "Excursion":

> The appearance, instantly disclosed,
> Was of a mighty city — boldly say
> A wilderness of building, sinking far
> And self-withdrawn into a boundless depth,
> Far sinking into splendour — without end!

But the city vanished, only to give place to another isle, where the most beautiful forms of foliage appear, imaging a paradise in the distant and purified air.  The sun, wearied of the elemental commotion, sank behind the green plains of the West.  The "great eye in heaven," however, went not down without a dark brow hanging over its departed light.  The rich flush of the unearthly light had passed, and the rain had ceased when the solemn church bells pealed, the laughter of children rang out loud, and, joyous after the storm, was heard with the carol of birds; while the forked and purple weapon of the skies still darted illumination around the Starling College, trying to rival its angles and leap into its dark windows.

Candles were lighted.  The piano strikes up.  We feel it good to have a home, good to be on earth where such revelations of beauty and power may be made.

## THE RASCALS AT WASHINGTON[1]

New York *Tribune*, January 26, 1854

If the traitorous men at Washington who are plotting the surrender to slavery of the free territory west of the Mississippi believed that a majority of the North would fail to sustain the movement, they would instantly cease their clamor and skulk back and we should hear no more about it.

But they have adopted the belief that the passage of the compromise measures of 1850, and the triumphant election of Frank Pierce, have taken all the spirit out of the North, and that the mass of the voters are now ready to wink at any party iniquity, and sustain any party measure, whatever its iniquity. . . .

There has been no time during the last seven years when the Whig and Freesoil parties have not been in a clear majority in nearly all the Northern States. The only ground upon which any doubt can be thrown on this presumption is the result of the last presidential election. But the vote of the Freesoil party in that contest was only partial, being but the ineffectual remonstrance (and so felt to be) of the more earnest of the Freesoilers against the settlement of the Compromise measures. And the vote of the Whigs in the North was notoriously the vote of a party divided against itself. It was a contest utterly balked by cross purposes. The presidential election of 1848, and the congressional elections of 1850, furnish the only grounds of any just judgment as to the real strength of the anti-slavery sentiment in the country; and these elections justify the statement that in every Free State that sentiment, whenever it could be fairly reached, would prove to be predominant.

Assuming this to be so, the only question to be answered is, whether that sentiment can be aroused and consolidated and brought to bear in solid phalanx against the atrocious proposition in consequence. The fools in Washington believe it cannot. We believe it can. And we further believe that this is by no means the whole strength of the North that will be brought into the field against this infamous project. We shall have the whole conservative force of the Free States of all parties against it. We shall have all the men who do not believe in violating contracts nor in repudiating solemn engagements on the side of earnest opposition. The moral stamina of the Free States will be set against the measure. Fair dealing and honest purposes will everywhere frown upon such faithlessness and

[1] Stephen A. Douglas's Kansas-Nebraska Bill, repealing the Missouri Compromise, was introduced into the Senate on January 4, 1854. Throwing open all the Territories to slaves, and leaving the question of their ultimate exclusion to "squatter sovereignty," or the vote of the actual settlers, it intensely angered all Free Soilers. Greeley's editorial is a scorching expression of that anger.

fraud. Sober-minded men who have leaned to the side of the South in the late contests, on the ground that the Abolitionists were the aggressors, will turn and resist this movement as a gross outrage and aggression on the part of the South.

## IS IT A FRAUD?[1]

### New York *Tribune*, February 15, 1854

We are charged by some of the active and open promoters of, as well as by the more cowardly and timid connivers at, Douglas's meditated repudiation of the Missouri Compromise, with using harsh and uncharitable language with reference to that scheme and its abettors. Our answer to the charge is, that no other language than that we use would faithfully express our sentiments or do justice to our convictions. Were it simply a bad measure, we might speak of it calmly and measuredly; but as an act of deliberate bad faith, impelled by the most sordid motives and threatening the most calamitous results, we must treat it as we do other gigantic perfidies and crimes. The conflagration it threatens is not to be extinguished by jets of rosewater.

*Is* it a fraud? That is the first question to be considered. Did the country, did Congress, did Mr. Douglas, understand when the Adjustment of 1850 was under consideration, that its success would repeal the Missouri Compromise and open the Territories from Missouri, Iowa, and Minnesota, westward to the Rocky Mountains, to the introduction of human slavery? That is a question which certainly admits of a definitive answer. If that *were* the understanding, then there *must* remain some contemporaneous evidence of the fact. It cannot be that this tremendous consequence was involved in the Adjustment of 1850, and yet that no Southern advocate thereof, though sorely pressed to justify his course against the assaults of Jeff Davis, Soule, Mason, Hunter, Butler, the Richmond *Examiner*, and so on, ever deemed it worth his while to mention this virtual repeal of the Missouri Restriction as among the advantages gained for slavery by the Compromise, and that no Northern Seward, Hale, Dayton, Beecher, or other anti-compromiser, ever enumerated it among the losses to Freedom by that settlement. In view of the notorious, acknowledged, unbroken silence in 1850 of all parties upon this point, is not the fundamental assumption of Douglas & Co. not only a fraud, but one most impudent, shameless, audacious?

---

[1] As the historian Rhodes says, this editorial bears in its autobiographical passages plain evidences of Greeley's authorship; and it is an unanswerable exposure of the hollowness of Douglas's claim that the Compromise of 1850 had been really a repeal of the Missouri Compromise, and that his own bill merely underlined that repeal. Greeley utterly destroys this argument.

Consider how sternly this Compromise was resisted by Calhoun, Butler, and every Representative from South Carolina — by the two Senators and most of the Democratic Representatives from Virginia — by the delegations from Arkansas and Mississippi (Senator Foote only, we believe, excepted) — by Venable and Yulee, and nearly every extreme pro-Slavery man in Congress. What did they all mean, what *could* they mean, if the adjustment they sought so savagely was to have the effect which Mr. Douglas now ascribes to it?

We were among the first, after it became evident that no bill affirming the Wilmot Proviso could be carried through the Senate, to suggest and advocate the devising of some practicable middle ground whereon moderate men of the North and South might unite in effecting an organization of the newly acquired Territories. Though we did not approve the connection therewith of topics palpably extraneous, such as the rendition of Fugitives and the District Slave-Trade, we did support Mr. Clay's Omnibus Bill defining the boundary of Texas, admitting California as a Free State, and organizing New Mexico and Utah as Territories without restriction as to slavery. We know Henry Clay did not deceive us with regard to *his* views and purposes in urging that Compromise; we are morally sure that no idea of repealing or "superseding" the Missouri Compromise entered into *his* mind. Others may have been deeper in his confidence; but he deceived no man, and he discussed the whole subject freely with us, and ever regarded it as one wherein the Territories were to enure to Free Labor, and that the practical business was to save the South from all needless and wanton humiliation. And so Senator Butler of South Carolina, when the Senate adjourned after defeating the Omnibus, said to us as he passed exultingly from the chamber, "I don't wonder at *your* support of this bill, for it would give you all you seek" — that is, the practical exclusion of slavery from the new Territories. How would he have been astounded by the information that the passage of that bill would repeal the Missouri Restriction, and open all the remaining Louisiana Territory to slavery!

But look at the Douglas proposition in another aspect — that of the numerous and serious transformations to which it has been subjected by its author since he first introduced it. First, it was a mere organization of Nebraska which quietly and ambiguously ignored the Missouri Restriction; next, it declared that Restriction "superseded" by the Adjustment of 1850 — which if true need not have been thrust into an act of Congress; and so it has been worked over and over, until at last we have a pointblank proposal to repeal the Restriction — but a proposal with a glaring falsehood appended by way of apology — or as Truman Smith forcibly terms it, "an enactment with a peroration." Is this the way honest and straightforward enactments are urged?

Suppose you were standing in your garden, and a rough and ready half-acquaintance should stalk in, make himself extra familiar, and meanwhile busy himself with eating up half of some rare and precious fruit which you had just brought to maturity, then cram the residue into his capacious pockets and bid you a cordial good day; you would have your own opinion of his breeding, but you could not consider him a thief. But suppose you were sitting out of sight in an arbor, and should see such a customer crawling and sidling up to your rear garden wall, dodging from the shelter of one shrub to another, and worming himself along the sinuosities of a Virginia fence, until he finally got within reach of your Seckels or Apricots — you might let him have a stone or a charge of peas with a moral certainty of hitting nothing short of a scoundrel.

It is our earnest conviction that the bill of Douglas, in so far as it proposes to disturb the Missouri Compromise, involves gross perfidy, and is bolstered up by the most audacious false pretenses and frauds. If we are wrong in this conviction, let it be shown, and we stand condemned; but if we are right in our view of it, who can truly say that we speak of the plot and its contrivers more harshly than they deserve?

## [STEPHEN A. DOUGLAS AS THE VOLUNTEER EXECUTIONER]

New York *Tribune*, February 22, 1854

Some years ago, several localities of the South were terribly agitated on the subject of Abolitionism. It was at the time that Mr. Van Buren sanctioned the opening of private letters and packages by postmasters in their search for "incendiary documents." In a place we care not to name the opposition to the anti-slavery sentiment ran so high that a Committee of Safety was appointed, and before this dread and irresponsible tribunal were arraigned all who could in any way be suspected of entertaining anti-slavery sentiments. Our soul sickens at the scenes of brutality that were witnessed there; but the reign of terror was for the moment triumphant. . . . A poor, miserable, half-witted and degraded wretch, who consorted with the negroes because he found no other willing associates, and what is most singular, a native born citizen of the very place we write about, was arrested and tried for using inflammatory expressions before the negroes. The poor creature could not comprehend his situation; born and reared in the place, he had no idea that any harm was intended him; and he listened to the charges on the trial with a silly laugh, and heard himself condemned to be hanged as if it were a joke.

The moment that sentence was pronounced, there went up a clamor for the execution, and from the tribunal the prisoner was hurried to the fatal tree. In a few moments a limb was selected, the rope adjusted, and the cart was driven beneath it. So far, all had been action, and consequently there was a want of time for reflection; but the moment that an executioner was needed, the moment that the fearful responsibility of taking life could not be distributed out among the multitude, there was a holding back, an irresolution, a fear that the act was not right.

In the meanwhile the victim sat on the edge of the cart, his hands tied behind his back, almost able to see the miserable cabin in which he was born, silent — speechless with terror. His life was trembling in the balance. A moment more and there would have gone up in the crowd a cry, "Let him go," "Let him go;" but at this critical moment a person unknown to the crowd was seen to move toward the cart. Springing upon it and rudely seizing the dangling rope, he turned round to the astonished spectators and said: "If none of you will act as hangman, I will. Damn the Abolitionists!" In another instant the fatal cord was adjusted, the cart driven off, and there was seen suspended between heaven and earth the trembling— the dead — form of an innocent man. The body in due time was cut down and hastily buried beneath the fatal tree, and the crowd dispersed with horror depicted upon their faces, and dark and before unknown passions of destruction awakened in their hearts.

Now who was this hangman? Who was this fierce defender of the peculiar institution? Was he a Southern man? No. Was he a citizen identified with the South? No. It was on the contrary a Northern man, from a free State — in fact, one who had been but two days in the place. It seemed as if, suspecting his own principles, revolting in his heart at slavery and afraid that in the excitement of the hour he might next be arraigned, he took this fearful and terrible office of executioner in order to place himself, as he supposed, on "high Southern ground." Thus, by one glaring act, wherein he violated his conscience — his early education — every law, in fact, of God and man — he thought to identify himself as a defender of slavery, and have his soundness placed above suspicion.

And here is to be seen reflected the true picture of Mr. Douglas's turpitude. Southern men may have in the madness of the hour conceived such iniquity as is embodied in the Nebraska bill. They may have prepared the halter for the neck of the Missouri Compromise — but the last fatal act would never have been undertaken had not the Senator from Illinois volunteered to act as executioner, been willing to mount the scaffold, and call down the infamy of murdering liberty upon his own head.

Thus it has ever been in Congress whenever the rights of man have been violated. Southerners, from the necessity of defending their local interests, are compelled to advocate principles repugnant to their consciences, but they would never press them upon the people of the North if there had not always been volunteers, like Douglas, willing to do the foul work that Southern men themselves revolt at, while feeling toward these ready tools of tyranny a contempt that is ever extended toward the traitor, whatever may be the advantages they reap from the treason enacted.

## [THE INTOLERABLE KANSAS-NEBRASKA ACT]

### New York *Tribune*, May 18, 1854

"We are in the midst of a revolution," said Mr. Clay on a memorable occasion. We are in the midst of a revolution, is our response to the proceedings at Washington on the Nebraska bill. The attempted passage of this measure is the first great effort of slavery to take American freedom directly by the throat. Hitherto it has but asked to be allowed to grow and expand side by side with that freedom, until now, at what is believed a favorable moment, it springs from its lair and clutches at the life of its political associate in the government. It engages in a *coup d'état*, and by the aid of Northern traitors to liberty attempts the most intolerable usurpation.

Should success attend the movement, it is tantamount to a civil revolution and an open declaration of war between freedom and slavery on the North American continent, to be ceaselessly waged until one or the other party finally and absolutely triumphs.

If Nebraska passes, the two parties must immediately marshal themselves in hostile array. The North will go on as it has done, to oppose every step toward making the Northwest pasture-ground for African slavery. It will oppose the introduction of slavery into Kansas and Nebraska as much after the passage of the bill as before, and should it gain foothold there, it will make open and direct war upon the institution within their limits now and henceforth. It will fight against the admission into the Union of either as a slave State, and in doing this it will necessarily be compelled to carry the war into Africa, and will fight against the admission of new slave States from any quarter whatever. Soundness upon this question will be made a test in the election of every Northern Representative. The popular branch of the government must be speedily purified, and no man elected thereto from the North who is not firmly committed against the admission of more slave States. A President must be elected by the Free States who will cordially support and earnestly respond to these views. There will be no other course but this open to the Free States, excepting one of abject, slavish submission to the iron rod of the Southern slave-drivers, and the more despicable domination of Northern flunkeyism. The passage of the Nebraska bill will arouse and consolidate the most gigantic, determined, and overwhelming party for freedom that the world ever saw. We may already see in the future its gathering groups on every hill side, in every valley, and on every prairie in the free States. We hear the deep and ominous murmur of the earnest voices of its myriad slowly-moving masses. We behold in their faces the unalterable determination of their purposes in behalf of freedom. We see the gigantic array gradually approach, closing its thick ranks, and moving onward with a force that no merely human power or human institution can resist. It sweeps along with the force of the tempest or the tornado. The spirit of liberty animates, the spirit of progress impels, and a spirit of solemn religious duty inspires and leavens the whole mass. This invincible army bears aloft the motto, "God with us!" Its immediate duties are plain. We have indicated them in the gross. Details will adjust themselves. What ulterior duties may be in store for this great party of Liberty time only can discover. The decisive events of history come but slowly. They have their source, as the great rivers have theirs, in the little rills that trickle in the hidden recesses of the plain and the mountain. But we cannot hide from our vision the vital fact that this party, once aroused, and consolidated on a platform sufficiently wide and substantial to afford a sure basis for its operation, such as the passage of the Kansas-Nebraska bill will furnish, will not hesitate in its course, or fail in its duties, however radical and sweeping those duties may become.

For the mole-eyed squad of little Northern men of Washington who are accidentally the controlling political force of the government at this junction of public affairs, lighting the torches of civil discord and vainly dreaming that no conflagration is to ensue, we have but pity for their blindness and fatuity. They are under the lead of men of gross and grovelling purposes, base instincts, and narrow vision. They are but blind followers of the blind.

To avert the throes and convulsions which must inevitably follow this infamous act, we have labored and shall labor, and as a last resort to this end, if there shall prove to be a majority of the House in favor of the final consummation of this scheme, we advocate the determined resistance of the minority to that consummation.

This bold and astounding assault upon the cause of liberty and of progress should be met by Northern representatives in Congress in the spirit with which freedom in its most lofty mood has ever resisted oppression. It is a solemn duty which devolves upon them, without agency of theirs, to bring about the crisis that enjoins their action. We know that it is easier to shirk it than to discharge it. But in so clear a case it were culpable to refuse to engage in the only procedure which gives any hope of arresting the infamous measure. For whatever results shall follow such a course we cheerfully court our share of the responsibility. Whatever that result shall be, we unhesitatingly say, Let it come. There are greater evils than a conflict between two parties in the legislative branch of the government — greater evils than temporarily blocking the wheels of public affairs, or than producing a shock which shall precipitately send the members of Congress home to their constituents. And clearly among them, in our estimation, are the fatal and far-reaching consequences of the passage of the Nebraska bill.

## SLAVE–CATCHER'S TRIUMPH[1]

### New York *Tribune*, June 3, 1854

The fugitive Burns is delivered into slavery. A man as much entitled to his freedom as any other man on the soil of Massachusetts has been seized in that State by other men, manacled, and consigned to hopeless bondage. The people of that great Commonwealth, containing a million of inhabitants, every one of them knowing the act to be a gross and unpardonable exercise of tyrannical power, a criminal outrage upon the inalienable rights of man, have suffered it to be done without interposing force to prevent it. That there was opposition to the act is seen, however, in the means employed for its consummation. Burns was not torn from the soil of freedom and consigned to slavery by any ordinary methods of imprisoning malefactors. He was not taken by a constable or sheriff, or even a whole police force of a great city. All these were insufficient. It took all the police of Boston, three companies of United States troops, one company of cavalry, and an entire battalion of militia, together

[1] Anthony Burns, a fugitive slave, was arrested in Boston on May 24, 1854; and a futile attempt at rescue, led by Theodore Parker, Wendell Phillips, and Thomas Wentworth Higginson, was made on the night of the 26th. On June 2 the slave was marched to the wharf through a crowd of fifty thousand jeering and groaning people, and placed on board a Federal revenue cutter to be taken back to the South. To guard the streets that day the authorities used the Boston police, twenty-two companies of Massachusetts soldiers, a battalion of Federal artillery, four platoons of marines, and a large civil posse. The cost of remanding the prisoner southward was nearly $40,000. The episode was an impressive demonstration of the revolt of the North against the Fugitive Slave Act.

with several pieces of artillery, to secure the capture of this citizen and remand him to slavery. It is said that this was an experimental case of slave-catching, got up especially for the purpose of showing how readily the North would acquiesce in the Nebraska bill, and succumb to the aggressions of the slave power. We trust the managers of the performance are satisfied. What do they think of the prospect of performing the same feat over again?

This cowardly capture of an innocent man, and consigning him to the horrors of a servile bondage, necessarily provokes some reflection. We desire to ask the principals in the affair, the leading Nebraska conspirators, and the Executive Government at Washington, what was the use of the ostentatious display of artillery charged with grape-shot that were planted in Court Square on the occasion? Do they not know that the discharge of that cannon upon the Boston multitude there assembled would have been the signal for fifty thousand men of Massachusetts to fly to arms? Do they not know that they did not dare discharge that artillery upon the friends of freedom in that commonwealth? Why, then, did they indulge in this piece of intimidation? Was it for the luxury of an unmeaning taunt? It may be that they cannot see that through all this Burns trial the public peace has been slumbering upon the edge of a volcano. If they cannot, perhaps they had better devote themselves to a closer scrutiny of the existing state of the popular pulse.

There has been the most imminent danger of a violent and armed outbreak during this late tragedy. And suppose it had taken place? Who would have quelled it? Who would have restored the public peace when once broken? Burns has been taken away, but let us tell the slave power that nothing has been accomplished by that capture but to deepen the resolution that slaves shall not be taken on the soil of the Free States. Nothing has been accomplished by it but to arouse the Northern mind to a determination to resistance to such scenes in the future. This time men have been unarmed. Another time it may be otherwise. We are but at the beginning of the resistance to the arrogant domination of the slave power. Things are but in the bud, in the gristle. Nothing has been done in this case but to declare against the proceeding. Not an arrangement to rescue the fugitive has been made. Nothing which savored of earnest resistance has been attempted. But it will not be so always. Some such event as a forcible rescue will yet take place, and when that takes place in Massachusetts, the fugitive will not be sent to Canada. He will be held upon her soil, and a note of defiance sounded to let them come and take him who dare.

The future is big with events such as these unless something is done to allay the public excitement produced by the proceedings of the slave power, backed by our rulers.   The fugitive slave law, as it now stands, can no longer be enforced without jeopardizing the public tranquillity to an alarming extent.   We again call upon Congress to give their earnest and immediate attention to this grave subject.   If there can be no repeal of the law at this session, which we think is quite certain, let us at least have the trial by jury.   A modification of this sort is absolutely demanded unless the country is to be precipitated upon insurrection, and perchance civil war.

## [THE ERROR OF ARMING THE KANSAS FREE–SOILERS] [1]

*The Liberator,* April 4, 1856.

What are the facts respecting Kansas?   Briefly these: "squatter sovereignty" has turned out to be repeated invasions of the Territory by armed bandits from Missouri, who have successfully made it a conquered province, manufactured a Territorial Government, enacted a code of laws worthy of pandemonium, and trampled the civil and political rights of the *bona-fide* settlers under their feet; and for one sole object — to make Kansas a slave State.   Hence the appeal, in self-defence, to the people of the free States for men, money, and arms;   hence the justification for the employment of Sharp's rifles against the "border ruffians."   It is said to be a struggle for liberty;   and earnest appeals are made to the hearts and the pockets of all who desire to see liberty victorious.

We burn with indignation at the insults and outrages to which the settlers have thus been subjected, and acknowledge their position to be a most trying and perilous one.   But we deny, in the first place, that they are acting upon principle, or contending for equal rights.   They resent as a foul slander the charge of being abolitionists;   they proclaim a truce on their part with slavery where it now exists;   they are pro-slavery in spirit and position, with regard to the millions who are now grinding in the Southern house of bondage;   they have meanly and wickedly proscribed every man of color, and made it illegal for him to be a resident in the Territory;   they do not object to slave-hunting on their soil, but recognize it as a constitutional obligation which they have no disposition to annul;   they go for *all* the pro-slavery compromises of the American Constitution;   they are contending for their own rights *as white men,* not for the rights of all, without distinction of caste or color;   they have pursued a shuffling and compromising policy throughout;

[1] William Lloyd Garrison wanted to see Kansas free soil; but he did not believe in fighting to make it so.

they have consented to make the existence of liberty or slavery in the Territory dependent upon the will of the majority, fairly expressed, and *to abide by the result*. The retribution now meted out to them is divinely ordered: having sown the wind, they are reaping the whirlwind. It is for them to say to one another, as did the treacherous brethren of Joseph: "We are verily guilty concerning our brother, in that we saw the anguish of his soul when he besought us, and we would not hear; therefore is this distress come upon us." And while they are yet standing, in common with the great body of the American people, with their feet upon the necks of four millions of chattel slaves — and while, to propitiate the proslavery spirit, they have banished from their presence all free colored emigrants, at the very time they are complaining of having their own rights wrested from them — with what face can they ask for the sympathy and coöperation of those who are battling for the cause of freedom on a worldwide basis? "Let the dead bury their dead."

Again, if such men are deserving of generous sympathy, and ought to be supplied with arms, are not the crushed and bleeding slaves at the South a million times more deserving of pity and succor? Why not, first of all, take measures to furnish them with Sharp's rifles? Their wrongs are beyond description; in comparison with which, those of the people of Kansas are utterly insignificant. Why strain at a gnat, and swallow a camel? If every "border ruffian" invading Kansas deserves to be shot, much more does every slaveholder, by the same rule; for the former is guilty only of attempting political subjection to his will, while the latter is the destroyer of all human rights, and there is none to deliver. Who will go for arming our slave population?

## [THE ABOLITIONISTS AND THE FRÉMONT CANDIDACY]

*The Liberator*, November 4, 1856

To these inquiries [Horace Greeley's question "whether you will personally vote, and advise those who agree with you to vote, for Col. Frémont"] we shall make categorical replies. 1. Personally, we shall not vote for Frémont. 2. We do not advise those who agree with us to vote for him, because he goes for perpetuating "the Union as it is" — we for its immediate dissolution as "a covenant with death." 3. The language attributed to us by such lying journals as the *Pennsylvanian* and the Boston *Post*, being torn from its connection and basely garbled, does not truly represent our views. We said: "If there were no moral barrier to our voting" (but there

is), "and we had a million of votes to bestow, we should cast them
all for Frémont as against Buchanan and Fillmore" — not because
he is an abolitionist or a disunionist (for he is neither, any more
than was Washington, Jefferson, Webster, Clay, or Jackson, occupying precisely their ground), but because he is for the non-extension
of slavery, in common with the great body of the people of the
North, whose attachment to the Union amounts to idolatry.

Well, the Presidential struggle will terminate on Tuesday next,
with all its forgeries, tricks, shams, lies, and slanders.  *Laus Deo!*
Whatever may be the result, upon our banner will still be inscribed
in ineffaceable characters the motto: "No Union with Slaveholders!"

## IMMIGRATION — POSITION OF THE DEMOCRATIC PARTY[1]

### Richmond *Enquirer*, April, 1855

Not to arrest immigration by absolute prohibition, but to suffer
foreigners to come hither and then to deny them the privileges of
citizenship, is so foolish and fatal a policy that it is difficult to understand how any man of ordinary intelligence can assent to it.  A
repeal of the laws of naturalization will not sensibly diminish the
flow of immigration.  By so harsh and illiberal a policy, we may
repel some of the prouder, brighter, and more aspiring spirits, who
might seek freedom and distinction in this country; but as the vast
mass of immigrants come here only in quest of peace and bread,
they would not be driven away by exclusion from office or the polls.
The tide would continue to flow with undiminished impetuosity;
but the character of the immigration would be sadly deteriorated.
And the effect of the Know-Nothing policy would be such that in
a few years the community would be divided into two distinct and
aristocratic classes of privileged patricians and disfranchised
plebeians.  The native would be haughty and overbearing, from a
sense of personal consequence and the distinction of caste.  The
foreign-born population, detached and dissociated from the community; exasperated by consciousness of wrong and degradation;
bound by no interest to the state; driven into compact array by
the blows of oppression, and animated by exclusive sympathies
and hopes, would be indeed an alien people in a foreign country;
and instead of being, as they are now, an element of wealth in
peace and of strength in war, they would become a source of distrac-

---

[1] During 1855 the Whig Party and the Know-Nothing Party seemed drawing
closer in the North, and in 1856 they nominated the same Presidential candidate,
Millard Fillmore.  The Democratic Party was at pains to make its hospitable attitude toward newcomers from Europe clear.  The *Enquirer's* editorial is a good
Southern expression of this attitude, and an attack on Know Nothing policy.

tion, disease, confusion, and inconceivable calamity. If, therefore, our foreign population be a pest, let us not strengthen them for evil, while we inflame their passions and exasperate revolt. The true policy is either to mitigate the evil, or else eradicate it by some sweeping and efficient remedy. Rather than pursue the insane policy of Know-Nothingism, it would be better by arbitrary enactment to expel our foreign-born fellow-citizens from the country, and to prohibit further immigration.

But the Democratic party denies that the foreign population is a pest. Without regard to the accidental abuses of immigration or naturalization, we contend that our foreign-born fellow-citizens have contributed incalculably to the power and glory of the country — that they have imparted a prodigious impulse to the development of its resources and to its progress in wealth and refinement. On the other hand, they have done nothing to retard the growth or to dishonor the name of America. Why, then, the proposition to proscribe and degrade them? Is it from the apprehension that they would ultimately subvert the liberties of the country? To this suggestion the Democratic party responds, "Sufficient unto the day is the evil thereof." When our foreign-born fellow-citizens manifest a disposition to overthrow the government and destroy the country, it will be time enough to fetter them with disabilities and to treat them as traitors. Meanwhile we maintain that any tendency to excessive immigration will be corrected by the irresistible laws of nature, or rather by the kind care of Providence. So long as the tide of immigration flows hither, it shows that the country is in want of labor — and when that is not the case, the current will turn without an artificial impulse, and run in another direction. The law of supply and demand, which is, in political economy, what the principle of gravitation is in the physical universe, will correct the evils of immigration. Indeed, we may already perceive that the tide of immigration is ebbing, and beginning to flow in the contrary direction.

## THE PROSPECT FOR KANSAS [1]

### New York *Tribune*, April 18, 1855

The unmitigated villains who have just overrun Kansas aim to gain the support of the more moderate and sensible men of the South by laying before them calculations showing that slavery

---

[1] During 1855 the Kansas struggle grew rapidly in intensity. Both the slavery forces and the Free Soilers formed governments; Emigrant Aid Societies in the North did everything in their power to promote the flow of settlers. When Greeley wrote his editorial, a legislative election had just been held (March 30), to which about 5,000 Missourians crowded from across the boundary, casting illegal ballots and carrying everything before them. The Northern press was naturally filled with indigation by this high-handed outrage.

there must be profitable.  These calculations are not, however, of a character very speedily to captivate men who are looking to their private interests, or likely to induce any very sudden rush, or indeed any rush at all, into that Territory by the slaveholders with their chattels.  The calculations are that slaves can be made very productive in raising hemp, wheat, corn, oats, and tobacco.  Now in ordinary times, the raising of these commodities in the latitude of Kansas is a starving business for the masters.  The estimated profits in the raising of these articles are based upon the fictitious price which hemp has borne under the recent unparalleled stimulation of the shipping interest, and upon the past and present famine prices of breadstuffs.  All of these prices must sooner or later recede, and be followed, through an inevitable law, by a corresponding depression below the average rate.  The business of slave-breeding alone saves them.  But a new State cannot be a slave-breeding State.  A virgin country revolts, through an instinctive rigor of nature, against all attempts to devote it to such loathsome uses.  The infamous occupation of breeding men and women for sale, flourishes only in the feculent muck accumulated from the corruptions of whole generations of squalid servitude and incompetence and slothful cupidity; such, for example, as the foul currents of slavery have deposited over the moral and physical wastes of Maryland and Virginia.  Their principal trade cannot be rivalled by Kansas.  We do not, therefore, fear for Kansas so much because slavery can be made so very profitable there as to induce a speedy slave immigration as we do from the efforts of slavery, as a political power, aiming at universal control on this continent.

The slaveholders of Missouri and of other States are determined to secure Kansas to their uses.  They will occupy it to as great an extent as they are able — not for money-making, but for political purposes.  They have rushed upon the Territory in the most outrageous manner in the late election.  They stand ready to do the same thing at every step of its political organization, till a Constitution establishing slavery is secured.  But these efforts, it should be remembered, are but fitful, from the nature of the case, and may be overborne and successfully resisted by the steady, natural current of immigration, if the flow of that current does not suffer itself to be hindered by the clamorous threats of the slaveholders to establish slavery.  Kansas is to be saved to freedom by a steady, persevering emigration thither from the Free States.  What we need now is time to get a foothold.  We require a great mass of free emigrants there — too great to be outvoted by a few thousand ruffians from Missouri, who at a given signal intend to rush in and extemporize a State Constitution, as they have extemporized a Legislature.  Give us the masses there before slavery shall be allowed to affix its black seal to the fundamental law of the State. Kansas without slavery is our motto; and she must wait for admission as a State until this is her established condition.

## THE TEMPER OF THE SOUTH

Montgomery *Mail*, July, 1855

Concerning the slavery question, the South has not been for many years in so quiet a mood. There is a perfect placidity of sentiment throughout the slave States. We have no indignation meetings, no torrents of declamation and denunciation, no fiery threatening resolutions. For all these there is a deep, deep calm. And the reason is that at length, after decades of bickerings, the whole section is agreed that the day is at hand. At length — at length, and for the first time in many a long year — the South occupies her true position, untrammeled by thrice accursed "compromises," and looking only to the Constitution for the measure of her rights. For the first time, too, she sees her fanatical enemies clothed with full power to do their will, in the House of Representatives of the United States. And thus there is made, for the first time, the true issue between the North and the South. How it will be decided is another question, but it is glorious that it is to be decided; that a few short months will give the conflict its culmination; and that whether the hordes of Free-Soilers and abolitionists are driven back impotent, overpowered by the innate conservatism of the whole people, or the South is compelled to withdraw from a government which is fast becoming her greatest enemy — in either event, our real relations with the antagonist section will be brought out in bold relief. The day of hypocrisy and duplicity will be over; our friends will be our friends and our enemies our enemies.

## SOUTHERN RETALIATION AGAINST MASSACHUSETTS

New Orleans *Bulletin*, July, 1855

Under the Massachusetts "personal liberty law" no open action as yet has taken place. Even the public gazettes have scarcely noticed the subject, so far as I can ascertain. Our people are scattered for the summer, hundreds spending their money in pleasure excursions or purchases in Massachusetts. No, my good friends of Bunker Hill and Lexington (and long may I be permitted to address you as such), there has been as yet no open action. Some of our bees and butterflies have fluttered off among you, but we who are toiling here at home consult together about your "liberty law," and other movements, and I have leave to tell you some things which are more than hinted at if such laws are to be enforced.

*First.* — Excluding your ships.

*Second.* — Excluding your manufactures.

*Third.* — Ceasing our visits to your borders, already unsafe and more or less unpleasant.

*Fourth.* — Requiring your citizens trading here at least to take out licenses, perhaps to furnish bond for good behavior.

How will such laws suit you? Of course not at all. They trench on that provision of the Constitution which declares that the citizens of each State shall be entitled to all the privileges and immunities of citizens in the several States. They certainly do, my conscientious friends, and such laws operate against all other rights the people of the several States have in other States under the Federal Constitution. We know it! but we also know that this is precisely our objection to this "liberty law," which has made all the trouble, and that its unconstitutionality has been pronounced by our highest tribunals.

All your reasoning would have done very well, so long as you held to your bargain — so long as you yourselves submitted to the paramount law, and recognized our rights under its guarantees — so long as Massachusetts held to her obligations and place in the great American family. But now you have repudiated a right of vital importance to us, and passed a law to fine and imprison as felons our citizens who may claim their rights under that Constitution. Why wait for a formal rupture and separation from you? You have not done so. Our compact is broken by *you*. There is little obligation on us to respect the rights of your citizens or their property, when you openly trample on ours. There is as little to restrain a mob from taking possession of one or more of your ships, as there was to restrain your mob in the case of the negro Burns from their assaults on the court and its officers, and from murdering the marshal Batchelder.

## THE BLESSINGS OF SLAVERY [1]

*De Bow's Review*, July, 1855

Divine Providence, for its own high and inscrutable purposes, has rescued more than three millions of human beings from the hardships of a savage state, and placed them in a condition of greater comfort than any other laboring class in the world; it has delivered them from the barbarous idolatries of Africa, and brought them

[1] An excellent illustration of that new doctrine of the beneficial nature of slavery of which Calhoun was the most distinguished exponent.

within the blessings covenanted to believers in Christ. At the same time it has provided the whites of the Anglo-Norman race in the Southern States with the necessary means of unexampled prosperity, with that slave labor, without which, as a general rule, no colonization in a new country has ever or ever will thrive and grow rapidly; it has given them a distinct and inferior race to fill a position equal to their highest capacity, which in less fortunate countries is occupied by the whites themselves. A large class — often the largest class — living from day to day by the labor of their hands, exists and must exist in every country; and it is impossible, as a general thing, for the persons of that class to have time or even inclination for much mental improvement. The force of peculiar genius may raise one in ten thousand to a higher place in society, but such cases become more and more infrequent as wages diminish with the progress of population, and the care of providing food grows more engrossing.

The whole question therefore resolves itself into this: Shall the laboring class be of an inferior race, so controlled and directed by the superior minds of the whites as continually to progress in material and moral well-being, far beyond any point it has ever shown a power of attaining in freedom? Or shall that laboring class be of whites and equals, capable of becoming "gods, as one of us," and yet condemned to a slow but sure increase of want and poverty — the slaves of society instead of individuals — isolated from their employers by the invisible but impassable barriers of customs, alien from their hearts, and utterly separated in manners, information, opinions, and tastes? Between the Southern master and his slave there is a fellow-feeling in sorrow and in joy, a mutual dependence and affection, which calls into play all the finer feelings of man's nature. What of all this is there between the Northern capitalist and his day-laborer? They have not known each other from infancy, nor been partners through good and evil fortune. Perhaps the tide of emigration brought them together yesterday and will hurry them apart tomorrow. The laborer does not look to his employer as his natural protector against the injustice of the powerful, or as his refuge in sickness or in old age. He must find that in the almshouse. If the laborer is a factory operative — perhaps a girl, or even a child, for in manufacturing societies the children of the poor never know the plays or freedom of childhood — he is regarded as but a part of the loom he attends to. Factory labor becomes more and more divided, the employments more and more monotonous, with each improvement in machinery. There is none of that variety of occupation and those frequent calls upon the discretion and intelligence of the laborer, which make the work upon a plantation in the South at once the most improving, the healthiest, and the most delightful species of manual labor. The factory operative, on the contrary, is chained to some single minute employment, which must be repeated thousands of times without the least variation. Nothing worse for the intellect can be imagined.

Idiocy and insanity multiply under their influences. In 1840, while the proportion of idiots and insane to the whole population was only 1 in 1,100 in the slave States, it was 1 to 900 in all the free States, and as much as 1 in 630 in New England alone. The effects of factory life on health are quite as bad. The cotton factories, the dyeing and bleaching factories, are hotbeds of consumption and disease of the lungs. At Sheffield a dry-grinder, no matter how vigorous his constitution, is never known to live beyond the fated age of thirty-five. In Massachusetts, according to her own statistics, factories shorten the life of the operative one-third! According to the evidence taken before the committee of the House of Commons it has taken but thirty-two years to change the operatives of Manchester from a race more vigorous than those of New England now are — a well-fed, well-clothed, moral population — into demoralized, enervated, feeble beings. As one of the witnesses says, "their life has been passed in turning the mule-jenny; their minds have been weakened and withered like a tree." How many years will it require to produce these effects in the North, when the span of man's life is already so much shortened? The very severity of the labor undermines the constitution. What wears out the human body is not the greatness of any exertion, but its duration. But the spinner has to move silently from one machine to another for twelve or fourteen hours a day, the attention never to flag, the mules never to rest. It has been calculated that the factory girl walks in this way twenty miles a day! The system is equally pernicious for the morals. We always find, first, illegitimate births and then prostitution, as well as drunkenness and crime, increase in great manufacturing districts. How should it be otherwise, when the family is broken up and the factory boarding-house substituted in its place; when children and girls are separated from their parents at the most critical period of life, crowded in heated work-rooms with a promiscuous herd of strangers, lost to all the conservative influences of home?

In what regard is such a condition of labor superior to Southern slavery? Let the free States begin within their own borders; let them place their white slaves in as good a condition, moral and physical, as the negroes, and then they may talk to us. The increasing hosts who live by toil in factories, the paupers who belong to the State, and the still greater number who drag out a wretched existence in the crowded haunts of want and vice in their great cities, form more than an offset to anything that can be said of negro slavery. We have no patience with this meddling philanthropy, which does not take the beam out of its own eye before it takes the mote out of its brother's, at the imminent risk of his eyesight; whose charity is all for show, and never grows warm except for objects at a distance; which overlooks want and misery at its own gate, in its eagerness to reform countries it has never seen, and institutions it cannot understand. It is the crying vice of our age; this desire to attend to everybody's business but our own, to perform any duties but those that lie immediately before us. Instead of making the most of our opportunities, we waste our time in vain wishes that the opportunities were greater.

## THE OUTRAGE ON MR. SUMNER [1]

New York *Evening Post*, May 23, 1856

The friends of slavery at Washington are attempting to silence the members of Congress from the free States by the same modes of discipline which make the slaves unite on their plantations. Two ruffians from the House of Representatives, named Brooks and Keith, both from South Carolina, yesterday made the Senate Chamber the scene of their cowardly brutality. They had armed themselves with heavy canes, and approaching Mr. Sumner, while sitting in his chair engaged in writing, Brooks struck him with his cane a violent blow on the head, which brought him stunned to the floor, and Keith with his weapon kept off the by-standers, while the other ruffian repeated the blows upon the head of the apparently lifeless victim till his cane was shattered to fragments. Mr. Sumner was conveyed from the Senate chamber bleeding and senseless, so severely wounded that the physician attending did not think it prudent to allow his friends to have access to him.

The excuse for this base assault is, that Mr. Sumner, on the Senate floor, in the course of a debate had spoken disrespectfully of Mr. Butler, a relative of Preston S. Brooks, one of the authors of this outrage. No possible indecorum of language on the part of Mr. Sumner could excuse, much less justify an attack like this; but we have carefully examined his speech to see if it contains any matter which could even extenuate such an act of violence, and find none. He had ridiculed Mr. Butler's devotion to slavery, it is true, but the weapon of ridicule in debate is by common consent as fair and

[1] The famous assault by Preston S. Brooks, a member of the House of Representatives from South Carolina, upon Senator Sumner of Massachusetts, raised a cry of Northern execration. This editorial is unmistakably Bryant's.

allowable a weapon as argument. The *Journal of Commerce* of this morning apologizes for the brutality of Brooks and his confederate, by saying that Mr. Sumner was guilty of "wholesale denunciation and bitter personalities;" and quotes what the Washington *Star* says of the character of Mr. Sumner's speech. What the Washington *Star* may say is nothing to the purpose; the question is what Mr. Sumner said, and as this has been published, the *Journal* should have placed it before its readers, that they might judge for themselves. It prudently, however, keeps the provocation, whatever it might be, out of sight. Our readers have already had the speech, and we leave it to them to say whether there is any wholesale denunciation or bitter personality in it; whether it contains anything which goes beyond the fair decorum of debate. There is surely, no wholesale denunciation — for Mr. Butler is assailed on one point only, his insane devotion to slavery; there is no bitter personality in it, for his character as a man in the ordinary relations of life is left unquestioned. We agree fully with Mr. Sumner that Mr. Butler is a monomaniac in the respect of which we speak; we certainly should place no confidence in any representation he might make which concerned the subject of slavery, and we say this without any expectation of an attempt being made upon our lives, or even of having our heads broken, for our boldness.

Has it come to this that we must speak with bated breath in the presence of our Southern masters; that even their follies are too sacred a subject for ridicule; that we must not deny the consistency of their principles or the accuracy of their statements? If we venture to laugh at them or question their logic, or dispute their facts, are we to be chastised as they chastise their slaves? Are we too, slaves, slaves for life, a target for their brutal blows, when we do not comport ourselves to please them? If this be so, it is time that the people of the free States knew it, and prepared themselves to acquiesce in their fate. They have labored under the delusion hitherto that they were their own masters.

Even if it were true, as it is not, that there were "wholesale denunciation and bitter personalities" against Mr. Butler in Mr. Sumner's speech, the denunciation should have been repelled and personalities rebuked by some of the fluent speakers of the powerful majority to which Mr. Butler belongs, and the matter should have ended there. The sudden attack made with deadly weapons upon an unarmed man in the Senate Chamber, where he could not expect it or have been prepared for it, was the act of men who must be poltroons as well as ruffians. It was as indecent, also, as it was cowardly; the Senate floor should be sacred from such outrages; or if they are common, if at all, it should only be by Senatorial blackguards.  It is true that the Senate had just adjourned, but the members were still there, many of them in their places;  it was their chamber, and this violence committed in their presence was an insult to their body.  Yet we have no expectation that the Senate will do anything to vindicate the sacredness and peace of their chamber, or the right of their members not to be called to account for words spoken in debate.  There will be a little discussion;  some will denounce and some will defend the assault, and then the matter will end.

The truth is, that the pro-slavery party, which rules in the Senate, looks upon violence as the proper instrument of its designs.  Violence reigns in the streets of Washington;  violence has now found its way into the Senate chamber.  Violence lies in wait on all the navigable rivers and all the railways of Missouri, to obstruct those who pass from the free States into Kansas.  Violence overhangs the frontiers of that territory like a storm-cloud charged with hail and lightning.  Violence has carried election after election in that territory.  In short, violence is the order of the day;  the North is to be pushed to the wall by it, and this plot will succeed if the people of the free States are as apathetic as the slaveholders are insolent.

## SLAVERY AN ECONOMIC NECESSITY

### Richmond *Dispatch*, May, 1856

The whole commerce of the world turns upon the product of slave labor.  What would commerce be without cotton, sugar, tobacco, rice, and naval stores?  All these are the product of slave labor.  It is a settled fact that free labor cannot produce them in sufficient quantities to supply the demands of mankind.  It has been said that one free laborer is equal to five slaves.  If this be so, why has not free labor been employed in the production of the above staples?  It has been attempted, and in every case in which it has been introduced has failed.  The world follows its interests, and if free labor was more valuable than slave, it would be employed at this moment in the United States, Cuba, and Brazil, which are all open to free labor.  And herein note the greater liberality and self-reliant strength of the slave States over the free States.  The former freely permit the Northern capitalist to come in with his free labor and compete with slave labor.  The latter pass laws prohibiting the Southern capitalist from coming in with his slaves to compete with Northern labor.  Their prohibitory laws are passed because they are afraid of slave competition;  whereas the South, in the face of the pretence which has been handed down from Wilberforce to these times, that one white laborer is equal in value to five

slaves, throws her door wide open and invites free labor to walk in
and try its hand, and it dare not come. What would become of
England, the arch-agitator of abolitionism, but for cotton, by the
manufacture of which she has waxed fat and strong, while she curses
the system by which it is produced? By the way, will someone inform us why the English conscience has never suffered as much
from slavery in Brazil as slavery in the United States?


## SOUTHERN THREATS OF DISUNION[1]

New York *Evening Post*, October 6, 1856

It will be seen in looking over Mr. Botts's letter to the editor of
the *National American*, which we give today, that he imputes the
threats of disunion contained in the speech which Governor Wise
delivered the other day at Richmond to a disordered mind. That
Wise is not perfectly sane may be true enough — a more well-
balanced mind than his might be overset by the excitement and
want of sleep of which he complained so pathetically at Richmond;
but all this blustering about disunion is simply a deliberately laid
plot to frighten the North. If any votes for Buchanan can be
obtained by it, if Frémont can be deprived by it of any votes, its
object will be effected; if not, no harm will be done, and the politicians of the slave states will submit as quietly as they did when
General Jackson enforced the laws of the Union in spite of the
nullifiers, and as when Mr. Banks was elected Speaker of the House
of Representatives.

Our readers may rely upon it, therefore, that Mr. Botts is too
charitable. They who make this threat of disunion are more knaves
than madmen. Mr. Forsyth and Governor Wise, and the men
who speak through the Washington *Union*, if they were absolutely
mad, might make a serious attempt to carry their project into effect;
but not one of them all, at present, has any more thought of attempting a dissolution of the Union than of attempting a dissolution
of the solar system. With the election of Colonel Frémont impending
over them, not the slightest preparation has been made on their
part for the event which they so studiously with one voice represent
as inevitable.

[1] In an effort to frighten Northern voters into casting their ballots for either
Buchanan or Millard Fillmore in 1856, numerous Southern leaders declared during the campaign that if Frémont were elected by the Republicans, the South
would secede. Governor Henry A. Wise of Virginia and John Forsyth of Alabama
were two of those who made the fiercest threats; and John Minor Botts of Richmond
was a Virginian who defended the idea of an indissoluble Union. Though Bryant
scoffed at these threats, they led many men to vote for Buchanan. This was particularly true in Pennsylvania, a pivotal state.

## [THE GROWING DEMAND FOR SECESSION]

New Orleans *Bulletin*, August, 1856

Secession is a foul and rank weed which finds no culture or sustenance in this uncongenial soil. Such being the universal sentiment predominant in this community, our people have always been slow to credit the fact of the existence of an opposite feeling in any part of the country. The wild and irrational ravings of the abolition press proper were supposed to be confined to a few fanatics, small in number and despicable in character, and by no means representing the opinions of the Northern people in the aggregate. Most unfortunately, different impressions begin to prevail. We cannot beguile ourselves any longer with such delusive hopes. The fact cannot be disguised or circumvented that this feeling of hostility to the institution of slavery, and to the section of country where it exists, is getting to be widespread, bitter and insatiable. The most discreet, conservative, and patriotic men of the North are openly taking sides on the sectional issue, which if it be their design to agitate until it is disposed of, can be terminated in no other way than by a dissolution of the Union. This is the only *finality* of the vexatious and embarrassing question which the factious disputants who persist in agitating it expect or hope for.

*De Bow's Review*, November, 1856

But, it is said, the South will not dare to leave the Union; that the sentiments of anti-slavery will pursue them into whatever political connection they may seek a refuge, and that the only ark of their political safety is in association with the North. This we doubt, and will give a brief consideration to this aspect of the subject.

It is said that anti-slavery will war upon us more than ever, but we doubt it. Under the forms of a political connection they can now disturb us with impunity. Tied by the ligaments of a common government, with a preponderance of legislative power against us, they can treat us as they please and laugh at our indignation. They can vote away the common fund; they can impose whatever impost duties upon foreign fabrics may be best calculated to build up interests among themselves, and while outraging every feeling of affection, can determine for us what discrimination in reference to our own interests will best subserve their ends. Possessed of this security, it is a cheap oppression to war upon the South — to disturb our social institutions — to circumscribe us in extent — to set the world against us and exercise the common incidents of merely vulgar despotism. But possessed of the functions of political sovereignty; at liberty to treat the North, not as it may please them but as it may please us; to hold them strictly responsible for their conduct, and cause them to feel that for every unwarrantable act we will make them pay the penalty in such discriminations as we shall have the power to use against them, and it is by no means certain that aggression will continue.

## THE CONSPIRACY AGAINST THE WORKING CLASS[1]

New York *Evening Post*, October 29, 1856

That those who are attached to the party of Mr. Buchanan by official ties should give him their support does not surprise us; it is the infirmity of human nature to cheat itself with the idea that what is for our present interest must be right. That those who own slaves at the South, and those at the North who are connected in any way with the slave-holding class by interest or other affinities, should support him, is quite natural; he is the slave-holders' candidate. But that any man who depends on the labor of his own hands for subsistence, who wishes that honest labor should be honored, and that the great West should be open to him and the class to which he belongs, and to their children, as a region in which they may exercise their calling without social degradation — that any such man should stand ready to give his vote for Buchanan, is what we cannot account for.

There are, we believe, very few farmers and mechanics at the North who are not fully aware that if slavery goes into the Territories, free labor must go out. When they look at the map of the United States, they perceive that the slave States are one-fourth larger in their areas than the free States. When they look at the census of the United States, they perceive that the number of white inhabitants in the free States, though their area is so much less, is more than twice the white population of the slave States. They perceive that slavery is an engrossing, encroaching institution, a greedy devourer of land, requiring three or four times as much space as free labor. They perceive also another important fact, that the less wealthy part of the Southern population are constantly migrating to free territory or to the western free States, where labor is held in honor, and where they can till the soil, or toil in other callings requiring bodily exertion, without being regarded as an inferior class. We published the other day a letter from Professor Hendrick, of North Carolina, in which he spoke feelingly of this constant necessity of removal to free territory, a necessity which forces his old friends and neighbors to leave their homes, and keeps down the natural

[1] Typical of the appeal by the Republicans in 1856 for the votes of Northern workingmen and of newly arrived immigrants.

increase of population in his native State.   The census shows that a large proportion of those who settle the free States of the west come from slave States.   Go where you will in the new settlements, you meet the emigrant from Virginia, from Kentucky, from Tennessee, from North Carolina.   We have ourselves frequently partaken of the hospitality of those sons of the South in their cabins on the prairies.   Southern Ohio, Illinois and Indiana are peopled by them and their descendants;  they follow up the rivers to Iowa, to Wisconsin, to Minnesota, to Nebraska;  they help to swell the population of Cincinnati, Chicago, Madison, and the other flourishing towns of the free West.   Thus it is the South casts out her offspring;  she keeps slavery, and parts with her children, who should make her strength and her honor.   Free labor cannot live by the side of the oligarchy which tills the soil by the hands of its bondmen, and sells carpenters, blacksmiths, and masons under the hammer.   The free white laborer of the South finds that in a thin population, public schools cannot be supported.   The planter, with a domain of from three to ten thousand acres, can send his children to some private school or keep a tutor;  but the poor man must see his children grow up in ignorance.   No wonder that he should remove to a place where education is brought to his door, and where labor is no longer a badge of degradation.

If, therefore, slavery is introduced into the Territories, as the Southern politicians, with the co-operation of all that party at the North now supporting Buchanan, are attempting to introduce it, we see what the effect must be.   We of the free States may enter those Territories with the purpose of settling there, but if we do not become slaveholders we must go out again.   The farmers who go thither to work with their own hands must consent to be looked down upon by the planters, with their domains of thousands of acres and their hundreds of work-people whose muscles and bones are their property.   The white farmer will take his place by the negro field-hand;  the white carpenter will be looked upon as a proper companion for the black carpenter who is sold at auction.   In going to such a community the farmer from the free States must renounce the advantage of schools;  he must see his children brought up as the poor population of Missouri are brought up, in utter ignorance, and with the propensity to debauchery which is nourished in those who have no intellectual resources.

They cannot live in such a community.   They will come thronging back to the new free States, as they now come from Virginia and North Carolina, driven out by the stinging sense of degradation which at the South is connected with poverty, and by the frightful dearth of the means of education, which makes this degradation

more complete. They will come back to us with their families, all
the worse in mind and morals for their sojourn in a land which to
them and their children will have been like the land of Egypt to
the Israelites.

## [THE REAL ISSUE OF 1856]

Springfield *Republican*, November 4, 1856

The real abstract question between the two parties is, whether
Congress shall control the destinies of the territories, and dedicate
them as of old to freedom, or whether they shall be left for bitter
and bloody struggles between the settlers, like those which in Kansas
now shock the moral sense of civilization everywhere. Practically
the question is whether the influence of the national government
shall be used to extend slavery, and aggregate its political power,
or to limit its bounds and weaken its hold over the politics, the
business, and the religion of the nation. Were the issue thus plainly
known of all men, there would be no dispute of the result. The
American party stepped in at an inopportune moment, overwhelmed
the true issue before the country, and turned aside the minds of
many men by the glittering success which it momentarily won.
And if the Republican party fails today to inaugurate that revolution
in the national government which must come ere this generation
passes away, or the government itself perishes, the responsibility
cannot be escaped by the American organization. To its door
must the defeat of John C. Frémont and the election of James
Buchanan be laid. By implanting in many minds a weak substitu-
tion for the strongest issue, and by keeping temporarily in the Democratic ranks many who but for their opposition to Americanism
would have rallied around the Republican standard, it has given
fresh strength to the Democracy, and enabled them to contest this
election with a fair prospect of success. . . .

The result of the struggle is in grave doubt, and the eagles of
victory are as likely, perhaps, to perch on the one side as on the other,
tomorrow morning. Of the two contestants, the Republicans can
alone afford to be beaten. With the Democracy, defeat is destruction. The party is only held together by its alliance with the national
treasury and the slaveholder. Separated from one, it becomes useless to the other, and its power is gone. But a reverse cannot break
the Republican column. It has an enduring vitality in its principles,
and a glorious destiny, as sure as the Republic has an existence.
Whether it enters upon the affirmative exercise of its mission now,
or four years hence, is to all seeming the only question of today.
Time will only vindicate its truthfulness, its necessity, and its
strength. It can afford to wait, if the country and the world can

afford to have it.   But the country cannot afford to wait for its
healing, peaceful mission, and though we look not upon the day's
struggle with confidence of victory, we await its result with a
buoyant hope that the day and the hour of redemption have come.

## THE ELECTIONS OF YESTERDAY

New York *Evening Post*, November 5, 1856

The battle is over, and we are all waiting for the smoke to clear
away that we may see the exact position of the armies which have
been engaged in the conflict.   The present aspect of the field is
disastrous for the cause which we have supported.   We will not
undertake to say at present that all hope is lost; we will not affirm
that it is impossible that the reports we are yet to hear from Pennsylvania may change the apparent defeat into a victory;  we will not
yet affirm that there is no chance that the election may be carried
into the House of Representatives.   The chances for Fillmore in
Kentucky and Louisiana were thought a week since to be as good
as in Maryland, which it is said has been carried for the Fillmore
electoral ticket.

But taking it for granted that Buchanan has succeeded, we confess
that there are considerations which, with us, mitigate the pain of
disappointment.   If we have not carried the United States, we have
obtained heavy majorities in a part of the Union which stands high
in the confederacy for intelligence and prosperity, and which,
through these characteristics, exercises a powerful influence on
public opinion.   We have at least laid the basis of a formidable and
well-organized party, in opposition to the spread of slavery — that
scheme which is the scandal of the country and of the age.   In
those states of the Union which have now given such large majorities
for Frémont, public opinion, which till lately has been undecided
and shuffling in regard to the slavery question, is now clear, fixed
and resolute.   If we look back to 1848, when we conducted a
Presidential election on this very ground of opposition to the extension of slavery, we shall see that we have made immense strides
towards the ascendancy which, if there be any grounds to hope for
the perpetuity of free institutions, is yet to be ours.   We were then
comparatively weak, we are now strong; we then counted our
thousands, we now count our millions; we could then point to our
respectable minorities in a few States, we now point to State after
State — to powerful old States on the Atlantic, and flourishing
young States in the West — which rally with us under the banner
of resistance to the extension of slavery.   The cause is not going
back — it is rapidly going forward; the Freesoil party of 1848 is the

nucleus of the Republican party of 1856; but with what accessions of numbers, of strength, of illustrious names, of moral power, of influence, not merely in public assemblies, but at the domestic fireside!

## MR. DELAVAN'S PROHIBITION LETTERS[1]

*Albany* Atlas and Argus, *March 10, 1857*

The day has gone by when individuals or parties are to be denounced as the enemies of temperance because they resist unconstitutional legislation. That game has been played out. When Governor Seymour was in the gubernatorial chair, the Whigs (so called at that day) sent to him for approval, a prohibitory law, which even the advocates of prohibition, in nine months afterwards, admitted violated the Constitution. Of course he vetoed it, as his duty and his official oath required. Straightway a howl was set up against him and the party which sustained him, charging both with hostility to the cause of temperance. The Chambers, the Burleighs, the Raymonds, the Greeleys, and the whole tribe of Whig politicians, suddenly became zealous reformers, and many of them over their cups drank success to prohibition and Sewardism. Governor Clark, a quiet and respectable citizen of Canandaigua, solely for the purpose of securing temperance votes, was taken up and set astride the prohibitory hobby. Raymond, giving a pledge to the temperance people which he violated before the ink was fairly dry, submitted to the humiliation of mounting behind and riding on the crupper. The coalition was successful. Mock philanthropy and corruption rioted at the capitol. To preserve a decent appearance of faith, a prohibitory law was passed in direct violation of the Constitution, which in less than a year fell before the judgment of the Court of Appeals.

The Democratic party opposed all this — the sham benevolence, the corruption, the violation of the Constitution — and now all disinterested men, even many of the actors in the shameful farce, concede the correctness of its action.

---

[1] In several Northern States during the fifties, including Massachusetts, Michigan, and New York, prohibitory laws were enacted but declared unconstitutional by the courts. The slavery excitement and Civil War arrested the spread of prohibition. Horatio Seymour, who was elected Governor in 1852, vetoed a prohibition bill on the Maine model. The result was the election, by a majority of a few hundred votes, of an ardent prohibitionist, Myron H. Clark, as Governor on the Whig ticket. This was in 1854. In 1855 a new prohibition bill was passed. As the *Argus* states, the Court of Appeals promptly declared it unconstitutional. This disposed of the issue in New York.

## PRENTICEIANA[1]

Louisville *Journal*, 1830–1859

The editor of the *Ohio Statesman* says more villainy is on foot. We suppose the editor has lost his horse.

James Ray and John Parr have started a Locofoco paper in Maine, called the *Democrat*. Parr, in all that pertains to decency, is below zero; and Ray is below Parr.

Whatever Midas touched was turned into gold; in these days, touch a man with gold and he'll turn into anything.

Have I changed? exclaims Governor P——. We don't know. That depends on whether you were ever an honest man.

The Washington *Globe* says that such patriotism as Mr. Clay's will not answer. True enough, for it can't be questioned.

The editor of the —— speaks of his "lying curled up in bed these cold mornings." This verifies what we said of him some time ago — "he lies like a dog."

Wild rye and wild wheat grow in some regions spontaneously. We believe that wild oats are always sown.

The *Globe* says that Mr. Clay is a sharp politician. No doubt of it, but the editor of the *Globe* is a sharper.

Men are deserters in adversity; when the sun sets, and all is dark, our very shadows refuse to follow us.

A well known writer says that a fine coat covers a multitude of sins. It is still truer that such coats cover a multitude of sinners.

Messrs. Bell and Topp, of the North Carolina *Gazette*, say that "Prentices were made to serve masters." Well, Bells were made to be hung, and Topps to be whipped.

## THE NEW FEDERAL CONSTITUTION[2]

New York *Evening Post*, March 9, 1857

Some of the journalists who support the cause of the Administration are pleasing themselves with the fancy that the decision of the Supreme bench of the United States in the Dred Scott case will put an end to the agitation of the slavery question. They will soon find their mistake. The feeling in favor of liberty is not so easily smothered; discussion is not so readily silenced. One specific after another has been tried, with the same view and with the same suc-

---

[1] George D. Prentice, who founded the Louisville *Journal* as an organ of Clay and the nascent Whig Party in 1830, became famous for his brief editorial paragraphs, a collection of which was issued under the title "Prenticeana" in 1859. Prentice died in 1870.

[2] Bryant's fiery editorial is typical of the refusal of Northern newspapers to accept any of the main implications of the Dred Scott decision, and to hold it null and void.

cess. The Fugitive Slave Law, we are told, was to quiet all agitation, but it did not; the Nebraska bill was to stop all controversy on the slavery question, but it proved to be oil poured on the flames. The usurpation of the government of Kansas by the inroad from Missouri was thought for a time to be a blow to the friends of liberty which they could not survive, but it only roused them to greater activity. The election of Mr. Buchanan as President in November was to put an end to the dispute, but since November the dispute has waxed warmer and warmer. It will never end till the cause of liberty has finally triumphed. Heap statute upon statute, follow up one act of executive interference with another, add usurpation to usurpation, and judicial decision to judicial decision, the spirit against which they are levelled is indestructible. As long as the press and speech are free, the warfare will be continued, and every attempt to suppress it, by directing against it any part of the machinery of the government, will only cause it to rage the more fiercely.

This has been the case hitherto. The more our Presidents have meddled with the matter, the more the majority in Congress have sought to stifle the discussion, the more force has been employed on the side of slavery — whether under the pretext of legal authority, as when Mr. Pierce called out the New Jersey troops to enforce the pretended laws of Kansas, or without that pretext, as when armed men crossed the border of that territory to make laws for the inhabitants — the more determined is the zeal by which the rights of freemen are asserted and upheld against the oligarchy. It will not cool the fiery temper of this zeal to know that slavery has enlisted the bench on its side; it will rather blow it into a stronger and more formidable flame.

Here are five slaveholding judges on the bench, disciples of this neologism of slavery — men who have espoused the doctrines lately invented by the Southern politicians, and who seek to graft them upon our code of constitutional law — men who alter our Constitution for us, who find in it what no man of common sense, reading for himself, could ever find, what its framers never thought of putting into it, what no man discerned in it until a very few days since it was seen with the aid of optics sharpened by the eager desire to preserve the political ascendency of the slave States. We feel, in reading the opinions of these men, that local political prejudices have gained the mastery of that bench, and tainted beyond recovery the minds of the majority of the judges. The Constitution which they now profess to administer, is not the Constitution under which this country has lived for seventy years; it is not the Constitution which Washington, Franklin, and Jefferson, and the abler jurists who filled the seat of justice in the calmer days of our republic, recognized; this is not the Constitution to which we have so long looked with admiration and reverence; it is a new Constitution, of which we never heard until it was invented by Mr. Calhoun, and which we cannot see adopted by the judges of our Federal court without shame and indignation.

Hereafter, if this decision shall stand for law, slavery, instead of being what the people of the slave States have hitherto called it, their peculiar institution, is a Federal institution, the common patrimony and shame of all the States, those which flaunt the title of free as well as those which accept the stigma of being the Land of Bondage; hereafter, wherever our jurisdiction extends, it carries with it the chain and the scourge, — wherever our flag floats, it is the flag of slavery. If so, that flag should have the light of the stars and the streaks of running red erased from it; it should be dyed black, and its device should be the ship and the fetter.

Are we to accept, without question, these new readings of the Constitution — to sit down contentedly under this disgrace — to admit that the Constitution was never before rightly understood, even by those who framed it — to consent that hereafter it shall be the slaveholders' instead of the freemen's Constitution? Never! Never! We hold that the provisions of the Constitution, so far as they regard slavery, are now just what they were when it was framed, and that no trick of interpretation can change them. The people of the free States will insist on the old impartial construction of the Constitution, adopted in calmer times — the construction given it by Washington and his contemporaries, instead of that invented by modern politicians in Congress and adopted by modern politicians on the bench.

## IMMIGRATION AND SLAVERY [1]

### Albany *Atlas and Argus*, January 28, 1857

(Official immigration figures of the Port of New York for the year 1856 show that a total of 141,625 immigrants entered then, bearing $9,642,104 in cash means. Of these 56,055 with $2,150,656 named New York as their destination; 13,327 with $1,984,126 Wisconsin. — *News Item*).

The portion of these new-comers who went to the old States were doubtless to a great extent laborers of both sexes, and show a less average amount of means per head. But it does not follow that they are less valuable, or perform less important functions in the great body politic. They fill a place in society which must be filled by a population of some description, either bond or free. They are

[1] A prominent place among the "doughface" newspapers — Northern newspapers with Southern views or principles — was long occupied by the Albany *Argus*, which here appears in the role of apologist for slavery.

the laborers of our nation. Their hands dig our canals, build our railroads, furnish the muscle in the erection of our houses, stores and various structures, aid the movements of commerce upon our docks, till our fields and gather our harvests, do the domestic service of our houses, and in brief, perform the great mass of the mere manual labor and physical service in all these Northern and Western States. The effect is to elevate our native population above the mere drudgery of physical labor, and give them a higher position in the scale of society, to make them the employers instead of the employed, to give them the position in the social and economical structure which depends more upon the exercise of mind than of muscle.

The speculation as to what would have been the condition in the present free States without the introduction of this vast mass of foreign labor, opens an interesting field of thought and inquiry. Without this foreign supply, who would now be our laborers and our domestic servants? Would all these places be filled by our own native population? Would they have discharged and continued to discharge all the various offices and duties which this foreign element has met? We doubt it. At the South the black population has supplied precisely the want which we should have experienced without the aid of immigration. The blacks are the laborers and the domestic servants of the South. Will it do for us to boast so much upon our superior philanthropy and humanity as to be quite certain that we should have released our hold upon the African race, had not this press of foreign bone and muscle been at our doors, soliciting employment and ready to do for us all that a system of compulsory service supplied and to do it better and cheaper? The motives of our action are not always quite apparent to ourselves. The human heart can easily persuade itself that it yields to the promptings of humanity or the stern demands of duty, when in fact it only follows the lead of self-interest. Radical changes in the social and political condition of a people are much more commonly conceded to the latter, than to the former. Without intending to depreciate or undervalue the influences of the former, we think the latter must be set down in any sound system of political economy as a far more controlling principle of human action.

## [HOW SLAVERY IMPOVERISHES THE SOUTH]

New York *Tribune*, March 15, 1858

Senator Hammond occupied the greater part of his speech on Lecompton with an exposition of the capacity of the slave States to establish and maintain what he called "a separate political organization." This is a common topic of abstract inquiry with South Carolinians, and we do not object to it, though its special relevancy to the question of admitting Kansas into the Union under a fraudulent Constitution we do not perceive.   In this review Mr. Hammond went over the old ground of Southern theorists, and reproduced with little change and no novelty the various considerations going to show how admirably a Southern slave-holding government would work in practise.   For our part, as a general proposition, we have no hesitation in admitting that the Southern States are able to maintain, in one way or another, an independent government of their own.   How powerful it would be or how prosperous is a question upon which there will be diversity of opinion.   Governor Hammond has the good sense to admit that its strength would not consist in its fighting power.   He gives it a high prospective rank among the nations, however, on the ground that, as he declares, "Cotton is king," and a king with whom none can afford to go to war.   The reign of this monarch will thus, as Governor Hammond thinks, be not only eternal but eternally pacific.

But we cannot allow one fallacy of Governor Hammond to go unreproved and unexposed, especially as it is one that the slave-holding statesmen are forever putting forward.   We mean the notion that foreign exports are the measure of a country's wealth and power.   We cannot understand how it is that gentlemen of intelligence can so tenaciously insist on this dismal fallacy.   What can be plainer than that it is the aggregate production of a country that constitutes its wealth, and is the real measure of its power? Exports are nothing but the exchange of products that are produced, for products that are not produced by the exporting country. Diversify production in any country, and no exports or exchanges with foreign countries are necessary.   Simplify production by confining it to one or two staples, and exchanges for foreign productions or exports must be proportionally large.   But is this to be taken as any evidence that the country that has a varied production is poor, and the country that has not is rich?   Yet such is substantially the deduction of economists who count exports as evidence of wealth. If they were right, then an island in the ocean whose entire population was engaged in the oyster or whale fishery, and who by dint of hard work and poor fare were able to make both ends meet at the end of a year, could point to the exports wherewith they bought their pork, and hard bread, and tarpaulins, as an evidence of their abundant prosperity, because their earnings were comparatively so large.   This is just the kind of prosperity the South exhibits in her reported surplus.   She raises cotton, but she can neither eat nor spin it, and hence it goes abroad to buy what she wants to eat and to wear.

But this is not all. A country where industry is not diversified, but where production is confined to one or two, or a very few staples, is constantly in a precarious condition. A failure of its chief crop for a single year spreads bankruptcy and famine. A threatened war fills it with dismay; an actual one with ruin. The country of large exports in proportion to its production is thus the weakest of countries rather than the strongest. The country whose products are the most varied, and the gross result of whose industry is the largest, is that which has the greatest amount of all the elements which constitute wealth, even though its exports may be comparatively small.[1] But if the Southern economists reject so sound a test of the wealth and resources of a people, they surely cannot object to estimate them by the earned surplus on hand in the form of taxable property. If this be done, how stand the slave and free States in a comparative estimate? The State of Massachusetts, with a population of 994,514 in 1850, possessed personal and real estate to the amount of $573,342,000. The valuation of the State of Virginia, with a population of 1,421,661, at the same period, was $391,646,000; and this comparison can be almost indefinitely extended between the free and the slave States.

What then becomes of the labored attempt of Governor Hammond and his coadjutors to show the comparative wealth and power of the slave States, by exhibiting their exports as contrasted with the free? And when we can demonstrate, as we did lately, that the aggregate production of the largest of the slave States is not equal to its annual expenses of living by $14,000,000 per annum? This one fact exhibits the wastefulness, weakness, and poverty inherent in the system of slavery in a more striking light than volumes of theoretical illustration. It shows, too, why it is that commercial capital does not accumulate in the South as it has done in the older free States, and why a never-ending succession of bankruptcies seem always necessary to extinguish the indebtedness which the South is constantly incurring at the North. It shows why it is that the banks of the South are so long in showing recuperative power after their suspension. If Virginia is any evidence, and even Maryland any evidence, of the working of the system of slave labor, none of the slave States are paying the expenses of their own living. They do not support themselves, they do not pay their own way, but live, to a greater or less extent, according to situation and circumstances, off the industry of the rest of the country. In fact, the slavery of the South is a positive pecuniary burden upon the free States — an absolute tax upon the free labor of the country.

[1] It is unquestionably true that a great part of the annual surplus produced by the South went to the North. It was used there to pay for tools, clothing, household wares, and food bought by the South.

## [ASPECTS OF AMERICAN SOCIAL HISTORY, 1858][1]

*Harper's Weekly*

*What Will You Do With Her?:* January 30.

In the little neighboring town of Orange, Mrs. Lucy Stone, a woman of intelligence, sense, and spirit, declines to pay her taxes. Why?

Because, she says, there should be no taxes without representation.

That was good doctrine on Bunker Hill and in Boston Harbor some eighty-four or five years ago. It remains to see how it will work in Orange.

She is undoubtedly a woman — but the tax-gatherer can hardly push that argument very far — for she is also a peaceable, useful citizen; and it must be a very eloquent tax-gatherer indeed who could persuade sensible people in Orange that so good a citizen ought to be taxed without representation.

It is, in fact, a brave little *coup d'état* in favor of Woman's Rights; and its success would hardly peril the prosperity of Jersey: for even if the Lords of Creation should graciously allow their female slaves to vote, there are very few of them who would take the trouble to exercise the right.

*Prohibitive Legislation:* February 13.

A *bona fide* attempt has recently been made, by the Mayor of New York, to put down gambling houses. Policemen, duly armed with authority and prepared to execute the laws, have made descents upon well-known gambling establishments; they have not, in any single instance, found anything to justify a seizure. When they made their appearance the most notorious dens of gamblers presented an aspect of primeval innocence. After heroic exertions they have been compelled to confess themselves beaten, and the Mayor's aim has, for the time, been defeated. It is needless to add that, after a convenient delay, the gambling houses will resume operations without let or hindrance.

The last Mayor of New York, Fernando Wood, began his career with a like display of virtuous vigilance. He, too, undertook to execute the laws and abate nuisances. But the desire did not last long. He soon abandoned a hopeless and thankless contest with the vices and propensities of the people. We are doing no injustice to Mayor Tiemann when we say he will follow the example. He will discover, before a fourth of his term has elapsed, that the evils

[1] By 1858 *Harper's Weekly*, now a year old, was popular and influential; the best of these editorials are from the pen of George W. Curtis, already a regular contributor.

against which the laws we have enumerated are directed are beyond
the reach of law and police to eradicate. And, like a sensible man,
he will confine his efforts to the pursuit of objects and reforms which
are humanly feasible. . . . We have, in large cities, certain habits
and modes of thought and action; these can not be altered or
modified by any act or statute. The only effect of prohibitive
legislation in reference to these settled and inherent vices is, first,
to induce concealment with its obvious concomitant evils, and
secondly, to engender a contempt for the law. There is no instance
where a rooted habit among the people of a large city has been
eradicated by legislation.

*Reopening of the Slave Trade:* March 13.

It seems that while the eyes of Northern politicians have been
steadily fixed on Kansas, the practical men of the South have been
quietly increasing their stock of negroes by vigorous importations
from Africa. At least such is the statement of the New Orleans
*Delta*, which journal avers that the plantations of Mississippi and
other Southern sea-board States are plentifully supplied with negroes
fresh from Africa. The story derives a plausibility from the bill
which has just passed the Legislature of Louisiana for the importation of negro apprentices from Africa, and from the agitation
which has existed for two or three years in South Carolina, Tennessee, and one or two other Southern States, in favor of the reopening
of the slave trade. It is a pity that some one does not suggest some
practical means by which the difficulties which now impede the
acquisition of labor by the South could be overcome. All admit,
and the steady increase in the value of negroes proves, that the great
want of the South is labor. If in the North our supply of foreign
labor were suddenly cut off, the country would receive a shock in
comparison with which the late revulsion would seem utterly insignificant. Yet the natural increase of our laboring population is
greater than that of the negroes.

*Physical Decay in the United States:* February 27.

There seems to exist among the people of the United States a
decided aversion for field sports and open air exercise. Among the
people of the large cities physical exercise is never considered for a
moment. No athletics, exercises, or sports are popular. We have
cricket clubs, at which the bulk of the players are Englishmen. We
have no hunts, with horses and dogs; a few enthusiastic persons
shoot a little in the season, but the sport can not be said to be general. As a general rule the New Yorker never takes a gun in his
hand except when he goes out on those doleful processions called

target excursions, which are usually equal parts of dullness and drink. New Yorkers do not ride. Their idea of horse exercise is sitting in an uncomfortable wagon behind a fast trotting horse, and swallowing several pounds of dust on a road covered with flash men and flash teams. There are several gymnasia in the large cities. They are frequented by very few acolytes, and after a few months' patronage these generally desert them. In fine, it may be said broadly that, after our people reach manhood, they never seem to think that it is necessary to exercise their muscles.

Lastly, the first and ruling consideration of every American is business. Walk up Broadway and listen to the conversation of the people whom you pass — ninety-nine out of a hundred are talking of dollars, percentages, and premiums. The same is true of the groups of men assembled in drawing-rooms, hotel parlors, and bar-rooms. Wherever two or three Americans are gathered together there you may be sure that business and dollars are on the tapis. There are a few boys whose prime aim in life is billiards, cigars, gloves, and drink; but they are an exception. The bulk of our people have no time to be vicious. They are too busy to sin. As Dr. Watts teaches, they shame the Evil One by the intensity of their application to the serious things of life. An English merchant works seven hours a day, goes home, eats a hearty dinner, and plays with his children till bedtime. A Frenchman drops into his office before breakfast, returns home at eleven, goes back to work at two, and dines at five, after which he may be seen at an opera or in a ball-room. An American begins work before he is dressed in the morning, and never stops till he goes to bed.

*Effects of the Atlantic Telegraph:* August 14.

That ocean steam navigation has tended to enlarge the social mind of the peoples of Great Britain and of the United States no one will be inclined to dispute. It has helped the two nations to know each other better, to get rid of ignorant prejudices, to share each other's progress. A volume would be required to describe the benefits which each nation has conferred on the other — through the agency of steam navigation — in respect of new inventions alone. This mutually improving process will be further developed by the telegraph. Hourly intercourse with Europe will familiarize us with the progress of the European mind, and efface the last remains of provincialism here. Regular morning and evening bulletins from the United States will open the eyes of Europe to the real state of society here, and will dispel that ignorance and prejudice which to this day disgrace so many enlightened Europeans. It is said that one of the most sagacious statesmen of continental Europe has been from the first opposed to the telegraph; he foresaw that regular announcements of the working of our system of self-government would exercise no small effect on the popular mind of Germany and France.

### The Great Prize-Fight:  October 30.

Without doubt the leading event of last week — to a large mass of the people of New York and the other large cities  — was the prize-fight which took place between Morrissey and Heenan not far from the city of Buffalo.  Other events there were, of no small import — Congressional nominations, speeches of political aspirants, début of Mlle. Piccolimini, the success of "Miles Standish," arrival of steamers from Europe, departure of war vessels from Paraguay — but all of these were overshadowed and swallowed up by the great boxing-match at Long Point.  On Thursday, especially, there was nothing heard of — uptown, downtown, and in the country — but the great prize-fight and the wonderful skill and science, and luck and pluck, and gentleness and behavior generally, of Morrissey and his antagonist, the Benicia Boy. . . . The rush for the paper which happened to contain the only report of the fight was frantic.  Copies were in demand at a shilling apiece, and at 10 A.M., in some parts, as the financial reporters would say, the market for *Heralds* was buoyant at a quarter.  The prize-fight was, we venture to assert, the only topic discussed that morning in bank parlors, counting rooms, and offices generally throughout the city — to say nothing of bar-rooms, and places of like character.  What are we to infer?  That the brutal element in our nature is simply vailed over by social habits, but that it will tear away the vail under adequate provocation?

### Coffee Displacing Tea in the United States:  October 30.

For the past six or eight months at least, the sales of imported teas at this port (which is the type of all the ports) have been unusually small, and the prices ruinous to the importer.  Just before the revulsion of last year teas — having been imported in excess — were selling at a severe loss.  The war with China suddenly imparted vitality to the market.  There was a possibility that our supply of tea might be cut off for years, and the price rose, in a very short space of time, to a point which left a profit on the importation.  But what happened?  People throughout the country were poor, and sought to retrench.  As if by concert with each other, families throughout the North and West began to dispense with tea — at the advance in price — and in many cases to adopt coffee as a substitute.  This was only discovered when the great tea-houses, which had been holding their cargoes throughout the long depression of 1856-7, attempted to realize on them at the advance in price. They found it impossible. Nobody wanted tea. . . . The spring and summer of 1858 passed. From time to time the pulse of the market was felt by auction sales. No advance worth mentioning was realized. The stock of tea in the interior must have been exhausted long since, and yet at the present moment the demand is so small that teas are actually selling in this market at 40 and 50 per cent loss on the cost of importation. In a word, a people who are in the habit of importing and consuming annually over 20,000,000 pounds of tea, have been content this year with one-fourth of that amount. Tea-drinking for the present has almost ceased.

On the other hand, coffee has been in steady demand throughout the year. It soon recovered from the depression caused by the financial crisis, and has been active, at a fair price, almost ever since.

## DEATH OF BENTON[1]

### New York *Tribune*, April 12, 1858

In the death of Mr. Benton the country loses one of its marked public characters. He was a man of great force, but that force was of a personal rather than of an intellectual nature. An intense individuality characterized all that he said and did. His frame was large, his health robust, his nature burly. He was truculent, energetic, intrepid, wilful, and indomitable. He always wore a resolute and determined air, and, simply viewed as an animal, possessed a very commanding aspect. He strode into public life with these qualities all prominent and bristling. Whenever he shone he shone in the exhibition of them. His intellectual powers always appeared as subsidiary; they never took the lead, never appeared to be the propelling force in any of the marked epochs of his life. The leading points of his career were his land-reform measure; his opposition to the old United States Bank; his expunging resolution; his war on Mr. Calhoun after his disappointment in the succession to the Presidency; and his hostility to the Compromise measures of 1850. In all these contests, at least in all but that for the reform of the land system, he bore himself as a fighting man. He carried this so far as to allude, in one of his later senatorial exhibitions, to a pair of pistols, which he said had never been used but a funeral followed.

Mr. Benton had been ten years in the Senate before he was known to the country as a prominent debater. The discussion on the United States Bank question brought him out fully, and was of a

[1] This admirable characterization is typical of Greeley's style at its best.

character to exhibit his powers to the greatest possible advantage. It was a question that touched the feelings and the private interests of individuals deeply, and roused the intensest ardor of all partisan politicians. The debates were heated and fiercely personal. A hand-to-hand political encounter overspread the country. This contest suited Benton exactly. He loved the turmoil and the war, and he rose with each successive exigency until he became, par excellence, the champion of General Jackson's Administration in its contest with the Bank. On one occasion, in 1830–31, he made a speech of four days. At the close of the fourth day Mr. Calhoun sarcastically remarked that Mr. Benton had taken one day longer in his assault on the Bank than it had taken to accomplish the revolution in France.

The intellectual strength of Mr. Benton's efforts never impressed his great adversaries, Clay, Calhoun, and Webster. They never regarded him as belonging to their class intellectually. Yet they always appreciated and dreaded his great personal force. In no case did this peculiar Bentonian ability manifest itself more clearly or more offensively than in the passage of the expunging resolution. General Jackson had been censured by the Senate in a resolution drawn by Mr. Clay for acting "in derogation of the Constitution." Mr. Benton set about to remove the censure by expunging it from the records. He has told how he accomplished this in his "Thirty Years' View." The story is fairly told and illustrates the man perfectly. The whole transaction bears the marks of a haughty, domineering, and repulsive spirit. The reader, as he peruses Mr. Benton's account of it, feels the triumph to be of a coarse and vulgar character, the work of ill-temper and passion, with not a single flash of intellectual or moral elevation in the whole proceeding.

In his political career Mr. Benton often showed himself a fierce and malignant, but never, we think, a generous adversary. It is said that on his deathbed he has done full justice to Mr. Clay in finishing his abridgement of the debates of 1850, and it is pleasant to hear it. We do not doubt that his temper was mollified in later years, as he found himself rapidly approaching the termination of his life. In that debate he came directly in collision with Mr. Clay, and was the only man, indeed, who offered or was able to offer anything like real practical resistance to the impetuous and overbearing march of that great parliamentary leader. In the great debate of 1850 in the Senate, Mr. Clay crushed at will all effective opposition but that of Mr. Benton. On that occasion Benton did not, however, furnish the brains of the debate any more than on previous occasions. Mr. Seward and others of the opposition had done that much more strikingly. But in parliamentary tactics, in the exhibition of personal intrepidity, and in individuality and manner — which in every legislative contest are important elements — Mr. Benton rose superior to every ally. His temper was roused, and he hurled wrath and defiance at his enemies. On a question of parliamentary law he came in immediate conflict with Mr. Clay, who had the majority of the Senate with him and was determined to carry his point. Mr. Benton met him with equal resolution, and with a bulldog ferocity that caused his antagonist to recede and yield the point from considerations of expediency. Mr. Benton was allowed his way after hours of violent struggle and a night's deliberation of the majority. It was, to a very great extent, a triumph of his fighting qualities. Foote, of Mississippi, entered very largely into that debate, and persisted in dogging and attacking Benton. Benton at last bade him stop, he would bear no more of his insults. Foote continued in the same strain. Benton rose from his seat and strode directly toward Foote, as if to throttle him on the spot. Foote fled, and Benton was checked; but Foote never referred to Benton afterward in the Senate. On another occasion Mr. Benton laid himself out to attack Mr. Calhoun. He did it with ability, but his bad blood, his ill-temper, his violence of manner and gross personalities were the predominant characteristics of the attack. There was no pleasure to be derived from it merely as an intellectual demonstration. On the contrary, it only impressed the hearer as repulsive and disgusting.

In all these examples we see where Mr. Benton's power lay as a parliamentarian, a debater, and a man. He never carried his point by winning or convincing, or by pure mental effort. He never reached his objects nor accomplished his successes by mere force of oratory or intellect. He never impressed his audience or the public by sheer strength of mind. It was his intense individuality and animal force, acting upon an intellect of common scope and character, that gave him all his triumphs. His industry was great and his memory remarkable. His knowledge was large, but it was in the domain of facts. He never rose to the consideration of scientific principles, and perhaps never even to the commoner field of philosophic generalization. For himself he claimed to be a man of "measures" rather than of principles or ideas. We should further qualify this claim by saying he was chiefly a man of "facts." His ideas of currency and the "gold" reform, which occupied him for many years, were very crude; and so far as we know, were never improved by after-study or reflection. They found expression in the existing sub-treasury system. Another favorite measure of his was a road to the Pacific, across the continent. His services in establishing the preëmption system in the disposition of the public lands were conspicuous, and their results have been eminently beneficent, but we think the record of his principal "measures" must stop here. . . .

Mr. Benton's moral character as a public man is deserving of very high praise. In his public acts we believe he always followed the dictates of an honest purpose. He did not legislate for popularity nor for pay, nor for any individual advantage in any way. He advocated and opposed public measures on the ground of what he considered to be their merits. His judgments may have been clouded by passion or partisan feeling, as no doubt at times they were, but we believe he was always true to his convictions. Of venality and corruption in legislation he had an instinctive abhorrence, and during the thirty years of his senatorial life we do not think the perfect integrity of his votes on all subjects, whether of a public or private character, was ever impugned. In this respect his example is worthy of the attention of all our rising public men, who, in these budding years of corruption, are likely to be tested by severer temptations than the statesmen of the past. Whatever else is unattainable in reputation to a legislator, the proud distinction of integrity is beyond no man's reach, and it is a virtue that is not likely to lose any of its lustre by being too common.

## MR. POLLARD'S "MAMMY"[1]

### New York *Tribune*, May 18, 1859

There are many instances of filial piety recorded, and very properly recorded, in history. The reader will please recall that which has most warmly touched his sensibilities, or most closely captivated his memory — of some Athenian son or Roman daughter, illustrious for obedience or devotion — and when contemplation has warmed him into an admiration of the Ancients and an inclination to depreciate the Moderns, we shall triumphantly bring forward Edward Pollard, of Washington, in the District of Columbia, Esq., as the champion, in this behalf, of the present day. Mr. Pollard has printed a pamphlet in defence of the proposition to re-open what may be most properly called the African Man-trade. Of Mr. Pollard's arguments in this production we cannot speak, for many reasons, the chief of which is that we have not seen them. But what Mr. Pollard may think of the slave-trade is of small consequence when compared with his filial devotion; and the expression of that feeling we have seen, for it has been disintegrated, if we may say so, from the main work, and, in the highly respectable character

[1] By C. T. Congdon, who wrote many of the most pungent and exasperating of the editorials which helped to provoke the Civil War.

of an Elegant Extract, is now making a fashionable tour through the newspapers.

We trust that the Reverend Doctor Adams has seen this wandering small paragraph; that it has rendered moist his venerable eyes, and warmed the cockles of his ancient heart. For it appears that when Mr. Edward Pollard was a boy, his father had not merely the happiness to possess such a son, but in addition to this blessing in tunics, Mr. Edward Pollard's father — not to put too fine a point upon it — owned niggers. As Mr. Edward Pollard lives in Washington, and is therefore, *prima facie*, an impoverished office-holder, the presumption is that the black diamonds are no longer retained as heir-looms in the Pollard family, but have been sold by papa Pollard, and sent to enjoy themselves upon the sugar-plantations, or to paddle and splash in the rice-swamps. Edward Pollard, Esq., has therefore the inestimable privilege of indulging in the Pleasures of Memory, and the way in which he does it is creditable to his heart. He sighs not for the stalwart field-hands, worth one thousand dollars apiece; he mourns not for the yellow hand-maidens with taper waists and languishing eyes; he weeps not for the coachman who guided his father's chariot; the laundress who got up his infant linen; the cook who prepared the domestic hominy; or the scullion who scrubbed the ancestral floor.

From these treasures, worth, in the aggregate, a very handsome sum of money, Edward Pollard, Esq., turns to drop a tear upon the grave of his "mammy." "Mammy" was Edward Pollard's nurse. From the sable heart of "mammy" he first drew his snowy sustenance. In the dark arms of "mammy" he tasted the titillation of his first dandle. From the black hand of "mammy" he received his initial corn-cake. Her voice chanted his vesper lullaby and summoned him to his matin ablutions. Mr. Pollard "confesses" — although, under the circumstances, we do not see the necessity of the qualification — that he is not ashamed of his affection for his "mammy." She died; for all "mammies" — even the "mammy" of Mr. Pollard — were or are mortal. Then came her sepulchral honors. Wiping the copious tears from his eyes, Mr. Pollard informs us that "in his younger days" he made "little monuments over the grave of his mammy." How many he made he does not inform us. What material he used, we are not told; but we know that infant architects have a partiality for mud.

And now Mr. Pollard, discarding the sentimental, waxes savage. Standing over the grave of his "mammy," and suddenly getting angry without any apparent occasion, he cries: "Do you think I could ever have borne to see her consigned to the demon abolitionists?" There is really no need of all this vehemence. We perfectly

understand the case.  We appreciate Mr. Pollard's feelings.  We
know that he could not have borne it.  For who then would have
ministered to his necessities?  Who would have darned his juvenile
hose?  Who would have rocked his cradle?  Who would have "run
to catch him when he fell and kissed the place to make it well?"
And, moreover, had "the demon abolitionists" caught Mr. Pollard's
"mammy," he is perfectly certain that they would have "consigned
her lean, starved corpse to a pauper grave."  From which we infer
that in addition to the mud memorials heretofore mentioned, as
erected by Mr. Pollard, in the first gush of childhood's sorrow, he
has since placed over the grave of "Mammy" something very splendid in the way of a mausoleum.  For, as we have already noticed,
"mammy" is no more;  and Edward Pollard, Esq., to use his own
most charming language, can "only look at her through the mist of
long years."  She died without the aid, assistance or cruel commerce
of "the demon abolitionists," and Mr. Pollard, who appears to be
an elderly gentleman, has to pay a washing-bill every Saturday, and
as he d—ns the laundress in respect of buttons, remembers "mammy"
and conjures up the image of "the dear old slave."  He recalls how,
when his mother scolded him, his "mammy" protected and humored
him; and seems, in his desolation to have come to the conclusion that
this is rather a weary world.  There appears nothing to do but to
put Edward Pollard, Esq., out to nurse — dry-nurse or wet-nurse, according to circumstances—and to strive by every tender art to divert
his mind from the distracting memory of the original "mammy."
Of all the poor white people in Washington, he seems to be in the
lowest spirits — if we except Mr. James Buchanan.

Whether the result of Mr. Edward Pollard's grief for his "mammy"
will re-open the African Man-trade, is more than we can determine.
The connection between his bereavement and that branch of commerce we have been somewhat at a loss to discover.  We have been
able to conclude only that there now exists at the South a dearth of
"mammies," and that Mr. Pollard, having felt through long years
the want of that useful article, seeks to replenish the market by the
importation of what we may call the raw material.  Left himself
an orphan in respect of "mammy," at a tender age, with his locks
unkempt, with his face dirty, with his mouth pitifully gaping for
gruel, and with his trousers torn, he looks forward to future Pollards
— still, if we may use the figure, mere shrubs in a like condition
of emptiness and squalor.  He seeks, like a true philanthropist, to
provide for this great want; and when the importation commences,
"mammies" will, we suppose, be regularly quoted in the Prices
Current.  Meanwhile, Mr. Pollard's case must be attended to by
the charitable.  A pair of "mammies" — one for him and one for
the White House — should be purchased at once by subscription.

## THE DEFENSIVE SQUARE OF AUSTRIAN ITALY[1]

New York *Times*, July 16, 1859

The main merit of Peschiera is that this fortress lies on an island, and was captured by the Duke of Genoa in 1848. At this time the Sardinians crossed the Mincio after several hours' hard fighting; and if we follow the windings of the Mincio we shall find countless elbows formed in the elbows of the regular army, at places like Salianza, Molini, and Borghette. These places make up the base of the allied army. The line of the Mincio is the base of the new campaign we are about to open.

Almost at the southern end of the river Mincio lies the strong fortress of Mantua, the only Gibraltar of Austria in Italy guaranteed by the treaties of 1815. Mantua, as we have said, lies on a lake of the river Mincio. In spite of the labors spent on it, Mantua still holds the next rank to Verona. It is a post of danger for the army shut between its walls, rather than for the enemy without. After a battle of several hours' duration, the Sardinians at Goito gave way; and, if we follow up the course of the Mincio, we shall find innumerable elbows formed by the sympathy of youth. Defended by Wurmser in 1797, Austria surrendered to Napoleon III in 1859. Notwithstanding the toil spent by Austria on the spot, we should have learned that we are protected by a foreign fleet coming up suddenly on our question of citizenship. A canal cuts Mantua in two; but we may rely on the most cordial Cabinet Minister of the new power in England.

## CORRECTION

New York *Times*, July 18, 1859

We owe it to our readers to say that, by a confusion of manuscripts, sent up at a late hour on Friday night, our leading article of Saturday on the "Austrian Defensive Square" was rendered perfectly unintelligible. The article appeared correctly in our second edition, but we reprint it today in another column. As our extremely ridiculous blunder afforded matter for much legitimate and good-natured merriment to our contemporaries of the Sunday press, and a happy occasion for airing a little envy, malice, and uncharitableness to the less respectable among the daily journals, the newspaper world is indebted to us for making it, and our apology is addressed to the world of readers alone.

---

[1] By W. H. Hurlburt, a brilliant if dissipated writer long with the *Times* and later with Manton Marble on the *World*. This editorial was written after a somewhat too gay evening party in honor of a friend departing for Europe.

## JOHN BROWN AND A SLAVE INSURRECTION[1]

New York *Evening Post*, October 18, 1859

The stories connecting the name of "old Brown of Ossawatomie," as he is called, with the leadership of this fanatical enterprise are, we are induced to think, well-founded; and in that event the whole affair might be regarded as a late fruit of the violence which the slaveholders introduced into Kansas. Brown was one of the early settlers in that territory; he was a conspicuous object of persecution all through the troubles; his property was destroyed; he and his family were cruelly treated on several occasions; three or four of his sons were killed by Southern desperadoes; and these many exasperations drove him to madness. He has not been regarded since, we are told, as a perfectly sane man. He has been known to vow vengeance against the whole class of slaveholders for the outrages perpetrated by their representatives in Kansas, and this insurrection, if he is at the head of it, is the manner in which he gluts his resentments. Frenzied by the remembrance of his wrongs, his whole nature turned into gall by the bitter hatreds stirred up in Kansas, and reckless of consequences, he has plunged into the work of blood.

Passion does not reason; but if Brown reasoned and desired to give a public motive to his personal rancors, he probably said to himself that "the slave drivers had tried to put down freedom in Kansas by force of arms, and he would try to put down slavery in the same means." Thus the bloody instructions which they taught return to plague the inventors. They gave, for the first time in the history of the United States, an example of the resort to arms to carry out their political schemes, and dreadful as the retaliation is which Brown has initiated, must take their share of the responsibility. They must remember that they accustomed men, in their Kansas forays, to the idea of using arms against their political opponents, that by their crimes and outrages they drove hundreds to madness, and that the feelings of bitterness and revenge thus generated have since rankled in the heart. Brown has made himself an organ of these in a fearfully significant way.

No one can think of the possible results of an outbreak of this kind, should it become general, without shuddering; without calling up to his imagination the most terrible scenes of incendiarism, carnage, and rape. In nearly all the Southern States the negroes greatly preponderate in number. Many of them, it is true, are too ignorant and stupid to take any effective part in an insurrection;

---

[1] John Brown began his famous raid into Virginia to free the slaves and excite an insurrection on October 16, 1859; he was captured on the 18th, severely wounded, and after trial in the Virginia courts, he was found guilty of treason and publicly hanged on December 2.

## AMINADAB SLEEK AT JONES' WOOD.

"My Friends, there is no patriotic duty on earth more gratifying to my feelings than to make a speech over Mr. Lincoln's political grave. [Loud cheers.] I do not make this remark out of any unkindness to Mr. Lincoln, but I believe that the good of his own country requires it."—*Douglas's Speech, Wednesday, September 12th, 1860.*

From *Vanity Fair*, October 13, 1860.

others, too, are profoundly attached to their masters or their families; but these excepted, there are yet thousands able and willing to strike for their emancipation. It has been impossible to keep them in entire ignorance of the blessings of freedom, and of the possibility of attaining it by force of arms; the fugitive slaves of the North have found means of communicating with their old comrades; the Abolitionists have spoken to them by pictures, if not by language; Democratic orators have told them falsely that the entire North was engaged in a crusade against the South for the sake of the slaves; and as servants in the cities they have heard the talk of the parlor and barrooms, and in innumerable other ways have been made to think and to desire. When the hour comes, therefore, they will not be found either so incapable or so docile as the slaveholders seem to suppose.

But what a condition of society is that in which half the population constantly menaces the other half with civil war and murder; in which the leading classes go to sleep every night, carelessly, it may be, over the crater of a volcano; and in which the dangers do not lessen, as in other societies, with time, but grow with its growth until an explosion becomes as inevitable as the eruptions of Etna or Vesuvius! What a condition of society, to be extended over the virgin territories of the West, the seat of our future empire, and for which politicians should clamor and sear their consciences, and desperadoes should fight!

How insane the policy which would recruit and extend this form of social existence, even while it is becoming unmanageable as it is! Open the gates to the slave trade, cry the Southerners, who are as great fanatics as Brown; tap the copious resources of Africa, let new millions of blacks be added to the enormous number that now cultivate our fields, let the alarming disproportion between them and the whites be increased; it is a blessed institution, and we cannot have too much of it! But while they speak the tocsin sounds, the blacks are in arms, their houses are in flames, their wives and children driven into exile or killed, and a furious servile war stretches its horrors over years. That is the blessed institution you ask us to foster and spread and worship, and for the sake of which you even spout your impotent threats against the grand edifice of the Union!

## [JOHN BROWN OF OSSAWATOMIE]
### Springfield *Republican*, 1859

*Brown's Character:* Oct. 19, 1859.

He is so constituted that when he gets possessed of an idea he carries it out with unflinching fidelity to all its original consequences, as they seem to him, hesitating at no absurdity, and deterred by no unpleasant consequences to him personally.   He is a Presbyterian in his faith and feels that it is for this very purpose that God has reared him up.   This is evident in the answers given in his catechism, as he lay chained and bloody, with fierce eyes against him and hearts thirsting for his blood.   His perfect coolness and self-possession, his evident truthfulness and transparent sincerity, and the utter absence of fear in his manner, commanded the respect of all about him.   The universal feeling is that John Brown is a hero — a misguided and insane man, but nevertheless inspired with a genuine heroism.   He has a large infusion of the stern old Puritan element in him.

### An Unfair Trial: Oct. 24.

The whole manner in which the trial is conducted shows that the Virginians have not recovered from their original fright.   They scent a rescue in the air, surround their poor wounded and worn prisoners with bayonets, and promise to bring them to the gallows within thirty days.   Let them go ahead in their crazy cowardice and see if their "ain roof-trees" are any firmer for it.

### Brown's Speech on Receiving Sentence: Nov. 4.

In calm dignity, in the conscious rectitude of good intentions, in an honest and hearty faith in Christianity, it has in it heroic elements that elevate it toward the sublime. . . . If he had been a weak man or a wicked man, a felon in the common acceptation of that word, when the sentence was pronounced upon him there would have been a general and tumultuous demonstration of satisfaction in the Charlestown court-room.   Instead of that, the impressive silence was broken only by the clapping of a single pair of hands, and the people were shocked and mortified that even one man should have been found in Virginia who appreciated so poorly the character of the prisoner and the nature of his condemnation.   This scene shows the wonderful impression made by Brown upon those about him.   It is this great sincerity and heroic self-sacrifice to what he believed to be right that gave him such influence over the men who enlisted in his scheme, and that has so impressed the Virginians with respect, from Governor Wise down, and that will make it a difficult thing to hang him.

### Awaiting Death: Nov. 12.

We can conceive of no event that could so deepen the moral hostility of the people of the free States to slavery as this execution.   This not because the acts of Brown are generally approved, for they are not.   It is because the nature and spirit of the man are seen to be great and noble, and everybody feels that he acted from feelings that do honor to human nature, and that are to be condemned only because they were not directed by wisdom and soundness of mind. John Brown is neither a traitor nor a murderer in intention. His death will be a result of his own folly, to be sure, but that will not prevent his being considered a martyr to his hatred of oppression, and all who sympathize with him in that sentiment will find their hatred grow stronger and deeper as they contemplate his death. Nobody can respect an institution to the safety of which the death of the too ardent lover of liberty is essential. If Virginia were wise she would see this and be magnanimous; but she is neither wise nor magnanimous in anything that concerns her property in human brains and bones, and so we suppose the appointed hanging will occur.

*The Day After the Execution:* Dec. 3.

John Brown still lives. The great State of Virginia has hung his venerable body upon the ignominious gallows, and released John Brown himself to join the "noble army of martyrs." There need be no tears for him. Few men die so happily, so satisfied with time, place, and circumstance, as did he. . . . A Christian man, hung by Christians for acting upon his convictions of duty — a brave man hung for a chivalrous and self-sacrificing deed of humanity — a philanthropist hung for seeking the liberty of oppressed men. No outcry about violated law can cover up the essential enormity of a deed like this.

## THE HELPER BOOK [1]

### New York *Tribune*, January 12, 1860

"The stars in their courses fought against Sisera." The slavery question cannot be discussed, even in the most commendatory manner, without inuring to the advancement of the cause of truth and righteousness. The Congressional denunciations of Helper's book are producing the most astonishing effect in promoting its circulation. The orders flow in for it from all quarters, in all quantities, from a single copy up to three hundred in a bunch. We do not know how many copies have been ordered, but we have reason to believe the number already exceeds one hundred thousand. The price is now reduced to about eighteen dollars a hundred in conse-

[1] Hinton Rowan Helper, a "poor white" of North Carolina, published "The Impending Crisis of the South, and How to Meet It," in 1857, and by 1859 it attained an enormous circulation. It attacked the oligarchy of the wealthy slaveholders in the South as a fatal impediment to the advancement and happiness of the millions of whites who had little or no property. Slavery, Helper argued, would have to be abolished in order to give the whites a proper economic and social position, to stimulate industry and commerce, and to encourage cities and schools.

quence of the extensive sale. The work goes everywhere, through all sorts of channels, to the North, East, South, and West. Old fogy Union-saving merchants in the Southern trade stand aghast at the sly requests slipped in all over the South, in the shape of notes and postscripts for goods, for "that Helper book that is making such a fuss in Congress." Innocent bales, bags, boxes, and barrels bound for the South, looking for all the world as though they contained nothing more inflammatory than coffee, calico, hardware, and other similar commodities, have each a copy of Helper tucked furtively away in the hidden centre of their contents. In this way the work is penetrating the whole South in a manner that no hunter for incendiary pamphlets would suppose or can possibly arrest. If we go about the streets of this most conservative city, ten to one we are delayed at the first crossing by a hand-cart or wheelbarrow load of Helper. It is Helper on the counter, Helper at the stand, Helper in the shop and out of the shop, Helper here, Helper there, Helper everywhere. It looks now as though every man, woman, and child in the United States was bound to have a Helper before the year is out. There never was a political pamphlet that had such a rushing demand and sale before, with the exception, perhaps, of the Life of Scott issued in the Presidential campaign of 1852. For the extraordinary impetus thus given to the sale of this highly valuable and interesting work we renewedly tender our heartfelt acknowledgments to the "Gulf Squadron" of members of the Federal House of Representatives at Washington. We certainly never expected them to do so much for the cause of their country, and we dare say they are equally astounded and sorry to have aided it so essentially. Let them be thankful that they have been the means of public enlightenment on an important topic, and that they have widely contributed to the spread of anti-slavery sentiment. It shall be gratefully remembered by the children of· oppression, and be chiselled on their tombstones.

> *The meanest reed that trembles in the wind,*
> *If Heaven select it for its instrument,*
> *May shed celestial music on the breeze,*
> *As clearly as the pipe whose notes*
> *Befit the lip of Phœbus.*

## [SLAVE LIFE PREFERRED BY NEGROES]

### De Bow's Review, April, 1860

A few days ago, Ben H. Baker, Esq., says the Montgomery *Mail*, visited the city and caused to be introduced a bill in the legislature by which twelve free negroes are allowed to become slaves. The bill passed both houses and was signed by the Governor; the speedy transaction of the affair being caused mainly by the entire confidence which members of both houses have in the personal integrity and fine intelligence of Mr. Baker. The facts are briefly these: These negroes, men, women, and children, have been reared by Mr. Young Edwards, of Russell County, and have always lived with him as servants. Lately someone informed these negroes that, being free, the sheriff would be required to expel them, under a provision of the code, within thirty days. At this they were greatly alarmed, and protested that they were unwilling to leave their master, and were perfectly willing to remain his slaves, and in fact preferred it. Mr. Baker visited the negroes, and explained to them their position and rights fully; and the upshot was, they induced him to come and lay their case before the Legislature, asking it to allow them to become the slaves of Mr. Edwards. The bill was accordingly passed. It provides that the probate court of Russell shall have the negroes brought before it, and diligently take testimony to ascertain if any undue influence has been used to obtain their consent to become slaves; and upon being satisfied that they, wittingly and with full knowledge of their rights, desire to enter a state of servitude, shall decree them to be the slaves of the person they may choose to be their owner.

These negroes know what their own best interest is. They will be better fed and clothed than ever Horace Greeley or Lucy Stone was, before these worthies made money by shovelling the filth of fanaticism; they will be better rewarded for their labor than any operative in any cotton mill in all Lawrence; and in sickness and old age, forever, will be tended carefully and surrounded with all necessary comforts. And so they don't choose to go into the wretchedness, privation, and squalor of free negro life in the North.

## THE ISSUES OF THIS CAMPAIGN

Springfield *Republican*, August 25, 1860

The South, through the mouth of many of its leading politicians and journals, defies the North to elect Abraham Lincoln to the presidency. It threatens secession in case he shall be elected. It arrogantly declares that he shall never take his seat. It passes resolutions of the most outrageous and insolent character, insulting every man who dares to vote for what they call a "Black Republican." To make a long matter very short and plain, they claim the privilege of conducting the government in all the future, as they have in all the past, for their own benefit and in their own way, with the alternative of dissolving the Union of the States. Now, if the non-slaveholding people have any spirit at all, they will settle this question at once and forever.    Look at the history of the last two administrations, in which the slave interest has had undisputed sway. This sway, the most disgraceful and shameless of anything in the history of the government, must not be thrown off or else the Union will be dissolved.    Let's try it!    Are we forever to be governed by a slaveholding minority?    Will the passage of four years more of misrule make it any easier for the majority to assume its functions?

There are many reasons why we desire to see this experiment tried this fall.    If the majority cannot rule the country without the secession of the minority, it is time the country knew it.    If the country can only exist under the rule of an oligarchy, let the fact be demonstrated at once, and let us change our institutions.    We desire to see the experiment tried, because we wish to have the Southern people, who have been blinded and cheated by the politicians, learn that a "Black Republican" respects the requirements of the Constitution and will protect their interests.    Harmony between the two sections of this country can never be secured until the South has learned that the North is not its enemy, but its best friend.    We desire to see it tried, that the whole horde of corrupt officials at Washington may be swept by the board, and something of decency and purity introduced there.    We desire to see it, that the government may be restored to its original integrity.    And any Northern man who has not pluck enough to stand up and help do this thing is a poltroon.    It will be tried, and our minority friends may make up their mind to it.

## THE HOME OF JOHN C. CALHOUN

*De Bow's Review*, September, 1860

We saw Mr. Calhoun first in Greenville District, South Carolina, in 1838, and heard him, in the presence of an assembled multitude, discourse of the independent treasury, and meet in debate the Hon. Waddy Thompson, who had then the hardihood to splinter a lance with him.    How the eyes of the old man flashed and his form towered, and how the welkin rang with the loud plaudits!    He was a guest that night at the simple farmhouse where we resided.    Next we saw him in the old theatre at Charleston, which was thronged from pit to dome.    "If ever," said he in opening, and the multitude stood without a pulsation, "if ever a representative had just reason to be proud of his constituents, I am that representative and you are those constituents."    Again, and this time we were companions on that memorable trip to the West (it was our first trip, from which we did not return, and hence the *Review*), it was our never-to-be-forgotten privilege of witnessing the ovations which, all along the banks of the great river, from New Orleans to Memphis, were paid to him by assembled hosts. At Vicksburg, Jefferson Davis addressed the great statesman, who, embarrassed by the compliment, said in reply that he was "unaccustomed to speak without a subject," which caused some merriment. On the part of the beautiful ladies who came on board, it was remarked that it was a custom established on the river by Mr. Clay that they had the right to kiss any great man who chanced to be passing by. "I dare not pretend," said Mr. Calhoun, "to vie with Mr. Clay in gallantry." Hereupon his son, a chivalrous young army officer, peace to his ashes, remarked to us aside, provoked by his father's austerity, "the old gentleman would do better to make me his deputy in the matter." A plain homespun countryman exclaimed on approaching, quite audibly, "Great God! It is old Jackson!" and another, somewhat inebriated, in attempting rather roughly to approach, was struck aback by the imposing presence, but rallying himself, at last found words, which the reader, we trust, will forgive us for repeating — "Mr. Calhoun, I have sworn by you all my life, and next to the Almighty, you are the greatest man in the world." But now the great Memphis convention is in session, and its president has risen from the chair to speak upon the questions at issue. Not a breath stirred the vast auditory. Oratory such as this, which spellbinds and yet deals not in the lightning and the thunderbolt, is a new revelation at the West; but when the words come, in speaking of the old Mississippi, that it is "an inland sea," there goes up a shout which is like the roar of Niagara, and rising from their seats, and waving their hats in wild enthusiasm, these men of the West give cheer after cheer to the Palmetto Chief. Not soon did the turmoil cease. In 1847, we took tea with him at Washington, and heard him speak of his intended treatise upon government, which, he said, would not be appreciated for twenty-five years; and when the smoke of Buena Vista had cleared away, and men began to agitate the nomination of its hero for the Presidency, there came to us at New Orleans, through the mail, one of those laconic dispatches which Mr. Calhoun only could indite, and which we remember nearly word for word, and will give, in remarkable illustration of his capacity for condensation:

I see that General Taylor's arrival among you is announced, and it is said he will run for the Presidency. How stands the fact, and what are understood to be his opinions in regard to party nominations for the Presidency, the "Wilmot Proviso," and the Tariff of 1846?

But space compels me to pause in these, to us, interesting reminiscences. They are recalled by everything around us. We are on classical ground. We tread the halls which so long answered only to *his* step. We are in his library, and here are the books which he read, and this is his writing desk, and his lamp, and his chair, and his walking-cane, as he left them. Here is a portrait, which shows him worn by the grim advances of age and disease, and another, a glorious picture, new to us at every point, showing him in those proud days of early manhood, when he was the very master-spirit of the Monroe Cabinet! Near by hangs the portrait, the first we have seen taken in his prime, of his friend and almost twin-brother in fame, George McDuffie.

Fit abode for such a man! — from its grand scenery and as grand historic associations. Just here was the site of Fort Rutledge (hence the name which Mr. Calhoun changed from "Fort Place" to "Fort Hill"), a relic of which we find in an old, now filled-up well. Tradition has it that this well was dug by the white inhabitants who were besieged and cut off from the river by innumerable savage hordes, and in their attempt afterward to escape, were surprised and ruthlessly put to death. One alone of the whole party remained to tell the tale. Tradition has it also, and Mr. Calhoun was wont to tell it himself, on the authority of his father-in-law, the story being confirmed to him by a well-informed Indian historian, that in the far remote past, ere yet the white man had been anywhere seen, a giant struggle took place at this very point between the Cherokees, who inhabited the country, and a tribe of Northern Senecas, who, victorious over every tribe in the Southern marches, were first brought to a stand here on the banks of the stream which thence took the name of Seneca, and were driven back with fearful slaughter. May not future history have in store a like record of other *Northern* tribes?

## THE PERIL OF THE SOUTH [1]

### Charleston *Courier*, November, 1860

Immediate danger will be brought to slavery in all the frontier States. When a party is enthronged at Washington, in the executive and legislative departments of the government, whose creed is to repeal the fugitive slave law, the underground railroad will become an overground railroad. The tenure of slave property will be felt to be weakened; and the slave will be sent down to the cotton States for sale, and the frontier States enter on the policy of making themselves free States.

[1] The *Courier* was the mouthpiece of Robert Barnwell Rhett and the extreme secessionists of South Carolina.

With the control of the government of the United States, and an organized and triumphant North to sustain them, the abolitionists will renew their operations upon the South with increased courage. The thousands in every country who look up to power and make gain out of the future will come out in support of the abolition government. They will organize; and from being a Union party to support an abolition government, they will become like the government they support, abolitionists. They will have an abolitionist party in the South of Southern men. The contest for slavery will no longer be one between the North and the South. It will be in the South, between the people of the South.

If in our present position of power and unitedness we have the raid of John Brown, and twenty towns burned down in Texas in one year by abolitionists, what will be the measures of insurrection and incendiarism which must follow our notorious and abject prostration to abolition rule in Washington, with all the patronage of the Federal government and a Union organization in the South to support it? Secret conspiracy and its attendant horrors, with rumors of more horrors, will hover over every portion of the South; while in the language of the Black Republican patriarch, Giddings, they will "laugh at your calamities, and mock when your fear cometh."

Already there is uneasiness throughout the South as to the stability of its institution of slavery. But with a submission to the rule of abolitionists at Washington, thousands of slaveholders will despair of the institution. While the condition of things in the frontier States will force the slaves on the market of the cotton States, the timid in the cotton States will sell their slaves. The general distrust must affect purchasers. The consequence must be that slave property will be greatly depreciated. We see advertisements for the sale of slaves in some of the cotton States for the simple object of getting rid of them; and we know that standing orders for the purchase of slaves in this market have been withdrawn, on account of an anticipated decline of value from the political condition of the country.

We suppose that, taking in view all these things, it is not extravagant to estimate that the submission of the South to the administration of the Federal government under Messrs. Lincoln and Hamlin must reduce the value of slaves in the South $100 each. It is computed that there are 4,300,000 slaves in the United States. Here, therefore, is a loss to the Southern people of $430,000,000 on their slaves alone. Of course real estate of all kinds must also partake in the depreciation of slaves. Slave property is the foundation of all property in the South. When security in this is shaken, all other property partakes of its instability.  Banks, stocks, bonds, must be influenced.  Timid men will sell out and leave the South.  Confusion, distrust, and pressure must reign.

The ruin of the South, by the emancipation of her slaves, is not like the ruin of any other people.  It is not a mere loss of liberty, like the Italians under the Bourbons.  It is not heavy taxation, which must still leave the means of living or otherwise taxation defeats itself.  But it is the loss of liberty, property, home, country — everything that makes life worth having.  And this loss will probably take place under circumstances of suffering and horror unparalleled in the history of nations.  We must preserve our liberties and institutions under penalties greater than those which impend over any people in the world.

## THE CRISIS AND THE REMEDY [1]

New York *Herald*, January 5, 1861

Let the people, therefore, speak.  Of the five millions of voters in the United States, it is within bounds to say that four million three hundred thousand are conservative in sentiment and prepared to concede to the South their reasonable demands.  A constituent convention of the Southern States is already impending.  The effervescence which has resulted in mob rule, violence, the seizure of national fortresses, custom houses, postoffices, and arsenals in South Carolina is generally disapproved of, even in slaveholding communities.  If similar acts are committed elsewhere they will be isolated and irresponsible, and the popular voice will fail to sanction them.  The general idea at the South, as is apparent from a study of the advices from the separate States, is that each aggrieved member of the confederation should secede, but that, once having passed acts of secession, they should leave relations with the Federal government as they are, and have recourse to a constituent convention of the Southern States to decide upon future definite action.

It is from such a Southern constituent convention that welfare to the Union may yet proceed.  It will be assembled, necessarily, to the comparative exclusion of the small fry of mere sectional politicians, and the guarantees which it asks will be sensible, reasonable, and such as must commend themselves to the common sense of the masses of the people in the Central and Western States.  They will insist upon the recognition of the property rights of their citizens everywhere;  upon the needful stipulations which intolerance

[1] A number of the New York newspapers, including the *Day Book*, *Daily News*, and the *Journal of Commerce*, were opposed to any coercion of the seceding States; but none went to the length reached by James Gordon Bennett's *Herald*.

has hitherto denied; upon full liberty to carry slaves into the common territory, and upon the recognition of universal toleration of opinion respecting slavery as a social institution in the several States of the Union.   They will submit these different conditions, as amendments to the Constitution, to the Northern States, earnestly inviting acceptance of them, and assigning a period, similar in principle to that which was appointed for the ratification of the Constitution in 1787, when all States which shall have agreed to them shall be considered as forming thenceforth the future United States of America.

It cannot be doubted for an instant, by those who have carefully analyzed the vote at the last Presidential election, and considered the reaction in the Republican ranks which has since taken place, that the people of the North and West will respond at once to the rational requirements of their Southern fellow-citizens.   They will not pause in choosing between the happiness and prosperity which will flash upon the country out of concord, and the misery which perseverance in the chaotic byways of Abolition would produce. But, in order to be prepared to act with the promptitude which the occasion demands, the voice of the Northern States ought to be raised now, without the procrastination of an instant, in calling for constituent State conventions by legislatures north of the Potomac. The propositions of the South must be submitted to the non-slave-holding States separately, and these States should hold themselves ready to consider them.   It is not an issue of parties.   It is the people only who, "like the voice of many waters," must overpower and drown beneath a deluge of patriotism the anti-Union heresies which infect the republic.   Let massmeetings everywhere call upon our Northern State Legislatures to summon together constituent State conventions.   If New York begins, Pennsylvania, New Jersey, Michigan, Illinois, Indiana, will speedily follow their example, and a contagion of those sentiments which lighted the fires of Bunker Hill, and stained with blood the ice-blocks of the Delaware, will spread from the Atlantic shore to the log-cabin of the most distant squatter in Nebraska.   "The Union must and shall be preserved" will be echoed and reëchoed far and near, and may even produce its rebound in the frozen consciences of Massachusetts and Vermont.

In a constituent Southern convention, and in constituent State conventions, assembled at the call of massmeetings everywhere by our Northern State Legislatures, to consider the amendments to the Constitution which the exigency of the times demands, is to be found the remedy of every evil.   It is possible that States east of the Connecticut River may reject the propositions which the South presents; but if they do so let them act upon their own peril.   Let them elect Garrison, Greeley, or Wendell Phillips as the president of a rigid Abolitionist republic; let them annex themselves to Canada; let them feed upon their own provincial self-conceit, love for isms, hatred for everybody but themselves, and console themselves in the enjoyment of a petty, intolerant, hard-bargaining, lawless, clergy-beridden nationality, with the reflection that not only the Southern, but the Middle States, are glad to get rid of them, and have regarded them as an incubus upon the Union for over a quarter of a century. Meanwhile, let the action of the Union-loving States be prompt. There is no time to be lost. With proper diligence massmeetings may initiate action on the part of all our Northern legislatures within the present month. In February the South will be ready to present its propositions, and before the period has arrived for the inauguration of Mr. Lincoln the tempest that now threatens so menacingly may have been entirely dispelled from our political horizon.

## THE INAUGURAL ADDRESS OF MR. LINCOLN

New York *Herald*, March 5, 1861

It would have been almost as instructive if President Lincoln had contented himself with telling his audience yesterday a funny story and let them go. His inaugural is but a paraphrase of the vague generalities contained in his pilgrimage speeches, and shows clearly either that he has not made up his mind respecting his future course, or else that he desires, for the present, to keep his intentions to himself. The stupendous questions of the last month have been whether the incoming Administration would adopt a coercive or a conciliatory policy towards the Southern States; whether it would propose satisfactory amendments to the Constitution, convening an extra session of Congress for the purpose of considering them; and whether, with the spirit of the statesmen who laid the cornerstone of the institutions of the republic, it would rise to the dignity of the occasion, and meet as was fitting the terrible crisis through which the country is passing. The inaugural gives no satisfaction on any of these points. Parts of it contradict those that precede them, and where the adoption of any course is hinted at, a studious disavowal of its being a recommendation is appended. Not a small portion of the columns of our paper, in which the document is amplified, look as though they were thrown in as a mere make-weight. A resolve to procrastinate, before committing himself, is apparent throughout. Indeed, Mr. Lincoln closes by saying that "there is no object in being in a hurry," and that "nothing valuable can be lost by taking time." Filled with careless *bonhomie* as this first

proclamation to the country of the new President, is, it will give
but small contentment to those who believe that not only its prosperity, but its very existence is at stake.

The inaugural opens by deliberately ignoring the true issue between the Southern and Northern States. It declares that the
slaveholding members of the confederation have no grievances;
that "nobody is hurt," or will have a right to imagine himself hurt,
until the peculiar institution is actively invaded when it exists.
"Apprehension," he says, "seems to exist among the people of the
Southern States, that their property, and their peace and personal
security, are to be endangered. There has never been any reasonable cause for apprehension. Indeed, the most ample evidence to
the contrary has all the while existed, and been open to their
inspection." The same spirit runs through the whole speech. He
quotes the Chicago platform resolution against John Brown, as
though that were an all-sufficient reply to his objections, and elsewhere exclaims: — "Is it true that any right written in the Constitution has been denied? I think not." Yet, in the line and a half
which is all that he thinks proper to devote to the momentous
question of the common Territories, out of which has grown the
sectional strife which convulses the Union, he virtually kicks to
pieces the whole groundwork of Republican aggressions, and confesses the untenableness of their past claims. "Must Congress,"
he says, "protect slavery in the Territories? The Constitution does
not expressly say."

A couple of paragraphs devoted to the Fugitive Slave law contain
acknowledgment of his duty to enforce it, but while emphatically
promising to do so, the President quibbles respecting the manner
of carrying out the law, and interpolates for the benefit of his
abolitionist friends a query respecting free negroes which is completely out of place. "Might it not be well," he asks, in their behalf,
"to provide by law for the enforcement of that clause in the Constitution which 'guarantees that the citizens of each State shall be
entitled to all the privileges and immunities of citizens in the several
States?'" This is a covert fling, of course, at South Carolina, whose
recent legislation on the subject of free negroes is thus held up for
reprobation. . . .

In a word, the inaugural is not a crude performance — it abounds
in traits of craft and cunning. It bears marks of indecision, and yet
of strong coercive proclivities, with serious doubts whether the
government will be able to gratify them. It is so clearly intended
to admit of a double, or even of any possible interpretation, that
many will content themselves with waiting for the progress of events,
in the meanwhile seeking in it for no meaning at all. It is neither

candid nor statesmanlike; nor does it possess any essential of dignity or patriotism. It would have caused a Washington to mourn and would have inspired Jefferson, Madison, or Jackson with contempt. With regard to the ultimate projects of Mr. Lincoln, the public is no wiser than before. It is sincerely to be trusted that he is yet ignorant of them himself.

## THE POLICY OF THE ADMINISTRATION DEVELOPED

New York *Herald*, April 9, 1861

It is becoming too evident that, so far as a vicious, imbecile, demoralized Administration possesses power, the hideous horrors of civil war are about to be forced upon the country. The deliberations of Mr. Lincoln and his advisers have been shrouded in mystery; but the very concealment they have affected has betrayed their iniquitous purposes. Amid the contradictory reports that have lately prevailed, unmistakable facts have compelled a tardy and reluctant acquiescence in the conviction that aggressive measures are contemplated against the seceding States, and that hostile demonstrations, upon an extensive scale, have for many weeks formed part of the design of the government. Ominous and painful uncertainty has, at length, given place to the fearful prospect of an internecine strife between the North and the South, which is inevitable unless the troops that are being sent southward, more patriotic than their leaders, shall emulate the example of French soldiers when ordered to fire upon the people, and refuse to imbrue their hands in the blood of their fellow-citizens. The factious pressure upon the President for the adoption of a definite coercive policy has been crowned with success. The doors of the temple of Janus have been thrown open, and if, which is doubtful, proclivities for peace ever existed, they have been buried out of sight. Mr. Lincoln has fallen back upon the war doctrines of his inaugural, or his still less ambiguous utterances during the memorable journey from Springfield to Harrisburg.

"Irrepressible conflict" has thus succeeded in developing the outlines of a fearful shadow over the land; but it is to be hoped that the very armies which are soon to be brought face to face will shrink from permitting it to acquire a bloody substance. Far better that the Union should be dismembered forever than that fraternal hands should be turned against one another, to disfigure the land by slaughter and carnage. The masses of the population reprobate the blood-thirsty imbecility of the Washington government. They are forewarned, by the gigantic footsteps with which anarchy has

been progressing, that a military despotism is imminent, which may
reduce the country to the lowest place in the scale of nations. In
the annals of history there would be found no parallel of a people,
from such a height of prosperity as the United States have attained,
so recklessly plunging its future destiny into an abyss of ruin, if the
present mismanagement of affairs is allowed to continue. The
popular sentiment is everywhere peaceful, and the time cannot be
distant when the shameful manner in which Mr. Lincoln and his
Cabinet are sacrificing the welfare of the land, and betraying its
most sacred interests, will call forth an outbreak of indignation
before which even Republican fanaticism and intolerance will
tremble.

## THE WAR AGAINST THE GOVERNMENT OF THE UNITED STATES[1]

New York *Times*, April 13, 1861

The Disunion conspiracy, which has for the last twenty years
been gnawing at the heart-strings of the great American republic,
has at last culminated in open war upon its glittering and resplendent
flag.   For the first time in the history of the United States, an organized attempt is made to destroy, by force of arms, the government which the American people have formed for themselves — to
overthrow the glorious Constitution which has made us the envy of
the world.   The history of the world does not show so causeless an
outrage.   Amid all the rebellions against government which have
stained the annals of civilized and Christian nations, not one can be
found which had not more provocation than that which yesterday
opened a war at Charleston upon the government and the forces of
the United States.   Not a solitary act of oppression — not a single
act of wrong — not the faintest possible trespass upon Southern
rights can be urged in extenuation of this infamous rebellion.
Whatever may be the result of the war which the South has now
begun, it will stand on the pages of history, for all time to come, as
the blackest and most dishonoring outbreak of irrational and fero-
cious passion which has ever marked the checkered annals of national
progress.   Whatever the leaders of this conspiracy may believe, the
civilized world will have but one opinion of their conduct; they
will be greeted with the indignant scorn and execration of the
world. . . .

One thing is certain.   Now that the rebels have opened the war,
the people will expect the government to defend itself with vigor
and determination.   There is no room for half-way measures now.

[1] The bombardment of Fort Sumter began on the morning of April 12; the
garrison surrendered the following day.

There can be no further talk of a pacific policy — of measures of conciliation — of fears of exasperating the people of the Southern States. The day for that has passed. *The South has chosen war, and it must have all the war it wants.* The issue is not made by the United States government. It is made by the South. The Administration has gone to the very verge of pusillanimity in its forbearance. It has endured wrongs and tamely submitted to outrages which no other government on the face of the earth would have endured for an hour. It has done everything consistent with honor, and many things which it is very hard to reconcile with a proper feeling of national self-respect, to avert this horrible alternative which is at last thrust upon them. For no other offence than that of trying to relieve its soldiers from starvation, the batteries of the Southern Confederacy have been opened upon the government of the United States. The flag of the republic is to be lowered in disgrace — or the issue of war is to be met.

The President of the United States must not hesitate an instant as to the policy he will pursue, nor must he spare anything of vigor and energy in the manner of putting it into execution.

## [ON TO WASHINGTON!][1]

Richmond *Examiner*, April 28, 1861

Washington is the weak point with our enemies — their fears and their preparations prove that they feel and know it. It is to Washington that the Northern rabble is summoned. Cannot Virginians and other Southerners reach Washington before this multitudinous and disorderly rabble arrives? Let not individuals, or companies, or regiments wait for orders, but proceed to Alexandria, where they are sure of a hearty welcome; nor wait for arms; *furor arma ministral* — brave men will always find something to fight with, or, that failing, find useful occupation in aiding those who are properly equipped for fight. If companies, and regiments, and individuals, from Richmond and Petersburg and Charlottesville and Warrenton, and from the counties between the James River and the Blue Ridge and Potomac, will hurry on to Alexandria, they will soon be joined by large forces from the Southern Confederacy. Soon, very soon, Davis and Beauregard, and Lee of Virginia, will be there to lead them on. And Scott, too, with his towering form and worldwide fame, unless the report be true that Scott has been arrested and imprisoned by the base and treacherous powers at Washington.

[1] The Confederate army was organized with great rapidity. Jefferson Davis called out 100,000 volunteers as early as March 6. They poured in with such celerity that some had to be turned back because arms were not available. Full of confidence, many Confederates felt in April that the war was in their hands.

## [ON TO RICHMOND!]

New York *Tribune*, June 3, 1861

Next to Charleston, there is no city in the rebel States whose occupancy by the Union forces would strike more dread to the hearts of the traitors, and so encourage the loyal citizens of the South, and so elate the masses of the loyal States, as that of Richmond. For years it has been a den of conspirators, plotting the destruction of the Republic. Affecting to act with more calmness and candor, with more deliberation and judgment, with more dignity and discretion, than its impulsive, fiery Palmetto sister, it has really been more guilty and far more despicable than she, because while committing the same offences against the public weal, it has assumed an air of virtue and innocence, attempting to cloak insidious treason under the guise of patriotic devotion to the doctrines of the fathers of the republic. In a word, and not to put too fine a point upon it, Richmond has been striving to do the dirtiest and most degrading work of the conspiracy, in a dignified and courtly manner. She has been the Robert Macaire of the plot, putting on mock airs and a shabby-genteel costume, and affecting to despise the Jacques Strops of the Gulf States, while in fact being the real leader of the conspirators.

Mr. Jeff. Davis has summoned his Congress of Confederate rebels to meet in Richmond on some day in July. Ere that time, we trust its capital will be the headquarters of the commander-in-chief of the Federal forces.

## THE NATION'S WAR–CRY[1]

New York *Tribune*, June 28, 1861

*Forward to Richmond! Forward to Richmond! The Rebel Congress must not be allowed to meet there on the 20th of July!* By That Date the Place Must Be Held by the National Army!

## BEATEN FOR A DAY — NOW TO CONQUER FOR ALL TIMES

New York *Tribune*, July 23, 1861

We have fought and been beaten. God forgive our rulers that this is so; but it is true and cannot be disguised. The Cabinet, recently expressing in rhetoric better adapted to a love-letter a fear

---

[1] Charles A. Dana, and not Greeley, was responsible for this foolish war-cry of the *Tribune*, and it was actually written by one of the editorial staff, Fitz-Henry Warren, who later joined Dana on the *Sun*. Bull Run was lost on July 21.

of being drowned in its own honey, is now nearly drowned in gore; while our honor on the high seas has only been saved by one daring and desperate negro, and he belonging to the merchant marine. The sacred soil of Virginia is crimson and wet with the blood of thousands of Northern men, needlessly shed. The great and universal question pervading the public mind is, "Shall this condition of things continue?"

A decimated and indignant people will demand the immediate retirement of the present Cabinet from the high places of power which, for one reason or another, they have shown themselves incompetent to fill. Give us for the President capable advisers, who comprehend the requirements of the crisis, and are equal to them; and for the army, leaders worthy of the rank and file, and our banner, now drooping, will soon float once more in triumph over the whole land. With the right men to lead, our people will show themselves unconquerable.

Onward, then, to victory and glory! But let not those who hold places of responsibility disregard for a day longer the means requisite for success. Our government is instituted and intended for the general good; and no private interest or personal ambition should be permitted to remain an obstacle to the achievement of that great object. The people will insist upon new heads of Executive Departments; and then upon a half million troops and the best qualified and ablest captains, colonels, and generals whom the country can furnish. All these must be had, and without delay.

## JUST ONCE[1]

### New York *Tribune*, July 25, 1861

I wish to be distinctly understood as not seeking to be relieved of any personal responsibility for urging the advance of the Union Grand Army into Virginia, though the precise phrase "Forward to Richmond" is not mine, and I would have preferred not to iterate it. I thought that that army, one hundred thousand strong, might have been in the rebel capital on or before the 20th inst., while I felt that there were urgent reasons why it should be there if possible. And now, if anyone imagines that I, or anyone connected with the *Tribune*, ever commended or imagined such strategy as the launching of barely thirty thousand of the one hundred thousand Union volunteers within fifty miles of Washington against ninety thousand rebels enveloped in a labyrinth of strong intrenchments and unreconnoitred masked batteries, then demonstration would be lost

[1] The shock of Bull Run, and his own sense of personal responsibility, were so great that Greeley fell under a severe attack of brain fever, and was confined to his bed for several weeks.

on his closed ear. But I will not dwell on this. If I am needed as a scapegoat for all the military blunders of the last month, so be it! Individuals must die that the nation may live. If I can serve her best in that capacity, I do not shrink from the ordeal.

Henceforth, I bar all criticism in these columns on army movements past and future, unless somebody should undertake to prove that General Patterson is a wise and brave commander. He seems to have none to speak his praises; so if there is anything to be said in his behalf, I will make an exception in his favor. Other than this, the subject is closed and sealed. Correspondents and reporters may state facts, but must forbear comments. I know that there is truth that yet needs to be uttered on this subject, but this paper has done its full share — all that it ought, and perhaps more than it could afford to — and henceforth stands back for others. Only I beg it to be understood — once for all — that if less than half the Union armies directly at hand are hurled against *all* the rebel forces that could be concentrated — more than double their number — on ground specially chosen and strongly fortified by the traitors, the *Tribune* does not approve and should not be held responsible for such madness. Say what you will of the past, but remember this for the future, though we keep silence.

Henceforth, it shall be the *Tribune's* sole vocation to rouse and animate the American people for the terrible ordeal which has befallen them. The Great Republic imminently needs the utmost exertions of every loyal heart and hand. We have tried to save her by exposing breakers ahead and around her; henceforth be it ours to strengthen, by all possible ways, the hands of those whose unenviable duty it is to pilot her through them. If more good is thus to be done, let us not repine that some truth must be withheld for a calmer moment, and for less troubled ears.

The journal which is made the conduit of the most violent of these personal assaults upon me attributes the course of the *Tribune* to resentment

"against those who have ever committed the inexpiable offence of thwarting Mr. Greeley's raging and unsatisfied thirst for office."

I think this justifies me in saying that there is no office in the gift of the government or of the people which I either hope, wish, or expect ever to hold. I certainly shall not parade myself as declining places that are not offered for my acceptance; but I am sure that the President has always known that I desired no office at *his* hands; and this not through any violation of the rule above stated, but through the report of mutual and influential friends, who at various times volunteered to ask me if I would take any place whatever under the government, and were uniformly and conclusively assured that I would not.

Now let the wolves howl on! I do not believe they can goad me into another personal notice of their ravings.

HORACE GREELEY.

July 24, 1861.


## [BULL RUN: WHO IS RESPONSIBLE?]

New York *Times*, July 25, 1861

The great blunder of Sunday lay in fighting the battle which ended so disastrously. Under no circumstances is it ever justifiable, in a military sense, for an inferior force to attack a superior when the latter has his own choice of position and is strongly intrenched. The chances are fifty to one against success. In this instance General McDowell was perfectly aware that the rebel forces either outnumbered his own, or could easily be made to do so by reinforcements which they had every facility for bringing forward. To use his own expression, the night before the battle, it was with them simply a question of rolling stock and provisions. He knew, too, that they had labored zealously for three months, under skilful engineers, in a country adapted admirably to defence, to fortify their position.

General McDowell is not at all likely to have fought this battle on his own responsibility. General Scott is known to have been opposed to the whole scheme from the beginning, and his own declaration, repeated by Mr. Richardson in Congress yesterday, proves that he was utterly hostile to attacking the rebels at that time, and that he was overruled in this matter by his only superior, President Lincoln himself. No one who knows Mr. Lincoln will believe for a moment that he put his own judgment against that of General Scott in so important a matter as this. But there is not the slightest doubt that he yielded to the urgent and almost imperative representatives of that portion of his Cabinet whose views have been reflected by the *Tribune*, and who asserted from the beginning that 10,000 men could march from Washington to Richmond with the greatest ease. It is these men who have constrained the President for the moment to override the opinion and the wish of General Scott, and to order the battle which has resulted in so much of shame to the national arms.

It is known, and need not be longer concealed, that there is in the Cabinet an element of intense hatred of General Scott. Perhaps Mr. Montgomery Blair embodies and represents it more thoroughly than any other member. He has made no secret of it, but has often, in spite of the gross breach of official propriety which such an act involved, denounced the general in public places as utterly unfit for his high position. It seems to us quite time that the President should make his choice between General Scott and those members of his Cabinet who would substitute for his experience and military skill their own resentments and ignorant pretence. His Cabinet has been distracted and his own action weakened long enough by these presumptuous and disastrous counsels.

## THE BATTLE OF WILSON'S CREEK[1]

New Orleans *Picayune*, August 17, 1861

The victory in Missouri is gloriously confirmed; Lyon is killed and Siegel in flight and believed to be captured; Sweeney is killed, and Southwestern Missouri cleared of the national scum of invaders. All honor and gratitude to Ben. McCulloch and the gallant men with him, who met and scourged the minions of national tyranny.

The brave sons of Louisiana were there and foremost in the fight, as at Manassas. There was a panic, it seems, of the untried and probably half-armed troops of Missouri, but the steady discipline and dashing courage of the Arkansas and Louisiana regiments retrieved the day, and after a stubborn fight with the United States regulars, under their most vaunted generals, made a clean sweep of the field. The flying enemy, intercepted by Hardee, have laid down their arms, and the day of the deliverance of Missouri is nigh. These were the best soldiers which the United States had in the State and in the West. They were well drilled by veteran officers and confident of an easy victory in Missouri. They were the nucleus of the great Western army which was to hold Missouri in bondage as the basis of a grand movement for the subjugation of the States on the lower Mississippi. They have been broken and dispersed. Southwestern Missouri is free already. The southeast cannot long stand before the advancing armies of Pillow and Hardee, joined to those of McCulloch, and the next word will be: On to St. Louis! That taken, the power of Lincolnism is broken in the whole West; and instead of shouting, Ho! for Richmond! and for New Orleans! there will be hurryings to and fro among the frightened magnates at Washington, and anxious inquiries of what they shall do to save themselves from the vengeance to come. Good tidings reach us from the North and the West. Heaven smiles on the arms of the Confederate States; through the brightly beaming vistas of these battles we see golden promises of the speedy triumph of a righteous cause — in the firm establishment of Southern independence.

[1] The battle of Wilson's Creek, Missouri, was fought on August 9, 1861, between the Union forces under Nathaniel Lyon, and the Confederates under Price and McCulloch. The Confederates won a brilliant victory.

## [THE EFFECTS OF THE BLOCKADE ON THE SOUTH][1]

Richmond *Examiner*, September, 1861

Starch, soap, ink, paper, leather, cotton goods, yarn, and a hundred other commodities scarce, used up, or outrageously dear, in a country of "abundant resources" — among a people who "want nothing from abroad" and intend in future to "depend upon them-- selves"! We are often hearing the remark, "if the blockade outlasts three years, we shall be one of the greatest nations in the world"; and yet again, "the war may last three years, and while it lasts we are engaged in meeting its demands," is pleaded by many as an excuse for slowness. But are we to wait until the war is over before we begin to supply the demands of such attainable articles as cotton goods, soap, starch, and yarn? The truth is, we must become a more practical people before the above results are reached. We must pocket our pride, and if we cannot be lawyers and professors, give our attention to those occupations that *will* pay, and not leave it to successful though less aspiring Yankees to creep in and establish themselves in this or that craft, and pocket our money because we are too genteel to supply our own needs.

We as a people have been blessed with plenty, and our land is teeming with wealth; as yet we have not learned to economize. Our children have been reared in habits of wastefulness and extravagance. Our very servants despise saving, and have no notion of collecting scraps. Rags, sheets of paper, bits of twine, pens, pins, needles, bottles, are daily swept away, burned up, or cast on rubbish heaps, which they are too lazy to pick up, even to "sell for cash," and which in such times as these ought never to be on the floor at all. . . . And you, our gentlemanly Micawber cousins, rouse your inventive faculties and dip into your encyclopaedias for practical knowledge. "Necessity is the mother of invention," and how can you display your patriotism to better purpose, if not fighting, than by contriving, suggesting, and assisting to establish and improve the many manufactories which have been already, and must be still further, set on foot to meet the demands of the nation, who need neither watch for the raising of the blockade, nor wait till the war is over, before they begin to become "a great and independent people."

[1] President Lincoln at once proclaimed a blockade of Southern ports. By the fall of 1861 its pressure had begun to be felt painfully. Dry goods had become very scarce. The best women of the South were wearing homespun. Medicines were running low. Salt, bacon, butter, coffee, tea, and soap had advanced enormously in price. Surgeons felt severely the scarcity of lint and plasters. This appeal is typical of many addressed to Confederate citizens; but under the circumstances economy could avail but little.

## SLAVERY AND THE WAR: A BLOW THAT WILL BE FELT[1]

New York *Times*, September 2, 1861

There is no victory so complete as that which solves a great political dilemma which has rested like a pall upon the public mind, destroying all life and spirit, paralyzing all enterprise and action, and producing all the consequences of a disastrous defeat. It is a happy stroke of genius that can overstep the bounds of tradition or conventional rule, and show a clear path in a direction supposed to be beset with insuperable difficulties. Such is the service rendered the nation by General Frémont's proclamation, placing Missouri under martial law and visiting upon traitors the penalties due to treason, with all the celerity of military dispatch. The traitor is to be divested of property as well as life; and further, a blow is struck where it has long been seen it might fall, upon the institution which is both the cause and support of the rebellion. Self-preservation renders no other course longer possible. If we would save ourselves, we must take from treason every weapon by which it can strike the deadly blow. We must maintain the rights of loyal men intact, but take from those in arms against us the means of keeping them in the field.

It has long been the boast of the South, in contrasting its strength with that of the North, that its whole white population could be made available for the war, for the reason that all its industries were carried on by the slaves, in peace as well as war; while those of the North rested upon the very men who, in case of hostilities, must be sent into the field. For the North, consequently, to fight, would be the destruction of all its material interests; for the South, only a pleasant pastime for hundreds of thousands of men, who without war would have no occupation. The South was another Sparta, the Helots of which, a degraded caste, performed all the useful labor, leaving to the privileged one only the honorable occupation of arms. The vast host which the South has put into the field has, to a great extent, made good these words. With the enemy at our throat, we must strike from under him the prop upon which his strength rests. It is our duty to save every life and every dollar of expense in our power. By seeking to put down the rebellion only by meeting the enemy in the open field, is uselessly to sacrifice hundreds of thousands of lives, and hundreds if not thousands

---

[1] Frémont's proclamation, freeing the slaves of all Missouri rebels taken in arms, and issued on August 30, 1861, met the approval of nearly the whole Northern press and of many public men, but was disapproved by Lincoln because of his fear of its effect upon the border States.

of millions of money, and perhaps after all accept a disastrous defeat as the result.

In this crisis General Frémont has sounded the keynote of the campaign that will be echoed wherever we have a soldier in arms. He has taken a step which cannot fail to produce a very marked effect throughout the South. He has declared that every slave who may be employed or permitted by his master to aid in the rebellion against the United States, shall be *free*. This, it will be seen, is no general act of emancipation. It has nothing to do with that general crusade against slavery which many have urged as the proper means of carrying on the war. It simply confiscates the property of rebels employed against the government. It does not touch the slaves of loyal citizens, nor affect the institution in any way, except as those responsible for it may choose to identify its fate with that of the rebellion itself. But just so far as slavery actively supports the rebellion must it become the object of attack. . . . It is very clear that Frémont's proclamation is, up to this time, by far the most important event of the war.

## [DISENTHRALMENT OF SOUTHERN LITERATURE]

*De Bow's Review*, October, 1861

While much has been gained by the withdrawal of Southern youth from the colleges of the North, still more good might be accomplished by raising those of the South to the position of universities in the proper acceptation of the term. Many of the latter are already universities in name, but in name only — being really inferior, in many respects, to the best high schools of which England can boast. Perhaps the only exception to this remark is afforded in the University of Virginia; and its success has shown that the lack of institutions of the highest order, in the South, has not been owing to a want of ability to sustain them. We have had, within the last two years, some cheering prospects in other quarters, which we sincerely hope may not be blighted by the existing war; for, with the establishment of Southern universities of equal grade with those of Europe, we may anticipate the dawn of a new era in Southern literature.

In the next place, we must rid ourselves of Yankee newspapers and periodicals. How is this to be accomplished? We cannot, by expostulation or command, prevent booksellers from selling, or the thoughtless among us from buying, this ephemeral trash of the North. We must resort, if possible, to the method of supplanting it by superior publications of our own. This, we think, can be readily accomplished by the proper action on the part of the reading men

and women of the South.  It is apparent that if our best Southern
journals be inferior to the Northern, the inferiority consists not in
tone, authenticity, or editorial ability; for, in the first two particulars, our journals have decidedly the advantage, while in the last
they are at least the equals of their Northern contemporaries. . . .
What, but the persistent efforts of Yankee periodicals, could have
given the prosaic Longfellow a wider circle of readers on this side
of the Atlantic than Tennyson, Campbell, or Burns?  What, but
they, could have convinced anybody out of New England, and in
his senses, that John Greenleaf Whittier — that most uninspired of
fanatics — was capable of aught in metre but the veriest doggerel?
or that the stuff manufactured from the brain of James Russell
Lowell was any more like genuine poetry than the taste of wooden
nutmegs resembles that of the real article?

## THE CONFEDERACY: PRESENT AND FUTURE

*De Bow's Review,* December, 1861

There will be peace; will they offer to negotiate for it?  We can
propose no terms, but we must demand them.  We desire nothing
that is not right and just, and we shall submit to nothing that is
wrong.  But no peace will be acceptable to the people that permits
the Lincoln Government to hold its abolition orgies, and fulminate
its vile edicts upon slave territory.  Much valuable property of our
citizens has been destroyed, or stolen and carried off by the invaders;
this should be accounted for, and paid.  The Yankees were shrewd
enough to cheat us out of the navy, but we must have half of the
war vessels and naval armaments in possession of the North at the
commencement of this war.  We should enter into no commercial
alliances or complications with them, but assume the entire control
of our commercial policy and regulations with them, to be modified
at our own discretion and pleasure.  They have closed against us
all navigation and trade on the Mississippi, Missouri, and other
rivers; it is our right and duty hereafter so to regulate the navigation
of these streams as may best conform to our own interests.  It
cannot be expected that we should permit the free navigation of the
lower Mississippi to the West after they have closed it against us
above, without the most stringent regulations.  There is no palliation in the pretence that the blockade above was a war measure;
they cannot so claim it unless we had been acknowledged as belligerents, and hence they have forfeited all right to free navigation as a
peace measure.  If, then, permission be given to the free States of the
West to navigate the lower Mississippi, it should be under such
restrictions as to afford a commensurate revenue to the Confederacy,

and the strictest rules regulating the ingress and egress of passengers, officers, and hands. . . .

We have conquered an outlet to the Pacific which must be maintained, though we can desire no dominion on the Pacific coast but such as may be sufficient to secure the terminus of our great Pacific railroad through Texas and Arizona. Toward the north and east, the Maryland and Pennslyvania line, including Delaware, is our true landmark. Kansas, on the other side, must be conquered and confiscated to pay for the negroes stolen from us, abolitionism expelled from its borders, and transformed into a slave State of the Confederacy. Perhaps, after we have done with Lincoln, this arrangement may be very acceptable to a majority in Kansas, without force. We will have no desire to disturb Mexico so long as she conducts herself peaceably toward us, and as a neighbor, maintains good faith in her dealings with us. Central America must remain as a future consideration; and instead of the acquisition of Cuba, she becomes our *friendly ally*, identified with us in interests and institutions, and so long as she continues to hold slaves, connected to us by the closest ties.

## EMANCIPATION: THE QUESTION OF THE DAY

New York *Tribune*, December 13, 1861

It is utterly idle to talk of ignoring questions affecting slavery while providing for the prosecution of the War for the Union. They *will not* be ignored; indeed, they *can not* be. We should be willing to refrain from discussing them; but we are not allowed our choice. Those who openly sympathized with and justified secession last spring, and who now loudly proclaim themselves the only hearty supporters of the government and the war, keep up a deafening clamor against any interference with slavery which they mean to have mistaken for public opinion. Silence on our part is acquiescence in gross misrepresentation under circumstances which stamp such acquiescence as cowardice. We propose once more to elucidate the position and vindicate the sagacity of those who maintain that it will not be possible to uphold both slavery and the Union.

I. We insist, that, in the present crisis, neither slavery nor abolition, per se, has any right to consideration at the hands of the government. One loyalist thinks slavery a good thing; another deems it entitled to legal protection so long as the slaveholders are loyal citizens; a third deems it an unmitigated evil and nuisance. Each of these has a right to his own opinion, and to its free and hearty expression. But when the question of saving or losing the republic presents itself, all others must give way. If upholding slavery tends to insure and hasten the vindication of the national authority, the saving of the Union, then it may plausibly be unheld; otherwise, No.

II. The questions in issue concern the slaves of *rebels*, and those only. Loyal slaveholders are a class by themselves — "small but respectable." With them, we would have the government nowise interfere, unless for their protection. But rebel slaveholders should have been warned at the outset that they could not persist in treason without losing their slaves, and striking a heavy blow at slavery. And had they been thus warned, we believe many, if not most, would have stood aloof from rebellion. And now, had they been seasonably notified that no one may persist in rebellion after the first of January next without forfeiting his slaves, we think many would conclude that rebellion is not likely to pay, and would give it up.

III. On the side of the rebels, confiscation is the order of the day. *All* the property of loyalists — slave or otherwise — is mercilessly swept into the strong-box of Jeff. Davis and Company. There is no talk in *that* quarter of confiscating only the slaves who work on the Union defenses or are found serving in our armies — they go the whole hog. . . .

IV. But we are reminded by the New York *Times* that "the objects of legislation are *practical*." The suggestion may be profound, but its novelty is not striking. Let us, therefore, once more enlighten the *Times* and those whom it guides as to the *end* we would accomplish.

Four millions of sturdy bondmen, nearly all residents of the rebel States, stand waiting and wondering what is to be *their* part in this contest, what their advantage therefrom. They form a majority of the people of South Carolina and nearly or quite a majority of those of several other revolted States. They are about one-third the population of Jeff Davis's dominions. Their interest in the struggle *is practical* — very practical indeed. They want many things, but before all else, Liberty. They are willing to work for it, run for it, fight for it, die for it. There cannot be a rational doubt of the ability of the government to enlist the sympathies and the efforts of these four millions of Jeff's subjects on the side of the Union by simply promising them freedom. Talk of confiscation does not move them, for it involves the idea — to their minds, at least — of deportation and sale to new masters. Talk of confiscating, or even freeing, those only who have been employed in the rebel armies, does not much affect them; for it seems partial, timid, and selfish. But say to them that all whose masters are involved in the rebellion shall be Free, and they will feel that their day is at last dawning. They will not hasten to throw away their lives by mad, senseless insurrections; but they will watch for opportunities to escape and come within our lines, bringing information certainly and perhaps arms and other material aid. And the bare fact that their slaves are watching their chances to get away and over to the Union side will immensely weaken the rebels.

We are not proposing that Congress should take any particular action in the premises. We indicate no time at which decisive action would be desirable, or beyond which it would be likely to prove fruitless. We do not propose to abandon the ship unless it is sailed according to our chart. We shall render a hearty support to the war for the Union, whether conducted according to our views or otherwise. But our conviction is very strong that the Unionists cannot afford to repel the sympathies and reject the aid of Four Millions of Southern people.

## THE AGRICULTURAL COLLEGE ACT[1]

New York *Tribune*, June 23, 1862

We print herewith the act recently passed by Congress providing, by grants of public lands, a fund in each State for the establishment of one or more colleges for the education of youth in agriculture and the mechanic arts, and the sciences auxiliary thereto. It is not often that a measure of such promise is carried by majorities so overwhelming as this — after years of struggle and debate — has commanded. We hail in this triumph an augury of wide and lasting good.

The benefits of such a measure cannot be speedily realized. Probably two years will elapse before any State will have so perfected the preliminary formalities and guaranties most wisely required by this act as to be able to avail herself directly and palpably of its benefits. Colleges must be organized, buildings erected, faculties chosen, etc., etc., before opportunities can be proffered under this act for the thousands of youths who would gladly combine Learning with Labor, and master the sciences which will make them eminent farmers and mechanics rather than those which would impel them into the already overcrowded professions. But the time *will* come — it will not be delayed beyond three years in some States, especially if institutions already commenced, such as the Farmers' College of Pennsylvania, shall be taken as the basis and nucleus of the larger and better seminaries which this act is intended and calculated to secure. Some States may possibly decline to accept the grant proffered them under the rather stringent conditions imposed by this act; some may fail even in hearty and well-meant efforts to popular-

[1] The Morrill Land Grand Act for the endowment of universities and colleges giving instruction in agriculture and the mechanic arts was passed by both houses in June, 1862, and signed by President Lincoln on July 2.

ize science and render the useful arts liberal and even learned pursuits; but it is not possible that *all* should fail. And if the net result of this measure is the establishment of *five* colleges in so many different States which shall within five years succeed in placing within the reach of our youth an education at once scientific and practical, including a knowledge of the sciences which underlie and control the chief processes of productive labor, all the cost of this measure will have been richly repaid.

## [THREE HUNDRED THOUSAND MORE]
### New York *Tribune*, July 3, 1862

We publish today a call from the President for 300,000 more men as an additional force to the armies of the Union. The President hopes that they "will be enrolled without delay, so as to bring this unnecessary and injurious civil war to a speedy and satisfactory conclusion." This wish will be responded to by every loyal heart in the land.

The call is made at the urgent request of all the Governors of the loyal States, with four exceptions. Whether these omissions are accidental, or because for some personal reason the signatures are withheld, we do not know; but these States, which have sent quite as large a number of their sons to the war, in proportion to their population, as the rest, will not, we are sure, be backward in responding to the President's call. The signers to the letter urging this appeal to the country very truly present, we have no doubt, the feeling of the people whom they represent. A "speedy conclusion" of the war is what the nation demands.

### New York *Evening Post*, July 16, 1862 [1]

*We are coming, Father Abraham, three hundred thousand more,*
*From Mississippi's winding stream, and from New England's shore;*
*We leave our ploughs and workshops, our wives and children dear,*
*With hearts too full for utterance, with but a silent tear*
*We dare not look behind us, but steadfastly before:*
*We are coming, Father Abraham, three hundred thousand more.*

*If you look across the hilltops that meet the Northern sky,*
*Long moving lines of rising dust your vision may descry;*
*And now the wind, an instant, tears the cloudy veil aside,*
*And floats aloft our spangled flag in glory and in pride,*
*And bayonets in the sunlight gleam, and bands brave music pour:*
*We are coming, Father Abraham, three hundred thousand more!*

[1] Contributed to the editorial columns by the financial editor, John S. Gibbons.

## THE TIME HAS COME[1]

The *Independent*, August 14, 1862

The way to make war is to destroy slavery. The way to secure peace after war is to destroy slavery. If any have scruples about interfering with Southern rights, their scruples are too late. We have already done it. War is supreme interference. We have violated State sovereignty as much as it can be done. What State sovereignty is there under an imposed military governor intruded upon New Orleans, Nashville, and Newbern?

The only question is whether we will use that lawful intrusion for the ends of health and peace, or whether we will go on with a timid and fatuous policy, designed to roll over upon future times tenfold greater disturbances than those which we have suffered.

Is it not time for us to ponder the meaning of God's providence?

With what energy did men resist the anti-slavery discussion of the past thirty years! But it prevailed and covered the land. With what desperate energy did the North resist the legislation of 1850 and the infamous Fugitive Slave law! But it was in vain. With what fierce indignation did the whole North resist the abrogation of the Missouri Compromise! But it was broken up and the Kansas volcano uncapped. Then came the fiery campaign between Frémont the Eagle, and Buchanan the Owl. In the days of him whom the Conservatives elected as safe and prudent, came Secession. When it was threatened, we refused to believe that it would happen. We were all mistaken. We then refused to believe that there would be war. But it has flamed over half a hemisphere.

Thus far, the conservative North has been striving to conduct this war so as not to meddle with the so-called Southern right of slavery. But in spite of every scruple, events have crowded men to the necessity of confiscation and emancipation. There is one more step. It is the last sublime step toward National safety and National Christian glory. It is IMMEDIATE AND UNIVERSAL EMANCIPATION!

Ah, men of America! Patriots! Christians! Could you but cleanse your native land of the inconsistency with her own vital principles, and give to her coming times undiseased with slavery, bright with the immortal beauty of liberty, would it not be worth all treasures and all suffering?

It may be done. Let every man in his place rise up and demand it! Each man's voice is but a breath. But let breath mingle with breath, and the current begin to move, as a storm marches which, gathering force as it goes, moves the very deep and shakes the land. Then, when the earthquake of War shall have been felt, and the

[1] By Henry Ward Beecher.

great and stormy voice of the People, our rulers will peradventure hear the still small voice of God, speaking with irresistible authority— "Let my people go!" — and bow down, and obey!

## THE PRAYER OF TWENTY MILLIONS

New York *Tribune*, August 20, 1862

*To Abraham Lincoln, President of the United States:*

Dear Sir: I do not intrude to tell you — for you must know already — that a great proportion of those who triumphed in your election, and of all who desire the unqualified suppression of the Rebellion now desolating our country, are sorely disappointed and deeply pained by the policy you seem to be pursuing with regard to the slaves of Rebels. I write only to set succinctly and unmistakably before you what we require, what we think we have a right to expect, and of what we complain.

I. We require of you, as the first servant of the Republic, charged especially and preëminently with this duty, that you EXECUTE THE LAWS. Most emphatically do we demand that such laws as have been recently enacted, which therefore may fairly be presumed to embody the *present* will and to be dictated by the *present* needs of the Republic, and which after due consideration have received your personal sanction, shall by you be carried into full effect, and that you publicly and decisively instruct your subordinates that such laws exist, that they are binding on all functionaries and citizens, and that they are to be obeyed to the letter.

II. We think you are strangely and disastrously remiss in the discharge of your official and imperative duty with regard to the emancipating provisions of the new Confiscation Act. These provisions were designed to fight Slavery with Liberty. They prescribe that men loyal to the Union, and willing to shed their blood in her behalf, shall no longer be held, with the Nation's consent, to persistent, malignant traitors, who for twenty years have been plotting and for sixteen months have been fighting to divide and destroy our country. Why these traitors should be treated with tenderness by you, to the prejudice of the dearest rights of loyal men, we cannot conceive.

III. We think you are unduly influenced by the counsels, the representations, the menaces, of certain fossil politicians hailing from the Border Slave States. Knowing well that the heartily, unconditionally loyal portion of the white citizens of these States do not expect nor desire that slavery shall be upheld to the prejudice of the Union — (for the truth of which we appeal not only to every Republican residing in those States, but to such eminent loyalists as H. Winter Davis, Parson Brownlow, the Union Central Committee of Baltimore, and the Nashville *Union*) — we ask you to consider that slavery is everywhere the inciting cause and sustaining base of treason: the most slaveholding sections of Maryland and Delaware being this day, though under the Union flag, in full sympathy with the Rebellion, while the Free-Labor portions of Tennessee and of Texas, though writhing under the bloody heel of Treason, are unconquerably loyal to the Union. So emphatically is this case, that a most intelligent Union banker of Baltimore recently avowed his confident belief that a majority of the present Legislature of Maryland, though elected as and still professing to be Unionists, are at heart desirous of the triumph of the Jeff. Davis conspiracy; and when asked how they could be won back to loyalty, replied — "Only by the complete abolition of slavery." It seems to us the most obvious truth, that whatever strengthens or fortifies slavery in the Border States strengthens also Treason, and drives home the wedge intended to divide the Union. Had you from the first refused to recognize in those States, as here, any other than unconditional loyalty — that which stands for the Union, whatever may become of slavery — those States would have been, and would be, far more helpful and less troublesome to the defenders of the Union than they have been, or now are.

IV. We think timid counsels in such a crisis calculated to prove perilous, and probably disastrous. It is the duty of a government so wantonly, wickedly assailed by Rebellion as ours has been to oppose force to force in a defiant, dauntless spirit. It cannot afford to compromise with traitors nor with semi-traitors. It must not bribe them to behave themselves, nor make them fair promises in the hope of disarming their causeless hostility. Representing a brave and high-spirited people, it can afford to forfeit anything else better than its own self-respect, or their admiring confidence. For our government even to seek, after war has been made on it, to dispel the affected apprehensions of armed traitors that their cherished privileges may be assailed by it, is to invite insult and to encourage hopes of its own downfall. The rush to arms of Ohio, Indiana, Illinois, is the true answer at once to the Rebel raids of John Morgan and the traitorous sophistries of Beriah Magoffin.

V. We complain that the Union cause has suffered, and is now suffering immensely, from mistaken deference to Rebel slavery. Had you, sir, in your inaugural address, unmistakably given notice that, in case the Rebellion already commenced were persisted in, and your efforts to preserve the Union and enforce the laws were resisted by armed force, *you would recognize no loyal person as rightfully held in slavery by a Traitor*, we believe the Rebellion would therein have received a staggering if not fatal blow. At that moment, according to the returns of the most recent elections, the Unionists were a large majority of the voters of the Slave States. But they were composed in good part of the aged, the feeble, the wealthy, the timid — the young, the reckless, the aspiring, the adventurous, had already been largely lured by the gamblers and negro-traders, the politicians by trade and the conspirators by instinct, into the toils of Treason. Had you then proclaimed that Rebellion would strike the shackles from the slaves of every traitor, the wealthy and the cautious would have been supplied with a powerful inducement to remain loyal. As it was, every coward in the South soon became a traitor from fear; for Loyalty was perilous, while Treason seemed comparatively safe. Hence the boasted unanimity of the South — a unanimity based on Rebel terrorism, and the fact that immunity and safety were found on that side, danger and probable death on ours. The Rebels from the first have been eager to confiscate, imprison, scourge, and kill; we have fought wolves with the devices of sheep. The result is just what might have been expected. Tens of thousands are fighting in the Rebel ranks today whose original bias and natural leanings would have led them into ours.

VI. We complain that the Confiscation Act which you approved is habitually disregarded by your generals, and that no word of rebuke for them from you has yet reached the public ear. Frémont's proclamation and Hunter's Order favoring emancipation were promptly annulled by you; while Halleck's No. 3, forbidding fugitives from slavery to Rebels to come within his lines — an order as unmilitary as inhuman, and which received the hearty approbation of every traitor in America — with scores of like tendency, have never provoked even your remonstrance. We complain that the officers of your armies have habitually repelled rather than invited the approach of slaves who would have gladly taken the risk of escaping from their Rebel masters to our camps, bringing intelligence often of inestimable value to the Union cause. We complain that those who *have* thus escaped to us, avowing a willingness to do for us whatever might be required, have been brutally and madly repulsed, and often surrendered to be scourged, maimed, and tortured by the ruffian traitors who pretend to own them. We complain that a large proportion of our regular army officers, with many volunteers, evince far more solicitude to uphold slavery than to put down the Rebellion. And finally we complain that you, Mr. President, elected as a Republican, knowing well what an abomination slavery is, and how emphatically it is the core and essence of this atrocious Rebellion, seem never to interfere with these atrocities, and never give a direction to your military subordinates, which does not appear to be conceived in the interest of Slavery rather than that of Freedom.

VII. Let me call your attention to the recent tragedy in New Orleans, whereof the facts are obtained entirely through pro-slavery channels. A considerable body of resolute, able-bodied men, held in slavery by two Rebel sugar-planters in defiance of the Confiscation Act which you have approved, left plantations thirty miles distant and made their way to the great mart of the Southwest, which they knew to be in the undisputed possession of the Union forces. They made their way safely and quietly through thirty miles of Rebel territory, expecting to find freedom under the protection of our flag. Whether they had or had not heard of the passage of the Confiscation Act, they reasoned logically that we could not kill them for deserting the service of their lifelong oppressors, who had through treason become our implacable enemies. They came to us for liberty and protection, for which they were willing to render their best service; they met with hostility, captivity, and murder. The barking of the base curs of Slavery in this quarter deceives no one — not even themselves. They say, indeed, that the negroes had no right to appear in New Orleans armed (with their implements of daily labor in the cane-field); but no one doubts that they would gladly have laid these down if assured that they should be free. They were set upon and maimed, captured and killed. . . . It was *somebody's* fault that they were so murdered — if others shall hereafter suffer in like manner, in default of explicit and public direction to your generals that they are to recognize and obey the Confiscation Act, the world will lay the blame on *you*. Whether you will choose to bear it through future history and at the bar of God, I will not judge. I can only hope.

VIII. On the face of this wide earth, Mr. President, there is not one disinterested, determined, intelligent champion of the Union cause who does not feel that all attempts to put down the Rebellion and at the same time uphold its inciting cause are preposterous and futile — that the rebellion, if crushed out tomorrow, would be renewed within a year if slavery were left in full vigor. . . . that army officers who remain to this day devoted to slavery can be but at best halfway loyal to the Union — and that every hour of deference to slavery is an hour of added and deepened peril to the Union. I appeal to the testimony of your Ambassadors in Europe. It is freely at your service, not at mine. . . .

IX. I close as I began with the statement that what an immense majority of the Loyal Millions of your countrymen require of you is a frank, declared, unqualified, ungrudging execution of the laws of the land, more especially of the Confiscation Act. That Act gives freedom to the slaves of Rebels coming within our lines, or whom those lines may at any time enclose — we ask you to render it due obedience by publicly requiring all your subordinates to recognize and obey it. The Rebels are everywhere using the late anti-negro riots in the North, as they have long used your officers' treatment of negroes in the South, to convince the slaves that they have nothing to hope from a Union success — that we mean in that case to sell them into a bitterer bondage to defray the cost of the war. Let them impress this as a truth upon the great mass of the ignorant and credulous bondmen, and the Union will never be restored — never. We cannot conquer Ten Millions of people united in solid phalanx against us, powerfully aided by Northern sympathizers and European allies. We must have scouts, guides, spies, cooks, teamsters, diggers and choppers, from the Blacks of the South, whether we allow them to fight for us or not, or we shall be baffled and repelled. As one of the millions who would gladly have avoided this struggle at any sacrifice but that of Principle and Honor, but who now feel that the triumph of the Union is indispensable not only to the existence of our country but to the well-being of mankind, I entreat you to render a hearty and unequivocal obedience to the law of the land.

HORACE GREELEY.

*New York,* August 19, 1862.

## PRESIDENT LINCOLN'S LETTER

New York *Tribune,* August 25, 1862

Executive Mansion, Washington
August 22, 1862.

*Hon. Horace Greeley:*

DEAR SIR: I have just read yours of the 19th, addressed to myself through THE N. Y. TRIBUNE. If there be in it any statements or assumptions of fact which I may know to be erroneous, I do not now and here controvert them. If there be in it any inferences which I may believe to be falsely drawn, I do not now and here argue against them. If there be perceptible in it an impatient and dictatorial tone, I waive it in deference to an old friend, whose heart I have always supposed to be right.

As to the policy I "seem to be pursuing," as you say, I have not meant to leave anyone in doubt.

I would save the Union. I would save it the shortest way under the Constitution. The sooner the National authority can be restored, the nearer the Union will be "the Union as it was." If there be those who would not save the Union unless they could at the same time *save* slavery, I do not agree with them. If there be those who would not save the Union unless they could at the same time *destroy* slavery, I do not agree with them. My paramount object in this struggle *is* to save the Union, and is *not* either to save or to destroy slavery. If I could save the Union without freeing *any* slave, I would do it; and if I could save it by freeing *all* the slaves, I would do it; and if I could do it by freeing some and leaving others alone, I would also do that. What I do about slavery and the colored race, I do because I believe it helps to save this Union; and what I forbear, I forbear because I do *not* believe it would help to save the Union. I shall do *less* whenever I believe what I am doing hurts the cause, and I shall do *more* whenever I shall believe doing more will help the cause. I shall try to correct errors when shown to be errors; and I shall adopt new views so fast as they shall appear to be true views. I have here stated my purpose according to my view of *official* duty, and I intend no modification of my oft-expressed *personal* wish that all men, everywhere, could be free. Yours,

A. LINCOLN.

### Mr. Greeley's Response

DEAR SIR: Although I did not anticipate nor seek any reply to my former letter unless through your official acts, I thank you for having accorded one, since it enables me to say explicitly that nothing was further from my thought than to impeach in any manner the sincerity or the intensity of your devotion to the saving of the Union. I never doubted, and have no friend who doubts, that you desire, before and above all else, to reëstablish the now derided authority and vindicate the territorial integrity of the Republic. I intended to raise only this question — *Do you propose to do this by recognizing, obeying, and enforcing the laws, or by ignoring, disregarding, and in effect defying them?*

I stand upon the law of the land. The humblest has a clear right to invoke its protection and support against even the highest. That law — in strict accordance with the law of Nations, of Nature, and of God — declares that every traitor now engaged in the infernal work of destroying our country has forfeited thereby all claim or color of right lawfully to hold human beings in slavery. I ask of you a clear and public recognition that this law is to be obeyed wherever the national authority is respected. . . .

Mr. President, I beseech you to open your eyes to the fact that the devotees of slavery everywhere — just as much in Maryland as in Mississippi, in Washington as in Richmond — are today your enemies and the implacable foes of every effort to reëstablish the National authority by the discomfiture of its assailants. Their President is not Abraham Lincoln but Jefferson Davis. You may draft them to serve in the war; but they will only fight under the Rebel flag. There is not in New York today a man who really believes in slavery, loves it, and desires its perpetuation, who heartily desires the crushing out of the Rebellion. He would much rather save the Republic by buying up and pensioning off its assailants. His "Union as it was" is a Union of which you were not President, and no one who truly wished Freedom to All ever could be. . . .

That you may not unseasonably perceive these vital truths as they will shine forth on the pages of history — that they may be read by our children irradiated by the glory of our National salvation, not rendered lurid by the blood-red glow of National conflagration and ruin — that you may promptly and practically realize that Slavery is to be vanquished only by Liberty — is the fervent and anxious prayer of

Yours, truly,

HORACE GREELEY.

*New York*, Aug. 24, 1862.

## THE PROCLAMATION OF FREEDOM[1]
### New York *Tribune*, September 24, 1862

In sacred and profane poetry, the epitome of all human wisdom, there is no truth more clearly recognized than that in the lives of nations and of men there comes sometimes a precious moment, a mere point of time, on the proper use of which depends salvation for that life, whether temporal or eternal. That moment has come to us. The proclamation of the President, which gives in a certain contingency — almost sure to occur — freedom to four millions of men, is one of those stupendous facts in human history which marks not only an era in the progress of the nation, but an epoch in the history of the world. Shall we recognize and use it wisely, or shall we, blindly and foolishly, refuse to see that we have now our future in our own hands, and enter upon that downward career which leads eventually to ruin and oblivion? . . . .

While we rejoice and hope for the best, we still tremble. There are among us men whose foolishness will not depart from them though it be brayed in a mortar — other men who will not cease from wicked ways while in the flesh. But the emancipation which the President has proclaimed is the emancipation of more than four millions of black slaves; it is the freedom of well-nigh twenty millions from a thraldom they have been taught to reverence. Have they learned aright the lesson of these last two years? Do they know now that they also have been in bondage, and will they accept this

[1] Lincoln's proclamation announcing emancipation was issued, following McClellan's victory over Lee at Antietam, on September 22, 1862.

great boon of freedom which a wise ruler offers them? We hope so; we devoutly pray that wisdom may enter into the hearts of all the people. Let the President know that everywhere throughout all the land he is hailed as Wisest and Best, and that by this great deed of enfranchisement to an oppressed people — a deed, the doing whereof was never before vouchsafed to any mortal ruler — he re-creates a nation.

For such indeed is the fact. By a single blow he has palsied the right arm of rebellion. Slavery is the root of the rebellion; he digs it up by the roots. Property in slaves, the appalling events of the last two years show, is dangerous to the existence of the nation; he destroys such property.. The Rebels are dependent for their daily subsistence upon their slaves; he makes these slaves freemen. As slaves they are the mere subjects of Rebels, to toil for them, to be used by them as beasts of burden; as freemen they are the loyal allies of a free government, asking only in return the protection which such a government gives to the humblest citizen. By a word the President transforms a State sunk in the semi-barbarism of a mediaeval age to the light and civilization of the Nineteenth Christian Century. As it is not extravagant to say that God had hid away this continent until the human race had reached its manhood and was fit to enter upon so fair an inheritance, so it is a simple statement of a truth to say that in all the ages there has been no act of one man and of one people so sublime as this emancipation of a race — no act so fraught with good for the sons of men in all time to come.

## LEE AND HIS ARMY[1]

### Richmond *Enquirer*, May 8, 1863

It is no disparagement to other great generals and gallant forces in our service to say that General Lee and his army of Northern Virginia may now be pronounced the most famous chief and army on earth at this day. No leader now in the world has won so many great battles. No army has stood so often or so long in such tempests of fire, nor borne off victory in the face of such terrible odds, and in the midst of such red carnivals of slaughter. The Confederacy may well be proud of such a host and such a leader: for the banners emblazoned with the names of the battles of Richmond, of Second Manassas, of Fredericksburg, and of the Rappahannock, fly higher at this day, and glow with a purer lustre than any battle standards that in this generation have been given to the winds over all lands and all seas.

[1] Published immediately after the battle of Chancellorsville, and before Lee's invasion of Pennsylvania.

The meagre and fitful snatches of news that have come to us from the last tremendous scene of conflict — gasped out, as it were, from amid the lurid war smoke and thunder, while our noble defenders are still panting and bloody with the desperate strife — inspire a feeling of proud and terrible joy, give a keen sense of the priceless value of that blessing that we pay for with oceans of so rich blood, and think it cheap. The events of such a war, stirring to the depths the inmost core of all hearts and kindling every generous and ennobling passion, cannot but elevate the whole character of a people, give it a higher purpose and a more intense love for all that is good and lofty in the world. It is war, not peace (war, we mean, waged in the righteous cause of liberty) that makes a nation great and good; that brings out the very best and purest qualities of manhood and womanhood, and intensifies that spirit of patriotism which is the true basis of a great national character. . . .

Who will not hereafter be proud to trace his descent from one of those who stood in the gaps at Fredericksburg with the glorious Lee? Will not the virtue and glory of such ancestors be a stimulus the more with their children's children even to the hundredth generation, to show themselves worthy of their forefathers? Even in our own day, when this horrible but needful work is done, and we can breathe freely with the sense that the land is redeemed and established forever, and is our own and our children's from the centre to the sky — who is there that will not feel within him a stronger spring of character, a purer impulse to the performance of all manly duty, from the very scenes of passionate struggle through which Providence has borne him safe; from the chivalrous friendships that will have been formed and cemented on the sanguinary fields where comrades have so often proved each other's manhood, relieved each other's weariness, and watched by one another's beds of pain!

Yes, our land shall be more opulent in every virtue, and one can scarce say whether she will be richer in her living or her dead, for it is by the dew of heroic blood that this ancient earth renews her youth forever, and by virtue thereof "the world is a world and not a waste." The daring imagery of Shelley holds a grand truth —

> "Still alive and still bold, shouted Earth —
> I grow bolder and still more bold —
> The Dead fill me ten thousand fold,
> Fuller of speed, of splendor, and mirth.
>
> "I was cloudy, and sullen, and cold,
> Like a frozen chaos uprolled,
> Till by the spirit of the mighty dead
> My heart grew warm —"

Such are the reflections that naturally throng upon us, as we seem to hear the crash of combat from behind the sulphurous clouds that cover the vale of the Rappahannock. — May God bless the banners of Lee and his immortal army!

## HOW TO EDIT A SOUND CONSERVATIVE UNION PAPER

New York *Evening Post*, May 20, 1863

It is a mystery to many readers how certain Democratic journals, which profess the warmest devotion to the Union, nevertheless, manage to play into the hands of the Secessionists. But the thing is easy enough — quite as easy as lying if you will only consider it for a moment. The editors of such journals are of course compelled to parade their Unionism, because of the overwhelming sentiment of the North; at the same time, however, by observing any or all of the following rules, they are able to do very effective work for the other side. The rules we give, by the way, are without charge to the parties concerned.

1st. All the military successes of the rebel armies should be magnified in their effects, while those of the North should be depreciated. If we lose ten thousand men, set it down at twenty-three thousand; while, if they lose eighteen thousand, set it down at eight. In this manner the superior gallantry and pluck of the Southerners may be gracefully insinuated into the popular mind until in the end it comes to be believed as a fact.

2nd. The war reports of the Southern papers should be paraded at great length, especially those which swell the number of their army, or which extol the exploits of their generals. But care must be taken to exclude their inflated despatches and leading articles, which are evidently, on the face of them, monstrous Munchausen-isms; for your readers must not be allowed to suppose that the rebel writers are ever guilty of inaccuracy or falsehood; as that would spoil their credit with the unsuspicious Northern public.

3rd. The efficient and energetic generals in the loyal service should be calumniated in every plausible way; insist upon it that they are plunderers and thieves; and above all, denounce them for utter incompetency. On the other hand, laud such Generals as have distinguished themselves for do-nothingism and a half-faced sympathy in the revolt; call them the master Generals of the age, whose prudence surpasses that of Fabius, while their impetuosity rivals Napoleon's; and above all, remark upon that pre-eminence of intellectual and moral quality which renders them the staunchest of conservatives.

4th. Whenever the Union army achieves a signal victory say very little about it; complain, perhaps, incidentally, at the slowness of the war, but whenever it suffers a reverse (as all armies do at times), ask boldly and indignantly whether it be not time that this patricidal and hopeless war should be brought to an end. Assert roundly that the people are weary of it; weary of paying their money and sacrificing the lives of their brothers; and that we can never hope to accomplish any result. It is scarcely necessary to suggest on this head that the fact that during the two years in which we have prosecuted the war we have made greater progress than during almost any other two years of war recorded in history, must be carefully concealed.

5th. The finances of the government may be made a fruitful topic of suggestion. Do not let your readers know, on any account, that our securities command better prices than they did in years of peace; do not show them what the exchequers of other nations have borne in times of war; do not appeal to the universal confidence our bonds inspire in commercial circles; but talk sneeringly of "greenbacks;" ask with a wink of the eye what has become of the gold; say that our debt must be two or three thousand millions by this time, is rapidly increasing, and can never be paid; and mutter of frightful times, bankruptcy, stock-jobbers, contractors and shoddy men. It would be well, if you could, to contrast the successful management of the rebel finances with ours; but as gold among them is about four hundred percent premium; as one of our notes will buy three of theirs; as their debt already equals ours; and as their taxation greatly surpasses ours, very little, we fear, could be made of the argument. Pass it over, therefore, in profound silence.

6th. In the abuse of Mr. Lincoln and his cabinet no regard need to be paid to the consistency of your charges. Pronounce them all weak, timid, vacillating, and utterly incapable, in one column; and in another, accuse them of tyranny, despotism, excessive rigor, and a determination to trample the rights of the masses into the dust. Some of your readers will believe one story, and some the other, and so the confidence of all sorts will be shaken. You need give yourself no concern about the truth of your charges, provided they look plausible, or can be made to stick. Be sure, however, to insinuate that the men in power are not attached to the Union, but that they prosecute the war only to compel the separation of the South. That part of the nation, it is well known, is so earnestly devoted to the national cause that nothing but the perverse obstinacy and hatred of the Administration keeps it from rushing into our arms in all the ecstacy of fraternal endearment. Mr. Lincoln and Mr. Seward do not wish the South to come back, and are fighting as hard as they can to keep it out. Claim for yourselves, at the same time, the title of the only true Unionists.

7th. As it does not hurt anybody very much in these days to call him a radical, while the bugaboo of abolitionism has lost its principal terrors, you cannot accomplish a great deal by reiterating those nefarious epithets. But you can protest vehemently against "nigger" brigades — against the atrocity of arming slaves against their masters, and against the still greater atrocity of putting black soldiers on a level with white. On that head you may be voluble, as considerable anti-negro prejudice still exists among our more ignorant classes. But in doing all this be somewhat adroit, and do not for the world let it slip out that the first negro troops were used by Governor Moore of Louisiana, that they are to be found in nearly all the rebel garrisons, and that their labors are sometimes assisted by Indians and blood-hounds. Should you reveal all the facts of the case, the common sense of the people might rush to the conclusion that, as negroes are to be used in the war inevitably by one side or the other, it will be better to use them on the side of the Union than against it, while it may also come to be considered that they are better adapted to the malarious regions of the semitropical climates. A few even may go so far as to calculate that the more negroes we put into the service the fewer white men will be exposed to the draft. Denounce, then, but avoid facts!

8th. The draft — the conscription — ah! That's your topic of topics, which can be played upon like "the harp of a thousand strings." Be careful, at the outset, not to imitate the foolhardy Fernando Wood and advise an open resistance to it: for Fort Warren frowns angrily in the distance. Nor yet let it be known that our enrolment act compared with the conscription laws of the rebels — of which there are three or more — is like the Sermon on the Mount compared to the Draconian code. But clamor against it in detail; intimate doubts of its constitutionality; concealing its benevolent exemption of all who have others dependent upon them, denounce the $300 clause; say that it make odious distinctions between the poor and the rich; and refer learnedly to the despotic military systems of Austria and France. As no man likes to be forced into any duty, and particularly into so dangerous an occupation as that of fighting, you will have a large audience to appeal to; their selfishness at least will be in your favor; and you may work not only upon that, but upon the affections of their wives and children, who very naturally desire to keep the head of the house at home. There is a fine field in which prejudices may be easily excited, and the law brought into the most unmitigated disgrace. Plough it and work it well, and it can scarcely fail to yield you much

By Thomas Nast

"CINCINNATUS"

From *Harpers Weekly*, Feb. 10, 1872.

H. G. the farmer receiving the nomination from H. G. the editor

fruit. The interests, the integrity, the honor, the glory of your country, can be quietly kept in the background, while you arouse the fears and touch the sensibilities of the mother and the wife.

By pursuing these rules, and others which we may hereafter prescribe, an excellent conservative journal may be published, orthodox in every respect at the North, and highly popular at the South.

## "TWO YEARS HENCE"
### Richmond *Enquirer*, June 16, 1863

In two years, as many persons hope, we may possibly have peace — that is, always provided we continue to repulse and defeat the invading enemy. The Yankee "Democracy" is certainly rousing itself and preparing for a new struggle (at the ballot-box) in the great cause of the "spoils," or, as they call it, the cause of constitutional liberty. Those Democrats are evidently beginning to raise a peace platform for their next Presidential election; and if they have the good luck to be helped on and sustained by more and more serious disasters of the Yankee army in the field, there is no doubt that the present devourers of the said spoils at Washington may soon be so discredited and decried that our enemy's country would be ripe for such peaceful ballot-box revolution.

It is sincerely to be hoped that those earnest champions of constitutional freedom will be helped on and sustained in the manner they require, namely, by continued and severe reverses in the field, and it is the first and most urgent duty of our countrymen so to help and sustain that Democratic party. It is nothing to us which of their factions may devour their "spoils"; just as little does it signify to us whether they recover or do not recover that constitutional liberty which they so wantonly threw away in the mad pursuit of Southern conquest and plunder. But it is of the utmost importance to us to aid in stimulating disaffection among Yankees against their own government, and in demoralizing and disintegrating society in that God-abandoned country. We can do this only in one way — namely, by thrashing their armies and carrying the war to their own firesides. Then, indeed, conscientious constitutional principles will hold sway; peace platforms will look attractive; arbitrary arrests will become odious, and habeas corpus be quoted at a premium. This is the only way we can help them. In this sense, and to this extent, those Democrats are truly our allies, and we shall endeavor to do our duty by them.

But armistice there will be none, and we are glad of it. Our sovereign independence is already won and paid for with treasures of brave blood. It shall not be sold by peddlers, to be built into a Yankee platform.

## THE GOOD NEWS

*Harper's Weekly*, July 18, 1863

After a long period of gloom and discouragement, we can again congratulate our readers upon good news. On 3d July, at five p.m., the broken masses of Lee's rebel army, recoiling from the shock of Meade's veterans, were flying to the mountains, throwing aside their guns and cartridge boxes, and strewing the plains of southern Pennsylvania with the materials of war; while on the one side the Army of the Potomac, flushed with victory and believing in its commander, was hotly pressing the fugitives in their retreat *northward;* and on the other the yeomen of New York and Pennsylvania, under Couch, fresh from peaceful pursuits but as steady as veterans, were pressing down on their flank and converting their attempted retreat into a rout. Not only did the rebels leave dead and wounded in our hands. The skulkers and stragglers from Lee's army — who fill every farmhouse and thicket in southern Pennsylvania and Maryland — are alone said to number one-fourth of the effective force with which he entered Maryland. Of the guns lost by the rebels and taken by us, the reports are thus far so conflicting that we do not care to repeat them. It is evident, however, that Lee must have lost in his hasty and disorderly retreat a great portion of his artillery; and if, as is reported, Meade came up with him at or near Williamsport on the 7th, and engaged him while he was preparing to cross into Virginia, his loss of guns will probably prove irreparable. Men may ford the river even in its present swollen condition, but guns cannot; and without an adequate artillery force Lee's forces will never get back to Richmond as an army.

Within twelve hours after the defeat of the rebels under Lee the garrison of Vicksburg surrendered to General Grant. We have as yet no details of the event — nothing, we may say, but a very brief dispatch from Admiral Porter to Secretary Welles. On this account the authenticity of the news has been questioned by some rebel sympathizers. We can see no good reason, however, for assuming its incorrectness. On the contrary, the last letters from Vicksburg, dated up to the 28th ult., all foreshadow the early surrender of the place, partly from the effect of our bombardment and mining operations, and partly from the want of provisions. Before these lines are read all doubts will be removed by the receipt of fuller intelligence, and we take for granted that this intelligence will confirm the present belief that we have taken Vicksburg with all its garrison and artillery.

It is assumed by some of our papers and many of our people that the defeat of Lee's army and the fall of Vicksburg involve the collapse of the rebellion. This may be so in one sense, inasmuch as the reopening of the Mississippi which follows as a matter of course from the capture of Vicksburg, and the overwhelming defeat of the rebel army in northern Virginia, render the further prosecution of the contest by the pro-slavery insurgents absolutely hopeless. The capture of Vicksburg secures the capture of Port Hudson, bisects the rebel country, and leaves General Grant's army free to operate in conjunction with Banks against Mobile, or in conjunction with Rosecrans against Chattanooga — the geographical and strategical centre of the Confederacy; while on the other hand the defeat of Lee uncovers Richmond and the railroad system of Virginia, and if properly turned to account by our people, will compel the so-called government of the Confederacy to seek refuge in North Carolina — where, according to last accounts, they are not very likely to be welcome. In this point of view, the news which we have, if confirmed, may be said to involve, sooner or later, the collapse of the pro-slavery insurrection, and the restoration of the authority of the United States government over the whole territory of the United States.

But it will probably prove a mistake to expect the actual surrender of the rebels, so long as Bragg, Beauregard, and Johnston have armies under their control. By falling back into the uplands of Carolina and Georgia; by concentrating their forces and their supplies; by increasing their cavalry force and devoting their energies to cavalry raids into the North, and the destruction of the long lines of communication which we shall have to maintain with our armies in the heart of the South; by distributing guerrillas and partisan companies along the banks of the Mississippi and the other great rivers of the Confederacy; a contest may be carried on even for years which, though hopeless and ineffectual to produce any good result, may yet avail to prevent our being able to claim that the rebellion has been crushed or peace restored. This, we take it, will be the policy of the rebel leaders. They are not the kind of men who "give up." They know that they have nothing to gain by penitence. Disgrace and exile are the mildest rewards they can expect. A halter from their own outraged people will be a more likely end to their career. The authors of the greatest rebellion in history — a rebellion equally remarkable as being a rebellion not only against the government of their own country, but against the plainest principles of truth and justice and Almighty God himself — they will not, they cannot, sue for terms as other vanquished combatants might. They will fight to the bitter end; fight so long as they can persuade a single deluded white man or wretched negro to shoulder a musket in their cause.

## THE DRAFT RIOTS

*Harper's Weekly*, August 1, 1863

The outbreak was the natural consequence of pernicious teachings widely scattered among the ignorant and excitable populace of a great city; and the only possible mode of dealing with it was stern and bloody repression. Had the mob been assailed with grape and canister on Monday, when the first disturbance took place, it would have been a saving of life and property. Had the resistance been more general and the bloodshed more profuse than it was, on Thursday, the city would have enjoyed a longer term of peace and tranquillity than we can now count upon.

It is about as idle now to argue the question of the $300 clause in the Conscription Act as it is to debate the abstract right of secession. Before Monday night the riot had got far beyond the question of the draft. Within an hour after the destruction of the Provost-Marshal's office the rioters had forgotten all about the $300 question, and were engrossed with villainous projects of arson, murder, and pillage. It was not in order to avoid the draft that the colored orphan asylum was burned; that private houses were sacked; that inoffensive colored persons were beaten, mutilated, and murdered; that Brooks's clothing establishment and a score of smaller stores were pillaged; that private citizens were robbed in the open daylight in the public streets, beaten, and maimed; that the metropolis of the country was kept for nearly a week in a state of agonizing terror and suspense. For these outrages the draft was merely the pretext; the cause was the natural turbulence of a heterogeneous populace, aggravated by the base teachings of despicable politicians and their newspaper organs.

Some newspapers dwell upon the fact that the rioters were uniformly Irish, and hence argue that our trouble arises from the perversity of the Irish race. But how do these theorists explain the fact that riots precisely similar to that of last week have occurred within our time at Paris, Madrid, Naples, Rome, Berlin, and Vienna; and that the Lord George Gordon riots in London, before our time, far surpassed the New York riot in every circumstance of atrocity? Turbulence is no exclusive attribute of the Irish character: it is common to all mobs in all countries. It happens in this city that, in our working classes, the Irish element largely preponderates over all others, and if the populace acts as a populace Irishmen are naturally prominent therein. It happens also that from the limited opportunities which the Irish enjoy for education in their own country, they are more easily misled by knaves, and made the tools of politicians when they come here, than Germans or men of other races. The impulsiveness of the Celt, likewise, prompts him to be foremost in every outburst, whether for a good or for an evil purpose. But it must be remembered in palliation of the disgrace which, as Archbishop Hughes say, the riots of last week have heaped upon the Irish name, that in many wards of the city the Irish were during the late riot stanch friends of law and order; that Irishmen helped to rescue the colored orphans in the asylum from the hands of the rioters; that a large proportion of the police, who behaved throughout the riot with the most exemplary gallantry, are Irishmen; that the Roman Catholic priesthood to a man used their influence on the side of the law; and that perhaps the most scathing rebuke administered to the riot was written by an Irishman, James T. Brady.

It is important that this riot should teach us something more useful than a revival of Know-Nothing prejudices. We ought to learn from it — what we should have known before, but communities like individuals learn nothing from experience — that riots are the natural and inevitable diseases of great cities, epidemics, like smallpox and cholera, which must be treated scientifically, upon logical principles, and with the light of large experience. In old cities where the authorities know how to treat riots, and resort at once to grape and canister, they never occur twice in a generation, one lesson being sufficient for the most hot-blooded rioter; in other places, where less vigorous counsels prevail, the disease is checked and covered up for a time, but breaks out afresh at intervals of a few months or years. The secret is, of course, that by the former method the populace are thoroughly imbued with a conviction of the power of the authorities, and of their ability and determination to crush a riot at any cost — a lesson remembered through life; while in the latter case, the half-quelled rioters are allowed to go home with a sort of feeling that they may after all be the stronger party, and the government the weaker. Hence it is that while the baton is the proper weapon of the policeman in times of peace and order, the rifle and the howitzer are the only merciful weapons in times of riot.

## [WARTIME PLEASURE–MAKING: THE RUSSIAN BALL]

*Harper's Weekly*, November 21, 1863

The Ball is over, the music is hushed, the dances ended, the wine drunk, the costly laces and diamonds put back to their places. And now that the sounds of the revel are dying out it occurs to us that we have a headache, and we are saying wisely to each other that the ball was not, after all, so very sensible a thing; and that, when

our brothers and our sons are dying on battlefields, and thousands
of brave Union soldiers, prisoners at Richmond, are being starved
to death by the Southern chivalry, it is hardly decent for us here to
be dancing, and making merry, and throwing away fortunes on
diamonds. There is something in the idea. Should this number of
*Harper's Weekly* fall into the hands of some poor wounded fellow at
Chattanooga, or some half-starved Union prisoner at Richmond,
the contrast between his own condition and that of the scented and
perfumed dancers who figure in the ball picture may not improve
his temper. "They are fiddling while I am dying," is the remark
which would not unnaturally occur to him, and it would leave a
bitter taste behind.

"What then?" says Shoddy. "Are we all to put on sackcloth and
ashes because of the war? Are Mrs. and the Misses Shoddy not to
have an opportunity of displaying their beauty — to say nothing of
the splendid dresses and the magnificent diamonds which I bought
them with the proceeds of paper money — simply because we are
engaged in a war? The notion is monstrous! I pay for the war:
taxes on my income, taxes on my clothing, taxes on my house, horses,
carriages, silver, and everything that I've got; I send my blood
relations to the war to fight and die; I give money for bounties
and money to the Sanitary Commission; I vote to support the
government. Having done all this, I submit that my duty is fulfilled, and that I may, if I choose, get up balls for Mrs. and the Misses
Shoddy, and that they may enjoy them as becomes their age, their
means, and their spirits. Dancing and balls are not bad things, by
any means. It is good that young people should enjoy themselves
while they can. They will all find sorrow enough in life by and by.
Besides, our Russian Ball had a political significance, and may
render good aid to the Union cause."

Thus much Shoddy. And though his reasoning is likely to seem
very shallow and very selfish to the brave suffering men on Belle
Isle or in Castle Thunder, it must fairly be admitted that, in past
time, balls and battles have often jostled with each other, and the
dying sounds of the dance have often mingled with the blast of the
bugle. "There was a sound of revelry by night" within a few hours
of the battle of Waterloo, and the dance was never more popular
in Europe than during the Napoleonic Wars. The Preacher gives
the key to the apparent paradox when he says, "Let us eat, drink,
and be merry; *for tomorrow we die.*"

And now — good Shoddy, fair Mrs. Shoddy, and sweet daughters
of the Shoddy house — that you have had your dance, and flirted
with your Cossack, and flashed your diamonds in a thousand envious
eyes; now that you have spent, so they say, over a million of dollars

for one night's enjoyment; have you time and do you care to think of a suggestion by which your pleasure and our suffering heroes' needs may both be satisfied?

There was a time, not many years ago, when a commercial crisis precipitated the poor of New York into great suffering. At that time large-minded men and women gave their thoughts to the subject, and while soup-kitchens were established by A. T. Stewart and others, fashionable ladies gave a series of calico balls, the rule of which was that every lady present donated the dress she wore to the poor. By this means thousands of poor girls and women, who would otherwise have gone half-clad that bitter winter, were furnished with clothing. What say you now, ladies, to a

## DIAMOND BALL,

the jewels worn to be given after the ball to the Sanitary Commission, which has our wounded soldiers in charge?

If, as is stated, a million of dollars' worth of diamonds were worn at the Russian ball, a million of dollars might be procured by such a Diamond Ball as we suggest — enough money to secure every comfort required by our wounded soldiers, and probably to save hundreds of lives which are now sacrificed for want of suitable attendance, clothing, and food. Could the jewels be put to a nobler use? Would not their radiance, in such a cause, flash not only from wall to wall of the ballroom, but down through the vale of time to the most distant age, lighting the fame of New York women, and proving that they were worthy wives and daughters of the brave men who are dying for their country?

## GETTYSBURG [1]

### Harper's Weekly, December 5, 1863

The solemn ceremony at Gettysburg is one of the most striking events of the war. There are graveyards enough in the land — what is Virginia but a cemetery? — and the brave who have died for us in this fierce war consecrate the soil from the ocean to the Mississippi. But there is peculiar significance in the field of Gettysburg, for there "thus far" was thundered to the rebellion. This it is which separates it from all the other battlefields of this war. Elsewhere the men in the ranks have fought as nobly, and their officers have directed as bravely; but here their valor stayed the flood of barbarism, and like the precious shells that the highest storm tides strew upon the beach, showing how far the waters came, so the

---

[1] Harper's Weekly and the Springfield Republican were the two outstanding journals which recognized at once the greatness of the Gettysburg Address.

dead heroes of Gettysburg marked the highest tide of the war. Therefore shall their graves be peculiarly honored, and their memory especially sacred; and all that living men can bring of pomp and solemnity and significance to hallow their resting-place shall not be wanting.

The President and the Cabinet were there, with famous soldiers and civilians. The oration by Mr. Everett was smooth and cold. Delivered, doubtless, with his accustomed graces, it yet wanted one stirring thought, one vivid picture, one thrilling appeal.

The few words of the President were from the heart to the heart. They cannot be read, even, without kindling emotion. "The world will little note nor long remember what we say here, but it can never forget what they did here." It was as simple and felicitous and earnest a word as was ever spoken.

Among the Governors present was Horatio Seymour. He came to honor the dead of Gettysburg. But when they were dying he stood in New York sneeringly asking where was the victory promised for the Fourth of July? These men were winning their victory and dying for us all; and now he mourns, ex officio, over their graves.

When the war is over and the verdict of history is rendered, it is not those who have steadily perplexed the government in every way — those who first incited and then palliated massacre and riot — who will be known as the friends of the soldiers, but those whose faith was firmest in the darkest hours, and who did not falter though the foe were at the door.

## THE UNION NOMINATIONS

*Harper's Weekly*, June 25, 1864

The Baltimore Convention met and organized on the 7th of June, and on the 8th, in one session, laid down its platform, nominated Abraham Lincoln and Andrew Johnson with enthusiastic unanimity, and adjourned.

There was never a convention which more truly represented the people, and upon the first opportunity offered, it showed its purpose in the most unmistakable manner. No one who watched its deliberations, or who has read its proceedings, but must feel that it expressed the strongest popular determination of the unflinching prosecution of the war by every efficient method. Its settlement of the Missouri question, by admitting the radical delegation from that State and excluding the other, by a vote of 440 to 4, was the indication that the vast mass of Union men in the country have parted company with the hesitating and doubtful course which has been associated with the name of Blair. The resolutions, clear, incisive, and full, are to the same result, and leave no doubt in any mind that the "Border State policy," having served its purpose, and a purpose with which we are not disposed to quarrel, is no longer the policy which the people of the country approve. This decision is emphasized by the nomination of Andrew Johnson, a lifelong Democrat, who has been educated by fire and sword straight up to the necessities of the crisis.

Of Abraham Lincoln we have nothing to change in the views often expressed in these columns. That he unites perfect patriotism and great sagacity to profound conviction and patient tenacity, and that his conduct of our affairs has been, upon the whole, most admirable and wise, we are more than ever convinced; and that no public man in our history since Washington has inspired a deeper popular confidence we have no doubt whatever that the result of the election will establish. Of Andrew Johnson it is enough to say that there is no man in the country, unless it be Mr. Lincoln himself, whom the rebels more cordially hate. He fought them in the Senate, when they counted upon his aid, and he has fought them steadily ever since and with untiring energy. It is pleasant to record, of our personal knowledge, that one of the wisest and truest patriots in the country, who has sacrificed not less than Johnson himself, says of the contingency of Johnson's succession to the chief magistracy, that the country and the cause of American liberty could then not be in safer hands.

The reception of the nominations is what might be expected of a people which had virtually ordered them to be made. The copperhead journals, the late supporters of John B. Floyd & Co., denounce the convention as a corrupt body; and seeing in the nominations the most tremendous proclamation of the loyal citizens of the United States to all enemies at home and abroad that the cause of the American Union is to be fought out along this line, they renew their old cry that our liberties have been lost in the effort to maintain them. The real copperhead regret is, not that liberty has been lost, but that slavery has not been saved. The Union journals which have considered Mr. Lincoln badly advised, timid, and hesitating, still cordially applaud the platform, which they properly regard as a body of instructions from the people for increased and continual vigor. They are entirely satisfied with the resolutions and Andrew Johnson, but wish the Presidential nomination had been left dependent upon the result of the campaign. That is a view of the situation which seems to us peculiarly erroneous, and fraught with the utmost danger. The reliance of every patriot is and must be upon the sturdy good sense and purpose of the people — a faith not to be shaken by disaster, and a purpose which demands that the

Chief Magistrate, in such a time as this, shall be a tried and not an untried man.

It is remarkable that journals which we have always supposed were truly and not technically "democratic," because believing in the general wisdom and instinct of the people, while they regret to see that Mr. Lincoln has been renominated, confess that he is beyond any question the man and the choice of the people.

## LINCOLN

### Richmond *Dispatch*, April 7, 1864

Lincoln alone harmonizes in himself all those qualities which are essential to a representation of average Yankeeism. He has no education beyond that of the common schools and the attorney's office, and is rich in moral and immoral features which distinguish the genuine son of the Puritan from the rest of mankind. He is shrewd, energetic, shallow, cunning, selfish, egotistical, hard-hearted, vulgar, hypocritical, and fanatical. Every one of these qualities he has manifested from the moment when he marched into Washington in a freight car, until the American people would be false to their own instincts if they did not recognize him as their true representative man. We shall be greatly mistaken if he is not the reëlected candidate for the Presidency.

## THE PEACE BLONDINS AT NIAGARA

### Harper's Weekly, August 6, 1864

The late Peace performance at Niagara Falls was not very mysterious. It was simply a movement of the rebels to help their friends the Copperheads. It was a notification, to whom it might concern, that if the government of the United States were handed over to the friends of the rebels, then the rebels would lay down their arms. It was a confession that the rebel leaders are sorely pinched, that they foresee disaster, and that they are perfectly willing to have us give them by our votes the victory which they despair of obtaining by their arms.

The conduct of the President was simple and proper. Informed that there were accredited agents from the rebel chiefs who wished to treat of peace, he consented that they should visit Washington. But when they confessed that they had no authority whatever, the President, in order that there should be no apparent justification even of the assertion that he had refused to listen to overtures from the rebels, issued a notice, to whom it may concern, that the government of the United States is always ready to hear and consider any authorized proposition from the rebel leaders involving the restoration of the Union and the abandonment of slavery. To this the discomfited and self-appointed rebel agents reply in a manifesto intended to represent the President as an autocrat and a despot, etc., and expressing their own resolution never to submit to conquest, etc. It is interesting to learn from this paper that in a region where every man between fifteen and sixty-five is dragged into the ranks, and exempt soldiers are legislated back to serve as long as they are wanted, there is no military autocrat; and that, in a section where the most hopeless terrorism prevails, social institutions, established constitutions, and priceless hereditary self-government are not overthrown, subverted, or bartered away. Mr. Clement Clay's letter is but a poor specimen of our own copperhead orations and editorials. But it is not without value, for it shows to the dullest mind the perfect sympathy in sentiment between Copperheads and rebels.

It is suggested that the Constitution does not authorize the President to make any condition such as the abandonment of slavery. Those who say so honestly are mistaken. There may be a question of policy, which we think the President has rightly resolved; but there is no constitutional question. The Constitution defines treason, authorizes making of war, appoints the President commander-in-chief, and authorizes the suspension of the writ of *habeas corpus* in case of rebellion and invasion. There is nothing in any of these provisions which deprives the government of the right of exercising its common sense, or compels it to lay down its arms at the will of rebels or foreign enemies. The government is the judge when a foreign war is over or a domestic rebellion quelled. Nor is there in the Constitution nor in reason any obligation upon the government to connive at its own destruction. The government of the United States is bound by every consideration to secure peace; and peace is impossible while the active cause for war remains, watching for its opportunity. The cry that the President can not constitutionally require the destruction of that cause as a condition of peace is but another effort of the enemies of the country to prolong the war indefinitely. When the government was established the cloud of slavery was as large as a man's hand. Four years ago it was a tempest, blackening the heavens and raining fire. And now we are told that it is proper to put up an umbrella to keep off the wet, but unconstitutional to erect a lightning rod to draw the fire harmless to the ground. It is idle to shirk the vital point of the whole war, and imagine that peace can be made with slavery. To that point the public mind has advanced. If a truce should be called and the question opened for debate, the truce would soon disappear in fresh cannon-smoke. Liberty and slavery are fighting for and against this government. Is he a wise man who affects to think that by omitting the name we can avoid the thing?

## THE CHICAGO DEMOCRATIC CONVENTION

*Harper's Weekly*, September 10, 1864

The platform of the Chicago Convention will satisfy every foreign and domestic enemy of American Union and Liberty. It declares that the government of the United States is guilty of resisting rebellion, and that the American people cannot maintain the authority of their laws. It has no word of righteous wrath against the recreant citizens who have plunged the country in the blood of civil war, but lavishes its fury upon the constituted authorities which have steadily defended the Union. It has no censure for any act of rebellion, but the war measures taken by the Administration, under the authority of the Constitution, are branded as tyrannical and despotic. There is not a word in it that can cheer any soldier or sailor fighting for his country; not a syllable that stirs the blood of a patriot. It is craven, abject, humiliating. It confesses the defeat of the Union cause, and covertly implores the mercy of Jefferson Davis and his crew.

And this at a moment when stout old Farragut is thundering at Mobile; when the inexorable Grant clutches at the Weldon Road, which, as an officer of the army writes, is "like touching the cubs of a tigress;" when Early's Shenandoah invasion is too late for success; when Sherman is closing around Atlanta; when State after State is supplying its quota of fresh soldiers; when gold steadily declines; when a universal public confidence is awakening; and when the rebels are plainly, palpably struggling to hold out only long enough to see if the election, by the elevation of the Chicago candidate, will not turn to their advantage.

Never again will this nation have a fairer chance of maintaining its constitutional authority than it has now. For three years it has, at every disadvantage, battled against this formidable conspiracy, and never was the conspiracy in so desperate a strait. The country has it by the throat. A little more force, a closer pressure, and the monster falls strangled, dead forever. A little less force, a relaxed hold, a wavering purpose, and the scaly folds of rebellion thrill with hope to the extremity; it renews its strength, it recruits its venom, and darts a deadlier blow at the life of the country. . . . The issue is simple and sublime. It is the life or the degradation of the nation. It is to show that a government of the people is equal to every exigency — ready for taxation, ready for military service, ready for endurance, ready for forbearance — that it is as strong as any government in the world, and stronger — that in war it is as powerful and resolute and orderly as in peace it is industrious and prosperous. There seems to us but one way in which this can be shown, but one way in which utter national humiliation can be avoided, and that is by the steady and strong hand of war until the rebels confess the authority of the government. That is the policy which is personified in Abraham Lincoln and Andrew Johnson, and which we shall most strenuously support, for it is the cause of the peace and happiness of the American people.

## [McCLELLAN'S CANDIDACY]

Springfield *Republican*, September 18, 1864

With respectable talents, a pure character, and patriotic purposes, he is wanting in that high moral sense that perceives the truest truth, and that high moral courage that does and dares in its behalf. He waits, he hesitates in the presence of great opportunities; he compromises with time and with truth; and he is no fit man to deal with the sharp exigencies and the sublime occasions of this hour. He wants and would try to save the country; but he would hinder rather than help the people, who *will* save it in the long run, despite their own occasional fickleness and faint-heartedness — because he fails to see and use quickly the moral and material agencies by which it is to be saved, and because he is no match for the men who are bent on its ruin. . . .

The platform is weak in words and wicked in intention. It lacks vigor, sharpness, and high principle. The breaking purpose shines through every sentence. Its words for the Union are hesitating, guarded, shuffling; while its clamor for experiments that would endanger it, its want of condemnation for those who have struck at it, and still hold aloft the bloody flag of disunion and destruction, and its petty arraignment of those who are wielding the power of the government to sustain and secure it, all show that the real sympathy of its authors is with the enemies rather than the defenders of the Union.

## NEGROES AS REBEL SOLDIERS [1]

Richmond *Inquirer*, October 6, 1864

The general order for the revocation of details will be found in this issue of the *Inquirer*. This step has been taken by the government to fill up the army. It is necessary and proper, and if this

[1] The question of arming the slaves was increasingly discussed throughout the South during 1864; the Confederate Congress that autumn authorized the hiring of slaves from their owners; and President Davis's message of November, 1864, recommended that the government be empowered to buy them for war use, and, if it liked, to emancipate them at the end of the struggle. The Confederate Secretary of War at the same time went farther and advocated making soldiers out of large bodies of slaves. When this editorial was written, however, such a proposal was considered extreme doctrine.

order is properly enforced the increase of the army will be speedy and rapid. We should like to see steps taken to promptly enforce the law of Congress for the employment of negroes as teamsters, etc. The law of Congress on this subject is plain, and though it does not go far enough, yet by promptly enforcing its provisions, many soldiers will be returned to their commands, and the army very greatly strengthened. The details should come forward promptly; their services are greatly needed, and if they are speedily collected and sent to the front there will be no danger at Richmond, and the condition of the country will present the most encouraging aspect. It is useless to seek to conceal that more men are greatly wanted.

The President has emphatically announced the startling fact that two-thirds of the army are absent from the ranks. There would be no need of reinforcements but for this most disgraceful straggling and deserting. But as the fact exists, and the evil must be repaired, the details are called upon to do service. How long their service will be required cannot now be said. Sixty to ninety days will terminate the active operations of the campaign, and then details may be resumed; but, at present, all are needed, and all must come forward. Those that delay or shirk will be hunted down, and permanently sent to the army.

The law of Congress authorizing the employment of negroes, if fully carried out, would give ten thousand men to the Army of Northern Virginia. The slaves and free negroes can be impressed just as any other property, and the law provides for their support and clothing, and pays the owner soldier's wages.

The question of making soldiers of negroes, of regularly enlisting them, and fighting them, for their own safety as well as our own, must have presented itself to every reflecting mind. Because the Yankees have not been able to make soldiers out of their drafted negroes, it does not follow that we cannot train our slaves to make very efficient troops. We believe that they can be, by drill and discipline, moulded into steady and reliable soldiers. The propriety of employing negroes as soldiers we shall not at present discuss; but whenever the subjugation of Virginia or the employment of her slaves as soldiers are alternative positions, then certainly we are for making them soldiers, and giving freedom to those negroes that escape the casualties of battle.

We should be glad to see the Confederate Congress provide for the purchase of two hundred and fifty thousand negroes, present them with their freedom and the privilege of remaining in the States, and arm, equip, drill and fight them. We believe that the negroes, identified with us by interest, and fighting for their freedom here, would be faithful and reliable soldiers, and, under officers who would drill them, could be depended on for much of the ordinary service and even for the hardest fighting. It is not necessary now to discuss this matter, and may never become so, but neither negroes nor slavery will be permitted to stand in the way of the success of our cause. This war is for national independence on our side, and for the subjugation of the whites and the emancipation of the negroes on the side of the enemy. If we fail the negroes are nominally free and their masters really slaves. We must, therefore, succeed. Other States may decide for themselves, but Virginia after exhausting her whites, will fight her blacks through to the last man. She will be free at all costs.

## THE FINAL RESULTS OF THIS WAR

Philadelphia *Public Ledger*, November 7, 1864

In the North no person can step into a railroad car but the rapid change which is going on will be apparent to him. Many are travelling who never travelled before on cars and steamboats, so that the character of the travelling masses is quite different from what it used to be. Formerly only merchants and professional men and persons of wealth and leisure travelled, but now the whole country, as soldiers, fathers, brothers, sisters, mothers of soldiers, are passing to and fro in every train. Those depths of society which are usually least disturbed by ordinary movements have been agitated and wakened into a life and activity unparalleled in history. There is hardly a family but has some of its sons with one or more of our armies in the South, and all this enlarges the mind and expands the ideas amazingly. What must and will be the result of such a war as the present, where soldiers go a thousand or two miles home on furlough and write letters by every post such as no other nation can parallel? Every newspaper conveys the latest telegraphic news and the minutest features in the domestic life of every town and village visited by our forces. Men are thrown together in masses who formerly lived sequestered, and by comparing their observations educate each other. All this may produce an intellectual activity for which the past affords no precedent. Already the best schools and institutions of learning, especially for young ladies, are crowded to excess, and academies and even colleges show such increased numbers that the effect of the draft is not felt upon them. The abundance of money is increasing the demand for education to such an extent that this war produces no injurious effect. This is, we believe, unprecedented.

What the effect of the war will be on the South eventually, who shall predict? But the masses of the poor whites will be much enlightened by all they have passed through, and by their contact with Northern minds. They will be no longer controlled by a few wealthy leaders. Northern energy and intelligence will be diffused in various ways throughout those Southern sections whose fertility is incalculable. When the present rebellion is put down the progress of the country as a whole will probably be very much more rapid than at any former period, and the history of a new life will begin from the present war. The whole world will be affected by it most sensibly. The wealth of Germany and the population of Ireland will be found transported to a wonderful extent to our shores. The privileged classes of the old world will see in our success, as Professor Goldwin Smith well remarked, their own downfall. But the masses of the people of all Europe will find it the prognostic of their own progress in liberty.

## THE DEATH OF LINCOLN [1]

New York *Evening Post*, April 20, 1865

*Oh, slow to smite and swift to spare,*
*Gentle and merciful and just!*
*Who, in the fear of God, didst bear*
*The sword of power, a nation's trust.*

*In sorrow by thy bier we stand,*
*Amid the awe that hushes all,*
*And speak the anguish of a land*
*That shook with horror at thy fall.*

*Thy task is done; the bond are free:*
*We bear thee to an honored grave,*
*Whose proudest monument shall be*
*The broken fetters of the slave.*

*Pure was thy life; its bloody close*
*Hath placed thee with the sons of light*
*Among the noble host of those*
*Who perished in the cause of right.*

[1] Contributed to the editorial columns by the editor-in-chief, William Cullen Bryant.

PART THREE

THE AMERICAN PRESS AND PUBLIC OPINION
1865-1900

# THE AMERICAN PRESS AND PUBLIC OPINION
## 1865–1900

When the Civil War ended the great veterans of journalism were about to pass from the stage, and in their places a new group of editors — to most observers it seemed a weaker group — was about to become prominent. Raymond died in 1869, at the untimely age of forty-nine; Greeley followed him in 1872; Bryant, now an old man, occupied himself in travel and in translating Homer, and left the *Evening Post* chiefly to a succession of managing editors; while Samuel Bowles ended his career in 1878. But before even the first of this constellation had been extinguished, two new stars had begun to attract general attention. E. L. Godkin, founding the *Nation* in 1865, showed at once a distinctive style, a refreshing penetration, and a skill in ironic analysis never before equalled in American journalism. Charles A. Dana, taking charge of the New York *Sun* after a disastrous experiment in Chicago journalism, gave that newspaper a liveliness in the presentation of news which lent vigor to its editorial columns. Other men were to follow. Greeley was succeeded in editing the *Tribune* by Whitelaw Reid, and the first Samuel Bowles had partly given way, even before his death, to the second eminent editor of that name.

As the greatest rôle in the leadership of opinion in the generation preceding the Civil War had been played by Horace Greeley, so the greatest single part in the next generation was with little doubt that of E. L. Godkin. This was the final verdict of more than one acute observer. Henry Holt declared at the close of the century that Godkin had taught the country more than any other man in it. "To my generation," wrote William James, "his was certainly the towering influence in all thought concerning public affairs, and indirectly his influence has assuredly been more pervasive than that of any other writer of the generation, for he influenced other writers who never quoted him, and determined the whole current of discussion." From 1865 until 1899 Godkin was editor-in-chief of the *Nation;* from 1881 to 1883 he was one of the three editors of the *Evening Post,* the others being Horace White and Carl Schurz; and from 1883 till the end of 1899, he was editor-in-chief of the *Evening Post*, of which the *Nation* became editorially a weekly edition.   Directly, he never addressed more than 35,000 subscribers to the two publications, but indirectly, as filtered down through other journals, through pulpits, through college chairs, and by word of mouth, his opinions affected almost every corner of the land.

Godkin was in almost every respect a new and strange apparition in the field of American journalism.   The previous masters of public opinion had been representatively democratic in education and views;  Godkin was essentially aristocratic in both.   Cobbett, Gales, Bennett, Greeley, and Bowles had been men of the people, and the two latter had appealed to the masses in the language of the masses;  Godkin was an Anglo-Irishman, a college graduate, a man of aloof, reserved temper, and one who, though a philosophical liberal, had no real sympathy for the struggling manual worker, for the farmer or laborer, or for those rougher aspects of American life which were the product of frontier conditions.   Upon many of the salient issues of the day his views were admirable, and he did the republic great service by his trenchant advocacy of civil service reform, of sane tariff legislation, of a sound currency, of reconciliation between the North and the South, and of higher cultural and moral standards in society.   No one fought corruption in government more effectively than he.   He had a faculty of penetrating to the raw in the hides of men who seemed impervious to censure, until the most brutish politicians would wince.   He arraigned the shady politicians of Grant's Administration savagely;  his campaign against Blaine in 1884 was witheringly effective;  and in the eighties and nineties he fought the Tammany heelers of Hugh Grant and Richard Croker until they feared his vitriolic pen more than they did newspapers of ten times the *Evening Post's* circulation.   But he always seemed slightly, and sometimes decidedly, outside the main current of American opinion — something that could seldom be said of Greeley or Raymond.

Godkin was essentially an editorial writer, not a manager, though the whole of the *Evening Post* was subtly informed by his intellectual pride, his integrity, his thoughtfulness, and his moral austerity.   In some respects his writing has never been equalled in America.   He was bold to the point of rashness, never feared libel suits, denounced men stingingly by name, and often plunged the *Evening Post* into hot water.   He was as combative as Cobbett.   A rich allusiveness pervaded his work, and it reflected the mind of the scholar like St. Loe

Strachey's editorial writing for the London *Spectator*. Yet it was never heavy. For one thing, he had a gift for observing the picturesque in social or political events; for another, he could always lighten his paragraphs with humorous images, pungent epithets, and strokes of caustic wit. "At daybreak this morning," he wrote when the news of Cleveland's triumph in 1884 finally came through, "everybody conceded Cleveland's election save the *Tribune*, which remains in doubt. If it persists in declaring Blaine elected there will be two inauguration ceremonies on March 4, one of Cleveland in Washington and one of Blaine on the steps of the *Tribune* building, the oath of office being administered by William Walter Phelps." Godkin used the parallel column with a skill that had never yet been approached. His articles had the merit of being full of ideas, for he never tolerated the commonplace in himself or his colleagues. Though not sententious, he joined grace with a remarkable compactness of expression. As Lord Bryce wrote, "every word had its use and every sentence told"; as Lowell put it, he combined in eminent degree "a lightness of touch and a weightiness of judgment."

To an extent previously unknown in American journalism, Godkin satisfied the intellectual classes — the lawyers, physicians, professors, clergy, authors. Yet even they, so frequently did he use irony, so atrabilious sometimes seemed his temperament, and so plainly limited were his sympathies with common men and common things, often tacitly rebelled a little against him. They complained that the *Nation* gave them mental dyspepsia. They told the story of the old lady who, living alone in the country, felt safe because the carrier threw the *Evening Post* on her porch at dusk, and "it just lay there and growled all night"; and they quoted Joseph Choate's remark about "that pessimistic, malignant, and malevolent sheet — which no good citizen ever goes to bed without reading!" It was always stimulating, but even its warmest admirers found it sometimes a bit irritating.

Charles A. Dana's greatness as an editor lies chiefly in his conduct of the news departments of the *Sun*, and little if at all in his formal relations with public opinion. He believed that a newspaper should not merely be enterprising and comprehensive; he held that it should also be vivaciously written, and filled from beginning to end with human interest. Under his editorship the *Sun* acquired the most brilliant staff of reporters, special writers, and correspondents in the nation, and became "the newspaperman's newspaper" — a breezy, witty, somewhat sensational, and vividly alert journal. Editorially its staff was also able. But Dana was responsible for a tone of cynicism, levity, and sometimes sheer perversity which destroyed a great deal of the influence over public opinion which the general merits of the *Sun* might have commanded. He assailed Grant in 1872 with unsparing rigor, and yet simultaneously poked fun at the candidacy of "Dr." Greeley, whom he was nominally supporting; he followed Rutherford B. Hayes with unremitting hostility as "The Fraudulent President"; he lost no opportunity of assailing Grover Cleveland, and in 1884 he fatuously supported Ben Butler on the Greenback ticket for the Presidency, thus losing the *Sun* tens of thousands of buyers. He did not believe in labor unions, and never failed to attack their strikes; he derided civil service reform; he constantly supported schemes of annexation and territorial expansion, calling for the acquisition of Canada, Cuba, and San Domingo. In fact, to honest and liberal leaders of journalism his course often seemed Machiavellian, and they condemned it as such.

Yet Dana's editorial page did possess certain decided merits. Now and then it attacked a wrong or espoused a noble cause for reasons which did not seem sardonic or rooted in love of the spectacular. Among Dana's editorial writers were men of distinction, the best being Edward P. Mitchell, who succeeded him in control of the *Sun*, W. O. Bartlett, Henry B. Stanton, and Francis P. Church. These men, like Dana himself, had a knack of swift biting phraseology. The characterization of Hancock in 1880 as "a good man, weighing 240 pounds," is one of the memorable hits of American political journalism; the jingle, "No king, no clown, To rule this town," was equally effective; and by mere reiteration some apt cries, like that in Grant's Administration, "Turn the rascals out," were printed deep into the public consciousness. Moreover, these men were expert in the composition of sparkling brief essays, humorous or literary, which in their kind have not been surpassed in American journalism. After the death of Dana in 1897 the *Sun's* editorial page retained this sparkle and pungency, and in political matters showed an enhanced sobriety and devotion to principle. Indeed, E. P. Mitchell, though without Dana's intense personal interest in politics, was his equal in cultivation — which is saying a great deal — and excelled him in style, in color, and in a broadly human interest in life.

Much closer to the essential American tradition than the work of Godkin and Dana — much steadier than the *Sun*, much more sympathetically liberal than the *Nation* — was the editorial page of the

Springfield *Republican*.  The elder Bowles distinguished himself during the Reconstruction period by his demand for a generous policy towards the South, opposing the enfranchisement of the negroes, the carpetbag looting, and the bayonet governments.  Unlike the *Nation*, the *Republican* stuck hopefully to the Liberal Republican movement of 1872 even after Greeley was nominated, and in 1876 it gave another evidence of stern political independence; for though it supported Hayes till November, it held after the election that Tilden had been legally chosen.  Some of the elder Bowles's observations upon the Erie Ring were so unpleasant that in 1868 he was thrown into jail, during a visit to New York, by Jim Fisk and his Tammany allies, and kept there without bail for a night.  When the younger Bowles succeeded his father in 1877, he carried on the tradition of complete independence.  It was most signally exercised in 1884, when the *Republican* joined with gusto in the mugwump revolt against Blaine, and in 1884 and 1892, when it again supported Cleveland.  Though the editorials of both the elder and younger Bowles lacked the combative purgency and the superb literary finish of Godkin's work, they were often finely persuasive pieces of argument; all the more persuasive for their moderation, their human sympathy with the poor, and their cordiality for such movements as prohibition and equal suffrage.

The *Republican* maintained its special distinction as the best all-round provincial newspaper; but there were other journals in widely scattered cities which, in the generation after the Civil War, became only less well known.  One was Henry Watterson's *Courier-Journal*, a newspaper made notable by the rich and expansive personality of its editor rather than by any great intellectual distinction.  Taking charge of the Louisville sheet just after the Civil War, Watterson enjoyed until 1919 an unhampered control of its editorial policies, in which he could say just what he pleased with all the exuberance, the eloquence, and the occasional extravagance which he liked — and which his Southern constituency liked also.

Watterson was fortunate in his time and place.  He became prominent in the dark days of Reconstruction, when as the chief editor in a loyal border State he could interpret each section to the other.  He had also a gift for practical politics, and from the days of Horatio Seymour to those of Woodrow Wilson, was one of the rather incalculable leaders of the Democratic party.  In some respects he was an editor of aggressively liberal views.  Thus in his reminiscences he could justly boast that he had striven not merely for reconciliation between North and South, but to make the South respect the rights of the negro, and face honestly the duties of the new era opened by emancipation. He sympathized with labor. His editorial page, rhetorical, full of personal memories, and containing signed or initialled articles which not infrequently ran to five or six columns, was never a model of style. But it was respected and it was important because it spoke of old "Marse Henry" himself. He was often wrong-headed, and some of his policies — his attacks upon Cleveland and Wilson, and his hatred of the League of Nations — are difficult to explain; but his heart was always in the right place. His best work was done late in life, when his ripe experience, his cosmopolitan knowledge of the world, had largely atoned for his lack of real intellectual discipline in youth, and when his writing, as orotund as ever, showed an extraordinary knowledge, verve, and range.

The only other great Southern editor, a man whom Watterson long outlived, was Henry W. Grady of the Atlanta *Constitution*. A Georgian, the son of a major killed at Petersburg, he was a fine representative of the new generation of his section. Journalistic service for the New York *Herald* gave him the means in 1879 to buy a quarter interest in the Atlanta *Constitution*, and he impressed himself upon every part of the South before his sudden death in 1889. At the height of its fame, the *Constitution* was edited by a talented triumvirate, for associated with Grady were Clark Howell and Joel Chandler Harris. Before him Grady kept always an ideal of social and industrial regeneration for the South, and in his editorials, glowingly eloquent, he drew constant attention to the material resources of the region, and the rich results that would follow their development. He was oratorical; he played alternately upon chords of humor and pathos; and to sophisticated readers much of his work now seems too sentimental and too sonorous. But he possessed a broadly statesmanlike view, and he exercised a large and wholesome influence. A man of similar position but of very different character, far in the Northwest, was Harvey W. Scott of the Portland *Oregonian;* a man who held his editorial chair for forty years, and displayed remarkable scholarship in that position. He also was keenly interested in the development, material and moral, of his section, and he labored fruitfully during a long generation for the upbuilding of the whole Pacific Coast.

In a somewhat subordinate category, a wide variety of newspapers held or gained a hearing of more than local scope in the generation after the war. The Chicago *Tribune* was one: it reached the apex of its editorial career when, Joseph Medill having been elected mayor of Chicago, the direction of the paper passed to Horace White. It was already the chief Republican journal of the West. White, an advocate of tariff, currency, and civil reform, a warm sympathizer with the abused farmers of the West, and a fighter for decent government without respect for party, rapidly raised the *Tribune* to a position of great and healthful authority. He was one of the independent editors who turned from the Republicans to the Liberal Republicans early in 1872. Unfortunately, in 1874 Medill resumed control, announced his intention of repairing the "mischief" which White had wrought, and brought the paper back to its old character. The chief Cincinnati newspaper became the *Commercial*, which was edited by the picturesque Murat Halstead: an ill-educated, energetic, muscular man, who won a reputation by his somewhat reckless attacks upon men and measures — especially Democratic men and measures — and by his crude but forcible language. In New England a respectable place was held by the Boston *Transcript*, and one more than respectable by the Hartford *Courant*, which came under the control of General Joseph R. Hawley and Charles Dudley Warner. They worked together harmoniously, and the journal reflected both Hawley's liberalism of outlook, and Warner's exceptional literary gifts.

More important than almost any of these papers — much more important than the staid, decorous, dull Philadelphia *Public Ledger*, which George W. Childs edited for the banking firm of the Drexels, or the Philadelphia *Times*, which Alexander K. McClure, an independent politician, founded in 1875 — were certain of the weeklies of the day. The *Independent* and the *Outlook* (originally the *Christian Observer*) were potent in church circles; but preëminent among these publications stood *Harper's Weekly*, the pet enterprise of the publisher, Fletcher Harper, which within a few years after its establishment in 1857 had climbed to the extraordinary circulation of 120,000. Its period of power dates from 1863, when George W. Curtis, previously a regular contributor, became its political editor. Curtis, a graduate of Brook Farm, had become known early in life as the author of some charming books of travel and social comment, but had been caught up by the great moral onslaught upon slavery, and dedicating himself fervently to it, had finally abandoned his absorption in pure literature. He instantly became one of the outstanding editors of the time. His convictions upon the war, the proper attitude of the government toward slavery, and the questions of Reconstruction, were clearly defined. Writing for the most part with a clear, direct, and even Doric style, he occasionally revealed the charming essayist vein, full of wit and grace, for which he was distinguished. As his biographer has said, his editorials were like the talk of a highly cultured, very earnest man of the world, abounding in point, allusion, and humor. "He seemed to have his reader as clearly in his mind as if he were sitting before him, and he reasoned with him, appealed to him, suggested to him, as he would have done had their eyes met."

In the fight against Tammany at the beginning of the seventies, Curtis's pen was not merely reinforced but was far outweighed by the pencil of Thomas Nast, whose work after more than a half century remains the supreme example of the power a cartoonist may exercise upon public opinion. Such pictures as "Tweedledee and Sweedledum," showing Tweed and Sweeny dispensing the public funds to their supporters, or "Who Stole the People's Money?", in which Tweed and his Ring associates are formed in a circle, pointing accusingly to one another, or "The Tammany Tiger Loose," were better than dozens of editorials. A representative of the Ring called upon Nast and offered him first $100,000, then $200,000, and finally $500,000 in gold to go abroad, take a rest, and study art; but Nast replied that "I made up my mind long ago to put some of those fellows behind the bars, and I'm going to put them there!" It was his work and that of the editors of the *Times* which furnished the basis for the destruction of the Ring. A dozen years later, in the Blaine-Cleveland campaign of 1884, *Harper's Weekly* again achieved a position of national eminence and struck a powerful blow for governmental reform. Curtis had gone to the Republican convention in Chicago as a delegate; returning, he bolted the ticket, and with the support of the Harper firm, trained the guns of the *Weekly* upon Blaine's candidacy with telling effect. Neither he nor Nast ever did better work than during this campaign summer.

The decade 1880–1890 was that in which three new figures, influential till long after the end of the century, came into prominence in American journalism: William Rockhill Nelson, who established the Kansas City *Evening Star* in 1880, Joseph Pulitzer, who purchased the New York *World* in 1883, and William Randolph Hearst, who took charge of the San Francisco *Examiner* in 1887. Nelson was especially interested in municipal improvement, and in his campaigns for honest transit arrangements, city parks, better homes, boulevards, and a municipal auditorium, he demonstrated what a splendid instrument for civic betterment a newspaper may be. Outside the municipal sphere the *Star* had slender influence, but it was always staunchly independent. In turn Nelson supported Cleveland, McKinley and Roosevelt, and Woodrow Wilson. Like the *Courier-Journal*, the *Star* expressed perfectly the robust personality of its editor — a fighting editor till the end of his days. "I've tried to be gentle and diplomatic," he remarked after one hard battle, "but I've never done well in my stocking feet." But he had no facility with the pen, and was never a writing editor; his ideas were expressed for him on the editorial page by members of his own staff, and he worked so much more effectively through the news columns than the editorial columns that it was only in times of crisis that he gave emphasis to the latter.

Greatest of all the new moulders of public opinion emerging near the close of the century was Pulitzer, the Hungarian-German of half Jewish descent who, after accumulating a small fortune in St. Louis journalism, purchased from Jay Gould the unprofitable New York *World*. He quickly made it commercially successful by reviving and extending the sensational treatment of news which had marked the *Herald* under the first Bennett, and to some extent the *Sun* in the early years of Dana's editorship. Indeed, his screaming headlines, his diagrammatic sketches of murder-scenes, his lavish uses of pictures, shocked intensely the conservative part of the public. Yet at the same time, Pulitzer imbued his handling of the news with a marked reformative temper, and immediately began using all departments of his paper in "crusades" which were usually of high public benefit. As for the editorial page, it quickly became a thing apart from and above the rest of the journal. It was aggressive, accurate, high-minded, scholarly in a pungent way, and immensely effective. Pulitzer supported Cleveland in 1884, 1888, and 1892; yet in 1895 he denounced the President savagely for his conduct of the Venezuelan dispute, and in the same year forced the Administration to market publicly the bonds which it had proposed to sell to a private syndicate of bankers. In 1896 he made the *World* one of the most vigorous opponents of Bryan and free silver. The course of the newspaper in the events leading up to the Spanish-American War was less creditable; but to the aberrations of this period it was partly prompted by the competition of Hearst's New York *Journal*, which had outdone the *World* in sensationalism without showing any of its merits in editorial energy and liberalism.

## [AN INDICTMENT OF ANDREW JOHNSON] [1]
### The Nation, April 5, 1866

There has been such a glamour thrown round the Presidential office by the war that a great many people seem totally to have forgotten the precise nature of the President's relations to Congress and the country. And it is because they have forgotten it that the present conflict between the legislature and the executive possesses much political importance. We are, in reality, witnessing at this moment, in the difference which convulses the country, the legitimate result of the departures from constitutional usage into which we were driven in the excitement and confusion of 1861. Nobody can, perhaps, be fairly blamed for the irregularities into which the Government then fell. They were the natural result of the alarm and anxiety and distrust of everybody and everything by which the nation was pervaded. But there is no denying the fact that our political machine received a severe jar on the day when Mr. Lincoln was allowed, of his own mere motion, the power of suspending the *habeas corpus*. Congress ought not to have lost a moment after its meeting in asserting its sole exclusive authority to meddle for any purpose whatever with the safeguards placed by the common law and the Constitution round individual liberty. The tameness with which it suffered this prerogative to be taken from it, and with which it submitted to divers other assumptions by the Executive of functions peculiarly legislative, are now bearing their legitimate fruit. People begin to see at last that disregard of the forms of law is a two-edged sword, and that although it may in the hands of a good man strike great blows for freedom, it may on the morrow and in the hands of a bad man strike almost as effective blows for slavery. . . .

At the close of the war Mr. Johnson appointed provisional governors. So far all was well; executive officers of some sort there had to be to prevent anarchy. He went further, and called conventions to reorganize the governments. This, too, was not open to objection. He was still acting within his sphere as commander-in-chief. The various States needed to have some means of expressing their wishes. But this is as far as we can go with him. He had no business to make discriminations between classes of the citizens. He, as commander-in-chief, had nothing to with State policy or State laws. His duty

---

[1] Until the publication of this editorial the *Nation* had criticized President Johnson with restraint, and had repeatedly reminded its readers of the fact that he had "in times past been tried and not found wanting in patriotism, in devotion to the Union, in faithfulness to his obligations." Now it began to deal with him more severely; in 1867 it advocated his impeachment, and in 1868 it was disappointed by his acquittal.

was to see that all had a hearing; when he decided who should vote and who should not, he *legislated* and consequently was guilty of usurpation. But at all events, once the conventions had met, he was as a holder of the war power *functus officio*. He should then have called Congress together and said: "The rebellion is over; the South is at your mercy. I have re-established order; I have provided the people of the revolted States with the means of addressing you. You are the legislature of the United States; in your hands the Constitution has lodged the power of initiating all laws and all schemes of policy. My duty, the duty assigned to me by the Constitution, is to report to you and make suggestions to you, and to carry into execution such laws as you may pass, either with my approval or in spite of my disapproval. I recommend to you to treat the South leniently; to receive the return of the revolted States to the Union with as little humiliation to them as possible; but it is for you to decide I shall express my opinion in the constitutional way on such bills as you may send for my signature; should my objections to them be deemed by you insufficient, I shall not forget that I am your executive officer; that 'all legislative (that is, all law-making) powers' are, by the Constitution, expressly 'vested in the Congress of the United States (Sec. 1) and that Congress consists of the Senate and House of Representatives;' that all I have to do with the lawmaking is to 'recommend to your consideration such measures as I shall judge necessary and expedient.'"

He, however, did nothing of the kind. He did not call Congress together. He did not wait for its coming together. He set to work to make laws with great assiduity. He issued edicts with a rapidity equal to that of Louis Napoleon in December, 1851. He first of all arbitrarily excluded all colored men from voting. He next arbitrarily excluded all persons from voting who had taken part in the rebellion, thus, on his own authority, inflicting a penalty of the highest kind on persons who had been neither tried nor convicted of any crime whatever. He then — we beg the reader's attention to this point — began to exact certain qualifications from revolted States as conditions of their readmission to the Union. He insisted that they should formally abolish slavery, that they should repeal the ordinances of secession, that they should repudiate the rebel debt. Now the power that makes such requirements as these of any people must be either a conqueror exercising the naked authority of the sword on conquered soil, or a legislature exercising a constitutional right. The first of these Mr. Johnson has always stoutly denied that he is or can be; the second the Constitution does not permit him to be; so that on every theory that has yet been propounded by himself or his friends, or that can be devised, of his position and duties, the whole reconstruction process, as he has carried it on, has been one long piece of usurpation, in which we are satisfied few loyal men at the North would have thought for one moment of acquiescing, if most of us had not been frightened by the war into forgetfulness or indifference to the true relations between the different branches of our government.

The whole work of reorganizing the South and restoring its relations with the Union is the most important kind of work on which a government can enter. It consists in lawmaking in the highest sense of the word. In a free country it is the legislature only which is capable of it. In this country the performance of it is expressly forbidden to anybody but the legislature. The phrase, "the President's policy," which is now heard so often, is a solecism of which no American who knows the nature of his own institutions ought to be guilty. The President has *opinions;* he ought not to have a policy. It is for Congress to frame a policy; it is for him to carry it out. As matters stand, he not only framed a policy without consulting Congress, but he went to work to carry it out, and when Congress met, they found the work half done. This was bad enough in all conscience; but this was not all. When they met, and took the state of the South into consideration, they came to the conclusion that the conditions he had imposed on the revolted States were not sufficient, and proceeded to impose others. But they have found that not only has he arrogated the power of imposing conditions himself, but he maintains that any attempt of the legislature to add to his list is an usurpation, against which he feels it to be his duty to offer every opposition in his power. He denies the right of Congress to revise his work or amend it; tells them to their faces that, if they presume to legislate about the South, they must take Southern representatives into their councils, just as if he consulted Jefferson Davis when *he* was about to draw up *his* conditions of restoration. He appeals to the Constitution as coolly as if the Constitution authorized the President to dictate to constitutional conventions the provisions of the organic law which they were to frame, or authorized him to drive from the polls at local elections whole classes of men who had been neither indicted, tried, nor convicted, or to maintain martial law in time of peace, or, in fact, to do any one of the acts by which he has sought to bring back the Southern States to their old position.

We confess that for our part we think the public acquiescence in the unwarrantable assumptions of power on which the President's whole interference with the Reconstruction process is based, has gone far enough. Whatever excuse there might have been for it three years or even one year ago, there is none now. It is too late to undo the irregularities committed during the war; but it is not too late to force every branch of the government to betake itself once more to its own business, and confine itself to the sphere traced out for it by the Constitution. We want no "deliverers" or "restorers" or "chieftains" or "Moseses"; no great man with a "mission" to get us out of our difficulties. If the legislative branch of our system be not equal to the present crisis, our institutions are a failure. But the people have not come to the conclusion that the old machinery is not still equal to the work that may be required of it. It is not probable that the confusion which now pervades the minds of a portion of the public regarding the President's duties can last very long. It would probably not have lasted even as long as it has were it not that the present controversy is one which touches the negro more nearly than the white man, and the influence which the negro exerts in bemuddling the intellects and blunting the perceptions even of the most sensible people is one those of things which, as we have often remarked before, we are glad to say it is not our duty to explain.

## A CALM REVIEW[1]

### New York *Sun*, May 19, 1868

The Republican party may fairly claim the credit of the most signal impartiality in the conclusion of the impeachment trial.

The President was impeached by the act of the Republican majority in the House of Representatives. He was arraigned before the Senate, and tried with patience and intelligence. The Republicans in the Senate were numerous enough to convict him. The country generally desired to see him ousted. It was felt that it would bring peace where there is now doubt and discord, and that it would tend powerfully to the speedy restoration of the Union and the revival of industry and business. We may even say that the world expected his conviction. It was the first time that the supreme executive officer of a nation had been brought before a tribunal, established by the people, for regular trial, and for peaceful deposition from office in case of conviction. Europe looked on with awe at this novel proceeding. Of course it was not supposed in these monarchical countries that any other result than the removal of the obnoxious executive could possibly follow.

Notwithstanding all this, the trial has ended in acquittal. Mr.

[1] President Johnson's trial before the Senate began March 4, 1868; the first and test vote was taken May 16. Seven Republicans joined twelve Democrats in voting "not guilty," and made the President's acquittal certain. Of the New York newspapers, the *Evening Post*, *Times*, *Herald*, and *World* were against conviction; Dana's *Sun* also, though mildly, approved the verdict; but the *Tribune*, which had denounced Johnson as "an aching tooth in the national jaw," was angered and embittered by the result.

Johnson still exercises all the powers of his great office. In spite of party feeling and party pressure, there are seven Republican Senators who have said on their oaths that the evidence and the law would not justify his conviction. It is creditable to these Senators that they have had the firmness thus to decide. Why dislike Mr. Johnson? They detest his character and his policy. But they will not swerve from the line of their convictions on that account. In their judgment he is not proved guilty, and so they declare.

This is the highest instance of impartiality and honesty in all political history. It is a glory to the institutions of the republic. It will excite new admiration in the breasts of thoughtful observers in Europe. It is most honorable to the party by whose statesmen it has been displayed. The hot-headed and indiscreet may violently denounce it; but the philosopher who shall hereafter write the history of parties in this country will record it as one of the best titles of the Republicans to genuine and lasting renown.

## IMPEACHMENT

New York *Sun*, May 23, 1868

If there be any good reason for believing that Senators were bribed to vote either for or against impeachment, let it be sifted to the bottom; and if any person be found guilty, let him be punished; and if bribery shall be traced directly to the President, the whole country will demand his removal from office at the earliest possible moment. But, as to the remaining ten articles of the pending case, the public interests require that they be disposed of at the next sitting of the Court. Congress has spent three months upon this subject, and the business of the nation now demands that it devote its time to legislation. Nothing can be gained by a protracted struggle over ten articles. The eleventh was deemed the strongest for evoking conviction, and if any Senator was bribed to vote against it, he was doubtless bought up for the whole series. On the points involved in this long controversy between the President and Congress, the opinions of intelligent men are made up on the one side or the other; and the quarrel is now adjourned to a higher tribunal than the Senate — the great forum of the people.

What effect a verdict of acquittal will have on Mr. Johnson during the brief period that he will occupy the White House, it is impossible to say. For the past two years his course has been more damaging to his supporters than to his opponents. Men who feel a stain as a wound would not regard a vote of thirty-five ayes to nineteen nays, on a charge of high crimes and misdemeanors in office, as a cause for self-gratulation. But the President is happily organized to meet this exigency; his sensibilities are not keen, and his cuticle is thick; and if his vanity and self confidence shall impel him to continue to hurl defiance in the face of Congress, he will harm that body and the Republican party much less than he will himself and his friends. If, on the other hand, he shall pursue the even tenor of his way, while Congress devotes itself to legitimate legislation, and the people plunge enthusiastically into the Presidential canvass, Mr. Johnson will soon lapse into obscurity and be forgotten.

## KENTUCKY[1]

### Louisville *Courier-Journal*, December 25, 1868

A little after midday on the twenty-fifth of December, 1778, a group of ten or a dozen pioneers in buckskin knee-breeches and linsey-woolsey hunting-shirts gathered around a log heap in front of a cabin, which, from a high cliff, overlooked the frozen bed and snowy banks of the Kentucky River. It was very bleak and cold. The sun had not shown out since the second day of the month. The streams were everywhere choked with ice. The very springs were inaccessible, and game was scarce and powder scarcer still. Foremost among the little knot of woodsmen were Daniel Boone and James Harrod; and they had met, as they declared, to offer up their prayers to God on behalf of the "brave men and patriots" who were "fighting the battles of freedom beyond the mountains." They knelt down and prayed accordingly; they said a hymn; and then, having affirmed devotion to the cause of the colonies against the Crown, they dispersed, each going his several ways, but all inspired by the same good purpose and free-born spirit. . . .

We do not propose to review what followed. Kentucky was not one of the seceding States. She stood true to the principles which were enunciated in those memorable resolutions at which it is common to hear men sneer. Whatever may be said of these resolutions, they embody a just and true spirit, and mean nothing which is base, or sordid, or narrow, or slavish, or mean. Kentucky's head was with the Union and her heart was with the South; for it is the nature of a generous and manly people to sympathize with the weak in its struggle with the strong. The war closed. Kentucky alone of the free States that were left in the Union was true to herself and to the professions with which the war was begun. She proscribed no one. She gave welcome to all. Today she is prosperous, peaceful, happy. The laws are better enforced in Kentucky than in Indiana. There is less crime in Kentucky than in Ohio.

[1] By Henry Watterson; an excellent exposition of the attitude of moderate men in the Border States toward Reconstruction. Before the end of the Civil War the Democrats or "Conservatives" had triumphed in Kentucky. They remained in the saddle there, and for a time successfully opposed the abolition of slavery.

Tennessee is poor. Missouri is poor. Both are the victims of despotic power running roughshod over the liberties and disregarding the private rights of the people. In Kentucky there is no partisan militia. In Kentucky there are no franchise laws. In Kentucky there are no threats of confiscation. Public opinion is the only arbiter of public questions, and every man is allowed to hold office who obtains votes enough. As in Massachusetts, public opinion is very much one way. There the people are Republicans for the most part; vote the Republican ticket; decline to vote for Democratic candidates or Democratic measures, and are, we dare say, conscientious. Here it is exactly reversed. We are, for the most part, Democrats; we vote the Democratic ticket; we decline to vote for Republican candidates and measures; we are perfectly honest, and think we have a right, as free citizens of a free republic, to decide for ourselves.

For so doing and so thinking we are denounced as traitors to our country and a despotism is sought to be placed over us by those who claim that we ought to be forced to vote for Republican candidates and Republican measures, and who declare that if we do not, we are guilty of rebellion and should be punished therefor.

This was not the spirit of Boone and his companions who prayed God to bless Massachusetts on Christmas Day, 1778. It was not the spirit of the Kentuckians who fought the battles of the country from King's Mountain to the City of Mexico. It is a new-born spirit, the spirit of rapine and war, not of liberty and peace. That the people of Kentucky should regard it with detestation is reasonable and natural. That they should cling the more tenaciously to their original fastening as the pressure from without becomes more violent is also reasonable and natural. But they are not intolerant nor inhospitable, but kind, generous, peaceful, enterprising, progressive; faithful to the past; liberal with the present; hopeful of the future. The snows of nearly a hundred years have come and gone since the Christmas of 1778. Many a change has come also over the land. The canebrakes are all gone. The old pioneers are all gone. Their graves are deep-sunken under the plowshare, and are hid beneath the clover blooms. But the hardy manhood; the warm, impulsive love of freedom; the honest hatred of persecution; the keen sympathy with the weak and suffering, all these noble sentiments that honored the lives of the fathers remain and are illustrated by the children in the unanimity with which they resist the despotism set up over their brothers at the South. Remove this despotism, and we may divide on a thousand issues; but as long as it continues we are one in opposing it as unnecessary, tyrannical, and cruel.

## PRESIDENT GRANT'S FIRST CABINET[1]

*The Nation*, March 11, 1869

The general expectation with regard to Grant's Cabinet was that it would probably surprise nearly everybody, but that nobody but the regular politicians would be disagreeably disappointed by it. There is little question, however, that the first announcement of it did disappoint even his friends and admirers, and probably his friends and admirers rather more than his enemies. The firm front he had presented to the deputations urging the "claims" of States on the old-fashioned grounds, had no doubt somewhat prepared the politicians for his complete departure from the regular routine hitherto pursued in cabinet-choosing; but then it had also prepared his friends for an extraordinary display of sagacity in the work of selection — in fact, for the formation of an ideal cabinet. The appointment of Mr. Washburne to the State Department was, therefore, a somewhat severe shock to a great many people, because, although Mr. Washburne is a very able and useful man, his qualifications for the management of the foreign affairs of the government, in which the duties of the department mainly consist, are, if they exist at all, entirely unknown to the general public. In fact, to state the case plainly, there is a general, and apparently well-founded, belief that Mr. Washburne knows nothing about foreign affairs, except what the general public knows from the newspapers, and that his installation in the State Department would be the commencement of his intimate acquaintance with the precedents and principles of international law. . . .

The selection of Mr. A. T. Stewart for the Treasury is neither so bad nor so good as it seems. He is a better choice than Mr. Boutwell would have been, and we compare these two gentlemen because the popular belief is that the place was first offered to the latter. Mr. Boutwell is doubtless as sound as possible on all the leading financial questions, and is not without administrative ability; but he has for the last four years displayed so many marked symptoms of chronic mental inflammation, and such unswerving fidelity to party — the last evidence of it being his open support on the stump of the great apostle of repudiation, General Butler — as to leave the best judges in doubt whether he will ever be fit for any position in which a cool head is the first requisite, and scientific considerations the weightiest and most important. Of Mr. Boutwell's most marked

---

[1] A majority of Grant's appointments to his first Cabinet were a surprise. In the choice of A. T. Stewart for the Treasury he violated an Act of 1789 forbidding the appointment to that post of anyone interested in trade or commerce, and later substituted George S. Boutwell. The historian Rhodes concurs in Godkin's remarks upon Washburne.

defects no trace is to be found in Mr. Stewart. We doubt if any emotions on any subject have ever disturbed his mental equilibrium; and if the time has come for managing the finances of the country on a business rather than a sentimental basis, certainly few persons could be found for the work possessing the requisite coolness, and the requisite contempt for purely emotional views of great questions, in a higher degree. But then that which constitutes, in the eyes of many persons, and perhaps in General Grant's, his highest qualification — his business experience — is, we take leave to say, not necessarily a qualification at all, and may prove a hindrance. It is singular but true that no contribution of value has ever been made to the science of finance by a man engaged actively in trade. . . .

## [SENATOR SUMNER'S ANNEXATION SCHEMES][1]

*The Nation*, April 15, 1869

The accession of British America to the United States would not only mean the addition of a vast extent of fertile soil, but of several millions of a hardy and industrious population, of the same origin as our own, speaking the same language, and imbued with the same social and political ideas, and already used to self-government. That they would gain by annexation far more than the United States we readily believe, for their gain would be real, while that of the United States would be largely in the imagination; and that the annexation would close up one great fountain of contention between the English Government and ours is also true. But then to make the annexation a gain to the Canadians, their consent to it should be asked, and given; and to make it, as is proposed, a healer of the breach between this country and England, England should make it fairly and voluntarily, and not under compulsion. There is something a little comic in the position just now taken by those who are arguing for it, as a means of restoring a cordial relation between her and the United States. What they say to England is substantially this: "Your conduct has been villainous and depraved beyond description, and the amount of mischief you have wilfully and maliciously done is simply incalculable, and therefore we shall not allow you even to attempt to pay damages. We should give you a sound thrashing if we were not otherwise occupied just now, but our intention is to give you one at some future day, when we find you in a fix. However, if you make us a present of Canada — which we shall take from you by force if you don't — we shall look

---

[1] In a speech of April 13, 1869, Senator Sumner declared that British intervention had doubled the length of the war, and that England was therefore assessable for more than two billions of dollars in damages. He desired the cession of Canada to the United States in partial or full settlement of our claim.

upon it as full satisfaction for all the wrongs we have suffered at your hands, and shall not only not lick you, but shall greatly esteem you, and shall live with you through all coming time on the most cordial terms."

Now, nations sometimes do make cessions of territory after being addressed in this way, but it is when they are in bodily fear, and England may make a cession of Canada on the protocol which is now laid before the public by the advocates of the scheme; but to say that the foundation of a cordial understanding with her can thus be laid is simply ridiculous. To give the negotiation for Canada a chance for success, as a healer of wounds, it should be conducted on its own merits, and, in form at least, separate and apart from the Alabama question.

## MR. HENRY J. RAYMOND[1]

*The Nation*, June 24, 1869

As one of the three men who may be said to have given New York a metropolitan press, Mr. Raymond would have occupied a very prominent place in the history of American journalism, even if he had not played a prominent part as a politician during one of the most eventful periods in the history of the country. He made his appearance in the political arena just as the Republican party was in process of formation, he had a leading share in its organization, and he served it faithfully till the close of the war. He may be fairly said, indeed, to have come out of the war in the position of one of its foremost and most trusted leaders. Although he had never been a thoroughgoing party man, and had never been looked on by party managers as a person to be counted on in all contingencies, and had retired to his tent in a somewhat sour mood after the defeat of Frémont in 1856, there was probably nobody in its ranks who could, in 1865, when Lee surrendered, show stronger titles to its confidence. The reason is that, though he doubted much in debate, when it is allowed to the wisest men to doubt, when the moment for action came he never doubted at all. It is a good deal to say of a journalist in Mr. Raymond's position — that is, a position in which he was in such close relations with the men in power that he learned what the people happily did not know — that from the day on which South Carolina seceded till the day on which Richmond fell, he persistently, unceasingly, and vigorously preached the indissolubility of the Union, and the duty and possibility of saving it by force of arms. In other words, in the presence

[1] Raymond died June 19, 1869. Godkin declared in this same editorial that "the *Times* under his management probably came nearer the newspaper of the good time coming than any other in existence."

of the most tremendous problem statesmen have in any age or country had to face, he never hesitated about the course to be pursued, and advocated it as cheerfully and courageously in the darkest as in the brightest hours; and the course he advocated proved the best of all possible courses. When the fighting was over, his tendency to hesitate once more showed itself, and it showed itself, unfortunately for him, at a period when party freedom ran unusually high, and entire freedom from doubt on any political subject whatever was considered the highest qualification of a statesman. The consequence was that he fell from the party eminence the war had won him, and made no effort to regain it, satisfied by this time that the constitution of his mind unfitted him for the struggles of the political arena.

That he should have been seduced into taking part in them by his readiness and brilliance as a debater was his greatest misfortune, not only because he wanted the thoroughgoing temper which was necessary to victory, but because it in some degree interfered with his usefulness as a journalist. He was as an editor constantly trammeled by his sense of the necessities and limitations of his position as a politician, and the habit thus bred lasted after he had ceased to be a politician. But for this he would probably have been the most successful journalist that has ever been seen. As it was, it would be difficult if not impossible to find his equal — to say nothing of his superior.

## [WOMEN'S RIGHTS: A LIBERAL NEW ENGLAND VIEW][1]

### Springfield *Republican*, February 14, 1870

The great truth that we should all see and accept on this question is this: That in the revolutionary order of life, in the progress of society and of government out of the issues of force and toward the laws of a common brotherhood, in the multiplication of duties which this enlargement of our responsibilities brings upon society, in the steady education and elevation of woman to a social and intellectual equality with man, we have reached that point where it is both desirable and necessary that woman should assume her place as an integral unit in life, and take a larger and more independent share in all its duties and responsibilities. This proposition seems to us to flow naturally out of our civilization, out of the wonderful accumulation of work pressing upon every thoughtful and conscientious member of society, out of the enlarged capacity of women, out

[1] By Samuel Bowles, Sr. The Civil War had given immense impetus to the woman's movement.

of her yearnings for a fuller life, out of the overburdened condition of her husband, brother, sons, and father.

Putting aside the labor absolutely necessary by both men and women for their daily subsistence, few will deny how much more heavily the serious burdens of outward life fall upon the men — the maintenance of government in all its ramifications, the earning of money for comforts and luxuries, providing for education, for the development of art in all its branches, for the care of the sick and the poor and the wicked, for claiming and reclaiming the orphans of society of every grade and name, and generally, indeed, the feeding and filling the whole wide and rapidly widening spheres into which our life is opening. And yet how large a share of all these questions, of all these duties, women are or may easily become quite as competent as men to deal with! So of the more special work of modern individual life, the industries which go to make up our civilization, so different from those of former generations — how full these all are of labor equally fitted, much of it more fitted, for the hand of woman than of man. It is out of all this enlargement and diversification and multiplication of both the duties of society and the work of the individual that the call and the necessity for the new career for women has come.

This is simply what the new reform seeks — the opening of all these duties, all this work of life, to woman equally with man. It is not simply woman's right to do it, it is her duty. It is man's right, too, to have her share in this aggregation of responsibility which civilization with its master strides has forced upon him. Suffrage is but a token; legal equality is but an opportunity; these are the real, actual elements of the woman's movement. It means nothing if it does not mean that she shall take up and perform her share of all this work. Some of it, of course, she cannot do as well as man, other she certainly can do better; but it has become too big, too vast, too delicate, for man alone to perform; and it is not right, it is shame rather than sense, that, while he is thus over-burdened, women should sit idly in carpeted and pictured parlors, half listless from inanition, accepting life's bounties, but shirking life's duties.

Given, first, legal reform, making men and women, husbands and wives, equally responsible to each other, to their children, to their creditors, and to society, in all matters of authority, of property, of obligation; and secondly, equality of women with men in suffrage — and we have the real, outward, visible tokens of the pending revolution. The legal reform we regard as even more important and more practically pressing of the two. The need of that is clear; we are educated up to it; the effects will be at once beneficent;

while suffrage is not suffering for women nor women greatly for it; and the early results of its gift to them now before they are prepared for it and generally seeking it, are of doubtful flavor. But in a republic the ballot box stands for position, stands for responsibility, stands for power; and so, rather as a sign than as the thing itself, is it desirable, and is it naturally put in the front of the new movement. Every real onward movement in history is marked by growing consideration of woman. Civilization is but the advance of the feminine element in life and in government. Macaulay said there never was a great man without a good deal of woman in him. So it is and will be more and more with our civilization. The larger the proportion of the feminine element, the higher becomes its advance, the purer its life, the broader its aims. This cause is not only the cause of woman, but the cause of man and the cause of God.

## A STATUE FOR BOSS TWEED[1]

### New York *Sun*, December 12, 1870

Has Boss Tweed any friends? If so, they are a mean set. It is now more than a year since an appeal was made to them to come forward and put up the ancillary qualities to erect a statue to Mr. Tweed in the centre of Tweed Plaza; but as yet only four citizens have sent in their subscriptions. These were not large, but they were paid in cash, and there is reason for the belief that they were the tokens of sincere admiration for Mr. Tweed. But the hundreds or rather thousands of small-potato politicians whom he has made rich and powerful stand aloof, and do not offer a picayune. We propose that the statue shall be executed by Captain Albertus De Groot, who made the celebrated Vanderbilt bronzes; but we have not decided whether it shall represent the favorite son of New York afoot or a-horseback. In fact, we rather incline to have a nautical statue, exhibiting Boss Tweed as a bold mariner, amid the foretop-gallant buttock shrouds of his steam yacht. But that is a matter for future consideration. The first thing is to get the money; and if those who claim to be Mr. Tweed's friends don't raise it, we shall begin to believe the rumor that the Honorable P. Brains Sweeny has turned against him, and has forbidden everyone to give anything toward the erection of the projected statue.

[1] By Charles A. Dana, "writ sarcastic"; but an editorial which was then and has been till today persistently misinterpreted as serious. Dana's attitude toward corrupt Tammany leaders was frequently all too friendly, but he was far too shrewd to ally himself with Tweed. The "P. Brains Sweeny" here mentioned was Peter B. Sweeny. He was City Chamberlain with Tweed. Everyone regarded him as the best educated and most cunning of the Ring.

"NONE BUT THE BRAVE DESERVES THE FAIR."
Miss Columbia May to H. G. December. "Do you see any thing Green in my Eye?"

From *Harper's Weekly*, October 26, 1872.                    By Thomas Nast.

## [CORRUPTION HIDING BEHIND LEGALITY][1]

Springfield *Republican*, January 30, 1871

The great mistake of Mr. David Dudley Field, as that of his defenders, in this controversy is, that they wholly ignore the moral element in all these questions. . . . Here is the law, they say, here are the courts, and here are the lawyers — scientific machinery which civilization has set up to determine the conflicting rights of its citizens; and whatever this machinery accords to Mr. Field and Mr. Fisk, they are entitled to, and nobody has the right to dispute the integrity of the verdict. Even if Mr. Fisk seizes somebody else's property, and by Mr. Field's help is able to hold on to it, it is not to be presumed that the judges or jurors would grant it to him unless it really belonged to him — and when they have so granted it, the question is settled. The idea that courts may be bribed, or that the very forms of law, fashioned to protect innocence and to prescribe rights, may be so twisted as to do the opposite, is ignored, or supposed to be impossible, or, if admitted as a possibility, is to be regarded as one of the incidents or aberrations of an exact science, to be submitted to as we submit to the operations of planetary movements, or to too much drought, or too much rain in the grand healthy progress of nature.

Now, if the law *is* an exact science like geology or mathematics — if the elements that enter into it and administer it are divine — if one of Judge Barnard's injunctions is a decree of Providence, and an affidavit from Mrs. Lawler "a song of the angels" — if the Court of the Infinite is run by the New York code, and Field and Shearman are entitled to an arrest of judgment against the Ten Commandments — if, in short, the devil is as good as the average, and the sum of both divine and human wisdom is the French philosophy that no matter what happens, so long as it does not happen to yourself — all this being so, then these gentlemen are clearly right, Field, Barnard, and Fisk are the victims of unworthy prejudices, and the modern newspaper is indeed "a public nuisance," as the junior Field protests. But if human imperfection is to be recognized in law and lawyers — if we admit the moral element into their work — if there is such a thing as a private conscience, and a public conscience as well — they are all wrong, and the journalist's general view in this discussion is the correct one. In this instance the latter may have drawn the lines too broadly and too sharply here and

---

[1] By Samuel Bowles, Sr. The editor's caustic strictures upon David Dudley Field, a son of the Connecticut Valley who became notorious for his legal services to Tweed, Jim Fisk, Gould, and other corruptionists, brought him into collision with that astute lawyer. In a series of editorials Bowles drove home the difference — very great in the seventies — between illegality and immorality.

there; but, given the concession of the moral sense in human action, yield to public opinion the right to bring in the Ten Commandments and independent thought to bear upon law and courts and lawyers, and the case is up for Messrs. Field and Fisk and their apologists.

## NOTORIETY[1]

### *The Nation*, July 20, 1871

We are only saying what nearly everybody has either said or thought, when we say that by no means the least marked of the effects on modern society produced by the newspaper press, has been the increase and diffusion of the love for publicity through all classes and conditions. This it has accomplished by putting publicity within nearly everybody's reach. The love of fame is of course a passion as old as the race, but it differs essentially from the love of notoriety in this, that fame rests on respect and admiration, in greater or less degree, while notoriety rests simply on the lowest order of curiosity. Now, it would be useless and unfair to deny that the press has done and does much for fame, but it would be also useless to deny that it has done far more for notoriety, and in doing it — that is, in making it easy for a man to become widely known without having achieved anything which would justify his fellow creatures in occupying their minds about him — it has enormously stimulated the passion for being known and talked about, *no matter for what reason*, which seems to be inherent in a certain class of natures. . . .

If we were to say that [James] Fisk, and [George Henry] Train, and [Victoria] Woodhull, and [Tennessee] Claflin, and a dozen others we might name — whose visible influence seems to be small, but whose career, depend upon it, is producing its effect on the silent and invisible army of young men and women who are pouring into our great cities year by year in quest of fortune, and determined to be *known* somehow — were the legitimate and natural results of the insane culture of publicity in thought, word, and deed which has been a very prominent feature for some time back in religion, literature, and reform, we should, perhaps, seem guilty of extravagance, and yet we cannot help saying it, and have no doubt of its truth. It is a system which develops the coarsest side of human nature, and appeals to the lowest class of motives, and subjects conduct to the least reliable of tests, and naturally and inevitably opens a career to knaves and charlatans, which is full of

---

[1] "Jim" Fisk was a New York stock gambler who joined Daniel Drew and Jay Gould in looting the Erie Railroad, and who owned the Grand Opera House in New York. At this date he was at the height of his renown; the following year he was murdered.

prizes, and which every year is sure to be more crowded. Having once got into the habit of encouraging people to make themselves notorious, we cannot avoid rewarding them by notoriety, and notoriety has become, with the aid of the newspaper press, not simply a source of gratification, but of gain.

Take the case of Fisk. This man came to New York a few years ago, a smart, impudent and ignorant pedlar, without morals or manners, and with a good deal of animal spirits, and in search of two things — physical enjoyment and notoriety. The physical enjoyment he might have had with a little money, but notoriety he could only get with the help of the newspapers, and this help they gave him to his heart's content. He went incontinently to work to do strange, indecent, and outrageous things, and they went to work to chronicle them and denounce him for them. This was natural enough when he first showed himself on the scene as a swindler and blackguard, but when it was discovered that he was really indifferent to public opinion, that he had no shame and no sensibility, and really enjoyed his bad reputation, liked to be thought lewd and smart and knavish, the press at once began to treat him as a curious phenomenon, and laugh over him, chronicle his movements, record his jokes, give him pet names, and devoted an amount of time to the consideration of him as an entertainment simply, which proved the best advertisement any charlatan ever had, and gratified his dearest ambition. To be "in the papers" every day, to be thought smart by brokers and drygoods-men and railroad men, are what he of all things most desires. The treatment he received, too, helped all his speculations. It advertised his theatre, his steamboats, and his railroads; it made the box in which he sat, and the carriage in which he rode with his strumpets, the objects on which all eyes were fixed. His fame, in short, filled the continent, and has now filled the civilized world. At last, too, the jocose treatment of him resulted in making him look less disreputable than he was at the beginning; from laughing over him a good deal, people got to thinking him "not such a bad fellow after all"; and, finally, we came to see business suspended at midday in the principal thoroughfare of the commercial capital of the country, whose courts and legislature he had corrupted, in order to see him ride down as elected Colonel at the head of a regiment nine hundred strong, composed of respectable young Americans. As colonel of this regiment he, the other day, asked for a municipal invitation for himself and it from the city of Boston, and, amongst other things, expressed a desire to have "divine service" celebrated for his benefit on Boston Common. The newspapers, thereupon, took this up, and discussed it, and joked over it, and showed the absurdity of it in article after article, and paragraph after paragraph, as if Fisk was really trying to play the hypocrite, and was trying to pass himself off as a religious man, the fact being that he was merely gratifying a showman's love of making a sensation, and by the newspaper exposures of him as an impudent dog got all he wanted, and probably far more than he looked for. . . .

We cannot make Fisk a person of importance, and fill everybody's mind every morning with his doings and sayings, without making Fisk's career an object of secret admiration to thousands, and making thousands in their inmost hearts determine to imitate him. The newspapers ought to remember that, while for some offenders against public decency and security denunciation may be a proper and effective punishment, the only way of reaching others is not to mention them.

## TWO THIEVES [1]

### New York *Times*, July 19, 1871

We published on the 8th inst. an article compiled from Connolly's (*alias* Slippery Dick's) own books, showing the frauds which are perpetrated at the expense of the public in relation to the city armories alone. We gave the official lists of the armories, the rents paid for them, and the rents they were actually worth. We sent this article to Connolly, and gave him the opportunity of correcting or denying it; but he could not do either.

Tomorrow morning we shall publish a still more important document, also compiled from Connolly's own books. We shall *prove,* and we challenge Connolly or any other of the city authorities to deny a single fact or figure in our statement, that the public are robbed of several millions a year under the head of armory accounts alone. We shall show that not less than NINETY MILLIONS a year pass through the hands of Hall and Connolly, and that they and their fellow conspirators steal a large part of the money. We have openly charged Dick Connolly with being a thief, and we shall now prove him to be one. We shall do the same with Mayor Hall. We undertake to place before the public *proofs* which would be sufficient to convict any man in a court of law, and we earnestly trust that the public will closely look into these proofs for themselves, and form their own judgment upon them.

Our article tomorrow, though of great importance, will be exceeded in interest by a *true copy* which we shall shortly publish of the money paid on warrants during 1869 and 1870 for the new Courthouse. These figures will convince any man beyond a doubt that Hall and Connolly, who signed the warrants, are SWINDLERS,

[1] With this editorial the *Times* initiated its courageous and effective exposure of the thefts by the Tweed Ring.

and as such we once more arraign them before the bar of public opinion.

We again ask the public to study for themselves the first of the two promised articles in tomorrow's *Times*.

## WILL IT "BLOW OVER?"

New York *Times*, July 31, 1871

Both Hall and Connolly knew that it was absurd to sign a warrant for $431,064, in favor of George Miller, for carpenter work done in ten lofts and stables in the course of nine months. They knew that "Ingersoll & Co." were not entitled to $170,729.60 for chairs supplied to the armories. They knew that the plastering had not cost $190,330. But they drew the warrants for these amounts, and divided the money among each other. We have, however, not yet begun to tell the story. What will the public think when they see that Ingersoll has received nearly $5,000,000 in two years for furniture supplied to the new Court-house? He is put down in the Controller's accounts as having received that sum, but of course only a small fraction of it actually passed into his hands. The system is this: A man does some work for the city authorities, and charges $5,000 for it. When he presents his bill, one of Connolly's agents says to him: "We can't pay this, but make the amount $55,000, and you shall have your money at once." A warrant is drawn for $55,000 and endorsed by the presentor of the bill over to J. H. Ingersoll. He then receives five $1,000 bills, and the Ring pockets the $50,000. That this is done every day, and done on a scale which will startle the most listless and indifferent, we shall prove beyond all doubt before we have completed our extracts from Connolly's books.

## [TILDEN AND BOSS TWEED][1]

*The Nation*, November 2, 1871

Mr. Samuel J. Tilden has brought Tweed's guilt home to him by a remarkable piece of work, which fully justifies what we said last week of the unpleasantness, if one had been erring, of being pursued by him. The Ring got inserted in the city charter a clause creating a county "Board of Audit," consisting of their precious selves. The "Board" met once for but ten minutes, and turned the whole "auditing" business over to Tweed. This sounds like a joke, but it is true. Tweed then went to work and "audited" as hard as he

[1] As legal agent and investigator for the Committee of Seventy which was formed to destroy the Tweed Ring, Tilden — assisted by Charles O'Conor and Andrew H. Green — made possible the conviction of the principals.

could, Garvey and other scamps bringing in the raw material in the shape of "claims," and he never stopped until he had audited about $6,000,000 worth. Connolly's part in the little game then came in, and that worthy citizen drew his warrants for the money, which that simple-minded "scholar and gentleman" the Mayor endorsed, without having the least idea what was going on. Another citizen named Woodward, holding a subordinate place in the Supervisor's office, but living in luxury at Norwalk, Connecticut, then took the warrants down to the Broadway Bank, having forged on the back of them any names of which his own or Garvey's graceful fancy had suggested the insertion in the body of the document. Here he divided up the sum among the confederates by making deposits to their credit. Unluckily for Tweed, he, Garvey, and Ingersoll kept their accounts at the same bank as Woodward, and Mr. Tilden, getting hold of the books of the bank, "decomposed" the deposits, as he says, and brought Tweed's share of the plunder home to him — about $1,000,000 in all. The Joint Committee have reported on the condition of the city's finances, and declare that the discoverable stealings of three years are $19,000,000, which is probably only half the real total.

## [THE ERRORS OF RECONSTRUCTION] [1]

*The Nation*, December 7, 1871

It is comparatively easy to reform the tariff or the civil service, or reduce the taxes, or return to specie payments, or civilize the Indians, or protect the immigrants, or get the overdue instalment from Venezuela, or bring Mexico to reason on that matter of the "free zone"; but it is almost as hard to give order, peace, and security to the southern half of American society as medicine to a mind diseased, or pluck the rooted sorrow from the brain. We do not need to tell any of our readers what the state of things in that region is. It is not simply that men suddenly raised from a condition of bestial servitude, inheriting the weaknesses of barbarism, aggravated by the weaknesses of slavery, have been admitted to participation in the rights and responsibilities of free society; it is that they have been put in full and exclusive control of that most delicate and complicated piece of mechanism known as the government of a civilized State, with its debts, its credits, its system of taxes, its system of jurisprudence, its history, its traditions, its thousand

---

[1] In the year 1871 the follies of Reconstruction reached their height. This was the year of the second Enforcement Act, placing Congressional elections at the South under Federal control; of the Ku-Klux Act, giving the President military powers to deal with Klan outrages; and of President Grant's suspension of the writ of habeas corpus in a large part of South Carolina.

knotty social and political problems. We say "exclusive control," because we do not call the division of power which the negroes have made with the Northern carpetbaggers a real division. The carpet-bagger . . . has got employment from the Southern negroes . . . with the firm determination of making all he can out of the job, and with no other determination whatever.

The condition of the negro after emancipation — that is, his ignorance and want of experience, combined with his position of estrangement from or hostility toward his white neighbors — attracted the carpet-bagger as naturally as a dead ox attracts the buzzard. The lower class of demagogues scents an unenlightened constituency at an almost incredible distance, and travels towards it over mountain, valley, and river with the certainty of the mariner's compass. But then we hastened his coming by our legislation. We deliberately, and for an indefinite period, excluded all the leading Southern men from active participation in the management of their local affairs, by a discrimination not unlike that which would be worked in this city, but very much worse, if every man who had not at some time belonged to the Tammany Society were declared incapable of holding office. It was before the war the time-honored custom of the Southern States, and a very good custom too, to put their ablest men, and men of the highest social standing and character, in office. The consequence was that it was these men who figured most prominently in the steps which led to the rebellion and in the rebellion itself. When the war was over we singled these men out, and not unnaturally, for punishment by the Fourteenth Amendment and other legislation, but we forgot that, as the President points out, they were no worse, so far as disloyalty went, than the rest of the community. They broke their oaths of allegiance to the United States, but the other white men of the South would have done the same thing if they had got the chance of doing it by being elevated to office, either under the United States or under the Confederacy. We forgot, too, that when putting a mutinous crew under irons, the most justly indignant captain leaves at liberty enough able-bodied seamen to work the ship.

There were, in short, two ways, and only two, of dealing with the South after the war, neither of which we adopted. One was to treat the whole community as hostile or diseased and disorganized, and take charge of it from top to bottom, administer its justice, manage its finances, provide it with security of life and property, until such time as we were satisfied that it was competent to take charge of itself. This was the course which the highest statesmanship prescribed, but there were grave constitutional and political difficulties in the way of resorting to it, and, although we have at various times

# THE ERRORS OF RECONSTRUCTION

advocated it, we have never been disposed to find fault with the majority in Congress for shrinking from it.

The other way was to treat the whole community as made up of unfortunate Americans, equally entitled to care and protection, demoralized by an accursed institution for which the whole Union was responsible, and which the whole Union had connived at, and, down to 1860, had profited by; rent and desolated by a bloody war; disorganized by the most radical social and industrial revolution ever witnessed. The first view was European, rather than American; this was purely American. It had no constitutional difficulties, or at least not so great constitutional difficulties, in its way, and it accorded in all respects with the habits and temper of the people and the machinery of the Government. We adopted neither plan, however, but a combination of the two, and the worst possible combination, the results of which have been positively infernal. In the idea that we were befriending the negroes, we gave them possession of the government, and deprived them of the aid of all the local capacity and experience in the management of it, thus offering the States as a prey to Northern adventurers, and thus inflicting on the freedmen the very worst calamity which could befall a race newly emerged from barbarism — that is, familiarity, in the very first moments of enfranchisement, with the processes of a corrupt administration, carried on by gangs of depraved vagabonds, in which the public money was stolen, the public faith made an article of traffic, the legislature openly corrupted, and all that the community contained of talent, probity, and social respectability put under a legal ban as something worthless and disreputable. We do not hesitate to say that a better mode of debauching the freedmen, and making them permanently unfit for civil government, could hardly have been hit on had the North had such an object deliberately in view. Instead of establishing equal rights for all, we set up the government of a class, and this class the least competent, the most ignorant and inexperienced, and a class, too, whose history and antecedents made its rule peculiarly obnoxious to the rest of the community.

Out of this state of things Ku-kluxing has grown as naturally as Whiteboyism grew out of Orange rule in Ireland, and Klephtism out of Turkish rule in Greece. We condemn the Whiteboys, the Klephts, and the Ku-klux; we read the patriotic, humanitarian, and law-loving denunciations of the last, which appear in the loyal papers of the North, with proper concurrence and approval. We cannot gainsay anything anybody says of the atrocity of riding about the country at night with one's face blackened, murdering and whipping people. But we confess we condemn Ku-kluxing

very much as we condemn the cholera. . . . There is no more use in
getting in a rage with Ku-kluxery, and sending cavalry and artillery
after it, than of legislating against pestilence, as long as nothing is
done to remove the causes.

## [THE NOMINATION OF GREELEY][1]

Springfield *Republican,* May 4, 1872

No persons more thoroughly than Mr. Greeley's brethren of the
press recognize his great worth, his large and varied ability, the vast
obligations the country is under to him; but they object to his high
protectionism, to the manner in which his nomination was secured,
and to the miserable set of small and jobbing politicians and often
corrupt speculators that have so long and so thoroughly surrounded
him, and influenced him alike strongly and perversely in much of
his political conduct. They fear the continued power of these influences over him in the larger sphere in which he is now invited
and exposed. . . .

The Irish will respond to this nomination as to no other. The
workingmen will, by genuine instinct, recognize in Mr. Greeley
their steadfast friend and co-laborer. The negro vote will be more
than divided in his behalf. The farmers of the West have read,
studied, and profited by Mr. Greeley too long and too much not to
feel the impulse to rally around him. Mr. Adams's strength would
have worked from the rich and cultivated and business classes down.
Mr. Greeley's will develop from the laborer, the poor and discontented, up. He is, perhaps, the ablest representative of the
American workingman. His fellow workingmen will recognize
him as such, and they will break the bonds of party. They will
ignore the circumstances of his nomination; they will forget the
weaknesses of the man and the dangerous influences that will surround him in a greater or less degree in the White House; they will
laugh at the jokes and caricatures at his expense, and they will vote
for and elect him. He does not stand for all the reforms that the
country demands, but he represents many and the largest and
noblest of them — the return to peace and its offices and instruments,
the reorganization of parties, the reduction of the cost and the power
of the army and navy, the multiplication of the means by which
government blesses the people and ministers to their everyday
comfort, the increase of official respect for popular opinion, the
decrease of the influence of mere partisanship in our government,

[1] This is an editorial dispatch sent by the elder Samuel Bowles to the *Republican*
from the Cincinnati Convention. See George S. Merriam, *The Life and Times of
Samuel Bowles.* II, 187.

and the limitations of the power of the executive over its offices and patronage — and his election will freshly illustrate and powerfully advance the cause of representative government.

## THE LAST BLOW[1]

### New York *Sun*, November 30, 1872

One of the most painful and affecting circumstances in the last days of Horace Greeley is the fact that the blow which seems to have finally overthrown his reason was struck by his own assistant in the conduct of the *Tribune*, Mr. Whitelaw Reid, who had been interested in the control of that journal while its chief editor was engaged in the Presidential campaign.

The election took place on Tuesday, Nov. 5, and on the Thursday following, only two days afterward, the subjoined card was conspicuously published in the *Tribune*:

"The undersigned resumes the editorship of the *Tribune*, which he relinquished on embarking in another line of business six months ago. Henceforth it shall be his endeavor to make this a thoroughly independent journal, treating all parties and political movements with judicial fairness and candor, but courting the favor and deprecating the wrath of no one.

"If he can hereafter say anything that will tend to heartily unite the whole American people on the broad platform of universal amnesty and impartial suffrage, he will gladly do so. For the present, however, he can best commend that consummation by silence and forbearance. The victors in our late struggle can hardly fail to take the whole subject of Southern rights and wrongs into early and earnest consideration, and to them, for the present, he remits it.

"Since he will never again be a candidate for any office, and is not in full accord with either of the great parties which have hitherto divided the country, he will be able and will endeavor to give wider and steadier regard to the progress of science, industry, and the useful arts, than a partisan journal can do; and he will not be provoked to indulgence in those bitter personalities which are the recognized bane of journalism. Sustained by a generous public, he will do his best to make the *Tribune* a power in the broader field it now contemplates, as, when human freedom was imperilled it was in the arena of political partisanship.

"Respectfully,     HORACE GREELEY.
"New York, Nov. 6, 1876."

[1] To the terrible accusation made in this editorial, Whitelaw Reid made no real answer, though his apologists have tried to do so. Greeley died November 29, 1872. Whitelaw Reid acquired certain outstanding options on the *Tribune* property, and immediately had himself elected publisher and editor.

In this card then is nothing to indicate mental derangement. On the contrary it is the language of one somewhat depressed perhaps by a great political disappointment, but yet in the full possession of his intellectual faculties and uttering himself in manly and not discouraging language. But on the same day with this card and following after it in the editorial columns of the same paper Mr. Whitelaw Reid published the subjoined astonishing article:

### "CRUMBS OF COMFORT"

"There has been no time, until now, within the last twelve years, when the *Tribune* was not supposed to keep, for the benefit of the idle and incapable, a sort of Federal employment agency, established to get places under government for those who were indisposed to work for their living. Any man who had ever voted the Republican ticket believed that it was the duty and the privilege of the editor of this paper to get him a place in the Custom House. Every red-nosed politician who had cheated at the caucus and fought at the polls looked to the editor of the *Tribune* to secure his appointment as postmaster, or as army chaplain, or as Minister to France. Every campaign orator came upon us after the battle was over for a recommendation as Secretary of the Treasury or the loan of half a dollar. If one of our party had an interest pending at Washington, the editor of the *Tribune* was telegraphed in frantic haste to come to the Capitol, save this bill, crush that one, promote one project or stop another. He was to be everybody's friend, with nothing to do but to take care of other folk's business, sign papers, write letters, and ask favors for them, and to get no thanks for it either. Four-fifths of these people were sent away without what they wanted, only to become straightway abusive enemies: it was the worry of life to try to gratify one demand in a dozen for the other fifth.

"The man with two wooden legs congratulated himself that he could never be troubled with cold feet. It is a source of profound satisfaction to us that office seekers will keep aloof from a defeated candidate who has not influence enough at Washington or Albany to get a sweeper appointed under the Sergeant-at-Arms, or a deputy-sub-assistant temporary clerk into the paste-pot section of the folding room. At last we shall be let alone to mind our own newspaper without being called aside every hour to help lazy people whom we don't know, and to spend our strength in efforts that only benefit people who don't deserve assistance. At last we shall keep our office clear of blatherskites and political beggars, and go about our daily work with the satisfaction of knowing that not the most credulous of place-hunters will suspect us of having any credit with the appointing powers. That is one of the results of Tuesday's election for which we own ourselves profoundly grateful."

This article was read by Mr. Greeley, as by many other sane persons, with horror and disgust. It was in effect a gross insult to the millions of voters who only two days before had given him their suffrages, and to the many distinguished and patriotic gentlemen, Democratic and Republican, who had cordially and unselfishly supported him throughout the canvass. No man felt this more keenly than Horace Greeley, and his first act was to go down to the *Tribune* office and write a disclaimer utterly denying any responsibility for this article. He had never been consulted respecting it; he had never seen it; he had no idea that anything of the sort was to appear; and in every respect he repudiated the sentiments and the language of the article.

This disclaimer was sent up by Mr. Greeley to the printing office to be published the next day at the head of the *Tribune's* editorial columns; but after he had left the office, Mr. Whitelaw Reid suppressed it and would not allow it to appear. The next day Mr. Greeley did not come down to the *Tribune* office, but he sent another paragraph containing a similar disclaimer, and this paragraph was also suppressed by Mr. Whitelaw Reid.

When it is remembered that Mr. Greeley had not only gone through the herculean labour and exciting agitation of the canvass, but had for weeks been in almost sleepless attendance at the bedside of his dying wife, is it surprising that this refusal of his own subordinate to allow him to disclaim in the *Tribune* sentiments which were repugnant to his heart and most injurious to his reputation, should have been followed by disorder of his mind and the collapse of all the physical stamina which still remained in his constitution?

## THE EFFECTS OF THE GREAT PANIC[1]

### *Commercial and Financial Chronicle*, December 27, 1873

The panic was remarkable in many respects. It came on suddenly. Everybody was surprised, and none more so than Jay Cooke & Co. themselves, when the towering columns of their financial reputation fell, and the imposing fabric, reared with so much skill, crumbled in a moment to ruins. Next the panic was remarkable for the depression of Stock Exchange values, which fell to a degree without precedent since the war, while the mercantile community seemed in large measure exempt from its influence, except indirectly and as a secondary consequence of later developments. Thirdly,

[1] The panic of 1873 was precipitated by the failure on September 18 of Jay Cooke & Company.

the panic was even still more remarkable for the slowness of its recovery and for the languor which it has left behind it.

## HAS THE GRANGER MOVEMENT FAILED?

Chicago *Weekly Tribune*, January 28, 1874

It is idle to talk of the failure of a movement which has gained the political control of the States of Wisconsin and California; which is dictating terms to the old parties in Iowa and Kansas; which has carried a majority of the counties of Illinois, and bids fair to carry the State at the next general election; which is making rapid headway in Minnesota and Michigan, and which has secured so fearless and able a leader as Gov. Booth in the United States Senate. . . . If there is any healthier political organization anywhere than that which the farmers have originated in the West, we do not know what name it is called by. . . . The main significance of the farmers' movement is that it offers to those who desire reform in public administration, and who have sought and failed to secure it in the old dividend-paying parties, an opportunity to accomplish something for the benefit of the country at large — not for the farmers merely, but for all who live by their industry, as distinguished from those who live by politics, speculations, and class-legislation.

## GRANT'S LETTER [1]

New York *Sun*, June 1, 1875

General Grant's letter on the third term is evidently all his own production. It is cunning; and it tells a good deal more than the author supposes.

The first intimation respecting the third term did not come from the press; it came from the White House. A person there, whose relations we need not more specifically define, said, just before the election of 1872, that "the great difference between General Washington and General Grant, as they would appear in history, would be that Washington had only two terms as President, while General Grant would have three." All that the press ever did in regard to this subject was to call attention to the unconcealed am-

[1] Dana's *Sun* had by 1870 become completely opposed to President Grant and his Administration. It naturally fought the talk of a third nomination vigorously. In 1875, a convention of Pennsylvania Republicans was ready to endorse Grant for a third term. On hearing of this, Grant wrote the president of the convention a reply, in which he declared: "I would not accept a nomination if it were tendered, unless it should come under such circumstances as to make it an imperative duty — circumstances not likely to arise." Censorious critics declared that there was a string to this refusal. In December the House of Representatives passed by an overwhelming vote a resolution against a third term for any President.

bition of Grant, thereby rendering its success impossible. About the fact of the ambition and the existence of the design there can be no question.

There is too much humbug in this letter. "I don't want the third term," he says, "any more than I wanted the first." Yet everybody knows how much he wanted the first. The only doubt in his mind was whether he should run as a Democrat or a Republican. He intrigued for the Democratic nomination, and failed, before he determined that he would be the Republican candidate; and now in this letter, when he says that he does not want the third term, he carefully leaves the door open in the hope that, after all, it may be given to him; and he ingeniously argues the constitutional point that the people have a right to elect a man President as often as they wish.

However, the thing is ended. The press settled it, and the Pennsylvania resolution registered the decree. When the Republican Convention meets to nominate a candidate for President, there will not be a man in it who will even think of nominating Grant.

## WHAT GRANT WILL DO ABOUT IT
### New York *Sun*, June 7, 1875

With scarcely an exception, the Democratic press regard Grant's recent letter as a sly argument in favor of his election for at least one more term. A small portion of the Republican newspapers take the same view of it, and are openly hostile to its object. Another small section of the Republican journals are either ominously silent or speak in doubtful phrase; and these are unquestionably desirous of giving Grant a third term.

But in spite of the plain drift of the letter, an influential majority of the Republican press affect to discover in it Grant's unqualified withdrawal from the list of candidates for 1876. Of course they will be successful. The Republican conventions in the leading States, and especially in the North and West, will follow the example of Pennsylvania and Ohio, and adopt resolutions against a third term. This will complete his destruction at the nominating convention next year, if he shall venture to appear there as a candidate.

But Grant will do his best to inflict summary retribution upon the party which thwarts his aspirations for a third term. What Tyler and Fillmore were to the Whigs in 1844 and 1852, that Grant will be to the Republicans in 1876. He will not play so bold and manly a game as Tyler did to defeat Clay; he will rather practise the foxy subtle policy of Fillmore, whose officeholders and confidential friends did their best to use up Scott.

The vengeance of a President whose party has refused to renominate him when he had set his heart upon it was illustrated in the conduct of so calm and urbane a gentleman as Martin Van Buren. Defeated in the Sub-Treasury issue in 1840, he claimed to be compensated by a renomination in 1844. He was overcome in the convention of that year by the friends of General Cass, although Polk became the candidate. Van Buren would have beaten Polk in that campaign had not Silas Wright, his confidential adviser and the author of the Sub-Treasury measure, been the candidate for Governor of this State, and had not Benjamin F. Butler (not of Lowell), the bosom friend of Van Buren, been promised a seat in Polk's Cabinet.

But in 1848, the Barnburner delegation from this State was excluded from the national Democratic Convention, and Cass was nominated! The hour for Mr. Van Buren to punish his enemies had now come. He had no patronage to bestow and no officeholders to marshal in line. But he was never at a loss for expedients. His personal followers assembled at Buffalo, and in conjunction with the Abolitionists and some anti-Taylor Whigs, gave him an independent nomination for President on the popular platform of Free Soil. The result was the overthrow of Cass, the regular Democratic candidate — an ample vengeance for his conduct in preventing Van Buren's nomination four years before.

Grant is not enough of a politician to employ the tactics of Van Buren; nor has he sufficient prestige as a statesman to last four years after he is turned out of office. Not even in the coming year would any faction bestow upon him an independent nomination. His only chance to strike will occur in the next campaign after the Republican Convention has rejected him. He will improve it; and the cunning, slippery tactics employed by Fillmore when he defeated General Scott, will be in his natural reliance. If the Democrats are wise, they will need no aid from him; but all that Grant can do will then be done in their behalf.

## [THE EMERGENCE OF SAMUEL J. TILDEN]

*The Nation*, October 7, 1875

The people are in a very puzzled and despondent state of mind about the political situation, and have got beyond the point at which they look for the appearance of the ideal statesman uniting the purest motives with the highest ability. They can get the pure motives, and they can get the high ability; but somehow, owing to no matter what circumstances, to get a man who unites both into a leading place in the government is a task of such difficulty that most people have given it up (at least for the present) for a bad job, and are willing to content themselves with any man who, for whatever motive, will do good work. It so happens, too, that the work to be done at this moment is not work which calls either for the highest order of genius or the highest aspirations. A man may do it very well without being either a Moses or a Washington — without, in short, being either a prophet or a hero. He has neither to lead a race out of captivity nor call a nation into existence. The task before the American politician of today is the simple and somewhat homely one of preventing public officers from stealing and dividing the public money, and of preventing the government from cheating its creditors; and when a man offers himself for this work, there is no general disposition to ask whether he is a statesman of the first rank, or whether his political judgment has always been sure, or his voice has always been heard on the right side. In fact, they go so far as to say that to make capital in this way is a good thing to do, and they wish all politicians to engage in it. They are ready to forbear all curious inquiries into the motives or antecedents of men who will undertake to put an end to cheating and stealing. In fact, the voters of the country are sticking notices up offering the highest offices in their gift, and "no questions asked," to anybody who will bring in a few plunderers of the state. Mr. Tilden has achieved his present success simply owing to his having, before anybody else of his class, understood the exact nature of the situation. He perceived sooner than his competitors that the time had come to stop preaching, and to begin making arrests and drawing up indictments. He now finds, and his competitors find, that his acuteness has rendered him the highest service, and his enemies actually play into his hands.

## [THE BABCOCK VERDICT][1]

### New York *World*, February 26, 1876

*From the New York Herald (Independent).* — But, while coinciding with this verdict, the country will say that the man who is pliable enough to allow thieves and conspirators to draw him into this most unfortunate position is not the man to enjoy the confidence of the President.

*From the New York Tribune (Republican).* — General Babcock may plead in extenuation of his imprudence that he has been no more reckless than the President. Keeping bad company is the besetting sin of General Grant's Administration.

[1] Orville E. Babcock, Grant's private secretary, became the centre of the Whiskey Ring scandal of 1875–1876; he was indicted and placed on trial in St. Louis, and though the evidence seemed heavily against him, he escaped — largely because of a deposition by President Grant in which the latter vigorously asserted his belief in Babcock's innocence.

*From the New York Times (Republican).* — All this was much too slender a basis on which to convict General Babcock of conspiracy, but it leaves enough of his conduct open to unfavorable comment to render highly necessary that "frank, full, and straightforward statement" which his friends in Washington expect him to publish.

*From the New York Evening Post (Independent).* — General Babcock takes the benefit of a doubt. It has cleared him before the St. Louis jury, but it may prove fatal to him before the country.

*From the New York Sun (Independent).* — The jury of St. Louis has acquitted Babcock. This is not surprising. The whole power and influence of the President and his nearest friends have been earnestly applied to produce such a result. But the facts proved on the trial are not obliterated and will not be forgotten. Now wait and see Secretary Bristow driven out.

*From the Boston Globe (Independent).* — It was a case of "easy virtue," of which we have had too much in our politics, and which, while it will not steal outright, never considers it worth while to be overfastidious on the score of honesty. General Babcock has profited by his connection with the "public improvements" in the city of Washington in a way which shows that he does not disdain the "opportunities" of public life. He may also have been willing that his friends should find some profit in it.

*From the Springfield Republican (Independent).* — General Babcock goes out of the St. Louis courthouse a more suspected and condemned man than he went into it. He does not longer deserve the confidence of the President; he has neither that nor the respect of the American people. If, under the circumstances, he was only what he confesses himself, the dupe of the whiskey-ring, that is enough for so much of condemnation.

*From the Philadelphia Times (Independent).* — No one will say that General Babcock is a simpleton; that he was deceived by designing men who simply used him to advance their peculations. He is not a fool, and the world will look in any other direction than that for the solution of his strange and at times jubilant dispatches to those who made him their chief agency to keep the government from dogging them in their paths of crime.

*From the Philadelphia Press (Republican).* — The fact of the arraignment of a gentleman of such high position on suspicion, and the rigid judicial investigation of the case at the hands of a common jury of a rural neighborhood, is what the Presbyterians would call a public "deliverance" of the people. It is a vote of instruction of the people to their official servants and leaders, admonishing them to integrity, honesty of action, and purity of motive.

*From the Baltimore Gazette (Independent).* — Let those who are able to believe in his innocence do so. If he was guilty there are others higher still who are also guilty and who cannot be reached. The rest can be left to history. A decent respect for an outraged public opinion requires, however, that Babcock be relieved of duty at the White House.

*From the Baltimore American (Republican).* — In brief, General Babcock was rightfully acquitted by the jury which passed upon his case, but he cannot recover from the evidence which in the minds of men has convicted him of holding a guilty connection with corrupters and defrauders of the government. He is legally innocent and morally criminal.

## [THE DOWNFALL OF SECRETARY BELKNAP][1]

*Harper's Weekly,* March 18, 1876

The tragical tale of the fall of Secretary Belknap naturally affected the country like a national calamity. The feeling with which it was received at once explains the conduct of General Hamilton, when Secretary of the Treasury, in preferring to confess a domestic crime rather than allow any imputation to rest upon his official honor. The disclosure in regard to Secretary Belknap was the more astounding because there had been no suspicion. He had been long a member of the Cabinet, and although not the most eminent among his colleagues, he bore from his service in the army, and as an officer in the internal revenue, an unsullied reputation. The suddenness and the completeness of the evidence against him were startling, and the universal condemnation with which he was greeted is a sign of the essential rectitude of the public mind which is the only final security of popular government. His offence, however, is not new in political history. Official jobbery is the most familiar fact in the political annals of England, for instance, from the purchase of place by bribes to the Duchess of Kendall, the mistress of George the First, and the frank corruption of Robert Walpole and the open sales under George the Third, to the securing of commissions by payments to the mistress of the Duke of York fifty years ago. Through English history jobbery of this kind has been gross and shameless. But the general sense of grief and horror with which the offense of General Belknap has been received, shows that whatever may be the uneasy fear that immense official corruption exists, the indisputable evidence of it falls upon the country with a heavy shock of consternation and shame.

[1] William W. Belknap, Secretary of War under Grant, was proved by a House committee to have accepted bribes from a post-trader in the Indian Territory. He was impeached but at once resigned, and the Senate refused to convict him because some members doubted their jurisdiction.

How is the fall of the Secretary to be explained? He was confessedly a brave and upright man. There were no whispers or insinuations against him. The report of his crime was incredible to the Representatives of his own State in Congress, and when the story was first told, all who personally knew him felt sure that the truth would prove to be that the offence was not his, but that of one very dear to him. A few hours, however, resolved all doubt, and left bare the dismal and degrading fact of his corruption. The Secretary's fall is a natural result of the relaxed tone of political honor and character, which is not peculiar to any party, but which weakens our whole political and social fabric. There is a too general and accepted maxim that all is fair in politics, that the ordinary laws of morality are suspended in the political sphere, that to insist upon common honor and honesty in party and political relations, to hold that a lie is a lie and a theft a theft in the awarding of contracts and the general conduct of administration, is to be visionary and impracticable and theoretical and fine-spun; there is a too general acceptance of the maxim that traditional practice is official common law, that what other men have done may be done as of course, and that, in fine, hay must be made while the sun shines. This feeling is the inevitable result of a system of the civil service which makes mere party servility and party influence the condition of appointment and the tenure of office. And it leads to a confusion of all moral distinctions, to apologies and palliations of flagrant offences, and to the social countenancing of knaves, thieves, and rascals of every degree.

This is the corroding atmosphere in which General Belknap, like every other public man and every man who actively engages in politics, has lived, and it unquestionably demands a certain firmness of moral fibre to resist its action. Those who have not strength and courage and constant watchfulness are in perpetual danger. It is a danger to be moderated and averted only by a process of purification, and that process does not consist in saying that good and honest and able men should be appointed, but in providing reasonable means to secure their appointment. The peril of official political life at the capital is immensely increased by the "great pace" of society. The profusion and splendor and reckless expense are captivating and fatally alluring. The imagination and ambition and rivalry of women are inflamed to passion. A Cabinet officer is in the highest social position. The temptation falls upon his family with enormous power — and he has ten thousand dollars a year salary.

The fall of Secretary Belknap is not a party disgrace; it is a national shame. It warns men of every party that a higher tone of political honor and morality is indispensable to the public safety and national life. It points sternly to the only way in which political success is possible in the election of the year, and that is the nomination of candidates whose characters and careers are the earnest of practical faith in an honesty of administration that avoids even the appearance of evil.

## PRESIDENT GRANT AND THE CABINET[1]

*Harper's Weekly*, August 5, 1876

The peremptory removal of the Postmaster-General without a word of explanation, and without the suspicion of any kind of misconduct or even of personal alienation from the President, is an insult to the country which he served efficiently, and to the party which elected the President. It is another illustration of General Grant's inability to understand that the Presidency is not a personal perquisite, but a great public trust. The method of the dismissal of Mr. Jewell assumes that a member of the President's Cabinet is a kind of body-servant or groom, whom his master may dismiss upon the spot, and without reason rendered. The members of the Cabinet are, indeed, nominated at the President's sole pleasure, and the Senate confirms as of course. But under our form of government there are moral conditions in the relation, implied if not expressed, which can not properly be disregarded. This is not an autocracy of any kind, but a government of the people, divided into parties. When a President is elected by one of the parties, that is, by a majority of the people preferring or acquiescing in a certain policy, he is bound to consider the terms of the trust, which are that he shall do what he can to promote that policy. That principle is to govern him in appointing the high political officers of administration, including the heads of departments. They are not to be boon companions whom he may personally like, but the necessity and reason of the case require that they shall be men publicly known to be friends of the general policy which the people have approved. "Should the gentlemen," wrote Jefferson after his probable election to the Presidency, and upon this very subject of Cabinet appointments — "should the gentlemen who possess the public confidence decline taking part in their affairs, and force us to take persons unknown to the people, the evil genius of this country may realize his avowal that he will beat down the Administration." With this primary condition, integrity, ability, efficiency, are of course to be

[1] Following the acquittal of Babcock, Benjamin H. Bristow, Secretary of the Treasury, who had accumulated the evidence against him and whom Grant for that reason disliked, resigned. Postmaster-General Marshall Jewell had sided with Bristow, and Grant immediately asked for his resignation also.

expected; and the nature of the relation with the chief executive officer is such that the members of the Cabinet must be upon pleasant personal terms with him.

The President must decide when the relation should end, unless the Secretary voluntarily resigns. But it ought never to end for any reason that can not be stated to the country. General Jackson, indeed, turned out several of his first Cabinet because the members' wives would not visit Mrs. Eaton. But Jackson was an ignorant, arrogant, and passionate man, who had no comprehension of the real character of the government or of official propriety. Nor was the dismissal of McHenry and of Timothy Pickering by John Adams in any sense whimsical or inexplicable. But the sudden and peremptory dismissal of a Cabinet officer against whom no kind of misconduct or inefficiency is alleged, and who to the very moment of his removal had been upon the most friendly personal terms with the President, and dismissal without a word of explanation except that it is the will of the President, is a degradation both of the Presidency and of the Cabinet. It exposes the officer so removed to the most injurious suspicion, and it convicts the Executive of a disposition wholly unbecoming the Chief Magistrate. What self-respecting gentleman would consent to take an office, however apparently elevated or honorable, if he knew that he was liable to be dismissed without alleged reason or warning?

The President, after all the revelations at St. Louis, retained General Babcock as private secretary until he was criminally indicted, and it is not known that he has yet dismissed him; he parted with Mr. Belknap with a note of regret; with Mr. Delano with a letter of sympathy; he nominated Mr. Shepherd to be Commissioner of the District of Columbia just after Congress had abolished the government of the District to get rid of him, and Mr. Fisher to a judicial post after the complicity of his office with the safe-burglary conspiracy. But he permits Mr. Bristow to leave the Cabinet without a word, and immediately turns out the most efficient of his subordinates in the prosecution of public frauds; dismisses without explanation the Postmaster-General, who by common consent is the best officer the country has had in that place for many a year; and compels the resignation of Mr. Commissioner Pratt of the internal revenue, because of his approval of tried and thoroughly efficient subordinates. And all this is done on the eve of an election in which the Republican party has approved the policy of these very officers, and has engaged to administer the government in their spirit. The President by his own action places himself under the pointed censure of the party that elected him, and his conduct, therefore, can not be honestly assumed to be that of the party. It is with sincere regret that we say it. Instead of loyally coöperating with the general spirit and policy declared at the late convention, his action apparently shows that he has fallen under those malign influences which have already sorely imperilled the Republican party, and which are compelling those who would gratefully remember him to fix their eyes solely upon his military career.

## [THE CUSTER MASSACRE][1]

*Harper's Weekly*, August 5, 1876

The fate of the brave and gallant Custer has deeply touched the public heart, which sees only a fearless soldier leading a charge against an ambushed foe, and falling at the head of his men and in the thick of the fray. A monument is proposed, and subscriptions have been made. But a truer monument, more enduring than brass or marble, would be an Indian policy intelligent, moral, and efficient. Custer would not have fallen in vain if such a policy should be the result of his death. It is a permanent accusation against our humanity and ability that over the Canadian line the relations between the Indians and whites are so tranquil, while upon our side they are summed up in perpetual treachery, waste, and war. When he was a young lieutenant on the frontier, General Grant saw this, and watching attentively, he came to the conclusion that the reason of the difference was that the English respected the rights of the Indians and kept faith with them, while we make solemn treaties with them as if they were civilized and powerful nations, and then practically regard them as vermin to be exterminated. The folly of making treaties with the Indian tribes may be as great as treating with a herd of buffalo. But the infamy of violating treaties when we have made them is undeniable, and we are guilty both of the folly and the infamy.

We make treaties — that is, we pledge our faith — and then leave swindlers and knaves of all kinds to execute them. We maintain and breed pauper colonies. The savages who know us and who will neither be pauperized nor trust our word we pursue and slay if we can at an incredible expense. The flower of our young officers is lost in inglorious forays, and one of the intelligent students of the whole subject rises in Congress and says, "The fact is that these Indians, with whom we have made a solemn treaty that their territory should not be invaded, and that they should receive supplies upon their reservations, have seen from one thousand to fifteen hundred miners during the present season entering and occupying

[1] General George A. Custer with 264 men was cut off in Montana by an overwhelming force of Sioux on June 25, 1876, and the entire command was destroyed.

their territory, while the Indians, owing to the failure of this and the last Congress to make adequate appropriations for their subsistence, instead of being fattened, as the gentleman says, by the support of the government, have simply been starved." The Red Cloud investigation of last year, however inadequate, sufficed to show the practise under our Indian policy, and we regretted then that ex-Governor Bullock of Massachusetts declined the appointment upon the commission, because there was evidently the opportunity of an exhaustive report upon the whole subject, which should have commanded the attention of the country, and would sooner or later have led to some decisive action.

It is plain that so long as we undertake to support the Indians as paupers, and then fail to supply the food; to respect their rights to reservations, and then permit the reservations to be overrun; to give them the best weapons and ammunition, and then furnish the pretext of their using them against us; to treat with them as men, and then hunt them like skunks — so long we shall have the most costly and bloody Indian wars, and the most tragical ambuscades, slaughters, and assassinations. The Indian is undoubtedly a savage, and a savage greatly spoiled by the kind of contact with civilization which he gets at the West. There is generally no interest whatever in him or his fate. But there should be some interest in our own good faith and humanity, in the lives of our soldiers and frontier settlers, and in the taxation to support our Indian policy. All this should certainly be enough to arouse a public demand for a thorough consideration of the subject, and the adoption of a system which should neither be puerile nor disgraceful, and which would tend to spare us the constant repetition of such sorrowful events as the slaughter of Custer and his brave men.

## CAN THE REPUBLICAN PARTY AFFORD IT? [1]

New York *Sun*, November 12, 1876

The proposition of the crazy and reckless Republican managers, like Zachariah Chandler and Jay Gould, is that all three of the disputed States shall be declared to have voted for Hayes, and that he shall be declared elected President upon this basis. But can the Republican party afford this?

If Mr. Hayes should be declared elected in this way, by a majority

[1] The returns of the election of November 7, 1876, gave Tilden 184 certain votes, with 185 needed for victory. Hayes believed that he had been defeated; but the day after the election Zachariah Chandler, chairman of the Republican National Committee, boldly claimed all the disputed votes of Louisiana, South Carolina, Florida, and Oregon, and the New York *Times* posted the bulletin: Hayes 185, Tilden 184. Dana never ceased to believe that Hayes was "the Fraudulent President."

of one electoral vote only, with the great majority of the popular vote against him, and with the almost universal conviction that the declaration was procured by fraud, would it be a situation such as the Republican party should desire? And would Mr. Hayes, under such circumstances, be able to perform the duties of the President effectively, successfully, and happily?

The taint of fraud would inevitably be attached to such a declaration that Mr. Hayes is elected. It would have to proceed upon the unquestionable fact that the vote of Louisiana was given to him by Kellogg's Returning Board: that the vote of South Carolina was given to him by Chamberlain's Board of Canvassers, and the vote of Florida by the officers of that State, whose own reëlection would thereby be determined by themselves, all in defiance of evidence that those States have really voted the other way. Thus while the local returns of Louisiana would demonstrate that the vote of that State had really been given to Tilden, Kellogg's Returning Board would declare that it had been given to Hayes. Now, the history of this Board is so well known, and its action has been so often stigmatized even by the Republican majority in the United States Senate as baseless and illegal, that no one could have any confidence in such a declaration, if the Board should now make one. So, too, in South Carolina, though the State Canvassers are not affected by the same universal notoriety as Kellogg's Board, yet should they assume to set aside and reverse the figures of the local returns from the different counties, nobody could believe them, because nobody could forget that they represent some of the very men who have done the most to bring the Prostrate State into its present condition, and that the first effect of their declaration would be to keep those men in power and save them from the hand of justice. In Florida, also, any declaration proceeding from the Republican office-holders of the State and giving the vote to Hayes, would not merely be tainted, but, in the judgment of the sensible people elsewhere, would be absolutely pervaded and filled with fraud from top to bottom and from centre to circumference.

Now the case in these three States stands just as we have described it; and if, following the lead of men like Zachariah Chandler and Jay Gould, themselves objects of distrust and suspicion all over the country, the Republican party should now force a declaration that Hayes is elected, and should endeavor to hold and carry on the government of the country on that declaration, what would be the verdict of the world upon it? That verdict, we think, would be that this once great party, having begun its career as the champion of freedom and the destroyer of negro slavery, had sunk through the depraving influence of the long possession of power, and had finally completed its history by bringing the whole people into a far baser kind of slavery by installing a President whom the people had not chosen. Can the Republican party afford this?

## SHALL THE GOVERNMENT BE STOLEN?

New York *Sun*, November 16, 1876

To count Hayes in fraudulently is probably the most monstrous political crime ever committed in this country. If successful, it would be the murder of the republic. It would be the end of official accountability to the people — the end of elections. Thenceforth our rulers would be named for us by those in power at Washington.

Who are the conspirators? Governor Hayes is not or at all events was not originally, one of them. When the insolent claim upon the electoral votes of the three States in the grip of Grantism was first put forth, Governor Hayes discountenanced it, apparently with a full knowledge that it portended, if it meant anything more than a mere gambler's device, a stupendous fraud. If Governor Hayes holds a different attitude now, it is because he has been admonished in the interval; and if he ultimately becomes a passive instrument in the hands of men attempting to seize the Government in his name, the fact will be only another and unnecessary proof that he is anybody's man but his own. No such purpose was ever born in his own heart, or contemplated without a mental protest.

Nor do we believe that any other Republican leader who has heretofore borne a respectable character is in the plot. We see no pure white hand anywhere in all this manipulation of returns, and all these mysterious telegraphic messages. We see here and there only the great black paws of Ring thieves and desperate political gamblers — of Chandler and of Gould, of Cameron and John Patterson, of Kellogg and Packard.

Republican statesmen and the rank and file of the Republican party are as much interested in the perpetuation of free institutions as Democrats are; and if Mr. Tilden is fairly elected, they will never permit another to be seated in his place. But this class had little or nothing to do with the management of the late campaign, and they are not now being consulted by the daring men who are plotting the hitherto unimagined crime of a usurpation of the Federal Government.

On the day after the election, when the nation was rejoicing over its deliverance from Grantism, and when the news from all parts — including Louisiana, Florida, and South Carolina — was favorable to Mr. Tilden's election, Zachariah Chandler began to freight the wires with mysterious messages in cypher, some of which have fallen into the hands of honest men and been translated. Some are addressed to Grant, and the rest to Grant's Marshals and carpet-bag Governors in the three States now in dispute. The prompt response is "more troops" from Grant, and confident assurances from the Southern marauders that the returning boards which they have created, hold, and manage, will present ample Hayes majorities.

Mr. Tilden has an enormous majority of the popular vote, and a good majority of the electoral votes. If this be true, and he is not inaugurated President on the 4th of March next, the republic is no more and the empire has arrived. But will the people of the United States suffer their Government to be stolen from them by Zachariah Chandler, Jay Gould, and Don Cameron? That may prove the most momentous question ever put to a people in all the tide of time.

## THE PUBLIC GOOD SENSE

*Harper's Weekly*, December 2, 1876

"We are all Republicans, we are all Federalists," said Mr. Jefferson in his inaugural address. In the same sense we may now say, we are all Republicans, we are all Democrats. That is, while our party preference is strong, our love of country is stronger. We do not mean that party spirit shall destroy our government, and with it the reasonable hope of popular liberty in the world. A French wit described the "liberty" of French republicans as the doing whatever the laws forbade. That is not American liberty. Americans make their own laws by their representatives, and obey them even to their own cost. We have earnestly desired the election of Mr. Hayes as the surer means of promoting the public welfare. But General Grant, who upon great occasions has more than once said most fitting words, spoke for us and for all true Republicans in saying, "No man worthy of the office of President should be willing to hold it if counted in or placed there by fraud. Either party can afford to be disappointed in the result. The country cannot afford to have the result tainted by the suspicion of false or illegal returns."

The American cleverness and readiness to meet an emergency were shown both in the suggestion of the President and the action of the Democratic Committee. "It is to be hoped," said the President, "that representative and fair men of both parties will go" and see "a fair count of the vote actually cast." To make the plan wholly satisfactory, the chairmen of the two National Committees should have united in inviting a few conspicuous and thoroughly trusted men in each party. The next best thing was done, however, in the President's invitation on the one side, and that of the chairman of the Democratic Committee on the other. The action was indicative of the ready good sense and patriotism which may be trusted to avert trouble. The report of the gentlemen on both sides who went to see fair play will be received with great interest. Should they agree, there is no doubt that the country will accept their verdict without question. Should they disagree, we shall at least have precise and authentic statements on both sides, instead of mere "claims" and "estimates" and "reports." In any case, there will be no rash action, and if we continue as we have begun, the public peace will not be disturbed.

## [ASPECTS OF AMERICAN SOCIAL HISTORY, 1876–78]

### The Nation

[*The Exposure of Political Corruption*]: April 27, 1876

The panic of 1873 suddenly sobered people, and turned their eyes to the position they were in and the road they were travelling. The "shrinkage of values," as it is called, and the disappointment of hopes consequent upon the panic, brought to light a great number of transactions which would not bear the light, and which, but for the panic, would never have seen the light, and exhibited a good many leading men in relations in which certainly no one ever expected to find them. It is not surprising that under these circumstances the temper of the public should be fierce, fretful, and doubting, and if it should call upon even the most respectable men in political life to give an account of themselves. We view with a sort of melancholy satisfaction the process of liquidation, as it is called, which is going on in the commercial world. We console ourselves, looking at the long lists of frauds and failures which are presented to us every month, by the reflection that, to borrow the phrase in common use, "the rotten concerns are being rapidly weeded out," that "we are getting rid of the dead wood," that "we shall soon touch bottom," and that the process of healthy recovery will then set it. Now, the public sees no reason why there should not be "liquidation" in politics as well as in business, why embarrassed statesmen should not submit their books and file their inventory and retire as well as embarrassed traders, or, at all events, why a politician any more than a merchant should object to having those who trust or employ him look into his affairs; and the public is not far wrong. This is not a time for great touchiness, and is certainly not a time when any man can safely take his stand on his dignity. We have a general mixture of all classes and conditions. All trades and callings run into all others. There has been a complete breakdown of the conventional barriers which formerly restricted men in their modes of making money. It is with the utmost difficulty that the press has succeeded, after years of hard fighting, in getting the government to stamp with reprobation the promotion of a joint-stock company by a national Minister in the country to which he was accredited. We have seen a doctor of divinity whose whole life was passed in pastoral duties, accept unblushingly a commission from the Treasury, which he must have known was a job, at a high salary, for performance of duties for which he knew he was totally unfitted. We have seen religious newspapers, for a commission, helping speculators to sell worthless bonds to some of the poorest people in the community. In fact, it has seemed at times of late years as if a man had only to call a thing a "business transaction" in order to release himself in carrying it through from all the restraints hitherto imposed by religion, morality, and manners.

Under these circumstances, it is not surprising and it is not improper that the public should call upon every man who offers himself or is offered by his friends as a candidate for high office, to tell how much money he has and how he got it.

[*Southern Violence*]: August 17, 1876.

The devotion of the Southern whites to the pastime of massacring the laboring population of the South since the Civil War has sadly interfered with the development of the old duello. The superior attraction of the new sport cannot be denied, inasmuch as it is much safer, being practised chiefly against unarmed males or women and children, and frequently without any opposing combatants at all, and its only drawback — the fear that excessive indulgence in it might lead to a diminution of industry and consequent yield of the arable soil — being entirely removed by the extraordinary fact, proved by experience, that the carnage and slaughter of the laboring population has a beneficial effect on the crops, especially cotton, the yield of which, year by year, shows a steady increase exactly proportionate to the increase of murder and arson. The duel was, however, a more picturesque sport, and it is pleasant to see that there is some chance of a revival of it in journalistic circles of South Carolina. Mr. R. B. Rhett, Jr., of the Charleston *Journal of Commerce*, a newspaper devoted to the "straight-out" policy, and therefore "antagonizing" the *News and Courier*, has published a card accusing Mr. F. W. Dawson — whom he refers to as the "aggressive member" of the staff of the latter paper — of accusing *him* of lying, and adds that it would naturally be assumed that any "manly man" who did such a thing would be prepared to give "that redress which honorable men are accustomed to seek as their protection and that of society against a repetition of such aggression." . . . It looks as if blood only could wipe out such a quarrel as this.

[*The Lesson of the Railway Riots*]: August 30, 1877.

In our time, with our vast accumulations of wealth and population at various points, our great cities have become reservoirs into which there flows from all parts of the country and from all parts of the world a steady stream of miscarriage and misfortune; of blameless men who have failed in everything and are embittered by it; of lazy men who have tried everything but industry, and against that have their faces set like flints; of visionaries who have their hearts set on a social state from which hard work will be banished, and who would wade through torrents of blood to achieve it; and of disappointed schemers who, unstable as water, after many failures, have sunk into a dull and pertinacious hatred of the successful and of all the tokens of success. Every class and condition of society furnishes its contribution to this mass of envious discontent, and the laboring class, as might be expected, the largest of any. Preaching does not reach them, because they have a gospel of their own, and the advice even of the well-to-do only exasperates them; and no arbitration or legislation or equitable division of profits, which is based on the obligation of steady labor and of fidelity to engagements, can at all touch them. They naturally congregate most largely in the great cities, because it is there easiest to live by one's wits, and to find auditors for one's plaints; and it is in the great cities only that rioting is most effective for destruction and disorganization — that even half an hour's work by a well-led mob can dissipate a hundred fortunes and suspend great branches of production. To leave society exposed to such risks, through a sentimental horror of "bayonets," is to be simply puerile.

[*Eastern Money-Lenders and Western Farmers*]: November 8, 1877.

Large sums of money have been lent in the last year on the frontiers of Minnesota and Kansas, in districts where there is no satisfactory security, the value of land being merely speculative. The rates of interest in these districts have been from 15 to 20 per cent, and agents handling capital at 10 per cent have charged from 10 to 20 per cent for their commissions. Indeed, 10 per cent is still or was till very recently charged all borrowers by the agents of one great investing company, though its officers must be aware that this commission effectually prevents their making any first-class loans, since, as a general thing, no first-class borrowers have for some years paid any such commissions. To call the method in which this great business is done reckless, scarcely describes it. . . .

The remedy is a simple enough one. It is merely to do business in a businesslike way. No loan should be made until the security has received the personal inspection of a salaried officer of the company, a man of established character and skill, whose sole interest is the welfare of the company. A few such men could travel over a whole State; and the enormously expensive commission agencies should be discouraged and applications sought direct from the farmer. The best security and nine or ten per cent interest could probably even now be obtained if the borrower were relieved of the commission and expenses, which sometimes, on small loans, eat up one-fifth before the loan reaches him.

[*The City and the Country*]: November 29, 1877.

Work on a farm is more or less repulsive to all men, from its severity and exposure to the weather. There is hardly anybody engaged in it who would not like to exchange it, if he could, for occupation needing less muscle, and capable of being pursued under cover, and with greater neatness and cleanliness, and with more company and greater opportunities for amusement. The young farmer, therefore, generally longs to "clerk it" in the nearest town, and having "clerked it" a while, and become used to clean hands, warm rooms, the theatre, and the concert-room, he will submit to almost any privation rather than go back to the hoe and the plough and the windy field.

What with these influences, and the facility for travel afforded by the railroads, the drain of "smart" youngsters from the country would probably have been very great, even if the high tariff of the last seventeen years had not put a high premium on city pursuits, a premium so great as to outbalance the inducements on the other side offered by cheap land and greater security. In the early colonial days, and for thirty years after the Revolution, the proportions between agriculture and the other pursuits were healthy because they were natural. Agriculture was then, as it is now, the great industry of the country, but the more active-minded, ingenious, and restless spirits overflowed from it naturally to the degree that was desirable into fisheries, commerce, mining, spinning and weaving. All these things flourished marvellously (witness Burke's description of New England enterprise) in spite of the exactions and discouragements of the mother country. The recent fiscal policy has been a powerful political and social disorganizer. It offered inducements to people to quit agriculture and engage in manufactures so powerful as to fit them rather for dull, unenterprising, and tradition-bound peasants like the Russians, than an active, eager, and easily-moved population like Americans, and while thus stripping the farms of their most intelligent and energetic men, it with curious fatuity shut them out from foreign commerce and the carrying trade, so that when the collapse came — and it *had* to come — they were absolutely cooped up in the cities, and unfitted to become tillers of the soil.

[*The Demagogue Kearney*]: August 1, 1878.[1]

The reception of Kearney, the California agitator, in Boston by a crowd of workingmen, the careful reports of his speeches by the press, and the editorial comments on him by all the leading papers, form altogether a spectacle that must delight Thomas Carlyle, if he still pays attention to contemporary politics, for Kearney is probably the lowest type of demagogue that has yet appeared in history. All his predecessors of which there is any record have laid claim to some of the qualities which are supposed to distinguish civilized man from the savage, but Kearney makes no pretence to anything which the reading, thinking, and remembering part of the human race has hitherto considered respectable. He simply does what the naked Bushman does — curses, calls names, and threatens death. Nevertheless, he has in one of the foremost communities of the modern world a considerable following, and is an object of interest, and even of deference, to most of our politicians. He is worth study because he is a kind of animal for which neither American politics nor manners have hitherto made the slightest preparation, and because he is the first to assert a claim which has been long in the air — viz., the claim not simply of the poor man to rule the state, but of the brutal, ignorant, blaspheming ruffian to have his way with the frugal, industrious, prudent, and religious; and assuredly we have not seen the last of his kind. Let us add — and without any wish to raise a question of party politics — that the moral and religious people of the North, in using their influence and the force of the Federal authority to procure and maintain for several years the government of great civilized communities of the South by the grossly ignorant portion of the population, and to discredit the intelligent portion for political purposes, have been sowing the seed from which the Kearneys spring. If Kearney makes the well-meaning believers in nose-counting as an efficient means of administering human affairs a little more thoughtful and cautious, he may yet prove a useful blackguard.

[1] Dennis Kearney was the "sand-lots orator" of San Francisco who led the workingmen in a violent movement against "oppressive" wealth and the competition of the Chinese. But while Kearney himself was a disreputable and vicious agitator, the discontent behind him deserved respectful treatment. Great corporations largely controlled the government. The best land was monopolized by large estates. Taxation was highly inequitable. The agitation helped bring about a constitutional convention in 1878–79, and this effected many reforms of a salutary nature. Of all the sound arguments which Kearney might have used, but did not, Godkin had nothing to say. The general social discontent of the time in California was connected with the labor rioting treated in the next editorial.

## THE RIOTS AND THE COMMITTEE OF SAFETY[1]

San Francisco *Bulletin*, July 31, 1877

In a sense San Francisco appears to better advantage in a social storm than at any other time. It is then that the qualities which have rendered her history so exciting are displayed in relief. In the usual calm flow of events there is not often an exhibition of what may be called public spirit. Men hurry to and fro absorbed in their own affairs. Not unfrequently they have not the time to exchange the ordinary courtesies of life. One would suppose, on a cursory view, that there was nothing here but an intense individuality which would render concert of action difficult, if not impossible, in an emergency. But deeper down there is a love of order and a faculty of prompt organization which is not observable anywhere else.

The troubles in this city commenced on Monday night of last week. They may be said to have come upon us unexpectedly. There was no strike among the laboring classes, and everything was moving in the accustomed channels. The sudden attacks on Chinese laundries and the incendiarism which accompanied it, at once exhibited the turn which things were going to take. Monday was a night of general alarm. The events that transpired showed plainly enough that if our citizens did not take matters instantly in hand there was no knowing what was going to happen. On Tuesday they began to organize with the old quietness and determination. On Wednesday they appeared on the scene in force. On Thursday they had the town completely under their control. On Thursday the rowdyism, with which we were for three nights confronted, ceased. The firebell but once broke the stillness of the night. No sound fell on the ear but that of the marching battalions of citizens.

Two days — more properly speaking a day and a half — were all that were required to bring into existence an organization of upwards of 7,000 men divided off into companies and regiments. Had our troubles gone on increasing there would be 50,000 enrolled today. There was no lawlessness possible which this great power could not have crushed like an eggshell at a single blow. This organization, called forth as it were by the wave of a magician's wand, was not only military but civil. It had its deliberative council and executive. Its headquarters were in communication with the official headquarters. Another mayor in fact stood by the side of the official personage, holding in his hands the whole power of the community. This mayor may be said to hold his power in

[1] The great railway strike of July, 1877, was accompanied by riots in Baltimore, Pittsburgh, Chicago, and other cities· in San Francisco a Vigilance Association restored order.

permanence. But he comes to the front only when anarchy begins to rear its head. W. T. Coleman is a man of great executive ability—calm, firm, and helpful in case of danger. The faculty of organization which he exhibits is something wonderful. Under his experienced lead everything moved like clockwork.

Our method of dealing with social disorder will attract a great deal of attention abroad. Already the organs of public sentiment elsewhere are pointing to the way San Francisco has of confronting rioters. They are expressing the most unlimited admiration, not unmixed with wonder, for it. But this means the youngest city of consequence in the world, and made up of the most heterogeneous materials, becomes the one in which order is most firmly established. Our city has secured a projection in this direction which will last it for a generation. Instant organization for the suppression of lawlessness has become a habit. This is the feature which the men who founded this city stamped upon its social structure; and this is the feature which it will longest retain.

## [A REVIEW OF TWEED]

### The Nation, October 18, 1877

It cannot be denied, we think, that in a certain sense he is indeed "a man of the times," and from one point of view, therefore, entitled to recognition as a representative man. His insatiable greed for money was accompanied by a good share of capacity for control. Not very many years ago, therefore, under a somewhat different civilization, he would have been, without doubt, a freebooter or brigand, and, at the head of a troop of followers, would have robbed upon the highway or plundered villages or laid towns under tribute. But in a different generation, when brigandage had changed its form and become possible only as modified into carpet-baggery, Credit Mobilier companies, freedmen's savings banks, forgeries, and all the peculiar manifestations of the speculative era which ended (or at least came to a crisis) four years ago, Tweed took his position by a sort of natural selection or fitness for the times, and his career was such as might have been prophesied by a wise observer of the man and his opportunities. He was as dependent upon his surroundings as, in a somewhat analogous way, the Italian brigand is, or until recently was, dependent upon the villagers around him. Tweed could have done nothing without the Watsons, Keysers, Joneses, and Garveys who abetted him, as well as the Halls, Connollys, Sweenys, and other members of his band who plundered with him, without legislators willing to be bribed as well as tradesmen willing to connive. Tweed was an amazing villain, but was nevertheless a legitimate outcome of his time, and his present complacency, or absence of conviction of sin, as our clerical friends might express it, is readily explainable in view of his associates and opportunities.

But has his day gone by? His particular hour is undoubtedly past, but we are not so sure that the day of great criminals is ended. The ever-increasing complexities of modern civilization furnish greater opportunities alike for saints and devils. Our social forces are so powerful that a slight derangement of them, sure to be taken advantage of by the criminal class, works infinite mischief. As civilization tends to make wars less frequent, but — owing to the invention of more highly destructive agencies, and the enormous expensiveness of vaster armaments, with the attendant financial derangements and interference with commercial relations — makes them more terrible than ever before, it is probable also that, in a somewhat analogous sense, civilization is reducing the number of criminals, but, for the time being, furnishes opportunities for greater crime, and the production therefore of more amazing criminals than ever before. Whether highway robberies, larcenies, and the like are diminishing or not may be an open question, with the chances in favor of an affirmative decision, but of more stupendous crimes — forgeries, defalcations, breaches of trust, swindles, and systematic peculations — we have witnessed recently a plentiful amount.

## SPRING FEVER FANCIES[1]

New Orleans *Item*, March 16, 1879

Together with the languor and dreaminess begotten by the spring's fragrance and its tepid winds, there comes to many, year after year, in whatever climate or country, but especially perhaps in our own, that vague longing for other lands and strange places — that thirst for the solitude of other lands, so romantically called by Curtis the Camel-spirit.

Imagination, in this age, has developed this strange feeling to a remarkable degree, and the most imaginative are those most cursed, or blessed, perhaps, by its influence.

Yet it may seem curious that at no other period of the year is the feeling so potent as at this time. It is not winter that inspires dreams of brighter and deeper skies, of whiter moons and larger stars, of sunsets more golden and winds more witchingly fragrant, of feathery-crested palms and strange poisonous flowers that slumber by day and open their pale hearts only to the tropical moon.

In winter the fancy seems at least restrained by the local boundaries of familiar places. It hibernates in a species of psychological

[1] By Lafcadio Hearn.

torpor. The call for daily duty, the strong necessity for active exertion, the hope inspired by present success, occupy the mind with material images and numb the fancy. The stream of Romance is bound up also in the rime of frost, however shadowy the frost-crystals.

Then the spring comes with its burst of roses, its magical perfumes, its genial warmth: — faint gossamers float up, like phantom Icarii vainly struggling toward the sun; — and all the long-pent-up vapors of fancy float upward with them! The heart feels heavy with a vague and mysterious sadness, the walls of the city seem constraining barriers, the wild clouds seem pregnant with omens, and the winds, pure as the heaven of amethyst, seem to bear the dreamer ghostly kisses from lands "where it is always afternoon."

It is a homesickness, yet without memories of home; a thirst for freedom, yet there is no sense of imprisonment; a sort of world weariness too vague for physical analysis. It is as though one might wish to wander through blue deeps of eternity to reach a rosy paradise in some far-sparkling world. Ideas of preëxistence, wild theories of metempsychosis and avatars throng upon one at such times.

Of what is this strange sickness born? Have philosophers written of such things, or are such things unknown to the arid reasoner though familiar to the heart of the poet?

Darwinism does not teach us yet whether some remote and antediluvian relationship may be found between man and the bird; yet one is almost tempted to fancy that man's spring fever of unrest had its origin in the palpitation of a bird's heart. The spring cometh; and the voice of the turtle is heard in the land. The wild birds fly north in the spring; southward in the autumn; happier than we, they may fearlessly gratify the Unspeakable Unrest.

Perhaps our Aryan ancestors, wandering in ages dimly prehistoric — traversing strange lands with their horn-bows at their backs — seeking softer climes and richer strands, may have bequeathed to us from forgotten years this feverish unrest of spring, this vague and undefinable longing for faraway lands.

## INGERSOLL'S DISREGARD OF THE UNIVERSAL RELIGIOUS SPIRIT[1]

Portland *Oregonian*, April 22, 1879

Robert G. Ingersoll, better known as "Colonel Bob Ingersoll," continues at intervals his lectures on theological subjects in different parts of the country; and now and then a member of the clergy

[1] By Harvey W. Scott. Robert G. Ingersoll had now become the most famous leader of the American agnostic movement.

takes a hand in answering him.  Ingersoll attacks with sneers and is repelled with denunciation.  On one side is contemptuous, unfair, and exaggerated treatment of the subject, and on the other epithetical abuse.  Ingersoll has power, undoubtedly, but it lies mainly in his tricks of words.  When he talks on theological subjects he always takes care to state the position he attacks, whether it be found in the words of the Bible or in scholastic authority, in a way that makes it both absurd and ridiculous.  Smart parody, clever travesty, or grosser burlesque, with occasional use of the lighter weapons of satire and wit, give a popular fervor to an address, and the orator carries off large honors.

Undoubtedly a great part of the power for which Ingersoll is noted is his very remarkable oratory.  He is not a great thinker, but he is a great speaker.  Those who remember when — until then an almost unknown Western lawyer — he took the platform, amid the buzzing of the great assembly that filled the Cincinnati Exposition Hall, and nominated James G. Blaine for President, will never forget what a revelation of oratory and influence it was.  Without having any phonographic statistics to go by, we should judge that Ingersoll speaks at least one-third faster than other first-class orators of the country.  The words, clear, distinct, and perfectly enunciated, come forth like a torrent.  It is as if he had so much to say that he must haste to get it all out, lest the hour-glass should cut him short before he is done.  The effect of this is to impart some portion of his own enthusiasm to his audience.  The torrent, if they give themselves up to it, takes away their understanding.  This is peculiarly the case when he delivers one of those singular cumulative sentences with which his orations or lectures abound.  It is hard to describe one of these artful combinations of words in which one phrase is tacked on to another, then another and another, until the whole is ended off with a stroke of assertion or wit that resounds through the audience like the crack of a whip.

An example may, perhaps, give the idea:

> For thousands of years men have been disputing about trifles, they have argued about sacrifices and altars, about circumcision and concision, about the cleanness and uncleanness of meats, about initiations and renunciations, about ablutions and baptisms, about the person of the deity and the substance of the Trinity, about original sin and the origin of evil, about consubstantiation and substitution, about the supper in one kind or in both kinds, about justification by faith, the damnation of infants, the location of hell.

This, delivered with increasing intensity and rapidity, inevitably has the effect on the audience of making them, at least for the moment, believe that men have actually been occupying themselves, for the last few thousand years, with trifles, and are only now about to awaken to really important things at the trumpet call of Apostle Ingersoll. Only the cooler heads will reflect that there is nothing in all this dogmatism. But, as Johnson said of Junius, he who attacks received opinions shall never want an audience. Ingersoll, and such as he, are at once the product of and a rebound from a hard, speculative, and in many respects unreasonable theology, which belongs rather to former generations than to this one.

## THE MISTAKES OF THE BIBLE

### Portland *Oregonian*, July 8, 1879

The student of history is impressed with nothing so much as the slowness which with men change their opinions on any subject, and the peculiar slowness with which they change the most deeply-rooted of all their opinions, namely, their religious beliefs. The "mistakes" which Ingersoll seems to think he has discovered were pointed out thousands of years ago, have again and again been proclaimed by a series of the most brilliant intellects the world has ever seen, and have never been fully explained by anyone; and yet the Christian Church has flourished and grown steadily till this time, and is growing yet. Nothing, therefore, could be more absurd than Ingersoll's supposition that in a few years more the whole splendidly-organized fabric will fall to pieces. Science no doubt will continue to modify it; the doctrine of hell is undergoing change, and the doctrine of the inspiration of the Scriptures, likewise, is presented with modifications, or rather, perhaps, with new definitions. But religious beliefs depend largely on the emotional nature of man, which will not be argued with; and so long as the Bible enters into the deepest experience of human lives, and its great utterances give consolation and hope to millions in their hours of pain and sorrow, so long will men — even "intelligent men" — not give it up. And that will be an indefinite length of time beyond the furthest survival of any remembrance or record of Ingersoll's rhetoric, brilliant as it is.

## THE REPUBLICAN PARTY AND REFORM[1]

### *Harper's Weekly*, April 3, 1880

The New York *Times* lately said: "If ever a party was fairly and deliberately committed to any object, the Republican party has been and is committed to the reform of the civil service. And we

[1] Civil service reform, long advocated by Carl Schurz, George W. Curtis, Lyman Trumbull, Dorman B. Eaton, and others, received its first fair chance under Presi-

may add that no party was ever more bound by expediency as well as by honor to redeem its pledges." The *Times* then remarks that notwithstanding this fact, it did not find in the reported speeches of Republicans in the House upon the bill prohibiting assessments upon office-holders "even the faintest recognition of the party obligation," and adds that "the cynical indifference" of Republican Representatives to the whole matter is "a blunder which amounts to a political crime." These words are well worth heeding. Far from decreasing within the party, the demand for reform is becoming the first and most positive principle of the younger Republicans, upon whom the traditional issues of the party have a fainter hold, and the number of intelligent citizens who see in the reform the obvious remedy for alarming political evils is constantly and rapidly enlarging. Reform of the civil service is in fact the reform of machine politics, because it is the abolition of the patronage which is the root of political corruption. Eight years ago Republican ascendency was at its height. President Grant was understood to favor reform. State Republican Conventions approved it, and the National Convention which renominated General Grant made this declaration:

> "Any system of the civil service under which the subordinate positions of the government are considered rewards for mere party zeal is fatally demoralizing, and we therefore favor a reform of the system by laws which shall abolish the evils of patronage, and make honesty, efficiency, and fidelity the essential qualifications for public positions, without practically creating a life tenure of office."

This demand for laws to abolish the evils of patronage, and to secure certain essential qualifications, covered the reform, and pledged the party. After the election, however, this pledge was forgotten, and nothing practically resulted from it. There was no reform, nor was the failure surprising, because, as it seemed to us then, and as it seems to us now, the Republican Administration was not prepared effectively to carry out such a declaration, and so far as we know, none of the recognized leaders of the party were in favor of it.

Nevertheless, the reform spirit spread rapidly among the Republicans. It was quickened by events during the second administration of General Grant, and the National Convention of 1876 reiterated the declaration of 1872, but in a manner so guarded as to be really non-committal. The reason of this is significant. It was that the

dent Hayes. He courageously based his appointments upon merit, and asked for a good Civil Service Act. In his final message of December, 1879, he gave several pages to a review of the history of civil service reform. But it required the murder of Garfield to galvanize Congress into action.

From *Harper's Weekly*, Nov. 9, 1872.     By Thomas Nast

"HOME-STRETCHED"

(Greeley, as the candidate of the Liberal Republicans and Democrats in 1868, carried only six border and Southern States against Grant.)

From *Harper's Weekly*, 1879.     By Thomas Nast

"STRANGER THINGS HAVE HAPPENED"

(In this cartoon the Donkey and Elephant symbol first appear together. Senator Bayard is represented as saying to the Donkey: "Hold on, and you may walk over the sluggish animal up there yet.")

reform could be treated no longer as mere buncombe, because if the party were successful it was known that the Administration would be held by reform Republicans to some honest effort at reform. This necessitated caution upon the part of the managers. The letter of acceptance of Mr. Hayes, however, and his inaugural address, were entirely satisfactory to Republicans who favored reform. But the vacillations and inconsistencies of the Administration upon the subject, and the surrender of last autumn by Mr. Evarts and Mr. Sherman to the enemies of reform in New York, were mortifying and inexplicable, although it is undeniable that in proving, at the very headquarters of the old system, the perfect practicability of the new, an immense service has been rendered by the President to reform. Indeed, there can be no doubt whatever that if the Administration had grappled with Mr. Cornell at once when, as Naval Officer, he defied it, had pursued its reform policy firmly at every point, and had extended the system which has been proved, so far as applied, to be completely successful in the New York Custom House, to every Custom House in the country, the Administration would have been more highly respected, and machine politics would have been terribly demoralized. The reason that this was not done probably was that the Cabinet was not agreed upon the subject, while Republican members of Congress and Republican politicians in general were "cynically indifferent." . . .

The Republican is the only one of the present parties whose general character and intelligence encourage the hope that it may yet make this reform honestly a part of its policy. The *Times* holds that the party is even now "fairly and deliberately committed to it." But the *Times* will agree with us that so long as the chief leaders of the party in Congress are men like Messrs. Cameron, Logan, and Conkling, and in this State such gentlemen as Messrs. Cornell, Arthur, Smyth, Platt, Dutcher, Murphy, Payn, Patterson, and other gentlemen who, however sound upon honest money and Southern outrages, yet cordially despise reform, the party will be in no sense whatever a reform party. The *Times*, which is a veteran leader in the contest for reform, and which dealt the fatal blow at the most dangerous and powerful political conspiracy in our State history — the Tweed Ring — says truly, "Though the party may, by the insane stupidity and recklessness of its opponents, carry this year's elections on issues unconnected with reform, the sentiment which demands reform is not a transient one, or one which is likely to become less." Here it touches the very point of the contest which is now going on in the Republican party, and it is not a contest that can be compromised. As new questions become more pressing, and old ones less important, a party must represent the new, or it will be rent asunder. This has been the history of every political organization. The Whig party refused to become a liberty party and it went to pieces. The Democratic party rejected its free-soil element and it was wrecked. The party leaders would not see, or they did not understand, the danger signals that were set high and unmistakable. Are there no danger signals flying now? Is the position which the Republican party has taken upon this subject to be evaded as the Whig party evaded the slavery question in 1852? Four years later, in 1856, the Whig party was gone. It cast 874,534 votes, against 1,838,169 Democratic and 1,341,364 Republican votes. We agree with the *Times* that chronic Republican indifference to the vital administrative evils which demand reform would be a blunder amounting to a crime.

## "BOSSES"

*Harper's Weekly*, September 25, 1880

It is a signal illustration of the condition of the Democratic party, and one which throws great light upon the general defection from that party, that Mr. John Kelly has become its supreme "boss" in New York and General Butler in Massachusetts. It is unnecessary for Republicans in either State to describe either potentate, because the Democratic papers during the last few years have exhausted the language in pointing out what they have called their treacheries, knaveries, and general worthlessness. General Butler, for instance, has been a standing Democratic argument against the Republican party, while the "regular" Democratic press of New York has depicted Mr. John Kelly as a vulgar Judas or clownish Guy Fawkes plotting to sell or to blow up his party.

General Butler, having now fully satisfied himself that the Republican party has done with him, announces himself a Democrat, and at once takes command of the party in his State, apprising Judge Abbott and Mr. Charles Francis Adams and Mr. Leverett Saltonstall and the other gentlemen who have recoiled with loathing from all political contact with him, that they will now obey his orders. The General thereupon graciously notifies Judge Abbott that he may be an elector-at-large, and he permits Mr. Adams to be a fellow vice-president of the State convention, and next year he will compel them to support him for the chief magistracy of Massachusetts. Of Mr. John Kelly's course we gave some account last week. After a long conflict with Mr. Tilden, who has the credit of being the most astute as well as the richest and most experienced of Democratic politicians, and who has been sustained by the respectability and "regularity" of the party, Mr. Kelly, who has bolted the nominations and defeated his party at the polls, has now forced Democratic respectability and regularity to his feet, and has dictated the terms upon which he will give his party its only chance of carrying the State of New York. If the Democratic party united were sure of carrying the State, and if the bargain lately concluded were sure to unite it, the Democratic prospects would be encouraging. But we have already shown, both from the electoral figures and the situation, that this is mere assumption; and while New York is always a doubtful State, the chances this year are wholly with the Republicans.

But in a national contest to be decided by the public judgment of the general character and probable course of the two parties, the ascendancy of "bosses" like Butler and Kelly becomes a very important element. Even if the election were a mere choice between "bosses," the chances would certainly favor the Republican side, for the simple reason that the last few months have shown in this respect both Republican independence and Democratic subserviency. One of the powerful and successful inducements for the independent vote to support Mr. Tilden in 1876 was the Democratic nomination of Mr. Adams as governor of Massachusetts. Following the nomination to the Presidency of Mr. Tilden, the "reform" governor of New York, this was accepted as an indication of a real Democratic regeneration, and it gave an immense impetus to the Democratic canvass. But now that after the dismal revelations of the cipher conspiracy, and the extra session, and the Garcelon infamy, Mr. John Kelly turns up as the Democratic boss in place of Mr. Tilden in New York, and General Butler in place of C. F. Adams in Massachusetts, while tissue ballots and false counting are the Democratic reliance in the Southern States, it is not surprising that intelligent voters . . . support the Republican nominations.


# RALPH WALDO EMERSON [1]

### Century Magazine, July, 1882

The idea of extent — of great length and breadth — the idea of large numbers, both of miles and inhabitants; the idea of enormous products; of gigantic mountain ranges; of big trees in immense forests; of endless rivers and unbounded prairies — this idea of extent and quantity is the one most commonly associated with the name of America. Our inventions are myriad; our bridges, our public buildings, our factories, our railroad systems, our charities, are enormous. Our national capital is a "city of magnificent dis-

[1] By Richard Watson Gilder; Emerson died April 27, 1882.

tances." Besides this, we used to have, and we have not yet quite lost, a reputation for loudness of voice and manners and a spirit of braggadocio based upon the general largeness of all things American.

It is a curious thing that the aesthetic products of America, those even that are considered most individual to the country, and some of those which have had the widest foreign vogue, are characterized rather by their condensation of manner and subtlety of thought and expression, than by that other more obvious American quality of physical force and extent. In America the arts have a strong tendency to refinement and even spirituality. We have had only two or three painters of "big pictures." We have eight or ten painters, at least, whom it would be hard to surpass in any one country of Europe today in the rarer qualities of technique. It is in America that wood-engraving has been carried to the highest delicacy of expression, and that the art of making stained glass has reached a delicacy and richness that well nigh equals, and a variety that surpasses, the best epochs of glass-making.

The only thing enormous about American literature is the "great daily" system, which has reached its culmination in our western cities. Longfellow, Lowell (except in his humorous works), and Holmes, are mainly regarded abroad as scholars and citizens of the world. Poe, Hawthorne, Emerson, Bret Harte, names like these, stand preëminently for American literature to the foreign audience; and how intense, condensed, and subtle the art of these writers! Even Whitman, with all his rank virility, writes about, but not for, the populace. Where is there more subtle description of out-of-doors nature than in the books of Thoreau and Burroughs? Holmes is regarded by competent foreign critics as the first living English master of the delicate art of what is rather vaguely called *vers de societé*. Bret Harte is the American humorist most widely quoted at home and abroad. The humor of Warner is most refined and elusive. Our later novelists, James, Howells, and Cable, are famed for the delicacy of their observation and style. American writers have long produced the best "single number" stories; while the English have, until very lately at least, been ahead of us in the production of first-class serial novels. A great danger, indeed, of the tendency of all American art is over-refinement, over-subtlety, resulting sometimes in self-consciousness and pettiness of execution.

Geographically speaking, it would seem as if America should have given birth to Carlyle, with his prodigality of expression, rather than Emerson with his brevity, reticence, and subtlety of phrase. And yet Emerson is the natural as well as the finest flower of our new-world life. His thoughts, by their sympathetic national quality, have taken hold of the minds of the thinking part of our vast population, as have the thoughts of no other man.  He has inspired our men of action.  He has inspired the inspirers — the ministers of every creed, the schoolteachers, the writers.

But other men of thought;  other wits (and some, like Bryant, regard Emerson chiefly as a wit), other preachers will arise and do their work in other epochs of our national life.  As a prophet and preacher he may be supplanted, temporarily at least.  In fact, there must always be some living preacher whose message will come to our hearts with peculiar directness and authenticity.  The continuance of Emerson's fame and power as an author will depend upon the verdict of posterity as to his art.  No one can authoritatively predict what that verdict will be.  But it is not presumptuous to discuss the point and to give one's own convictions.  It seems to us that Emerson's thoughts, expressed either in prose or verse, are packed tight for a long journey.  Especially does this seem clear with regard to his poetry.  Harsh and limping as much of his verse may be, there are lines, couplets, stanzas, and whole poems that have about them the flavor of immortality.  Hating jingle, he sometimes stumbled into discord — but for all that there is no poet who has written on this side of the water, who has produced so many lines of poetry not only weighty with deep and novel thought, but beautiful in form and texture;  with a beauty like Shakespeare, like Shelley (whom he underrated), like Keats.  When Emerson's line is good, it is unsurpassably good;  having a beauty not merely of cadence, but of inner, intense, birdlike sound;  the vowels, the consonants, the syllables are exquisitely musical.  It may be said of Emerson as of Michael Angelo, when he "deigns to be beautiful," how piercing the quality of beauty!

## THE BURNING OF THE DEAD [1]

New Orleans *Times-Democrat*, March 30, 1884

The strong feeling in favor of cremation both at home and abroad is a sign of the times.  It is true that this feeling is by no means that of the great majority as yet;  but it is the feeling of a very intelligent and imposing minority which has the power to make converts rapidly in multitudes.  The mind of the nineteenth century is undergoing a reaction in favor of ancient funeral rites and pagan common sense.  Is this because we are growing skeptical — because the old superstitions and the Folklore of the Dead are passing away?  Certainly the feeling against cremation is most strong where superstitions do most survive.  But the vanishing away of certain dark

[1] By Lafcadio Hearn;  a characteristic subject, treated with Hearn's superb command of sonorous diction and of imagery.

forms of belief, and the tendency of the times to abandon old customs and old ideas, are themselves due to those vast economical changes which have already modified the face of the world, and broken down barriers between nations. The skepticism of the period is a cause, perhaps — but only a subordinate cause, for the open advocacy of cremation. The great primal cause is the enormous industrial progress of the period, enabling countries to maintain populations ten times larger than could have found support some centuries ago. The world's markets are becoming more colossal than was ever Babylon or Egyptian Thebes; cities of a hundred thousand people spring up every few decades in the midst of what were previously wildernesses; and towns of insignificant size receive sudden nourishment from railroads and swell to metropolitan proportions. In many American cities population doubles itself at astonishingly brief intervals; and the intervening lands are cultivated to their utmost extent by a rapidly increasing race of sturdy farmers. In Europe the increase of population is slower by far, but it is nevertheless astounding when compared with the populousness of the sixteenth and seventeenth centuries. A generation ago London had barely three millions of inhabitants; she has now almost five millions. All the great capitals are becoming more populous. Science and invention have enabled the human race to multiply extraordinarily. But with the increase of life there is the inevitable increase of disease; and the work of Death is becoming so gigantic that the living can scarcely find place for his harvests. Cemeteries are too quickly filled; the city grows out to them and beyond them; the expenses of extra-mural burial increase continuously; the earth is overfed with corpses until she can no longer digest them; and the air of each metropolis becomes heavy with odors of dissolution. Inhumation can no longer meet the demands of hygiene: — Science has taken alarm, and seeks to summon Fire to the assistance of Earth. Fire, the All-Producer, as personified in the Sun — (Surya, 'The Begetter') — is also the All-Purifier. Fire, not earth, shall devour the dead in centuries to come as in centuries that have passed away. Cremation will become at last not a choice but a necessity. It may first be established as optional; it will then become obligatory. These are the declarations and predictions of its advocates.

Elsewhere we publish extracts from an excellent article on that subject, which appeared in the Paris *Figaro*. The author, who is a devout Roman Catholic, admirably points out the absence of any potent religious argument against the incineration of the dead, while he also dwells upon the horrors of the decomposition and the involuntary yet inevitable condemnation of thousands to a *living burial.* But there is also a poetical side to the sinister question, which might be dilated upon — the swift restoration of the substances of being to their primal source of light and air — the remelting of the body into the pure and luminous elements which formed them. The body soars with the rising of the flame which enwraps it, soars toward that blue to which all eyes turn at times with an indefinite longing — as though there were something of the bird in every human breast.

"The earth," poetically says a Vedic poet, "receives the dead even as a mother wraps the fold of her robe about the weary child who sinks to slumber in her arms." The thought seems beautiful, but its words are untrue. For the earth is a cannibal: — she devours her children as hideously but infinitely more slowly than the python devours his prey; so hideously that only the bravest soldiers of Science have ever dared to peer into the processes of her digestion — as did Orfila. Perhaps it would be well if certain sentimental opponents of cremation should behold that indescribable treatise of his upon Juridical Exhumation with its frightful colored plates, whose horrors surpass the most loathsome conceptions of madness and the most appalling monstrosities of nightmare. One glance at these secrets of the tomb were enough to convert the bitterest anti-cremationist! And how slow the decay! Sometimes in five years the earth has not consumed its food. Poets may write touching pantheistic madrigals concerning the ultimate blending of all flesh with that "Universal Paste formed of the shapes that God melts down"; but has the poet ever dared to raise the coffin-lid and observe the ghastly transmutation for an instant? Could even the philosopher dare so much? — for the breath of the tomb is fatal. Death permits only the high priests of science to study that ghastly chemistry and live! Surely the noblest works of God are wrought in fire; — in flame were born all the hosts of heaven, and of flame is the visible soul of stars: — fire is the creative force of nature; and to fire alone rightfully belongs the task of redissolving that which it first warmed and shaped into life. Modern respect for the dead is really superficial; it stops at the surface of graves, and at the entrances of vaults. To abandon the body of a friend, of a child, of a woman beloved, to worms and to all the frightful fermentation of the tomb, seems, when we reflect upon it, barbarous — hideous! Even the Parsee Towers of Silence, with their vultures and birds of carrion hovering in spiral flight, contain naught so frightful as do our fairest sepulchres; — better surely abandon the dead unto the birds of heaven than to the worms of earth. Death was not a nightmare to antique civilizations; it became so only when the funeral pyres had ceased to flame, and the funeral urns had ceased to be.

There was nothing sinister, nothing awful, about the tombs of the Greek and the Roman dead — only the graceful vases containing the "pinch of scentless and delicate dust" gathered from the pyre — "the dust of the soul's own butterfly wings," as it has been so daintily called.

## GROVER CLEVELAND

*Harper's Weekly*, July 19, 1884

The nomination of Grover Cleveland defines sharply the actual issue of the Presidential election of this year. He is a man whose absolute official integrity has never been questioned, who has no laborious and doubtful explanations to make, and who is universally known as the Governor of New York elected by an unprecedented majority which was not partisan and represented both the votes and consent of an enormous body of Republicans, and who as the chief executive of the State has steadily withstood the blandishments and the threats of the worst elements of his party, and has justly earned the reputation of a courageous, independent, and efficient friend and promoter of administrative reform. His name has become that of the especial representative among our public men of the integrity, purity, and economy of administration which are the objects of the most intelligent and patriotic citizens. The bitter and furious hostility of Tammany Hall and of General Butler to Governor Cleveland is his passport to the confidence of good men, and the general conviction that Tammany will do all it can to defeat him will be an additional incentive to the voters who cannot support Mr. Blaine, and who are unwilling not to vote at all, to secure the election of a candidate whom the political rings and the party trainers instinctively hate and unitedly oppose.

So firm and "clear" and independent in his high office has Governor Cleveland shown himself to be that he is denounced as not being a Democrat by his Democratic opponents. This denunciation springs from the fact that he has not hesitated to prefer the public welfare to the mere interest of his party. Last autumn, when the Democratic district attorney of Queens County was charged with misconduct, the Governor heard the accusation and the defence, and decided that it was his duty to remove the officer. He was asked by his party friends to defer the removal until after election, as otherwise the party would lose the district by the opposition of the attorney's friends. The Governor understood his duty, and removed the officer some days before the election, and the party did lose the district. This kind of courage and devotion to public duty in the teeth of the most virulent opposition of traders of his own party is unusual in any public man, and it shows precisely the executive quality which is demanded at a time when every form of speculation and fraud presses upon the public treasury under the specious plea of party advantage.

The argument that in an election it is not a man but a party that is supported, and that the Democratic party is less to be trusted than the Republican, is futile at a time when the Republican party has nominated a candidate whom a great body of the most conscientious Republicans cannot support, and the Democratic party has nominated a candidate whom a great body of the most venal Democrats practically bolt. Distrust of the Democratic party springs from the conduct of the very Democrats who madly oppose Governor Cleveland because they know that they cannot use him. The mere party argument is vain also because no honorable man will be pulled in to vote for a candidate whom he believes to be personally disqualified for the Presidency on the ground that a party ought to be sustained. No honest Republican would sustain his party for such a reason, and the honest Republicans who propose to vote for Mr. Blaine will do so because they do not believe, as the protesting Republicans do believe, that he made his official action subserve a personal advantage. Nothing is more hopeless than an attempt to persuade such Republicans to sustain their party by voting for an unworthy candidate. Should they help to reward such a candidate by conferring upon him the highest official honor in the world, they could not reasonably expect the nomination of a worthier candidate at the next election, and they could not consistently oppose the election of any candidate whom their party might select. The time to defeat unfit nominations is when they are made, not next time. The nomination of Grover Cleveland is due not so much to the preference of his party as to the general demand of the country for a candidacy which stands for precisely the qualities and services which are associated with his name.

## MR. CLEVELAND'S PRIVATE LAPSE AND PUBLIC CANDIDACY[1]

*The Nation*, August 7, 1884

"Well, but," we shall be asked, "does not the charge against Cleveland, as you yourselves state and admit it, disqualify him, in your estimation, for the Presidency of the United States?" We answer frankly: "Yes, if his opponent be free from this stain, and as

---

[1] Much was made by Cleveland's opponents of a long-forgotten liaison of his with a married woman of Buffalo. In this editorial defence Godkin was betrayed into some rash statements. There is no evidence whatever that a historian would accept against the chastity of either Washington or Jefferson.

good a man in all other ways." We should like to see candidates for the Presidency models of all the virtues, pure as the snow and steadfast as the eternal hills. But when the alternative is a man of whom the Buffalo *Express*, a political opponent, said immediately after his nomination, "that the people of Buffalo had known him as one of their worthiest citizens, one of their manliest men, faithful to his clients, faithful to his friends, and faithful to every public trust," and of whom the Buffalo *Commercial*, another political opponent, said that, in opposing him, "it would not detract one jot or tittle from the well-earned fame of the distinguished gentleman who honored the opposition by bearing its standard," a good son and good brother, and unmarried in order that he might be the better son and brother, against whom nothing can be said except that he has not been proof against one of the most powerful temptations by which human nature is assailed; or, on the other hand, a man convicted out of his own mouth of having publicly lied in order to hide his jobbery in office, of having offered his judicial decisions as a sign of his possible usefulness to railroad speculators in case they paid him his price, of trading in charters which had been benefited by legislation in which he took part, and of having broken his word of honor in order to destroy documentary proof of his corruption — a man who has accumulated a fortune in a few years on the salary of a Congressman — then we say emphatically no — ten thousand times no. We should be ashamed of ourselves if we had any other answer to make, and are amazed to hear that there are scores of clergymen all over the country advising people who care for morality to choose the trickster and jobber because he is chaste before the honest man, faithful to every public trust, because he has been weak before a passion of which everybody knows the force.

We had supposed the reason for this was so obvious that it did not need to be stated. Cleveland's virtues are those which bind human society together, and in which states are founded and maintained. There has been no great benefactor of the human race who has not been truthful, faithful to his trusts, disinterested, self-denying. There have been very few who have been chaste, Blaine's vices are those by which governments are overthrown, states brought to naught, and the haunts of commerce turned into dens of thieves. The standard by which some ministers now propose to exclude Cleveland from high place would have prevented Washington, Franklin, Jefferson, Hamilton, not to go any further, from taking any prominent part in the foundation of the American republic. It would have excluded from office in England nearly every great statesman or reformer of the last hundred years, except, perhaps, Romilly, Wilberforce, and Gladstone. It would have visited nearly every prominent politician in the Republican party since 1860 with popular odium. It would, had the Democrats chosen to apply it, have defeated one Republican candidate for the Presidency by charges worse by far than Cleveland's, in that they added the sin of broken vows to the sin of incontinence.

We are not defending incontinence. Chastity is a great virtue, but every man knows in his heart that it is not the greatest of virtues, that offences against it have often been consistent with the possession of all the qualities which ennoble human nature and dignify human life and make human progress possible. It ought to be preached and practised by every man to the utmost of his ability, but no one ought to preach it with any other motive than the spread of virtue, and least of all for the purpose, as in the present case, of making some of the basest of vices — the vices which sap everything which is valuable in society and politics — seem respectable. Preaching of this sort, at this time, is cant, and cant in its most loathsome form, for it fills every household in the land with filthy suggestions and insinuations, turns the press into a common sewer, and converts scores of editors into hypocrites, who must blush in secret over their own ridiculous sermons and their simulated righteousness. We will not for our part support the Republican party at this crisis in an attempt to capture the Presidency for a trickster, as Joshua captured Jericho, by the aid of a harlot. Great as its faults are, it deserves a less ignominious end than this.

## GROVER CLEVELAND'S UNFITNESS[1]

### The Independent, September 4, 1884

The Democratic papers, in resorting to various forms of apologetic casuistry for the offence, not only concede the substantial truth of the main charge, but also the necessity of making an apology for it, in order to break, as far as possible, its force as an objection to the candidacy of Governor Cleveland. We then assume as a fact, admitted and known to the people, that some ten years ago Mr. Cleveland, when he was about forty years of age, was guilty of the offence imputed to him, and that he is the reputed father of a bastard son, now living in Buffalo, and who, to the day of his death, will be stamped and humiliated with the disgrace of his illegitimacy.

The question then is not whether God or man will or should forgive Mr. Cleveland for his sincere repentance for this sin, but whether, with a private character stained with this disgusting infamy, he should by the deliberate act and voice of the people, be

[1] As a religious publication the *Independent* followed great numbers of the clergy in refusing to support either Blaine or Cleveland.

made the Chief Magistrate of this great nation. That is the question which every voter must face. If the facts were not known, or if there were grounds for a reasonable doubt about them, the case would be entirely different. The facts, however, are known. There is no pretence of any denial or refutation of the chief facts in the case; and if the people of the United States who are in favor of sound morality follow our advice, they certainly will not bestow the honors of the Presidency upon Grover Cleveland. His election would argue a low state of morals among the people, and be a burning shame and never-to-be-forgotten disgrace to the nation. No man with such a private character as is shown in respect to him is fit to fill any office in the gift of the people.

## THE NEW MULLIGAN LETTERS

*Harper's Weekly*, September 27, 1884

The publication of the last series of Mulligan letters completes the national humiliation of the nomination of Mr. Blaine. Had the letter written by him to Mr. Fisher on the 16th of April, 1876, inclosing a letter which he asked Mr. Fisher to copy and return to him as his own voluntary act, been made public before the Republican convention, it is impossible that Mr. Blaine could have been nominated, unless the Republican party has really fallen as low as its Democratic opponents assert. It is now plain enough why Mr. Blaine was so alarmed when he heard during the investigation that Mr. Mulligan had arrived in Washington with the letters which he supposed to have been destroyed, and why the passionately excited scene with Mr. Mulligan followed. Mr. Blaine supposed that the letter proposing that Mr. Fisher should tell a falsehood to protect Mr. Blaine himself was among them, and he knew that the publication of that letter would necessarily be fatal to his hopes of the Presidential nomination. The letters previously published seemed to us sufficiently to show the unfitness of Mr. Blaine for the highest official trust in the government. But no honest man can escape the conclusion of those now made public. They convict Mr. Blaine beyond question of taking "44,000,000 people into his confidence," and deliberately telling them a series of falsehoods. They leave him exposed as trading upon his official position as Speaker for his own gain. They complete the most amazing and painful disclosure that was ever made of a candidate for the Presidency of the United States.

From these letters, all of which we publish elsewhere, we select for illustration this point of deliberate falsehood. By referring to the letters the reader will see that on the 16th of April, 1872, Mr. Fisher writes to Mr. Blaine:

"You obtained subscriptions from your friends in Maine for the building of the Little Rock and Fort Smith Railroad. Out of their subscriptions you obtained a large amount both of bonds and money, free of cost to you. I have your own figures, and know the amount. Owing to your political position, you were able to work off all your bonds at a very high price, and the fact is well known to others as well as myself."

Mr. Blaine's contract as agent is dated Sept. 5, 1869, and has been published. That it was carried out is shown by the memorandum with his "own figures" in his own handwriting which was produced by Mr. Mulligan in Mr. Blaine's presence before the committee, and Mr. Blaine was silent. Yet while he was scheming for the nomination in 1876, before anything was known to the public, and the vague rumors of his railroad transactions first filled the air, Mr. Blaine wrote to Mr. Fisher, enclosing the draft of a letter which he wished Mr. Fisher to return to him as his own, and asked him, in the face of what is now known to be the truth, to say:

"You [Mr. Blaine] became the purchaser of about $30,000 of the bonds on precisely the same terms that every other buyer received, paying for them in installments running over a considerable period, just as others did. The transaction was perfectly open, and there was no more secrecy in regard to it than if you had been buying flour or sugar. I am sure that you never owned a bond of the road which you did not pay for at the market rate. . . . Your action in the whole matter was as open and as fair as the day. When the original enterprise failed, I knew with what severity the pecuniary loss fell upon you, and with what integrity and nerve you met it. Years having since elapsed, it seems rather hard at this late day to be compelled to meet a slander in a matter where your conduct was in the highest degree honorable and straightforward."

This letter was sent by Mr. Blaine to Mr. Fisher on the 16th of April, 1876. Mr. Fisher, however, did not return the letter as his own, and so, on the 24th of April, a week later, Mr. Blaine in the House made the statement for himself, and he emphasized the assertion that he paid the usual rate for his bonds by saying:

"I never heard and do not believe that the Little Rock Company ever parted with a bond to any person except at the regular price fixed for their sale. Instead of receiving bonds of the Little Rock and Fort Smith Railroad as a gratuity, I never had one except at the regular market price."

All this is untrue. At the time the speech was made we said, in common with other journals, that in the absence of further evidence it was a complete vindication. The other evidence has now appeared, and the statement is plainly untrue. Mr. Blaine represented himself as a simple investor. He alleged that he had bought securities in open market. He concealed totally and intentionally the fact that he was a broker in the securities of a road which owed its value to Congressional legislation, and which value he boasted that, as Speaker, he had saved, making the boast in order to secure a further pecuniary interest in the speculation. The Blaine organs have the hardihood to assert that the letter of Mr. Blaine enclosing the draft to Mr. Fisher, which he asks him to regard as strictly confidential, and not to show to anyone, and to burn, and which he sends to the Parker House for greater secrecy, although he knows that Mr. Fisher is at the Commonwealth Hotel, and telegraphs him there to call at the Parker House and get the letter — this letter, they say, is a simple request to Mr. Fisher to attest the truth on behalf of Mr. Blaine. The reader, however, will have seen that it asks Mr. Fisher to state as the truth what Mr. Fisher himself had already declared to Mr. Blaine to be untrue. But, much more than this, the request is that Mr. Fisher will copy Mr. Blaine's letter and send it to Mr. Blaine to be read as the unsolicited letter of Mr. Fisher. Whatever the letter contained, therefore, the letter was in itself a falsehood. It would have had no effect if it had been known to be Mr. Blaine's letter. It was to be presented to the country, therefore, as the spontaneous testimony of an old friend to a business associate.

There is but one point in this shameful business. The amazing correspondence will be everywhere read, and considering all its revelations and implications, its falsifications, its prostitution of official power and influence, its debasing view of public morality, and the deep disgrace that it casts upon the American name, it is hard to believe that a public officer who has trafficked in his place as these letters show, and has then besought a friend to perjure himself in order to deceive the country, can be called by the American people to the chair of Washington and Lincoln.

## SENATOR HOAR FOR THE DEFENSE

*Harper's Weekly*, Sept. 13, 1884

The friends of Mr. Blaine have at last seen the folly of attempting to persuade Republicans by praising the Republican party and denouncing the Democratic party to support a Presidential candidate whom they hold to be unworthy. Such Republicans have praised one party and denounced the other quite as warmly as their fellow-Republicans who propose to vote for Mr. Blaine. But the higher

the standard of official conduct and of party principle and character is raised, the more difficult it is to show them that for the sake
of the party they ought to do something which in their judgment is
entirely unworthy of the party. All the Blaine speeches, therefore,
for the first three months of the campaign, were totally futile to
win or to drive back protesting Republicans, and at last the Blaine
advocates began to treat the real question, the official conduct of
Mr. Blaine when Speaker. But they speak only to show how wise
was their silence, for their reluctant and unwilling explanations do
not explain. It may be safely assumed that Senator Hoar's letter
is the best defense that can be made for Mr. Blaine's railway transactions. The Senator undertakes to traverse the speech of Mr. Schurz
at Brooklyn. But in a cogent reply Mr. Schurz has conclusively
disposed of the Senator's defense. He shows from Mr. Blaine's
own letters and from undisputed facts the inaccuracy of Senator
Hoar's statements, and he points out the extraordinary character
of the Senator's ethics.

Thus Mr. Blaine's persistent and repeated reminder to Caldwell
and Fisher that his ruling had virtually saved the road — a reminder which was renewed and reiterated for the purpose of aiding
him in obtaining a pecuniary interest in the speculation — Mr.
Hoar treats as a perfectly natural and casual allusion to an interesting
coincidence. Casual allusions to interesting coincidences are never
suspicious, and require no demonstration. But persistent references
to past official action as inducement for pecuniary favors are not
casual allusions. They are intimations of a kind which Senator
Hoar would no more give with the purpose of private gain than he
would do any other discreditable act. As Mr. Schurz truly says:

"When the Speaker says to a railroad man, 'I rendered you
and your road in a perfectly proper way a great favor, and I am
glad I did it,' that is one thing. But when the Speaker says to
a railroad man, 'I did you such and such a service by the exercise
of my power, and now I want you to give me a valuable interest
in your enterprise; I know I am not going to be a deadhead in
it, and I see various channels in which I can be useful' — is not
that quite another thing? But that is just what Mr. Blaine did."

Senator Hoar also says that "Mr. Blaine is not charged with any
corrupt, improper, or wrong act whatever." This is a curious
misapprehension, or a very singular use of words. How does Mr.
Schurz in his speech put the case?

"Here we find the Speaker of the House of Representatives in
a businesslike way participating and urgently asking for a greater
share in larger enterprises, the pecuniary success of which is in a

great measure dependent on the action of the same House over which he presides, and in which he wields great power — *for the purpose of getting rich.* We find him pointing out the exercise of his official power as a channel in which he already has made himself useful, in order to obtain more of a valuable interest in such an enterprise, thus literally trading upon his official trust and opportunities. To cover up these things we find him resorting to all sorts of barefaced untruths, deceptions, and concealments on the most solemn occasions. The concealments resorted to, and the side perspectives opened by the official investigation, are fully sufficient to justify the inference that the case disclosed is only one of many. We find that he did get rich while in office, without any other regular business. His most devoted friend publicly admits his fortune to be about half a million, while the estimates of others go far beyond that. But the lowest estimate, half a million, is wealth not only to anyone starting with nothing, but to all of our countrymen except a few. This is the character of the case."

Is there no improper or wrong act here? Is not such conduct in the strictest sense an act, and can it be truly said that to be charged with such conduct is not to be accused of wrongful acts? The Speaker's conduct is to be judged by the whole of it, and by all the circumstances. Senator Hoar's view is that it was "simple, natural, and honest." The Senator is capable of bitter sarcasm. Are the misstatements of the speech of April 24, the excited apprehension about the letters, the seizure and retention of them in violation of a pledge, the circumstances of reading them, the trick of the Caldwell telegram, the refusal to show the letters, the failure to insist upon the completion of the investigation, all "simple, honest, and natural"? Was the conduct of Mr. Blaine throughout the whole affair that of a man consciously innocent, and anxious that everything should be known, or that of a man desperately determined that everything should not be known? We advise every voter in the land, young or old, to read together Mr. Schurz's speech, Senator Hoar's reply, and Mr. Schurz's answer. They will then understand why so many Republicans refuse to vote for Mr. Blaine, and they will see the best defense that the most honest of Republicans can make for him. Senator Hoar, however, as if conscious that his defense does not really defend, adds to it a plea to vote for Mr. Blaine in order to support the party. But if his defense is satisfactory to any Independent Republican voter this plea is unnecessary, because if such a voter's objections to the candidate are removed, he will, of course, vote for him. If they are not removed, the party plea is futile, because it is simply an exhortation to support the candidate because of the party. If the question were merely of personal preference, this plea would be good. But as a plea to support a candidate whom the voter believes to have "marketed his official power for private gain," the reply to it is that of the Massachusetts Republican Convention of 1879, that the duty of party men to support a nomination is reciprocal with that of party conventions to make nominations fit to be supported.

### [ONE OF MR. BLAINE'S FALSEHOODS][1]

New York *Evening Post*, October 18, 1884

Mr. Blaine has resumed letter-writing, and has constructed a fresh denial of his Hocking Valley interests, but with a material variation from his first denial. The second letter is addressed to the Hon. William McKinley of Canton, Ohio, and is dated Bellaire, Ohio, October 4. We reproduce the two denials and the stock subscription in the deadly parallel columns.

| *Full Falsehood* | *Proof* | *Limited Falsehood* |
|---|---|---|
| Letter to Bundy. | Stock Subscription. | Letter to McKinley. |
| Bar Harbor, Maine, July 22, 1884. | Senate Chamber, Washington, December 30, 1880. | *Third* — I do not own and never did own, an acre of coal land |
| Hon. H. S. Bundy: | Dear Sir: Find enclosed my draft for $25,000 in payment of my subscription to the Hope Furnace enterprise. Touching the interest, I have to ask that, whatever it may amount to, you will permit its payment to be postponed until some matters between Mr. Lee and myself are definitely adjusted. | or any other kind of land in the Hocking Valley or in any other part of Ohio. My letter to the Hon. Hezekiah Bundy in July last *on this same subject* was accurately true. — Very Truly Yours, |
| In answer to your recent favor, I beg to say that I *am not and never have been* the owner of any coal lands or iron lands, or lands of any character whatever in the Hocking Valley, or in any part of Ohio. Nor have I *at any time owned a share of stock in any coal, iron, or land company in the State of Ohio.* . . . | | |
| J. G. Blaine. | Very Resp'y, J. G. Blaine. Mr. Denison. | J. G. Blaine. |

It will be seen that Mr. Blaine does not deny in his letter to McKinley his ownership of stock, but only his ownership of land.

[1] By E. L. Godkin; an excellent illustration, triple-barrelled, of his favorite device of parallel columns.

## "RUM, ROMANISM, AND REBELLION"

*New York World*, October 30, 1884

The rock-ribbed Republican clergymen who waited on Mr. Blaine yesterday to assure him of their loyalty and allegiance were presided over by the Reverend Dr. Burchard, of the Murray Hill Presbyterian Church. Before receiving Mr. Blaine these reverend gentlemen, ministers of the gospel of love and charity, adopted a series of resolutions in which, emulating the malicious lying and slandering of scurvy politicians, they assailed the character of the Democratic candidate, Grover Cleveland, an honest, upright, truthful man, and beslavered with unctuous praise the notorious self-convicted corruptionist and "continental" liar, James G. Blaine.

When Mr. Blaine entered the room the chairman received him and said: "We are happy to welcome you to this circle. We are Republicans and do not propose to leave our party and identify ourselves with the party whose antecedents have been Rum, Romanism, and Rebellion."

How do the Democrats, and especially those of Irish birth and descent who are said to be willing to support Mr. Blaine, relish this picture of the party to which they have adhered for years? How do they like the idea of an association with hypocrites and bigots who denounce the faith of their fathers as Romanism and place it on a par with "rum" and "rebellion"? Mr. Blaine and his friends in their eagerness to clutch at every chance of making political capital have not hesitated to inflame religious prejudices, and to drag creeds into politics. They have appealed to all religions and to all nationalities in their reckless struggle for votes. But their ingrained intolerance speaks out through the voices of their less trained and less politic adherents.

"The party of Rum, Romanism, and Rebellion!"

The designation is an insult to a great majority of the people of the United States.

## THE FATAL ERROR[1]

*Harper's Weekly*, November 22, 1884

Mr. Blaine himself furnished the weapons in the destructive campaign against his election. His desperate efforts, seconded by his orators and newspapers, to raise a false issue of protection, and of wrongs to the colored race, failed, and the fight was forced upon

[1] The election of 1884 gave Cleveland a popular plurality of about 23,000 votes over Blaine; carrying New York by a plurality of only 1,149 votes, he had 219 votes in the electoral college against 182 for Blaine. Four years earlier Hancock had received only 155 electoral votes against 214 for Garfield. Many elements entered into the overturn, but the issue of integrity was one of the chief. George W. Curtis could say "I told you so."

the one paramount point of official integrity. The response to the Independent appeal was worthy of the old Republican party and the American people. The figures of the election returns show how totally mistaken were the Republicans who sneered at the demands for honesty in the Presidential office as "particular" and "finicky," and who were sure that a "dashing, smashing" leader would sweep the country. Like the *habitues* of London clubs who laughed at Gladstone as a moral prig, but who were taught what the opinion of the real England was when Beaconsfield was overthrown, the airy gentlemen who really supposed that a knot of New York politicians associated with Mr. Elkins and certain notorious capitalists carried Republican principles literally in their breeches' pockets have at last heard from the Republican party.

There were four doubtful States, upon whose votes the election turned; but Mr. Blaine did not carry one of them. Massachusetts is the original and representative Republican State. In three Presidential elections the average Republican majority had been 56,000; but Mr. Blaine got less than half of the votes cast, and except for the diversion of his ally Butler, he would have lost the State. Four years ago Garfield carried Michigan by 53,000. This year, a week after the election, it was not clear that Mr. Blaine had carried it at all. Iowa gave Garfield a majority of 78,000. Mr. Blaine may receive a majority of 18,000. Illinois cast 40,000 majority for Garfield. It has possibly given Mr. Blaine 23,000. The Garfield majority in Wisconsin was 29,000. The Blaine majority may be 5,000. Garfield carried Indiana by 6,600. Mr. Blaine loses Indiana by 7,000. In no State, we believe, except Colorado and Maine, is the Republican majority increased, and it would not be surprising if the final result should show a falling off of nearly a half of the Garfield majorities. But to this must be added the immense number of Republican votes most reluctantly and protestingly cast for Mr. Blaine before the significance of the whole situation is perceived.

Even if it could have been clearly shown that Mr. Blaine had a plurality of a few hundred votes in New York, and he had so scratched into the Presidency, the folly of the nomination would have been thoroughly exposed. But with the actual result it is seen to have been an appalling folly. After a dominance of a quarter of a century, and with as noble a history as any party can show, the Republican party loses the Presidency on an issue of official honesty.

## THE ROAR OF A GREAT CITY[1]

New Orleans *Times-Democrat*, November 30, 1884

When Hogarth painted his story of "The Enraged Musician," whose music was drowned in the thousand cries and noises that surrounded him; when Chambers described "The Roar of a Great City," the blending of a thousand noises, it was of the city of the past they told. Since then this roar has been growing louder and louder, until now, miles away, even before you see the smoky coronet that surrounds the modern city, you can hear a wild growl like that of some enraged beast. Neither Hogarth nor Chambers dreamed of the fierce whistle of the steamboat and locomotive, of the rattle of engine and machinery, of the cannonade as a cotton float flies over the granite pavement, of the stunning noise of the New York Elevated Railroad. All these have come of late years.

The electric light, the telephone and telegraph wires have added new music to our city. When the winds blow at night one can hear a sombre, melancholy music high up in the air — as mysterious as that of Ariel himself or the undiscovered music of the Pascagoula. If you want to hear it in perfection go some of these windy nights we have lately enjoyed to Delord or Dryades, or some of the streets in the neighborhood of the electric light works, where the wires are numerous and the houses low, and where there is a clean sweep for the wind from the New Basin to the river. There the music becomes wild and grand indeed. The storm whistling and shrieking around some sharp corner never equalled it. Above, around, in every direction can be heard this music, sighing, mourning like the treetops, with a buzzing metallic sound that almost drowns your conversation. There is something in it weird and melancholy — it is like the last wail of a dying man, or the shriek of the angel of death as he clasps his victim to him.

If such it is today, what have we to hope for in the future? If the city is already a monstrous spider web, a great Aeolian harp, what is its destiny with several new telephone and telegraph companies, and thousands of new poles, and millions of new wires promised us? If this aerial music increases, this shrieking and moaning and wailing will reach such a pitch that we will greet the rattle of the floats and tinkle of the street-cars as tending to drown the new noise, and welcome the roar of the city as likely to muffle its meaning.

---

[1] By Lafcadio Hearn. The telephone, patented by Alexander Graham Bell in 1876, had by this time come into wide use. The business genius of Theodore N. Vail, who became general manager of the Bell Company, made the device a national institution. Not until the nineties were steps generally taken by the large cities to force the wires underground. The result was the network and the "roar" described by Hearn.

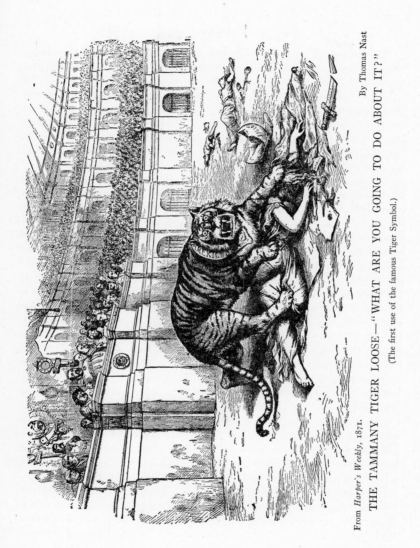

From *Harper's Weekly*, 1871.
By Thomas Nast

THE TAMMANY TIGER LOOSE—"WHAT ARE YOU GOING TO DO ABOUT IT?"

(The first use of the famous Tiger Symbol.)

## OUR OFFICE CAT[1]

New York *Sun*, January 12, 1885

The universal interest which this accomplished animal has excited throughout the country is a refutation that genius is not honored in its own day and generation. Perhaps no other living critic has attained the popularity and the vogue now enjoyed by our cat. For years he worked in silence, unknown, perhaps, beyond the limits of the office. He is a sort of Rosicrucian cat, and his motto has been "to know all and to keep himself unknown." But he could not escape the glory his efforts deserved, and a few mornings ago he woke up, like Byron, to find himself famous.

We are glad to announce that he hasn't been puffed up by the enthusiastic praise which comes to him from all sources. He is the same industrious, conscientious, sharp-eyed, and sharp-toothed censor of copy that he has always been, nor should we have known that he is conscious of the admiration he excites had we not observed him in the act of dilacerating a copy of the *Graphic* containing an alleged protrait of him. It was impossible not to sympathize with his evident indignation. The *Graphic's* portrait did foul injustice to his majestic and intellectual features. Besides, it represented him as having a bandage over one eye, as if he had been involved in a controversy and had had his eye mashed. Now, aside from the fact that he needs both eyes to discharge his literary duties properly, he is able to whip his weight in office cats, and his fine large eyes have never been shrouded in black, and we don't believe they ever will be. He is a soldier as well as a scholar.

We have received many requests to give a detailed account of the personal habits and peculiarities of this feline Aristarchus. Indeed, we have been requested to prepare a full biographical sketch to appear in the next edition of "Homes of American Authors." At some future day we may satisfy public curiosity with the details of his literary methods. But genius such as his defies analysis, and the privacy of a celebrity ought not to be rudely invaded.

It is not out of place, however, to indicate a few traits which illustrate his extraordinary faculty of literary decomposition, so to speak. His favorite food is a tariff discussion. When a big speech, full of wind and statistics, comes within his reach, he pounces upon it immediately, and digests the figures at his leisure. During the discussion over the Morrison bill he used to feed steadily on tariff speeches for eight hours a day, and yet his appetite remained unimpaired.

When a piece of stale news or a long-winded, prosy article comes

[1] By Charles A. Dana.

into the office, his remarkable sense of smell instantly detects it, and it is impossible to keep it from him. He always assists with great interest at the opening of the office mail, and he files several hundred letters a day in his interior department. The favorite diversion of the office boys is to make him jump for twelve-column articles on the restoration of the American merchant marine.

He takes a keen delight in hunting for essays on civil service reform, and will play with them, if he has time, for hours. They are so pretty that he hates to kill them, but duty is duty. Clumsy and awkward English he springs at with indescribable quickness and ferocity; but he won't eat it. He simply tears it up. He can't stand everything.

We don't pretend that he is perfect. We admit he has an uncontrollable appetite for the *Congressional Record*. We have to keep this particular publication out of his reach. He will sit for hours and watch with burning eyes the iron safe in which we are obliged to shut up the *Record* for safe-keeping. Once in a while we let him have a number or two. He becomes uneasy without it. It is his catnip. With the exception of this pardonable excess he is a blameless beast. He mouses out all the stupid stuff and nonsense that finds its way into the office, and goes for it, tooth and claw. He is the biggest copyholder in the world. And he never gets tired, his health is good, and we have not deemed it necessary to take out a policy on any one of his numerous lives.

Many of our esteemed contemporaries are furnishing their offices with cats, but they can never hope to have the equal of the *Sun's* venerable polyphage. He is a cat of genius.

## ATLANTA'S SILENT VISITOR [1]

### Atlanta *Constitution*, August 2, 1885

Like all her Confederate sisters, Atlanta was ready to die in the last ditch.

She found the last ditch something more than a lurid figure of warlike rhetoric. Literally it was a bloody chasm, and when she tumbled into it the swarming legions of Sherman surged around and about it, and then rolled resistlessly onward, a mighty blue wave shooting straight to the sea.

It was months before the shattered victim struggled to her feet again, and stood amidst the ashes of her ruined temples. The tremendous tidings of Appomattox failed to stir her pulse or thrill her breast. Slowly, as the seasons glided away, her strength was

[1] By Henry W. Grady. Written a few days after the death of Ulysses S. Grant.

renewed, her olden courage revived, and the hum of industry and the clatter of traffic were again heard in her long-deserted mart.

The last days of Sixty-five found the Gate City a busy chaos. The old thoroughfares were just beginning to straggle out from under the ashheaps, and a tumultuous mushroom growth of temporary structures spread out in every direction. The dismantled redoubts circling the city told their story of the famous siege of forty days. There were other disagreeable suggestions of disaster and defeat. Victorious foemen flushed with triumph jostled the sad-faced citizens in the street, and filled the air with their martial clangor. On almost every corner stood an ebony statue, a frowning menace to civilization, in the shape of a black soldier, with a bayonet in one hand and a spelling book in the other.

# I

These discordant elements and evidences of peace and war, of destruction and reconstruction, wore their usual grim look one gloomy December day. So thought a silent stranger whose quiet gray eyes took in the scene as he drove with a companion through the ragged streets, past blackened ruins and over piles of débris left over from the siege.

Leaning back in the top buggy with the laprobe well drawn up to keep off the pelting, sleety rain, the stranger pulled his slouch hat down over his brow and took a thoughtful survey of the situation. He listened attentively to his companion, a military-looking man, but said little in return. The few people hurrying to and fro on this inclement day dismissed the silent man with a glance. They saw only a middle-aged man of business, evidently a plain citizen. His careless attire, his apparently listless manner and his hat slouched over his eyes, made him anything but a conspicuous figure. Those who took a second glance noted that this stolid person was squarely and solidly built, with square shoulders, a square head, and a square face covered with a closely trimmed brown beard. In his square, firm mouth was a cigar which he puffed industriously.

The presence of this visitor, unknown, perhaps, to more than a score of persons, was a notable event. It did much to decide the fate of Atlanta and the South.

This was the first and last time that the hero of Appomattox ever looked upon Atlanta.

Throughout that dreary December day General Grant quietly devoted himself to the object of his mission. He was making a tour of the South, at the request of President Johnson, and his brief sojourn in Atlanta was for the purpose of ascertaining the sentiment and temper of the people and their leaders.

Federal officers, ex-Confederates, Union sympathizers, and the unreconstructed talked to the statuesque soldier. To one and all the general listened with grave attention. Indignant loyalists told him that the rebels hated the old flag and threatened violence to the Unionists.

"It is natural," was the only comment that could be drawn from the general.

Some wild schemers suggested confiscation, disfranchisement, and military rule.

"We don't do that way in America," was the calm reply.

An old man referred feelingly to the bad blood engendered by the war.

"It can't last," said the general.

## II

The next morning the silent visitor with his inevitable cigar was on his way to Washington to report to the President. Over his own signature he assured the government and the country that "the masses of the thinking men of the South accept the situation in good faith."

Against that calm judgment it was useless to struggle. It broke the full force of the cruel legislation then in progress, and the enemies of the prostrate South were compelled to modify their programme. The demagogues were powerless when the Man of Appomattox barred their reckless march.

## A QUESTION[1]

New York *World*, January 9, 1887

The Interstate Commerce bill is opposed by Jay Gould;
    By C. P. Huntington;
    By the Western cattle rings;
    By Philip D. Armour;
    By stock jobbers, large and small;
    By corporations generally;
    By Leland Stanford, the millionaire and corporation Senator.
It is favored by
    The Western farmers;
    The Eastern merchants;
    The boards of trade and transportation;

[1] The Cullom Act for the regulation of interstate commerce became law in January, 1887, and was the outstanding piece of legislation in Cleveland's first term.

Anti-monopolists in general;
The people.
Ought the Interstate Commerce bill to become a law or to suffer
defeat?

## A GREAT SENTIMENTALIST [1]

New York *Sun*, March 10, 1887

The death of Henry Ward Beecher brings out in a very striking
way an ordinary phenomenon of American life, that indiscriminate
praise of distinguished men which begins with their death and continues after their death. It is a saying of Bacon that "death openeth
the gate to good fame." In the United States, at least, the saying
is true. The tendency to say nothing but good of the dead is carried
to excess. No matter what bitter truths are said of an American
public man when living, little but praise is said of him when he is
dead. This is particularly the case in politics. Not merely is the
ordinary public appreciation of dead public men full of indis-
criminating eulogy, but usually the biographies of conspicuous
American politicians are devoid of just criticism. Everything is
subordinated to the desire of projecting upon the public mind a
great and faultless character.

In regard to Mr. Beecher's death, it would seem that an incorrect
impression of his character is studiously presented by most of the
organs of opinion. Mr. Beecher was not strong either on the intellectual or the moral side. He had the orator's gift of suddenly
identifying himself with popular or unpopular sentiments. The
presence of a great audience filled him with all its passion. He
became in its presence something greater than himself, the eye of
all its half-seen intentions, the voice of all its half-spoken feeling,
the representative and vehicle of its wishes. He was an orator whose
power cannot be judged from any of his written words. The
stenographers corrected many slips of syntax, but their best and most
laborious efforts give no idea of his speech. He was himself a
stenographer of emotion and sentiment, a reporter of feelings deeper
than he experienced himself. Yet this is only half the truth. His
temperament was at the start sincere, and in his best time he moved
others because he was moved himself. Since Wendell Phillips he
was the greatest of the old school orators. That is, he was at once
the moulder of his audience and was moulded by it. He was not a
thinker. He was not a student. The great movements in science
which have altered the face of both the history of the past and the
uncertainty of the future to many thoughtful men, did not affect

[1] Dana and the *Sun* had been convinced of Henry Ward Beecher's guilt in the
Tilton-Beecher adultery case, and had treated the preacher with unremitting enmity.

him except in the most superficial manner. He was not orthodox, but he was unorthodox not from thought, but from a certain flippancy, and a volatility of temperament which was not agreeable. He was a voice and not a brain. It is hardly fanciful to trace in him a certain degeneration or falling off which finally affected most of the men concerned as he was in the anti-slavery movement. When that movement was ended by the war — and in the war it played nearly no part at all — there was nothing for its survivors to do. They had been used to a life of agitation and to the employment of strong language. Some of them took up total abstinence, some greenbackism and the labor movement, some woman suffrage. Mr. Beecher fell into the besetting weakness of popular preachers, and illustrated a not unusual but regrettable type, the Puritan decayed. He was always rather a surface than a source of emotion, and the moral ruin of his latter years was perhaps not alien to a certain indolence and weakness of his nature. When the genuine part of his emotion was exhausted, he degenerated into sentimentalities of whose fatal folly of expression it may be unkind but not unjust to speak.

One service he gave to his country. His passionate oratory, and his interesting personality were of value in keeping the Exeter Hall people in line with the Union cause. With the intellectual part of England he never came into relations.

It would have been better for his fame, in one sense, if he had died earlier. As it is, he will be remembered more for the greatness of his fall than for any height he fell from. Genius associated with frailty is undoubtedly attractive to the mass of men. Frailty is sometimes even more attractive than genius. The confession of Francesca da Rimini touches the heart of men and women more than all the great intellect and burning thought of Dante. But Mr. Beecher made no other confession than that found in his letters.

## ROSCOE CONKLING [1]

### *Harper's Weekly*, April 28, 1888

After prolonged and acute suffering, during which he seemed characteristically to defy and fight death, Roscoe Conkling died on the 18th of April, in his fifty-ninth year. Courageous, honest, tenacious, ardent in friendship and in enmity, proud, imperious, and absolutely undisciplined, he was one of the most picturesque and conspicuous figures in the political annals of the country. From the beginning of his career in 1850 to his death he was constantly in the public eye. His character was simple and of definite outline, easily comprehended, and appealing strongly to popular admiration.

[1] By George W. Curtis, personally familiar with all aspects of Conkling's career.

He came to Congress in his thirtieth year, and during the Grant epoch he was the chief spokesman of the President, whom the vehement, unbending, and able Senator fascinated and counselled. During this period he easily became the Republican autocrat of New York, his alertness and audacity, his sparkling rhetoric, his undaunted self-confidence, and his brilliant and aggressive personality totally eclipsing and overwhelming his urbane, smooth, feline rival, Mr. Fenton. Mr. Conkling had some signal qualities of leadership, but equally fatal defects. With his vigor, his unhesitating readiness, and his fertility of resource, he was imperious, irascible, impatient, intolerant; and while his ardor and wit and the charm of an affluent memory held fast his associates, he exacted implicit obedience, and repelled those whom he could not command. Under his sole leadership the Republican "machine" in New York was brought to an efficiency which recalled the old Albany Regency. The Regency was an oligarchy, but the Conkling rule was a despotism. He chose his lieutenants with skill, and always from those who could not aspire to rivalry. His supremacy was absolute, repressing independence and aiming at party dominance by rigorous discipline and the power of patronage, with which personally he was disinclined to meddle, but which was carefully controlled in his interest by his agents.

Upon the general field of politics he maintained with unquestionable ability the great measures of his party, while it cannot be said that he was a constructive legislator or a guide of the public mind and conscience. Indeed, the higher plane of statesmanship he never trod. Among great Republican leaders he does not stand, and he never stood in the same rank with Lincoln, Seward, Sumner, and Andrew. Mr. Conkling knew well the lower but not the loftier motives of human action. The generous instincts, the noble impulses, the unselfish purposes, which inspire multitudes of men and which in the long run control human affairs, he distrusted. Public spirit in its large and comprehensive sense seemed to him a romantic fiction, a delusion, or an arrant hypocrisy. He did not conceive politics that were not personal. He was largely surrounded by sycophants, parasites, and flatterers, and he resented independence as a personal wrong. The word reform exasperated him, and he ridiculed it with the scornful bitterness of Dr. Johnson and Sir Robert Walpole in defining patriotism and describing patriots. From this constitutional defect of perception it resulted — although it may seem a paradox to say it of a prominent and powerful party leader — that he did not understand his own party. The party chafed under his leadership. There were protests, then open opposition in conventions, and at last general insurrection, when, proudly relying upon the perfection of party discipline, he resigned the Senatorship upon a question of patronage, in absolute confidence of prompt and triumphant reëlection, and of carrying the mandate of Republican New York to require the submission of the President. He miscalculated and overthrew himself. His course had alienated the party, and the constituencies forbade the representatives to reëlect him.[1]

The sudden end of his political career in the prime of his life and powers is one of the striking romances of politics. So immediate and complete a catastrophe of the kind is without a parallel except from some delinquency. To a man so self-absorbed and so sensitive to ridicule the overwhelming disappointment and sharp mortification of the event must have been inconceivable. No man could have suffered more from such a reverse. But no man could have hidden it more completely. The pride which was an imperial robe in the day of triumph, giving to power a princely air, was an all-concealing cloak when the change came. He made no other sign than that of total withdrawal from the sphere of activity in which alone he had lived. From that time till his death he took no part in politics, and evaded every attempt to draw from him a positive or definite expression upon political affairs. Yet so faithful was the personal devotion that he inspired that in these opening days of a Presidential contest clubs had been organized bearing his name, and proposing him as a Presidential candidate. But had his interests been public rather than partisan, had politics been a method of patriotism rather than a personal game, could powers so adapted by taste and long experience to the public service have been wholly diverted to other pursuits? It is Mr. Conkling's praise that in an epoch of great public corruption he was incorruptible. Whatever may be thought of his views of politics, he did not make them in the mercenary sense a trade for himself. Yet the power of patronage, upon which his whole system of practical politics rested, is essentially bribery; and it was, as we have said, upon a question of patronage that his public life ended. But to all differences among honorable men death calls a truce. The last days of Mr. Conkling's life moved the deep sympathy of all his countrymen. Like his life, his death was profoundly pathetic. As often to the memory of the dying return the hours of childhood in undimmed brightness, so by the deathbed of those who have borne a stormy part in the great strife of life only their kindly and generous qualities are remembered. The contest is ended, but its history remains, and its thoughtful student will pause long and sadly at the name of Roscoe Conkling.

[1] In 1881, President Garfield appointed a political enemy of Conkling's, William H. Robertson, collector of the port of New York. The Senate confirmed this appointment in the face of Conkling's opposition. He and Senator Thomas C. Platt thereupon resigned. They expected reëlection, but were disappointed.

## THE RENOMINATION OF MR. CLEVELAND[1]

*Harper's Weekly,* June 16, 1888

The Democratic party in renominating the President merely ratifies the verdict of the country upon his general course. Indeed, to have hesitated or to have set him aside would have been to declare that a magistrate so acceptable did not represent his party, and a party capable of such folly would have been overwhelmed. The Democratic party owes very much more to Mr. Cleveland than to any other leader of this generation, for he alone has removed from it that stigma of profound distrust and alarmed apprehension which justly attached to it for so many of the most critical years of our history. He has impressed the country as an upright patriot of conservative temperament, and of a wise but not Quixotic or factitious courage, who while of course a party man, seeks first the public welfare through his party, and who, while yielding upon some points to an evil pressure, has upon the whole commanded his party by character and courage, giving it a distinct policy, dispersing serious party opposition, uniting it as no leader since the war has been able to unite it, and receiving a renomination without a whisper of dissent, and by enthusiastic acclamation. How his personality reacts upon his party is seen in the speech of Mr. Collins, the president of the convention. It was set in the high party key, but such a speech in a Democratic convention, showing so just a sense of what at least a party must now be believed to be in order to hope for success, has been hitherto unheard. *Harper's Weekly* has not disguised its regret and disappointment at the course of the President in regard to civil service reform. Had he been more firm and consistent he would in our judgment have been stronger in the canvass. But while we have frankly acknowledged that his Administration could not be called distinctively a reform Administration, we have pointed out the falsity and injustice of the charge that nothing has been accomplished. Very much has been accomplished. The President has purified the political atmosphere, and the increasing interest in the question and the demand for reform have been stimulated and confirmed by his known conviction and desire. No man who has the reform at heart can regret that Mr. Blaine was defeated, nor anticipate that any candidate who is likely to receive the Republican nomination would advance the reform.

[1] The Democratic National Convention in St. Louis renominated Cleveland for the Presidency early in June, 1884. This was despite the opposition of Tammany and part of Gov. D. B. Hill's supporters. The platform was drawn up by Cleveland. Though the President had made some bad political appointments, his record was on the whole admirable.

## THE REPUBLICAN NOMINATION [1]

*Harper's Weekly*, June 30, 1888

Upon the platform into which the convention had put Mr. Blaine, and which we consider elsewhere, it has placed General Benjamin Harrison of Indiana. His name is known in political circles, but his personality is not familiar to the country. He is a man of high character, of excellent abilities, and a leader of the bar in Indiana. He was a brave soldier and a diligent Senator, and since the death of Mr. Morton he has been the Republican chief in his State. He was strongly urged as a candidate who would make Indiana sure for the Republicans, and he has been regarded as a safe man, who if he could not arouse enthusiasm, would be a perfectly respectable representative of his party. Upon the issue of extreme protection he is in harmony with the platform. Upon the question of reform in the civil service we gather from a speech made by him in the Senate after the inauguration of Mr. Cleveland, in which he described the President's course in Indiana, that he condemned him not for removing his political opponents, but for pretending that such removals were made in the interests of reform. We are not aware of anything that General Harrison has said or done which shows that his administration would be governed in this respect by sound principles of reform.

As the representative of the platform which we describe elsewhere, no friend of a reduction of the surplus by moderating the tariff tax upon the necessities of life and raw materials could support General Harrison unless he feared some grave peril from the success of Mr. Cleveland. This is an apprehension, however, which although strong and natural in 1884, has now disappeared. Mr. Cleveland made his own platform in his message, and there has been nothing in his administration which has alarmed the business interests of the country. General Harrison appears in the canvass as the representative of higher and higher protection, and of free whiskey and tobacco, rather than of a lighter duty upon any class of articles produced in this country. In other words, he is for an average tariff tax of 47 per cent instead of forty per cent, and of a profuse and consequently demoralizing expenditure of a surplus, instead of leaving it in the pockets of the taxpayers.

[1] The nomination of Benjamin Harrison and Levi P. Morton by the Republicans at Chicago in 1888 gave *Harper's Weekly* an excellent opportunity to return to the Republican party, but it stuck to Cleveland. Cleveland had devoted his entire last annual message to a demand that the tariff be revised downward. The Republicans at once accepted this challenge. Revision became the main issue of the campaign. Cleveland's course was courageous, for he would have kept many votes by remaining silent.

## "PRIVACY"[1]

*The Nation*, September 6, 1888

Mr. Henry James, who has cultivated perhaps more than any novel-writer of the day the art of pointing contrasts between the minor morals of Europe and of the United States, has in his last book, "The Reverberator," undertaken to compare European and American ideas on the subject of privacy — using that term to designate the exemption of private individuals and families from newspaper criticism, comment, or description. In fact, the book may be called a study of the American "newspaper man," as he is known to American society — that is, the man to whom the most important thing in the world is news, and to whom news is something which, whether true or false, people must have, and to whom the great function of the intellect is to be "newsy," "breezy," chatty, and to whom its highest achievement is the production of a very salable "gossippy letter" or a column of "Stroller's paragraphs." . . .

Privacy in the best sense of the term is the virtue or the luxury of an old society. In all very new communities, the desire to live to one's self and keep one's affairs to one's self, and see only a restricted or in some manner selected circle, is considered more or less an affectation, and resented accordingly. There is a very good story of a traveller from one of the Eastern States hanging his shirt across the window of his room in the hotel of a mining town in the Rocky Mountains, in order to protect himself during his toilet from the gaze of some loafers on the piazza. It was soon thrust aside from without, and when the traveller asked the head which appeared at the opening what the intrusion meant, he was informed that they wished to know "what there was so darned private going on in there." In the first stage of civilization there is no privacy; it grows as the community becomes larger and more complicated. But it is kept down, even in our great cities, by the newspapers working in combination with the large class which loves notoriety. The journalist who starts out with a sense of the sacredness of a man's personality and private affairs is very apt to have his reverence for them greatly blunted, if not actually destroyed, by finding that the lovers of publicity appear to the journalistic eye to be in a majority, so numerous are those who dread nothing so much as obscurity, and would sooner be known for anything than for nothing at all. It is among these people that many of our young journalists obtain their experience of public tastes and needs, and it is not surprising that they soon become hardened explorers of private life, and cynical disbelievers in professions of dislike for the public gaze.

[1] By E. L. Godkin; typical of his pungent comments upon aspects of the American social scene.

## [THE SACKVILLE–WEST LETTER: DIVERGENT VIEWS]

*Public Opinion*, October 24, 1895

*Denver News* (Populist): — Sir Lionel Sackville-West was the British minister to this country from 1881 to 1888. During the very exciting Presidential campaign of 1888 the English diplomat received a letter from a supposed person named Murchison, making inquiries as to his feelings regarding the pending contest. Wholly unmindful of his position as a foreign ambassador, he penned a reply in which he expressed strong views in favor of Cleveland's reëlection. The letter was a decoy, Murchison was a purely mythical person, and the epistle fell naturally into the hands of the Republican National Committee and was published. The affair at once created a storm of excitement. It was an unheard-of thing for a diplomat to interfere in the politics of the nation, and the Republican managers made the most of the prejudice created. If an English minister desired the reëlection of Mr. Cleveland, that constituted the best argument in the world why Americans and particularly Irish-Americans should vote against him. By direction of Mr. Cleveland, Secretary Bayard sent the minister his passports, which was the proper thing to do and all he could do under the circumstances. Now after a lapse of some years Lord Sackville writes and prints a pamphlet for private circulation in regard to the affair. It can hardly be called a defense, since he admits that his letter was an "incautious" one, but he makes his dismissal the basis of a wholesale attack on American statesmen, and American parties, and is especially severe on ex-Secretary Bayard, now minister to England, whom he accuses of duplicity and untruthfulness. If the Murchison incident did not furnish ample grounds for the assertion that Lord Sackville has no sense, this pamphlet does.

*Springfield Republican* (Independent): — When Lord Sackville comes to the Murchison letter which entrapped him, he tells no more or less than the truth. There was no Murchison, no anxious voter of England nationality, in Pomona, Cal., who wanted to know how he ought to vote in the interest of England. A fellow was hired by the Republican managers to sign such a letter, which was written by some particularly shrewd politician. Lord Sackville credits the publication of the letter and his answer to "one Quay, a Senator and chief of the Republican wire-pullers." It is very likely, such things being quite in Quay's line. This is of the same character as the notorious Morey letter with which the Democrats tried to entangle Garfield. There is probably no country in the world where such devices are so frequent or so characteristic. And as to his arraignment of our subservient politicians, and their course in respect to the Irish vote in the campaign of 1888, he is no more than just. He makes some minor mistakes, and overweighs the expressions of political organs as well as of politicians; but the truckling of Blaine to the Irish and the cowardice of Democrats in the same direction are patent to all who read the history of those years.

St. Louis *Globe-Democrat* (Republican): — Sackville-West ought to keep his tribulations dark. The little episode in 1888 in which he figured unpleasantly while minister to the United States was discreditable to every person connected with it — to West for his blindness in walking into the trap clumsily set for him, to trapsetter "Murchison" for his duplicity, to the Republican National Committee for its imposture in lending itself to this fraud, and to the Democratic President for his cowardice and silliness in. being stampeded by it. Out of the 11,000,000 votes cast in 1888 probably not more than 11 were changed by the foolish "Murchison" letter.

## THE SALOON IN POLITICS
New York *Evening Post*, November 18, 1888

The candidacy of David B. Hill for Governor of New York as the champion of the saloons was so open and flagrant an exhibition of subservience to the liquor interest, and its effect upon the national election was so obvious, that the public is in danger of overlooking some other manifestations of the same influence in politics which are hardly less important. This tendency is strengthened by the fact that Republicans find party advantage in fixing attention upon the discredit which the Democrats of this State brought upon their organization throughout the country by yielding to the demand of the saloons for Gov. Hill's renomination, and thus claiming that the Democratic party is always and everywhere the liquor party.

But the idea that the saloons are Democratic any more than Republican in politics, or that the liquor interest cares anything for politics at all, except as it can make either party serve its ends, is altogether wrong, as has been proved by elections held in other States. We have more than once referred to the fact that, while the Republicans of New York were inveighing against the Democrat, David B. Hill, as the friend of the saloons, the Republicans of Connecticut were trying to elect to the governorship of that State Morgan G. Bulkeley, who has long been equally notorious among his neighbors as the friend of the saloons. The saloons of Connecticut, without regard to party, were as stoutly opposed to the Democratic candidate for Governor of that State as the saloons of New York were to the Republican candidate for Governor of this State.

Still more striking was the influence of the saloon in the politics of Missouri. This is a State long controlled by the Democrats, and where, according to the theory of the New York Republicans, one would expect to find the liquor interests controlling the government through the Democratic party. On the contrary, Missouri was one of the first States to accept the doctrine of high license, a law of that sort having passed the legislature several years ago and been maintained against all attempts to weaken it. In the chief city of the State a Democratic mayor, David R. Francis, has enforced the Sunday Closing Law, and secured St. Louis the quietest Sundays it has ever known. . . . With the same impartiality in the matter of parties as was exhibited in New York and Connecticut, the saloons in Missouri waged war upon their enemy. Mr. Francis having been nominated for Governor by the Democrats, the saloons of St. Louis, which are chiefly beer-saloons, threw their whole influence against him, and carried the city for the Republicans by a large majority. The *Republic*, the chief Democratic newspaper, says that they "polled at least 8,000 votes, and polled them as a unit, demonstrating the power of the beer-saloon in politics as it has never been demonstrated before until this election, when we have similar evidence of it in the vote for Hill in New York."

The saloon showed equal impartiality in national politics. Mr. Gallus Thumann, the head of the Literary Bureau of the United States Brewers' Association, tells a reporter that "the Republicans were beaten in 1884 because they nominated a man for President from the great prohibition State of Maine, whose record on the prohibition question did not suit the Germans. I know what I am talking about," he added, "for I myself made an investigation of his record. I found that Mr. Blaine, while a drinker himself, had been hypocritical enough to be an ardent advocate of the Maine law in his own State. That lost him the German vote, and cost the Republican party the election." But the Republican managers changed front this year, and so won back the German vote and carried the election. "They found out their mistake," Mr. Thumann went on, "and in 1888 they nominated a man who had no objectionable prohibition record, gave the Prohibitionists the cold shoulder, and adopted a resolution copied after the utterance of the National Liquor-Dealers' Association. The consequence was that the Germans came back to the party and Harrison is elected."

The great advantage which the saloon has in all these controversies is the fact that its favorite, when once nominated by one of the great parties, is sure to be supported by a large percentage of the opponents of the saloon, simply because he is the regular candidate. Most of the Democrats in this State who deplore the power of the drink evil voted for Hill as the Democratic nominee, just as most Republicans of like mind in Connecticut voted for Bulkeley as the Republican nominee. In other words, so long as the saloon can nominate its man in a close State, it can rely upon a large share of the churches to help elect him.

## ["GOD HELP THE SURPLUS!"] [1]

### Atlanta *Constitution*, April 20, 1889

Corporal Tanner, who holds the position of Pension Commissioner by virtue of his being the most earnest champion of pension extravagance in the United States, is, in the administration of that office, astounding even those who believe that the country ought to be bankrupted, if necessary, to pension every man, woman, and child who had any connection with the Union army during the late war. He has, so to speak, taken the bit in his mouth, and is running the office independent of precedent and of any other principle than that the surplus must be emptied into the pockets of all those who want pensions, whether deserving them or not. Only a few days ago he made a decision that will take several million dollars annually out of the Treasury, in ordering that the mothers of runaway slaves who were injured while in service in the Federal army should receive pensions, as having been deprived of a means of support. And now comes another decision even more absurd. The Pension Commissioner has, in his application of one of the pension rules, virtually decided that whenever any soldier who served in the late war dies of delirium tremens, those dependent on him should be pensioned, because, he argues, the inference of the law is that he contracted his love of liquor as a soldier, and that as he died from the effect of drinking, the deprivation of his family of their means of support is the clear result of his service as a soldier. If Corporal Tanner continues the work he has begun, the country will not be bothered about the surplus very long. But he is going even too fast for a Republican Administration, and the probability is that the President will find it necessary to pull him in if he continues his present gait. Let us hope that the Administration will sit upon him, if only to demonstrate that he is not a bigger man than the Administration.

[1] President Harrison appointed a favorite of the Grand Army of the Republic, James Tanner, to be head of the Pensions Bureau. His activities in re-rating the pensions — he is said to have remarked "God help the surplus!" — resulted in a rebuke by the Secretary of the Interior, and shortly thereafter in his removal by Harrison. But a general dependent pension bill for all disabled old soldiers was passed in 1890. The total annual pensions expenditure quickly mounted above $100,000,000. Harrison had unwisely said that it was "no time to be weighing the claims of old soldiers with apothecary's scales."

## [CIVIL SERVICE REFORM: THE CHINESE IDOL] [1]

New York *Sun*, August 13, 1889

Before skipping gayly away to his Dakotan ranch, where, in the words of Mr. Joseph Addison, "the zephyrs and the heifers their odoriferous breath compare," Mr. Theodore Roosevelt, the life of the Civil Service Commission, wrote a letter to the Boston *Journal* in praise of the reform into which he is putting so much elbow grease. It is a longer letter than the letters of recommendation and "inflooence" he sent to the police commissioners of this town, but it isn't half so good. It is difficult for him to be slow, but with such a tedious, spavined old nag as civil-service reform he cannot but fall into a prosing pace. There is nothing new for him to say. Beating a gong in front of a Chinese idol is monotonous work. Mr. Roosevelt's letter is thus, through no fault of his, deeply uninteresting. We cull one little bouquet of assumptions, however, as a specimen of the jauntiness wherewith the Mandarins of the Green go on arguing from premises which ninety-nine hundredths of the American people do not admit:

> I do not see how any man can watch the effects of the spoils system, both upon the poor unfortunates who suffer from it and the almost equally unfortunate men who deem that they benefit by it, without regarding the whole thing in its entirety as a curse to our institutions. It is a curse to our public service, and it is a still greater curse to Congress, for it puts a premium upon every Congressman turning spoilsmonger instead of statesman.

Now, to most Americans it seems that the public service is well conducted under the spoils system, and they are satisfied with it. They do not regard it as a curse to our institutions or to Congress, or to anything or anybody except the civil-service reformers, whom it seems to affect with positive mania. Congressmen curse the civil-service law, not the spoils system. Statesmanship requires an endowment of intellect, courage, experience, and tact. A statesman who keeps his eye on the offices and looks out for his friends is not likely to have his head in the clouds or to suffer from fatty degeneration of the sense of responsibility to his party.

---

[1] Characteristic of Dana in form and matter. Previously Dana had spoken of Roosevelt as "a very good fellow, though somewhat bumptious." The Republican platform of 1888 had urged the extension of civil service reform, which had been "auspiciously begun under the Republican Administration" of Chester A. Arthur. Harrison's appointment of Roosevelt to the Civil Service Commission was a notable contribution to the cause. Roosevelt vigorously met the attacks of the spoilsmen.

## INTERNATIONAL COPYRIGHT [1]

*The Nation*, May 22, 1890

The discussion over international copyright has now been going on for half a century, and the pros and cons of the question have been thoroughly canvassed. It may be said that, as a rule, all intelligent Americans who acknowledge that there is such a thing as literary property at all, have ranged themselves on the side of those who are willing to provide legal protection for the foreign author in this country, in return for similar protection for our authors in foreign countries. A very marked feature in the controversy has been the increasingly prominent part which the question of right or wrong, as distinguished from the mere question of commercial expediency, has been made to play in it. In other words, international copyright has, as the years have gone by, been more and more urged on the ground that the publication and sale of an author's works without his consent and without paying him any compensation, by another person for the purpose of making money by it, is theft or fraud in the sense in which these offences are forbidden in the commandment, "Thou shalt not steal."

The answer usually made to this by the opponents of international copyright is, that to give the foreign author property in his books on this side of the water would make them dearer, and that cheap books are so important for the American people that it is lawful to steal them from a foreigner, if they cannot be got cheap in any other way. It has been, in fact, maintained in terms, that it is far more important that an American should be well read and intelligent than that he should be honest. One member, in the late debate, told with pride a story of his having himself paid nine dollars a volume for the "Encyclopaedia Britannica" when it first came out, a work requiring an immense expenditure of brains and capital, for which the publishers paid British and American authors equally. Going to spend the night at the house of a farmer friend in Illinois some time later, he found on his shelves a pirated edition which came from Philadelphia and only cost $2.25 a volume. On this he (Mr. Payson) made the astonishing comment:

> But there, sir, in an humble room in my county, in the sitting room of an humble farmer, is a library in itself, made possible by the laws under which you and I live, and I am content with them. (Applause.) I am just now advised that a reprint of that work is out at $1.25 a volume. And so with other books.

This is exactly what a Norse statesman in the ninth century might have said after passing a night in a farm-house on one of the fjords,

[1] Equally characteristic of Godkin in form and matter.

and having seen it filled with rich plunder from the coast of England and France. "Thank God," he would observe, "under the
laws and customs of our happy country, when the poor husbandman
wants a new set of furniture and some new ornaments for his bride,
he can man his galley and run across the sea, and slaughter a Saxon
family, and fit up his humble home with comfort and decency
from the sack of their house; and yet there are canting rascals who
say piracy is wrong."

## THE LEADER OF SOCIETY

*The Nation*, October 2, 1890

Rumor has it, and it is not an improbable rumor, that Mr.
Ward McAllister has been offered $50,000 by Mr. Abbey for a
winter's course of lectures on Society. Whether Mr. McAllister
will refuse remains to be seen, but we should say that the chances
were that he would accept. The offer is a very flattering one, and
evidently by no means an empty compliment. Mr. Abbey backs
his opinion of Mr. McAllister's popularity with a mighty sum, and
Mr. Abbey is no mean judge of what takes with the American
people. We believe there is today no man in the country who excites
so much popular curiosity, especially in the West, as Mr. McAllister,
simply because he is supposed to hold the key to what a vast body
of people consider an enchanted land, the region called "Society,"
or more particularly "New York Society." The eagerness to get
into it, and the desire to know how to get in, and how to behave
when in, are every year ravaging a greater and greater number of
American bosoms; and the pressure on the barriers is becoming
every year more and more dangerous. In no capital is Society as
hard to enter as it used to be. In every capital a crowd of almost
uncontrollable newly enriched people are jostling each other fiercely
at the golden gates, and offering the porter fabulous sums to let
them squeeze through. But the crowd is kept down in European
cities by the greater slowness with which fortunes are made. Curiosity, too, about Society, is much less there than it is here, because
nearly all aspirants have either had glimpses of it before they
actually became candidates for admission or have received through
mere filtration from above, in the course of their previous lives, more
or less acquaintance with its uses. There is hardly a newly enriched
man or woman in England, struggling to get into the upper circles,
who has not had, before he actually came to close quarters with his
problem, a certain familiarity with dinner-giving and ball-giving,
perhaps on a scale of some luxury. What he gains by social promotion is therefore, in most cases, simply more distinguished company
at his entertainments.

In the United States the conditions are different. Here, as a rule, the candidate for admission to Society arrives at the barriers with hardly any equipment but his checkbook. Neither he nor his wife knows anything about dinner-giving or ball-giving, or about etiquette in general. The way "Society ladies," "club men," and others behave when in each other's company is a great mystery to them both, which they are dying to solve. Hence the demand for "manuals of etiquette," and hence the minuteness of the directions about the minor morals into which these works have to descend. Very often they have to begin with such elementary matters as cautions against spitting on carpets, or using the dinner-knife as a shovel.

The number of these people who have acquired enough money to get into Society, especially in the West, is enormous. Every year makes additions to the army of them who, having already "travelled extensively in Europe," are dying to "bring out their girls" or marry their boys among the haughty aristocrats who, they fondly believe, fill the mansions in Fifth and Madison Avenues. To this rather helpless and simple-minded multitude Mr. McAllister appears as a kind of Moses, who can lead them into the land of promise. They think he can decide who is fit for "Society," and who is not, and that he may be propitiated into indulgent views about manners and general outfit if properly approached. The report that he had said that there were only 400 "Society people" in New York, sent a thrill through the mass which has hardly subsided at this hour. They had no idea the number was so small, and the announcement excited both their hopes and fears to the highest pitch. What he really did say, we are informed on all but the highest authority, was that there were only about four hundred people in New York, not "fit for Society" — God forbid! — but who were in the habit of giving dinners and other more or less costly entertainments.

The history of this speech of his has been very droll, and furnishes a striking illustration of the place he fills in the popular imagination. It was treated by the newspapers as something very like the Venetian "Closing of the Council," that is, a final determination who were the ladies and gentlemen of this community. "Official" and "semi-official" list of them were concocted, sold, and read with great delight or deep depression, as the case might be; and the "Four Hundred" has actually passed into popular parlance as a not wholly humorous designation of the beginnings of an American aristocracy. The fortune of the selection abroad was even more illustrious. In the London *Daily News* the other day we saw the Four Hundred of New York described as the descendants of a body of "Old Dutch

From *Harper's Weekly*.                                      By W. A. Rogers

A CARTOON WHICH KILLED A BAD BILL AT ALBANY

Burghers," who lived absolutely to themselves and constituted one of the most exclusive societies in the world.

Of course Mr. McAllister is not responsible for this nonsense. He knows better than anybody the curious material of which his world is made up, and the smallness of its pretensions to any distinction but that of wealth. All he claims is, that there is something in New York called Society, in which people eat and dress well, and amuse themselves expensively, and that he has more to say than any other one person about the time and manner in which the newcomers can be admitted to it. Some of those who were in it before he appeared on the scene flout his pretensions, it is true, and in moments of excitement call him a "cad"; but to the aspirants he is the very glass of fashion and mould of form, the most interesting and for certain purposes the most powerful American.

## [A BRICKBAT FOR SENATOR INGALLS]

*The Nation*, November 13, 1890

Conspicuous on the list of the slain in the great battle should be placed the name of John J. Ingalls, Senator from Kansas, and author of the following celebrated statement of modern political ethics:

> The purification of politics is an iridescent dream. Government is force. Politics is a battle for supremacy. Parties are the armies. The Decalogue and the golden rule have no place in a political campaign. The object is success. To defeat the antagonist and expel the party in power is the purpose. In war it is lawful to deceive the adversary, to hire Hessians, to purchase mercenaries, to mutilate, to kill, to destroy. The commander who lost a battle through the activity of his moral nature would be the derision and jest of history. This modern cant about the corruption of politics is fatiguing in the extreme. It proceeds from the tea-custard and syllabub dilettantism, the frivolous and desultory sentimentalism, of epicenes.

There has never been any doubt that the author of this passage was a charlatan and a corrupt man. He has been more than suspected of having bought his seat in the Senate, yet he has been able to get that seat for three successive terms, and though his most conspicuous characteristic as a debater is his foul mouth, he has been elected repeatedly to the presidency of the Senate by the Republican majority. At last the "moral nature" of Kansas has shown sufficient "activity" to put an end to his career. A political revolution has taken place in the State, and a Legislature has been chosen which, according to the chairman of the Republican State Committee, "is conceded to have an anti-Ingalls majority." It is believed to be too large for him to buy — a circumstance which will doubtless make this "modern cant about the corruption of politics" more "fatiguing" than ever. It will be an incalculable gain to the moral atmosphere of the Senate chamber to have this vulgar ranter tipped out of its chairman's seat.

## [ARGUMENTS AGAINST LODGE'S FORCE BILL] [1]

### Savannah *News*, December 20, 1890

Nothing would give the Southern people greater satisfaction than the entire disappearance of sectional animosity. They think that the feelings of bitterness engendered by the Civil War ought to have disappeared long ago, and that the people of the North and South should work together harmoniously for the prosperity of the whole country. The resolutions relative to sectional animosities introduced into the Asheville convention are indicative of the sentiment which prevails in the South; and if the people of the North would meet the people of the South half way, there would be no more sectional legislation and no more exhibitions of sectional bitterness. And there is no good reason why there should be a political line dividing the North and the South. There would be no such line if the Republican leaders would cease their efforts to use the South to keep their party in power. These leaders, ever since the Civil War ended, have not only misrepresented the South with the view of keeping the Northern people hostile to her, but they have insisted that the South should be dealt with as if she were not loyal to the government. What is the Force bill but an effort to put the Southern people under bayonet rule and humiliate them? That the bill would be productive of race disturbances, and retard the South's prosperity, no thinking man, who fully understands what the effect of the bill would be, for a moment doubts. There is no necessity for such a bill, but the attempt to pass it leads the Northern people to think there is.

### Cleveland *Plain Dealer*, December 21, 1890

Senator Stewart said that the bill ought not to pass, because it would never be enforced; because it would consolidate the Southern whites; because it would bring further misery upon the Southern blacks, and because it would increase sectional animosities and kindle

---

[1] Henry Cabot Lodge's odious Force bill, for Federal supervision of Southern elections, helped the Democrats to carry the Congressional elections of 1890 with a tremendous sweep; the House in 1891 numbered 235 Democrats against 88 Republicans.

anew the discords of party. Whatever, said the Republican Senator,
was done in the matter of protecting suffrage at the South, unless it
was done through the voluntary action of the people of that section,
would have to result in one of two things: if the negro were protected by force, the same force would inevitably be driven to the
necessity of destroying his enemy. That involved the enslavement
and final extermination of the whites. It was the deliberate judgment of Senator Stewart that no assumption of party necessity could
justify such an act. Senator Stewart is justified in his view of the
effect the Force bill would have in the South by the statements of
leading Republicans and colored men in that section. Isaiah T.
Montgomery, one of the ablest colored men of Mississippi, who was
chosen by his people to represent them in the late constitutional
convention, said: "The solution offered by the Force bill is a solution that does not solve — it is a remedy that does not cure." If
two men, he added, live neighbors to each other, they will find some
basis on which they will agree; if not one basis, then another; but
they will find some basis. But if a stranger comes in and takes the
part of one against the other, the stranger must stay there all the
time in order to preserve the situation.

## [THE ITALIAN LYNCHINGS IN NEW ORLEANS] [1]

St. Louis *Republic*, March 15, 1891

It has never been proved that the chief of police of New Orleans
was assassinated either by the Italians who were murdered by the
mob, or by any other Italians. The circumstantial evidence made
it probable that the murder was committed by order of the Sicilian
vendetta society, the Mafia, and on this unproved probability the
spirit of vengeance was aroused to its highest pitch. As long as
the Sicilians killed each other, there was a complete willingness to
"let justice take its course." There was neither blind rage against
them, nor blind "public spirit" demanding a blood-sacrifice for
society. Only when it was supposed that the Sicilians had carried
their vendetta beyond their own ranks was this public spirit aroused,
and as aroused it manifested itself from the start in the thirst for
retribution, for the blood of Sicilians enough to avenge Hennessy.
So the eleven prisoners were lynched yesterday on proof of being
"dagos" and on the merest suspicion of being guilty of any other
crime.

[1] A band of Italians in New Orleans had been accused of murdering the chief
of police, Hennessy, who had tracked them down for previous misdeeds. A jury
acquitted six of the prisoners and disagreed in the case of three more; whereupon
a mob lynched eleven Italians held in the jail. Congress ultimately voted $25,000
to the relatives of the dead men.

New Orleans *Times-Democrat*, March 15, 1891

Villainy came to the front and saved the miserable miscreants' necks from the hangman's noose; the briber and the perjurer once again defrauded justice of her prey. And then the patience of the people was exhausted; and they resolved quietly but firmly that justice must be satisfied somehow, if not by ordinary, then by extraordinary, methods. All ordinary methods had been tried fully and fairly, and had failed; extraordinary methods must be had recourse to, to remedy the failure. They were had recourse to — and with effect. In the violation of the ordinary routine of justice to which the citizens in complete and admirable self-control resorted yesterday, they were doing merely for law and for the administration of justice what law and the administration of justice had confessedly been unable to do for themselves. To vindicate law which had repeatedly been mocked and to reinstate oft-outraged justice again upon her throne, the people took defiant crime by the nape of the neck, and strangled it and threw it in the gutter. This is the lesson of the thrilling events of yesterday, March 14. The short, sharp, and decisive drama of yesterday had in it, moreover, a warning for another class besides the wretched and brutalized aliens who think they can import their secret assassination schemes into this country and graft them upon our free institutions, which stand before the world the high watermark of human liberty. We have among us a class of jury-fixers, who are expert in getting at talesmen and jurymen, and in filling the jury-box, partially or wholly, with men pledged to consult above all things the interests of the criminals. . . . The events of yesterday are a significant hint to these men.

## [THE HOMESTEAD STRIKE: AN ANTI–LABOR VIEW][1]

Detroit *News*, November, 1892

The Homestead strike, which has at last, after a most pitiful failure, been declared off, should not pass out of mind with the workingmen of the country until they have made a careful review of the transaction, and endeavored to strike some sort of balance on the account. There has been abundance of fuming and fretting;

---

[1] A wage reduction by the Carnegie Steel Company at Homestead, Pa., had provoked a strike; the Carnegie officers employed a force of private guards, rioting broke out, and there was a two-day battle, with much loss of life. The episode offered a striking instance of the lawlessness of great corporations, and made the private militia system highly unpopular. It also showed a protected industry cutting wages at the very time that Republican orators were preaching the blessings of the McKinley Tariff Act.

there have been expressions of indignation and sympathy without limit; the demagogues of the country on the stump and in the press have been liberal in verbal encouragement of the strikers, and denunciations of the Carnegies and Fricks. A Presidential campaign was on, and these expressions were very cheap pay for the votes they were expected to bring. But the election is over now, the politicians have got their returns, they have figured up their realized profits, and the poor strikers, feeling instinctively that they are no longer of much account, sink helplessly into the pit of pauperism which they digged for themselves. The shops which they quitted are filled with strangers who have just the same right to earn their bread that the strikers have; the wheels of industry which they hoped to paralyze are being turned as deftly and as rapidly as ever by other hands recruited from the vast army of surplus labor with which the country is overrun. All that has resulted, so far as labor is concerned, is a displacement. A portion which was employed has become idle, and a portion which was idle has been employed. The Amalgamated Association of Iron Workers withdrew itself from the place it occupied, and tried to dam up all approaches to the spot. But the sea of idle labor rushed in upon it, filled up the petty vacuum, and still surges with superfluous force in mighty waves in every channel of employment in the country.

If there is any fact conspicuous in the situation it is this. It is not the trusts or corporations, the Carnegies or Fricks, who made this sea of labor which is dashing against the door of every factory in the country, and which fills at once every vacuum made by a strike. Nor is it they who give to this surplus labor the right to accept work which strikers refuse. That right is inherent in our laws, the most sacred right which humanity enjoys, without which freedom would be a sham and a delusion, government a fraud, and civilized society impossible. The great employers of labor, whether they be corporations or individuals, are in no way responsible for the abundance of it or for its cheapness, and it is the supreme point of folly to demand or expect that they shall pay more for it than the lowest price at which it is offered. It is not human nature for them to do so, and there is no law or power on earth that can make them do so. There is not an orator nor an editor in the land, nor a mechanic nor a laborer, how eloquently soever he may denounce the big employers such as Carnegie or Frick, who does not follow precisely the same rule as they in every purchase he makes, whether it be merchandise or labor in which he is dealing. Of what use then is it, except to the politicians and office-seekers in a campaign, to waste breath in denouncing individuals or corporations who differ from others in their relation to labor only in that they employ more of it?  If a scapegoat must be found, if the wrath of labor must be expended upon something or somebody, it would be wiser to do a little calm thinking first, so as to come nearer the mark.

Who, then, should the workingmen of Homestead blame for the pitiful position in which they now find themselves — after five months of voluntary idleness, their resources squandered in a hopeless struggle, many of them having to answer to the law for criminal acts, facing a hard winter with no employment and no hopes of it? Who but the blind or knavish leaders who deceive them?  Who, but the men they obey so blindly to their own ruin?

## [THE HOMESTEAD STRIKE: ANTI–CAPITALIST VIEWS]

*The American Nonconformist* (Indianapolis), November, 1892

This result settles nothing at all.  It has proved to be one of the most seriously contested battles between the contending forces, but no thoughtful observer will believe that either side has brought all its forces into the contest, or that either has exhausted its reserves. Capital is still organized, and labor is still organized, or perhaps more properly speaking, labor has all the elements of organization and effective combat still intact.  The only thing that may be said to be fully demonstrated is that the present organization of the power of the State is entirely in the interests of the rights of property. The defeat of the men at Homestead is due to the presence of the militia and the prostitution of all the power of the courts.  It is demonstrated that as far west as Pittsburgh the man who will not work on the terms of organized capital shall be declared an outlaw and hounded by all the power of the State to submission or starvation.

*Kansas City Journal*, November, 1892

Over eighty, some say fully ninety, per cent of these Homestead workers are not American citizens.  How, then, did they come to be there?  For several years now, iron men, railroad builders, coal miners, coke burners, and such interests have been importing labor from the most destitute populations of Europe, to the injury and exclusion of American labor, and of the voluntary immigration from the skilled or self-respecting labor of the Old World.  And the turbulent and lawless scenes from the Molly Maguires down to the violence of these imported men in the coal, iron, and coke regions of the country, are from these contract labors almost exclusively.  We have no bowels of compassion for the employers. For mercenary ends they have brought these masses to compete with and drive out the legitimate labor of the country, and they have to pay the penalty. The trouble is that these men can be dangerous in the hands of the enemies of capital, as capital has made them dangerous to the legitimate labor of the country.

Indianapolis Sentinel, November, 1892

Aside from the effect that may be produced from economic questions, there is no room for question that this strike has had an extraordinary effect in a political way. Coming as it did when the protection issue was already fixed before the country, and when the Republican party had made a special bid for the votes of working-men by declaring for a tariff sufficient to cover the difference between American and European wages, it called attention forcibly to the fallacy that lies under the theory of protection "for American labor." It made clear the fact that while protection gave the manufacturer such profits that he might pay his employees liberally, it had no binding force to make him pay more than the lowest market rates.

Louisville Courier-Journal, November, 1892

The strikers at last realize, what others have long believed, that their efforts have failed. This strike would have been a notable one at any time, but its importance was much enhanced by the fact that it occurred near the beginning of a Presidential campaign in which the tariff was the dominant issue, and in which the relations of the tariff to wages were necessarily attracting great attention. For this reason the most strenuous exertions were made to break the force of the object lesson which the strike afforded. That these efforts were not very successful may be inferred from the result of the election, and from the reduction of the Republican majority in Pennsylvania by one-fourth.

## [SPEAKER REED ON A "CHEAP AND NASTY" COUNTRY]

New York Evening Post, October 20, 1890

Speaker Reed has not "caught on" to the new Republican defence of the McKinley Law and its higher prices. He is arguing on the ground first assumed by its defenders, that the law has, to quote the language of Belden's Congressional Republican campaign document, "in no case raised the cost of necessary supplies to the American consumer." In other words, he is maintaining that "cheapness" is a desirable thing, and that the McKinley Law has given us a great deal of it. We place a passage from his speech at

Buffalo on Wednesday evening side by side with a passage from Mr. McKinley's speech in Kalamazoo on the previous evening.

| *McKinley, October 14, 1890* | *Reed, October 15, 1890* |
|---|---|
| Well, now they say you would have things cheaper if only you had a Democratic revenue tariff. Cheap! I never liked the word. "Cheap" and "nasty" go together. The whole system of cheap things is a badge of poverty, for cheap merchandise means cheap men, and cheap men mean a cheap country, and that is not the kind our fathers builded. Furthermore, it is not the kind their sons mean to maintain. | They also ask me if I know of any article which has been lowered in price by the tariff. I could spend the entire evening in giving the facts showing that articles have been lowered in price. I can remember the time when I had to pay $1.45 a yard for ingrain carpet. Now you can buy it for 45 cents a yard. I remember when you had to pay $6 a keg for nails. Now you can get the same nails for $3 a keg. The Democrats say it is invention that lowers prices. Is invention the gift of God? In my opinion it rests upon protection. It is the protective tariff which tempts our inventors to work at inventing cheaper processes of manufacturing. |

According to Mr. Reed, the McKinley Tariff Law is working to make what McKinley calls a "cheap and nasty country" filled with "cheap men."

[THE JUSTICE OF MR. CLEVELAND'S STAND] [1]

Indianapolis *News*, December 24, 1895

Whether or not Lord Salisbury is right in insisting that the Monroe Doctrine, as originally formulated, does not apply to the present difficulty, it is not now necessary to inquire. Nor does it much matter whether or not he is right in speaking of "the strange development which the doctrine has received at Mr. Olney's hands." We say these matters are of comparatively minor importance, for

---

[1] For several years the boundary dispute between Great Britain and Venezuela had excited the concern of the American government, and President Cleveland had tried to bring it to arbitration, which the British government resisted. On December 17, 1895, Cleveland electrified the world by a step which for a few days seemed to mean war. He submitted the correspondence, including a new refusal by Great Britain, to Congress, asked for money for the expenses of an American commission to determine the true boundary line, and stated that it would be "the duty of the United States to resist by every means in its power" any violation of that line by the British. Congress immediately appropriated $100,000.

the reason that in Lord Salisbury's dispatch may be found ample support for the position assumed by the United States. It is not necessary to go beyond the British Premier's own words. He says:

> The United States have a right, like every other nation, to interpose in any controversy by which their own interests are affected, and they are the judges whether those interests are touched, and in what measure they should be sustained.

That covers the whole case. We have decided that any attempt on the part of Great Britain to rob Venezuela of her territory is something which affects our interests, and Lord Salisbury admits that we have the right so to decide. What will be the outcome it is not necessary now to inquire. One thing, however, is certain, and that is that there will be no backdown on the part of the United States. The sensible people of this country have a deep-seated abhorrence of war, and they will pray to be delivered from such a calamity. But they will fight if right and principle cannot otherwise be established. There is no use in trying to disguise the gravity of the situation. It may be that the commission which the President recommends will find that England is in the right. But unless it does so find, the indications all point to a forcible resistance on our part to British aggressions — unless England shall admit that she is in the wrong.

## [THE INJUSTICE OF MR. CLEVELAND'S STAND]

New York *World*, December 23, 1895

President Cleveland's message is a serious blunder. It is a blunder because it is based upon a wrong conception, because it is not sustained by international law or usage, and because it places the United States in a false position. The President in his message, like Secretary Olney in his dispatches, assumes that the policy of Great Britain in Venezuela involves a menace to this country. The assumption is absurd. And with it falls the structure of ponderously dramatic rhetoric reared by the President. It is a grave blunder to put this country in the attitude of threatening war unless we mean it and are prepared for it and can appeal hopefully to the sympathies of the civilized world in making it. Do these conditions exist? Will any of the Senators who applauded the President's message yesterday seriously affirm that they do? If these conditions do not exist, what remains for us except a few weeks or months of bluster and a more or less graceful backdown? President Cleveland either means war in the contingency which he has foreshadowed or he does not. If he does not he is playing with fire. If he does he has assumed the gravest responsibility for the slightest cause of any President that the country has ever had. He has evoked either a storm of war or a storm of ridicule. Blaine lost the Presidency by his jingoism. That was the last straw that broke the people's confidence. Has history really lost the habit of repeating itself? Can the remnants of the third term load bear the addition of a "brilliant foreign policy"?

## [WHAT ARE PRESIDENT CLEVELAND'S MOTIVES?]

Milwaukee *Sentinel*, December 20, 1895

The President's newspaper supporters in Boston and New York have often said that he is not what is called a jingo, but essentially a man of peace. We are inclined to think that this description of Mr. Cleveland was correct until the desire for a third term came upon him, and made him warlike. The few persons who will not think Mr. Cleveland capable of wanting a third term may interpret the message as the cornerstone of an Olney boom.

## [PRESIDENT CLEVELAND'S VENEZUELA MESSAGE]

Springfield *Republican*, December, 1895

President Cleveland's message presents to the Congress and the American people the most momentous issue which the generation now predominant in public affairs has had thrust upon it. Never was such magnitude of possible combat projected from such frail foundations! It is idle to conceal the seriousness of the situation. No arbitration now. Britain has refused arbitration. We will therefore decide what her boundaries in that country will be, and then compel her to accept the limits so prescribed. Deeming it beneath her dignity to arbitrate, how will this great nation beyond the seas relish an enforced marking of the boundary lines of its colonies in America by another nation? Such is the stand taken by this government. Such is the humiliating position into which we are to force the strongest power of Europe. These two great peoples, common in origin, laws, and language, foremost in the march of civilization, mightiest of all nations — are they to fight in the broad light of nineteen centuries of Christian progress — fight over a beggarly plot of land which is "not room enough or continent enough to hide the slain"? We cannot believe it. The British Government has made a mistake in admitting a legitimate interest of the United States in the Venezuela matter and then refusing to submit its claims to an impartial tribunal. It now owes to the peace of the civilized world a compromise of its dispute with a weak and defenceless nation. A war such as this quarrel contemplates would be the greatest calamity to civilization of the century, if not of the Christian era. The sober judgment of two great and kindred peoples will not permit it.

We are not of those now ready to assert that Great Britain is wholly or even partially right in the controversy. That nation, in our judgment, is indefensibly in the wrong. Let any doubting one read the statement of apparent facts contained in Mr. Olney's note to Mr. Bayard. Let him further note the evident craft of Her Majesty's government in drawing various boundary lines from time to time, as if to raise a fog of doubt under cover of which the full extent of its greed for territory might be satisfied. And this in the full knowledge of the attitude and feeling of the American people on the subject! What more natural than that the United States should feel affronted at this flagrant disregard of our duly expressed desires and concerns? In refusing to arbitrate, history is going to condemn Lord Salisbury. So far we can follow the President. But we cannot endorse his extreme attitude in declaring in advance that the findings of the commission are necessarily to be supported by this government by force of arms. The President here has made a great mistake. He has needlessly placed the British Government in a position where retreat is difficult if not impossible.


## THE END OF THE FIGHT[1]

Emporia *Gazette*, June 20, 1895

There came through Emporia yesterday two old-fashioned "mover wagons," headed east. The stock in the caravan would invoice four horses, very poor and very tired, one mule, more disheartened than the horses, and one sad-eyed dog, that had probably been compelled to rustle his own precarious living for many a long and weary day. A few farm implements of the simpler sort were loaded in the wagon, but nothing that had wheels was moving except the two wagons. All the rest of the impedimenta had been left upon the battlefield, and these poor stragglers, defeated but not conquered, were fleeing to another field, to try the fight again. These movers were from western Kansas — from one of those counties near the Colorado line which holds a charter from the State to officiate as the very worst, most desolate, God-forsaken, man-deserted spot on the sad old earth. They had come from that wilderness only after a ten years' hard, vicious fight, a fight which had left its scars on their faces, had beat their bodies, had taken the elasticity from their steps, and left them crippled to enter the battle

[1] By William Allen White.

anew. For ten years they had been fighting the elements. They had seen it stop raining for months at a time. They had heard the fury of the winter wind as it came whining across the short burned grass, and cut the flesh from their children huddling in the corner. These movers have strained their eyes watching through the long summer days for the rain that never came. They have seen that big cloud roll up from the southwest about one in the afternoon, hover over the land, and stumble away with a few thumps of thunder as the sun went down. They have tossed through hot nights wild with worry, and have arisen only to find their worst nightmares grazing in reality on the brown stubble in front of their sun-warped doors. They had such high hopes when they went out there; they are so desolate now — no, not now, for now they are in the land of corn and honey. They have come out of the wilderness, back to the land of promise. They are now in God's own country down on the Neosho, with their wife's folks, and the taste of apple butter and good corn bread and fresh meat and pie — pieplant pie like mother used to make — gladdened their shrunken palates last night; and real cream, curdling on their coffee saucers last night for supper, was a sight so rich and strange that it lingered in their dreams, wherein they walked beside the still waters, and lay down in green pastures.

## A KINGDOM COMING

### Emporia *Gazette*, June 29, 1895

This has been a corn-growing week, sunshine sandwiched in clouds, and sprinkled here and there with lightly falling rain; the corn is for the most part "laid by" now, and the dark green of the sturdily curved blades stretches far down from the uplands into the bottoms, shading darker and ranker as the roots find the richer loam of the river drift. It is a glorious sight, an inspiring sight, the view from some light eminence upon the "gently rolling prairie" across the upland and over the sagging bottom, where the thousands and tens of thousands of rows of green-clad sentinels stand guard for the homes of Kansas. No one looking over the scene, as it is duplicated from the Missouri to the Cimarron, can fail to do homage to King Corn. There is something royal in the magnificence with which King Corn adorns his great throne room: the sculptured hills, the tracery of the river winding around the border of the throne, the glorious ever-changing canopy of blue and white and gray, and — at the sunset and in the morn — purple and graceful natural curves, and dazzling color schemes, all point to a regal custodian, all call for a reverential homage. Corn is King.

## "THRIFTY MERCHANT — PRODIGAL SON"[1]

New York *World*, July, 1895

Philadelphia, July 27. — The trouble among the employees of ex-Postmaster General Wanamaker over the low wages and petty tyranny of the floor bosses is serious. Since the publication of the employees' grievances and their steps to organize for self-protection, detectives have been employed in Wanamaker's store to find out the employees who have joined the union. The new labor league, which numbers over one thousand, threatens to go out in a body if any of their number is discharged. The league, which is known as the Retail Employees' Protective Association, claim that they are paid but $4 a week, and are subjected to petty and unnecessary fines for trivial faults. The delegates from the different leagues have formed a mutual protection agreement with the Knights of Labor, and at a meeting of District Union No. 1120 K. of L., a resolution was passed pledging moral and financial support to the employees in their efforts to obtain more liberal wages and conditions of labor. It is common knowledge in Philadelphia that the Wanamaker employees below a certain grade have fewer privileges and have to bear greater exactions than employees of any other dry-goods firm.

Paris, July 27. — All Paris is talking of the prodigal extravagance of Rodman Wanamaker, the young son of ex-Postmaster General Wanamaker, of Philadelphia, who spent $20,000 this week on a single dinner to 22 guests. Even in this city of sumptuous dining it is doubtful whether so much money was ever squandered on a single feast. It was given in the Pavilion d'Armenonville, a famous restaurant in the Bois de Boulogne. Twenty-two of the finest equipages called at the same moment at the residences of the guests and brought them to the banquet hall. The decorations were marvelous. Luminous fountains planted upon great blocks of ice kept the air cool. It was not one dinner but 22 independent dinners, separately served, one to each guest. Each guest had before him a whole leg of mutton, a whole salmon, truffled fowl, a basket of peaches, and a double magnum of champagne, besides bottles of wine of sacred vintage and fabulous cost. After the banquet costly jewelry was distributed to the guests, among whom were a number of young titled Frenchmen. Paris newspapers speak of the banquet as magnificent, but in bad taste.

---

[1] An effective exemplification of Joseph Pulitzer's policy, as stated in 1883, of making *The World* an institution that should "never lack sympathy with the poor."

## A FREE–COINAGE CATECHISM[1]

*The Nation*, July 9, 1896

Q. — What is the fundamental contention of the free-coinage advocates? A. — That the amount of money in circulation has been decreasing since the demonetization of silver, and that this decrease has caused a general fall in prices.

Q. — Is it true that the money supply has been decreasing? A. — It is not.

Q. — What are the facts? A. — So far as the United States is concerned, there has been an enormous increase. In 1860 the money in circulation in this country was $442,102,477; in 1872 it was $738,309,549; by the Treasury bulletin, at the beginning of the present month of July, it was $1,509,725,200.

Q. — What does this show? A. — It shows that our money supply has increased 240 per cent as compared with 1860, and 104 per cent as compared with 1872.

Q. — Has the money supply increased faster than the population? A. — Very much faster.

Q. — How do you prove this? A. — By dividing the total money in circulation at each date by the total population of the country at the same date, and thus finding the circulation per capita.

Q. — What does such a process show? A. — The per capita circulation of the United States on July 1, 1860, was $14.06; on July 1, 1872, it was $18.70; at the beginning of July in 1896 it was $21.15.

Q. — But has not the money supply of the world at large been decreasing? A. — On the contrary, it has been increasing rapidly.

Q. — How is this proved? A. — By the statistics of new gold production.

Q. — How large has this production been? A. — The reports of the Director of the Mint, which are acknowledged authority, show that from 1873 to 1894 inclusive the world's total new gold production has been $2,526,834,900.

Q. — Is this new product of gold increasing or decreasing? A. — It is increasing with enormous rapidity.

Q. — Give the figures. A. — In 1873 the world's gold production was $96,200,000; in 1880 it was $106,436,800. In the year 1890 it was $118,849,000. In 1894 it was $180,626,100. In 1895 the exact total is not yet compiled, but it is closely estimated at $199,500,000.

Q. — What does this mean? A. — It means that the amount of gold annually added to the world's money supply has more than doubled in the last twenty-three years.

[1] By Alexander Dana Noyes, financial editor of the New York *Evening Post* and the *Nation*.

Q. — Is not this annual rate of production liable to decrease? A. — On the contrary, all experts in the American, Australian, and South African gold fields look for a further and very heavy increase over the present rate of production.

Q. — But has not the disuse of silver with full coinage privileges cut down the total annual addition to the world's metallic money supply? A. — It has not.

Q. — Why? A. — In 1873 the world's gold production was $96,200,000; its silver production, $81,800,000; total, $178,000,000. Last year the production of *gold alone* was $199,500,000.

Q. — Was not the combined annual production of gold and silver larger than this in the "bonanza days"? A. — It was not.

Q. — What was the highest record of that period? A. — Between 1856 and 1860, the world's average annual production of gold was $134,083,000; of silver, $37,618,000; total, $171,701,000, or less, by $27,800,000, than last year's production of gold alone.

Q. — What are we to say, then, of the argument that the money supply, since silver free coinage was abandoned, has been contracting? A. — That it is utterly false as applied to the world at large, and especially so as applied to the United States.

Q. — Is it true, nevertheless, that the price of wheat and many other farm products has fallen heavily? A. — It is.

Q. — How are such declines, in wheat for instance, to be explained? A. — By the enormously rapid increase in grain-growing area throughout the world.

Q. — Has this increase been especially rapid since 1872? A. — The increase in grain-growing area in this period, especially in North America, South America, and Asia, has never been approached in any equal period in the history of the world. . . .

Q. — Has there been an increase in the United States itself? A. — An enormous increase.

Q. — How large? A. — In 1875 there were 26,381,512 acres of wheat cultivated in this country; in 1891 there were 39,916,897, an increase of 50 per cent. The yield in 1875 was 292,136,000 bushels, a heavy increase over preceding years. In 1891 the yield was 611,780,000. Even last year, with a greatly reduced acreage and a partial crop failure, the yield was 467,100,000 bushels.

## THE CHICAGO NOMINATION [1]

New York *World*, July 11, 1896

The expected happened in the Chicago platform. The unexpected happened in the nomination for President. Lunacy having dictated the platform, it was perhaps natural that hysteria should evolve the candidate.

Mr. Bryan was not seriously considered for the first place until his speech in favor of the free-silver platform threw the convention and the galleries into a state of hysterical frenzy. This effect was a tribute to Mr. Bryan's eloquence, but it was not favorable to the calm judgment required for the wise selection of a Presidential candidate.

As the party is doomed to defeat by its platform, the ticket is of minor consequence, except as it bears upon the future of the party. A political organization can survive being made odious. There is peril in making it ridiculous. The nomination of a "boy orator" for the White House at this junction of the nation's affairs, domestic and foreign, when the ripest experience, the best-tested wisdom, the broadest patriotism, and the greatest executive ability are required, comes perilously near taking this fatal step from the sublime.

It is to the future that *The World* looks in considering the effect of this convention. There is no doubt as to the result of the election, except as to the size of McKinley's popular and electoral majorities. To question this is to doubt the intelligence, the underlying honesty, and the public morality of the people. Opinions as to the result, upon the issue which the free-silver monometallists have forced, are a test of faith in the people. *The World* believes — it *must* believe — in the abiding good sense and the active conscience of the American people. It is absolutely confident that the proposal to debase the currency to a standard of a few semi-civilized countries, against the standard and the experience of the most enlightened and prosperous nations, cannot stand the trial of a four months' discussion. It is confirmed in this opinion by the observation of John Stuart Mill: "The voters of the United States have several times, in dealing with financial questions, apparently been about to do the wrong thing, but always at the critical time the great common sense of the people has asserted itself, and the wrong thing has been put down and the right thing made to prevail."

But *The World* remembers that the Democratic party has blundered frightfully in the past, and has survived and recovered from

---

[1] William Jennings Bryan made his "cross of gold" speech at the Democratic Convention in Chicago on July 9, 1896, and was nominated on July 10.

the effects of its unwisdom. We desire to see the old and splendid historic organization left after defeat in such a condition that the fragments can be made to cohere again in 1900.

## [THE REPUBLICAN CAMPAIGN OF VILLIFICATION] [1]

New York *Journal*, July 13, 1896

The manner in which the opponents of the Democratic ticket nominated at Chicago have begun their campaign must rouse the profoundest resentment of every American regardful of the interests and jealous of the honor of his country. The representatives of half of the American people have been denounced in delirious language as anarchists, cutthroats, and swindlers. This crusade has been one of reckless misrepresentation from the start. The libelers of the late convention know that the Chicago platform is not anarchical. In most respects it is inspired by enlightened progressiveness. The anarchical elements in the convention — Tillman and Altgeld — were distinctly frowned upon. The condemnation of the practise of substituting government by injunction for the old, orderly processes of courts and juries, so far from being revolutionary, is a vindication of the ancient rights of the English-speaking race against a novel and dangerous innovation which deserves the name of anarchy much better than anything done at Chicago. Moreover, the silver plank in the Chicago platform does not deserve the frantic vituperation levelled against it. If its authors were mistaken in their methods, its aim was to introduce bimetallism, and bimetallism is a scientific theory with too much expert authority on its side to brand its advocates as lunatics or incendiaries. Nor is it possible with any more sincerity to call Mr. Bryan a demagogue. He follows the truth as he sees it, though it lead him to political destruction. His spirit is rather that of a prophet. On the other side we have William McKinley, bound hand, foot, and tongue to the most corrupt combination that ever exhibited itself openly in an American Presidential campaign. His election would put the resources of the government at the disposal of the Hanna syndicate. Nobody who realizes what is at stake in this campaign can vote to abandon government of the people, by the people, for the people, in favor of government of McKinley, by Hanna, for a syndicate.

[1] Alone among the New York newspapers, the *World* having bolted the ticket, Hearst's *Journal* supported Bryan. There was much justice in what it said of the "villification." Thus the New York *Tribune* spoke of Bryan as "the wretched, addle-pated boy," who was leader of a "league of hell." Dr. Parkhurst called Bryan's campaign "accursed and treasonable." Another minister termed him "a mouthing, slobbering demagogue." Many employers told their workmen that if Bryan won the business would be closed down.

## WHAT'S THE MATTER WITH KANSAS? [1]

Emporia *Gazette*, August 15, 1896

Today the Kansas department of agriculture sent out a statement which indicates that Kansas has gained less than two thousand people in the past year. There are about 225,000 families in the State, and there were about ten thousand babies born in Kansas, and yet so many people have left the State that the natural increase is cut down to less than two thousand net.

This has been going on for eight years.

If there had been a high brick wall around the State eight years ago, and not a soul had been admitted or permitted to leave, Kansas would be a half million souls better off than she is today. And yet the nation has increased in population. In five years ten million people have been added to the national population, yet instead of gaining a share of this — say half a million — Kansas has apparently been a plague spot, and in the very garden of the world, has lost population by ten thousands every year.

Not only has she lost population, but she has lost money. Every moneyed man in the State who could get out without loss has gone. Every month in every community sees someone who has a little money pack up and leave the State. This has been going on for eight years. Money has been drained out all the time. In towns where ten years ago there were three or four or half a dozen money-lending concerns stimulating industry by furnishing capital, there is now none, or one or two that are looking after the interest and principal already outstanding.

No one brings any money into Kansas any more. What community knows over one or two men who have moved in with more than $5,000 in the past three years? And what community cannot count half a score of men in that time who have left, taking all the money they could scrape together?

Yet the nation has grown rich, other States have increased in population and wealth — other neighboring States. Missouri has gained over two million, while Kansas has been losing half a million. Nebraska has gained in wealth and population while Kansas has gone down hill. Colorado has gained every way, while Kansas has lost every way since 1888.

What's the matter with Kansas?

There is no substantial city in the State. Every big town save

[1] This editorial was reprinted in almost every Republican newspaper of the country, and Mark Hanna used it more widely than any other campaign document. Directed at the Populist ticket, it did not prevent its election. Mr. White years later referred to the editorial as representing "conservatism in its full and perfect flower."

one has lost in population. Yet Kansas City, Omaha, Lincoln, St. Louis, Denver, Colorado Springs, Sedalia, the cities of the Dakotas, St. Paul and Minneapolis and Des Moines — all cities and towns in the West have steadily grown.

Take up the government blue book and you will see that Kansas is virtually off the map. Two or three little scrubby consular places in yellow-fever-stricken communities that do not aggregate ten thousand dollars a year is all the recognition that Kansas has. Nebraska draws about one hundred thousand dollars; little old North Dakota draws about fifty thousand dollars; Oklahoma doubles Kansas; Missouri leaves her a thousand miles behind; Colorado is almost seven times greater than Kansas — the whole West is ahead of Kansas. Take it by any standard you please, Kansas is not in it.

Go east and you hear them laugh at Kansas, go west and they sneer at her, go south and they "cuss" her, go north and they have forgotten her. Go into any crowd of intelligent people gathered anywhere on the globe, and you will find the Kansas man on the defensive. The newspaper columns and magazines once devoted to praise of her, to boastful facts and startling figures concerning her resources, are now filled with cartoons, jibes, and, Pefferian speeches. Kansas just naturally isn't in it. She has traded places with Arkansas and Timbuctoo.

What's the matter with Kansas?

We all know; yet here we are at it again. We have an old mossback Jacksonian who snorts and howls because there is a bathtub in the statehouse; we are running that old jay for governor. We have another shabby, wild-eyed, rattle-brained fanatic who has said openly in a dozen speeches that "the rights of the user are paramount to the rights of the owner"; we are running him for chief justice, so that capital will come tumbling over itself to get into the State. We have raked the old ash-heap of failure in the State and found an old human hoopskirt who has failed as a business man, who has failed as an editor, who has failed as a preacher, and we are going to run him for Congress-at-large. He will help the looks of the Kansas delegation in Washington. Then we have discovered a kid without a law practise and decided to run him for attorney-general. Then for fear some hint that the State had become respectable might percolate through the civilized portions of the nation, we have decided to send three or four harpies out lecturing, telling the people that Kansas is raising hell and letting the corn go to weeds.

Oh, this is a State to be proud of! We are a people who can hold up our heads! What we need is not more money, but less capital, fewer white shirts, and brains, fewer men with business judgment, and more of those fellows who boast that they are "just ordinary clodhoppers, but they know more in a minute about finance than John Sherman"; we need more men who are "posted," who can bellow about the crime of '73, who hate prosperity, and who think because a man believes in national honor, he is a tool of Wall Street. We have a few of them — some hundred and fifty thousand — but we need more.

We need several thousand gibbering idiots to scream about the "Great Red Dragon" of Lombard Street. We don't need population, we don't need wealth, we don't need well-dressed men on the streets, we don't need cities on the fertile prairies; you bet we don't! What we are after is the money-power. Because we have become poorer and ornerier and meaner than a spavined, distempered mule, we, the people of Kansas, propose to kick; we don't care to build up, we wish to tear down.

"There are two ideas of government," said our noble Bryan at Chicago. "There are those who believe that if you just legislate to make the well-to-do prosperous, the prosperity will leak through on those below. The Democratic idea has been that if you legislate to make the masses prosperous their prosperity will find its way up and through every class and rest on us."

That's the stuff! Give the prosperous man the dickens! Legislate the thriftless man into ease, whack the stuffing out of the creditors and tell the debtors who borrowed the money five years ago when money "per capita" was greater than it is now that the contraction of the currency gives him a right to repudiate. Whoop it up for the ragged trousers; put the ragged, greasy fizzle who can't pay his debts on the altar, and bow down and worship him. Let the State ideal be high. What we need is not the respect of our fellow men, but the chance to get something for nothing.

O, yes, Kansas is a great State. Here are people fleeing from it by the score every day, capital going out of the State by the hundreds of dollars; and every industry but farming paralyzed, and that crippled, because its products have to go across the ocean before they can find a laboring man at work who can afford to buy them. Let's don't stop this year. Let's drive all the decent, self-respecting men out of the State. Let's keep the old clodhoppers who know it all. Let's encourage the man who is "posted." He can talk, and what we need is not millhands to eat our meat, nor factory hands to eat our wheat, nor cities to oppress the farmer by consuming his butter and eggs and chickens and produce. What Kansas needs is men who can talk, who have large leisure to argue the currency question while their wives wait at home for that nickel's worth of blueing.

What's the matter with Kansas?

Nothing under the shining sun. She is losing wealth, population, and standing. She has got her statesmen, and the money power is afraid of her. Kansas is all right. She has started in to raise hell, as Mrs. Lease advised, and she seems to have an overproduction. But that doesn't matter. Kansas never did believe in diversified crops. Kansas is all right. There is absolutely nothing wrong with Kansas. "Every prospect pleases, and only man is vile."

## A SPLENDID TICKET — DON'T VOTE FOR IT
### New York *Sun,* September 17, 1896

The Indianapolis Gold-Democratic nominations are admirable. The platform on which General Palmer and General Buckner stand is clear, strong, and satisfactory in its main feature; and in this unparalleled contest for the defence of a single principle of supreme concern, minor points of difference are not vital. With what zeal, energy, and hopefulness the Democracy of the Union could rally to the support of Palmer and Buckner and honest money, under circumstances other than those attending the present crisis! But there is another consideration of surpassing importance to every Democrat who is first of all a patriot. Magnificent as a protest, valuable as a framework for a future home for regenerated Democracy, the Indianopolis organization does not change the present duty of the individual Democrat who abhors repudiation and desires to safeguard the national honor against the assaults of the revolutionists. Admire the spirit displayed at Indianapolis, take off your hats to John McAuley Palmer and Simon Bolivar Buckner, cheer them to the top of your voice, not only as fine old types of Northern and Southern Democracy, but also as the advance guard of a Democratic column starting out for further victories; and then go to the polls and clear the way for the new Democracy by firing directly at Bryan a ballot for William McKinley!

## A TRUE VICTORY FOR BOTH PARTIES
### New York *World*, November 5, 1896

Not since the fall of Richmond have patriotic Americans had such cause for rejoicing as they feel today. Then the integrity of the Union was secured. Now its honor is preserved. Indeed in one sense the peril was greater now than then. The success of secession would have given us at the worst two republics. The success of repudiation, with the accompanying denial of the sovereign authority of the nation and the proposition to prostitute the Supreme Court, would have destroyed the very essence of the republican idea. This great deliverance is not a party triumph. It is a triumph of morality and patriotism.

Democratic votes, guided by conscience and independence, gave to the magnificent column in favor of sound money, law, order, and national authority these States, all of which voted for the Democratic candidate in 1892: Connecticut, Delaware, Illinois, Indiana, New Jersey, New York, Maryland, Wisconsin, Kentucky, and West Virginia. Never before has there been such a test of Democratic conscience and courage. It was easy for Republicans to support McKinley, because he represented their principles and embodied their policy. But it was most difficult for Democrats to support him, because it required them not only to go against their party but to accept the Republican who was most odiously opposed to their principles on every point save that of sound money. They had no other motive for their action than that of pure patriotism and public spirit.

The victory means far more than the election of Mr. McKinley. It means peace and security for four years. It goes beyond the seas and all over the world as a declaration that the institutions of human freedom and political equality are absolutely secure. It is a splendid vindication of the republican system. It justifies the faith of the fathers in the ability and the virtue of the people, and their capacity for self-government. There is no longer a "solid South," and there never will be again. The issues that made it solid have "gone glimmering among the things that were," and on a new issue of vital importance the dividing line between North and South is completely rubbed out.

## TIMELY COUNSEL AND WARNING

New York *World*, November 18, 1896

Carl Schurz and William L. Wilson are men everywhere honored for their statesmanship, for absolute sincerity of mind, and for exalted patriotism. It is significant that these two men have on the same day felt it incumbent upon them to deliver to the country the same strenuous message of counsel and warning.

That message in brief is this: There are real wrongs, real grievances, real oppressions to be righted. Behind the late outbreak of Populism there was a cause deeper than any reckless whim, more earnest than a mere desire for change. It would be "irrational to suppose," said Mr. Wilson, "that all the millions of American voters who massed behind the flag of free silver were conscious advocates of repudiation and disaster, or less patriotic than the mass of their countrymen."

The fact that Mr. Bryan received so large a vote as he did, says Mr. Schurz, "is a result which certainly was not owing to popular ignorance and blind partisanship alone," but "to the existence of discontents not entirely groundless, the causes of which should be examined with candor, care, and courage."

All this is what *The World* earnestly urged upon attention early in the campaign. But for the existence of real and grievous wrongs the elements of discontent dominant at Chicago would have been powerless to control a party convention or to enlist even a respectable support for their cause.

And the real grievances, the actual wrongs that cry out for remedy, are not far to seek. There is no doubt that in this Republic, based as it is upon simplicity and ideas of equality before the law, there are growing inequalities of privilege and increasingly offensive encroachments and vulgarities of the rich.

The trust combinations are fostered by tariffs that protect them from foreign competition. They grow every year more arrogant, more despotic, and more oppressive in their exactions. Yet the laws against them are not only not enforced, but no honest effort is made to enforce them.

The Attorney-Generals of two Administrations — one Republican and the other Democratic — refused to do anything to check the rapacity of these conspiracies of greed against need. The one neglected the law. The other mocked and jeered at it and was promoted for his pains.

In the same way the people have seen bargains made in secret between the Treasury authorities and a Wall Street syndicate for the sale of millions of bonds for 15 cents on the dollar less than their open market value — in other words, for the direct transfer of many millions of the people's money to the pockets of the banker friends of the Administration, without any consideration whatever.

They have seen State legislatures of both parties dominated by corporations so that no measure of relief from wrong done by corporations could become law. They have seen legislators purchased or corrupted by the political influence of corporations. They have seen great railroad combinations put their own agents in the Senate of the United States. They have reason to believe that rich men have even bought seats in that body.

In brief, money is too largely usurping the power and influence of manhood. The people may perhaps exaggerate the facts in their fear of plutocratic rule, but there ought to be no such facts for them to exaggerate.

The election of McKinley and a Congress that will support him carries with it a broader commission than ordinary. He and it were elected not by a party for partisan purposes, but by the people of both parties for the purpose of averting threatened disasters. But if those disasters are to be permanently averted, the causes of the discontent that was so narrowly defeated in its programme of destructiveness must be carefully sought out and removed before another Presidential year should come round. Otherwise the discontent will continue and the disaster will threaten again in some other form.

This is the message of Mr. Schurz and Mr. Wilson. It should fall upon attentive ears.

## IS THERE A SANTA CLAUS?[1]

New York *Sun*, September 21, 1897

We take pleasure in answering at once and thus prominently the communication below, expressing at the same time our great gratification that its faithful author is numbered among the friends of *The Sun*.

> Dear Editor: I am eight years old. Some of my little friends say there is no Santa Claus. Papa says "if you see it in *The Sun* it's so." Please tell me the truth, is there a Santa Claus?
>
> Virginia O'Hanlon.
>
> 115 West 95th Street.

Virginia, your little friends are wrong. They have been affected by the skepticism of a skeptical age. They do not believe except they see. They think that nothing can be which is not comprehended by their little minds. All minds, Virginia, whether they be men's or children's, are little. In this great universe of ours man is a mere insect, an ant, in his intellect, as compared with the boundless world about him, as measured by the intelligence capable of grasping the whole of truth and knowledge.

Yes, Virginia, there is a Santa Claus. He exists as certainly as love and generosity and devotion exist, and you know that they abound and give to our life its highest beauty and joy. Alas! how dreary would be the world if there were no Santa Claus. It would be as dreary as if there were no Virginias. There would be no childish faith then, no poetry, no romance, to make tolerable this existence. We should have no enjoyment, except in sense

[1] By Francis P. Church.

and sight. The eternal light with which childhood fills the world would be extinguished.

Not believe in Santa Claus! You might as well not believe in fairies! You might get your papa to hire men to watch in all the chimnies on Christmas Eve to catch Santa Claus, but even if they did not see Santa Claus coming down, what would that prove? Nobody sees Santa Claus, but that is no sign that there is no Santa Claus. The most real things in the world are those that neither children nor men can see. Did you ever see fairies dancing on the lawn? Of course not, but that's no proof that they are not there. Nobody can conceive or imagine all the wonders there are unseen and unseeable in the world.

You may tear apart the baby's rattle and see what makes the noise inside, but there is a veil covering the unseen world which not the strongest men, nor even the united strength of all the strongest men that ever lived, could tear apart. Only fancy, poetry, love, romance can push aside that curtain and view and picture the supernal beauty and glory behind. Is it all real? Ah, Virginia, in all this world there is nothing else real and abiding.

No Santa Claus! Thank God! he lives and he lives forever. A thousand years from now, Virginia, nay, ten times ten thousand years from now, he will continue to make glad the heart of childhood.

## PASSPORTS FOR MINISTER DE LOME[1]

### New York *Evening Journal*, February 9, 1898

This country has endured much from the Spanish Minister at Washington. It has seen him maintain for three years a gigantic system of espionage and corruption, with its headquarters at our capital. It has seen the effect of his subterranean machinations in the dumb palsy that has afflicted men who before they came within the range of his influence were free-spoken Americans, in touch with the sentiment of their compatriots. It has known him for a private slanderer of the people whose hospitality he has enjoyed and abused. But not until this morning, when the *Journal* presents the documentary evidence of his insults to the head of the government to which he is accredited, has it been possible to convict him by his own handwriting of offences justifying a demand for his recall.

[1] Senor Dupuy de Lome, the Spanish Minister in Washington, wrote a letter to a friend in Havana declaring that McKinley was a weakling and a "cheap politician" who was catering to the jingoes of the country. When the *Journal* published the letter, stolen from the Havana postoffice by a spy, De Lome had to resign.

Mr. De Lome once wrote a book in which he impartially libelled everything American, including our women.  He has been trying ever since to live that down, excusing himself on the plea that the book was written before he was old enough to know better.  He will find it hard to make a similar excuse cover his letter to Mr. Canalejas, which was written less than two months ago.  This is the Spanish Minister's opinion of the President of the United States:

> The message has undeceived the insurgents, who expected something else, and has paralyzed the actions of Congress, but I consider it bad.  Besides the natural and inevitable coarseness with which he repeats all that the press and public opinion of Spain had said of Weyler, it shows once more what McKinley is, weak and catering to the rabble, and besides a low politician who desires to leave a door open to use, and to stand well with the jingoes of his party.

There it is, signed, sealed, and absolutely irreparable.  What possible explanation can De Lome make?  He may denounce the emissaries of the Cuban Junta for abstracting his private letters, but that will not alter the fact that he considers President McKinley "a low politician," "weak and catering to the rabble."   What is written is written, and now that the President knows the Spanish Minister's opinion of him, nothing can restore the old fiction of their mutual regard.

The *Journal* has to thank Mr. De Lome for correcting the mis-representations of certain pro-Spanish newspapers regarding its Cuban correspondence.  The Minister warns his friend in Havana that "I do not believe you pay enough attention to the rôle of England.  Nearly all that newspaper canaille which swarms in your hotel are English, and at the same time that they are corre-spondents of the *Journal* they are also correspondents of the best newspapers and reviews of London.  Thus it has been since the beginning."  The envious contemporaries that have had so much to say about the "lies of the irresponsible reporters of the *Journal*" in Cuba will please take notice of Mr. De Lome's statement that the best newspapers and reviews of London depend upon *Journal* correspondents for information about Cuban affairs.

The Minister exposes the humbug of the reciprocity negotiations by which it has been hoped to stifle American sympathy for Cuban patriots.  "It would be most important," he tells Mr. Canalejas, "that you should agitate the question of commercial relations, even though it would be only for effect, and that you should send here a man of importance in order that I might use him, to make a propaganda among the Senators and others in opposition to the junta and to win our exiles." Now that the President knows that these commercial negotiations are carried on "only for effect," will he continue to allow himself to be used as a Spanish stoolpigeon?

Minister De Lome's usefulness to his employers is ended. If he have any sensitiveness in his composition, or any feeling of personal dignity, his correspondence will be enlarged forthwith by two more letters, one to his chief at Madrid tendering his resignation, and the other to the Secretary of State of the United States announcing his immediate departure for home without leavetaking. In default of the second of these communications it will be the duty of our government at once to send the Minister his passports and decline to hold any further communication with him.

Mr. De Lome has had a long rope, but he has reached the end of it at last. He has insulted women, slandered men, and arrogantly interfered with the administration of our laws. We have endured it all, but even our meek and lowly government can hardly be expected to continue to hold relations with a Minister who describes its Chief Magistrate as "a low politician," "weak and catering to the rabble."

## SPAIN'S VICTORY OF PEACE [1]

### New York *Journal*, February 17, 1898

To five hundred thousand Cubans starved or otherwise murdered have been added an American battleship and three hundred American sailors lost as the direct result of the dilatory policy of our government toward Spain. If we had stopped the war in Cuba when duty and policy alike urged us to do so the Maine would have been afloat today, and three hundred homes, now desolate, would have been unscathed.

It was an accident, they say. Perhaps it was, but accident or not, it would never have happened if there had been peace in Cuba, as there would have been had we done our duty. And it is an accident of a remarkably convenient kind for Spain. Two days ago we had five battleships in the Atlantic. Now we have four. A few more such accidents will leave us at the mercy of the Spanish fleet.

Two years ago our naval superiority over Spain was overwhelming. Two successive Administrations have waited patiently for Spain to overcome that disadvantage by buying and building ships enough to bring her navy up to an equality with ours. That process proving too slow, it is now being hastened by the accidental

[1] The *Maine* was sunk in Havana harbor on February 15, 1898.

reduction of the American fleet. At this rate it ought not to take long for Spain's naval strength to surpass our own.

As to the immediate cause of the disaster that has bereaved so many American households and robbed the American navy of one of the most valued elements of its fighting strength, we heed Captain Sigsbee's appeal to suspend judgment. The government has set an investigation on foot, and the *Journal* has independently undertaken another. Between them the truth will soon be known. If it be found that the Spanish authorities have brought about this calamity, so propitious to themselves, no power from the White House to Wall Street will be able to restrain the American people from exacting a terrible retribution. And Spain's innocence must be clearly proved. All the circumstances of the case fix the burden of proof upon her. The Maine was lying in one of her harbors, under the guns of one of her fortresses, with her warships at hand. The removal of the Maine meant a tremendous reduction in the odds against her in the event of the conflict that all Spanish Havana desired. The chances against such a removal by accident were millions to one, and yet the removal occurred. In such circumstances polite expressions of regret count for nothing. The investigations must clearly disclose Spain's innocence or her guilt will be assumed.

But while we must wait for definite evidence before formally charging Spain with the shameful treachery of which all the world is ready to suspect her, we need wait for nothing before instituting such a change of policy as will relieve us of the fear of future troubles. The anarchy in Cuba, which for three years has reached the sympathies of all Americans but the dehumanized stockjobbers of Wall Street, has become an intolerable evil to American interests. It has destroyed three hundred millions of dollars' worth of American trade and scores of millions of American property; it has kept business in a state of continual anxiety or semi-panic. It has checked the restoration of prosperity; it has distracted the attention of the American people from their own pressing concerns; and now, at last, it has robbed us of a magnificent battleship and the lives of three hundred seamen. We have endured it long enough. Whether a Spanish torpedo sank the Maine or not, peace must be restored in Cuba at once. If we cannot have peace without fighting for it, let us fight and have it over with. It is not likely that the entire Spanish navy would be able to do us so much harm in open battle as we suffered in Havana harbor in one second of a state of things that was neither peace nor war.

The investigation into the injuries of the Maine may take a week, but the independence of Cuba can be recognized today.

The Spanish Government can receive today such a notice as fired Mexico when it was addressed to Louis Napoleon. The Vesuvius can be recalled today from her odious work of doing police service for Spain against Cuban patriots and sent to join the defenders of America. The American fleet can move on Havana today and plant the flag of the Cuban Republic on Morro and Cabanas. It is still strong enough for that in the absence of further "accidents." And if we take such action as that, it is extremely unlikely that any further accident will appear.

## [THE CLAMOR FOR WAR WITH SPAIN] [1]

### Washington *Star*, April 8, 1898

The postponement of a President's message which promised to lead to hostilities on the ground that the lives of Americans would not be safe in the territory of the prospective enemy after its transmittal is in itself a savage indictment of the anarchical and barbarous condition of the Spanish so-called government in Cuba, which it has become the duty of the American republic to correct and reform by the expulsion of Spanish rule from the island.

### Kansas City *Times*, April 12, 1898

The message was not what the country had a right to expect from its President. It contains no new information, unless it be the official confession of diplomatic failure. One can readily see the impatience and disgust with which it was received by a patriotic Congress. The first reference to the Maine affair was calculated to create the impression that an outspoken declaration would follow. What does follow is in reality a recital of facts understood by all the people, which show that the Spaniards are incapable of ruling a people in this hemisphere, and an argument against every step proposed for giving permanent relief to this same people. The great men who gave this country its Constitution must have anticipated some such opportunity for the nation's betrayal when they vested in Congress the only authority to declare war. That Congress will not betray the people is almost certain. Cuba will be free, and in her battle for freedom she will have every material assistance which the United States can offer. In our settlement with Spain we will not forget the *Maine*. We have a score to settle, and the vacillation of our President will not prevent us from settling it rightly.

[1] President McKinley's message advocating forcible interference as the only way to end the inhuman conditions in Cuba, and declaring that "the issue is now with Congress," was, after a slight delay, sent to Congress on April 11, 1898.

## [WAR IS DECLARED: TWO CONFLICTING VIEWS]

Brooklyn *Eagle*, April 19, 1898

For hundreds of years the flag of red and yellow has floated over Morro Castle. Its brutal supremacy is doomed. It has fluttered at the gates of a colossal slaughter-house, an emblem of government by the sword, and of the control of a country whose watchword, says Senator Cullom, has been blood, and whose inspiration death. There is scant precedent for what has just been added to the pages of American history. Intervention comes in response to sentiment which has swept the country, if not the continent, so that the voices which were heard in protest have been shamed into whispers rarely audible and worth little of the breath that is spent upon them. In the laws which govern intervention the academicians are welcome to all the satisfaction they can find. While they are quibbling over the arid technicalities which contribute to the mustiness of international statute books, the people of the United States have answered their President with the voice of thunder. He asked that in the name of humanity and of civilization and in behalf of endangered American interests he be empowered to act, to include if necessary blood and steel in the catalogue of his resources, and to ask no nation on the earth what it thought about the matter. From every State in the Union came the reply, telling of union in every State, talking not of cost or consequence and passing upon the Spaniard sentence that can know neither commutation nor suspension. The bolt has fallen. It would be as easy to recall the ball which has belched from the muzzle of a cannon as to arrest the movement which began on Monday, April 18.

New Orleans *Times-Democrat*, April 15, 1898

Few who consider the matter seriously will justify such a war. Men who would not hesitate a moment, if their country was invaded or its honor and good name were at stake, to offer their lives to save it, have not been able to see any justification for this war of sympathy with Cuba. They fail to see why they should sacrifice their lives and those of their sons for such sympathy. They fail to understand why it is necessary to fill this land with widows and orphans out of sympathy to the Cubans. They do not see why their commerce should be destroyed, their great industries paralyzed, and their leading agricultural products go begging for buyers, all because of a sympathetic sentiment for the Cubans. Such a war, quixotic and unnecessary as it is, becomes a binding obligation upon the patriotism of every citizen from the moment that the government turns loose the forces of death and destruction. The first hostile gun fired at an American ship by the Spaniards compels every patriot in the United States to range himself under its flag and against its foes, and he will fight with the best and bravest; but he will know all the time that he has been driven into an unjust and unnecessary war, to satisfy the demands of men who, for political purposes solely, have desired to plunge the republic into foreign war.

## THE REALITIES OF THE EXPANSION PROGRAM[1]

Baltimore *News*, December 13, 1898

Whether the line adopted by Senator Vest — which is also, judging by his past utterances, that which will be taken by Senator Hoar — is the one best calculated to produce results, is open to serious question. That the Constitution could be invoked with irresistible power to prevent the annexation if annexation could be shown to be in clear conflict with the Constitution, we entertain no doubt. The American people are not so bent upon taking in those islands that they would sanction, for a moment, an overriding of the fundamental law of the land for the sake of getting them. It is doubtful whether the majority, or even any large fraction of the people, want them at all. We feel pretty well assured, for our own part, that the great bulk of the people are simply in a state of suspense upon the subject. The belief that the Constitution was to be violated for the purpose of acquiring the Philippines would convert this great mass of doubters into ardent opponents of annexation.

The trouble is that the strictly Constitutional objection has not enough definiteness or solidity to operate as an effective force. You cannot rouse public sentiment to the point of action by declaring that in your judgment the Constitution would be violated by a certain course of action, unless you are able to make it plain to the wayfaring man wherein the violation consists. The Constitution does not forbid the acquisition of territory; nobody pretends that it does. It is only contended that the Constitution does not empower the United States to acquire territory except for the purpose of ultimately adding it to the group of States of the Union. Unfortunately, it is impossible to rest this contention upon any words of the Constitution itself. High judicial authority may be cited in support of it; strong public men of today may declare it to be their own view; but after all, it must remain a mere matter of personal opinion, and cannot be laid down with the impressive-

[1] By Fabian Franklin.

ness which would be necessary to produce a real and vital effect on public opinion. It is interesting to recall how completely the alleged unconstitutionality of a protective tariff was relegated to the rear when the real fight on that issue came on in President Cleveland's time.

A real leader in the anti-expansion fight must take it up from the point of view of the actual effect that the carrying out of the "imperialist" programme may be expected to have upon the institutions and the traditions of the country. His cause would be strengthened, not weakened, by throwing away the clumsy shield which the Constitution is supposed to furnish in the shape of an inferential limitation of power. Let the objection be based, not upon what it may be argued that the fathers intended, but upon what it may be expected the sons will feel to be a real danger to the inheritance which those fathers handed down. It is true that Senator Vest essays to do this also, to some extent, in his speech. But he is encumbered by the weight of a Constitutional argument which is more marked by heaviness than by strength. Let the next Senator who speaks against expansion take it on its merits, pure and simple. Let him show how the government of such a dependency as the Philippines would tend to destroy the simplicity of our political principles, to burden us with tasks to which we are unsuited, to impose on us vast expenses for which the returns are extremely doubtful, to complicate our domestic problems and to invite foreign difficulties, to weaken our position in American affairs as embodied in the Monroe Doctrine. Let these and other objections to annexation be put forward on their merits, with all the logic and all the eloquence that can be commanded, and let the expansionists be challenged to meet them if they can. If you tell them that their policy is not permitted by the Constitution, all the reply practically necessary is a denial of your assertion; if you waive your right to a Constitutional challenge, and attack their policy on its merits, they are bound to meet you on your own ground and make real answer to your arguments.

## [ASPECTS OF AMERICAN SOCIAL HISTORY, 1897–1904]

Emporia *Gazette;* Springfield *Republican*

### [*Let's Have the Joints*]: *The Gazette,* May 17, 1897

Here are the five joints in town — one at the corner of Sixth and Mechanics, two on Commercial between Third and Fourth Avenues, and two down by the depot. They are nice, clean, respectable joints. They sell good, wholesome, health-giving beer and delicious, bracing, gladsome whiskey. The ladies and gentlemen who conduct these homelike emporiums have high ideals, and their love of the glorious profession of liquor-selling spurs them on to make their places of business cheerful, cosy resorts where tired men and boys may find a few moments' rest from their loved employ each day.

Perhaps the *Gazette* has been wrong in arguing that these joints be closed. If so, here is another proposition: let's have the joints — let them run openly. No city of any importance survives without whiskey selling.

So let's have the joints. Let's license them. Then we can get some money with which to pay policemen to bring our boys and our fathers and our brothers home drunk. It is horrible to see them coming home beastly sober night after night.

Let's have the joints and then we can have some variety in town. An occasional murder — a nice, interesting wife murder that will give us something to talk about. Maybe we could educate some of the boys — if we had joints — so that they would loaf around low dives, and that would make the mothers of the town happy.

By all means, let's have joints, so that some of our girls growing up in Emporia schools may have a chance to marry drunkards and reform them and come running out of their homes in their night dresses to the neighbors for protection a few months after the wedding. Little episodes like this would make life worth living. As it is the town is slow, humdrum, prosy, stupid. Let's have the joints. They are illegal. Their presence violates the law. The dignity of the courts is torn down. Mob law is encouraged. Lawbreaking in other lines is stimulated. Disregard for property rights and other fossil notions of civil integrity are bred. We might have some delightful lynchings, some charming gambling, followed by ennobling embezzlement, if we had the joints.

*[Carrie Nation and Things]*:  *The Gazette*, January 28, 1901.

Carrie Nation is wrong — dead wrong. Many people who are right are wrong. John Brown was. So was Christ, for that matter. Probably if the *Gazette* had been published in Jerusalem 2,000 years ago, it would have stood by the social order and the dignity of the law, and would have cautioned people to keep away from the mob that followed Christ over the country, listening to his spurious doctrine. Probably the *Gazette* would have referred to the Sermon on the Mount as "incendiary talk" delivered to the "ragtag and bobtail yesterday out on Mount Tabor." The *Gazette* also probably would have referred to his charlatan tricks in serving free lunch, and would have advised the people "to keep their heads and not be led into foolishness by an unknown fellow who goes about the country imitating the fakirs of India and stirring up dissension with the established church." . . .

Now, as to Mrs. Nation! She is crazy as a bedbug. There is no doubt about that. And she won't stop the sale of beer by her foolish crusade. Also by appealing to anarchy she discredits the very law which she would have the jointist respect. She has, by her unwomanly conduct, forfeited every claim she may have had to respect as a woman, and she deserves richly everything she has got — and more, too.

But still that is merely her personal side of it. There is also this side: she is giving a great big horse-type object lesson which tells the people in simple, homely words of one syllable that a man who sells whiskey illegally, or a man who encourages him, has no moral right which a white man is bound to respect. It's just as well to keep that lesson in view — even if it takes a crazy woman to carry the banner.

*[Crop Diversification in the West]*: *The Gazette*, July 19, 1901.

The drought, which is a sizzler and frier and boiler, is a good thing for Kansas. It shows the people of the State what Kansas can stand, and never faze her. The drought probably will kill most of the corn and the grass. Fifteen years ago corn and grass made the entire list of Kansas assets. Today Kansas has a dozen other sources of revenue. There are thousands of bushels of old corn in the Kansas cribs. There are thousands of acres of alfalfa and tame grass, which the drought will not destroy. There are millions of chickens and turkeys and dairy cows, which will bring in a big revenue to Kansas farmers without checking on the steer's account. Kansas is not a one-crop State. A drought doesn't hurt Kansas now any more seriously than it hurts Iowa, Missouri, or Indiana.

So brace up, gentle reader. Leave off groaning over the mulligrubs. Stop weeping and wailing and wearing the enamel off your good store teeth. Merchants should stock up. If they don't, Sears, Roebuck, and Montgomery Ward will sell thousands of dollars' worth of truck which should be sold in Emporia.

*[A Negro Burned in Leavenworth]*: *The Gazette*, January 16, 1901.

No possible crime that may be committed justifies cruelty or barbarity in punishing the offender. To exterminate a fiend is the duty of society. To pen up a man who can't pen up his passions is the only protection civilization has. To execute murderers, human beasts, train wreckers, and the like is necessary. But revenge has no place in civilized conduct, and barbarous cruelty in public executions only breeds cruelty and barbarism in private deeds. Leavenworth is a thousand times more dangerous a community to live in than it was before the savage act was performed yesterday. The film of human sympathy is thin enough over the heart of the brute in man at best, and when it is wantonly scraped off by such an act of merciless, vicious, depraved vengeance as that which occurred in Leavenworth yesterday, the animal in man is uncaged, and the community temporarily has gone back to savagery.

The lesson which the mob intended is lost. A mob which could stand by and see a live dog — even a vicious live dog — roasted to death is made hard and cruel and hellish at heart. What must a mob be which could roast a live man to death — no matter what he did! Torture is a reversion to the demon in man. It is as unjustifiable as the crime that prompts torture.

[*On Anarchists*]: *The Gazette*, December 7, 1903.

Anarchists are wrong. Their theory of leveling by destruction is opposed to all principles of building known to science. To level permanently one must build up. There is no other way around it. But —

Supposing the case: Suppose you worked hard till your back ached every night in dirty, grimy work, that made you look like the devil. Suppose the standard of living had been increased — through no apparent fault of yours — so that the best you could get out of a day's work was a little house in an unpleasant part of town, and that your children were not so warmly clad as you would like, and your wife had to go without a girl at those times when it tore your heart to see her bending over the washtub. Suppose that when she was sick she had to work right along, and that death came to her and took her from you when a few dollars at the right time would have saved her. Suppose, then, that when you were at work some man whom you knew came to work at nine o'clock and went away at half-past three, looked at you at your grimy work with that horrible leer of patronizing pity that heartless, spotless men give to their fellows in the mire; suppose that you knew his wife and children were alive by reason of their money; suppose you should overhear a remark which that spotless chap made which indicated that he didn't think of you as a human being, but as a unit of labor, merely a working animal. . . .

In your anguish at death, in your place from below, wouldn't you curse God and man and law and society and the scheme of things?

[*The Supreme Issue: Which?*] *The Republican*, January 29, 1904.

Not long ago a doctor of divinity, writing in a weekly magazine, hit upon the capacity of the American people for crazes and fanaticisms, like Dowieism, as the most formidable peril of the nation. Get rid of the fool isms and civilization is saved — was his view. There are those who differ from him. Senator Lodge seems to regard our supremest danger as unrestricted foreign immigration. Mr. Bryan evidently still believes the gold standard to be the deadliest enemy of the interests of the common people. President Eliot sees our national life almost hanging by a thread for want of a more richly subsidized school system. Rum, in many eyes, is the one over-shadowing curse of mankind. Brooks Adams thinks that Anglo-Saxon civilization depends upon the appropriation or the control of certain vast iron and coal deposits in China by the English-speaking nations. Corsets are, in the opinion of some very estimable persons, the chief issue of the time. And "race suicide" is accounted by others the problem of problems, at least in the best-fed circles of society.

[*One Blow at American Juvenility*]: *The Republican*, January 20, 1904.[1]

The agitation thus early begun in Massachusetts to secure a saner observance of the Fourth of July should have its result on the next celebration of the nation's birthday anniversary. Springfield's experience of last year proved that public sentiment was ready for better things than gunpowder, noise, and lawlessness, with their train of accidents and general nerve prostration. The appeal to local pride was well directed, and while it could not be expected that all would join in the effort to make the celebration a sensible and happy one, a good start was made. It should be possible to improve on the observance from year to year until the hoodlumism and deviltry of a festive few have no place in the day's program.

## THE DEWEY CANDIDACY

*The Nation*, April 12, 1900

At any time from the 1st of May, 1898, to the 3d of October, 1899, Admiral Dewey was in a position to command a nomination to the office of President of the United States by either political party; and by simply holding his peace, he might from that time onward have equally commanded an election at the polls. On the first of these dates the battle of Manila was fought. On the second the admiral had his triumphant reception in New York. There has been no hero as popular, no idol so worshipped, since General Grant received the surrender of Lee's army at Appomattox. Nor was this idolatry based upon mere success in battle. It had a more

[1] The city of Springfield, inspired by Samuel Bowles of the *Republican*, was the leader in the national movement for a safe and sane Fourth.

respectable foundation in the belief that Dewey was a man without political ambition, but not without clear views and convictions concerning the war he was engaged in, and a high purpose to promote the best interests of his own country and of the inhabitants of the Philippine Islands.  His dispatches were models of brevity, clearness, and modesty.  His declaration, more than once repeated, that the Filipinos were better fitted for self-government than the Cubans, and that he spoke from knowledge of both, was hailed with joy by all who were opposed to the subjugation by arms of our late allies.  In short, Admiral Dewey had exhibited those qualities of decorum, equipoise, and sterling sense, in addition to those of the naval hero, which were well calculated to impress the reflecting portion of the community as well as to capture the imaginations of the unthinking.  If he had not come home at all, but had pursued the even tenor of his way, a nomination for the Presidency, and perhaps more than one, would have followed him to the other side of the globe.  He was the terror of the machine politicians, and most especially of the McKinley machine, from the day of Manila until long after his return.

The first thing that opened people's eyes was the signing of the report of the Philippine Commission by Admiral Dewey just before the election of last autumn.  This report was in open conflict with his previously expressed opinions as to the capacity of the Filipinos for self-government.  It was accompanied by no explanation of his change of opinion.  It left those who had admired his previous straightforward course speechless with astonishment and regret. Nor has any explanation yet been offered, but the fact gradually leaked out that he signed the report without reading it, regardless of the fact that the public attached more importance to his share in it than to those of all the other members taken together.  It is needless to say that the Anti-Imperialists had no further interest in Admiral Dewey when they found that he could not be depended upon to stand firm for the opinions he had originally proclaimed. Until the signing of that report, he had the destiny of the country in his hands.  He could have turned it, or rather have held it, true to the principles of self-government.  He did not do so.  What he did was not a conscious betrayal of principle;  it was an act of thoughtlessness which proclaimed him unfit for grave national responsibilities.

The events of the past week have confirmed this view of his character.  He has announced himself a candidate for a Presidential nomination.  When asked which party he prefers and what principles he espouses, he replies that he is at the service of any party, and that it is not for the candidate to frame the party's platform, but to stand on it. The duties of the Presidential office, he thinks, are to execute the laws of Congress, and not to have a policy of his own. He recalls a President who announced that he had a policy and who came to grief in consequence. He knows enough to avoid the example and the fate of Andrew Johnson. He ends by admitting that he is a Democrat.

The manner in which this announcement has been received by the people, has done much to reveal the true political sentiment of the country. The first feeling was that the frank, almost childlike sailor had, by the manner of his reference to the Presidency, cheapened a great office. But did he, after all, do anything more than express in words the theory of the Presidency on which Mr. McKinley has consistently acted? "It's easy enough to be President," said the naïve admiral, after narrowly observing for some months the way in which the present Executive discharges his duties; "all you have to do, I see, is to take orders from Congress, and I have been obeying orders all my life." If Dewey cheapens the Presidency by his conception of it, he is only following the model now in the White House. It is but one more compliment to Mr. McKinley. Mr. Bryan puts the same ideal of the Presidency into his voluble promises to be nothing but the people's "hired man," if he is ever chosen President. . . . Because the main object just now is the restoration of the Presidency to its ancient and intended vigor and dignity; because what we want in the White House is a leader of men, not a tool of tools; because we desire not merely to beat Bryan and McKinley, but to banish their type altogether, we cannot but regard as gratifying the coolness and regret which Admiral Dewey's aspirations have met from the country. A man is wanted more than ever — no crouching figure, stooping low to go under the bars which the politicians raise in front of men of large moral stature; but we sorrowfully perceive that the Admiral is not the man for the hour.

## THE RENOMINATION OF McKINLEY

*The Nation*, June 7, 1900

It is now proposed to renominate for the Presidency the most unmoral of all the occupants of that high office. Time was when public sentiment would not have tolerated the spectacle of a *first* candidacy engineered by the millionaire who had paid the debts of his puppet, and who bought the rotten-borough votes of States in which the party had no other ground for existence than to traffic at nominating conventions, and secure a share of the Federal spoils. But that spectacle is past, and past is another, hardly less revolting

From the New York *Journal*, 1900.

By Frederick B. Opper

McKINLEY, ROOSEVELT, HANNA, AND THE TRUSTS

to the healthy tone of the republic, McKinley's repayment of Hanna with a Senatorship. The same machinery has been set in motion for a second term. The accidental great man who lost the empty honor of the Speakership to win the consolation prize of leader of the House, and so attached his name to a measure not his own, comes smiling to the front, and asks for the seal of party and popular approval after three fateful years of administration.

We have called McKinley unmoral, but our definition of that term would take a paradoxical form. As was said of a certain Swiss folk by one of their countrymen, he is not without morals, but he has no principles. The clergy and high officials who have been lauding him to the skies will hold up their hands at this. Well, let them point to one single line of conduct steadfastly pursued, one single doctrine maintained independently of personal or party interest. Shall it be the currency question? He has lately signed the bill establishing the gold standard for the United States. Did the action give him one ray of pleasure greater than he felt in voting for the free coinage of depreciated silver dollars in November, 1877; or in voting to override Hayes's veto of the Bland-Allison bill in February, 1878; or in voting, in January of the latter year, in favor of Stanley Matthews's concurrent resolution declaring all bonds payable in silver at the option of the government? Notoriously in 1890 he supported the Sherman silver-purchase act, which disastrous measure, by the testimony of Senator Teller and Speaker Reed, was the barter for the tariff bill fathered by him. He openly contended for the use of all our silver product as money. In 1891, he had two voices — that of February, when he accused President Cleveland of dishonoring silver; and that of August, when he opposed free coinage. Again veering, in September, 1893, he sought to embarrass President Cleveland's constraint of Congress to repeal the Sherman Act, and was still condemning the repeal in 1894. On the eve of the St. Louis convention, he was opposed to the 16-to-1 ratio, as he told Mr. Kohlsaat, but equally objected to the use of the word gold in the platform. While ministers were testifying to his churchgoing habits, he either was silent about his real views on the currency, or veiled them in ambiguous language as long as possible. On July 30 he let drop the word gold at Canton, and had the effrontery on August 12 to quote Hayes in favor of sound money. Then, after his election but before he took office, in order to propitiate the Republican silver States, he fell in with Senator Wolcott's scheme for a roving wild-goose European bimetallic mission. Installed as President, he sacrifices currency reform to the tariff, and delays till the tag-end of the session his proposal of a currency commission. Can any candid mind review this revelation of character and conclude that McKinley has had a particle of principle from the beginning to end of the struggle for an honest and stable currency and unsullied national credit?

Consider next his attitude towards civil service reform. It is true that in 1890, as chairman of the Ways and Means Committee, he spoke manfully of the existing law, and held the Republican party to its solemn pledges. Once in the White House, however, he gave notice that his Presidential patronage would be dispensed, not on grounds of fitness, but as per agreement of the Senators immediately concerned. Typical examples of this practise were the appointments of Roberts to be Treasurer of the United States, and Bidwell to be Collector of the Port of New York, both creatures of Platt. To oblige Senator Elkins, he gave the Fish and Fisheries Commissionership to Bowers; and he ratified Hanna's corrupt bargain with Wimberley by which this Louisiana politician got the Collectorship of the Port of New Orleans, in return for having voted at St. Louis for McKinley instead of Reed. For the same reason he made Demas Naval Officer at New Orleans; but this was too much even for the Senate to confirm. The nomination of Hazel to be district judge in western New York is a flaming scandal. It is true that the President, on July 28, 1897, issued an order bringing a large number of new places within the classified service, and forbidding removals in that service except for cause and with charges filed in writing. But it is also true that, in less than six months, his message to Congress foreshadowed that wholesale removal of places from the classified service consummated in May, 1899, without conference with the civil service commissioners, and with no attempt at public justification of it. After this, they must have been confiding indeed who looked for Executive prosecution or censure of the Ohio Republican machine's violation of the law, last November, by soliciting money from Federal officeholders all over the country.

On every question of public policy, McKinley's want of a settled opinion or of good faith has been manifest. In April, 1897, he sent a Jingo and annexation minister to Hawaii, after warning the country in his inaugural address against "the temptation of territorial aggression." He assured the Japanese Minister that no treaty of annexation was in preparation or contemplation; then, in his December message, favored such a treaty, made it an administration measure for the sake of warding off a reciprocity treaty menacing the tariff, and carried it when the war with Spain had paralyzed the power of the country to resist. The Cuban insurrection being on the eve of expiring, he came to its rescue, and declared that forcible annexation would be criminal aggression. When the Philippine insurrection was on the eve of succeeding, he declared taking possession of the islands a responsibility imposed by the Almighty, at whatsoever cost in blood and treasure to victor and vanquished.  He proclaimed it our plain duty to extend our interstate freedom of trade to Porto Rico;  at the command of the protected interests, he took the opposite view with the same bland and righteous expression, and forced the Foraker bill through Congress.  In short, as was said of Queen Elizabeth, "wherever his hand is visible there is always vacillation, infirmity of purpose, and general dishonesty."

His perfidy to the sound money Democrats who insured his election was not more prompt or odious in his coquetting with the silverites than in his using his power for an aggravated protective tariff. The art of cheating the Filipinos of the fruits of victory won at Manila by their assistance, he had learned by Aguinaldoing his political allies at home.  So his excuse for silence about his own convictions, because he would not forestall the party platform (which he was secretly dictating), was a fit precursor of his pretence to have no policy of war or expansion beyond the will of Congress. When that body was not in session, he shaped events so as to preclude its freedom of action and to encourage it to abdicate its function;  when it was in session, he would have everything left to his wisdom and discretion, whether as President or as Commander-in-Chief.  In this way he played fast and loose with the country; disarming suspicion, cooling public sentiment, and gaining time for the imperial mould to set, with commission after commission. He posed as the victim of Destiny in seizing the whole of the Philippine group, although he entered upon the Paris Treaty with intent to demand Luzon alone.   He admitted at Pittsburg, on August 28, 1899, that we had no authority beyond Manila till the treaty was ratified, yet seven weeks in advance of that event he issued, on December 21, 1898, that infamous proclamation of a war of subjugation to the death which even Gen. Otis had to modify in the interest of decency.

That McKinley's renomination, a fortnight hence, is inevitable, we cannot doubt;  nor do we judge the probabilities of his reëlection according to our hopes.

> "It may succeed;  and if our sins should call
> For more than common punishment, it shall."

## REFORM  BY  SOCIAL  STIGMA

*The Nation*, January 18, 1900

What social results may we expect to follow from the recent revelations in the financial and political world?  Will anybody "ostracise" the bankers who went on their knees to Platt to get a government deposit? Will the men who let Payn and Sheehan have enormous loans, with a well-understood political attachment, find their fellows looking askance at them?

Even our political corruptionists we are at last recognizing socially. The moral harm that Gov. Roosevelt and President Low have done by sitting down amicably to breakfast with Platt is incalculable.[1] He was almost as much of a social outcast as Hill, before these social eminences recognized him as an equal. But the power of discrimination in these matters seems almost gone; and our "society" will soon deserve George William Curtis's burlesque account of the rich noodle in Newport, looking about him at the ball and saying complacently and innocently, "Well, I see all the parvenus are here!" The churches have a terrible esponsibility in the matter. Who does not remember the Presbyterian coquetting with Jay Gould? What Protestant church in this city would refuse a present of $50,000 from Platt to support a vested choir? What Catholic church would turn on Croker, bearing gifts, with an indignant "Thy money perish with thee"? The pious Quay has founded a church in Pennsylvania, and we do not doubt, would endow a theological seminary if necessary. At a certain stage of his career every wealthy corruptionist is said to fairly pine for a theological seminary to take his money. And what do the ecclesiastical — yes, and the educational — authorities do in such cases except to imitate the old Scotch minister who told the dying skinflint that he could not guarantee that a gift to the church would save his soul, but that "the experiment was well worth trying"?

But when all this is said, we repeat that President Hadley (in his address at Denver) is on the right track. He speaks for the ideal of society. What society should be is the great moral and reformatory power he alludes to. It should be separate and touch not the unclean thing. It should smite the evil-doer, though he be rich, with open scorn, and pass a decree of perpetual banishment against him. We greatly need a quickening of our social sensitiveness, and the best way to induce it is to show what a power for good it might be made. Matthew Arnold said there could be no human perfection without society; and it is our business to make society the deadly foe of human imperfection, so that illegitimate wealth shall have the brand of social disqualification burned into it, and political tricksters, together with those who strike hands with them and hire them as bravoes and panders, shall be made to lie in social outer darkness.

[1] Roosevelt in his Autobiography states that the "tom-fool reformers" did not see "that my series of breakfasts with Platt always meant that I was going to do something he did not like, and that I was trying, courteously and frankly, to reconcile him to it." But many men refused to regard Platt as a gentleman.

## [AMERICA IN CHINA AND IN THE PHILIPPINES]

*The Nation,* July 26, 1900

Gov. Roosevelt caught up in his speech at St. Paul the idle chatter (to borrow a favorite phrase of his own) of the newspapers about our course in China being on all fours with our course in the Philippines. Conversely, he said, the Anti-Imperialists who condemn what has been done in the Philippines, ought also to condemn, instead of praising as they do, the policy of our country in China. That they do not is simply because they are not "logical," asserted the Rough Rider and the still rougher reasoner. Now, what is our present policy in China? It is, after doing what we can to rescue and protect our own citizens, to find a native government with which we can coöperate, and to which we can turn over responsibility and the work of administration. Secretary Hay has clung to this determination from the start. He has done it in the face of ridicule and opposition, both at home and abroad. Where was his Chinese Government? If none existed, we must create one. The idea of division and of foreign control of local government was monstrous. It would mean millions of treasure and rivers of blood. We must stand on one side and let China be governed by the Chinese. To that ultimate policy this country, and with it apparently the European Powers, is committed. But did we search for a native government in the Philippines? Yes, but only to strangle it! Did we look anxiously for native leaders able to take up the work of local administration? Yes, but only to hunt them to the mountains like wild beasts! If we could discover such a body in China now, we should declare it a crime against civilization for the Powers not to utilize and support it. But we wiped the Malolos Congress out of existence. What we profess to be seeking in China with the deepest anxiety, we had ready to our hands in the Philippines, and there raged against it and destroyed it as if *we* had been Boxers.

## A SOCRATIC DIALOGUE [1]

*The Nation,* July 12, 1900

"I think I got some capacity for cross-examining witnesses, which was very useful to me afterwards, from reading Plato's dialogues and getting familiar with Socrates's method of reducing a sophist *ad absurdum.*" — (Senator George F. Hoar in his *Scribner* article on "Harvard College Fifty-eight Years Ago.")

SOCRATES REDIVIVUS — Well met, Gorgias. I have been anxious to hear you explain, as your friends tell me you can with an unrivalled

[1] Senator George F. Hoar of Massachusetts had opposed the acquisition of the Philippines, but he supported McKinley for reëlection in 1900.

mastery of the rhetor's art, a passage in your oration to the Ephors which puzzled my poor understanding.

GORGIAS HODIERNUS — What passage was that, Socrates?

SOCRATES — The one where you said that it was "due to Mr. Bryan, more than to any other man," that the treaty of Paris was not defeated, or at least amended so as to put the Philippines on the same basis as Cuba.

GORGIAS — It is true, Socrates, I made that statement to the Ephors, and by Ammon, the god of Cyrene, I will defend and maintain it in all places.

SOCRATES — Then you would say that a man who does not defeat an evil deed is more guilty than the man who plans and carries it through by all the means in his power?

GORGIAS — What do you mean, Socrates? What I said is clear and certain. If Mr. Bryan had not persuaded the Democratic Ephors, the treaty would have been rejected or amended. Therefore the guilt is on his head.

SOCRATES — Well, let us follow the argument, Gorgias. Who is the real housebreaker, the man who plots a violent entry for robbery, or the man who fails to eject him?

GORGIAS — It would be the former, Socrates.

SOCRATES — And you would say the same of political robbers?

GORGIAS — I do not know what you mean, Socrates.

SOCRATES — Well, I would ask you what you would say if a Spartan general should agree with a Persian satrap to corrupt the Lacedemonian state by introducing Persian customs — whom would you blame, that general or a private citizen who weakly acquiesced in his plot?

GORGIAS — The general would be the man, Socrates.

SOCRATES — That is, you distinguish between the principal and the accessory?

GORGIAS — All men do, Socrates.

SOCRATES — Then, by the dog of Egypt, tell me who was the principal in the matter of the Paris treaty. Was it Mr. Bryan?

GORGIAS — No, but he frustrated the attempt to defeat it.

SOCRATES — But President McKinley might have frustrated the treaty itself, might he not? He negotiated it, did he not? When you were opposing its ratification, he was urging it, night and day, was he not?

GORGIAS — I cannot deny it.

SOCRATES — Then, in the name of Zeus and Athene at once, how can you, who denounce the accessory, praise the principal? How can you say that the man who is chiefly responsible for what you describe as an attempt to "change our republic into an empire," is the "best beloved President who ever sat in the chair of Washington"?

GORGIAS — But I expressly said that I had never questioned the honesty of purpose of President McKinley.

SOCRATES — Yes, but you do question Mr. Bryan's honesty?

GORGIAS — How so, Socrates?

SOCRATES — You said you thought he wanted the treaty ratified so as to "keep the question for an issue in the campaign."

GORGIAS — Yes, I said that, Socrates.

SOCRATES — But how could the deed of an honest and beloved President be an issue in the campaign?

GORGIAS — It might seem, nevertheless, bad for the state.

SOCRATES — Then an honest and beloved man might yet ruin the republic?

GORGIAS — That is so, Socrates.

SOCRATES — A dishonest and hated man might save it?

GORGIAS — It would seem so.

SOCRATES — Then it is better to be right than to be beloved?

GORGIAS — Better in a public man, I admit. Mr. Bryan, however, was both wrong and disliked. He was for ratifying the treaty, and that meant a continuation of the war.

SOCRATES — Yet he said he wanted to end the war, did he not?

GORGIAS — He did.

SOCRATES — And he urged his friends to vote for the joint resolution putting the Philippines on the same footing as Cuba?

GORGIAS — Even so, Socrates.

SOCRATES — And they did so?

GORGIAS — They did.

SOCRATES — You voted for it yourself?

GORGIAS — Assuredly, Socrates.

SOCRATES — And it would have ended the war, if adopted, and prevented the republic from becoming an empire?

GORGIAS — I have no doubt of it.

SOCRATES — Yet McKinley was against it? All his friends among the Ephors were against it? It was defeated only by the casting vote of the Vice-President? Are not all these things so?

GORGIAS — They are.

SOCRATES — Then must you not admit that Bryan and his friends wanted to end the war and save the republic, and that McKinley and his friends were really the ones who prolonged the war and threaten now to convert our state into an empire?

GORGIAS — No, Socrates, I do not admit it. By Here, I never will admit that!

SOCRATES — But why not, if truth and argument compel you?

GORGIAS — Because I am a Republican, Socrates.

# PART FOUR

# THE AMERICAN PRESS AND PUBLIC OPINION
## 1900–1928

# THE AMERICAN PRESS AND PUBLIC OPINION

## 1900–1928

Since 1900 American journalism has been largely transformed by a half dozen sweeping tendencies. The publication of newspapers, especially in large cities, has become a capitalistic enterprise involving large protective resources, a heavy dependence on advertising, and a fierce competition for the circulation upon which advertising is based. One result has been a disproportionate emphasis upon the business side of journalism, overshadowing the editorial side. Another has been a steady process of consolidation, crushing out newspaper after newspaper in the large cities, giving national prominence to such a wrecker of journals as Frank Munsey, who destroyed six in New York City alone, and leaving many cities with but one morning publication. Newspaper chains have sprung into prosperity, some owned by individuals, like Munsey and Hearst, and some by companies organized upon a joint-stock basis, like the Scripps-Howard (formerly the Scripps-McRae) chain. Few new journals have come into existence. The most remarkable of these have been the tabloid newspapers, which first appeared immediately after the World War — the *Illustrated Daily News* in New York was founded in June, 1919 — and which achieved a popular success in inverse ratio to their merits, either as news media or organs of opinion. Among the better tendencies of the time have been astonishing mechanical advances; an increased breadth of appeal; and a new professional consciousness, manifested in the creation of excellent schools of journalism, in a more rigid self-respect, and in organized efforts to protect journalism against "propaganda" and unclean or dishonest advertising.

The general commercial tendency of the time, and the extinction of many newspapers of old repute and influence, have led some observers to take a dark view of the relation between the press and public opinion. They complain that the forces of the period are unfavorable to powerful editors; that large sections of the country are without any fresh, intellectual, and independent imprint upon the public mind; and that the influence of the press is visibly declining. While there is much to support these views, they are often overstated. The most pessimistic of the critics commonly underestimate the number of really good editorial organs today; they invariably exaggerate the merit of the newspapers of the past, drawing too roseate a picture of the good old times of the editorial giants — Greeley, Raymond, Bryant, and Dana. Actually there has never been a time when the American newspaper press did not excite any number of Catos and Jeremiahs. John Adams in 1800 and Thomas Jefferson in 1810 spoke of it as the prey of a pack of malignant, ignorant, and mendacious scribblers. A generation later the penny papers, the *Sun* and *Herald*, were the detestation of all moral and educated people, while the slangwhanging of party organs like the *Globe* and *Telegraph* somehow seemed to make journalism a field for rowdies rather than gentlemen. In Civil War days the flightiness of Greeley, the lukewarm temper of the *Times*, and the frequent thinness of the *Evening Post*, aroused constant criticism; and after the conflict Dana's *Sun*, so often eulogized today, was reprobated and attacked on every hand. Godkin spoke in the harshest tones of the press as it existed in 1860, and in the nineties, viewing its new "yellow" phases, he believed that it was rapidly going to utter perdition.

The renascence of the New York *Times*, which has been perhaps the most important single feature of American journalism since 1900, has counted for more in the news field than editorially; yet even in the latter it has been of far-reaching value. When Adolph S. Ochs, a Chattanooga newspaperman, assumed control in 1896, the *Times* had fallen upon evil days, its net circulation being only 9,000, and its influence negligible. By enterprise, shrewdness, and emphasis upon sound quality, Mr. Ochs pushed the circulation above 100,000 by 1901, and above 200,000 by the end of 1903; while a quarter century later it was steadily approaching an average of 450,000. Unlike many of his competitors, the owner rigidly excluded mere features, mere entertainment, and mere frills. His policy was to furnish information — which comprehended not only ordinary news but book reviews, magazine articles, and criticism of music, art, and drama — and editorial comment, and to offer them quietly, conservatively, and accurately. He insisted that the *Times* should at all costs be an "independent newspaper," which would "tolerate no tampering with the news, no coloring, no deception," and that it should stand preëminent "for the fullness, trustworthiness, and impartiality of its news service." Always a little fuller than its rivals, always prompt, always ready to sacrifice advertising space to public documents in order to be a newspaper of record, the *Times* has acquired the most truly national circulation in American history, and has become an educational institution of unsurpassed value — in some respects the foremost newspaper not merely of America, but of the globe.

Under one editor of sound common sense, Charles R. Miller, and another of high intellectual distinction, Rollo Ogden, the editorial page of the *Times* has perfectly accorded with its news columns. It has not been aggressively liberal; it has never been imbued with a crusading spirit; in some issues presented by labor troubles and even governmental corruption it has seemed excessively conservative; but in the main it has been upon the right side, and its utterances have carried increasing weight. For one cause, the cause of an American policy of international coöperation, the *Times* has fought with a devotion and effectiveness not surpassed by any other newspaper; and it has never ceased its vigilance for the betterment of State and municipal administration. In politics it has been staunchly independent. But in those years since 1910 during which most highly capitalized and business-colored newspapers have been Republican, the *Times* — largely because of its belief in the League of Nations and in international coöperation — has tended to take the Democratic side.

While the *Times* was becoming preëminent in the treatment of news, the New York *World* was assuming a similar primacy in that field of aggressive editorial leadership which Joseph Pulitzer had marked out for it. During the nineties and later Pulitzer's nervous energy and quick, unresting brain were the life of the *World*, even though he was blind and an invalid. The newspaper was fortunate in that, when he died, there was at hand an editor of rare sturdiness, courage, and force. Frank I. Cobb was selected by Pulitzer himself: a young Detroit journalist whose simple and vigorous style could take on a sledge-hammer force when he was aroused. The two men were of contrasting type, for Cobb had none of Pulitzer's extraordinary mental agility and subtlety, as Pulitzer lacked Cobb's directness, bluntness, and intuitive political sense. In remarkable degree, Cobb had the elemental, homely, telling qualities which gave Cobbett and Greeley their greatness; he was a writer of more self-control and consistency than the Englishman, and of far steadier wisdom in matters of statesmanship than the founder of the *Tribune*, but in important respects he resembled both. During the dozen years that he was in chief control of the *World*, he accustomed his readers to look each morning for a forthright and emphatic leader which rendered some aspect of the central question of the day as clear as light, and expressed the paper's opinion upon it with precision and emphasis. He was honest, he was fair-minded, he was enthusiastic in his likes and hatreds, and he hated a trimmer; no one went to the *World* for an elaborate and profound analysis of public questions, for that was beyond his power, or for a fine literary style, for at that he did not aim; but for the forcible expression of a simple, logical opinion he was in his own generation unapproachable.

More than that, Cobb and his associates fought the *World* as a good captain and his crew fight a battleship. When the newspaper undertook a crusade, like the exposure of Roosevelt's course in the Panama affair, or the attack on Republican campaign finances in 1904, or the assault upon the crooked management of the New York, New Haven & Hartford in 1912, or the battle for the League of Nations in 1918–19, every department was called into action. That had been one of Joseph Pulitzer's chief contributions to journalism, and it was one of the chief of the factors which continued to make the *World* a national power. In the various successive fights for decent government in New York, under Mayors McClellan, Gaynor, Mitchel, and Hylan, Cobb was always in the forefront, and in so complicated and technical a matter as the ratification of the dual subway contracts his opposition was later completely justified by events. During the World War he stood close to President Wilson, who wrote later that he valued his "peculiar genius for giving direct and effective expression to the enlightened opinions which he held," and that he considered his death an irreparable loss "to the liberal political policies which are necessary to liberate mankind from the errors of the past and the partizan selfishness of the present." The *World* did not hesitate upon occasion to disagree with Wilson, as when it criticized some of his Cabinet appointments, and his blunder in calling in 1918 for the election of a Democratic Congress. But in spite of being nominally independent, after 1908 it swung steadily toward the position of the chief Democratic journal of the nation. Upon the death of Cobb in 1925, control of the *World's* editorial page passed into the hands of one of the most brilliant younger men of journalism, Walter Lippmann, and it gained rather than lost in vigor.

The one other metropolitan newspaper of high distinction in this period, the *Evening Post*, was edited from 1903 to 1920 by Rollo

Ogden, and for four years thereafter by Simeon Strunsky; intellectual and rather austerely liberal, in the Godkin tradition, it had during much of this period the best-rounded and most brilliant editorial staff in the country. By 1912 this staff included with Mr. Ogden and Mr. Strunsky, Alexander Dana Noyes, Fabian Franklin, Royal J. Davis, Paul Elmer More, and Harold DeWolfe Fuller. The sale of the *Evening Post* to Cyrus W. Curtis of Philadelphia marked its eclipse after almost a full century of uninterrupted eminence in American journalism. A similar eclipse overtook the Springfield *Republican* shortly after the death of the third Samuel Bowles in 1915, although the journal remained in the possession of the Bowles family. He had been, in his retiring way, only a less able editor than his father, and under him the Republican had been admired from the Atlantic to the Pacific as a remarkably scrupulous, incisive, and informed newspaper, while it had furnished perhaps the best journalistic training school in the country. But in partial compensation there occurred, in the second decade of the century, a sudden and refreshing resurrection of two Baltimore newspapers, the morning and evening *Sun*. This resurrection was begun by Charles H. Grasty, who drew to the papers an able staff and gave them his own vision of independence, integrity, and enterprise, but who was himself shortly forced by business antagonisms to retire. By 1925 the morning *Sun* in especial was one of the most liberal and intelligent of American newspapers, widely known for its trenchant editorials, for the contributions of H. L. Mencken, and for the political articles of Frank Kent.

Western journalism was meanwhile producing an admirable small-city newspaper in William Allen White's *Emporia Gazette*, and another of somewhat lesser, more uneven merit in Edward W. Howe's Atchison *Globe*. Both White and Howe were men of unusual literary gifts, who have written fiction of enduring value. The former became editor of the *Gazette* in 1895, attracted national attention a year later by his swinging answer to the inquiry, "What's the matter with Kansas?", and developed a burly, genial, neighborly personality which endeared him to a wide audience. Loving his profession of country editor, to him Emporia was a microcosm of the world. He liked the opportunity his editorial chair gave him of surveying human weaknesses and virtues, of being teacher and helper to the whole community, of expressing his own audacious opinion today upon some problem which affected a single family or block, and tomorrow upon some issue of world importance. His informality, the trait of a really great and transparently sincere personality, was captivating, and in combination with his spontaneous literary talent, enabled him to touch chords of humor and pathos, and to rise to occasional levels of literary beauty, which would have been quite impossible under the restraints of ordinary urban journalism. In his outlook upon national affairs, he began as a conservative, but rapidly worked around to a vigorous political and social insurgency, which in turn gave way to a philosophic tolerance of liberal stamp. "Ed" Howe's *Globe*, which the Atchison "philosopher" controlled until 1911, showed a different set of qualities and never gained quite the repute of its neighbor; for its editor's distinction lay in his satiric gift, and his editorials and epigrams had a sardonic flavor which slightly repelled outsiders where William Allen White's frankness and dash of sentiment attracted them.

As the intellectual force and leadership of the daily newspaper seemed to lessen, a greater importance was attained by the weekly journal of opinion. Among the early evidences of this tendency was the appearance of several weekly organs of special shades of political opinion, established by men or organizations who lacked the capital to control newspapers. W. J. Bryan's *Commoner* (founded in 1900) for some time stood alone, but was followed by *La Follette's Magazine*, by the radical labor weekly *Solidarity*, and in 1911 by Max Eastman's socialist weekly *The Masses*. Each of these had its devoted following, and gave salutary expression to a definite set of news. The greatest influence in the weekly field, however, remained that wielded by publications of a broader character and appeal.

In this weekly journalism the period was marked by the total disappearance of *Harper's Weekly*, by a succession of changes in the character of the *Outlook* (which reached the height of its influence when Roosevelt became a "contributing editor"), by the transformation of the *Nation* into an aggressively radical publication, and by the founding of the *New Republic*. The last-named weekly, edited by Herbert Croly and a brilliant staff, came into existence in the closing months of 1914, just after the commencement of the World War. It announced itself simply as "an experiment," "a journal of opinion which seeks to meet the challenge of the new time." Actually it represented, in large part, the faith which had animated the founders of the Progressive Party, and stood for an advanced programme of social legislation, and for a stern effort to bring corporate greed under control. Always aloof from old-party entanglements, and supporting even Woodrow Wilson in a cautiously critical spirit, it appealed to a comparatively small body of intellectuals, and like the old *Nation*, affected general public opinion chiefly by indirect means. Yet it contained some of the best, if not the very best, editorial writing of the World War period and afterwards, and an examination of its files must impress every student with the sanity of its observations, and the accuracy with which later events bore out those interpretations which looked toward the future. Sanity and balance were qualities which the *Nation*, after Oswald Garrison Villard took complete control in 1916 and cast off the old connection with the *Evening Post*, often seemed to lack; and yet its insurgent spirit, its courage in protest, and its eloquence in behalf of the victims of brute strength or of thoughtless clamor, made it invaluable. Even when it was clearly wrong it was often of public benefit in arousing men to thought and to doubt.

At the other pole from the *Nation* the *Weekly Review*, which enjoyed a brief existence under Fabian Franklin and Harold DeWolfe Fuller, espoused the conservative side in the great issues of the post-war period. Also short-lived, the *Freeman*, edited by Albert Jay Nock, Francis Neilson, Van Wyck Brooks, and others from March, 1920, to March, 1924, was nominally a single tax organ. Actually, in its brilliantly erratic way, it was a radical publication (the editors preferred the word "liberal"), devoted to sharp criticism of the political and social order, attacking any movement toward European "entanglements," and displaying a somewhat capricious sarcasm in its treatment of both the Wilson and Harding Administrations. Its chief merits were the admirably crisp and pungent style of its sophisticated political articles, and the elegance and penetration of its literary criticism. Its influence was far slighter than that of either the *New Republic* or Mr. Villard's *Nation*, but its extinction was regretted by many even of those who read it only to take issue with its views.

Throughout the nation at large, in this period, the number of newspapers which attracted attention by displaying qualities of editorial independence and leadership was deplorably small; and it was noted as one of the grave evils of the time that the extinction of competition in many cities was accompanied by the disappearance of aggressive opinion. Journals which were to be bought by Democrats and Republicans, by poor and rich, by liberals and conservatives alike, had to refrain from anything but the most tepid and neutral editorial expression. Here and there a newspaper, for a longer or shorter time, stood out above its contemporaries. One was the Fresno *Republican*, ably edited for years by Chester Rowell in a manner recalling its namesake of Springfield. Another was the San Francisco *Bulletin* under Fremont Older, a crusading editor with a steadfast vision of social justice, who later was compelled to remove to the *Call*, a Hearst publication, but who refused to be quenched even there. Another was the Omaha *World-Herald*, a Democratic sheet ably edited, under the guidance of Senator Gilbert M. Hitchcock, in a Republican region; and still another, which has become one of the lights of present-day journalism in America, is the St. Louis *Post-Dispatch*, a property of the Pulitzer family animated by the same spirit as the New York *World*. In one special category, a place of honor must be given to the *Christian Science Monitor*, an unconventionally edited journal of high intellectual quality; in another special field, that of the foreign language press, equal distinction has been achieved by the *Vorwärts* of New York, a Yiddish journal that has become a great racial institution. These newspapers have been among the encouraging features of a period in which there is all too much that is discouraging.

## JUSTICE TO THE POPULISTS [1]

*The Commoner*, March 29, 1901

The Populist party, ridiculed by the Republicans and denounced by the Gold Democrats, has really been a great educator. It is an historical fact that many political organizations have been influential in moulding public opinion, even though they have never secured control of the federal government. The Populists have never had at any time more than a score of members of Congress, and yet they have given an impetus to several reforms which must ultimately be accomplished.

For years the Democrats preached tariff reform in States like Kansas, Nebraska, Colorado, and the Dakotas, but they seemed to make little progress because Republican prejudice was a barrier to Democratic doctrines. The Populists did not denounce a protective tariff in their platform, but in attacking the Republican party they weakened the protective sentiment among their members, and today tariff reform is much stronger in the West than it would have been without the assistance of Populism. The Wilson Bill, the only tariff reform measure passed since the war, could not have passed without the aid of Populist votes in the Senate.

The first national platform written by the Populists demanded

[1] By William Jennings Bryan.

the election of United States Senators by a direct vote of the people. That was before the matter received serious attention in Congress, but since then the House of Representatives has three times adopted a resolution proposing the necessary amendment. In 1900 the Democratic platform endorsed this reform, and it is now receiving the support of many prominent papers which until recently have been silent upon the subject or opposed to the change.

The Populist party is an advocate of the system known as the initiative and referendum, whereby the people can compel the submission of important questions and pass upon the acts of legislatures. This reform has been endorsed by many Democratic State conventions and was last year approved by the national convention of the party. South Dakota, at the 1898 election, adopted an amendment providing for the initiative and referendum, in spite of the fact that the Republicans carried the State by a considerable majority. Even more recently, a Republican legislature in Oregon has given its endorsement to direct legislation.

The Populists, as might be expected, oppose imperialism and trusts. They also unite with the Democrats in favoring arbitration and condemning government by injunction and the blacklist.

No one who understands the history of the last ten years can doubt the influence which the Populist party has exerted upon public affairs. It has been a great educational factor and the Democratic party has strengthened rather than weakened itself by endorsing a number of propositions which are called "Populistic." To repudiate our Populist allies and surrender to the corporate influences which now dominate the Republican party would be as impolitic as it would be unpatriotic. The Democratic party has no reason for existence except to champion the cause of the people; it must stand ready to coöperate with those who are fighting organized greed.

## "AT THE BAR OF HISTORY" [1]

*The Nation*, July 4, 1901

After keeping us for more than three years in the dark, the Administration has at last deigned to publish the diplomatic correspondence leading up to the war with Spain. This was at first promised in connection with the President's war message of April 11, 1898; but on second thought, it was stated, Mr. McKinley determined that it would not be "prudent" to give out the documents at that time. As we read them now, it is easy to agree that

[1] The facts contained in this harsh indictment of McKinley are accepted by many historians, including James Ford Rhodes, as proving that the Spanish War would have been found avoidable by a President of marked strength and determination.

it would have been a piece of terrible imprudence to give them to the world then, since they prove that the war was needless. This tardy publication of the dispatches makes it impossible to deny what, in fact, Minister Woodford and Senator Hoar and Congressman Boutelle openly asserted in 1898, that there would have been no war but for the violence of Congress and the weakness of the President. From the official correspondence we learn the truth of the statement made by Mr. Boutelle in explanation of his vote against the war — namely, that "Spain had conceded nearly every one of our demands, and seemed plainly disposed to meet them all," so that, but for the insane fury of Congress, before which Mr. McKinley fell terrorized, we should, as Minister Woodford said publicly in Boston in October, 1898, have seen the Spanish flag leave Cuba "without the firing of a shot or the loss of a life."

The proof is very simple. It lies on the face of the dispatches. Passing by all preliminaries, we find Secretary Day on March 27, 1898, telegraphing instructions to Minister Woodford to make three demands:

> First. Armistice until October 1. Negotiations meanwhile looking for peace between Spain and insurgents through friendly offices of President United States.
> Second. Immediate revocation of reconcentrado order.
> Add, if possible,
> Third. If terms of peace not satisfactorily settled by October 1, President of the United States to be final arbiter between Spain and insurgents.

Now what followed? On March 31 the reconcentrado order was revoked, and a special credit of 3,000,000 pesetas put at the disposal of Governor-General Blanco to care for the homeless Cubans. There was our demand number two promptly complied with. The offer to concede demand number one was cabled by Minister Woodford on April 5. It is the critical dispatch of the whole volume, and its suppression until now certainly shows an extraordinary degree of "prudence," and possibly something else, in the President. We publish it in full, and we ask for it the careful attention of those clergymen and church people who were driving Congress on to war:

"Should the Queen proclaim the following before twelve o'clock noon of Wednesday, April 6, will you sustain the Queen and can you prevent hostile action by Congress?

> At the request of the Holy Father, in this Passion Week and in the name of Christ, I proclaim immediate and unconditional suspension of hostilities in the Island of Cuba.

This suspension is to become immediately effective so soon as accepted by the insurgents of the island and is to continue for the space of six months, to the fifth day of October, eighteen ninety-eight.

I do this to give time for passions to cease, and in the sincere hope and belief that, during this suspension, permanent and honorable peace may be obtained between the insular Government of Cuba and those of my subjects in the island who are now in rebellion against the authority of Spain.

I pray the blessing of Heaven upon this Truce of God, which I now declare in His name, and with the sanction of the Holy Father of all Christendom.

April 5, 1898.

"Please read this in the light of all my previous telegrams and letters. I believe that this means peace, which the sober judgment of our people will approve long before next November, and which must be approved at the bar of final history.

"I permit the papal nuncio to read this telegram, upon my own responsibility, and without committing you in any manner. I dare not reject this last chance for peace. I will show your reply to the Queen in person, and I believe that you will approve this last conscientious effort for peace."

What could be more moving, more pathetic, more like an unexpected messenger of peace to be greeted with devout thankfulness by all Christian hearts? But how did President McKinley greet it? Why, he telegraphed Minister Woodford that he "highly appreciated the Queen's desire for peace," but that he could not "assume to influence the action of the American Congress." Yet if an armistice were offered, he would "communicate that fact to Congress." Yes, but how did he communicate it? Did he cite a syllable of the pious and exalted language of the Queen? Did he explain how the venerable head of the Catholic Church had exerted himself to prevent a wicked war? No, he simply added a couple of vague paragraphs at the very end of his message. Read the passionate, eager words of the Queen of Spain, read the solemn exhortations of Minister Woodford, and then read how President McKinley presented the matter to Congress:

Yesterday, and since the preparation of the foregoing message, official information was received by me that the latest decree of the Queen Regent of Spain directs Gen. Blanco, in order to prepare and facilitate peace, to proclaim a suspension of hostilities, the duration and details of which have not yet been communicated to me.

This fact, with every other pertinent consideration, will, I am sure, have your just and careful attention in the solemn deliberations upon which you are about to enter. If this measure attains a successful result, then our aspirations as a Christian, peace-loving people will be realized. If it fails, it will be only another justification for our contemplated action.

Congress, of course, paid not the slightest attention to this perfunctory tail-end of a message, all the previous trend and argument of which made for war. What the President should have done was to throw away the message which he had prepared, face the altered situation with an altered policy, and go boldly to the country with Woodford's dispatch, including the Queen's elevated proclamation. He could have truly hailed it as a great triumph of American diplomacy. Our two categorical demands were both granted, and the third conditional one would easily follow. The President could have appealed irresistibly to the sober sentiment of the country. He could have especially appealed to our Catholic population, on the strength of the Queen's references to religious motives, and the sanction of the Pope. He could have made peace certain. But alas, the "stop-watch" of Congress was held on him, he had promised his excited and alarmed fellow-partisans to send in a war message and not let the Democrats win an advantage, and so "this last conscientious effort for peace," as Minister Woodford called it, this grandest opportunity that ever came to a Christian President, was miserably neglected and the war ensued.

General Woodford urged President McKinley to think not only of "November" (that is, the election which the Republicans feared the Democrats would win if a war was not forced), but of "the bar of final history." It is to that tribunal, of course, that the cause must now go. After all the shouting and the flattery have died away, the historian will settle down to the documentary evidence concerning the Spanish War, and impartially and fearlessly assign praise or blame. We know, for example, what the historians now say of Polk and the Mexican War.[1] Will not their verdict on McKinley and the war with Spain be fully as unpleasant reading fifty years from now? We fear so. Partisan newspapers today will not even print the evidence. A busy and careless people will not read it. But history will do its whole duty, will let nothing escape it, will weigh motive and opportunity and responsibility, and will fix the stigma of cowardice, the shame of weak yielding to clamor, where it belongs; and will do it with the serenity and the certainty of all-judging Jove.

[1] In 1900 historians still took the view that the Mexican War was unjustifiably provoked by the Polk Administration. But later research, and particularly the books of George L. Rives and Justin Smith, have changed that view. The war is now generally held to have been justifiable and unavoidable. Numerous historians take the same view of the Spanish War.

By W. A. Rogers

"THE FIRST SPADEFUL"

From *Harper's Weekly*, 1903.

## PEGASUS IN POUND

New York *Sun*, July 28, 1901

Many students of contemporary American literature believe that Indiana is now its centre. Nowhere else in the United States is the output so rich and various in quality or so filling in quantity in proportion to population. Names like Wallace, Riley, Tarkington, Major may be said to be on every lip and on many billboards, and there are other Indiana authors who are not much less famous and revered. What lover of American poetry does not know by heart the works of Mr. James Byron Elmore of Alamo? He cultivates a farm as well as poetry. He also cultivates independence. Booksellers, those proverbial grinders of the faces of poets, are not allowed to come between him and the profits of the muse. He sells his books from door to door. Thus he shows himself to be a true descendant of the old minstrels and rhapsodists, the travelling men of song.

Far different from them, however, he is a solid citizen. He has a stake in the soil. His itinerary is but an avocation or a whim. His most pleasing poems, if not his greatest, are bucolic or idyllic. In the spring thousands of Hoosiers take his "Ode to Sassafras" as a delightful substitute for "spring medicine" or (cursed?) "sarsaparil." Read a stanza and be cheered and cured:

> "*In the spring of the year, when blood is too thick,*
> *There is nothing so rare as a sassafras stick;*
> *It cleans up the liver and regulates the heart*
> *And to the whole system new life doth impart.*
> *Sassafras, oh, sassafras,*
> *Thou art the stuff for me,*
> *And in the spring I love to sing,*
> *Sweet sassafras, of thee.*"

We defy anyone to read the last four lines without remembering them forever. They have the true haunting, magical melody. They are much better than any other kind of medicine. Yet in the opinion of some members of the Indianapolis Elmore Club, "Bessie, the Belle of Alamo," is more satisfactory. Here begins a fit:

> *Bessie, the belle of Alamo,*
> *She never flirts with transient people,*
> *Or swings on the gate for show,*
> *But lures by charms becoming*
> *The belle of Alamo.*

The news columns of the Indianapolis *Journal* are incorrect in describing Mr. Elmore as "best known as the poet-historian of the wreck on the Monon which so tangled up the plans of Tom Miaco's burlesque company, the members of which were passengers on the wrecked train." It is in the poem in which the wreck will go down through the ages that Mr. Elmore so impressively says:

> *"And in among the wreck I see*
> *A man that's pinned down by the knee,*
> *And hear him calmly for to say,*
> *Cut, oh, cut my leg away."*

Mr. Elmore will go down through the ages with his "Love Under the Mistletoe and Other Poems" in his hand; and "Cut, oh, cut my leg away" is in his first imitative manner, an unconscious reminiscence of "Take, oh, take those lips away." "Sassafras," and "Bessie of Alamo" are his greatest and most original works.

Prosaic and commonplace people are too likely to have a prejudice against poets, whom they call visionary and flighty. Will it be believed that Mr. Elmore's own brother, Jake, is having him prosecuted for breaking the Sunday law by tapping his sugar trees on Sunday? But right beats spite. No justice or jury will believe that so sweet a poet is obliged to tap sugar trees on Sunday or any other day.

## A PROPHECY THAT FAILED[1]

*The Commoner,* November 22, 1901

In the campaign of 1900 the Republican leaders denied that their party contemplated a permanent increase in the standing army. They asserted that a large army was necessary only because of the insurrection in the Philippines, and they boldly declared that the insurrection would cease immediately if the Republican ticket was successful. The Democratic platform and Democratic speakers were blamed for the prolongation of the war. "Just re-elect President McKinley," they said, "and let the Filipinos know they are not to have independence, and they will lay down their arms and our soldiers can come home."

Well, the Republican ticket was elected, and the Filipinos were notified that they were not to have independence, but a month after the election the Republicans rushed through Congress a bill authorizing the President to raise the regular army to 100,000, and

[1] To Bryan, editor of *The Commoner,* in 1900 imperialism had been the "paramount issue"; and he largely devoted his weekly to attacking it.

now, after a year has elapsed, the insurrection is still in progress and the end is not yet. Some of the worst losses of the year have been suffered by our troops within two months. General Chaffee reports that the Filipinos have profited by the deception practised upon them when Aguinaldo was trapped. He says that "insurgent soldiers in ordinary civilian dress have lurked about and among American garrisons," and he adds that "with deceptive cunning they obtained credentials from American authorities." We were assured a year ago that only a small fraction of the Filipinos were hostile to the American government. We were told that the great majority of the Filipinos welcomed the American government and were glad to be made subjects. The Chicago *Times-Herald* quotes General Chaffee as saying that "the whole people of the Philippines are engaged in waging war upon the United States." The *Times-Herald* (a Republican paper) adds: "The Filipinos who are friendly to the United States are said to be those holding office, and the officers who discussed the situation today assert that their loyalty will continue only so long as they have the opportunity of drawing American dollars."

After the Republican victory made it impossible for the imperialists to blame the anti-imperialists for the continuation of hostilities, the Republican leaders declared that Aguinaldo, actuated by selfish ambition, was compelling his countrymen to continue the war. But even after his capture and imprisonment — yes, even after his captors had secured from him an address advising his comrades to surrender — the insurrection continued. How long will it take the imperialists to learn that we can never have peace in the Philippine Islands? That we can suppress open resistance is certain, although the cost may be far beyond any gain that can be derived from a colonial government, but that we can ever make the Filipinos love us or trust us while we rule them through a carpetbag government, is absurd.[1]

If the Republicans had read the speeches of Abraham Lincoln as much recently as they did in former years, they would have known that hatred of an alien government is a natural thing and

[1] It is estimated that during three years of warfare between the Americans and the Philippine insurgents, some hundreds of thousands of Filipinos died from famine and pestilence. In March, 1901, Gen. Frederick Funston captured Aguinaldo. But resistance continued for many months, with much cruelty on both sides. On July 4, 1902, Roosevelt officially declared the islands pacified. Bryan expressed a resentment which many Americans felt. Particularly did the methods of some soldiers, like "Hell-roaring Jake Smith," excite indignation. Smith ordered his men to "kill everything over ten." For this he was courtmartialed and placed on the retired list. For some years the Moros remained exceedingly restive. The first civil governor of the islands, William H. Taft, was inaugurated on July 4, 1901. Thereafter a program of education and internal development was carried out.

a thing to be expected everywhere.  Lincoln said that it was God himself who placed in every human heart the love of liberty. Lincoln spoke the truth.  Love of liberty is linked to life itself and "whom God hath joined together let no man put asunder."

## [YELLOW JOURNALISM AND ANARCHY] [1]

Brooklyn *Eagle*, September 11, 1901

The journalism of anarchy shares responsibility for the attack on President McKinley.  It did not mean that he should be shot.  It only wished to sell more papers by commenting on and cartooning him as "a tyrant reddening his hands in the blood of the poor and filling his pockets and those of others with dollars coined out of the sweat and tears and hunger of helpless strikers, their wan wives, and their starving children."  Today the journalism or the oratory which may have inspired Leon Czolgosz to his deed is the most tearful, sympathetic, and grief-stricken journalism or oratory in America.  It editorializes, interviews, and moralizes on the lovableness of the man whom it lately and long and habitually portrayed as a monster, a despot, and a coward.  It is very scared, very sorry — or very politic, or would like to seem to be so.  Let us hope it is really sorry.  Then let us hope that its sorrow will last long enough to persuade it that the selling of more papers or the getting of more votes is not the chief end of journalism or of oratory, when it leads one to defamation as a delight, to villification as an industry, and to printed, pictorial, or platform blackguardism as a trade.

Chicago *Journal*, September 13, 1901

Who is it that makes the Goldmans and the Mosts, the Spieses and the Parsonses, whose writings and speeches thus incite men to assassination?  From whom do these teachers get their best encouragement in this country?  Whose teaching is it that anarchists think they only carry to its logical conclusion when they advise and commit murder?  Deliberately and without hesitation we say the "yellow journals" and the men behind them.  These are the wellsprings of discontent, class hatred, and anarchy.  Let us place the responsibility for this dastardly crime where it justly belongs. It is due to reckless, unscrupulous, unprincipled journalism such as has been seen daily in the pages of the New York *Journal*, the Chicago *American*, and the San Francisco *Examiner*, since William R. Hearst has controlled them.

[1] President McKinley was shot in Buffalo on September 6, 1901, by a German Pole who had been inflamed by the oratory of foreign anarchists; but the blame for the attack was unjustly laid by many upon the yellow journals which had been assailing McKinley.

## SAUSAGE AND SCRAPPLE

New York *Sun*, October 1, 1901

In Philadelphia the scrapple-making days have come, the gladdest of the year. From now until mid-March that ancient town will be devoted to the task of turning raw pig into bar scrapple and sausage string. Catfish-and-waffles is but a plaything and a toy of fancy to the Philadelphian. That takes his mind; his heart he gives to sausage and scrapple. These, says the Philadelphia *Press*, "have never before been popular." Then it is a judicious inference that Philadelphia now eats them four times a day instead of three, not counting nibbles between meals. To like, to love sausage and scrapple, especially scrapple, is as natural to a Philadelphian as swimming to a duck. A scrapple case is an even more necessary part of the baggage of a travelling Philadelphian than that receptacle which the Providence *Journal* forbids us to call a "dress-suit case" — an evening clothes bag, shall we say? As Dr. David Rittenhouse Bingham sings in his "Plectrum and Scalpel":

> "*O flower of all the flavors, O queen of all the savors*
> *That e'er to happy nostrils deliciously have rolled!*
> *My soul with rapture shivers when I see the perfect slivers*
> *Of kidney blent with livers, the scrapple hot or cold!*"

Our Philadelphia contemporary recounts joyously the details of the process by which the pig is transmuted and translated. It shows us in a corner of the sausage-and-scrapple studio the pen where the victims await their doom. We see them walking up the steep plank to the fatal platform. One brief flash of steel and squeal; then *kerflunk!* into the kettle of boiling water below. The future delicacy is kept in the hot bath for some hours. Then the scraping machine does its work. It is useless to try and disguise these details. They have their value as the raw materials of Dr. Bingham's ode. After the bath and the strigil, Lord Bacon is hanged, drawn and quartered, weighed, "cut up until he resembles mince-meat by blades, that whirl around in a huge chopping bowl, with incredible swiftness. After being cut up, the meat is placed in a mixing machine. Another machine then receives it and passes it through a narrow opening into the casing. They are then linked by hand and are ready for the market." The chain of sausages is complete. Now for the bar of scrapple:

After the sausages are made, all the meat and fat that is left over in the process is mixed together with savors, cut up fine, mixed with buckwheat flour, beaten into a sort of paste or mush, is set aside for a short time, and then formed into molds and sold as scrapple.

The Pennsylvania Dutch have many solid and useful qualities, and one of the most engaging languages known to man; as the inventors of scrapple, they have conferred upon Philadelphia and the rest of the world a priceless boon.

## [PRESIDENT McKINLEY'S BUFFALO SPEECH][1]

### Kansas City *Star*, October 8, 1901

In his Buffalo speech the President practically admitted that protection, in its application to certain industries, had outlived its usefulness, and that the time had come for such modifications of the tariff as would be calculated to encourage foreign trade. Never before in his Presidential addresses had Mr. McKinley expressed the least lack of confidence in the permanent efficacy of the policy of high protection.  In his Buffalo speech he declared that the statistics of trade were "almost appalling"; that it could not be well for the United States or for other countries that one should continue to sell in enormous quantities and buy little or nothing; that the "period of exclusiveness" was past; that "no narrow or selfish policy would subserve" the great business interests of the nation.  In other words, that the equilibrium of international trade is essential to the continuous and equitable prosperity of a great producing country like the United States.  He spoke frankly in favor of reciprocity treaties.  In short, he had come to a stopping place as a national economist, and was unwilling to drift further without pointing out some of the dangers that might lie ahead.  The committal recorded in this address may have an important bearing on the future policies of the Republican party.

### Chicago *Daily News*, October 9, 1901

It is not easy to reconcile these views with those of the William McKinley who as a Congressman a few years ago advocated tariffs regardless of their restraining effect on trade and boldly declared that the United States as a self-sufficient and self-sustaining power

[1] McKinley's last and finest speech, delivered the day before his assassination, was upon the subject of friendly coöperation with the other nations of the world. He was outgrowing his old doctrine of an exclusive tariff, and now he frankly confessed the fact.  "Commercial wars are unprofitable. . . . Reciprocity treaties are in harmony with the spirit of the times, measures of retaliation are not.  If perchance some of our tariffs are no longer needed for revenue or to encourage and foster our industries at home, why should they not be employed to extend and promote our markets abroad?"

had no need to seek foreign trade. The President's change of view, however, shows that he has followed the trend of events intelligently, and it is in following opportunities rather than in premising or creating them that Mr. McKinley is strongest. He has learned that as a nation we cannot maintain high-tariff barriers if we would hold a commanding position in the world's markets. The policy he advocates he now styles "reciprocity," but the principle which it proposes to apply calls for a broader name. Apparently it looks to a revenue tariff with liberal but incidental protective features rather than to a consistent protective system modified only in special instances to secure a better basis for trade operations. Mr. McKinley has outlived and outgrown the "McKinleyism" of his more callow statesmanship. That is a most hopeful sign of further progress and of enduring greatness for the nation which has also outgrown the protective system so long advocated by Mr. McKinley.

## E. L. GODKIN[1]

### *The Nation*, May 22, 1902

A great journalist has departed. His name, absolutely unknown to the American public in 1865, blazed up instantly upon the appearance of the *Nation*, at a moment when Bennett and Bryant, Greeley and Raymond, were approaching the end of their careers, leaving no successors. He was not a great editor in the sense of being an organizer or manager. The *Nation* was avowedly patterned after the London *Spectator;* the *Evening Post* was already in its ninth decade when Mr. Godkin joined Messrs. Carl Schurz and Horace White in assuming editorial direction of it. He had, strictly speaking, no business instinct, no faculty for details, nor any liking for the task of coördinating the departments of a daily newspaper. He was *par excellence* a leader-writer, with an astonishing productiveness, and a freshness in handling old themes which won even the hardened proof-reader's admiration. The prospectus of the *Nation* laid stress upon the advantages of a weekly over a daily newspaper in respect of leisure for ascertainment of the facts and deliberation in comment; and the argument was as incontrovertible in 1881, when Mr. Godkin became one of the editors of the *Evening Post*, as it was in 1865. The change might not have come about had the *Nation* prospered so as to warrant an enlargement of its staff. The strain of writing from three to

[1] E. L. Godkin died in Devonshire, England, on May 21, 1902. This editorial was written by Wendell Phillips Garrison, for many years the distinguished literary editor of the *Nation*.

five pages for it weekly was felt at last to be too severe as well as too unremunerative, in view of the scrutiny to which Mr. Godkin was subjected while all but single-handed.

Apart from the resultant greater conspicuity, the merging of the weekly editor in the daily was not a promotion, for the *Nation* had already placed him in the front rank of American journalists even during the lifetime of the veterans we have mentioned. It was a familiar flattery to have his articles made over at a safe interval in a metropolitan daily; and in the country at large the practise was still more common. The *Nation* was eagerly read in every newspaper office of importance, and its ideas filtered down without acknowledgment through a thousand channels. On the other hand, in his new position, Mr. Godkin became inevitably a greater target for censure and abuse; the more because a New York daily must needs come to close quarters with local corruption and misrule, and its editor be more exposed to pay with his person for incurring the wrath of organized iniquity. This Mr. Godkin did in his memorable campaign against Tammany.

Few journalists have labored less whose writing was of as high quality as Mr. Godkin's. His pen was fluent and ready, but his diction was never careless; rather it bore at all times the marks of training and culture of a high order. While able to develop a subject at any length, he had extraordinary aptitude for paragraph writing; his touch in either case was always light, his matter always pithy. His expression was very direct, vigorous, and trenchant; and he had an exceptional gift for descriptive narration. His style, indeed, was adequate for every use to which he applied it, and passed without effort from the journalistic to the literary vein, treating nothing that it did not adorn. Such adaptability is seldom encountered, and perhaps the nearest parallel to his is to be found in the writings of Harriet Martineau, long an editorial contributor to the *Daily News*. Mr. Godkin's humor, which

*"was ever*
*Lance and sword to him, and buckler and helmet,"*

perplexed the simple-minded, while it enraged his enemies. Its droll visualizing quality lightened every page that he wrote for the *Nation*. On this side he has never been surpassed, if approached, and the effectiveness of his humor as a literary weapon consisted in the freedom with which he directed it against the objects of a sham popular and partisan reverence. He owed this freedom, undeniably, to the foreign birth with which he was constantly reproached; but it was his humor which first pierced the glamour

and enabled him to see men and policies in a dry light.    Biting
as it might be, it was never cynical.    His conversation was naturally
playful and seasoned with a hearty laughter, and his daily com-
panionship most delightful.

As no American could have written Bryce's "American Commonwealth" or Goldwin Smith's "History of the United States,"
so it may be doubted if any native of this country could have
erected the standard of political independence which Mr. Godkin
set up in the *Nation* and maintained in the *Evening Post*.   He did
this, however, not as a foreigner, but as an American to the core.
A utilitarian of the school of Bentham, an economist of the school
of John Stuart Mill, an English Liberal to whom America, with
all its flagrant inconsistency of slaveholding, was still the hope of
universal democracy, he cast in his lot with us, became a naturalized
citizen, took an American wife — gave every pledge to the land of
his adoption except that of being a servile follower of party.   He
brought to his high calling sound principles of finance, with which
he fought the good fight of honest money, specie payments, and
currency reform;  of political economy, with which he combated
protection and its attendant corruption;  of popular government,
which stood by him in the removal of the Reconstruction scandal;
of office as a public trust, which made his journal the most potent
medium for the promotion of civil service reform and the exposure
of machine and boss government.    Nowhere is there such a body
of useful doctrine for serious-minded youth seeking to fit themselves
to be "perfect citizens" (as was said of the late John M. Forbes)
as the files of the *Nation* contain during Mr. Godkin's thirty-five
years' connection with it.    Nowhere can the historically minded
man more profitably turn for light upon our latter-day decadence.


## THE PLIGHT OF ST. LOUIS [1]

### *The Nation*, February 26, 1903

All students of politics and lovers of good government should
read an article by Mr. Lincoln Steffens in *McClure's Magazine* for
March, which is rather startlingly entitled "The Shamelessness of
St. Louis."   Why St. Louis should be considered shameless above
other cities that have let themselves be governed by scoundrels,
will appear when it is noted that in St. Louis alone has the cycle
of political corruption swung full, producing upon the machine and

---

[1] Lincoln Steffens's series called "The Shame of the Cities," running in *McClure's
Magazine*, exposed the governmental corruption in New York, Philadelphia, Chicago,
St. Louis, and San Francisco.   It was one of the earlier of those spectacular revelations which President Roosevelt later, at the Gridiron dinner of 1906, termed
"muckraking."

the quiet body of honest citizens alike its inevitable disintegrating result. In no other instance, on a large scale, has the machine been allowed to run its entire mortal course unhindered. New York cut down her Tweed in his heyday, and made it too hot for Mr. Croker before his dominion over the machine had fairly been shaken. Minneapolis has routed her boodlers, and is now dragging back ex-Mayor Ames to trial and apparently to certain punishment. In Philadelphia, perhaps, the powers of corruption have fortified themselves against internal dissension. But in St. Louis we have a complete and probably a unique example of ring government in its dotage and public opinion in its decrepitude.

How such demoralization has afflicted a proud city may be learned in Mr. Steffens's scornful pages. The "boodle" ring was like any other ring. Col. E. R. Butler and his associated "good fellows," during and after the year 1898, got control of the city government, and began a careful sale of illegal privileges. Gradually becoming stronger, they began to charge a tariff for all the services that the city was bound to render to the citizens. If a railroad wanted a switch, a financial house a franchise, a householder a permit to dig in front of his dwelling or for his block to be lighted — any of these ordinary rights had to be paid for handsomely. The holding up of corporations became a business, with its rules of procedure and etiquette. If there was a certain brutality in keeping the city dark for weeks until the bidders for the lighting contract had "come up" with $175,000, there was delicacy in the action of Councilman Uthoff, who, holding the boss's retaining fee of $25,000 to fight a traction contract, refused indignantly $50,000 from the contractor, finally accepted $100,000, and the next day returned the $25,000 to Boss Butler, because he "had not earned it."

This transaction is typical, and pointed to the dissolution of the Butler ring, which was already in a bad way with fatty degeneration before Circuit Attorney Folk took a hold. Col. Butler's gains were inordinate, and at the very time when he was making a mockery of party government by naming both Republican and Democratic candidates, his own fellows, weary of dividing a tithe against the boss's nine-tenths, began boodling on their own account. Butler was powerless to stop the mutiny; apparently he hardly cared to stop it; for when the sale of franchises and other city assets was running up to $50,000,000 worth, there was boodle enough for all. Great plans were on foot — the sale of certain markets and the transfer of the city water works to private hands. The rival "honest brokers" of franchises began to expose each other, and even to take legal proceedings that revealed wholesale bribery. A great mass of evidence against the ring was becoming accessible, but nobody cared to use it. The Republicans and Democrats, honest citizens generally, went on stolidly "voting the regular ticket," as the boodlers themselves uncovered the corruption of both parties. And this is the really appalling feature of the situation, as Mr. Steffens depicts it, that just as the machine was rickety from its own riotous living, the capacity for moral indignation which might have shattered it once for all was departed from the city.

One man did care, as everybody knows. Single-handed, Circuit Attorney Joseph Folk hammered at the ring, if he could not destroy it. Nobody knew much about him when the politicians nominated him. Certainly nobody suspected that he would fight the boodlers. It occurred neither to Col. Butler and his gang nor to the honest citizens of St. Louis that the boodlers could be fought. The sheer accident that a courageous man, who believed in the law he administered, was elected by the piratical fraternity, alone could have led to the exposures that now are a household tale. This mishap might easily have been prevented had it been anticipated, and today, while Col. Butler lies under conviction for bribery, his candidates are returned by the city of St. Louis, his creatures, frequently under conviction for crime, are kept by the law's delays in the City Council and State Legislature, and in Mr. Steffens's opinion the activities of the ring are merely suspended — for from this temporary discomfiture it may learn valuable lessons in the matter of making the power of public plunder genuinely cohesive.

New York city certainly has little right to assume airs of superior righteousness, but has much to learn from St. Louis. There was, two or three years ago, every probability that the more astute members of Tammany Hall would improve upon the old Platt-Croker alliance and control both the Republican and the Democratic organization. This process, of which there were only indications in New York, was actually accomplished by the St. Louis boodlers. Furthermore, there have been signs that both the inner Tammany ring and the police "system" have been going stale. The disproportionate gains of Croker and Devery were undoubtedly causing jealousy, and might have produced revolt. The inner rottenness of Tammany Hall was likely to impair its strength, just as the shamelessness of the franchise-jobbers of St. Louis made them vulnerable to Mr. Folk's attack. But the case of St. Louis shows that there could be no worse policy than to let political corruption perish of its own exceeding wantonness; for the cost of such a cure is the complete deadening of the sense of public decency.

## THE INJURY TO MR. HAY[1]

*The Nation*, December 24, 1903

One of the most unfortunate results of our Panama diplomacy is the damage it has done to the reputation of Secretary Hay. His prestige has been a matter of legitimate national pride. Not only by skill and address, but by pursuing policies at once humane and honorable, had he won fame abroad as well as admiration at home. His exemplary patience when the first Hay-Pauncefote treaty was defeated by American Jingoes, headed by Mr. Roosevelt, implied that he had that first of diplomatic virtues, the ability to say, "I can wait." But the rash and lawless course which the Administration, with Mr. Hay's advice or at least consent, has adopted in the Isthmian canal affair operates gravely to his injury.

The fundamental vice of our Colombian diplomacy is revealed afresh in the correspondence made public on Saturday. Apparently, neither President Roosevelt nor Secretary Hay thought Colombia entitled to her rights under international law. They never dreamed of treating her as an equal. They addressed demands to her which, if made to us by any other Power, we should have rightly regarded as a deep insult. Read the offensive dispatch which Mr. Hay sent on June 9. It stated that the rejection of the treaty would "seriously compromise the friendly understanding between the two countries," and might lead to action by Congress "which every friend of Colombia would regret." What right had the Secretary to say that? How could it be maintained that the constitutional action of the Colombian Senate in rejecting one of Mr. Hay's treaties was any more unfriendly than the similar action of the United States Senate in rejecting several of them? Clearly, Secretary Hay would never have thought of making so thinly veiled a threat to France. He would not have endured it an instant coming from England. Lord Lansdowne might, with as good warrant, have insisted that our Senate confirm the Hay-Pauncefote treaty. That was sought by use as directly as the canal treaty was by Colombia. Mr. Hay makes much of the fact that negotiations were "instituted by Colombia." The Hay-Pauncefote treaty was instituted by us. Indeed, it was publicly stated that Mr. Hay was allowed to write it just as he pleased. Yet the British Foreign Office never thought of reproaching or

[1] The "bloodless revolution" in Panama, resulting in the erection of that part of Colombia into an independent republic under American protection, occurred November 3, 1903. Under Roosevelt's orders, American vessels were near at hand; and two days after the revolutionary government was established (November 6) it was recognized by the United States. Criticism of Roosevelt was loudly voiced in the more liberal section of the American press, led by the *Nation*.

threatening our government on that account. We demand the treatment of an equal, but do not accord it to Colombia, though by law and treaty it should be hers.

The latest correspondence only makes the Panama case appear worse. It shows that the Administration was prepared to ignore Colombian sentiment, and to trample upon Colombian rights. And as for what this government actually did in connection with the Panama revolution, the dispatches now published are either irrelevant or further inculpatory. To show that we were long aware of trouble brewing, is a queer way of excusing us for acting with gross impropriety when it came. It does not leave us even the pretext of having been taken by surprise. Nothing that has yet seen the light can explain or defend the orders to our naval commanders, two days before the revolution, to prevent Colombia from suppressing it. That, as Senator Hoar maintained from his place in the Senate, was nothing less than an act of war, authority for which the President possesses neither in sound policy nor in the Constitution and laws which he is sworn to uphold. Besides being a diplomatic blunder, it was an open usurpation of power.

All this, we say, came with a shock to the friends of Secretary Hay and must prove a detriment to his fair fame. Nowhere has his sagacious and humane statesmanship been held in higher esteem than in England. But what are Englishmen saying now of the policy in which he has made himself *particeps?* The influential organs of English opinion express that verdict of posterity which is proverbially to be sought in the judgment of friendly and intelligent foreigners. The *Speaker*, the Liberal weekly, says that the Administration was guilty of an "act of brigandage" in Panama, and adds that "the United States has shaken the confidence of the civilized world in her honesty." It is the opinion of the *Scotsman* that Colombia has been "at the same time plundered and mocked." Says the Glasgow *Herald*, "Expediency has been stronger than morality." In the Manchester *Guardian* we read, "The United States Government, coveting the canal territory and unable to control it by treaty, has torn it off from Colombia by force." Our Panama diplomacy is called by the *Daily Graphic* "a very disagreeable page of American history." The *Globe* speaks of the "underground manoeuvring of President Roosevelt and Mr. Hay." Our course at Panama was, says the *Daily News*, in "complete disregard for the opinion of the civilized world." We could make many more citations to the same effect from representative and powerful English newspapers. Enough has been adduced, however, to show that the Colombian diplomacy for which Secretary Hay has made himself responsible incurs the condemnation of our well-wishers abroad. The result is, unhappily, not only a diminution of his own repute, but a tarnishing of his country's good name.

## MARK HANNA'S PUBLIC CAREER [1]

*The Nation*, February 18, 1904

We can see pretty clearly now what will be perfectly distinct to the acute historian in the future, that Mr. Hanna was the full flower of the spirit of commercialism in politics. He was, in this, but the child of his epoch. That was the reason for his success. He best embodied the tendency of the years in which he was militant. It was in Senator Hanna that the grosser and more repulsive policies of his own party beheld themselves as in a mirror. What was everywhere latent, he caught up and flashed forth. The apologies of others became his defiances; what they deprecated, even while profiting by, he gloried in. To invest money in politics as in a mine or railroad, and to look confidently for the pecuniary return; to appeal for votes on the basis of the sheer material advantage; to cry up prosperity as the be-all and end-all of government; to vulgarize politics by making its watchwords the cries of the market and the slang of the gambler; to make of the electoral struggles of a free people an exciting game with huge and glittering money-stakes — in a word, to put mercantile methods in the place of forensic, and to hold the best title to office to be the fact that it has been bought and paid for — this was the great political distinction of Mr. Hanna.

He set about the first election of President McKinley in this spirit, and with many of the devices of a financier planning a vast combination. In fact, there was an almost ludicrous resemblance between his campaign for the nomination of Mr. McKinley and a skilful reorganization of a bankrupt railway. Mr. Hanna took up a Congressman whose private fortunes were shattered and whose political prestige was broken. That looked like most unpromising material out of which to create a Governor, and later, a President. But Mr. Hanna saw the financial possibilities of the situation. A political reaction was upon the country. After years of depression a promise that the people were to be fed and filled and warmed was sure to be fetching. Mr. Hanna openly dangled that bribe in the nation's face. He set in motion, certainly in 1895, probably as early as 1894, an elaborate and heavily endowed organization to bring Mr. McKinley to the front. Just who furnished the funds, and in what sums, will not be known until Mr. Hanna's private records leap to life, if they ever do; but it was common

[1] Mark Hanna died of typhoid fever in Washington on February 15, 1904.

gossip in advance that such and such men were to have this office and the other for subscriptions received. It is to be said for Mr. McKinley that he honored every obligation of that sort. Financial good faith was kept. So was political. Not one of Mr. Hanna's "original McKinley men" went unrewarded, let clergymen and college professors protest against them as scandalous ill-livers if they choose. The whole ante-convention campaign was tinged with the merchandising spirit, and afterwards every note was met as it fell due.

Things fell out luckily for Mr. Hanna after McKinley and Bryan were fairly in the field in 1896. The contest turned into an assault upon the nation's financial credit. The result was to put vast sums at Chairman Hanna's disposal. This seemed necessary at the time, and the sound principle undoubtedly triumphed; but it was at the cost of a frightful extension of the spirit of commercialism in politics. For this, Mr. Hanna was too much responsible. We have heard men familiar with his methods say that his plan was to block out the contested states into small districts, and coolly figure out how much money it would take to make each safe. All this was bad enough at the time, but the doctrine of no peril without its price, no vote that could not be had for cash in hand, secured a fatal hold and was applied disastrously for years. It rose to its final pitch of vulgar effrontery in the Ohio campaign of last year, which resulted in an attempt to baptize the Republican party anew in the faith of the almighty dollar.

We wish to be entirely fair. Prosperity, rightly conceived and worthily striven for, is a national blessing. We do not doubt that Senator Hanna really wished to see everybody busy and contented. That went with his kindness of heart, as did also, we presume, the efforts to compose labor troubles to which he gave so much time and energy. But it was his misfortune to seem to make meat more than life. He identified his name with lavish and wasteful policies. Politico-financial promoters swarmed about him, as did also the unscrupulous politicians of whom he made use, and by whom he thought it a point of honor to stand in all their detected knaveries. Thus he exactly typified the baser tendencies of his party and his day. We had loud praises from him of the full dinner-pail and the swollen bank account, with money enough in the Treasury for every schemer; but when did he ever speak an echoing word for human liberty, or show that national honor was dearer to him than the jingling of the guinea, or separate himself from the category of those who, in Puritan phrase, "make Religion as twelve and the world as thirteen"? Mr. Hanna was a master of legions of "negro delegates," but real sympathy with the struggles of black men to rise he never betrayed in public. Asked last summer what was the intent of the Ohio plank about negro suffrage in the South, he replied that he was against having the party really take up that issue, and added, in the most matter-of-fact way, "There are 25,000 negroes in Ohio whose votes we want."

Senator Hanna rose as high as such a man could go in this country. It is unavailing for his friends to speak of what might have been had he lived — of disappointed ambitions. Verily, he had his reward. His support by the men who are in politics for the money they can make, and by the grand army of corrupt politicians, was the real and final measure of his success. The judgment of the people is just, in the long run; and it had already given Mr. Hanna his true place. A skilled political manager, yes; but a public man on whom Americans would delight to bestow their highest honors? Never.

## COLORED FOLK IN PULLMAN CARS

Springfield *Republican*, February 26, 1904

We recently noted the reported action of the Pullman car company in refusing accommodations to the colored Bishop Arnett and other prelates of the African Methodist Church who wished to go from Cincinnati to Mobile to attend a council of bishops. The report states that in order to travel in a sleeper car the bishop had to hire a whole car at a cost of nearly $100 additional to the regular transportation charge. It is said that the Pullman company is extending its exclusion of colored people all over the South — the method employed being that commonly used by hotels in turning away colored applicants with the statement that all the berths or seats are engaged, etc.

The practise of the Pullman company is flatly contrary to the act for the regulation of interstate commerce, and the company should be called to account for it before the interstate commerce commission. The case differs radically from the "Jim Crow" practises of the Southern railroads in reference to ordinary passenger transportation. Here the roads provide separate cars for whites and blacks, of supposedly equal convenience, comfort, and safety, and the commission has decided that this does not create an undue or unjust prejudice or preference. But the commission has also decided that "colored people who buy first-class tickets must be furnished with accommodations equally safe and comfortable with other first-class passengers" — and a colored man in possession of such a transportation ticket accordingly, under the law, stands on an equality with the white man when he applies for the extra accommodations furnished by the Pullman company. For this company is a common carrier none the less for not owning and operating the road over which it runs, and it falls under the interstate law the same as a railroad company in the case of its own cars.

The president of the Pullman company is Robert T. Lincoln, son of Abraham Lincoln, the emancipator. Can it be that this company is sharing in and aiding and abetting the revival of race prejudice in this country with the approval or consent of the son of Abraham Lincoln — going so far as to violate the law of the land in doing so? It would be well to hear from the president of the company on this point. But the appeal of the excluded colored people should be not to Mr. Lincoln, but to the national commission charged with the duty of enforcing the law which fits the case. The Pullman company need not necessarily receive white and colored passengers in the same car; it can provide separate cars or accommodations, and should be compelled to do the one thing or the other.

## THE NORTHERN SECURITIES DECISION[1]

New York *World*, March 15, 1904

The decision of the Supreme Court against the Northern Securities Merger is an event of vital and far-reaching importance. . . . So clear, so obvious, so important are the issues involved that wonder grows that a final decision in a case of the first magnitude was not reached until almost fourteen years after the passage of the Sherman Act.

What is the decision; what the circumstances that led up to it; what its probable effects?

*I — The Case.*

The first railway across the continent was necessarily a monopoly. As each additional line was opened an effort was made to prevent competition. This effort was particularly active in the Northwest, where the Northern Pacific and the Great Northern railroads were natural rivals.

The Burlington and the Union Pacific were other parallel lines. The Northern Pacific secured control of the Burlington by a stock-conversion deal. To protect their interests the masters of the Union Pacific set out to capture the Northern Pacific, and this led to the great Northern Pacific war and the panic of May 9, 1901.

[1] The Northern Securities case marked the launching of a new policy by the government in its relations with great corporations; an aggressive policy, intent upon law enforcement. On March 14, 1904, Justice Harlan handed down the decision of the Supreme Court dissolving the merger of the three railway companies involved.

The financiers of Wall Street met to restore peace and apportion the spoils, and out of their efforts grew the Northern Securities Merger, organized in November, 1901, under the laws of New Jersey, for the purpose of holding the stock of the Northern Pacific and Great Northern companies, including the control of the Burlington. It was modestly suggested that it might later take in the Chicago, Milwaukee, and St. Paul, the Chicago and Northwestern, and probably the Chicago Great Western and the Wisconsin Central.

It was said that the combination was legally unassailable; that all the railroads of the United States might presently be consolidated in the hands of a few great holding companies. This was a menace and a challenge.

*II — The Law.*

On March 3, 1902, Attorney-General Knox, urged thereto by President Roosevelt, filed a petition against the combination and its two constituent companies in the United States Circuit Court of Minnesota, under the Sherman Anti-Trust Act of 1890, which provides:

Section 1. Every contract, combination in the form of trust or otherwise, or conspiracy in restraint of trade or commerce, among the several States or with foreign nations, is hereby declared to be illegal. Every person who shall make any such contract or engage in any such combination shall be deemed guilty of a misdemeanor, and on conviction thereof shall be punished by a fine not exceeding $5,000, or by imprisonment not exceeding one year, or by both said punishments in the decision of the court.

Section 4. The several circuit courts of the United States are hereby invested with jurisdiction to prevent and restrain violations of this act; and it shall be the duty of the several district attorneys of the United States, in their respective districts, under the direction of the Attorney-General, to institute proceedings in equity to prevent and restrain such violations.

*III — The Decree.*

The case was vigorously pushed. One week later the Attorney-General alleged in a bill in equity filed at St. Paul that the Northern Pacific and Great Northern were "the only transcontinental lines of railway extending across the northern tier of States west of the Great Lakes . . . to the Pacific Ocean, and were (previously) engaged in active competition for freight and passenger traffic;" that by the merger the defendants were monopolizing interstate and foreign commerce in violation of the Sherman Act and that the Securities Company "was not organized in good faith to purchase and pay for" the roads it acquired, but "solely to incorporate the pooling of the stocks of said companies."

Mr. Knox added that if this were permitted the act of Congress could be set at naught and all the railway systems of the country could be "absorbed, merged, and consolidated, thus placing the public at the absolute mercy of the holding corporation."

This view was sustained on April 9 of last year by the United States Circuit Court of Appeals, Justice Thayer saying that Congress, after forbidding the "trusts" known at the time of the passage of the law —

> Evidently anticipating that the combination might be otherwise formed, was careful to declare that a combination in any other form, if in restraint of interstate trade or commerce, — that is, if it directly occasioned or effected such restraint — should likewise be deemed illegal.

### IV — The Supreme Court.

By a majority of five to four in the Supreme Court itself the decree of the Circuit Court is now confirmed. This is final. There is no appeal.

The decision, written by Justice Harlan, states that, than the holding company, "no scheme or device could certainly more effectively come within the prohibition of the Anti-Trust law." The law is not an interference with the right of the States to charter companies. The authority of Congress is supreme. Sweeping away by broad principles a maze of technicalities, Justice Harlan finds that the merger is "a combination in restraint of interstate and international commerce, and that is enough to bring it under the condemnation of the Act." If such a combination is not destroyed —

> The entire commerce in the immense territory in the northern part of the United States, between the Great Lakes and the Pacific at Puget Sound, will be at the mercy of a single holding corporation, organized in a State distant from the people of that territory.

### V — The Effect.

Of business interests the decision is conservative, not destructive, not obstructive. Because of it no wheel need cease to turn, no property is destroyed, no right of wealth invaded, no legitimate ambition assailed. The sun will rise and set as before, the rain will fall, the grain will grow as bravely in all that vast region which the merger sought to make subject in the important matter of transportation to one corporate will.

Mr. Morgan himself once pointed out that the real value in the railroads could not be destroyed by the courts. The very securities of the "holding company" which is forbidden have value as denoting ownership in the original railroad. More, or other, or greater value they could never have had save at the people's cost by "killing competition, and capitalizing the corpse."

Already there is talk of a campaign of education to secure the repeal of the Sherman Act. Against the folly of this attitude of an arrogant plutocracy cheated of its prey we enter protest. As *The World* said to Mr. Morgan three days after the filing of the decree: "You and your great trusts and combinations were in the position of a man with an incipient dangerous disease. When such a man disregards nature's warnings, ignores wise counsel, and continues his reckless life, he dooms himself. By recognizing the disease at an early stage and accepting a remedy he will recover. Obedience is life. Defiance is death."

No man of sense desires the destruction of all forms of capitalistic combination which the larger scale of modern industrial development demands. But the limit of safety is passed when the rights of the people are encroached upon. If there were no limit, the great railway systems, already consisting in some cases of 20,000 miles of track, could be combined in "holding companies," and these holding companies combined in still larger ones until the universal "merger" was reached; and a single man might thus control many times the amount of its capital and sway the transportation of the entire country.

The will of the people, as embodied in the law, is that this shall not be made possible. A "campaign of education," by all means; but let the school be opened in Wall Street, not on the farm!

## PRESIDENT CHARLES W. ELIOT'S WORK

Springfield *Republican*, March 18, 1904

To those who follow closely the educational movement of our time the story of President Eliot's work is a thrice-told tale; but the greater number of us need to be reminded of its salient points in order to comprehend its epochal nature. If we could reconstruct in our imaginations the condition of education in America when in 1869, at the age of 35 years, Dr. Eliot became president of Harvard, and were then to compare it with the condition of education today, the facts would seem, to the younger generation in particular, almost incredible. . . . He has recreated Harvard. That institution was still dominated by eighteenth century or rather mediaeval pedagogical ideas when he came to the front. The preceding president was the last of the clergymen in office; President Eliot had been a professor of chemistry, with a scientific bent, and full of new ideas drawn from his educational studies in Europe. Classicism ruled the curriculum. Although there were already a dozen elective studies, the four years' course was almost wholly prescribed. Science was a sickly, feeble plant, memorized from textbooks rather than seen and studied in laboratories. The seniors "finished" political economy. The freshmen still were drilled in the evidences of Christianity. The medical school was a monstrosity of incapacity, and the law school turned out an ignoramus with as much facility as a Choate. In 1869 any graduate of Harvard College, who had a "good moral character" and $5 cash, could buy a master of arts degree, after three years.

Within two decades a revolution had taken place. The elective system had been hammered into every department of instruction, and brought within the reach even of the freshman class. The old recitation system had given way largely to the method of instruction by lectures. Science and history were now reborn at Harvard through the insistence upon original experimentation and inquiry. Absolute freedom of investigation was encouraged in teacher and student in every department. The priceless worth of the differences in men was recognized, and the gospel of individualism in mental development was proclaimed as never had been possible in the days when all students, of whatever gifts or tendencies, were made to lie in the procrustean bed of the prescribed system of studies. The medical and law schools were lifted from their low level and given character, dignity, and high standing through the raising of the requirements for admission, the lengthening and enrichment of the courses, and the severity of the examinations which were prerequisites to diplomas. The divinity school was divorced from denominationalism, and made to serve as the handmaiden of all great ethical systems and religions. Thus Harvard became, as never before, truly American, for religious freedom is one of the cardinal principles of the republic. The great graduate department which now exists at the institution is entirely the growth of the Eliot period; indeed, it may be said to crown the elective system introduced in the undergraduate school.[1]

[1] Charles W. Eliot had been but one of several statesmen of higher education who appeared immediately after the Civil War. The others included Andrew D. White of Cornell, James McCosh of Princeton, James B. Angell of Michigan, and Daniel Coit Gilman of Johns Hopkins. But Dr. Eliot's administration was much the longest and the most fruitful. His achievements might fill up a much longer list than that here given.

## MR. ROOSEVELT AND THE CORPORATIONS[1]

New York *World*, October 1, 1904

Mr. President:

The Congress that created the Bureau of Corporations, which, you say, has been administered "with entire efficiency," gave you the unique, the extraordinary appropriation of $500,000 to enforce the existing laws against corporations.

What is your record in the expenditure of this money? About $26,000 of it has been spent for the purpose to which it was appropriated. The rest has been lying idle in the Treasury for 583 days.

You pressed the suit against the Northern Securities merger and established the constitutionality of the Sherman Anti-Trust law. That was a brave and admirable action, for which *The World* gave you and Mr. Knox unstinted praise — praise that your committee is now circulating as a Republican campaign document. But why did you stop there, and with your ineffectual injunction against the Beef Trust and certain railroad corporations? Why were not the beef case and the rebate cases advanced in court, as the law now permits? Was it, perhaps, because the corporations were willing to pay your campaign committee liberally for the non-use of this money? Was it, perhaps, because they could afford to pay ten times this appropriation into your campaign treasury in order to keep this corporation fighting fund in the United States Treasury? Was it, perhaps, because this money, together with the new acts of Congress and the decision in the Northern Securities case, could be made a veritable sword of Damocles and suspended over the head of every corporation engaged in interstate commerce? I do not assert it; I merely ask.

But will not publicans and sinners insist that this appropriation has been a two-fold war-chest, a double treasury, in your campaign for election? Will not skeptics and scoffers think that, while the use of a little of this money gained you great popular applause, the non-use of a great deal of it gained you princely contributions to further your election?

Your pretended record, in your own words, as to the effectiveness with which you have prosecuted these corporations, is set down in your letter of acceptance, where you say that the need of officials having the disposition and courage to enforce existing laws —

---

[1] This signed editorial by Joseph Pulitzer occupied the whole editorial page of the *World*. The extract here given represents its main idea. George B. Cortelyou had been Secretary of Commerce and Labor under Roosevelt 1903–04, but had resigned and become manager of the Republican campaign. Roosevelt's opponent in 1904, Parker, accused Cortelyou of using his official position and information to demand large campaign contributions from the big corporations; and Mr. Pulitzer energetically followed up this accusation.

has been met by the consistent and steadily continued action of the Department of Justice under the present Administration.

"The consistent and steadily continued action of the Department of Justice"! Indeed! Consistent in what? Steadily continued in what?

John Moody, a trustworthy and authoritative writer, states in his book "The Truth About Trusts," that there existed in February, 1904, a whole year after your Bureau of Corporations began its work, about 440 important trusts, with a total capitalization of nearly $11,000,000,000, including six great railroad groups, constituting as many trusts, with an additional capitalization of $9,000,000,000.

Here is $20,000,000,000 of combined capital about which your Bureau of Corporations, after 583 days, has not made public a single fact; not one single figure.

The only important and effective action against any corporation in these groups was taken against the Northern Securities Company. This one mangled merger represents substantially the sum total of that "consistent and steadily continued action" that you talk about. . . .

If you wished to keep your Administration free from suspicion, why did you select your corporation investigator [Mr. Cortelyou] to collect cash for your campaign fund? Do you not see the indelicacy of it, the impropriety of it?

If you did not wish your sincerity to be impeached, why have you never lighted the torch of publicity that Congress placed in your hand? What can you expect when people see the corporations and trusts that ought to be cowering in fear before your Department of Commerce contributing so generously to a campaign fund collected by a former Cabinet officer who knows their secrets?

Your Department of Commerce has been investigating the Beef Trust, and your Department of Justice has secured a temporary injunction against the Trust. Yet the Trust is supporting your candidacy.

Your Department of Commerce has been investigating the great life insurance companies. Whereupon John A. McCall, president of the New York Life Insurance Company, a lifelong Democrat, and Theodore Banta, another officer of the company, "who never voted for a Republican in his life," declare themselves in favor of your election on the ground possibly that the gold standard is not irrevocably established.

You smashed the Northern Securities Company and Wall Street threatened your political life. Yet E. Harriman, one of the controlling factors in the merger, says, "Nobody wants to put the Republicans out." J. Pierpont Morgan, the president of Wall

Street, another controlling factor in this merger, is supporting your candidacy, although he once threatened to destroy you. One of his partners, Edward T. Stotesbury, is collecting a campaign fund for you in Pennsylvania, and all the other partners are advocating your election.

Your Department of Justice has brought suit against certain railroads charged with violating the interstate commerce laws. Yet all the great railroad groups are supporting your candidacy.

The Standard Oil Company was strongly opposed to your Department of Commerce bill. Mr. Archbold is said to have sent telegrams to United States Senators requesting them in the name of Mr. Rockefeller to oppose it. Yet Mr. Stillman, president of the National City Bank, which is controlled by the Rockefellers, spoke in high terms of your letter of acceptance, and said: "I'm sure the sentiment of Wall Street is strong for President Roosevelt." Mr. Mellen, president of the New York, New Haven & Hartford, a railroad practically controlled by the Rockefellers, was a member of the committee that notified you of your nomination.

I doubt if you can find an intelligent citizen, Mr. President, Democrat or Republican, who believes that there is a single manufacturer of importance deriving profit from any of the 4,000 articles taxed under the Dingley tariff law who is not paying a tax for protection to your Mr. Cortelyou's campaign fund. Or one who believes there is a single great railway corporation which is not paying a tribute or tax to your Mr. Cortelyou's fund. Or one who believes that there is a single trust which is not contributing to your Mr. Cortelyou's campaign fund.

I have been told by a Western Republican friend that Mr. Hanna collected $5,000,000 in 1900 to elect Mr. McKinley and yourself, and that the sum was so much greater than he needed that part of the money was returned to the contributors. Mr. Hanna's $5,000,000 was trifling in comparison with the sum Mr. Cortelyou could raise if necessary to insure your election. In 1900 the Supreme Court had not affirmed the constitutionality of the Sherman Anti-Trust Act. There was no Department of Commerce. There was no Bureau of Corporations. There was no appropriation of $500,000 to enforce the anti-trust laws. The President wielded no such power over corporations as Congress and the courts have conferred upon you.

Can you wonder that your record of secrecy, silence, and solicitation of contributions has produced a painful impression upon some of your admirers, and that they seek in vain for suitable apologies for such official indelicacy? Can you be surprised if your opponents charge that instead of "publicity in the interest of the public" there has been only secrecy in the interest of Theodore Roosevelt?

I do not say that a Democratic Administration having your opportunities and moved by your consuming ambition to perpetuate itself in power would display a finer sensibility than you have shown. The power which you hold over so much of the organized capital of a nation is too great to be entrusted to any President — even a Jefferson — under present political conditions, where all the energies of a Chief Executive serving his first term are directed toward obtaining a second term. If our liberties are to be preserved intact as they came down to us from the fathers, I do not see how we dare maintain a system that places such despotic power in the hands of a President and such tremendous temptations in the way of his using it.

I sincerely believe that the reform measure most urgently needed in the United States is a corrupt practises act to forbid the receiving of national campaign contributions from corporations having business relations with the Federal Government or from corporations liable to punishment for violations of the Federal statutes regulating trade and commerce.

JOSEPH PULITZER.

## THE ELECTIONS AND MONEY

Springfield Republican, November 11, 1904

Elihu Root, speaking in New York Friday night, denounced as "foul and infamous" the charge that the great corporations have been in this campaign the special prey of the Republican money-gatherers, owing to the inquisitorial powers of the Federal bureau of corporations and to the connection with that bureau which Chairman Cortelyou has sustained while a member of the Cabinet. Mr. Root may have been fully justified in his language, but of paramount interest was his distinct admission concerning the practise of both parties in soliciting funds. Mr. Root said: "The same men — I know some of them — among the most prominent contributors, have been applied to by both parties. They were asked to contribute to the Republican fund and they were asked to contribute to the Democratic fund. They took their choice. And would it have been disgraceful for them if they had chosen the Republican fund, and praiseworthy if they had chosen the Democratic fund?"

These men who were thus approached by both sides, according to Mr. Root, were undoubtedly the heads of great railroad systems, industrial combinations, and consolidated banking interests. Both sides solicited and therefore hoped for the financial support of these grand moguls of capital. One party rather than the other was preferred by the money power, in this very practical test. The side that was not preferred was disappointed; the side that was preferred wished nothing said about it. Hence the uproar. But again let us cleave to the essential truth, which is that regardless of candidates and personalities, regardless of Mr. Roosevelt and Judge Parker, both honorable men, money is a mighty power in our politics.

Whichever way our sympathies may incline as between parties and candidates, let us not forget that the secret collection and secret use of enormous campaign funds, for whose control no one is responsible under the law, and about which, when once scattered, no one pretends to have the slightest knowledge — let us not forget that all this has become a national scandal, and confronts you and all of us as a deadly peril to the form of government and the institutions which we hold dear.

## THE SENTIMENT TO WHICH LAWSON APPEALS[1]

*The Nation*, December 29, 1904

The professional financiers who are indiscriminately lumped together in the term "Wall Street" are unable to comprehend the popular interest in Thomas W. Lawson's articles on "Frenzied Finance." On the other hand, the unsophisticated millions who devour these lurid tales of greed and gold are indignant that anybody should speak cynically or flippantly of a truly penitent stockjobber. Your banker or insurance-company president dismisses Lawson with the contemptuous comment that whatever in his stories is true has long been known, and that what is new is false. "Lawson," they say, "is obviously a blackguard; he confesses to complicity in swindling operations; he is possibly a blackmailer. Let him pass." But he still remains an obstinate fact to be reckoned with. More than one sincere communication has reached us deploring our lack of faith in the heroic Lawson. "He is doing a good work in his own way," they plead; "the least you can do is to respect his motives and let him alone."

This popular view of Lawson has its roots in certain large social and political sentiments that are but dimly apprehended in that part of Manhattan Island lying south of City Hall. Our complacent capitalists have heard faintly and from far off the wild talk of Populists and Socialists about the money devil; but they set this

[1] Thomas W. Lawson, a Boston financier, in 1904 published in *Everybody's Magazine* a series of articles on "Frenzied Finance," describing somewhat sensationally the alleged inner workings of "the system" by which manipulators fleeced the public.

down as the raving of ignorance and hysteria. The Populists and Socialists, however, have simply formulated into a political creed and voiced from the platform an unrest and distrust widespread among laborers, farmers, and persons of narrow incomes throughout the country. These men and women have seen our captains of industry accumulate enormous fortunes with a speed which is to them inexplicable except on the plausible theory of dishonesty. These plain people know that stocks are watered in the most shameless fashion in enterprises that remain solvent; and that the most barefaced swindling has been practised in bankrupt ventures like the Shipbuilding Trust — to cite one example in a thousand. Poor men and women have put their slow savings into companies presumably directed by men of intelligence and probity — the Amalgamated Copper, for instance — and have seen their petty provision for the future disappear in a night. Somebody has got away with that money; nobody is prosecuted by our fearless district attorneys. The question of the duped and enraged investor is, "Who is the thief?" Lawson is ready with an answer. . . . His descriptions of the panic-stricken Addicks, with eyes as dull as those of a dead fish, his account of blackmailing receiverships, of juggling with the judiciary, of buying the votes of five States, his charges of absolutely insatiate and conscienceless rapacity, fit in with the preconceived theories, and confirm the darkest suspicions of the unfortunates who were fleeced.

More significant than Lawson himself, who may soon be a spent rocket, is this sentiment to which he has made such a successful appeal. The people who are convinced that our laws are out of joint are — if we may judge by the recent Socialist vote — an increasing class. In a period of general prosperity they are quiescent; in the pinch of hard times they muster enough strength to be formidable in our politics. For this element the Lawson articles are fresh sinews of war. One of the shrewdest politicians of the Northwest remarked last summer: "Every grafter in Wall Street is against Roosevelt, and consequently we're for him." President Roosevelt was fortunate in having the financial support of Wall Street and the votes of those who hate it; but again in the future, as frequently in the past, there will be a sharp cleavage in politics. When that crisis arrives, such pamphlets as "Frenzied Finance," if skilfully circulated, may wreck a conservative party. Bryan's phrase about crucifying labor upon a "cross of gold" shook the whole fabric of our credit because men's minds were prepared to believe that it expressed a truth. The seed was sown in good ground. So long as financiers of repute lend their names and influence to speculations that may properly be characterized as "frenzied," just so long will "Down with the grafters of Wall Street!" be a potent battle-cry, just so long will the utterances of a Lawson be flame to the flax.

The enemies, then, which our great financial institutions, our railways, our insurance companies, and our banks, have chiefly to fear, are, so to speak, of their own household.   When the Goths and Vandals prepare a descent upon our "vested interests," their most terrible weapons will be drawn from the armories of New York, Boston, and Philadelphia.   The men who have promoted the vast and bottomless undertakings into which a credulous public has poured its dollars, are the real begetters of the Populistic and Socialistic parties.   From the victims of their rapine, when the day of political judgment dawns, they may expect no quarter.

## ROOSEVELT ON THE EVE OF HIS SECOND TERM

Baltimore *News*, March 4, 1905

It is much to be doubted whether any President has entered upon his term of office, either for the first or the second time, the object of a degree and kind of popular admiration such as that which greets Theodore Roosevelt today.   The comparison which most readily suggests itself is that of Andrew Jackson.   The hero of New Orleans and the fight against the Bank of the United States evoked a kind of popular idolatry not unlike that which President Roosevelt commands, and it was very much more intense.   But along with it there was an equally intense party and personal feeling directed against him; and his defeated opponent, Henry Clay, was a man who commanded such enthusiastic devotion on the part of his followers and admirers as has probably not been paralleled in the entire history of American politics.   Moreover, there was something of a class division there — Clay appealing rather to the intellect and wealth of the country, Jackson to the instincts of the masses. In Roosevelt's case, the remarkable phenomenon is presented of a man born to wealth and high family connections, a scholar and author, first conspicuous nationally as an advocate and prompter of that "aristocratic" measure, civil service reform, who is nevertheless above all a favorite with the great masses of the people, while remaining almost equally a favorite with the class in which he would himself naturally be placed; and, to complete the picture, he is a man who, while a thorough-going Republican partisan, enters upon his second term with Democratic party feeling against him reduced to such small dimensions as to be almost a negligible factor.

If other comparisons were desired, the first to present itself, going backward in point of time, would be Cleveland.   For our own part, we believe that if the popularity of a man could be *weighed* in some authentic way, instead of being merely indicated by *count*, no man in our time — Roosevelt not excepted — has had so great a measure of popularity throughout the country, and irrespective of party, as that commanded by Grover Cleveland from the close of his first to the opening of his second Administration. There was toward him something of the same popular appreciation of simple, sterling and cardinal qualities which forms the basis of Mr. Roosevelt's hold upon the people; and the feeling in Mr. Cleveland's case was more deep-seated, went farther down into the roots of character. But it was not so nearly universal as Mr. Roosevelt's case, nor was it a feeling so naturally manifested upon the surface. The cases of Grant and Lincoln present, of course, the anomaly of a divided, or recently divided, country, which puts them out of line for direct comparison. And when we go back to the instance of George Washington, we are confronted with the phenomenon of a feeling wholly different in kind from any that could be evoked by services other than those sublime and immortal works which the Father of His Country devoted to the making of the nation, in war and in peace. It is true he had bitter enemies and unrestrained maligners; but the feeling toward him on the part of the typical American was a feeling that transcends mere popularity, and has something in it which can hardly be called a personal feeling at all.

The tap-root of the remarkable popularity of Mr. Roosevelt, we feel sure, is the absolute conviction that there is nothing about him that is mean or sordid. All his feats of physical prowess, his Rough Rider exploits, his youthful ardor and effervescence, would have proved quite unequal to captivating the American people were there not behind these qualities, attractive as they are to the multitude, something that appeals more strongly to the national heart and conscience. The primary thing the people want in a President, before they will give him their applause or liking, is honesty; but that is not sufficient. They wish to feel that he has something about him that will not quietly accommodate itself, in a sordid spirit of comfortable ease, to things as they happen to be. The people feel about Mr. Roosevelt not only that he is honest but — we wish he had not so abused the word as to make it almost impossible to use — that he is strenuously honest. They feel that he is ready to assert himself in the face of the forces of plutocracy, so nearly omnipotent in the councils of his own party. They feel that there are great national questions upon which he is thoroughly in earnest, and in behalf of which he is ever ready to work with energy and enthusiasm. They like him in his capacity as a man, as the head of his own family, as an exponent of vigorous and youthful Americanism: but all this

would not avail to make him the national favorite that he is without
the solid foundation of a belief in sterling qualities which place him
above the common level of political thought and action.

One reflection that is forcibly suggested by these considerations
has a significant bearing upon the status of the national parties.
That Mr. Roosevelt was stronger than his party — as well as that
Mr. Parker was weaker than his — in the recent election is a proposition hardly open to dispute; but it is perhaps not sufficiently
recognized that the reason that he is stronger than his party is by
no means wholly a personal one. Mr. Roosevelt's special strength
lies largely in that part of him in which he is in marked opposition
to the dominant tendency of his own party. The people are not so
delighted with the prospect of a millionaire millennium as the
Republican magnates have often seemed to imagine. Mere wallow-
ing in prosperity — especially when that prosperity is so peculiarly
distributed — does not meet all the aspirations of the American
nature. Whether wisely and ably, or only vigorously and emphatically, Mr. Roosevelt has certainly entered an energetic protest
against a complacent acceptance of things as they are. He has
defied the "oh, well" sentiment of Wall Street magnates and their
Senatorial representatives. He stands for many of the things which,
only a short time ago, when proposed by Mr. Bryan, were howled
down as anarchistic. And the people like him the better for it —
not only the people who have been clamoring for a change all along,
and not only the people who are beginning to see that something
must be done sooner or later, but very many of the people who
think Mr. Roosevelt is specifically wrong but believe that the spirit
of what he is doing is wholesome. The great god Prosperity is not a
god whose worship can be continuously and completely satisfying.
A few years of it was quite enough to give soundly constituted
people a surfeit of it. Mr. Roosevelt has been supplying something
less gross to occupy the attention of the nation, and the nation is
thankful for it. The Republican party will either permit itself to
be affected by the virus that he has put into it or will find itself less
surely in possession of national power than it imagines.

# JOHN HAY[1]

### The Nation, July 6, 1905

The late John Hay represented to the full both theories of genius.
He had capacities so marked and versatile that everything he undertook was done with a kind of divine ease, and he had a special
training so laborious and protracted that his success might be ac-

---

[1] John Hay died at his summer home in New Hampshire on July 1, 1905.

counted for as the result of sheer application. What distinguishes him from a score of illustrious predecessors in the State Department is a certain literary, or if you will, artistic quality of temper. It requires flexibility of mind to write devil-may-care ballads after you have served in the legations of Paris, Vienna, and Madrid. It needs a ready sympathy to be forty-odd, to be an ex-diplomat and an Assistant Secretary of State, and then to make the literary sensation of the season with an anonymous novel on the labor problem, "The Breadwinners." In fact, it was because Mr. Hay so thoroughly represented what Bliss Perry has eulogized as the "amateur spirit," that he was a figure not only potent but fascinating in all of the many walks of life he entered. From his Jim Bludsoes to the epigones of the Metternich school, he was able to meet all sorts and conditions of men on their own basis; he prevailed through a superior imaginative quality, which he reinforced with an amazing variety of material information. That anecdote is characteristic which tells how a famous art critic, dining at Mr. Hay's table at Washington, displayed distress at a landscape by Constable which hung on the opposite wall. When his trouble had been noted and its cause asked, the connoisseur deprecatingly regretted that Mr. Hay had been taken in by one of the cleverer sort of forgeries. Unruffled, the host first pointed out the intrinsic marks by which the authenticity of the picture was established, and then observed, as if casually, that he had had it of Constable's heirs, and could trace it direct to the artist's studio. . . .

As ambassador to England Mr. Hay's success was personal rather than diplomatic, but as Secretary of State since 1898 his peculiar abilities have gained world-wide recognition. It was typical of his manner of thought that the sensational episode of the siege of the Peking legation did not suggest spectacular vindication of national honor, but hastened the execution of a humane plan, previously conceived, for the rehabilitation of the troubled Empire. By patient consultation with the European powers he succeeded in imposing the principle that China was no longer a field for spoliation, but was to be open on equal terms to the trade of the world, and was to have its opportunity for national reform and development. Mr. Hay's circular notes on the Manchuria question were the object of some mockery, as merely academic. That tone has changed since it has been perceived that the Japanese triumph is merely one interpretation of Mr. Hay's doctrine, and Mr. Roosevelt's humane mediation between the combatants another. These facts have completely borne out Mr. Hay's prophetic vision that the Chinese question is one in morals as well as in international politics, and that the time for European aggression has passed.

It would be unworthy of Mr. Hay's own great achievements and personal candor to point out that he had not only the qualities, but the defects, of the amateur spirit. His desire to illustrate his office, his quick imaginative response to distant situations, led him at times into empty undertakings, like the Rumanian circular against persecution of the Jews. His devotion to the project of the Panama Canal and to that of national expansion generally drew him into more than one equivocal transaction in the national behoof, as his admirers must acknowledge with averted faces. But his administration, taken broadly, was characterized by scholarship, dignity, and resourcefulness. In seven years he has raised the State Department from a condition of relative provincialism to a commanding position among the chancelleries of the world. Mr. Hay is most likely to be remembered for that magnanimous stand in the Far East which stemmed the tide of brutal aggression upon helpless China. His associates and our generation of brethren of the pen will remember with most affection the *litterateur* who, amid the gravest responsibilities, vindicated the practical value of the artistic imagination.

## THE NEW YORK LIFE ON THE STAND[1]

### *The Nation*, October 12, 1905

President McCall's previous testimony has led the public to believe him capable of much moral callousness, but his attitude and admissions on October 4 were more damaging than his worst enemy could have believed possible. If he has any defence at all, it must be along the line of Mirabeau's saying about his younger brother: "In any other family than ours, he would be considered a scapegrace." In any other business than that in which the Equitable's revelations had been made, Mr. McCall's confessions would be regarded as absolutely damning. It is true that no such palpable mismanagement, or outright looting, as marked the administration of the Equitable has been shown to exist in the New York Life; but the disclosure of its loose methods and reckless payments of huge sums for political corruption — avowed as they are with singular effrontery — has come with an especial and cumulative shock. We think that the country will be more stirred and feel more outraged by President McCall's latest evidence than by anything that has gone before.

Note, first, how the head of a great fiduciary institution acknowledges that $150,000 can be taken from its funds without a single

[1] The life insurance investigation of 1905 in New York, conducted by Charles E. Hughes, resulted in bringing the great life insurance companies under careful public supervision.

trace being left on the books. Apparently, President McCall's contributions to successive Republican campaign funds were not even hidden under that broad mantle which covers such a multitude of sins, "legal expenses." The $150,000 was taken from the policy-holders and left not a wrack behind. Mr. McCall had to confess with mortification that he had not been able to discover any book-keeping entry showing from what fund the money was withdrawn. It is presumed that "profits" were diminished by so much, though there is no record. But what every policy-holder will at once ask is, if $150,000 could thus disappear, why not $500,000? If money of the company can be taken for politics, and no telltale track left, why not for speculation, for gambling, for debauchery? In other words, the door for embezzlement seems to stand wide open. This is the implication of President McCall's statements; and it is almost more amazing than the gifts to politicians themselves, shocking and illegal as these were.

But the positively sickening thing is the final uncovering of the reptile fund to which President McCall has ordered such vast amounts paid from year to year. Within the past four and a half years, he swore, he had turned over $476,927 to a legislative jobber wholly without voucher. During that same period, he had paid out $1,103,920 in "law expenses," a good part of which, it is clear, must have been used to corrupt legislatures. Of course, Mr. McCall did not use the word "corrupt." His phrase was "produce results"; but he knows, and everybody out of the infant school knows, that the most abhorrent means might have been used, and doubtless in many cases were used, to secure the desired "results" and demoralize our public life. The President of the New York Life must be com-mended for greater frankness than he displayed when first testifying about his payments to Hamilton. Originally, he talked evasively about "real estate" transactions; now, the only inference from his acknowledgments is that the money was a legislative corruption fund.

Naturally, Mr. Hughes had to go through the form of asking whether any direct proposition to bribe a legislator was ever laid before him, and naturally Mr. McCall replied with indignation, "Never." But this deceives no one. Mr. McCall was bred at Albany. He knows from the inside the game that is played there. It is idle for him or any president of a corporation who gives money to Albany lobbyists to pretend that he does not know what is done with it. No member of the investigating committee could have kept his countenance if he had supposed that President McCall's prot-estations of ignorance and innocence were meant to be taken seri-ously. No, the facts stand out clear as noonday: the great insurance companies have poured out money like water to defeat or procure legislation. We have a blunt man out West who tells us just what to think about this business. Gov. Folk calls it crime. He says that President McCall's payment of trust funds to politicians is "embezzlement" — " just the same as if a public official in charge of the public funds were to put his hands into the public treasury."

## THE STRAIN ON THE CONSTITUTION [1]

### Baltimore *News*, January 7, 1907

The Constitution of the United States is being tugged at nowadays in a way that has not been paralleled since the great struggle of the Civil War. The question how far the Federal Government can go in the regulation of the industrial, commercial, and transportation interests of the country, as a consequence of the "interstate commerce" clause of the Constitution, is constantly to the front. This has, indeed, been the case ever since the passing of the interstate commerce law in 1887, and of the anti-trust law in 1890; but never has it occupied a position of anything like the prominence, or anything like the urgency, that now characterize it. That this is so is due not only to the active exertions of political leaders like Mr. Bryan and Mr. Roosevelt, but even more, of course, to the stupendous expansion of our great corporations, the menace of monopoly, and those amazing exhibitions of one-man power of which the disclosures concerning Mr. Harriman's operations furnish the latest example. In the face of a situation so wholly unlike anything that the framers of the Constitution could possibly have contemplated, and in view of the obvious fact that it is a situation with which the separate States are inherently unable to cope, it is not surprising that the effort has been made to exploit to the utmost such power as the Constitution of the United States places in the hands of the Federal Government to deal with the pressing questions of our present economic life.

The basis of all the interstate commerce legislation of the United States is to be found in just four words of the Constitution. Among the powers granted to Congress by that instrument is included the power "to regulate commerce with foreign nations, and among the several States, and with the Indian tribes." The original interstate commerce law, the anti-trust law, the recently enacted railroad rate law, the pure food law, and all the rest of our Federal legislation affecting conditions of manufacture, trade, and transportation stand upon this foundation. Just how much weight it can be made to carry must depend on the decision of the United

[1] By Fabian Franklin.

States courts, if we assume a disposition on the part of Congress and the President to press its possibilities to the utmost. At the present moment a most interesting stage has been reached in the determination of this most critical issue. On the one hand, the Senate has under consideration Senator Beveridge's bill prohibiting the interstate transportation of any goods in the manufacture of which the labor of children under fourteen years of age has been employed — a bill which manifestly extends the scope of the interstate commerce clause far beyond any previous application; and on the other hand, two United States district judges have independently declared the employers' liability act recently passed by Congress unconstitutional. If the decisions of these judges are sustained, on appeal, by the Supreme Court, this event will mark the drawing of the line very much on the hither side of legislation of the character of the Beveridge bill; if, on the other hand, the constitutionality of the employers' liability act is sustained by the Supreme Court, and if at any time in the near future such a bill as that of Senator Beveridge shall be passed by Congress, it would be impossible to assign any limits to the extension of Federal power, not simply under cover of those four pregnant words of the interstate commerce clause, but under cover of any of a dozen other phrases in the Constitution. . . .

Take, for example, such a proposition as that contained in the Beveridge bill. To prohibit the transportation, in interstate commerce, of goods in the making of which child labor has entered, is to use the power over interstate commerce simply as a weapon of coercion in the regulation of conditions of industry in the several States. The purpose may be ever so laudable, but the point is that it is a purpose having none but the most accidental — incidental is not a strong enough word — and far-fetched connection with interstate commerce, or commerce of any kind. If the power to regulate interstate commerce be held to justify an application so remote, what is to hinder its being used to prohibit the transportation of goods of any kind from a State in which child labor is allowed, or in which the sale of alcoholic liquors is permitted, or which does not maintain a State university? It may be that between the Beveridge proposal and such fantastic propositions as we have here imagined there is a wide gulf; but the point is that unless it be recognized that the power to regulate interstate commerce is to be construed as having such limitations as a reasonable attitude toward the meaning of written language would impose, we are landed in a situation in which the power of the Federal government to coerce the separate States upon any point of internal policy would be practically without limit. And even if it be admitted that the necessity of a great stretching of Federal power in industrial and commercial matters is a necessity of the times, it should be borne in mind that the process of changing the Constitution by orderly amendment is open to the nation. That this process is only a paper possibility, but is in practise out of the question, is a belief widely entertained, but it is in reality little better than a superstition. It is high time that the question were being seriously considered whether the unlimited stretching of the Constitution can be justified by the unwarranted assumption that legal amendment of that instrument is an impossibility.

## CHILD'S HISTORY OF KANSAS[1]

Emporia *Gazette*, July 4, 1907

A child lives his own life, and the world of grown-up is a thing apart. And when grown to man's estate, he recalls events that passed before his childish memories. Thus in Kansas, for instance, one child now living in a man's memory remembers the drought of '60, not by the anxiety on the faces of his parents, not by the waiting and watching for rain, but by the fact that a time was when they parceled out the biscuits at table, and a boy had to take his share and no more. The whole tragedy of the time to hundreds of men and women, when pride and want fought until want went to the "aid store" and took what was needed — all the bleakness and brownness of the land — these passed unnoticed under his eyes. For the things he saw were in the child's world. And so to one who came later into the world, history, as it was told by those who were a part of history, was told to a child, and recalled only with a child's understanding. Thus the child holds in his memory today not the stories he was told of the adventures of the army of the border, but he retains a curious wonder as to why those men had red legs. And of the statesman whose tragic end stirred Kansas in the early days, the child who heard the story of the dramas' beginning, rise, and close a dozen times recalls only that the man wore a buffalo skin overcoat, and that men said he had dark, piercing eyes. All other things the man has learned, he has read, and it is the man's memory and not the child's that rises. And of the war between the States, the child who must have heard the story a thousand times remembers best the songs — "Old Nicodemus," "The Year of the Jubiloo," "We Shall Meet but we Shall Miss Him," "Tramp, Tramp, Tramp," and the hanging of Jeff Davis to a sour apple tree. The tale that was told did not seem to stick; only the tale that was read found lodgment, but the songs cling like burrs to the memory.

[1] By William Allen White, who of course is the child here mentioned.

As the child grew into his own consciousness, he passed through the drought of '73 and the grasshopper year. But of that strange calamity, so little remains in his memory. He remembers that men stood in the street looking at the sky, and that he turned his face toward the sky and watched the shimmering cloud of insects floating above him. But he does not remember how they came, nor when they went. He remembers that there was a time when boys caught grasshoppers by the bottleful, and played with them, and made them "spit tobacco juice," and that for a certain number of pins another little boy would eat grasshopper legs; and that once the boys put up a fabulous purse of marbles and pins and precious treasure to get the little boy to eat them alive, and that he did eat a hopper and was very sick. But of the plague and its devastation the child remembers nothing, and of the drought of '74 he only remembers that the clouds were high and big and white and feathery one year, and the sky was bluer than ever, and the dirt in the road that passed before the house was warm to play in far after sundown. But of the withered corn and the starving cattle he remembers only that one day an antelope came up to eat with the cattle in the feed lot. Also there is a recollection that the bone yard grew that year, and that the boy was not allowed to play there for a long time.

Of the politics that moved men in Kansas in the early days of the '70's the child, who must have heard men talk politics many long hours, remembers only that when he wore a Greeley scarf, another little boy grabbed one end, and a big boy grabbed another, and choked the boy until he was black in the face, and the schoolteacher doused water in his face and brought him to. Later, when he was a big boy, he and four other big boys in the intermediate room at school, great hulks of fellows eight years old, lined up the four little Democrats in school one fall day, and threw watermelon rinds for Tilden one whole hour, and at recess again faced the school behind the woodpile for reform, and came in besmeared and bespattered but unconquered. "It was a famous victory." But what it was all about the boy did not know, except that his father was a Democrat, and that all Republican little boys were to be fought if they said much about it. It was years afterward that the boy knew what had become of Tilden, or why he smeared himself with watermelons in the lost cause. The fight in the boy world was a boy-world feud, and had only a remote connection with the contest in the world outside. Indeed, so confused was the boy's idea of the issues at stake in the upper world that he confused Tilden with the man whose name was linked with Beecher's, and when they began talking about Tilton, then he would be sent out of the room for something, and when he came back be sent away for something else, and then told to run and play.

From the Chicago *Tribune*, November 10, 1904          By John T. McCutcheon

THE MYSTERIOUS STRANGER

(Published the day after election returns showed that Missouri had gone Republican for the first time in history.)

# HISTORY OF SUNDAY LAW IN OREGON[1]

### Portland *Oregonian*, October 1, 1908

Long had the statute slept, under which a great many persons were arrested on Sunday last for selling small packages of fruits or peanuts to passers-by, or for shining the shoes or brushing the dust from the clothes of those who had need for the service. But last Sunday great numbers were accused of these "crimes." Close construction of the statute, it is said, requires this proceeding, for vindication of the majesty of the law, and for protection of public and private morals. Hitherto this small, this convenient traffic has been carried on under the exceptions permitted by the word "necessity." It belongs, indeed, to things that have become necessary through changes in conditions since the statute was enacted, forty-four years ago.

In 1864, when this statute was enacted, the most simple and primitive pioneer conditions prevailed. The population was small and sparse; there was no town above the rank of a small village; means of transportation on land did not exist, and on water were

[1] By Harvey W. Scott.

very limited; there was no railroad, and the steamboat schedules, when there were any, advertised trips once or twice a week. On Sundays people reposed at home, and most did little else on week days. It was easy for a few thousand people, scattered over a vast country that abounded in all the resources of nature, to get a living and be content. The habits of that time lingered long in the country and in some degree still survive, which is one reason why the progress of Oregon is slow and difficult. Habits and thoughts and customs of that time were fixed in statutes which have been regarded for years as obsolete; certainly are obsolescent. But even these statutes were protests, to an extent, against the beginnings of emergence from pioneer conditions. Particularly so was the one under present consideration.

The country was just beginning to move a little. Some stir out of the usual way began to be noticed, and when it appeared on Sundays it attracted unusual attention. Dealers began to offer little luxuries and necessities for sale on that day. In a small way there were Sunday amusements. Now and then a summer excursion was advertised for Sunday, and fruits and sandwiches and soda-water were sold. Booths for the sale of meats, fruits and vegetables were erected at or near camp-meeting grounds, and those less scrupulous about Sunday observance would buy on that day. These things, and similar ones, scandalized "the good people," and their resolve to stop them, and to prevent the growth of the custom that was "profaning the Lord's Day," led to this statute; which, however, in this special feature, has never been enforced, but in most places has lain dormant all these years.

It was no harm to let the old law, almost unnoticed when it was enacted, and practically forgotten years ago, continue to sleep; it is not possible to see any good result from the effort to revive it by literal enforcement of these provisions. Besides, questions will be raised before every jury under the exceptions provided in the act itself. Of course the law can be altered or repealed, if the people desire, but there are obsolete enactments that may just as well be ignored or let alone. Dead long since, there is no need of disinterment for new burial.

## COMPETITION IN POLITICAL PURITY

*The Nation*, July 23, 1908

In the lively contest in political purity between Mr. Taft and Mr. Bryan, Mr. Taft has just scored a point by announcing that the Republican National Committee will not accept contributions from any corporation. Mr. Bryan had already made a declaration to the same effect.  The honors between the two leaders seem now to be about even, though in view of the intimate relations between the Republican Committee and the corporations in recent campaigns Mr. Taft has made the greater renunciation.  The spectacle of the parties bidding against each other in the matter of opening the campaign subscription books and in spurning "tainted" money is as exhilarating as unexpected.  What Congress refused to do, what the Republican Convention shied at, has been brought about by the candidates.  Each of them has perceived whither public opinion is tending, and has sought to get into accord with it.  The first move was made when Mr. Taft sensibly and shrewdly took a position in advance of his party, and gave orders that an account of all moneys given to aid his election should be made public after the voting was over.  Then came Mr. Bryan, announcing that *his* publicity will begin on October 15, and extend over every day thereafter until the campaign closes.  This is in line with the McCall bill, which provided that a sworn return of funds obtained should be published before as well as after the election.  The arguments for such a course are obvious.  If we are going to have publicity at all, we may as well have it real and entire.

The great evils of secrecy in the raising and expending of money to carry elections are not confined to direct corruption of the suffrage by outright purchase of votes.  Far too much of that has been done.  When Harriman wrote that the $260,000 which he raised for Roosevelt in the closing days of the campaign of 1904 meant a change of 50,000 votes, he undoubtedly implied that they were bought like so many railroad shares.  In the two campaigns which Mark Hanna conducted so lavishly, doubtless an appalling amount of the coin found its way to the pockets of venal voters.  But even more demoralizing and shocking are the secret arrangements of the party managers with large contributors.  They are given, for their money, a first lien upon legislation, or are promised that they will be looked after when it comes to distribute good things in office.

## COUNTRY TOWN SAYINGS[1]
### Atchison *Globe*, 1877–1911

Families with babies, and families without babies, are so sorry for each other.

Don't be ashamed if you can't play the piano; be proud of it.

There never was a man so patient that it didn't make him mad to get a line under his horse's tail when out driving.

How good a yawn tastes at about ten o'clock in the evening, just before going to bed!

[1] By E. W. Howe, "the philosopher of Potato Hill."

A girl should be given an allowance every week, if it is not more than fifty cents. It will teach her how to handle the great sums intrusted to her care when she marries.

When a man buys a new hat he wants one just like the one he had before. But a woman isn't that way.

If you want to get a man very angry, get some one to pray for him.

Women like to attend weddings, to hear the big, sweet, juicy promises the bridegrooms make.

I once wondered how the banks made their money, but when I procured a loan I found out.

After a man has said grace at a meal some time is required for those around the table to become comfortable again.

Nearly every unsuccessful man we ever met was a good billiard player.

When a woman is on her last legs, she starts a boarding house; a man starts a fire-insurance agency.

When a friend is in trouble, don't annoy him by asking if there is anything you can do; think up something appropriate, and do it.

We have always found it a pretty good rule to avoid an "intellectual treat."

A Protestant preacher's idea of great success in his work is to convert a Catholic.

Some people never have anything except ideals.

The better a pie tastes, the worse it is for you.

Nearly every man says of his dog, "His father cost a thousand dollars."

How a little girl loves to say to a little boy, "Oh, you are going to catch it!"

With all its meanness and dirt, we rather like Chicago.

A man has his clothes made to fit him; a woman makes herself fit her clothes.


## THE ALDRICH TARIFF REVISION[1]

### The *Independent*, June 10, 1909

At the end of last week the Senate voted upon the Aldrich bill's increases of the duties upon cotton goods. These increases had been attacked with much force and persistence by the Republican critics of the Aldrich revision. Mr. Dolliver began the work some time ago, before the cotton goods schedule had been taken up. It was

[1] The Republican platform of 1908 promised "unequivocally" a revision of the tariff immediately after the election, and while a candidate Mr. Taft in various speeches called for tariff reduction. The Payne-Aldrich tariff of 1909, increasing rates, was universally regarded as a betrayal of this pledge, and Taft's approval of the law in his famous Winona speech marked the beginning of his political down fall.

renewed last week by himself and others, and a very notable contribution to the debate was made by Mr. La Follette, who laid bare the disguised and unwarrantable additions to the Dingley duties, item by item, using official figures and statements and showing a long list of increases, running up to 110 per cent, upon goods the importation of which is virtually prohibited even by the present rates.

That is to say, where the increase is 110 per cent, the imports last year were only $8,109, and where Mr. Aldrich proposes an addition of 98 per cent, the present duty permitted only $7,000 worth of goods to come in from abroad. And in one exceptional instance, the official statement indicated an increase of 460 per cent, designed to check an incoming flood represented by imports last year of $5,000! Of course, such additions are not to be made for protection. Surely, there is ample protection in the present duties. But such increases would enable combined domestic manufacturers to raise prices. Attack and exposure were made in vain. The provisions of the bill were approved. On every motion Mr. Aldrich had a majority of from 9 to 11, and the opposition of ten Republicans was easily overcome. This was regarded as a conclusive test of the "insurgent" strength, and now it is admitted that the bill will be passed in the form desired by the Aldrich majority. Those duties which have been withheld so long, for trading purposes or to keep uncertain men in line, will soon be brought forward and approved, together with the provisions for a costly and unnecessary Customs Court and the extraordinary maximum rates which, if enacted, will add 25 per cent, for a time at least, to the duties upon a considerable part of our imports, in some instances more than doubling the ordinary duties of the bill. It should not be forgotten that these maximum rates would, so far as they should be used, give 25 per cent more protection to domestic manufacturers and combinations of manufacturers.

As for the conference committee, to which it is said that Mr. Taft looks for relief, we venture to say that part of its work is already done. Does anyone think that the names of its members have not for some time past been known to Senator Aldrich and Speaker Cannon?

Will the country be satisfied with such a bill as, in all probability, is soon to be passed and sent to the President? We think not. The fact should not be overlooked that the character of the bill has been thoroughly exposed by Republicans, not by Democrats, whose arguments and attacks have little or no weight with the average Republican partisan. The unwarrantable increases, open or hidden, have been pointed out and denounced by men of exceptional force and ability, who are not only Republicans, but also protectionists. As a rule, they are willing to accept the present Dingley duties. They attack additions to these duties, and their work has been well done. We believe that a majority of their Republican constituents think that even the Dingley rates are too high.

## THE TRAGIC SENSE[1]

New York *Evening Post*, July 25, 1908

The strange return of Eberhard, the New Jersey murderer, to the scene of his crime and his distracted confession, and the mystery surrounding the death of Helen Drew of Troy, prove anew that the newspapers are dealing constantly in the raw stuff of tragedy. It is dangerous material to handle — this daily chronicle of passion and violence. For tragedy is one thing, and the raw material of tragedy is another. The spectacle of the one is a deterrent, of the other an incentive to crime. The process of transforming an unwholesome passage from the records of the police courts into something akin to tragic drama demands a deeply reflective mind. It must be admitted that the average newspaper reporter is wholly inadequate to the task, even if it were not quite aside from the purpose of his calling. It is unnecessary to say that the mind of the ordinary newspaper reader is as unequal to the transformation as that of the reporter.

The truly tragic, according to the Greek critic, stirs the soul with pity for the offender and cleanses it with terror for the offence. The perilous fascination exercised by the newspaper record of crime is due to its entire lack of tragic "purgation." By the newspaper men the divine terror of the "Agamemnon" would be reduced to the story of a brutal woman who trapped her husband in his bath and brained him with a hatchet. In that form the material is unedifying and unprofitable; but, unfortunately, in that form it is also the most generally palatable. The public, if we may judge by the circulation of the sensational papers, is most pleased when the major crimes are treated with apparent nonchalance or even with flippancy and gloating detail. What is desired is crude sensation, as in the voluminous accounts of the Thaw trial, without troublesome afterthought.

The moral purgation effected by tragedy is to be attributed in large measure to its constant relating of cause to effect — a thing which no reporter can do and which no self-indulgent sinner likes to do. Macbeth indulges in this weak or vicious thought today which

[1] By Stuart P. Sherman, who repeatedly served on the *Evening Post* staff during his summer vacations as professor at the University of Illinois. An excellent example of his power of giving depth to an ordinary subject.

will cause him to do that bad thing tomorrow which will lead to a bloody deed the day after — and so all our yesterdays have lighted fools the way to bloody death.    The tragic sense divines every link in the chain till the first is forged to the last.    The newspaper man's aim is clean contrary.    His object is to thrill and startle. Last night this man was worth millions;    this morning he has not a cent.    Interesting.    Yesterday this man was a pillar of his church; today he has two wives.    Amusing.    Last night he was a respected bank cashier;    this morning he is in Canada.    Alarming.    This morning she was selling lace in a big drygoods store;    tonight she is in the East River.    Shocking.    He quietly entered the house and put a knife into his wife and three children.    Horrible.    Horrible, shocking, alarming, amusing, interesting — sensations of the moment gradually accumulating into an abiding sense that this is a pretty nasty world;    that is the limit of instruction in the newspaper account of crime.    How different from the reflection of the villain Edmund in "Lear," when deep-dyed in evil he meets his end: "The wheel is come full circle;    I am here."

The newspaper records of crime weaken the will by reminding men of their moral insignificance;    tragedy strengthens it by reminding them of their moral greatness.    For, as the wisdom of the Greeks and the Elizabethans divined, tragedy can befall only a great man in whom good and evil elements are mingled.    In his destiny more than mortal powers participate.    When Oedipus died, the sky lightened and strange voices were heard.    When the devils contended for the soul of Faustus, Christ's blood streamed in the firmament. We no longer believe that tragedy is concerned only with the fates of lords and ladies.    Since Wordsworth found it in the shepherd, and Thomas Hardy in the dairymaid, we have come to recognize the tragic possibilities in the common man who every day does as mad things as a king.    But the common man towers to tragic proportions only when the contention of good and evil in him is related to superhuman powers — to the "something not ourselves which makes for righteousness," and to the something not ourselves which opposes it.    Into the pity and terror of that struggle the crime-monger never penetrates;    and it is not the least of our grievances against him that his public reveling in horrors blunts the keenness of our own tragic sense.

## THE INIQUITOUS PAYNE–ALDRICH TARIFF

*New York* World, August 5, 1909

For the first time in the history of the United States we now have a law whose avowed object is to "guarantee a reasonable profit to American industries."    The tariff bill which received executive approval yesterday is certain, therefore, to be celebrated no less for the candor of its authors than for the drastic provisions of its schedules.

When a governmental policy like tariff taxation becomes institutional it is interesting to consider the reasons advanced for its preservation and extension. The purpose of the tariff of 1789 was said to be "the protection of and encouragement of manufacturers," in which we may discern the infant-industry theory which afterward became highly popular. It is worthy of note that when our industries were in fact infants they were protected and encouraged by a tariff so low that a return to it now would be looked upon as a wild adventure in "free trade." After the infant-industry era we had the "home market" and the "American system."

It was not until 1840 that the wage question was definitely advanced as an excuse for monopoly tariffs. Before that period high wages in America were sometimes pleaded as an excuse for legislation favoring employers; afterward it became the fashion to insist that wages were high because of the tariff and could not be maintained without it. With increasing ardor this contention has been made the basis of the policy until now we find it coupled with the "guarantee of a reasonable profit to American industries."[1]

This departure originated in Ohio, possibly with President Taft himself. It was in the platform on which he was elected. It was scrupulously adhered to by him in nearly all of his speeches — even those in which he was most emphatic in demanding a revision downward. Remembering these things, we need not be surprised at the outcome. The law would have been worse if the President had not interfered, but the fact that it is disappointing in many respects must be attributed to his own avowal that government is to concern itself hereafter with the profits of selected business interests.

Where is this underwriting to end? No insurance company has an actuary keen enough to show how an enterprise of this kind could be carried on successfully by private capital. It would go to smash in a year, even with the sanction of Congress, if it were not grossly discriminating, if the richest country in the world did not furnish the resources, and if those who are wronged did not outnumber ten to one those who are favored.

---

[1] The Republican platform of 1908 declared that "In all tariff legislation the true principle of protection is best maintained by the imposition of such duties as will equal the difference between the cost of production at home and abroad, together with a reasonable profit to American industries." In repeated speeches Taft promised revision downward.

## ["TAINTED MONEY"] [1]

*The Independent*, March 18, 1909

The question is a practical one in Nebraska and elsewhere. The University of Nebraska might have accepted for its retired professors the advantage of the Carnegie pension fund, but Mr. Bryan appeared before the Legislature and protested against accepting on the ground that the money is tainted, because given originally by a noted trust baron and multimillionaire; and by the narrowest margin of votes the Legislature refused to allow the professors to take advantage of the fund. Mr. Bryan is very stern in this matter, much more so than Governor Johnson of Minnesota; but Governor Johnson is declared not to be so good a Democrat as is Mr. Bryan. Indeed, Mr. Bryan is the law and norm of Democracy.

Let us take another case. A man gets immense wealth by fraudulent control of a railroad. He dies and his property is divided between his children. A daughter — or a son — is like the good son of a bad man described by a Hebrew prophet, and she, or he, uses the money inherited in such a way as to gild with glory the shaded name. Is the money that she, or he, gives so worthily, so tainted that it cannot be received by good people for a good cause? Certainly not. No one will believe so. We have settled that by universal applause.

Now let us revert to the Nebraska case of the Carnegie pension fund. That money belonged to Mr. Carnegie, was acquired by him in the line of business methods which Mr. Bryan believes to be oppressive and wrong. But it passed out of his hands just as much as if he had died. It was given over to the Carnegie Foundation for the Advancement of Teaching, and Mr. Carnegie no longer owns it or has any control of it. The cause is a noble one. Does the alleged taint stick to the money still? Certainly no more than in the other case in which the original accumulator of the wealth has died. St. Augustine's principle applies. The light is not defiled; the money is not tainted; and Mr. Bryan simply lacks the clearness of vision to see the facts and their application. Let Nebraska freely allow her aged professors to receive their pensions.

## [EX–PRESIDENT ROOSEVELT ON THE TARIFF]

*The Nation*, September 8, 1910

In the rapid conversion of Mr. Roosevelt to beliefs which he used to denounce, nothing is more astonishing than his coming over to the idea that the tariff is a moral issue. In his Saturday's address at

[1] Washington Gladden, objecting to the ecclesiastical acceptance of gifts from John D. Rockefeller Sr., gave currency to the phrase "tainted money."

Sioux Falls he spoke with vehemence of "the scramble of selfish interests" which goes to the making of a protective tariff — the Dingley law as well as the Payne-Aldrich bill — and said that when "we get a crooked deal" in the tariff, as he admitted that the people had, "then it becomes very emphatically a moral issue." But this is what Roosevelt when candidate and Roosevelt when President could never be got to concede. The tariff then was a mere fiscal measure, with a lot of wearisome details, in which he could not be induced to take any interest because it was not a moral question. During all of the seven years of his Presidency he never once lifted a finger to remove the burdens and scandal of the then tariff in which, as he now confesses, the "general interest of the public" was "subordinated" to "the profit of the special interests." In the light of this experience it is clear that, in Mr. Roosevelt's case, we need a new definition of what is "moral." A thing is evidently moral when votes and popularity can be won by advocating it, but it is abysmally immoral if a man like Cannon goes to the White House and tells the President that he will hurt himself and his party by taking it up.

## GOVERNOR HUGHES'S WORK

*The Nation*, October 13, 1910

If we were to single out one other characteristic which marks off Governor Hughes's administration from all that had gone before it, we should dwell upon his free resort to the people over the heads of the members of the Legislature. He early foreshadowed this plan. In a speech at Albany shortly after becoming Governor he declared that if he could not persuade the Legislature to enact the reforms which he advocated, he should go directly to the constituencies. This he did in instance after instance, and with what effect the whole State knows. It was a new departure in the conception of a Governor's power, which was so striking and on the whole so victorious that it attracted attention and provoked imitation all over the country. Woodrow Wilson is today promising to do in New Jersey what Hughes did in New York — that is, to insist upon Statewide discussion of Statewide interests, and when necessary to go behind the Legislature to the people. It is one of those great changes that sometimes are wrought in the on-going of our government without statutory or constitutional enactment, and all owing to the initiative of a bold and self-reliant man who quietly puts old material to new uses. This goes well, too, with the rising assertion of the power of the States. One can distinctly see the coming of a New Stateism to offset or withstand the New Nationalism; and of that movement Governor Hughes has been a leading prophet and exponent.

Of him New York took leave last Thursday with sincere regret and a deep sense of indebtedness. The high example which he has set will make lapses from it more difficult and more unforgivable. How the good that he has done will live after his official life is over we get a hint in the way in which both parties have now been forced to adopt his despised and defeated plan for direct primaries. He will not be here at the final triumph, but it will be his triumph. And in many other ways the faithful and unflagging labor which he gave to the State will be fruitful after he is gone. No one but would wish him different in some respects; but we have to take men as they are, and so taking Charles E. Hughes, we gratefully acknowledge that he has ennobled our public life and quickened our hope in democracy.

## ROOSEVELT AND THE THIRD–TERM TRADITION[1]

### New York *World*, January 2, 1912

*The World* cannot agree with its old friend Henry Watterson that "the third-term tradition is all that stands between us and life tenure in the Presidential office."

The third-term tradition has undoubtedly had its uses; yet we think those uses have been greatly overestimated. The tradition is of less importance than the character of the President upon whom the third term is to be conferred. A third term for Washington or Jefferson or Jackson would not and could not have meant life tenure. Had Lincoln been spared, a third term in his case might have averted the terrible tragedy of reconstruction without diminishing by a single grain the sum total of American liberty.

A nation that is wholly fit for self-government, that respects its own institutions, that believes in due process of law and is still attached to the basic principles of human freedom, has little to fear from a third term or even a fourth term. Its political salvation is always in its own hands and it remains the strongest guarantee of its own liberties.

The menace of the Roosevelt campaign does not lie in the attack upon the third-term tradition but in the state of mind that could desire four years more of Theodore Roosevelt in the White House — four years more of personal government, four years more of Presidential lawlessness, four years more of autocratic rule, four years more of Executive contempt for Congress, courts and Constitution, four years more of centralization, four years more of jingoism, four

[1] By Frank I. Cobb.

years more of wanton extravagance, four years more of denunciation and demogogy — in the state of mind that wants the New Nationalism, that wants a Little Father, that wants a Federal interference with every form of human industry and activity, that wants the States stripped of their powers, that wants the minority deprived of all safeguards against the tyranny of the majority and bureaucracy substituted for the Bill of Rights.

This is a generation that has far too little insight into the meaning of its own institutions. It has forgotten how much blood and iron went into the making of the liberties which it inherited and which cost it nothing. It is a generation of no restraint upon its impulses and it passions. It regards itself as the Fathers and the Prophets. It thinks it has nothing to learn from the past and that the history of the human struggle for freedom carries no lesson to the century. Anything like Constitutions or courts or precedents which stand in the way of its immediate will is regarded as an obstacle to progress.

This sentiment alone is responsible for the recrudescence of Rooseveltism, and this sentiment constitutes the real menace to representative government and republican institutions. If the American people are determined to have the kind of government that Mr. Roosevelt represents they will get it regardless of third terms. If they do not take him they will find another Roosevelt.

The danger does not lie in popular indifference to the third-term tradition but in popular indifference to the fundamental principles of liberty upon which the Republic was established. If the American people, with all their knowledge of two terms of Roosevelt, want a third term of Roosevelt, they should allow nothing so flimsy as a precedent to stand in the way.

## BETRAYING A GREAT CAUSE[1]

### New York *World*, March 8, 1912

The United States Senate does not merely cut away the principle which gives life and force to the arbitration treaties with Great Britain and France. It adds insult to injury by ratifying the remains as if life were left in them.

No treaties are required to bring nations into an arbitration of questions which they are always mutually willing to arbitrate at the time of a dispute. What these treaties sought to do was to create an obligation to arbitrate a broad or justiciable class of questions which they might not be willing to arbitrate in the heat of contro-

---

[1] President Taft negotiated treaties of arbitration with Great Britain and France in the summer of 1911, and under the leadership of Henry Cabot Lodge the Senate promptly mangled them, as it had previously mangled arbitration treaties of Roosevelt's.

versy. So provision was made for joint high commissions of both parties to interpret disputed points and determine the arbitral character of issues arising.

The Senate strikes out this vital provision. It adds others for the further emasculation of the proposed conventions. And then in solemn mockery it adopts the Lodge resolution which was intended to overcome the objections thus enforced. It saw no harm to its own prerogatives four years ago in leaving to arbitration the interpretation of existing treaties. It now sees vital harm in leaving to arbitration any interpretation of these treaties.

It is not the Taft Administration which the Senate has injured. It is the Senate itself.

It is not the President who has been betrayed, it is the great cause of civilization.

## THE TARIFF[1]

Editorial by Theodore Roosevelt, *The Outlook*, September 14, 1912

It is not merely the tariff that should be revised, but the method of tariff-making and tariff-administration. Whenever nowadays an industry is to be protected it should be on the theory that such protection will serve to keep up the wages and the standard of living of the wage-worker in that industry with full regard for the interest of the consumer. To accomplish this the tariff to be levied should, as nearly as is scientifically possible, approximate the differential between the cost of production at home and abroad. The differential is chiefly, if not wholly, in labor cost. No duty should be permitted to stand as regards any industry unless the workers receive their full share of the benefits of that duty. In other words, there is no warrant for protection unless a legitimate share of the benefits gets into the pay-envelope of the worker.

The practise of undertaking a general revision of all the schedules at one time, and of securing information as to the conditions in the different industries and as to rates of duty desired chiefly from those engaged in the industries, who themselves benefit directly from the rates they propose, has been demonstrated to be not only iniquitous but futile. It has afforded opportunities for practically all the abuses which have crept into our tariff-making and our tariff-administration. The day of the log-rolling tariff must end. The progressive thought of the country has recognized this fact for several years, and the time has come when all genuine Progressives should insist upon a thorough and radical change in the method of tariff-making.

[1] While candidate for President in 1912, Roosevelt continued his contributing editorship of the *Outlook*. His contributions were called editorials, but were signed.

The first step should be the creation of a permanent commission of non-partisan experts whose business it shall be to study scientifically all phases of tariff-making and of tariff effects. This commission should be large enough to cover all the different and widely varying branches of American industry. It should have ample powers to enable it to secure exact and reliable information. It should have authority to examine closely all correlated subjects, such as the effect of any given duty on the consumers of the article on which the duty is levied; that is, it should consider directly the question as to what any duty costs the people in the price of living. It should examine into the wages and conditions of life of the workmen in any industry, so as to insure our refusing protection to any industry unless the showing as regards the share labor receives therefrom is satisfactory. This commission would be wholly different from the unsatisfactory tariff board which was created under a provision of law which failed to give it the powers indispensable if it was to do the work it should do.

## THE TAFT–WILSON TRUST PROGRAMME

Editorial by Theodore Roosevelt, *The Outlook*, September 21, 1912

During my first Administration and since, I have first directed and tested, and then studied, the working of the Sherman Anti-Trust Law. When I came into office that law was dead; I took it up and for the first time had it enforced.

We gained this much by the enforcement: we gained the establishment of the principle that the government was supreme over the great corporations; but that is almost the end of the good that came through our lawsuits.

Take the Northern Securities case. Under me that suit was brought to a successful conclusion. I at first thought that we had secured a definite and real solution of the difficulties, and my opponents thought so too at first and were very sore; but in the end it proved that all we had actually accomplished is what is said above. As one of the greatest magnates concerned afterwards remarked: "Well, when the smoke cleared away, I found that whereas formerly I had to prove my ownership by one bit of paper, I now have to prove it by two."

Take again the Standard Oil decision. The Standard Oil Company was nominally dissolved as a result of the suit against it. It was divided nominally into thirty-four different companies. For a moment there was a great deal of fright in Wall Street; and under the stress of that fright the big magnates for the time being thought that they would come round and advocate the

From *The Commoner*, April, 1905

By Guy R. Spencer

ROCKEFELLER THE TRUST GROWER

Based on a famous sentence in a speech by J. D. Rockefeller Jr., at Brown University: "The American Beauty rose can be produced in all its splendor only by sacrificing the early buds that grow up around it."

policy of control I had advocated, because while that control would really control them, would hamper and limit them, at least they thought that they would thereby escape death. Then they found that it was only make-believe death to which they were exposed. And as a result of the suit for dissolution Mr. Rockefeller's property rose in value to a higher degree than it had ever gone before, and to an already sufficient fortune he added some eighty or ninety millions of dollars, while the price of oil went up to the consumer. Men who purchased Standard Oil on the curb in New York tell me that the sole difference is that, while formerly the broker would give them one slip of paper, now he gives them an envelope containing thirty-seven slips — that's all.

You recollect Mr. Pierpont Morgan said, "You can't unscramble the eggs in an omelet." This particular instance of trying to unscramble them didn't help anybody but the owners of the eggs, for it increased the value of the eggs indefinitely and made the omelet cost more to the general public. Now our proposal is not to try to unscramble the eggs by a mere succession of lawsuits, but to exercise such administrative control by the government as will prevent the eggs from ever being scrambled.

Mr. Wilson in a recent speech in New York said that "no body of men would have the wisdom necessary to enable them to regulate the industrial processes of the country." I was much interested in that remark because it represents the exact attitude always taken by the respectable ultra-conservative in matters of this nature. Word for word it is what some of the great railway magnates used to say before the passage of the Interstate Commerce Law. They used to say that "no body of men alive could undertake to regulate the complicated railway business." Other big men used to say the same thing when the proposal was to establish Public Utilities Commissions.

I appeal from the prophet of today to the way the facts have refuted the prophets of yesterday. There is no more difficulty in regulating the Standard Oil or the Steel Corporation than in regulating a big railway. We have actually made the Interstate Commerce Law work. We have found by the test of actual work that the way to control the railways lies through increasing the power, and especially through increasing the application of the power, of the Interstate Commerce Commission, by regulating and controlling those railways, and not by any development of the Anti-Trust Law. Real control of the trusts can come only by the adoption of similar expedients. What I want to see done with our industrial concerns is to see an Interstate Industrial Commission established, which shall handle the Standard Oil, the Steel Trust, the Tobacco Trust, and every such big trust, through administrative action, just as the Interstate Commerce Commission handles the railways, and with a power extended beyond that of the Interstate Commerce Commission.[1]

[1] Both the Democrats and the Republican followers of Taft attacked Roosevelt's trust program as meaning a tyrannical and unworkable control of industry by bureaucrats. The Democratic program of a new Anti-Trust Act was carried out in 1914 by passage of the Clayton Act.

## [THE CAMPAIGN ISSUES: TWO VIEWS]

*The Outlook*, October 12, 1912

A valuable addition to campaign discussion has been made by two letters published in the New York *Times:* one by Charles W. Eliot, president emeritus of Harvard University, advocating the election of Governor Wilson; the other a reply by Albert Bushnell Hart, advocating the election of Mr. Roosevelt. The *Outlook* heartily welcomes the publication of these two letters. The writers have set an example which might worthily be followed by other leaders of thought. It is a great advantage not to have the campaign discussion carried on exclusively by candidates, professional spellbinders, and partisan journals. President Eliot thinks that there are two principal issues in the present campaign: the prompt and effective reduction of the high tariff, and the extent to which the Constitution of the United States ought to be modified by interpretation or in practise in order to enable the national government to deal with grave measures of social, industrial, and political reform. Governor Wilson and the Democratic party he thinks likely to accomplish a judicious and effective reduction in tariff rates, which he believes is not to be expected either from the Republican party under the leadership of Mr. Taft or from the Progressive party under the leadership of Mr. Roosevelt. The platforms of all three parties he regards as "much alike in promising a large number of social and industrial reforms, many of them long known to be desirable, but some full of difficulties and dangers." The Democratic party's platform and candidates, while less conservative than the Republican, are more promising than the Progressive, partly because "the public sayings of Governor Wilson are much more prudent and measured in regard to the proposed changes than those of ex-President Roosevelt." Mr. Roosevelt is regarded by Mr. Eliot as "an impulsive, self-confident, headstrong man, impatient of restraints and opposition," who has "shown himself capable while in power of taking grave public action — which of course seemed to him wise and right — in disregard of Constitutional legal limitations." Finally, Mr. Eliot objects to Mr. Roosevelt's candidacy because it involves "another constitutional change — the question of a third term in the Presidency."

Professor Hart defines the principal issue thus: "Is the American government to be really democratic, as democratic as human nature will admit, or the affair of a comparatively small class in the community?" The Progressive movement is the product of a determination to secure the birthright of which we have been deprived.

Single reforms in the direction of popular rights, such as commission government for the cities, the Australian ballot, primary laws, the popular election of Senators, have been accomplished in spite of the resistance of the political forces in control of the old parties. "The Progressive party is the first great national organization in our history to commit itself and all its voters to the programme of general reform." The dread of Federal centralization is not justified by national experience. "The Postoffice is one of the largest business enterprises in the world, and with all its defects, is as superior to the sacred express companies acting under State charters as Theodore Roosevelt is superior to Governor Dix." There is much more danger of usurpation by corporations than by a single President. Some kind of progress is inevitable. If the government stands still, powerful interests will make progress and create a private system and acquire vested rights difficult to disturb, and Socialism will make progress, and in a little while will elect a Socialist President of the United States, "which means that the Socialist National Committee will be President. There is only one way to head off the danger, and that is the formation of a party which will take over the reasonable part of the Socialistic programme." Mr. Eliot's estimate of Theodore Roosevelt is not justified. "Those who know Theodore Roosevelt intimately know how far his head or mind is from acting on impulse, or from acting without consultation and discretion." Mr. Roosevelt's strong language is both justified and beneficial; justified because "it is not easy to be calm and weigh every word when bandits are emptying your pockets;" beneficial because his vigorous representation of the country's need of reform has been one of the factors in creating a national progressive sentiment. "He is the political parent of Governor Hughes and Governor Folk and Governor Johnson and Governor Wilson. Not one of them would have been governor in our time but for the influence of Theodore Roosevelt." As for the third term, "not one voter in ten today is seriously influenced by the fear of the third term *per se*, or will vote against Theodore Roosevelt on that ground."

It is probably too much to hope that either of the political parties will publish both letters for general distribution; and the political millennium is not so far advanced that the two parties are likely to combine in such publication. We wish that the New York *Times*, which originally published these letters, would print them both in cheap pamphlet form and give them to both the National Democratic and the National Progressive Committees for distribution. That our own sympathies are wholly with Professor Hart may be taken for granted.

## PERVERTED SYMPATHY FOR GUNMEN[1]

New York *World*, April 11, 1914

Writing in *The World* on behalf of the condemned "gunmen," Mrs. Inez Milholland-Boissevain asserts that —

> Life, education, and environment have penalized these youths to the fullest extent, as evidenced by their every word and act.

With due respect to Mrs. Boissevain, this is sheer nonsense. These young men were penalized by themselves, and by themselves alone.

They came of decent, hard-working parents. They were born under exactly the same conditions that tens of thousands of industrious, law-abiding men in New York were born. They had the same educational opportunities. They had the same chance to make something of themselves. They did not become criminals by circumstance. They are not "warped and misshapen offspring of our present social conditions," as Mrs. Boissevain calls them. They elected a criminal career as the easiest way of making a living. Society did not lead them to the shadow of the death-chair. They blazed their own trail.

Mrs. Boissevain does not believe in capital punishment. That is a debatable question. But the death sentence over these "gunmen" is no more an argument against capital punishment than is the death sentence over Schmidt. Nor are their cases the kind over which Mrs. Boissevain need waste "sympathy and everlasting pity."

If any part of society is to blame for the fate of the "gunmen," however, it is the philanthropic and uplifting element with which Mrs. Boissevain is identified. For years various writers, agitators, lecturers, and social workers in this community have been preaching a gospel that is a gospel of disaster.

They have been teaching in effect that society owes everybody a living; that work is a bondage; that workers are wage-slavers; that all employers are oppressors; that civilization is a tyrant which grinds out the lives of the poor to create luxuries for the rich, and that nobody is responsible for anything he may do unless he happens to have been born with a silver spoon in his mouth.

What wonder that our Whitey Lewises, our Dago Franks, our Gyps the Blood, and our Lefty Louies drink in this contempt for honest labor, and for fathers and mothers and brothers and sisters who are content to earn their bread in the sweat of their faces! Why work when one can be a thug, a tin-horn gambler, a pimp,

[1] This editorial upon the murderers in the famous Rosenthal police case was written by Frank I. Cobb.

a cheap burglar and a criminal parasite upon society in general? That sort of doctrine is pounded into the ears of the youth of New York every day. Fortunately, most of them have too much sense and character to follow it. But that is not the fault of the social agitators who spare no effort to teach the degradation of labor.

Society owes neither reparation nor apology to the graduates of this school. Whatever sympathy *The World* has to give, whatever help it can offer, will not be wasted upon "gunmen" convicted of murder. Whatever measure of sympathy or help *The World* can extend to struggling humanity is reserved for the boys and girls, the men and women, who are seeking to make something of themselves, who are striving to be useful members of society, who are not afraid to do an honest day's work for an honest day's pay, and who try to do their duty as God gives them strength and light to see that duty. These are the people whose battle *The World* esteems it a high privilege to help fight, and we shall waste none of our time in blubbering over convicted "gunmen," the manner of whose death will be no more shameful than the manner of their life.

## BELGIUM, 1914

### By Theodore Roosevelt, *The Outlook*, Sept. 23, 1914

A deputation of Belgians has arrived in this country to invoke our assistance in the time of their deadly need. What action our government can or will take I know not. It has been announced that no action can be taken that will interfere with our entire neutrality. It is certainly eminently desirable that we should remain entirely neutral, and nothing but urgent need would warrant breaking our neutrality and taking sides one way or the other. . . . Of course it would be folly to jump into the gulf ourselves for no good purpose; and in every probability nothing that we could have done would have helped Belgium.

## WOMEN'S RIGHT TO VOTE

### New York *World*, March 14, 1915

Woman suffrage will not reform government in the conventional moral sense, although in the long run it will produce a more representative and responsible government. If we may judge the future by the past, the immediate effect of woman suffrage will be to disorganize government and add to its confusion. That is what has always happened when the franchise was extended. Each new influx of voters submerged the old order, and the former standards of public service deteriorated for the time being, much to the anguish of the Brahmin classes, but not to the permanent injury of society. Enlarging the suffrage does not purify government, but enlarging the suffrage stabilizes and strengthens democracy, and hence the ultimate influence is invariably for the general good. In a democracy the people do not exist for the government, but the government exists for the people, and every adult person subject to government may reasonably ask for a voice in ordering the policies of that government.

For women to demand suffrage on the ground that they are purer and nobler and holier than men is to argue against their own cause. An oligarchy of virtue would be only one degree less oppressive than an oligarchy of vice. Nobody has ever obtained the franchise on the mere pretext that he was pure in heart, and nobody ever will. The franchise is not granted in order that politics may be purified, but in order that the holder of the franchise may the better protect his life, liberty, property and welfare under the government to which he is responsible as a citizen.

Votes for women will not improve the quality of government, but it will make women more intelligent and more responsible, and hence society as a whole must inevitably benefit. The ballot box is a mighty university. It has proved so in the case of men, and it must prove so in the case of women, or the experience of history is false.

Moreover, the political influence already exerted by a few women makes it highly desirable that all women be enfranchised in order to reëstablish the balance. Under republican institutions power without responsibility is a grave evil. Women today have great power in government, but no responsibility. Various organizations of women, which probably do not represent ten per cent of the sex, maintain at times a veritable reign of terror in legislative bodies by pretending to speak in the name of all women. In consequence, half the country is now bedevilled by some form or other of harem government which in no respect is a true expression of public opinion. Legislators who are no better than they ought to be are forever making ridiculous concessions to women agitators on the theory that official sympathy with such moral yearnings is a shrewd method of diverting public suspicion. The statute books are loaded down with foolish laws dictated by a few crusading women and enacted in a spirit of "The ladies — God bless them!" An overwhelming majority of women have had no voice in this legislation, and they disclaim all responsibility for its results. But the statutes remain, the situation grows worse from year to year, and all laws fall more or less into contempt through this legislation bred of fanaticism and hypocrisy.

We know what would probably happen if government were in
the hands of women, and Anthony Comstock, Charles Edward
Russell, and the Anti-Saloon League were accepted as the spokesmen for all the disfranchised males. Yet something of that sort is
going on all the time in State capitals in the name of women.
The only antidote to the influence of some women upon government is the influence of all women upon government. When all
sex limitations upon suffrage have been removed the political
power of those women who are obsessed with the idea that government must assume the spiritual characteristics of a communistic
prayer meeting will be restricted to their own votes, and the votes
of those who are actually in sympathy with them.

But if the claim that votes for women will purify politics is
sentimental nonsense, the counter-claim that votes for women will
wreck the home is equally absurd. Protecting the home is one of
the favorite recreations of American Bourbonism. The home is
the oldest of human institutions. It is older than government. It
protects itself. It is not government that protects the home, but
it is the home that maintains government. It was because of
homes that governments were established. An institution that has
withstood the vicissitudes of centuries is not likely to collapse because the women of a community spend half an hour in the voting
booth on the first Tuesday after the first Monday in November.
If the home could survive St. Paul, it can survive the ballot.

Eliminating from the suffrage controversy all of its cant and
twaddle, the question is a straight issue of whether all the adult
citizens of the State shall be entitled to a vote in making the laws
to which all of them are subject, or whether this privilege shall be
the exclusive property of half of these citizens who gain their political power by the accident of sex.

Lincoln once said that this republic was founded upon the rule
of "root, hog, or die," and women are no less amenable to that
principle than are men. The amiable theory that it is man's
function to provide and woman's function to be sheltered is a
living lie, as millions of women wage-earners can testify. Sometimes man provides and sometimes he doesn't. The woman who
is sheltered today may be working in a factory tomorrow to support herself and her children. Hunger knows no sex. Want
knows no sex. Necessity knows no sex. Law knows no sex.
Property knows no sex. Only the ballot box knows sex.

But the ballot box once knew rank. It once knew land and
primogeniture. It once knew income and money and family. All
those paraphernalia of privilege have been swept away, and the
disability of sex will follow. In the steady sweep of democracy

the time will come when the present opposition to woman suffrage will seem as short-sighted and senseless as the former opposition to manhood suffrage now seems.

Democracies always move forward. That is their law of self-preservation. If they stand still or retrograde they are lost.

## THE STAR BOARDER'S WAIL[1]

Emporia *Gazette*, December 16, 1915

To the Editor of the Gazette.

Sir: I have been boarding with one landlady five years. I pay every Monday morning. In that five years we have had round steak fried hard for the noon meal every single weekday that we haven't had pork fried hard. In the name of all the gods of cooking, can't you start something? Respectfully,

A STAR BOARDER.

With all the fervor of an ardent nature we can try, O thou tortured soul! We can tell your landlady if she reads these lines that in the bright lexicon of cookery nothing — not even thick broiled porterhouse steak — costs so much as pork and round steak fried hard.

For less money than fried round steak costs she could give you broiled round steak, slightly underdone. It goes further, and makes more blood and strength. For less money than round steak costs she could give you shoulder or brisket of mutton with rice and curry. For half what fried hard round steak costs she could give you hamburger steak, with lots of meal and pimentos and onions mixed in it, served with gravy from the steak. For a third less than fried round steak or pork costs she could give you short ribs of beef, pot-roasted with onions, carrots and potatoes with oodles of brown gravy. For what round steak costs she could buy a shoulder of mutton, cover it with flour, rub garlic on it, and roast it, serving it slightly underdone, and make it go further than round steak, with lots of mutton gravy. And for less than round steak she could give you pig hocks boiled with cabbage and turnips and potatoes.

There is a list of edible food as long as the moral law that costs less and tastes better, for a change, than round steak fried hard or fried pork. The trouble with the boarding-house keeper is that she won't take the trouble to get out of the beaten track. It's easy to think up round steak fried hard or pork, and cooking is always a work of imagination and mental effort.

---

[1] William Allen White's campaign for culinary reform in "the fried steak belt" was carried on year after year with highly salutary effect.

## THE RAILROAD CRISIS AND AFTER[1]

*The New Republic*, August 26, 1916

As a statesman confronted with a great emergency, Mr. Wilson is compelled to break through the slogans which serve publicity rather than sense. The great fact before him is that the Brotherhoods have the power to call a strike which would bring such disaster and suffering to the country that it must be averted. The President knows that no matter how great the public sentiment against the men the strike could take place and would not be broken without riot and bloodshed and agony. Assume that the men were utterly wrong, assume that they deserve no sympathy whatever, it would still be out of the question for the President to coerce them. They have the power to strike and the legal right, and that fact cannot be argued out of existence. You may believe in "arbitration" world without end but if one party which has the power declares that an issue is not arbitrable, it is useless sentimentality to talk about arbitration.

The President has done, therefore, what the practical situation required. He has narrowed the issue down to the very lowest point which the Brotherhoods will accept, and has asked the managers to try the "eight-hour day" with the pledge that it will be studied in operation, that if it doesn't work the government will save the railroad from "ruin." A more sensible and statesmanlike proposal has not been suggested, and no sympathy is due the management for pretending that it will be ruined when there is a practical guaranty that the federal power will not allow it to be ruined. Through improvement in efficiency and through possible increase of rates there is an ample margin of safety. And if it is shown that the trains cannot be run on the schedules, the question can be reopened and readjusted. The railroads are not faced with the alternative of ruin or victory. The real alternative, as the President has shown, is between a strike and the trial of a new system subject to public inquiry and public guaranties. . . .

The railroads say they are thinking of the future and of the precedents which would be created. There they have hold of something which must occupy the inventive thought of the nation.

[1] The four railway brotherhoods — engineers, conductors, firemen, trainmen, comprising about 340,000 employees — had been for several years asking for an eight-hour day for freight-train workers, which through the operation of overtime rates meant an increase in pay. They called a strike in August, 1916; President Wilson, after futile efforts to adjust the dispute, went before Congress with a request for legislation to meet the men's demands. The result was hasty passage of the Adamson Act. Stoppage of railway traffic would not merely have meant a disaster to America, but possible loss of the war by the Allies, who were dependent on American shipments.

In fact, the most hopeful aspect of the whole matter is that from the President down there seems to be a clear idea that this calamity must not only be averted, but must be averted in such a way that better methods may prevail in the future.

There again the President's plan is both wise and imaginative. The proposal that the workings of the settlement be put to Federal inquiry is fruitful. Once a commission is created to study the wages problem on railroads we shall have an agency capable of growth. For arbitration in the crude sense does not meet the facts. There is no hope, we believe, in creating a tribunal to deal with an industrial dispute after it has become an out and out conflict. What we need is an administrative commission continuously in touch with the wage problem. It is just as impractical to arbitrate wages when everything is prepared for a strike as it was to deal with rates through the courts and legislature. No tribunal can handle the situation after the irritation has culminated in a national conflict. Great conflicts can be prevented only by breaking up big issues into small ones, and adjusting them from day to day.

## [PRESIDENT WILSON AND THE TRUSTS]

*The New Republic*, September 9, 1916

President Wilson's handling of the anti-trust legislation in his speech of acceptance is hard to understand. He accused the Republicans of enacting "anti-trust laws which hampered the very things they were meant to foster, which were stiff and inelastic and in fact unintelligible." This must refer to the Sherman law, which so far from being stiff and inelastic, embodied one of the most flexible and comprehensive legal formulas known to the history of Anglo-Saxon jurisprudence. In so far as it was unintelligible its unintelligibility was the result of its vagueness and elasticity. He went on to describe what the Democrats have accomplished in the following words: "The laws against the trusts have been clarified by definition, with a view to making it plain that they were not directed against big business, but only against unfair business." But the laws against the trusts have not been clarified by definition. In the Clayton Act nothing was done to restrict the operation of the Sherman law. Its definitions were only those which had already been substantially achieved in the judicial construction of the law. Least of all were the definitions made with a view to distinguishing between "big business" and "unfair business." Congress has still left it for the courts to settle whether and to what extent big business is bad business. The suits now pending against the Harvester and Steel trusts conspicuously raise the issue whether mere dangerous size offends the Sherman law or whether only the commission of actual public injury makes a combination illegal. This aspect of the law has never received explicit and complete definition, and the Clayton Act will do nothing to affect the decision one way or another. Do Mr. Wilson's words mean that the Democratic party has been finally converted to the position against which it has so long and strenuously protested: that public policy can ignore the question of how large a portion of any one business is concentrated under one management?

## HUGHES OR WILSON?

*The New Republic*, October 28, 1916

The unsatisfactory aspects of the alternative offered by Mr. Wilson and the Democrats [to Mr. Hughes] have made hesitation easy. The President's infirmities in action, the distrust inspired by his erratic and inflated phrase-making, his willingness to confuse the interest of the Democratic party with the public welfare, his scant sympathy with certain essential aspects of progressivism and his ignoring of progressives who were not Democrats until he needed their votes, the limitations of the social and administrative program outlined in the Democratic platform and in the President's speeches, and Mr. Wilson's own unqualified loyalty to the two-party system — these considerations tempted many liberals to look toward Mr. Hughes in the hope of getting something better. They craved a militant progressivism which would carry on the fight not only against partisan opponents but against partisan associates. Mr. Hughes was that kind of Progressive before his transfer to the bench. As governor of New York he had preferred to jeopardize the success of his local party organization rather than yield his own clear personal convictions. If his liberalism had grown during his retirement from active politics, if he had added to his passion for good government an equally lively passion for social amelioration, and if his program had waxed sufficiently aggressive and well defined to call for a relentless war on the reactionary influences in his own party, there might have been a sufficient justification for preferring Mr. Hughes to Mr. Wilson.

As soon as Mr. Hughes began to talk these hopes speedily vanished. His words were not those of a thorough-going Progressive for whom the great barrier to the increasing unity and momentum of American national life was the comparative impoverishment, alienation, and dependence of the huge wage-earning class. His spirit was not that of a militant who would fight hard, as Mr. Roosevelt had once fought, to transform the Republican party into the servant of democratic, political, and social aspirations. He declared himself to be a Republican first. His chosen method of redeeming Republicanism was that of ignoring as unimportant the quarrel of 1912 and of restoring a superficial, muddle-headed, and demoralizing harmony. So far as his speeches expressed any explicit vision of public policy, it was that merely of the more efficient conduct of private and public business. He gave no indication of associating in his own mind the needed efficiency with a tenacious social purpose and with a shift in the distribution of political and economic power. He was unable to understand why the solemn declaration of his own virtuous intentions was not a sufficient answer to every demand for a sharper definition of his own attitude toward the deeper controversies of the time. After such an exhibition an uncompromising liberal could support Mr. Hughes only by forgetting that liberalism meant anything in particular.

There remained Mr. Wilson's disqualifications; but formidable as they had once seemed, they began to look negligible in the light of the issue which Mr. Hughes had allowed Mr. Wilson to establish. The utterances of the Republican candidate, so far from redeeming the reactionary record of his party, had served as its partial confirmation. During the past year Mr. Wilson has been astutely striving to mould the Democracy into the national Progressive party, and by contrast to attach to the Republicans in the popular mind the stigma of being reactionary. Mr. Hughes has permitted him to succeed. His success and the acquiescence of his opponent created a living issue between the parties. No matter how necessary it may be eventually to combat the illiberal elements in the Democracy, it is of the utmost immediate importance to support its frank progressivism rather than the furtive standpatism of the Republicans. During the past few weeks the hesitation of many former Progressives has disappeared. With few exceptions that wing of the party which was primarily interested in social amelioration has rallied to Mr. Wilson, and what is equally significant, the example is being followed by many of the less doctrinaire and intellectually more independent Socialists. To their minds the result of the campaign has been the gradual emergence of a sharp and emphatic lineup between liberalism and reaction. The defeat of Mr. Wilson and the triumph of Mr. Hughes would be interpreted as a liberal setback and would increase the formidable obstacles to the success of the liberal cause.

The *New Republic* has come to share this preference for Mr.

Wilson and the Democratic party. The inevitable result of
Mr. Hughes's attempt to ignore the quarrel of 1912 has been to
reunite the Republican party, if at all, as a reactionary organ of government. He did not intend to accomplish any such result, but
he builded worse than he knew, because he failed to understand
the logic and spirit of the Progressive movement. Progressivism
cannot allow itself to be considered compliant and unimportant.
It can be made to triumph only by the use of aggressive tactics. It
would be the inevitable and dishonored victim of an attempt
to establish peace either in the party or the nation merely by
ignoring vital differences and extolling harmony. The certain
result of Mr. Hughes's leadership was to force liberals to support
a party which was definitely committed to a Progressive program
as opposed to a party whose program at best was not more than
non-committal.

## [WOODROW WILSON REËLECTED]
*The New Republic*, November 11, 1916

The reëlection of Mr. Wilson even by such a narrow margin is
one of the most extraordinary achievements in the political annals
of the United States. In 1912 his huge majority in the electoral
college was earned for him by an actual minority of the vote.
His supporters amounted to only about forty per cent of the
American electorate. His four years of office have been among
the most troubled in the country's history. He has had to deal
with a number of novel and critical problems which, no matter
how he handled them, obliged him to alienate certain of his former
supporters. Many thousands of Democrats among the professional
and business men of the country withdrew their allegiance because
of the infirmities of his foreign policy. Many thousands of the
Irish and German-Americans became his bitter and unscrupulous
enemies because of his benevolent neutrality toward the Allies.
One can only guess how much the default has amounted to, but
taking all the people with grievances together it could hardly have
been less than 500,000 votes. In order to win reëlection he was
obliged to convert into Democrats between 1,000,000 and 1,500,000
new voters; and the job was the more difficult because he could not
count upon the assistance of an expansive personality which the
ordinary American voter would understand and like. Yet he succeeded somehow in getting the necessary support. His gains were
chiefly among the farmers and women voters in those parts of the
country where Mr. Roosevelt's popularity had formerly been most
emphatic. Without the women voters, for the increase of whom
he has done so little, Mr. Wilson might have failed of election.

One outstanding fact about the election is the novel and significant distribution of the strength of the two major political parties. Mr. Hughes carried the East and the Middle West, Mr. Wilson the South and the Far West. In the case of every important industrial community except Ohio Mr. Hughes was victorious, although by widely different margins. Broadly speaking the lineup was between town and country, between industry and agriculture. The Democrats had expected to obtain a large measure of support from the wage-earners in the big industries of the country. It looks now as if they had received less than usual. The Republicans were apparently successful in the last two weeks of the campaign in holding a sufficient proportion of the votes of the laborers in the protected manufactures. But they lost much of their grip on the agrarian communities of the Mississippi Valley and the mountain States. The Democrats were saved from a severe defeat only by their success in making inroads on the normal support received by the Republicans from the farmers in the newer parts of the country. More than any election which has taken place since the Civil War, the old American territorial democracy, the democracy of Jackson and Douglas, has reasserted itself. Mr. Wilson has done what Mr. Bryan failed to do. He has recovered for the Democratic party the support of a great majority of the predominantly agricultural States. This support has not the same economic meaning as it had during the pioneer period, when the farmers in the newer parts of the country were in debt and thought themselves oppressed by the money power. The Far West is not aggrieved and rebellious as it was at the time of the "greenback" and "Populist" movements. But it still has a mind of its own, sharply defined from that of the rest of the country. In a combination with the solid South and with one or two other industrial States of the Middle West it is strong enough barely to swing a national victory.

## ROOSEVELT AND RIGHTEOUSNESS

*The New Republic*, January 13, 1917

In the current issue of the *Metropolitan Magazine* Mr. Roosevelt breaks loose in a violent onslaught upon the idea and the advocates of a League to Enforce Peace. His intention in publishing the article was to check the obviously increasing popularity of the agitation in favor of American participation in such a league, and its effect cannot fail to be mischievous because the article is loaded with the authority of an ex-President of the United States whose words always carry a certain amount of weight at home and abroad. But in this instance Mr. Roosevelt has overreached himself. The article will do more damage to Mr. Roosevelt's own reputation than it will to the popularity of a League to Enforce Peace. It is not a frank and well-informed discussion of the idea of a peace league, such as one has a right to expect from an ex-President who is peculiarly competent to deal with questions of foreign policy. If it were, it would deserve respectful consideration on its merits, no matter how sharp and how emphatic Mr. Roosevelt might be in his expression of an ultimately unfavorable verdict. It is a vindictive personal attack on the President and the ex-President of the United States who are the most prominent supporters of American participation in such a league, combined with a disingenuous attempt to explain away Mr. Roosevelt's own former advocacy of the principle underlying the plan. . . .

In the book entitled "America and the Great War," which he published in 1915, Mr. Roosevelt sought to indoctrinate his fellow-countrymen with what he believed to be the lessons for them of the catastrophe in Europe. The dominant idea which pervades the book is that of a necessary increase of American armaments for the protection of American liberties; but Mr. Roosevelt at that time expressly rejected the idea that American security could be guaranteed by armaments alone. He declared (page 107) "we ought not and must not rest content with working for our own defense." He reached this conclusion as the result of a careful analysis of the causes of the war. He pointed out (page 67 and following) that all "the peoples of the several European nations believe themselves to be fighting for righteous causes" connected with their national safety, and that if "we are to prevent a repetition of this world tragedy," the intensity of this conviction of national righteousness becomes "a prime factor for consideration." Mere preparedness will not prevail, because the European nations were prepared almost to the extent of their resources previous to the present war. On the contrary, Mr. Roosevelt uses phrases which imply that the greater the military preparedness the greater the danger of such catastrophes. It creates mutual fears, and these fears paralyze the forces which make for righteousness within a nation. "The fear among the plain German people of the combined strength of France and Russia made them acquiesce in the policy of the military party which was to disregard the laws of international morality" (page 73). "At present each nation has cause for the fear it feels. Each nation has cause to believe that its national life is in peril unless it is able to take the national life of one or more of its foes or at least hopelessly to cripple that foe." The causes of this fear must be removed or "these causes will bring about a repetition of the same awful tragedy."

After this analysis of the world war Mr. Roosevelt goes on to consider the remedy. The difficulty consists in the entire lack of "connection between force on the one hand and any scheme for securing international peace or justice on the other" (page 81). Such a connection can be established by creating some kind of an international police power to stand behind international sense of right as expressed in a competent tribunal (page 62). Mr. Roosevelt returns to this idea again and again, and it is not necessary to repeat his repetitions. In so far as he develops his plan in detail it differs in certain respects from the program which the advocates of a peace league are now recommending to the American people; but the object which Mr. Roosevelt was trying to accomplish in 1915 is the same as that which Mr. Wilson is trying to accomplish in 1917. Both were or are seeking the creation of a legal obligation on the part of powerful nations to use force for the guaranteeing of international security and justice. "Under such conditions," Mr. Roosevelt says (that is, if a peace league were instituted) "Belgium would be safe from any attack, such as that made by Germany, and Germany would be released of the haunting fear its people now have lest the Russians and the French smash their empire to pieces." He calls the alternative Utopian, but it is "a Utopia of a very practical kind," a working and realizable Utopia; and "the *only* alternative" to Utopia is the perpetuation of war or the perpetuation of hell.

Consider the situation in which Mr. Roosevelt is placed by the comparison between his argument of two years ago, and his attitude of today. In 1915 preparation for national defence was called insufficient because the more thoroughly nations prepared without establishing some connection between the use of force and the organization of international peace and justice, the more intense and dangerous became their apprehensions one of another. Today anybody who advocates American participation in this organization of international peace is "wicked" because the agitation may distract attention from the military preparedness which, in the absence of such organization, Mr. Roosevelt has himself declared to result in calamitous war. True, Mr. Roosevelt was as emphatic then as now in proclaiming the futility of American participation in the organization of peace, unless the nation were better prepared to contribute its share of the effective force by which the authority of a peace league would have to be sustained. But in the interval between 1915 and today such preparations have been begun. The government adopted in 1916 a program of naval construction whose cost exceeds that voted in one year before the war by Great Britain and Germany combined, and which aims to

make the United States the equal of any other naval power except
the British Empire. The program of military preparation adopted
in the same year is a failure for which the Administration is justly
censurable, but the nation has fully made up its mind to increase
its army, and so to add to the force which would be available
either for self-defence or to sustain the responsibilities of possible
American participation in a peace league. If it is "wicked" in
1917 to agitate for such a league, it was more "wicked" in 1915.
And what about the wickedness of advocating military and naval
preparedness which, according to Mr. Roosevelt's own testimony,
would result in hell unless it is accompanied by participation in
organization, now condemned by Mr. Roosevelt, to promote international security and justice? The truth is, of course, precisely the
opposite of what Mr. Roosevelt now proclaims it to be. What
takes the curse out of American naval and military preparedness
is the official support of the peace league. It is because we have
begun to prepare that the peace league should become part of
American foreign policy.

## AMERICA SPEAKS[1]

*The New Republic,* January 27, 1917

Everyone who stops to visualize the machinery of the approaching peace congress is appalled at the intricacy of the negotiations
which it will require. Nine Allies on one side, four on the other,
a score of vitally interested neutrals, life, prosperity, liberty and
security on four continents and the seven seas are involved. For
the first time in history the negotiation is to be conducted not by
a few men with autocratic powers but by envoys who must consider popular opinion. Obviously such a settlement cannot be
made suddenly, without preparation, and without a worldwide
background of ideas. The war came, it seemed, without warning;
peace cannot come that way. It must come after a gradual lift-
ing of the fog of war after an uncovering and illumination in which
some common understanding is created.

We have all of us to be educated through international discussion for the approaching peace. On December 18th the President,
using the prestige of his office, gave great impulse to the discussion.
He asked the warring powers to lay down their formulae of settlement and suggested that the United States would enter a league

[1] The month after the American people had endorsed his Administration in
1916, President Wilson addressed an identic note to the European belligerents
asking them for "such an avowal of their respective views as to the terms on which
the war might be concluded and the arrangements which would be deemed satisfactory as a guaranty against its renewal . . . as would make it possible frankly
to compare them."

of nations for the organization of security. After a few days of misunderstanding because he had used an unclear phrase, the note began to have its effect. The Central Powers answered curtly, and immediately lost whatever psychological advantage they had gained by the Chancellor's offer of peace. Their proposal of a blind negotiation, their dismissal of security as a secondary object, convinced the outer world that the offer was either insincere, or that they wanted merely a German peace, or that their own public opinion was in such bad condition that it could not be dealt with openly. The nine Allies by their reply won a great advantage. They specifically put the organization of security first, made territorial claims contingent upon it, and proposed a formula which was ambiguous enough to permit of wide negotiation. Mr. Balfour in his supplementary note reëmphasized the point.

Now in accepting the idea of a league, the nine Allies not only made it necessary for Germany to make another move, they made it necessary for the United States to move again. They asked quite rightly what there was behind the President's offer of American aid. To be sure, it was a plank in the Democratic platform and the Democrats won at the polls. The idea had been endorsed by Mr. Hughes, by Mr. Taft, and formerly by Mr. Roosevelt. It had wide non-partisan support. Still the peoples of Europe, faced by the immediate brutal fact of German aggression, knowing the traditional isolation of this country, were entitled to much greater assurance of American support.

It is this support which the President is now arousing. His address to the Senate on Monday is primarily a summons to the American nation to share the responsibilities of the peace. Mr. Wilson is asking his people to prepare themselves for the work which the world has begun to expect of them. It is the beginning of a popular campaign in this country designed to make it certain that when the time comes for a settlement of the war, America will be firm as to its purposes, unified in their support, and conscious of the responsibility. Mr. Wilson knows that he cannot ask the European powers to clear up the ambiguity of their aims without at the same time clearing up the ambiguity of our own. Not only abroad but here too the fog must be cleared away. He had sent a note to Europe asking for a definition of objects. On Monday he addressed the Senate and began to define ours.

No one supposes the work of definition is accomplished now or could be accomplished in one note or one address. The fog has lifted only a little; only a few big landmarks are as yet visible. Just as the reply of the Allies was merely a loose statement of principle, so is the President's address. But in essence it comes very close to the prime objects which the Allies have announced. We are as clear as the Allies; we both are clearer and more unanimous than the Germans. Not only has the President recognized Russia's claim to passage of the Dardanelles and Poland's claim to autonomy, he has set America against any attempt to annex occupied territory, and has recognized the justice of liberating peoples held in bondage. It is difficult to see how he could have gone further in accepting as American policy the liberal purposes of the Allied nations. . . .

The moment is not yet here when it is possible to conclude dogmatically upon all the difficult questions involved in the settlement. The discussion of the next few months will be concerned with them. For the moment the President is bent on creating an atmosphere of negotiation. In this effort he has had to say one thing which was not easy to say. He had to tell the world that America could not share in a settlement which was dictated by the victor to the vanquished. He had to say that only a peace negotiated in a spirit of give and take could be stable enough to justify America in the risks he was proposing. In making that point he used a phrase which will hurt deeply many whose support is required. He said that it must be a peace without victory.

It was an idea that had to be expressed, costly as it may be. So long as the people of the world believe that a lasting peace can be secured by dictation rather than by negotiation, the world will be where it always has been, at the mercy of a teetering balance of power. Peace has never been secured in Europe by that method and never will be, and the Allied spokesmen have generally recognized this. They have told us their object was to prevent Germany from winning anything by her aggression. They wanted her to go home with a sense of futility. They wanted to show that war does not pay, that nothing can be accomplished by it. The war will not end, and President Wilson, we take it, would not wish it to end, till that demonstration is complete. If the Germans think they are offering peace now because their armies are victorious, then the war will have to go on till the military situation changes.

But how long is it to go on after that? Is it to go on till the Allies can dictate a peace to a prostrate enemy? Are they to take the position that no peace is possible unless they have won an absolute decision in the field? Perhaps, but in that case Europe is likely to be so embittered with its sacrifices that any larger plan of security must fail. If Europe fights on in the belief that security can be had only by victory, then the foundations of a league will be shattered. It is likely to be the old peace which never lasted because it put all its faith in military power and ignored international organization.

The President has said that obviously we could not prevent Europeans from following this theory. The matter is in their hands. But if they did follow it, if they set their hearts on that rather than on a concert of power, America would not leave its isolation. A world organized on the creed of victory is a world in which America must arm to the teeth and pursue a purely national policy. Americans in the mass do not want to live in such a world, and they are preparing to do what they can to make it unnecessary.

Happily they have found a leader who can express that feeling nobly and eloquently, a man who knows his countrymen well enough to state the tremendous alternative before them. Organized security or armed isolation — that is the choice we have to make. The better choice takes courage, means risks and heavy responsibility. But the man would not be fit to live who failed to try it after the agony of these years. This thing must not be repeated if human power can prevent it. Our vitality, our strength and our potentialities are too great for the mere pursuit of our own interests. All that is valuable in our tradition cries out that we must not sit still in grudging isolation.

The President cannot succeed without the hearty support of the American people. With it he may succeed, and in that success he will have elevated the pride of American citizenship. It will be something to boast of that we have lived in a time when the world called us into partnership, and we went gladly, went remembering what we had always professed, and pledging ourselves to it in a larger theatre. At least it shall not be said that we were too selfish and too timid to attempt it, or that the sources of American idealism have run dry.

## 1796 OR 1917?[1]

### New York *World*, January 30, 1917

The policy of isolation that was urged upon the American people in Washington's Farewell Address was constructed upon this hypothesis:

> Europe has a set of primary interests which to us have none, or a very remote connection. Hence she must be engaged in frequent controversies the causes of which are essentially foreign to our concerns.

This was true in 1796 when the United States was a great experiment in self-government, when there was no steamship, no railroad, no cable, no wireless, when the republic was geographically as well as politically isolated from the rest of the world; but is it true today?

[1] By Frank I. Cobb.

Will anybody affirm that the primary interests of British democracy differ essentially from our own primary interests? Or French democracy? Or Italian democracy? Or even the mass of Germans for whom Maximilian Harden alone has the courage and vision to be spokesman? Various European governments may have interests which are foreign to our interests, but even there can we say that those interests do not concern us?

June 28, 1914, a double murder was committed in a street of Sarajevo, a town in Bosnia. Although the victims were an Austrian Archduke and Archduchess, nothing in 1796 would have been of less concern to the United States than a crime perpetrated in a Balkan province of Austria-Hungary.

Yet this murder in Sarajevo brought the United States to the verge of another civil war. It will cost the American people thousands of millions of dollars in taxation. It has set back for half a century the work of assimilating the immigrant population of this country. It has diverted the mind of the nation from its most vital domestic problems. It has all but embroiled us in the most ghastly war of human history. It has complicated our affairs with the whole world, disorganized all internal affairs, and in a way left us denationalized, divided into hostile camps of European tribesmen.

If the fundamental principle of Washington's farewell address still has vital force, what happened in. Sarajevo was "essentially foreign to our vital concerns." Nevertheless, we all know what has befallen us, and the question is whether we are to sit by and permit it to happen again without having anything to say about it.

Had there been almost any kind of council of the nations, this war could never have taken place. Conference and discussion alone would have averted it. The war was possible only because a secret and tortuous diplomacy made it possible. But had Vienna, dealing at first with Belgrade and then with Petrograd, known that it would have to reckon in the end with all the civilized nations, there would have been no ultimatum to Serbia.

This war marked the collapse of the system of entangling alliances intriguing for the balance of power. Civilization, in its own interest, is now compelled to take a step forward. Is American democracy to hold aloof? Have we no obligations whatever to the rest of mankind which would impel us to throw our influence into the balance to prevent a repetition of this war? Because George Washington in 1796 wisely decided that a policy of isolation was then for the best interest of the United States, must we refuse to admit that there has been any change in the world since 1796 and that our interests and obligations now are precisely what they were then?

The men who are against participation by the United States in a League to Enforce Peace on the ground that it conflicts with Washington's Farewell Address are spiritual brothers of the men who ardently defended the institution of slavery on the ground that George Washington was a slaveowner. What was moral in 1796 was still moral in 1860 to the Southern slaveholder. What was a wise foreign policy in 1796 is still a wise foreign policy to the mandarins of the United States Senate who can never believe that the world moves forward.

Before many months have elapsed the American people must decide for themselves whether the United States in relation to the other nations is living in the year 1796 or the year 1917. Are they ready to coöperate with the other great countries in the common interest, or are they by the policy of isolation to invite the other great countries to coöperate against them? It will inevitably be one or the other.

## VAE VICTIS[1]

Louisville *Courier-Journal*, April 7, 1917

Surely the time has arrived — many of us think it was long since overdue — for calling the braves to the colors. Nations must e'en take stock on occasion and manhood come to a showdown. It is but a truism to say so.

Fifty years the country has enjoyed surpassing prosperity. This has overcommercialized the character and habits of the people. Twenty-five years the gospel of passivism, with "business is business" for its text, has not only been preached — indiscriminately, oracularly — without let or hindrance, but has been rudely financed and potently organized. It has established a party. It has made a cult, justifying itself in a fad it has called Humanity — in many ways a most spurious humanity — and has set this above and against patriotic inclination and duty.

Like a bolt out of the blue flashed the war signal from the very heart of Europe. Across the Atlantic its reverberations rolled to find us divided, neutral, and unprepared. For fifteen years a body of German reservists disguised as citizens have been marching and counter-marching. They grew at length bold enough to rally to the support of a Pan-German scheme of conquest and a pro-German propaganda of "kultur," basing its effrontery on the German-American vote, which began its agitation by threatening us with civil war if we dared to go to war with Germany. Then followed the assassin sea-monsters and the airship campaign of murder.

[1] By Henry Watterson. War against Germany was declared April 6, 1917.

All the while we looked on with either simpering idiocy, or dazed apathy. Serbia? It was no affair of ours. Belgium? Why should we worry? Foodstuffs soaring — warstuffs roaring — everybody making money — the mercenary, the poor of heart, the mean of spirit, the bleak and barren of soul, could still plead the Hypocrisy of Uplift and chortle: "I did not raise my boy to be a soldier." Even the Lusitania did not awaken us to a sense of danger, and arouse us from the stupefaction of ignorant and ignoble self-complacency.

First of all on bended knee we should pray God to forgive us. Then erect as men, Christian men, soldierly men, to the flag and the fray — wherever they lead us — over the ocean — through France to Flanders — across the Low Countries to Köln, Bonn, and Koblens — tumbling the fortress of Ehrenbreitstein into the Rhine as we pass and damming the mouth of the Moselle with the ruin we make of it — then on, on to Berlin, the Black Horse Cavalry sweeping the Wilhelmstrasse like lava down the mountainside, the Junker and the sabre-rattler flying before us, the tunes being "Dixie" and "Yankee Doodle," the cry being "Hail the French Republic — hail the Republic of Russia — welcome the Commonwealth of the Vaterland — no peace with the Kaiser — no parley with Autocracy, Absolutism, and the divine right of Kings — to hell with the Hapsburg and the Hohenzollern!"

## THE GERMAN HORROR

Theodore Roosevelt in the Kansas City *Star*, May 2, 1918

The Hague conferences laid down a number of rules which the signatory powers, including Germany, agreed to observe in order to mitigate the horrors of war. Germany has with equal cynicism and brutality violated every one of these rules. She has waged war as it was waged in the Dark Ages. She has shown revolting cruelty toward soldiers and especially toward non-combatants, including women and children.

At this moment a great cannon is bombarding Paris. Not a soldier has been killed by it; it has not in the smallest degree affected France's military nor was it intended to do so. It was intended to terrorize the French civilian population by the destruction of churches, hospitals, and private buildings and the murder of women and children. On Good Friday one of the shells wrecked a church and killed a number of the little choir boys and a number of women who were at prayer. Among the killed were three American women whom I knew, who were abroad working for our soldiers. An American friend who saw the horror writes me:

Evidently the Germans do not worry over the fact that their shells descend on women and children kneeling in prayer on a Good Friday, before the crucifix.

Another American friend, a Red Cross woman, writes:

One shell burst in a maternity hospital, killing a nurse, a young mother, and a little baby. Several other mothers and new-born babies were injured.

The Zeppelins and airplanes are continually bombarding undefended English and French cities and have killed women and children by the hundreds. The submarines have waged war with callous mercilessness. Their crews have continually practiced torture on the prisoners they have taken. They leave women and children to drown. They shoot into the lifeboats. At this moment Americans are dying from the poison gas which the Germans, in contemptuous defiance of The Hague rules, have made an ordinary weapon of war. I have just been talking with an American soldier absolutely trustworthy, who himself saw the body of a Canadian whom the Germans had just crucified.

Every violation of the laws of war has been practiced by Germany. By her outrages on humanity she has made herself an outlaw among nations, and unless she pays heavily for her crimes, the whole world will be in danger. It is Germany, and only Germany, who is responsible for the hideous atrocities that have marked this war, atrocities which all civilized men outside of Germany believed to have been eliminated forever from civilized warfare. Germany has habitually and as a matter of policy practiced the torture of men, the rape of women, and the killing of children.

It was deeply to our discredit that during the shameful years of our neutrality we refused to protest against these hideous atrocities. Now at last this Nation has awakened and has gone to war against the enemy of America and of mankind. Let our people now keep steadily in mind just what kind of a foe we are fighting and just what kind of infamy that foe is habitually practicing. Then let us resolve that, come what may, we will fight this war through to a finish until the authors of this hideous infamy have paid in full and have been punished as they deserve. For in no other way can a peace worth having be obtained.

## [MOB VIOLENCE AND WAR PSYCHOLOGY]

*The New Republic*, August 3, 1918

The incompatibility between the American state of mind in 1916 and the American state of mind today is not so flagrant as it seems. Our existing pugnacity and intolerance is the reaction which an intensely patriotic and essentially political people would naturally pass through during the earlier stages of a war, participation in which it had for a while feared and shirked. The American nation is more bellicose, intolerant, and headstrong than its European allies, precisely because of its former irresponsibility. Two years ago it was trying to be indifferent to the moral issues involved by the war. Up to the end of 1916 the government, with the support of the preponderant element in American public opinion, was working on the assumption that American national unity depended on maintaining a neutral isolation with respect to the European war. In acting on this assumption the utmost latitude was allowed to all kinds of pro-Ally, pro-German, pacifist, militarist and nationalist, and Socialist propaganda and activities. In 1917 the nation was obliged suddenly to abandon this assumption.

After the German government forced war upon us American national unity came to depend upon a revolutionary reversal of feeling. Instead of preserving isolation we were committed to a policy of mortgaging the future productive ability of the American people and risking the lives of dearly beloved fellow-citizens in a quarrel of European origin which had to be fought out on European soil. Probably the needed revolution in feeling could not have taken place without some measure of calculated violence both in opinion and policy. At any rate, many Americans are now undoubtedly finding compensation for the neutral indifference and pacific irresponsibility of their former attitude toward the war by a disposition to be more European than the Europeans, more warlike than the Gauls, and about as intolerant of dissenting opinion as were the British Tories in 1800. This is particularly true of the Middle West, which in 1916 was most reluctant to enter the war on any terms. Typical journals such as the Chicago *Tribune*, which in 1916 did not consider it of any particular importance to beat the Germans, now consider anybody who questions the desirability of a one hundred per cent Allied military victory as a moral pervert and a traitor to civilization.

Other conditions peculiar to this country have contributed to the violence of this reaction. Our English friends should remember that there were domiciled in America thousands of aliens who were friendly to Germany, who were only too willing to contribute to American defeat. They should remember that the American Socialist organization was practically controlled by Germans, that American participation in the war was condemned as a crime by the American Socialist party, in spite of the international purposes for which America was fighting, and that a large amount of propaganda which was defeatist and pro-German in its effect was being circulated as Socialist party literature. No such conditions as these existed in any European country. The clear connection all during 1917 between much Socialist propaganda and at least an indifference to Allied or American victory had much to do with the rigor of the official censorship and the intolerance of American public opinion. Without palliating for one moment the excesses of this censorship and of the intolerance associated with it, these alien Socialists presented, it must be admitted, an obstacle to American political victory in the war which had to be suppressed by some measure of force. It was their own behavior which compelled the government to associate with respect for American national purposes a wholesome fear of American national power.

In so far as the foregoing account of the way in which the existing American war psychology originated is true, we may feel sure that its peculiar violence will gradually abate. Our fellow-countrymen suddenly became fearful that American national unity would not survive the disintegrating process which their revolutionary participation in a European war had started on its career; and in case we had entered this war for any purposes less democratic and disinterested than those laid down by the President, the fear might have been justified. As the result of the fear they yielded to panic and have gone further than was necessary in suspecting and in trying to stamp out dissenting views. At the present time the very violence of American opinion and policy has become itself an obstacle rather than an aid to our national moral unity. But the violence will not last. The essential unity of this country has been magnificently vindicated. America is more of a nation today than she has ever been in the past and her nationality is more firmly attached than ever to democratic domestic and foreign policy. It is this fact which will restore to Americans a feeling of national moral security, which will undermine the psychological causes of the existing mob violence and intolerance of dissenting opinion.

## [AMERICAN LEADERSHIP]

*The New Republic*, November 23, 1918

Beyond all republics in history, the American republic has been fortunate in having at its head in times of crisis great, serious men, with sympathies comprehensive enough to include all mankind, with vision clear enough to sweep even the remote past and the distant future. Athens in her hour of supreme trial was so ill-fated as to have for spokesman and leader the vile demagogue Kleon, scheming to consolidate his own ignoble political fortunes by whipping up the Athenian people to an atrocious fury of revenge upon civil populations fallen to Athenian mercies by the fortunes of war. The Roman republic, rising to immortal greatness, had her honor stained and her future compromised by the savage blood-lust of Marius and Sulla. We Americans read the spirit of revolutionary America in the words and acts of George Washington. Only the curious student of history knows that the revolutionary States were teeming with ignoble passions demanding the proscription of those who remained in their old loyalty and failed to espouse the new order's superior claim. Only the curious student of history knows that a clamor of revenge and inhumanity all but drowned the clear, wise, humane voice of Lincoln at the close of the Civil War. A hundred years from now the young American citizen will study the policy and read the utterances of President Wilson, and his heart will glow with the feeling that in her third time of trial America again gave proof not only of material greatness but of moral grandeur. He will not know that an obscene clamor arose in these great days, demanding that the helpless civil population of a vanquished state be left to perish in famine and anarchy.

## [PRESIDENT WILSON'S STORMY FUTURE]

*The New Republic*, November 30, 1918

The President is now just beginning to pay the price which he was always bound to pay at some time for the peculiar method adopted by him of running the country during the war. This method was in brief to promote a sound democratic purpose by means which were in certain respects autocratic and coercive. He used the intense patriotic feelings of one of the most patriotic peoples in the world in order to unite the nation during the war under his own leadership, but the unity which he obtained in this way was artificial and forced. He never sufficiently shared his responsibility with those of his fellow-countrymen who were entitled to share it, and he never built up a loyal following among the people whose support he most needed. Now when the war is over the forced unity disappears, and he is left dangerously isolated at the moment when the success of his policy is being challenged by enemies no less stiff-necked and hostile than the Germans. His own party is disgruntled; the Republican party is aggrieved and embittered; non-partisan liberals cannot get over his harsh and unnecessary suppression of freedom of utterance; Congress as a body resents the extent to which he has failed during the war to consult its leaders; the war bureaucracy does not inspire so much trust as it should; people find it hard to understand why he should surround himself with so many inferior men; and they find his frequent failure to take public opinion into his confidence equally a cause of suspicion. Finally, and most important, it is only too clear that his fellow-countrymen have not grasped the meaning of his international policy. He has not built up among his own people a body of public opinion which realizes the importance of a League of Nations, the obstacles to its realization, and the necessity of assuming such a grave future obligation. The suppression of discussion and the consequent stagnation of thought which the Administration favored has prevented any sufficient education of the American people in the significance of their own great enterprise.

During the next few months President Wilson will suffer severely from the partial loss of popular confidence, but that is all the more reason why good Americans who wish their own behavior to contribute to the moral unity of the American nation and the welfare of mankind should stand by and support as far as possible the large trend of his policy. The policy itself has been the supreme political gain of the war. It only needs to be carried out loyally and intelligently to become salutary during an era when the civilized world seems likely to need a great deal of saving. If during the next two years the spread of Leninism is to be checked and the road cleared for an orderly social advance, based on popular education and an enlightened public opinion, the western democracies must depend upon Wilsonism to do the job. But it must be a thorough-going Wilsonism, which can distinguish true from false democracy and is not afraid to trust the people to do many unprecedented things. The chief trouble with Mr. Wilson during the war was that he was not sufficiently Wilsonian. The only way in which he can get through the remainder of his Presidential term with credit to himself and benefit to his country is to trust still more completely to the virtue of his own principles and less to autocratic and unenlightened methods in seeking this realization.

## THOSE WHO LAUGH AT A DRUNKEN MAN [1]

### New York *Evening Journal*

How often have you seen a drunken man stagger along the street!

His clothes are soiled from falling. His face is bruised. His eyes are dull. Sometimes he curses the boys that tease him. Sometimes he tries to smile in a drunken effort to placate pitiless, childish cruelty.

His body, worn out, can stand no more, and he mumbles that he is going home.

The children persecute him, throw things at him, laugh at him, running ahead of him.

[1] The date of this editorial has been found unascertainable by the *Journal* staff or by its writer, Arthur Brisbane. It belongs to the prohibition movement which rose to its crest in 1918–20.

Grown men and women, too, often laugh with the children, nudge each other, and actually find humor in the sight of a human being sunk below the lowest animal.

The sight of a drunken man going home should make every other man sad and sympathetic. And horrible as the sight is, it should be useful, by inspiring in those who see it a determination to avoid and to help others avoid that man's fate.

That reeling drunkard is going home.

He is going home to children who are afraid of him, to a wife whose life he has made miserable.

He is going home, taking with him the worst curse in the world — to suffer bitter remorse himself after having inflicted suffering on those whom he should protect.

And as he goes home men and women, knowing what the home-coming means, laugh at him and enjoy the sight.

In the old days in the arena it occasionally happened that brothers were set to fight each other. When they refused to fight, they were forced to it by red-hot irons applied to their backs.

We have progressed beyond the moral condition of human beings guilty of such brutality as that. But we cannot call ourselves civilized while our imaginations and sympathies are so dull that the reeling drunkard is thought an amusing spectacle.

## THE ISSUE[1]

### *The New Republic*, December 14, 1918

On the eve of President Wilson's departure for Europe Senator Knox presented for the consideration of his colleagues a series of resolutions which demanded of every American interested in the victory of American war policy the most exact and the most earnest consideration. The preamble to the resolution recites that the United States entered the war in order to "vindicate the ancient rights to navigation as established under international law and in order to remove forever the German menace to our peace," that American aims are "expressed as restitution, reparation, and guaranty against the German menace," and that the surrender of Germany and Austria-Hungary has already realized or rendered enforcible the whole of those aims. It then goes on to declare that the policy of the United States at the Conference should be confined to the realization of the aims defined in the preamble, and to their future safeguarding by a definite understanding that, if the same necessity arises in the future, there shall be the same "complete accord and coöperation with our chief co-belligerents for the defence

[1] President Wilson sailed for Europe on December 4, 1918.

of civilization." The resolution ends by declaring in substance that projects such as a general league of nations or any sweeping "changes in the ancient laws of the seas" are irrelevant to the war aims of the United States and to the defense of civilization. They should be postponed for future consideration.

These resolutions define the issue between President Wilson and his opponents, between those who believe and those who do not believe in a League of Free Nations, with satisfactory sharpness and finality. If they are adopted they would imply the emphatic repudiation by the Senate of the whole war diplomacy of President Wilson and its contemptuous indifference to the idealistic leaven which the President has labored to infuse into the Allied war aims. In January, 1917, the French and British governments defined the objects for which they were fighting, in the very words of the Knox resolution, as restitution, reparation, and guaranties for the future. The definition was not considered satisfactory by liberal and democratic opinion throughout the world. All agreed upon the necessity of restitution and reparation, but what was the nature of the guaranties? The phrase could be used to justify a treaty of peace intended merely to deprive the German nation of future independence while at the time authorizing the Allied enemies of Germany to use a victory for the purpose of realizing their own nationalist and imperialist purposes. . . . Hence it was that the President in his declaration of the war aims of the United States restated the issue so as to infuse our war policy with the traditional American aspiration for some authentic organization of international right. He insisted that the guaranties should be general rather than specific, and should strike at the root of the international competition for power. The world was to be made safe not merely for France, Great Britain, and America as against Germany, but for democracy in all countries, for free people everywhere and under all circumstances. He proposed the League of Nations as the instrument of this general guaranty of future security. . . .

The Knox and Wilson programmes are not only sharply contrasted but they are mutually exclusive. The Senate resolutions disguise this incompatibility by proposing to postpone the attempt to establish the reign of law instead of entirely abandoning it. The implication is that an alliance among the victors, designed to secure permanent preponderance of power, would not prevent the subsequent organization of a League of Free Nations. The implication is not justified. If the war ends in an alliance of the victors intended chiefly to perpetuate their own supremacy, there will be no chance so long as the alliance lasts of forming an authentic League of Free Nations. For the decisive advantage of the alliance compared to the League of Free Nations could consist in nothing but the ability which the Allied Powers would obtain to ignore considerations of justice and the need of security for the vanquished in writing the terms of peace. If the Knoxes, the Lodges, and their analogues in Europe do not propose to consult almost exclusively the interest and the future power of the victors in writing the peace, why should they object so uncompromisingly to any subordination of the policy of the victors to the rule of impartial law? And if the treaty of peace does not embody the reign of law, based on the consent of the governed and sustained by the organized opinion of mankind, the indispensable condition of the subsequent formation of a League of Free Nations would be the dissolution of the Alliance and the abrogation of the reactionary treaty of peace.

The contradiction between the two programmes cannot be overcome and the ensuing issue cannot be escaped. It is born of the most fundamental needs of a war-exhausted world and of the essential nature of the obligations which, if the need is to be satisfied, the larger nations must assume. The peoples of the world want and need security. One condition of future security is the acceptance by every nation which signs the treaty of peace of a peculiarly binding promise to live up to its obligations. The engagements into which they enter as a result of the settlement will be pledges of the utmost solemnity which they must be ready to redeem at any cost to themselves and the redemption of which they must be willing, if necessary, to force on other signatories. The Knox resolutions, for instance, pledge the American people to complete accord and co-operation with their present co-belligerents should the "same necessity arise in the future," which is equivalent, of course, to a defensive alliance with those Powers to prevent any future violation of the treaty. Yet no matter how solemn the engagements are, they will not continue to be observed unless they express progressive and enduring principles of international association. The Allies cannot write a Treaty of Vienna, based upon the trafficking of power among themselves, and then seek to monument their structure by a Holy Alliance among the exclusively legitimate states. If the obligation to observe a treaty is to be authoritative and permanent, the treaty must be built of trustworthy materials, and it must deserve as much loyalty as it exacts. No democratic nation with the traditions of the United States can undertake such a solemn covenant without sufficient assurances that the specific provisions which it promises to enforce with all its resources, do not create popular grievances, provoke international dissension, and make ultimately for the exploitation of one nation by another.

The issue turns, consequently, the nature of the pledge which the American people will utter when they ratify the treaty of peace. If the informing principle of the treaty is, as the President proposes, a League of Nations which embodies the reign of law, based on the consent of the governed and sustained by the organized opinion of mankind, they will sign a document which is the realization of the noblest traditions in America's foreign policy, which will emancipate the American nation from the temptation of entangling foreign alliances, and which will earn hereafter the most complete and solemn loyalty of the American people. But if, as the Knox resolutions propose, the attempt to associate with the treaty of peace an instrument and a rule of impartial justice among nations is abandoned, the American nation by ratifying the treaty will renounce the greatest benefit which our forbears crossed the Atlantic in order to obtain, and the present American government will sign a pledge that some future government will repudiate. The Knox resolution would commit the United States to a hideously entangling alliance. It would pledge the nation to support all the French, British, and Italian interests involved in the settlement, no matter whether they proved to be justifiable or not. The United States might be placed in the impossible position, even from the point of view of power politics, of promising to fight for all the special national policies of its Allies but for none of its own, because none of its own would be embodied in the treaty.

## THE TRUTH ABOUT THE PEACE CONFERENCE [1]

*The Nation*, April 26, 1919

It has, of course, been everything but a peace *conference*. So far as the word is concerned, it is a palpable fraud upon the world. A small executive committee, first of ten men, then of five, then of four, has been parcelling out the globe in sessions so secret that their closest associates, the members of their own delegations, have not known what was going on. The very existence of this committee is the result of an arrogant, unauthorized assumption of power; for never and nowhere did the conference endow Messrs. Wilson, Orlando, Clemenceau, and Lloyd George with the authority to transact all business and come to all the decisions. The Germans need not complain if they are arbitrarily summoned to Versailles and told to take the treaty and sign it without discussion. They are only in the same category with all the various Allied delegates to the "Conference," except four. The Allied delegates too will be told, in the language of one of our captains of industry to his stockholders, to "vote first and discuss afterwards." Of all the groups

---

[1] Contributed from Paris by Oswald Garrison Villard.

of unemployed workers in France, none is so deserving of sympathy as the lesser delegates. Statesmen like Venizelos — and there are a few statesmen in Paris whatever the appearance to the contrary — have been graciously permitted to appear as expert witnesses whenever the question of the boundaries of their country was to be considered, but not otherwise. They are now informed that the treaty will be published on April 24, and that a complete copy will be handed to the Germans on April 28. Between those dates the puppets who are officially styled delegates will be given a chance to ratify the treaty, but that is all. They are to bow to the superior knowledge of the Big Four with the same obedience, the same abnegation of their reasoning faculties and of their conscience, as if they were the willing tools of a Tammany Hall.

How is it possible to procure a democratic peace or a lasting one under such conditions? A democratic peace, frankly, it can never be; a lasting peace it can be only if heaven shows an unexampled favor. When the Conference assembled, eleven wars were going on in which heavy cannon were being used; at the beginning of April, it was jestingly said at the Hotel Crillon (the American headquarters) that it was quite fitting that the wars had grown to fourteen, because there was thus one to each of the fourteen peace terms. But if the wars have multiplied, the fourteen peace terms have steadily grown less. One by one they have been abandoned by their originator until their very names have been almost forgotten. Who hears today in Paris of the freedom of the seas? Who, when he reads of the Saar basin, recalls the fine phrase about "no punitive indemnities or annexations"? Actually, we seem to have progressed but little since Napoleon. If there are today four Napoleons setting up new governments and redrawing the map, at least the great Emperor spared the world the hypocrisy of clothing his acts in language to charm — and to be discarded at will. And while the Big Four have wrangled, argued, reargued, and fought, Europe has come to the very edge of the abyss. It is civilization itself that is now trembling in the balance.

That Mr. Lloyd George, at least, sees this is at last apparent. In his speech last week in the House of Commons, he boldly declared that a new and more terrible enemy than the Germans has arisen in Europe, namely, hunger; but he forgot to explain why the menace of hunger, communism, and anarchy is so terrifying today as to overshadow everything else, or who is responsible for its growth to such vast proportions. It is the Big Four upon whom this terrible responsibility rests. The Big Four took from November until the end of March to lift the food blockade of Germany, and meanwhile Hungary and Bavaria, and now Vienna, have surrendered to communism or anarchy. It took them until April to decide that Russia should have food, thus trying a pacifist policy where the policy of imposing their will by bayonets had utterly and deservedly failed. Poland, Czecho-Slovakia, Rumania, Italy, these are a few of the states that are on the verge of revolution or collapse. . . .

As for the League of Nations, some of our foremost representatives in Paris have lost all interest in it, not merely because it has been the particular property of the President, or because it is a weak and dangerous proposal as it now stands, but also because they can really think seriously of nothing save the terrible plight in which all Europe finds itself. Of what use will a League of Nations be if· Europe is to flare up in a revolution in which all the states east of the Rhine will be joined in a veritable league to impose their extreme social policies upon the rest of the world? When sober men of long political experience are face to face with the possibility of a Europe relapsing into another Dark Age, they find it hard to take interest in a League of Nations which is foredoomed to failure by the insincerity of many of those who have accepted it, by the exclusion from it of the representatives of two thirds of Europe and all the black races, and which holds out few attractions to the small and the neutral nations. The strongest advocates of the League in Paris, men who have worked for a real League with all their strength, offer no argument for the Paris plan save that it is a half or a third of a loaf. "Try it," they say, "and out of it may come something worth while."

Something good may indeed come of it, but so may, and with more certainty, a good deal that is evil. Already by an autocratic counting of votes, the League is to come into being without recognizing the equality of the citizens of all of its members; and this at once will kill all Japanese interest in it. If the League is actually formed under the present draft, it will be in fact only another Holy Alliance. It will be a continuation of the present Entente with enormous power vested in the very men who are at present in the position of having brought Europe to the edge of the abyss while they talked and talked. There is in the League the possibility of a world dictatorship so odious as to make a revolution in Russian style seem almost tolerable. Even a third of a loaf may be of no value to a starving man if its ingredients are uneatable or poisonous; and if Mr. Wilson is now ready to agree to the giving of a special guarantee to France by Great Britain and the United States, he has dealt the *coup de grace* to his own creation and it is no longer worth discussion by serious-minded Americans. . . .

As for Mr. Wilson, it is not easy to describe exactly the part he has played. Without him the Peace "Conference" would have degenerated into an orgy of land-grabbing and imperialism. His idealism has been the saving grace if such grace there be. He has been the only one of the Big Four who has really desired to create a better world. But the old defects of his public character — his unwillingness to take counsel, his colossal egotism, his inability to hold at any cost to a principle which he has laid down, his readiness to compromise — together with his inability to translate beliefs into fact and action, and his refusal to take either the press or the public into his confidence, have forced him into the position of playing a lone and secret hand, and have already cost him the wondrous and all but overpowering confidence of the plain people of Europe which at first was his. When Mr. Wilson goes so far as to overrule a majority vote because it does not result as he wished, he need expect only criticism commensurate with the adoration which was his, beyond any other man's, a few months ago.

Yet it is far more than a test of the real moral force and character of President Wilson which we are witnessing. It is a far-reaching test of the value of war as the creator of moral values. Entered into on the part of the American public with the highest idealism, and with the confident belief that it was to be a war to end war and to make the world safe for democracy, the war thus far has made the world less safe for democracy than it has been at any previous period in modern times, and in addition has brought a brood of actual wars and the threat of others in its train. The struggle is ending at Paris with bitterness and hatred as well as with colossal hypocrisy. It is ending with the whole modern order of society on trial for its life; for nothing is plainer than that if the four men who have become the dictators of the world cannot produce a peace that is real, one that shall not only end war but do away with armaments, a deceived and disappointed world will try other ways and means. Can war be cured by more war, or is it to be cured by frankly trying to apply the doctrines of Christianity and the brotherhood of man? This is the question which is to be answered at Paris. Beside it the new Holy Alliance misnamed the League of Nations sinks into insignificance.

## VERY MUCH ALIVE

New York *Evening Post*, May 28, 1919

For a dead thing the League of Nations is displaying most offensive activity. Its demise has been solemnly proclaimed by Republican doctors. Senator Reed and Colonel Harvey have held a "coroner's quest" upon it. Yet the League, like the Irishman,

---

[1] By Rollo Ogden. President Wilson had secured the adoption of the League Covenant as the first article of the Peace Treaty on April 28, 1919.

if it is dead, is not conscious of it. It goes on functioning already in a dozen ways quite unfit for a dead man. More than that, it is displaying something like contempt for the Senate. While the latter is preparing to spend a few pleasant months debating the question whether the League shall be allowed to live in any form whatever, the League itself goes cheerfully ahead acting as if it were very much alive. From the standpoint of a Senatorial Dogberry, this surely is most tolerable and not to be endured.

Secretary Daniels yesterday threw over the Administration plans for the biggest navy in the world. And he did it explicitly on the ground that the League of Nations was going to bring about disarmament all round. It is undeniable that a League of Nations must be alive and kicking if it can lop off $500,000,000 from a naval bill. We do not say that this change of front by the Secretary of the Navy is gracefully effected. If his arguments for the biggest appropriation ever heard of were sound last December, they cannot have suddenly been made worthless by anything that has since happened. If he was, at the President's direction, going through a little manoeuvre then, it will be hard to deny that he is trying to get the wind of the Republicans now. They will have to make their choice — will have to legislate as if there were not going to be a League of Nations, or else, with Secretary Daniels, to assume its existence. The latter will seem wholly improper to Leader Lodge, yet will he care to have his party take the responsibility for voting hundreds of millions which the Democratic Secretary of the Navy declares not to be needed? It is a vexing dilemma.

Other signs accumulate that, whatever Senators may think, the rest of the world is quietly taking it for granted that the League of Nations will presently be established. The French Government has already designated its member. Sir Eric Drummond has accepted the appointment to the Secretariat. And now we read in the news that Lloyd George is hoping to come to this country so as to attend the first formal meeting of the League of Nations at Washington in October. The impudent Welshman! Doesn't he know that the most august assembly on earth has not yet made up its mind whether it will allow the League to come into being at all?

All these thickening indications that the whole world is "discounting" the coming of the League of Nations are a pretty good proof that it will come. When international agreements and governmental policies and appropriation bills are framed on the confident supposition that something is going to occur, it will occur. What people everywhere expect to get, it is fairly certain that they will get. It may be gall and worm-wood for some Senators to see mankind coolly ignoring their frowns and threats, but the inference they ought to draw is, not that everybody else is perverse and unpatriotic, but that their own activity has been misdirected. Even if they consider the organization of the League badly planned, and fear that in its present form it will not work well, this is not a reason for their fuming and fretting, but rather for doing their best to improve and strengthen the League. Any sort of League will do for a beginning. The London *Spectator* recently had an article severely critical of the amended draft of the League, but wound up by pointing out that the League, in any form, would have a splendid chance because of the certainty that for twenty or thirty years there will not be another big war. This interval can be used to make good the deficiencies of the League, as they may appear in actual working, and in time to make of it the hoped-for instrument for justice and peace between the nations.

## "PERILS" IN THE LEAGUE[1]

### New York *Evening Post*, June 7, 1919

A drop of sterilized water, a fragment of the purest food product on the market, when examined under a high-power lens, is apt to leave the ordinary man with little interest in drink or meat for some time to come. It is through such a multi-diameter scrutiny that the Covenant of the League is now being revealed as a thing of endless and pestiferous horrors. Its thinnest strand becomes a bulking serpent, its innocent network a monstrous snare, its invisible air-spaces yawning chasms and pitfalls. Enemies of the Covenant have gone even further. They have applied to the instrument a telemicroscope which projects the dread vision into an indefinite future and reveals the perils that may come if they are not yet there. Let it be said at once that if this is the kind of analysis which is to be brought to bear on the Covenant, the League will stand condemned, just as every historic document, just as every action in history would have been paralyzed from the beginning by the same test. But it is a test which will be rejected by every sensible man who realizes that the good of clean water compensates for the irreducible minimum of danger it carries, that the value of food outweighs its microscopic perils, and that the benefits of a leagued world can be obtained only on the same terms. Sensible men, if they are convinced that the League is worth striving for, will seek to make the League as good and clean as may be, and assume the inevitable hazards.

Article X of the Covenant has been a favorite subject with the

[1] By Simeon Strunsky.

microscopists. In its straightforward stipulation for the safeguarding of the territorial integrity and political independence of the members of the League against *external aggression* they have discovered all sorts of swarming dangers: America subjected to the beck and call of every little nation; a world frozen into immobility from the moment the Treaty is signed; a world put into a straightjacket; the fetters of slavery fixed in perpetuity upon every suffering people. Critics who rage against the conspiracy of aged diplomats and premiers now at work in Paris have themselves gone in for a minute legalism, an extravagant verbal hair-splitting, a breathless search after lethal commas and semi-colons that are all the world away from the fresh realities and the living facts for which they profess to stand. A clause which means that the United States expresses its condemnation in advance against an international crime like that which it took four years of war to beat down has been interpreted to mean that the United States will spring to arms against an oppressed people rising against a cruel master. We are asked to believe that when the application of Article X is invoked the United States will be stopped from exercising its reason and its judgment on specific facts, will be bound against inquiry into the moralities, the justice, and the common sense of a situation, and will be compelled to automatic action by a set of words meaning what the enemies of the League now discover them to mean.

How will Article X operate to keep the world in a straightjacket? By preventing righteous revolution, the opponents of the League argue. But revolution is not "external aggression"? True, they say; but see how it will work out. Suppose the Poles revolt against their present aristocratic Government and try to establish a Socialist régime. Suppose that an existing Soviet Government in Russia attempts to come to the help of its fellow-Socialists in Poland. Such action by Soviet Russia would be external aggression against Poland, and the United States would be pledged to come to the aid of the anti-democratic Polish Government. Or suppose the Slavs in the territories that now go to Italy rise in revolt and the Jugo-Slav armies come to the help of their unredeemed brothers. The United States would be pledged to intervene against a nationality bent on self-determination. Thus Article X freezes the world into immobility.

Much more powerful is the Hiram Johnson telemicroscope when trained on Article X as the foe of righteous revolution:

> In the construction of Article X it will require neither astute lawyers nor cunning diplomat to apply external aggression to any form of internal revolution which it was feared might be com-

municated to neighboring States. It was exactly upon this theory that internal revolution was held by Metternich and his associates to be within the jurisdiction of the Quadruple Alliance of a century ago.

In other words: If the Italian people should rise in revolution, the Jugo-Slav Kingdom would maintain that the Italian revolution threatens the peace of Jugo-Slavia and therefore the United States must intervene to put down the Italian revolution! And what Hiram Johnson would have us believe is that it needs only a skilled Jugo-Slav lawyer or diplomat to get the United States into war against Italian revolutionists by showing that revolution at Rome is external aggression against Belgrade. If this is one of the perils of the League, then by all means let us kill the League.

The simple fact is that the enemies of the League do not in the least share in the basic impulse which has made the League the hope of humanity. They do not want to see war checked. They believe in their own kind of war. The sympathizer with the Soviets wants no obstacle in the way of Soviet Russia's intervention in Poland to establish a Soviet Polish republic; he only shrinks with horror from a Russian Czar intervening in Poland to make Paderewski king. The professed friend of the Jugo-Slavs believes that a Jugo-Slav invasion of Italy in behalf of the Italian Slavs would be a righteous war; it is only an Italian invasion of Jugo-Slavia in behalf of the Italians of Laibach that would be a crime. Our radicals believed in the League of Nations to safeguard their kind of a world; but since the Treaty has failed to live up to specifications, we have no need of a League of Nations.

The peril which the enemies of the League foresee, in divers camps, is only the imperilment of their own ideas. The Great Peril, war, does not frighten them. Hiram Johnson does not shrink from the thought of war against Japan and possibly Mexico.[1] Radical opinion does not shrink from the thought of war brought on by new national or economic forces emerging into the field of history. They will not have the boundaries of the world permanently fixed against new nationalities striving forward in legitimate growth. Only that was precisely Germany's argument five years ago.

[1] Senator Hiram Johnson, reflecting much popular sentiment in California, had distinguished himself by his diatribes against Japan and the Japanese. His attitude on international questions was frequently only less chauvinist and bellicose than that of Henry Cabot Lodge, who later joined in an insulting prohibition of Japanese immigration.

## [PRESIDENT WILSON'S SPEECH TO THE SENATE][1]

*Harvey's Weekly,* July 19, 1919

It was the more unappropriate, to use no stronger term, for the President to present such stuff to the Senate because of two major reasons. One was the secrecy with which the Treaty had been made. In the first of his Fourteen Commandments the President spoke for "open covenants openly arrived at;" in his Farewell Address to Congress he said, "You will know all that I do;" and in last week's address to the Senate he said, "You have been daily cognizant of what was going on." But the fact is, as he knew right well, that the Covenant was not "openly arrived at," that Congress did not know all that he did, that the Senate had not been daily cognizant of what was going on; and that its lack of information was due to his own censorship over the news of the Conference. He thus came back to a Senate which he had kept in the dark, and he refused or at least failed to enlighten it.

The other reason was that there had been raised in the Senate certain very specific points of objection to the Treaty, upon which consideration of it was bound to dwell, and upon which final action upon it was bound to turn. The President knew that this was the case. He knew what these points were. He knew that they were what the Senate was most interested in. And he dodged them, every one. The Senate wanted to know why it was necessary to destroy the Monroe Doctrine by adopting a false characterization of it; and the President told them that "a cry had gone out from every home in every stricken land from which sons and brothers and fathers had gone forth to the great sacrifice, that such a sacrifice should never again be exacted." The Senate wanted to know why we should not be permitted to withdraw from the League of Nations at will; and the President said that "The only question is whether we can refuse the moral leadership that is offered us." The Senate wanted to know to what extent we were to be bound to meddle in every war or danger of war that might occur anywhere in distant parts; and the President vouchsafed the information that if we rejected the Covenant of Denationalization, we should "break the heart of the world."

A little later, with a select company of Democratic Senators and others he informally discussed certain of these points; and he announced his willingness to appear before the Foreign Relations Committee and give it whatever information it desired. But that

[1] By George Harvey. President Wilson returned from Europe to the United States at the end of June, 1919, to find the opposition to the Covenant already well organized.

did not and could not atone for his amazing failure to improve the great opportunity of his address to the Senate. It was more and worse than a failure to improve it. It was an egregious neglect to perform a public duty, if indeed it did not come perilously near to being a slight to a coördinate branch of the government. The Senate of the United States had no need of disquisitions upon the world's weariness of war; of a lecture upon the difficulties of diplomatic negotiation; or of exhortations to seek the good, the true, and the beautiful. It knows as much about such matters as — with all respect — the President himself, and has just as high ideals as he. What it wanted, what it was entitled to, was an explicit and practical report upon the President's extraordinary mission, and it did not get it. Instead, it got a rhetorical exploitation of the President and his peculiar doctrines. It wanted facts: it got "words, words, words."

## STRIKE OUT ARTICLE TEN[1]

*Harvey's Weekly*, August 9, 1919

If Article Ten of the League Covenant means what Mr. Wilson says it means, then it means nothing. If it means nothing, then its proper destination is the wastebasket. It should be stricken out *in toto* as so much sheer surplusage.

The first sentence of the Article provides that "the members of the League undertake to respect and preserve as against external aggression the territory and existing political independence of all members of the League." The second sentence provides that the League Council shall advise upon the means by which the obligation involved in the first sentence shall be fulfilled.

Mr. Wilson's interpretation of this second sentence, as presented in his message transmitting the Franco-American alliance treaty, is that after the League Council's advice has been duly given, the League members will do precisely as they please about following it. In the first sentence the members of the League solemnly agree to respect and protect each other as against external aggression. In the second sentence — according to Mr. Wilson's interpretation — a League member will act upon the League Council's advice in a given aggression case "only if its own judgment justifies such action." In other words, the second sentence of the Article completely cancels the first sentence, leaving zero as the remaining total.

[1] President Wilson formally presented the treaty and the Covenant to the Senate on July 10, 1919. Early in September, seeing defeat by the Senate to be almost inevitable, he set out on a transcontinental trip to rally public sentiment to his side.

Mr. Hughes said of Article X that it was an "illusory engagement." Mr. Wilson goes Mr. Hughes one better. He says, in substance, that it is no engagement at all, illusory or otherwise. The League Council may advise until it is black in the face, and the League members may go serenely on their respective ways without giving the slightest heed to this advice. And both League members and League Council will equally have done their full duty under Article X.

If Article X be interpreted to mean anything, that meaning necessarily is that we engage to send our armed forces wherever and whenever a super-government of foreigners sitting in Switzerland orders us to send them. If it be interpreted as Mr. Wilson interprets it, the foreign super-government's powers extend only to the giving of advice which we agree to heed or ignore as our judgment dictates. One interpretation is an insult to our self-respect as a nation. The other reduces the whole of Article X to a vacuum.

The way to treat Article X is to strike it out.

## "CONFINEMENT IN WASHINGTON"

*Harvey's Weekly*, September 13, 1919

Coming from a President of the United States who has broken all records for absence from his post of duty, Mr. Wilson's statement at Columbus that for a long time he has "chafed at his confinement in Washington," is a direct appeal to the American sense of humor.

Of the thirty months which have elapsed since Mr. Wilson's second inauguration, he has spent something like half a year in semi-royal progresses in foreign lands, including about a month on the high seas and something like five months of administration, or attempted administration, of his high office by transfer of our executive seat of government from the banks of the Potomac to the banks of the Seine. In addition to that, he is now on a 10,000 mile transcontinental excursion which is to consume a month more of time. Add to this the ordinary vacation absences and excursions of say another month, and we find that Mr. Wilson has been relieved from "chafing at confinement in Washington" for something like eight months, all told. This approximates four months a year vacation which the President has allowed himself with full salary and travelling expenses of half a million dollars or so out of the pockets of his employers, the patient, all-enduring taxpayers of the country.

The legality or illegality of the President's foreign travels during his term of office need not be discussed. The question has never been brought to an issue and probably never will be. As to the propriety of these foreign roamings, however, that is a question which already has been so definitely and for all time settled in the minds of the American people that it is wholly safe to say that never again will an American President attempt to follow the dangerous precedent in this respect which Mr. Wilson has made. Hereafter, no matter how badly in need of re-psychologizing may be the esteemed populations of the Hedjaz and Timbuctoo, we feel quite safe in saying that, so far as American Presidents are concerned, the job will be done by the absent treatment and not again by personal presence and the physical laying on of hand. If the heart of the world is going to break unless an American President starts on another globe-trotting expedition, then the heart of the world will have to go to smash. The day of peripatetic American Presidents is ended. From the end of the Wilson Administration on, they will stay in Washington and mind their own and the American people's business, irrespective of the cardiac symptoms of Europe, Asia, Africa, and Polynesia, and even irrespective of whatever chafing at confinement there may be entailed.

## THE TREATY ISSUE AS MADE[1]

### Chicago *Tribune*, March 2, 1920

The President is reported on good authority to have sent word to Administration Senators that he will accept no modification of Article Ten.

Senator Lodge counters with the declaration that the Republicans under his leadership will stand pat on the majority reservation.

Senator Hitchcock has a revised version of this reservation, but if the President is determined to accept no modification of Article Ten, Mr. Hitchcock's refinement upon the Lodge reservation is useless and we have a flat issue, not between the Lodge wording and Hitchcock's, but on the Lodge reservation itself.

Our readers may, therefore, like to have their memories refreshed on the exact phraseology over which this controversy turns. Although Mr. Wilson insisted at first on no change whatsoever in the inspired wording of the Covenant, it is believed that if he has to adopt an irreducible minimum, it is in regard to Article Ten, which is, in the English version of the treaty, as follows:

[1] The final vote on the treaty was taken March 19, 1920; it showed 57 ayes to 39 nays, the Wilson Democrats, spurning the Senate reservations, joining with the irreconcilable Republicans to defeat the instrument.

The members of the League undertake to respect and preserve as against external aggression the territorial integrity and existing political independence of all members of the League. In case of any such aggression or in case of any threat or danger of such aggression the Council shall advise upon the means by which this obligation is fulfilled.

To this Senator Lodge and his associates propose the following reservation:

The United States assumes no obligation to preserve the territorial integrity or political independence of any other country, or to interfere in controversies between nations — whether members of the League or not — under the provisions of Article Ten, or to employ the military and naval forces of the United States under any article of the treaty for any purpose, unless in any particular case the Congress which, under the Constitution, has the sole power to declare war or authorize the employment of the military or naval forces of the United States, shall by act or joint resolution so provide.

The President is understood to have asserted that this reservation "cuts the heart out of the treaty."

The issue is, therefore, in simplest terms this: The President demands that the Senate shall not declare we have reserved the right under the treaty to determine in each particular situation calling for military or naval action whether or not our soldiers or sailors shall take part.

Senator Lodge and his associates demand that Congress shall preserve this right and preserve it by explicit language embodied in the ratification so as to put the right beyond any possibility of mistake.

There has been much debate over what Article Ten means, what its scope is, how far it could or would bind us even if ratified as written. We need not go into these questions here. The issue has been made not on the Article, but on the reservation to the Article, and there is and can be no doubt whatsoever as to what it means.

The Democrats realize this and have very little stomach for taking this issue to the people. We think their reluctance is justified.

Who shall order our armies and warships to go forth to war? The League Council or the Congress? That is the issue. The defenders of Article Ten say it does not and cannot empower the League to send them forth. If that is true why does the President object to the Lodge reservation, which merely declares it?

We think the American people will not hesitate over such an

issue. When America's young manhood is asked to give its life for any cause, they will be summoned by their own government, not by any super-government as yet conceivable. That must be made clear in any treaty which bears the sign-manual of the United States.

## THOMAS HARDY AT EIGHTY[1]

*The Freeman*, June 16, 1920

That was a great crowd for Oxford, the 10th of last February. An enormous crowd was gathered in the theatre — all the fine youth of the University, those who had survived the war, those who had succeeded the dead, young men and young women with years of full life before them still, dons and their wives (breathing culture), and a few battered old travellers of life like myself. We had come partly to see a selection from the scenes of Thomas Hardy's "Dynasts," put on the stage by the Dramatic Society of the undergrads themselves. But chiefly we had come because it was known that the great poet himself was to be there. He was soon to be eighty, and youth longed to see him before he died. . . .

What a record lay behind that shy and delicate figure, that waxen and mournful face! There was the man who for fifty years had held the world entranced by the beauty of a mind capable of sharing all life's sorrow and some of its joy, and by the beauty of a style which was but the expression of that inmost mind — the style that is both the substance and the architectural form of thought. As one looked at him, one recalled the great pictures of life which he had created and described in prose — "Far From the Madding Crowd," "The Return of the Native," "Tess," and "Jude the Obscure," besides so many other beautiful and ironic scenes, so many other beautiful and tragic personalities. For eighty years those pale, sad eyes had looked steadily out upon the world, and like the poet Heine he could cry, "O ancient Earth, I've counted all thy sorrows." We thought of those immortal scenes — of Bathsheba and Trim, of Egdon Heath, of Tess christening her baby, of the Isle of Singers, and of Jude who gazed with yearning upon our very Oxford from the Berkshire downs. No writer had ever come so close to the heart of ancient England — of the south-land which is the ancient heart of England, with its peculiarly English strain of men and women, humorous, kindly, ironic, capable of profound emotions that lie restrained and dumb. No imaginative writer in prose, I think, had ever come so near the heart of Earth. It was as though he felt still bound to her by

[1] Contributed as part of a "middle" editorial article by Henry W. Nevinson.

the cord that binds a child to its mother's life. Looking at him, I saw the vision of Man passing across a wide and desolate moorland under the obscure light of a moon behind driving clouds. Sprung from Earth, he was soon again to return to her. Under his feet lay the stony relics of uncouth creatures that lived and died and had been obliterated uncounted ages before Man himself appeared. Above his head moved uncounted stars, speechless and unknowable. On one hand rose the gaunt monuments of the "Hanging Stones," where man once worshipped. On the other rose a gallows with clanking chains, and the ruins of a village church. Man's eyes were fixed upon the dubious path before him, leading to a destination he could not name, and perhaps to no destination of any kind. But in the heart of wandering Man burned a compassion which consumed him like a cruel rage, and in his brain moved thoughts that ranged beyond the flaming bulwarks of the stars.

## [A REVELATION OF AMERICAN IMPERIALISM]

*The Freeman*, September 1, 1920

These are the days that try the stoutest burlap in which cats were ever bagged. Hardly a day passes but some awkward little truth slips out into the air and is caught by industrious pencils and then, after many hazardous adventures, ending in a linotype machine, is born again; this time on fresh clean strips of paper which go out into all the ways of the world. Those precious moments when we meet face to face these wandering bits of truth, are fit to be treasured through a long life. Thus at Butte, Montana, a few days ago, the hills must have rejoiced and the mountains and valleys been exceeding glad when Mr. Franklin D. Roosevelt said:

The Republicans are playing a shell game on the American people. They are still busy circulating the story that [in the League of Nations] England has six votes to America's one. It is just the other way. As a matter of fact, the United States has about twelve votes in the Assembly. Until last week I had two of them myself, and now Secretary Daniels has them. You know I have had something to do with the running of a couple of little republics. The facts are that I wrote Haiti's Constitution myself, and if I do say it, I think it is a pretty good Constitution.

Mr. Roosevelt went on to say that Haiti, Santo Domingo, Panama, Cuba, and the other Central American countries, which have at least twelve votes in the League's Assembly, all regarded Uncle Sam as a guardian and big brother, and that this country practically would have their votes in the League. Now why, in the name of goodness, didn't President Wilson tell us. that himself long ago, and so have saved us all this bother?

Think now for a moment of how it will be when the League of Nations holds its first meeting with Uncle Sam joining in. All the nations will be there. The representatives of England and her five self-governing dominions enter the great hall together (the Labour premier of Australia and the Nationalist premier of South Africa casting sinister glances at the gentleman from Downing Street). Suddenly just outside the Assembly hall the sound of a sharp military command is heard. It is Captain W. W. Gilmer, of the United States Marines, until lately Governor of Guam, calling to attention the round dozen of diplomats representing Mr. Franklin D. Roosevelt's little Republics. "Now, then," he says briskly, "you fellows have got to do as you're told, and don't you forget it. No whistling here, you from Guam! Attention! Forward march!" And with fine military precision the little company walks in to take its place in the great Assembly of the Nations.

## THE TWO BROKEN OLD MEN

### Emporia *Gazette*, February 1, 1921

One at Washington, palsied and frail, who made war and brought a hundred million people into a great cataclysm that piled up debt for countless generations, and filled the land with hate and suspicion. In some future day the fruits of the war will ripen into righteousness, but now they are bitter persimmons. The war and all that it stands for — justly or unjustly — is accursed in the hearts of the people.

Another old man is working under the broiling sun in the federal prison at Atlanta. He stood up and denounced war — this war, all war — as God's curse upon the world. So the first old man sent the second old man to jail. The present, with its greed and suspicion and depression and hatreds, seems to justify this old man's curse upon war; yet he is in prison.

And on the other hand the future with its united world under a league of peace, "the federation of the world," for which the frail old man at Washington brought America into the war, will justify that old man. But the two broken old men, each despising the immediate endeavor and the immediate aims of the other, yet both working for the same brotherhood of man, present a strange concord of discords that will merge into ultimate harmonies. Wilson and Debs, two sad old men, wrecks of the world!

## THAT GREAT AND SOLEMN REFERENDUM

New York *Globe*, October 4, 1920

Senator Johnson of California and Senator Reed of Missouri both said that the covenant of the League of Nations as President Wilson brought it back from Paris was one of the worst pieces of merchandise that had ever passed the custom-house. Senator Johnson said that he wouldn't stand for such a flagrant abdication of American rights. Senator Reed said he wouldn't either. Both agreed that this was the paramount issue of the day.

The Republicans nominated Warren G. Harding, whom Senator Johnson has accepted as being quite right about the treaty. The Democrats nominated James M. Cox, in whose hands Senator Reed is convinced the honor and safety of the country will be safer than some people suspect. Senator Johnson has been campaigning for Harding. Senator Reed has been campaigning for Cox.

Is this the great and solemn referendum that President Wilson called for some months ago?

## THE REPUBLICAN PLEDGE

New York *Globe*, October 11, 1920

"The Republican party," said Mr. Hoover at Indianapolis on Saturday, "have pledged themselves by platform, by the doctrines of their majority in the Senate, by the repeated statements of Senator Harding, that they undertake the fundamental mission to put into living being the principle of an organized association of nations for the preservation of peace. The carrying out of that promise is the test of the entire sincerity, integrity, and statesmanship of the Republican party."

Johnson, Borah, Brandegee, Knox, Poindexter, and other Republican Senators who voted against the Lodge amendments are against any kind of League of Nations, and are supporting Harding on the League issue. They are as ready to assume that the Republican party's honor is pledged against an undertaking with other nations to prevent war as Mr. Hoover and his associates are to assume the contrary.

But there is this difference between Hoover and the irreconcilable Senators. They have a political future to consult and political jobs to cling to. Hoover has no political future as far as anyone can see, and does not need a political job. His opinion is an opinion, not a corn-plaster.

The Republican friends of the League take the obligation which

Mr. Hoover mentions with extreme seriousness. The party can betray its promises only at the cost of driving them out of its ranks and bringing down on itself moral and material ruin.

## WOODROW WILSON — AN INTERPRETATION

### New York *World*, March 4, 1921

*Hundreds of years hence Wilson's name will be one of the greatest in history.* — Jan Christian Smuts, Premier of the Union of South Africa.

No other American has made so much world history as Woodrow Wilson, who retires at noon today from the office of President of the United States. No other American has ever bulked so large in the affairs of civilization or wielded so commanding an influence in shaping their ends.

The great outstanding figure of the war, Mr. Wilson remains the great outstanding figure of the peace. Broken in health and shattered in body, Mr. Wilson is leaving the White House, but his spirit still dominates the scene. It pervades every chancellery in Europe. It hovers over every capital. Because Woodrow Wilson was President of the United States during the most critical period of modern history, international relations have undergone their first far-reaching moral revolution. . . .

No sooner had Congress declared war than Mr. Wilson proceeded to mobilize all the resources of the nation and throw them into the conflict. This war was different from any other war in which the United States had ever engaged, not only by reason of its magnitude but by reason of the necessity for coördinating American military plans with the plans of the Allies. The Allies were not quite agreed as to what they desired of the United States, aside from unlimited financial assistance, and the solution of the general problem depended more or less on the trend of events.

The test of any war policy is its success, and it is a waste of time to enter into a vindication of the manner in which the Wilson Administration made war, or to trouble about the accusations of waste and extravagance, as if war were an economic process which could be carried on prudently and frugally. The historian is not likely to devote serious attention to the partisan accusations relating to Mr. Wilson's conduct of the war, but he will find it interesting to record the manner in which the President brought his historical knowledge to bear in shaping the war policies of the country.

The voluntary system and the draft system had both been discredited in the Civil War, so Mr. Wilson demanded a Selective

Service Act under which the country could raise 10,000,000 troops, if 10,000,000 were needed, without deranging its essential industries. It had taken Mr. Lincoln three years to find a general whom he would intrust with the command of the Union armies. Mr. Wilson picked his commander-in-chief before he went to war, and then gave to Gen. Pershing the same kind of ungrudging support that Mr. Lincoln gave to General Grant. The Civil War had been financed by greenbacks and bond issues peddled by bankers. Mr. Wilson called on the American people to finance their own war, and they unhesitatingly responded. In the war with Spain the commissary system had broken down completely owing to the antiquated methods that were employed. No other army in time of war was ever so well fed or so well cared for as that of the United States in the conflict with Germany.

Mistakes there were in plenty, both in methods and in the choice of men, and errors of judgment and the shortcomings that always result from a lack of experience, but the impartial verdict of history must be that when everything is set forth on the debit side of the balance sheet which can be set forth, Mr. Wilson remains the most vigorous of all the war Presidents. Yet it is also true that history will concern itself far less with Mr. Wilson as a war President than with Mr. Wilson as a peace President. It is around him as a peacemaking President that all the passions and prejudices and disappointments of the world still rage.

Mr. Wilson in his "peace without victory" address to the Senate previous to the entry of the United States into the war had sketched a general plan of a coöperative peace. "I am proposing, as it were," he said, "that the nations with one accord should adopt the doctrine of President Monroe as the doctrine of the world." He returned to the subject again in his war address, in which he defined the principles for which the United States was to fight, and the principles on which an enduring peace could be made. The time came when it was necessary to be still more specific.

In the winter of 1918 the morale of the Allies was at its lowest ebb. Russia had passed into the hands of the Bolsheviki and was preparing to make a separate peace with Germany. There was widespread discontent in Italy, and everywhere in Europe soldiers and civilians were asking one another what they were really fighting for. On January 8 Mr. Wilson went before Congress and delivered the message which contained the Fourteen Points of peace, a message which was greeted both in the United States and Europe as a veritable Magna Charta of the nations. Mr. Wilson had again become the spokesman of the aspirations of mankind, and from the moment that this address was delivered the thrones of the Hohenzollerns and the Hapsburgs ceased to be stable.

Ten months later they were to crumble and collapse. Before the armistice was signed on November 11, 1918, Mr. Wilson had overthrown the doctrine of divine right in Europe. The Hapsburgs ran away. The Kaiser was compelled to abdicate and take refuge in exile, justifying his flight by the explanation that Wilson would not make peace with Germany while a Hohenzollern was on the throne. This was the climax of Mr. Wilson's power and influence, and strangely enough, it was the dawn of his own day of disaster.

For nearly six years Mr. Wilson had manipulated the government of the United States with a skill that was almost uncanny. He had turned himself from a minority President into a majority President. He had so deftly outmanoeuvred all his opponents in Congress and out of Congress that they had nothing with which to console themselves except their intensive hatred of the man and all that pertained to him. Then at the very summit of his career he made his first fatal blunder.

Every President in the off-year election urges the election of a Congress of his own party. That is part of the routine of politics, and during the campaign of 1918 Mr. Wilson's advisers urged him to follow the precedent. What they forgot and he forgot was that it was no time for partisan precedents, and he allowed his distrust of the Republican leaders to sweep him into an inexcusable error that he, of all men, should have avoided. The Sixty-fifth Congress was anything but popular. The Western farmers were aggrieved because the price of wheat had been regulated, and the price of cotton had not. The East was greatly dissatisfied with the war taxes, which it regarded as an unfair discrimination, and it remembered Mr. Kitchin's boast that the North wanted the war and the North would have to pay for it. There was general complaint from business interests against the Southern Democratic control of the legislative department, and all this sentiment instantly crystallized when the President asked for another Democratic Congress. Republicans who were loyally supporting the Administration in all its war activities were justly incensed that a party issue had been raised. A Republican Congress was elected and by inference the President sustained a personal defeat.

Misfortunes did not come singly in Mr. Wilson's case. Following the mistake of appealing for the election of a Democratic Congress he made an equally serious mistake in the selection of his Peace Commission.

To anybody who knows Mr. Wilson, who knows Mr. Lloyd

George, who knows Mr. Clemenceau, nothing could be sillier than the chapters of Keynes and Dillon in which they undertake to picture the President's unfitness to cope with the European masters of diplomacy. Mr. Wilson for years had been playing with European masters of diplomacy as a cat plays with a mouse. To assume that Mr. Wilson was ever deceived by the transparent tactics of Mr. Lloyd George and Mr. Clemenceau is to assume the impossible. It would be as easy to conceive of his being tricked and bamboozled by the United States Senate.

Mr. Wilson needed strong Republican representation on the peace commission not to reinforce him in his struggles with his adversaries but to divide with him the responsibility for a treaty of peace that was doomed in advance to be a disappointment. Although the popular sentiment in Europe was almost passionate in its advocacy of President Wilson's war programme, all the special interests that were seeking to capitalize the peace for their own advantage or profit were actively at work and were beginning to swing all the influence that they could command upon their various governments. It was inevitable from the outset that Mr. Wilson could never get the peace that he had expected. The treaty was bound to be a series of compromises that would satisfy nobody, and when Mr. Wilson assumed all the responsibility for it in advance he assumed a responsibility that no statesman who had ever lived could carry alone. Had he taken Mr. Root or Mr. Taft or both of them with him the terms of the treaty of Versailles might have been no different, but the Senate would have been robbed of the partisan grievance on which it organized the defeat of ratification.

Day after day during the conference Mr. Wilson fought the fight for a peace that represented the liberal thought of the world. Day after day the odds against him lengthened. The contest finally resolved itself into a question of whether he should take what he could get or whether he should withdraw from the conference and throw the doors open to chaos. The President made the only decision that he had a moral right to make. He took what he could get, nor are the statesmen with whom he was associated altogether to blame because he did not get more. They too had to contend against forces over which they had no control. They were not free agents either, and Mr. Smuts has summed up the case in two sentences:

It was not the statesmen that failed so much as the spirit of the peoples behind them. The hope, the aspiration, for a new world order of peace and right and justice, however deeply and universally felt, was still only feeble and ineffective in comparison with the dominant national passions which found their expression in the peace treaty.

All the passions and hatreds bred of four years of merciless warfare, all the insatiable fury for revenge, all the racial ambitions that had been twisted and perverted by centuries of devious diplomacy — these were all gathered around the council table, clamorous in their demand to dictate the terms.

Mr. Wilson surrendered more than he dreamed he was surrendering, but it is not difficult to follow his line of reasoning. The League of Nations was to be a continuing court of equity, sitting in judgment on the peace itself, revising its terms when revision became necessary and possible, slowly readjusting the provisions of the treaty to a calmer and saner public state of mind. Get peace first. Establish the League, and the League would rectify the inevitable mistakes of the treaty.

It is a curious commentary on human nature that when the treaty was completed and the storm of wrath broke, all the rage, all the resentment, all the odium should have fallen on the one man who had struggled week in and week out against the forces of reaction and revenge and had written into the treaty all that it contains which makes for the international advancement of the race.

Into that record must also go the impressive fact that the Treaty of Versailles was rejected by the United States Senate, under the leadership of Henry Cabot Lodge, not because of its acknowledged defects and shortcomings, not because it breathed the spirit of a Carthaginian peace in its punitive clauses, but because of its most enlightened provision, the covenant at the League of Nations, which is the one hope of a war-racked world.

When people speak of the tragedy of Mr. Wilson's career they have in mind only the temporary aspects of it — the universal dissatisfaction with the treaty of peace, his physical collapse, his defeat in the Senate and the verdict of the polls in November. They forget that the end of the chapter is not yet written. The League of Nations is a fact, whatever the attitude of the United States may be toward it, and it will live unless the people of the earth prove their political incapacity to use it for the promotion of their own welfare. The principle of self-determination will remain as long as men believe in the right of self-government and are willing to die for it. It was Woodrow Wilson who wrote that principle into the law of nations, even though he failed to obtain a universal application of it. Tacitus said of the Catti tribesmen, "Others go to battle; these go to war," and Mr. Wilson went to war in behalf of the democratic theory of government extended to all the affairs of the nations. The war is not yet won, and the commander-in-chief is crippled by the wound he received on the field of action. But the responsibility for the future does not rest with him. It rests with the self-governing peoples for whom he has blazed the trail. All the complicated issues of this titanic struggle finally reduce themselves to these prophetic words of Maximilian Harden: "Only one conqueror's work will endure — Wilson's thought."

Woodrow Wilson on this morning of the Fourth of March can say in the words of Paul the Apostle to Timothy:

*"For I am now ready to be offered, and the time of my departure is at hand. I have fought a good fight, I have finished my course, I have kept the faith."*

## A SINISTER EPISODE

New York *Evening Post*, October 14, 1920

The military record in Haiti is a blot on the Administration and a stain on the honor of the American people. The revelation that our marines engaged in the "unlawful, indiscriminate killing" of Haitian natives during the five years of our occupation of the island is a shock to those who have cherished the conviction that American military rule did not imitate the coercive methods of some more experienced and more callous governments. General Barrett makes it clear that this is not a new discovery. Over a year ago he himself wrote a letter to the present officer commanding an investigation. Nor does he confine his revelation now to evidence of killing. The Haitian natives have been oppressed by the revival of the old cower system of forced labor at road making outside their own districts.

Of the Haitian natives slain, more than half were killed in the repulse of an attack on Port-Au-Prince and during the military operations succeeding. An actual state of war existed during much of that period. This affords a partial justification of the unpleasant record. Moreover, the marines did some good things for Haiti; they protected cities, held native bandits at bay, and went far to restore order on many occasions. But it is not a question of arithmetic. "Indiscriminate killings" by American troops would be a horror if measured in units instead of hundreds. It is a record that calls for prompt and stern punishment of the guilty. General Barrett himself calls it "the most startling thing of its kind that has ever taken place in the Marine Corps."

We had a "bandit" problem with the Moros in the Philippines, and we solved it by combining determination with self-restraint and intelligence. We should have done the same in Haiti. Haiti has problems peculiar to its own people. No doubt much has been done there of which we may be proud. But we need to conceive our task as one calling for responsible, sympathetic guidance, and not for the free use of bullets.

## THE THIRTY–ONE FOR HARDING[1]

New York *Evening Post*, October 15, 1920

On June, 16, 1858, before the Republican State Convention of Illinois, Abraham Lincoln said:

There are those who whisper softly that Senator Douglas is the aptest instrument there is to over-throw the "power of the present political dynasty". . . . How can he oppose the advance of slavery? He does not care anything about it. His avowed mission is impressing the public heart to care nothing about it. Our cause must be intrusted to, and conducted by, its own undoubted friends — those whose hands are free, whose hearts are in the work, who do care for the result.

The statement issued yesterday in support of Harding by thirty-one eminent Republican friends of the League calls upon the American people to approach a great question in the opposite spirit from that of Abraham Lincoln. It is a call upon the voters to intrust the task of promoting world peace through coöperation to a man named Harding, who does not care anything about world coöperation and who has been doing his best to impress the public heart to care nothing. It is an invitation to let the great cause of world peace be conducted by a man whose hands are not free but are bound with the shackles of Hiram Johnson and Borah; by a man whose heart is not in the work; by a man who does not care for the result.

To prove that Harding will give us world coöperation for peace the thirty-one quote the Republican platform and Harding's speech of August 28. And we are free to confess that as a reminder to Harding of what he ought in honor to do the document is adroit. But as proof that Harding *will do his duty* the document has no force whatever. For Harding has cast aside the Republican platform and the speech of August 28. Since the speech of August 28, there have been other speeches, including a speech at Des Moines on October 7. And in these speeches Harding has made it plain

[1] Thirty-one leading Republicans, all friends of the League, and including Charles E. Hughes, George Wickersham, and Herbert Hoover, signed a manifesto in which they declared their faith that Harding would, if elected, bring America into coöperation with the rest of the world for peace.

that he is against a League and against a real association of nations. Harding uses the phrase, but he has said frankly that he does not know what it means. At different times his association of nations was to be the League with all that is good in it; it was to be the Hague Court with teeth in it; it was to be an association with nations "whose ideals are not the same as ours, never have been and never will be." And yesterday the association of nations became an association "with the other nations in which the mutual commercial and trade problems must be worked out"! So it is for a League of Nations to promote trade that men have hoped and labored and died.

Harding still speaks of an association of nations and the thirty-one have tried to show that it will be an association with a good deal of the League in it. But Johnson and Borah have seen to it, and will continue to see to it, that it shall be an association of nations with nothing in it.

Having whitewashed Harding's enmity to a League into friendship for a League, the thirty-one proceed to distort Cox's friendship for a League into the destruction of a League. This they do by asserting that the issue is whether we shall join under an agreement containing the exact provisions negotiated by President Wilson at Paris, or under an agreement which omits or modifies some of these provisions.

This is not true. The issue is between a man who said:

> We will accept any reservation that helps to clarify.
> We will accept any reservation that helps to reassure.
> We will accept any reservation that helps to strengthen.

and a man who has said:

> I do not want to clarify these obligations. I want to turn my back upon them. It is not interpretation but rejection that I am seeking.

Cox is not for the unmodified Covenant. Cox, if elected, will accept any changes necessary to get us into the League. If Cox is elected, the pressure behind him will not be Wilson pressure but the pressure of friends of the League who have been willing to pay any price to get the League started. In this city Mr. Cox is supported by the *Evening Post*, the *World*, and the *Times*. Last November the *Evening Post*, though believing that the Lodge reservations were dictated primarily by partisan enmity, called upon President Wilson to accept the Lodge reservations. So did the *World*. So did the *Times*. What we demanded of Wilson we would demand of Cox. If Cox is elected, Cox will be President.

And it is our firm belief that President Cox will get us into a League as it is our firm belief that President Harding will be blackmailed by Johnson and Borah into rejecting anything that bears the semblance of the League for which the world hopes.

As to the labor involved in scrapping the League and beginning negotiations for a new association of nations, Ambassador Davis repeated in masterful fashion last night what all men know. It means years of delay, years of uncertainty for the world, years for the forces of social dissolution to do their utmost. It is a herculean task if we approached it with the most ardent faith. It is a hopeless task if we approach it with the faith that is in Johnson and Borah. We are to have an association with nations whom Hiram Johnson denounced last night as spoliators, with nations of whom Harding says that their "ideals are not the same as ours, never have been, and never will be."

The statement of the thirty-one shows that Republicans are morally ill at ease. The document is not a clarion call. It is only a way out for men in an unhappy position. Life-long Republicans are deserting Harding. That is the reason why a fortnight before the election a former Republican candidate for the Presidency and former members of Republican Cabinets feel themselves compelled to issue an apologia for voting for Harding!

"Our cause," said Abraham Lincoln, "must be intrusted to, and conducted by, its own undoubted friends, those whose hands are free, whose hearts are in the work, who do care for the result."

## THE UNKNOWN SOLDIER[1]

New York *Herald*, November 11, 1921

. . . It is a common weakness of humanity to ask the questions that can never be answered in this life. Probably none to whom the drama of the Unknown Soldier has appealed has not wondered who, in the sunshine of earth, was the protagonist of today's ceremony. A logger from the Penobscot? An orchardist from the Pacific coast? A well-driller from Texas? A machinist from Connecticut? A lad who left his hoe to rust among the Missouri corn? A longshoreman from Hell's Kitchen? Perhaps some youth from the tobacco fields, resting again in his own Virginia. All that the Army tells us of him is that he died in battle. All that the heart tells us is that some woman loved him. More than that no man shall learn. In this mystery, as in the riddle of the universe, the wise wonder; but they would not know.

[1] From the editorial by Frank M. O'Brien on the day the Unknown Soldier was buried at Arlington; awarded the Pulitzer Prize as the best editorial of that year

What were his dreams, his ambitions?  Likely he shared those common to the millions:  a life of peace and honest struggle, with such small success as comes to most who try;  and at the end the place on the hillside among his fathers.  Today to do honor at his last resting-place come the greatest soldiers of the age, famous statesmen from other continents, the President, the high judges and the legislators of his own country, and many men who, like himself, fought for the flag.  At his bier will gather the most remarkable group that America has seen.  And the tomb which fate reserved for him is, instead of the narrow cell on the village hillside, one as lasting as that of Rameses and as inspiring as Napoleon's!

## THE IMPOSSIBLE THIRD PARTY

New York *Globe*, November 29, 1921

Stoughton Cooley, in the *Freeman*, gives a review of third parties calculated thoroughly to discourage anyone planning to start a new one.  Ruling out the Progressives as presumably nothing but a "Republican split," he demonstrates that the highest third party vote ever polled was the 1,041,028 showing of the Populists in 1892. The Socialists reached their high point with 915,302 in 1920. With the Prohibitionists and Farmer-Laborites they attracted only 5.2 per cent of the voting population from the two regular parties.

Mr. Cooley believes that a much larger body will never be attracted.  The American voter is a different kind of animal from the British or French or German voter.  He likes his party.  When he wishes to register disapproval of it, "he casts his vote for the opposition, where it will have double weight."  Therefore the bones of the Native American party, the Greenbackers, and the Populists along the road of national political struggles.  Therefore the sickly existence of the Prohibition, the Farmer-Labor, and Socialist parties today.  Real causes worm into the big parties and thrive or die there.  A third party by a kind of spontaneous combustion is a possibility, but should it be formed it would probably displace one of the old ones.

The course of American politics gives ammunition to anyone fighting for such a view, but no proof.  Examination of the minor parties here gives plenty of reason for their failure.  They have been built around radical-liberal or radical philosophy, or around freak programmes seeming to Americans of 1921 mere curiosities. The two-party system has persisted because these parties have never made an effective assault upon it.  Socialism in the United States has assumed a far more doctrinaire and far less practical form than in Europe.  The various forms of liberalism working outside

Democracy or Republicanism have killed themselves by resolutely turning their backs upon opportunistic effort. Local elections in New York, Montana, California, and Wisconsin have shown the possibility of appealing to the electorate from new parties. A new party with sane and enthusiastic organizers and promoters is possible at any time. A labor party may yet emerge. The agricultural bloc in Congress is a threat. The Non-Partisan movement in the Northwest, seeking not dissimilar ends from those professed by the Middle Western representatives, succeeded in agitating the entire country. A strong third party has never been born here. The past is no warrant for what will happen in the future. If a new political group took shape tomorrow the miracle would not be its presence, but the fact that it had failed to materialize before.

## SEEING RED

### Emporia *Gazette*, January 8, 1922

The Attorney General seems to be seeing red. He is rounding up every manner of radical in the country — every man who hopes for a better world is in danger of deportation by the Attorney General. The whole business is un-American. There are certain rules which should govern in the treason cases.

First, it should be agreed that a man may believe what he chooses.

Second, it should be agreed that when he preaches violence he is disturbing the peace and should be put in jail; whether he preaches violence in politics, business, or religion, whether he advocates murder and arson and pillage for gain or for political ends, he is violating the common law and should be squelched — jailed until he is willing to quit advocating force in a democracy.

Third, he should be allowed to say what he pleases so long as he advocates legal constitutional methods of procedure. Just because a man does not believe this government is good is no reason why he should be deported. Abraham Lincoln did not believe this government was all right seventy-five years ago. He advocated changes, but he advocated constitutional means, and he had a war with those who advocated force to maintain the government as it was. Ten years ago Roosevelt advocated great changes in our American life — in our Constitution, in our social and economic life. Most of the changes he advocated have been made, but they were made in the regular legal way. He preached no force. And if a man desires to preach any doctrine under the shining sun, and to advocate the realization of his vision by lawful, orderly, constitutional means — let him alone. If he is Socialist, anarchist, or Mormon, and merely preaches his creed and does not preach violence, he can do no harm. For the folly of his doctrine will be its answer.

The deportation business is going to make martyrs of a lot of idiots whose cause is not worth it.

## THE DECLINE OF JAZZ JOY[1]

### Emporia *Gazette*, November 10, 1922

The stated clerk of the Presbyterian General Assembly, who ex-officio is a preacher of parts, in a recent address declared that he could see a visible decline in the barbarous customs of American youth: the jazz orchestra, the caveman dances, the hip-pocket flask, the all-night functions with breakfast refreshments. The stated clerk is on the watchtower and should know the signs of the times. Let us trust that he is not merely watching the mirage of his hopes.

At any rate it is high time for youth to begin taking the slack out of its bad manners. A lot of bad manners, which looked like bad morals, but which were probably not what they seemed, followed the war, and took an excuse from the war. The war gave a lot of us an opportunity to pin on tails and climb into the trees. The profiteer who sandbagged his neighbors, the patrioteer who kukluxed his enemies, the desk soldier who swanked around afternoon teas while his betters were dying, the politician who let the drums do his thinking and the guns do his talking, the war worker who let his emotions govern his conduct and wasn't particular which emotion was running his behavior — all these let down a lot of bars which have kept society in bounds for hundreds of years. So there was more or less running hog-wild upon the once prim laws of orderly society.

No wonder youth got at it. And youth is not to blame for its jazz joy. Youth merely was imitating its elders. Instead of grabbing money and boycotting disagreeable people and swaggering in tin swords and lying to the electorate and flirting with middle-aged ladies in uniforms, youth went straight for those particular joys which interest youth most — the joys which are found down the "primrose path" beyond the twilight's purple rim. Hence the jungle dance, the petting parties, the all-night shindy, and the parked coupe. And what is more, so long as the old folks keep up their war activities and their warlike morals, the boys and girls will go the gait. The way to stop youth is to curb the old folks. It is the monkey of imitation in youth that has shocked its elders cold. And the imitations of youth are sad commentaries upon the morals of their parents.

[1] By William Allen White; a partial summary of the effect of the war on American morals.

## THE FARM BLOC'S RECORD[1]

Chicago *Tribune*, July 16, 1923

The agrarian bloc in the United States Senate and, to a lesser degree, in the House, became a notable factor in the last Congress. So powerful was this organization that there was much grave talk not only in Washington but throughout the country as to the possible dangers of bloc and class legislation. The difficulties of the deflated farmers of the nation were so pressing, however, as to bring about organization and a flood of legislation designed for their relief by such men as Capper, Norris, Ladd, Brookhart, La Follette, and Shipstead.

These representatives of the farmers put things over for the farmer in Washington with a notable whoopla and remarkable ease. The rest of Congress seemed to be more or less eating out of their hands. Acts to help the farmers included the Federal farm loan act, an act to amend the Federal farm loan act, an act to amend the amended farm loan act, an act to regulate interstate and foreign commerce in live stock and all live stock, dairy, and poultry products, an act to regulate the grain exchanges, an act to amend the War Finance Corporation act to provide relief for dealers in agricultural products, provision for a new system of farm loan bonds, and by no means least, both an emergency and a permanent tariff on farm products dictated entirely by the agrarians in Congress. That is not the entire list of legislation in behalf of the farmers, but it is enough to show the extent of the influence and efficiency of their agricultural representatives.

All these laws were designed to recoup the farmers' financial condition, which was admittedly bad when they were passed. They were hailed with delight. And what has it brought them?

On July 11 wheat and flour prices dropped to the lowest levels in eight years. Hogs are about $3 less than a year ago. Wages promise to be higher than ever. The protective tariff on industrial products which the farmer approved in order to get a useless tariff on his own products has kept up prices of necessities which the farmer must buy.

That is the situation after a full session of farm bloc dictation in Congress. Let the farmer ponder it.

[1] The 'agricultural bloc' first appeared in Congress in 1921, in the special session called by President Harding. Agricultural distress, however, continued acute throughout the Middle West. When a great number of minor legislative expedients failed — as the Chicago *Tribune* points out — to bring relief, many farmers turned to the McNary-Haugen bill. The result was a direct collision between the industrial East and the agricultural West.

## AMERICANIZE AMERICA
Chicago *Tribune*, August 21, 1923

The Chicago Association of Commerce has completed a census of the city which reveals that only 28 per cent of our population is American-born of American-born parents. Less than 25 per cent of our white population enjoys that distinction. There is a condition which cannot fail to impress the entire United States with the necessity of continuing for many years a restriction of foreign immigration at least as close, if not closer, than that under which we are now operating.

It is a perfectly natural and understandable thing for foreign-born parents to bring many of their national and racial prejudices and customs into this country, and to continue them in their children. Some of these characteristics may be good. Some of them are bad, as is indicated by the condition into which they have allowed these people to sink before coming to the United States.

Probably the figures would be similar in New York and not very dissimilar in Cleveland, St. Louis, Milwaukee, Boston, Pittsburgh, and other cities.

It is intelligent for us to restrict immigration for at least a full generation that the great mass of Americans shall be of American-born parentage. Then, and not until then, will we be on the way to becoming a homogeneous people.

## [THE UNITED STATES SHOULD KEEP OUT OF EUROPE]
*The Freeman*, September 26, 1923

Europe is not a country; it is an aggregation of not less than twenty-seven different countries. . . . This is the parti-colored agglomeration of peoples, governments, languages and international interests which ought really to be thought of when "Europe" is mentioned; an agglomeration with no social or political unity and with extremely little sense, so far as can be gathered from events, of common obligation. Some one will probably protest, however, that even if there is no organic political or social unity there are, nevertheless, certain common problems, and in particular certain common distresses, most of which owe their origin to the world war; and that it is to these that the United States is morally bound to address its benevolent aid. Take reparations, for example; is not that question keeping all Europe in turmoil? Or the war-debts; are not most of the European States entangled in these?

Or foreign exchange; is not every European country struggling with its depreciated currency? Here, surely, are things in plenty for the United States to take hold of, even if it does not care to tackle everything and launch a general clean-up. America ought to have a heart and "go in." Where there's a will there's a way.

Is there? Let us look a bit at that seductive appeal. America should help to settle the great European difficulties that have arisen out of the war. Lay that proposition athwart the map of Europe and observe the States upon which it falls. What do we find? To begin with, we shall discover that six important European States — the Netherlands, Denmark, Sweden, Norway, Switzerland, and Spain — contrived, to their everlasting honor, to keep out of the war, and were rewarded for their good sense by being also kept out of the peace conference. None of them has any reparations to collect or war debts of importance to repay; while their currencies, although depreciated, are at the present time in very much better condition than those of most of the former belligerents. Incidentally, they are all distinctly more pro-German than pro-Ally, and this also notwithstanding the war. Russia was out of the fray some time before the war ended; no other European Power seems particularly desirous to pick a quarrel with it; and its new gold-secured currency will shortly shift off into space the depreciated roubles in which a number of ardent patriots elsewhere have been speculating. Add together the populations of these seven States, and it will appear that about one-half the population of Europe neither needs nor desires American intervention, so far as anything immediately connected with the world war is involved.

How about the "Europe" of the one-time belligerents, of the nations which vowed before high heaven that they would act together until the great "enemy" was vanquished and an "enduring peace" enthroned? Are there any two of the former Allies that show much sign of agreement upon a method of handling the problems of reparations and war debts, for example? Even Belgium and France, which joined forces for the invasion of the Ruhr, have not been able to make joint replies to the various British notes; while Italy, notwithstanding that it has kept out of the Ruhr, is at odds with both Belgium and France because neither of those Powers will consent to tie together reparations and war-debts in the same bundle. About the only value of the British notes that Mr. Baldwin and Lord Curzon have concocted is their demonstration of British incapacity in the face of an international quarrel, and the manoeuvrings of the Cuno and Stresemann governments have wreathed no halo about the German mind; but the most convinced advocate of American intervention can hardly fail to see, if he will only reflect, that almost anything that any one of these mutually suspicious or openly hostile Powers liked, the others would be much disposed to reject. We have the ennobling spectacle of four great States, all agreeing that Germany ought to pay and ought to be made to pay, but wholly unable to agree as to how or how much it shall be made to pay, or how the payments, if any are obtained, shall be divided among the claimants; and this is the "Europe" which, it is insisted, America ought long since to have helped!

The whole plea for "doing something" in Europe is sentimental humbug and political claptrap; and it is mischievous into the bargain, because it is supported by men and women who know better, but who make no use of what they know. The only way in which the United States can intervene in Europe is by playing the game of some one of the quarreling Powers, and that is what every government that pleads for America to "come in" really wants. France would burn incense on every altar and light a bonfire on every hill if Mr. Coolidge would throw his arms about M. Poincare and call him brother; but if by any chance Mr. Coolidge were to embrace Mr. Baldwin, the mudslinging batteries of the subsidized French press would work overtime in hurling abuse. What would happen in Paris and London if the United States should express the opinion that the pressure on Germany ought to be relaxed, can better be imagined than described. There is no "Europe" that America can aid.

## PUBLIC SENTIMENT ON VOLSTEAD[1]

New York *Evening Post*, October 5, 1923

The stranger from Mars, when he reads of yesterday's declaration by the State Chamber of Commerce in favor of the modification of the Volstead law "to conform more nearly with the public sentiment," would be led to think that the Volstead law was enacted for the people of the United States by a super-Mussolini instead of by an elective and supposedly representative Congress. The reason for the existence of Congress is to translate public sentiments into law. If the Volstead law is modified by Congress it would mean that public sentiment demands such revision. If the Volstead law stands unchanged it means that public sentiment wants the Volstead law left alone. The efforts of the Volstead revisionists should be addressed not to Congress but to the people that elects Congress.

[1] The Eighteenth Amendment, for constitutional prohibition, was ratified January 16, 1919. The Volstead Act became law October 28, 1919.

It may be, however, that the Chamber of Commerce resolution was ineptly worded. Probably the intention was to urge Congress to modify the Volstead law so as to make it conform more nearly with local public sentiment. In New York, New Jersey, and Illinois the popular majority holds that light wines and beer are not intoxicating under the Eighteenth Amendment. These States should be permitted to have their light wines and beer. The argument is, of course, that under such a system we should be spared the present demoralizing spectacle of entire communities virtually repudiating a law that outrages the public sentiment in such communities.

The trouble with this apparently simple solution is that it overlooks the entire trend of events that gave us the Eighteenth Amendment and the Volstead law. The prohibition movement began and made headway as a local movement. Before the Eighteenth Amendment, prohibition had conquered the greater part of the country by towns, counties, and States. And then it happened with prohibition as things are obviously happening with the movement for the abolition of child labor. The separate States found themselves hampered in their domestic policies by divergencies among the States. Specifically, the dry States found that prohibition enforcement was rendered difficult by liquor importations from wet States. The sealed package led directly to the Eighteenth Amendment.

The present story of scotch and rye from Canada and the West Indies and Sandy Hook would be repeated on a magnified scale in the story of light wines and beer from New York and New Jersey. For good or ill, all the States of the Union have got into the habit of ultimately marching together on big issues. The proposition of a Volstead law so modified as to let New York and New Jersey have the light wines and beer they are supposed to want is a phantasy.

## CECILIA COONEY[1]

### New York *World*, May 8, 1924

For some months now we have been vastly entertained by the bobbed-hair bandit. Knowing nothing about her, we created a perfect story standardized according to the rules laid down by the movies and the short-story magazines. The story had, as the press agents say, everything. It had a flapper and a bandit who baffled the police; it had sex and money, crime and mystery. And then yesterday we read in the probation officer's report the story of Cecilia Cooney's life. It was not in the least entertaining. For there in the place of the dashing bandit was a pitiable girl; instead

[1] By Walter Lippmann.

of an amusing tale, a dark and mean tragedy; instead of a lovely adventure, a terrible accusation.

In the twenty years she has lived in this city she has come at one time or another within reach of all the agencies of righteousness. Five years before she was born her father was summoned to court for drunkenness and neglect; the Charities Department recommended then that her older brothers and sisters be committed to an institution. That did not prevent her parents bringing, with the full consent of the law, three or four more children into the world. Cecilia herself, the youngest of eight, came at four years of age into the custody of the Children's Society. Six months later, on the recommendation of the Department of Public Charity, she was turned back to her mother, who promptly deserted her.

She was next taken to Brooklyn by her aunt and for ten years or so attended parochial school. At the age of fourteen her mother brought her back to New York, took her to a furnished room, stole her clothes, and deserted her. A year later, aged fifteen, Cecilia became a child-laborer in a brush factory in Brooklyn, and was associating at night with sailors picked up on the water front. At sixteen Cecilia was back in New York, living with her mother, working as a laundress for a few months at a stretch in various hospitals. At twenty she was married, had borne a child, had committed a series of robberies, and is condemned to spend the rest of her youth in prison.

This is what twentieth-century civilization in New York achieved in the case of Cecilia Cooney. Fully warned by the behavior of her parents long before her birth, the law allowed her parents to reproduce their kind. Fully warned when she was still an infant, society allowed her to drift out of its hands into a life of dirt, neglect, dark basements, begging, stealing, ignorance, poor little tawdry excitements and twisted romance. The courts had their chance and they missed it. Charity had its chance and missed it. The church had its chance and missed it. The absent-minded routine of all that is well-meaning and respectable did not deflect by an inch her inexorable progress from the basement where she was born to the jail where she will expiate her crimes and ours.

For her crimes are on our heads too. No record could be clearer or more eloquent. None could leave less room for doubt that Cecilia Cooney is a product of this city, of its neglect and its carelessness, of its indifference and its undercurrents of misery. We recommend her story to the pulpits of New York, to the school men of New York, to the lawmakers of New York, to the social workers of New York, to those who are tempted to boast of its wealth, its magnificence, and its power.

## THEY  WENT  ON[1]

New York *Times*, July 7, 1924

While it is too soon to despair of government by party, many of us have become heartily ashamed of it. The sullen animosities of the Democratic strife are not ennobled even by their ferocity. Nor does the contrasting harmony of the Republicans offer much consolation; for the Democratic civil war began in a fight for a sound principle, while the Republicans attained harmony by ignoring it as beneath the notice of gentlemen.

Yet, from Madison Square Garden, look up to Everest. The unconquered mountain is not unconquerable. Perhaps it was conquered by those two men who disappeared in the mist, still going upward. They never came back — Irvine with the fiery dedication of his youth, Mallory whose battle with the mountain had become a personal combat. They knew, on that late afternoon just below the summit, with darkness closing in and bringing such cold as no man can resist, that they had climbed higher than men ever climbed before. But they had not reached the peak, so they went on. They knew that if they climbed higher they might never come back, yet they went on.

Man's victory over Nature is ancient history. Ever since thick-skulled, hairy men learned to defy the ice-sheet, Nature has been beaten. What the world has been wondering is whether Man can ever conquer himself, or if that self is worth conquering. Snarling Democrats and smirking Republicans say no. Mallory and Irvine say yes.

## THE  CHAMPION[2]

*American Mercury*, October, 1924

Of the forty-eight sovereign States of this imperial federation, which is the worst? In what one of them is a civilized man most uncomfortable? Over half the votes, if the question were put to a vote, would probably be divided between California and Georgia. Each, in its way, is almost unspeakable. Georgia, of course, has never been civilized, save in a small area along the tidewater. Even in the earliest days of the republic, it was regarded as barbaric by its neighbors. But California, at one time, promised to develop a charming and enlightening civilization. There was a touch of

[1] At a time when many Americans were disgusted with the oil scandal in the Harding Administration, the activities of the Ku Klux Klan in both parties, and the deadlock of the Democratic convention of 1924, word came that two lost members of the British Himalayan expedition had last been seen disappearing at dusk into the storm clouds that wreathed the pinnacle of Mt. Everest.

[2] Few if any of H. L. Mencken's chief prejudices are not expressed or implied in this editorial jeer.

tropical balm in its air, and a touch of Latin and even oriental color in its ideas. Like Louisiana, it seemed likely to resist Americanization for many years; perhaps forever. But now California, the old California, is simply extinct. What remains is an Alsatia of retired Ford agents and crazy fat women — a paradise of Rotary and the New Thought. Its laws are the most extravagant and idiotic ever heard of in Christendom. Its public officers, and particularly its judges, are famous all over the world for their imbecility. When one hears of it at all, one hears that some citizen has been jailed for reading the Constitution of the United States, or that some new swami in a yellow bedtick has got all the realtors' wives of Los Angeles by the ears. When one hears of it further, it is only to learn that some distinguished movie wench in Hollywood has murdered another lover. The State is run by its Chambers of Commerce, which is to say, by the worst variety of resident Babbits. No man of any dignity seems to have any part in its public life. Not an idea ever comes out of it; that is, not an idea beyond the grasp of a Kiwanis Club secretary, a Christian Science sorcerer, or a grand wizard of the American Legion. Twice of late, it has offered the country candidates for the Presidency. One was the Hon. Hiram Johnson and the other was the Hon. William Gibbs McAdoo! Only Vermont can beat that record.

The minority of civilized Californians — who recently, by the way, sent out a call from Los Angeles for succor, as if they were beset by wolves! — commonly lay the blame for this degeneration of a once proud commonwealth upon the horde of morons which has flowed in from Iowa, Nebraska, and the other cow-States, seeking relief from the bitter climate of the steppes. The California realtors have been luring in these hinds for a generation past, and they now swarm in all the Southern towns, especially Los Angeles. They come in with their savings, are swindled and sent home, and so make room for more. While they remain and have any part of their money left, they patronize the swamis, buy oil stock, gape at the movie gals, and pack the Methodist churches. Unquestionably, the influence of such vacuums has tended to degrade the general tone of California life; what was once a Spanish *fiesta* is now merely an upper Mississippi valley street-carnival. But it is not to be forgotten that the Native Sons have gone down the chute with the newcomers — that there is little more sign of intellectual vigor in the old stock than there is in the new stock. A few intransigents hold out against the tide of 100 per cent Americanism, but only a few. The rest bawl against the Reds as loudly as any Iowa steer-stuffer.

The truth is that it is unjust to blame Iowa for the decay of California, for Iowa itself is now moving up, not down. And so is Nebraska. A few years ago both States were as sterile, intellectually, as Guatemala, but both are showing signs of progress today, and in another generation or two, as the Prohibition lunacy passes and the pall of Methodism begins to lift, they will probably burst into very vigorous activity. Some excellent stock is in them; it is probably very little contaminated by what is called Anglo-Saxon blood. Iowa, even today, is decidedly more civilized than California. It is producing more ideas, and, much more important still, it is carrying on a much less violent war *against* ideas. I doubt whether any man who read the Constitution in Davenport or Des Moines would be jailed for it, as Upton Sinclair (or one of his friends) was in Pasadena. . . .

The case of Georgia is simpler. It happens to be the chief battleground between the poor white trash who have been in control of the whole South since the Civil War and the small but growing minority of civilized rebels. That battle is going on all over the South, but in Georgia it is especially bitter, for there the poor white trash are very strongly entrenched and desperately determined to beat their antagonists. They have many advantages. They control the legislature, they have the support of most of the newspapers, and they have produced a number of leaders of great boldness. Hence the Ku Klux Klan. Hence the prohibition of Darwinism. Hence the tax of $1,000 a performance on grand opera. But Georgia, though it is thus in the depths, is not hopeless. There are civilized Georgians, and they are by no means inactive. Today they carry on their fight against apparently hopeless odds, but if they keep their resolution they may win tomorrow. At all events, they keep on fighting, bravely and even gayly. But in California, as I have said, the civilized minority is in despair. In Los Angeles, indeed, it has gone so far that it has thrown up its hands and cast itself upon the Christian charity of the rest of the country.

## SESQUICENTENNIAL OF THE REPUBLIC:
### JULY 4, 1926 [1]

New York *World*, July 5, 1926

During the last century and a half the promise of America has held the imagination of the modern world in a way which is not unlike the spell cast by the memory of Rome upon the Middle Ages. The name America has been a symbol through which

[1] By Walter Lippmann.

western mankind expressed its sense of the future. The Middle Ages never ceased to believe that they would find fulfillment and peace in the restoration of the Roman Empire. The modern age has never ceased to think that in America the meaning of modernity would be most completely realized. Usually modern men have looked upon this fulfillment with great hope; now and then, more often in these later years, they have looked upon it with anxiety. But always by universal consent the word America has been something more than the name of a country and of a nation. It has been the name of an idea which hopefully or otherwise signified one of the possible destinies of the Western civilization.

The sense that the old civilization of Europe was born again on this soil has attended American history throughout its course. We have no long, slow, and vegetative history behind us. We have been very conscious of the significance of our history while we were living it. At the birth of the nation the men who signed the Declaration felt they were acting not merely as against the Ministers of George III, but in the presence of mankind. They knew and said that they were testing out in action the principles which men of the eighteenth century had forged for the revolution against the ancient régime. At Gettysburg during the climax of the war to maintain the Union Lincoln expressed again the sense that the outcome in America was in some profound way a test for mankind of the outcome of popular government. And once again at the climax of the World War the tradition of a conscious destiny was expressed by Woodrow Wilson when he announced the end of the era of isolation. On these three great occasions which marked the birth of the nation, the union of the nation, and its emergence as a world power, the idea has prevailed that the purpose of America had a significance that transcended the purposes of individual Americans. Certainly Jefferson felt that, Lincoln felt it, and Wilson felt it, and through the utterances of these three men the dim purposes and confused activity of events day by day have taken on historic form and an ideal meaning.

To those who live close to the details of a time and are addled by its complexities this form and meaning are hard to discern. The principles of the Declaration of Independence must have seemed remote and quaint to the men who were immersed in the confusion after 1783. Yet those principles, which are in many ways out of harmony with our own ways of thinking, played an immense part in the European revolution which ushered in the modern world. The words that Lincoln spoke at Gettysburg must have seemed shadowy and remote to the generation which was mired in the follies and corruption of Reconstruction. The words that Wilson spoke in April, 1917, are now submerged in the post-war confusion, the post-war selfishness, the post-war weariness of all high purpose.  But they too will survive, though in detail like Jefferson's Declaration they will seem quaint and archaic and verbal.  They will survive because, like the Declaration and like the Gettysburg speech, they herald an event of indubitable conse-quence to mankind.

## AMERICA EUROPE, AND THE WAR DEBTS [1]

### New York *World*, July 29, 1926

The fundamental reason why these great international war debts cannot be regarded as ordinary debts is that they are dead.  They do not represent capital invested in a living enterprise which pro-duces as it goes along the interest and the principal to repay the money which was loaned.  An ordinary debt is productive for the debtor, but these international debts are like bills submitted to pay for the damage done on a wild party by one's grandfather.  The payment seems to the debtor like a pure loss, and when it is paid by one nation to another it seems like tribute by the conquered to the conqueror.  Money borrowed to build a railroad earns money to pay for itself.  But money borrowed to fight a war pro-duces nothing, and if it has to be paid it becomes a dead mortgage superimposed upon all the living credits of a nation.

The United States has engaged itself to collect for the next two generations the sum of $400,000,000 a year on a dead debt.  Most of the veterans of the war will be gone.  Their children born after the war, knowing no more of its reality than an American college boy knows of the Civil War, will be elderly men, their children in turn will be approaching middle age, and still the huge payments will go on.  The last instalments will be paid out of the earnings of the great-grandsons of the men who directed the war.  Is it conceivable that for the rest of the century this thing will go on?  Does anybody really think he lives in a world where such things are possible?

Let us not deceive ourselves.  Mr. Coolidge and Mr. Mellon and Mr. Borah and Mr. Baldwin and M. Briand and the other gentle-men who have made these arrangements will not bind posterity nor mortgage the future in any such fashion as this.  To us the war was a great event.  But already there is a generation out in the world which has almost no knowledge of it.  In a few years those of us who lived through the war will seem like reminiscent old bores to young people who will have many better things to do

[1] By Walter Lippmann.

than hash over the rights and wrongs of 1914–18. Yet here we are deluding ourselves with the preposterous idea that from now until about 1984 people and governments are going to be bothered with carrying out what to them will be perfectly meaningless settlements. Already Mr. Mellon and Mr. Churchill can't quite remember what the money was spent for. The next generation certainly, our own if it is wise, will say in face of the endless bother and animosity that these settlements entail: Let the past be the past, let the dead bury the dead, let us forget, let us forgive, let us have peace.

## [ASPECTS OF AMERICAN SOCIAL HISTORY, 1927]

*The New Republic*

### [*The Ebb in Religion*]: August 24.

The Rev. H. K. Carroll says, in an official report, that the Protestant Churches of America are losing members at the rate of 500,000 a year. Mr. Carroll is secretary of the Continuation Committee of the Interchurch Conference, and ought to know what he is talking about. However, the reasons he assigns for this state of affairs are curious. He lays much blame on the American habit of moving frequently from town to town. But surely, to say this is to imply that church membership is, for many persons, not a pleasurable and voluntary association, but the result of community coercion, something to be avoided when removal to another city makes escape possible. Mr. Carroll also blames that good old scapegoat, the War. But with the end of the conflict now nine years in the past, it would seem that such an influence would have reached and passed its peak long ago. Moreover, the War is universally conceded to have caused a great revival of mysticism, and of religious emotionalism in general, in all countries. We believe a more important clue is to be found in Mr. Carroll's incidental remark that some of the clergy and churches have failed to keep abreast of the changing spiritual needs of their flocks. Here is a fruitful field for further, careful inquiry.

### [*Recklessness in Aviation*]: August 31.

Three persons were killed in the course of preparations for the recent civilian flight to the Hawaiian Islands for a $35,000 prize; and seven others are missing, with the chances overwhelmingly against their being found alive — five in two planes which were entered in the race, two in a plane which flew to hunt for them. It is now learned that the government strongly protested against the risks which were run. It sought to have the race postponed two weeks longer in order to prepare the planes; it urged that the course be altered so as to conduct the race over land, perhaps between the Pacific and Atlantic seaboards, or if this suggestion were unacceptable, that the planes be taken to Hawaii by ship, and the flight end in California. These proposals were all rejected; and the government lacked the authority to enforce its wishes. Two conclusions are forced upon us by the incident. Long-distance flights over the ocean are still hazardous in the extreme; and there is need of a Federal law giving the government power to see to it that fliers do not risk almost certain death.

[*Farewell to the Flivver*]: September 14.

The world pushes on, relentlessly discarding, in its dotage, instruments that once worked incalculably for its progress. In America the pace is swift. Men not yet old have but dim memories of things that helped them vanquish the frontier, and today lie discarded. These memories take an ever-deepening tinge of romance as they fade. There was the pony express. How we look upon it now! Ah, they were men, those riders, and they lived in a golden age of romance. All the sordid side of the pony express — and there must have been one — has been forgotten.

America has just discarded as outworn another great aid in the everlasting thrust against frontiers — frontiers not alone of our country but of the world. It is the Ford flivver, unlovely and almost ridiculous now, because it is so familiar. The days of the old Ford are ended. Production stopped some months ago, and, it is said, repair parts will be made only five more years. Soon after those five years, the Ford will join the covered wagon and the pony express and become a memory.

The pony express and the covered wagon began where the railroads left off, serving because nothing else would go where they went and do it so quickly. In 1903 Henry Ford put his car on the market. It went, too, went where nothing else would go so quickly. It pushed down great barriers. It brought utility and pleasure to millions. In nineteen years Henry Ford built fifteen million cars, as alike in their essential mechanism as peas in a pod. He built one of the greatest enterprises in the world. He fashioned a fortune so great it cannot be comprehended. Little has come from Ford himself in these days of transition, when the old car, outclassed now, is being abandoned for the new. But from a word here and there, it is apparent that Henry Ford is not laying aside the old Model T without a pang of regret. It was completely his, from first to last. Perhaps he, better than anyone else, knows that with its passing goes irretrievably a part of America.

[*Prosperity and Prizefights*]: September 21.

Mr. Gene Tunney is to receive a guarantee of one million dollars for his share in the little bout of fisticuffs with Mr. Jack Dempsey in Chicago on September 22. Mr. Dempsey is to receive $450,000. Mr. Tunney will get an additional sum of perhaps $250,000, because of a sliding scale arrangement based on the box-office receipts. These have already passed $2,500,000, and are expected to reach $3,000,000. And there are the movie rights. In addition to paying up to $40 each for their tickets (or more to speculators) many of the 100,000 persons who will see the fight will have spent additional hundreds of dollars each on railroad fare. This despite the fact that most of the seats in the arena promise only a remote view of the spectacle; despite the possibility of staying at home and hearing it described in detail on the radio; despite the notorious criticism of nearly every recent bout as having been crooked. In the decadent days of Rome, the citizens clamored for bread and circuses. Nowadays, we seem willing to omit the bread.

[*Can Radio Be Rescued?*]: October 26.

In the main, broadcasting in America is an advertising device. Other countries — Great Britain, for example — keep it under government control, and an official bureau is charged with the responsibility for giving the people just as good material and as much of it as they will tolerate; but in the United States, there are only two possible sources of revenue, the sale of receiving sets and the sale of other goods which can be popularized by having them described, or perhaps merely mentioned, over the air. Some stations are making a profit on their operations through the fees received from advertisers; and nearly all of them seek at least to diminish their deficit by that means. The formula is like that of the big-circulation magazines — a streak of reading matter, and then a streak, three times wider, of advertising. This takes the form of concerts broadcast "through the courtesy of" some manufacturer of soap or pickles or batteries; or the persistent announcer comes on the air between the movements of the symphony to urge upon you the merits of Glantz's bakery or the Helen's Beauty Parlor Special Facial. How much of this sort of street-begging-in-the-home the listeners will stand for, is still a question which awaits an answer.

An important movement in recent months corresponds to the development in journalism of chain ownership of newspapers. Radio stations throughout the country are now being leased or purchased, or their time bought, and linked up into systems with their material broadcast from a central source. The cost is paid by the owner of the system, and charged to advertising. One such chain of many stations is owned by a phonograph company, and others by a vaudeville theatre organization and a motion picture producer. The "circulation" reached by these chains, daily or nightly, presumably mounts into many millions. It is not unlikely that this process will go on until the little local station, with its home-talent programs and its advertising of home-town department-store bargains, will have been forced out of business. Naturally, the programs offered by the great national chains are very much better. They can afford to employ world famous musicians to sing or play to the microphone, while the local studio is still dependent, for the most part, on the ambitious amateur. If both programs are on the air simultaneously, the listeners will probably take the well-known stars. Ergo, advertising through the local station will no longer be profitable; ergo, the source of revenue will dwindle.

But the chain itself is confronted by the same deadly problem, in the long run. Can it keep people listening, not occasionally, but regularly? For if it cannot, the economic organization of broadcasting will break down. Every new owner of a receiving set listens faithfully, for a time, to no matter what trash, enthralled by the mechanical marvel; but in far too many homes there is today a silent set, resuscitated only when something comes along like a Dempsey-Tunney fight.

[*The Family Goes On*]: November 16.

The institution of the family will continue to exist. It is being altered, but is in no danger of being destroyed. That is the general opinion which prevailed at the recent conference "On Family Life in America Today," at which leading experts from all parts of the United States gathered to record their verdict on the present and future outlook for the home. . . .

The customary factors were cited as reasons for the declining importance of the home as an institution. It no longer has economic significance, since the manufacturing processes which once went on within its walls are now conducted elsewhere. Children in their late 'teens who still live at home, and even wives, tend increasingly to engage in outside remunerative work, and thus the dominance of the father, once backed by the club of grim necessity, has been much weakened. It has also been diminished by the general decline of authoritarianism, political and religious. The rising cost of land and residential construction make houses and apartments ever smaller, until there is hardly enough room for family life, in the old sense, and hospitality consists to an increasing extent in taking one's guests out to hotel, restaurant, or theatre. New sources of extra-mural activity are furnished by the automobile, the motion picture, the enormously increased popularity of dancing. As one speaker observed, modern life is so rich in recreational and cultural opportunities that the home needs to be more interesting and enjoyable than it often is, in order to compete. It simply doesn't put on a good enough show. The only cement which may be expected to hold the home of the future together (except as to very young children and their parents) is voluntary association, on a basis of mutual respect and affection; and even as to the infant, from cradle days on, these factors are of enormously increased importance. This change in the basis of the home is one which the experts contemplate without apprehension. Indeed, they feel that one of the great difficulties of the present is, not that the family is changing too fast, but that it is not changing fast enough. The necessity for a new type of relationship is insufficiently recognized, especially by parents, who often seek to maintain over their adult children a type of relationship now archaic.

# INDEX